Daniel Reiser

Imagery Techniques in Modern Jewish Mysticism

Studia Judaica

Forschungen zur Wissenschaft des Judentums

Begründet von
Ernst Ludwig Ehrlich

Herausgegeben von
Günter Stemberger, Charlotte Fonrobert,
Alexander Samely und Irene Zwiep

Band 101

Daniel Reiser

Imagery Techniques in Modern Jewish Mysticism

Translated by Eugene D. Matanky
with Daniel Reiser

DE GRUYTER MAGNES

This book was published with the support of the Israel Science Foundation (ISF) and with the support of Zefat Academic College Research Grants.

ISBN 978-3-11-071049-6
e-ISBN (PDF) 978-3-11-053588-4
e-ISBN (EPUB) 978-3-11-053408-5
ISSN 0585-5306

Library of Congress Cataloging-in-Publication Data

Names: Reiser, Daniel, 1976- author.
Title: Imagery techniques in modern Jewish mysticism / Daniel Reiser.
Description: First edition. | Boston ; Berlin : De Gruyter, [2018] | Series: Studia Judaica, ISSN 0585-5306 ; band 101 | Includes bibliographical references.
Identifiers: LCCN 2018022976| ISBN 9783110533941 (print) | ISBN 9783110535884 (e-book (pdf) | ISBN 9783110534085 (e-book (epub)
Subjects: LCSH: Imagery (Psychology)--Methodology--History--20th century. | Imagination (Philosophy)--History--20th century. | Visualization--Technique--History--20th century. | Mysticism--Judaism--History--20th century.
Classification: LCC BF367 .R45 2018 | DDC 153.3/2--dc23 LC record available at https://lccn.loc.gov/2018022976

Bibliografic information published by the Deutsche Nationalbibliothek
The Deutsche Nationalbibliothek lists this publication in the Deutsche Nationalbibliografie; detailed bibliografic data are available on the Internet at http://dnb.dnb.de.

This volume is text- and page-identical with the hardback published in 2018.
Printing and binding: CPI books GmbH, Leck

www.degruyter.com
www.magnespress.co.il

Acknowledgements

> Cinema... makes movement the immediate given of the image... It is only when movement becomes automatic that the artistic essence of the image is realized: *producing a shock to thought, communicating vibrations to the cortex, touching the nervous and cerebral system directly... Automatic movement* gives rise to a *spiritual automaton* in us.[1]

The status of the imagination has surged in contemporary culture, even being capable of preceding and dictating reality. People of imagination: artists, novelists, actors, and musicians, gain popularity and influence, while people of intellect: intellectuals, philosophers, scientists, and academics lose recognition and effect. Images produce a reality that further reflects these images. This development did not occur in a vacuum, but rather is a cultural aspect that germinated within and already characterized the modern era. A minority of religious authorities and figures were attuned to this development and employed it for their own purposes. I will discuss these select individuals in this work and demonstrate how they utilized the imagination as a means for religious and even mystical experience.

This study began as my doctoral dissertation, entitled, "'To Fly like Angels': Imagery or Waking Dream Techniques in Hasidic Mysticism in the First Half of the Twentieth Century," (Hebrew University of Jerusalem, 2011). This served as the foundation for my Hebrew book *Vision as a Mirror* (Los Angeles: Cherub Press, 2014), upon which I have expanded and inserted significant alterations. *Vision as a Mirror's* scope extends beyond hasidism, with an emphasis on examining and contrasting similar imagery techniques developed in both Jewish and non-Jewish contexts, such as the Lithuanian Musar movement, modern psychological studies, and the East. *Vision as a Mirror* was awarded the *World Union of Jewish Studies Matanel Prize* for the best book in Jewish Thought published during the years 2013–2014.

This current book, *Imagery Techniques in Modern Jewish Mysticism*, is not just a translation of the Hebrew book, but rather also includes revisions and updated research. In the last four years, new research has been published that has added more sophisticated perspectives on the subject of my study and I have engaged them in this book. Additionally, I have expanded and revised portions of the book in light of the constructive criticism which it received when originally published. My first book was meant for a Hebrew reading audience, whereas

1 Giles Deleuze, *Cinema 2: The Time-Image*, trans. Hugh Tomlinson and Robert Galeta (London: The Athlone Press, 1989), 156. Emphasis in original.

https://doi.org/10.1515/9783110535884-001

this current book is meant for an English reading audience. The change in audience also caused changes to be made in the book. I shortened entire sections that had received much attention in English-based studies prior to my Hebrew book, since it would be superfluous to restate them in this translation. Instead, I have sufficed with referencing the academic research, without expanding upon it. In contrast, the Hebrew concepts and terminology which served me in my research have been clarified in English.

I must express my deepest gratitude to my teachers and friends that have assisted me in every step of this work. First and foremost, Prof. Moshe Idel, under whom I wrote my dissertation. His many insights and conceptions are to be found strewn throughout this book. Without his critical comments and expansive knowledge, this work would have remained like a sheep without a shepherd. Prof. Jonathan Garb, who wrote and published a review of my Hebrew book and made important comments, which influenced certain changes made in this English edition. Prof. Daniel Abrams, the book series editor of Cherub Press, who not only encouraged me to publish my research and carefully edited the Hebrew version of this work, despite his many other pressing obligations, but who has also graciously allowed for its English translation.

I would like to acknowledge the generous support of my current academic homes, Zefat Academic College and its research authority, which supported this translation, and to Herzog Academic College's research authority and its director Dr. Amos Geula, who submitted this research successfully for an ISF book grant. I would like to express my sincere gratitude to the Israel Science Foundation (ISF) for their generous financial assistance in the publishing of this English translation.

A few of the chapters included in this work previously appeared in abbreviated form in the journal *Modern Judaism*. I would like to thank its editor, Prof. Steven Katz, for allowing them to be republished here. Likewise, chapter eight was improved upon in a research program of the Center for Austrian Studies, European Forum, at the Hebrew University of Jerusalem. I would also like to thank the City of Vienna Scholarship for its support.

I cannot express my thanks to Gene Matanky, the translator of the book. He is not just a translator, but a scholar in his own right, I am sure that we will see his own work in the near future. Over the course of this translation, Gene referred me to materials and sources that I had not come across, which have entered this work. The translation of this book became a shared learning experience in which he would ask and I would answer, and I would ask and he would answer. Our enjoyable and productive collaborative efforts have formed the book in front of you. I would also like to thank Sam Glauber who carefully edited the English manuscript and made important stylisic suggestions.

My gratitude to the Hebrew University Magnes Press, Jerusalem, and to the De Gruyter Press for publishing the English translation of my book.

May this book be an *illui neshamah*, an elevation of the soul, for my grandparents, Sigmund and Carole Reiser, and Aharon and Devora Rosenberg blessed be their memories, Holocaust survivors "brands plucked from the fire" (Zechariah 3:2); my great-grandparents, Binyamin and Feiga Reiser, Moshe Salamon, Yaakov and Leah Klamer, and Shmuel and Rivka Rosenberg, who were murdered by the Nazis, may their names be erased.

This book is dedicated to my parents, Prof. Benjamin and Rivka Reiser, who raised me with the love of Torah and scholarship (*Ḥokhmah*). They have always stood by my side and encouraged my work, and words cannot express my appreciation for all they have done for me.

Daniel Reiser, Zefat and Herzog Academic Colleges

Translator's Note

In this work, I have had to make use of many rabbinic texts and have relied upon different translations. The biblical text in this book has largely been quoted from the *New Jewish Publication Society* (*NJPS*). The Talmudic passages have made use of *The Soncino Talmud*. Midrash Rabbah translations have been primarily from or based on the *Soncino Midrash Rabbah*. The *Zohar* quotations have been primarily from or based on the *Zohar Pritzker Edition*, for the available sections. Other translations of rabbinic texts are mine, unless otherwise noted. All emphases within primary material, whether it be biblical, rabbinic, kabbalistic, or hasidic, is that of the author, unless otherwise noted. Transliteration has largely followed the guidelines found in *Encyclopaedia Judaica* and the *YIVO Encyclopedia*, however there have been exceptions due to a variety of factors. Eastern European towns and cities have been referenced in their current spellings with their Yiddish pronunciation in parentheses in their first occurrence, with some exceptions. The current translation is of *Ha-Mar'eh ka-Mar'ah: Ṭekniqat ha-Dimyun be-Misṭiqah ha-Yehudit ba-Me'ah ha-Esrim*. This translation has been carried out with the collaboration of the author.

Eugene D. Matanky

https://doi.org/10.1515/9783110535884-002

Contents

Introduction — 1
A The Study of Mystical Techniques in Jewish Mysticism — **1**
B The Study of Imagery Techniques — **5**

Section I: Imaginative Models

Chapter One: Models of Imagination — 17
A Models of Imagination in Western Philosophy — **18**
B Models of Imagination in Jewish Thought — **23**
R. Judah Halevi — **26**
Maimonides — **31**
R. Naḥman of Bratslav — **41**
C Conclusion — **47**

Section II: Parameters for Mystical Praxis

Chapter Two: Empowerment — 53
A Defining the Concept "Mysticism" — **53**
B Empowerment — **61**

Chapter Three: Prophecy, Ecstasy, and Mysticism — 67
A Two Models of Prophecy — **67**
The Notion of Biblical Prophecy in Rabbinic Literature — **75**
Biblical Prophecy through the Prism of Prophetic Kabbalah — **78**
Prophecy in the New Testament and Medieval Christian Theology — **79**
The Limitation and Expansion of Prophecy in Medieval Jewish Rationalist Thought — **81**
B Kalonymous Kalman Shapira's Conception of Prophecy: A Third Model — **83**
The Twentieth-Century Quest to Renew Prophecy in the Teachings of Shapira — **90**
Shapira's Attempts to Actualize Prophecy in the Twentieth Century — **93**
C Conclusion — **95**

Section III: Imagery Techniques

Chapter Four: Imagination as an Empowering Factor in R. Kalonymous Kalman Shapira's Thought — 99

A Introduction: Imagination in R. Kalonymous Kalman Shapira's Thought — **99**
- Biographical Introduction — **99**
- R. Kalonymous Kalman Shapira's Books — **102**
- Maḥshavah (Thought), Imagination, and Visualization in R. Kalonymous Kalman Shapira's Teaching — **103**
- R. Kalonymous Kalman Shapira's Imagery Techniques and His Imaginal-Literary Style — **107**

B Imagination as an Empowering Factor of Anomian Experiences — **116**
- Dance and Imagery — **117**
- Melody and Imagination — **126**
- Hitbodedut and Imagination — **133**
- Speaking Out Loud and Imagination — **137**
- Writing and Imagination — **140**
- Conclusion — **142**

C Imagination as an Empowering Factor in Nomian Experiences — **142**
- Introduction — **142**
- Torah — **145**
- Intensification of Biblical Stories — **146**
- Prayer — **149**

D Imagination as Empowering the Experience of Sacred Time: Sabbath and Festivals — **156**
- Introduction — **156**
- Sabbath — **160**
- Passover — **165**
- Hanukkah — **167**

E Imagination as Empowering Emotions — **170**
- The Imagination as a Self-Empowering Factor — **170**
- Visualizing Distress and Worry as Intensifying Factors for Seeking God — **173**
- Visualizing the Day of Death — **176**
- Spiritual and Theurgical Worry — **183**
- The Imagination as an Intensifying Factor of Self-Sacrifice Experiences — **186**

F Conclusion — **189**

G Addendum – *Ṣaddiq* Imagery Techniques: “One Longing to Seek God’s Face” — **191**
The *Ṣaddiq*’s Status in Shapira’s Thought — **191**
Visualizing the Ṣaddiq — **194**

Chapter Five: Imagination as a Prophetic Factor: The Yearning for Prophecy in the Twentieth Century — 198
A Preface — **198**
B Prophetic Imagination in the Teachings of R. Zadok ha-Kohen of Lublin and R. Abraham Isaac ha-Kohen Kook — **200**
C Imagination and Prophecy in R. Kalonymous Kalman Shapira’s Thought — **209**
Nefesh Geluyah (A Revealed Soul) — **209**
Gilui ha-Nefesh (Revelation of the Soul) and Prophecy — **211**
Prophecy and Imagination — **213**
Imagination as a Technique for Illustrating God — **219**
The Visualization of God and Corporealization in Shapira’s Thought — **226**
Heavenly Imagery Techniques: Imaginal Substitutions — **232**
“To Visualize the Holy Name”: Outflanking Imagination – Imagination within Imagination — **234**
Visualizing God’s Name as a Technique for the Acquisition of Prophecy — **239**
D The Silencing Technique — **241**
E Categorization of Imagery Techniques — **244**
F Conclusion — **248**

Chapter Six: A War of Imaginations: Imagery Techniques in R. Menaḥem Ekstein’s Teachings — 250
A Biographical Introduction — **250**
B The Book and Its Sources — **259**
C The Bifurcated Soul and Self-Awareness — **262**
D Self-Awareness and Imagination — **266**
E War of Imaginations — **267**
F Integration (Hitkallelut) — **275**
G Ecstasy and Amazement — **281**
The Sublime — **281**
The Sublime and the Sense of Astonishment — **284**
The Sublime and the Imagination in Ekstein’s Teachings — **288**

H *Raṣo va-Shov* (Running and Returning): Numerous Scenes and Their Successive Progression — 294
I The Technique of "Negative Commandments" (Lav) — 300
J Autoscopy and Self-Visualization in Menaḥem Mendel Ekstein's Teachings — 302
Autoscopic Phenomena — 302
Neurocognitive Models of Autoscopic Phenomena — 305
Autoscopy in Ekstein's Teachings — 308
The Heautoscopy Model and Its Characterization in Ekstein's Imaginal Self-Visualization Techniques — 310
K Between Kalonymous Kalman Shapira and Menaḥem Ekstein — 311
L Imagery Techniques in Twentieth Century Hasidism — 314

Chapter Seven: War of the "Senses:" Imagination in the Musar Movement — 318
A Introduction — 318
B The Conception of Imagination in Israel Lipkin of Salant's Teaching — 321
C Ecstasy and the Battle of the Senses: The Development of the Imagination in the Musar Movement — 324
D Between the Musar Movement and Hasidism — 340
E Conclusion — 340

Section IV: Adventures of Ideas: West and East

Introduction: Similar Thought Patterns — 345

Chapter Eight: "My Heart is in the East and I am at the Ends of the West": Imagery Techniques in Light of the West — 348
A Imagery Techniques in Light of Mesmerism and the Unconscious — 348
Franz Mesmer: His Life, Thought and Influence — 348
Mesmerism and the Jewish World — 354
Menaḥem Ekstein, Mesmerism, and Imaginative Technique — 359
Imagery Techniques and Modern Psychology — 363
Vienna: Authority and Mysticism — 367
Vienna: The Meeting Place of Hasidic Psychology and Western Psychology — 370

B Transformation of Traditional Concepts into Modern Concepts and the Translation of Kabbalah into Psychological Terminology — **373**
C The Unconscious and the Occult — **380**
D The Idea of the Unconscious in the Musar Movement — **387**

Chapter Nine: "A Voice Calls from the East:" Imagery Techniques in Light of the East — 396

Afterword — 406

Bibliography — 408
Primary Rabbinic, Kabbbalistic, Hasidic Sources — **408**
Philosophical and Secondary Sources — **413**

Index of Persons — 439

Subject Index — 442

Introduction

A The Study of Mystical Techniques in Jewish Mysticism

Until recently, the study of Jewish mysticism was methodologically dominated by the theological approach. According to this approach theology represents religion. This methodology was reflected in the diverse studies of kabbalah, zoharic literature, and hasidism, while the study of mystical praxis was neglected. As Moshe Idel writes, "Modern scholarship of religion had emerged out of attempts to describe, more emphatically, the systemic forms of thought, basically beliefs, myths, symbols while the ways of behavior, religious praxes and rituals attracted much less attention from the side of scholars."[1] In contrast to this approach, other scholars proposed to consider the possibility that different forms of religious praxes have the capability to provide key evidence of the mystical nature of that religion. Therefore, instead of solely relying on a detailed study of theologies that left their mark on a specific type of mysticism in order to discover if they allow for an extreme or moderate experience, these scholars suggested that mystical techniques and experiences should be researched as primary methods for sketching the schema of the mystical nature of a specific religion.[2]

The first fissures in the theological approach began to appear mainly in academic publications at the end of the 1980's and beginning of the '90s. These continued and flourished in the first decade of the twenty-first century, although rooted in work which appeared in the '70s. A pioneer of this revolution, Moshe Idel acknowledged:

> The image of kabbalah that arises from modern scholarship is too uniform... this homogenous image arose by ignoring a significant strand in Jewish esoteric teachings... the prophetic kabbalah... when the matter became clear to me, during the preparation of my doc-

---

1 Moshe Idel, "On Judaism, Jewish Mysticism and Magic," in *Envisioning Magic: A Princeton Seminar and Symposium*, ed. P. Schäfer H. G. Kippenberg (Leiden: Brill, 1997), 195. In this essay, Idel shows that the lack of attention to the characteristics of behaviors and actions excluded magic, which phenomenologically is at the heart of many subjects in Judaism due to the centrality of actions in this religion, from kabbalah scholarship.

2 Idem, *Enchanted Chains: Techniques and Rituals in Jewish Mysticism* (Los Angeles: Cherub Press, 2005), 31–33. For more about the importance of mystical and magical techniques in kabbalah see, idem, *Kabbalah: New Perspectives* (New Haven: Yale University, 1988), 74–111; R. J. Zwi Werblowsky, *Joseph Karo: Lawyer and Mystic* (Philadelphia: Jewish Publication Society of America, 1977), 38–83; Lawrence Fine, "Recitation of Mishnah as a Vehicle for Mystical Inspiration: A Contemplative Technique Taught by Hayyim Vital," *Revue des études juives* 141 (1982): 183–199.

https://doi.org/10.1515/9783110535884-003

> toral dissertation that was submitted in 1976, a gradual change began in my perception of the essence of kabbalah in general. On the one hand, my perspective on historical processes changed... and on the other hand, I came to a different phenomenological view, one which placed more importance on mystical techniques, devequt (communion), and unio mystica in kabbalah.[3]

He further wrote, at the end of the '80s, in relation to the research of kabbalistic praxis, "Like mystics of other faiths, Kabbalists used certain techniques in order to induce paranormal states of consciousness. But despite the great importance of these practices, their history and description have received only scant attention in the modern study of Jewish mysticism."[4] Idel claimed that "the raising of topics connected to mystical techniques to the researcher's consciousness will serve as a transition stage for understanding kabbalah as possessing experiential foundations."[5]

This new conception inspired a generation of students engaged in studying praxis. Such studies, although currently underway, have only just begun. For instance, Elliot Wolfson's guiding principle in zoharic scholarship is that it is impossible to understand the *Zohar* without taking into account that theosophic conceptions within the text are also practical means for achieving a state of ecstasy, namely that of *devequt* (communion).[6] In contradistinction to Gershom Scholem's scholarship, which presented the *Zohar* as only Jewish theosophy, Wolfson demonstrates that the zoharic text constitutes a means of ecstasy for

3 Even though Idel refrains from this term ("revolution") in relation to his research, see idem, "Old and New in the Study of Kabbalah," *Zion* 54 (1989): 506, "There is no revolution here"—I permitted myself to present it as such, for I see the transition of emphasis from theology to praxis as a revolution, and as a conception that effectually allows this current work. Ibid., "Old and New," 493–494.

4 Idem, *Kabbalah: New Perspectives*, 74. Indeed, the Hebrew translation is from 1993, whereas the original English was published in 1988. Also see, Jonathan Garb, *The Chosen Will Become Herds: Studies in Twentieth-Century Kabbalah*, trans. Yaffah Berkovits-Murciano (New Haven: Yale University Press, 2005), 6, "The research is limited by biases stemming from various agendas that until recently were accepted without question. One example of such a bias is the tendency to deal with ideas rather than with social structures or practices."

5 Idel, "Old and New," 498, n. 10. For more on this revolution, see Adam Afterman, "Afterword: A New Paradigm in Kabbalah Research," in Moshe Idel, *Enchanted Chains: Techniques and Rituals in Jewish Mysticism*, trans. Miri Scharf (Jerusalem: Shalom Hartman Institute, 2015), 221–232, concerning the paradigmatic shift that occurred in the field with the works of Moshe Idel and Yehuda Liebes.

6 Elliot R. Wolfson, *Luminal Darkness: Imaginal Gleanings from the Zoharic Literature* (Oxford: Oneworld Publications, 2007), 112.

the kabbalist. The zoharic text itself reflects an experiential state of *devequt* as well as an amalgamate state between the mystic's soul and divinity.[7]

The focus on praxis introduced a new definition of the term mysticism! Henceforth, mysticism itself is a derivative of praxes that constitute the central force for experiencing union with the divine. Praxis is that which actualizes the divine and mysticism is a spiritual phenomenon brought about by the praxes, "The term 'mysticism' in Jewish texts refers to spiritual and corporeal phenomena resulting from certain practices designed to ensure… a unitive experience. By 'unitive' I mean being in the immediate presence of God."[8]

It is important to note for the purpose of this study, which engages primarily with the hasidic world, that this conception led to a new definition and mapping of the hasidic movement. According to Idel, hasidism is not a popularization of kabbalah, psychological interpretation of Lurianic teachings, psychologization of kabbalistic symbols,[9] or a generic name for a number of congregations having a charismatic figure standing at their center.[10] In his opinion, hasidism is a unique spiritual configuration, constituting a continuation of previous thought patterns with certain changes. The vital mystical foundation of the hasidic movement is not the theological conception. Hasidic mysticism is connected more to the performance of mystical practices and techniques, the magical and mystical reasons for the commandments (*ṭa'amei ha-miṣvot*), and the testimonies of the *ṣaddiqim* (hasidic masters) regarding their mystical experience and magical activities.[11] This conception paved a new way in scholarship and made possible the

---

7 Ibid., 112–116. Also, idem, "The Hermeneutics of Visionary Experience: Revelation and Interpretation in the *Zohar*," *Religion* 18 (1998): 311, "Visionary experience of the divine is not only central to Zoharic theosophy, but that the act of textual study itself must be understood in the light of this phenomenon insofar as the text is nothing but the configuration of divine light." The entire article (ibid., 311–345, specifically, 317–325) proves this thesis with numerous examples.

8 Idel, *Enchanted Chains*, 4.

9 These definitions represent Scholem's views. See Gershom Scholem, *Major Trends in Jewish Mysticism* (New York: Schocken Books, 1954), 340–341. Also, idem, *Explications and Implications: Writings on Jewish Heritage and Renaissance* (Tel Aviv: Am Oved, 1982), 353–354. Also ibid., 365, that Scholem saw hasidism as a development within the framework of Lurianic kabbalah. In contrast to this view, Idel demonstrated the central influence of Cordoverian kabbalah on hasidism, Moshe Idel, *Hasidism: Between Ecstasy and Magic* (Albany: State University of New York Press, 1995), 11–14, 178–180.

10 The conception of Mendel Piekarz, *The Beginning of Hasidism: Ideological Trends in Derush and Musar Literature* (Jerusalem: Bialik Press, 1978), 392; idem, *Between Ideology and Reality: Humility, Ayin, Self-Negation and Devekut in Hasidic Thought* (Jerusalem: Bialik Press, 1994), 178.

11 Idel, *Hasidism*, 211; idem, "On Prophecy and Early Hasidism," in *Studies in Modern Religions, Religious Movements, and the Bābī Bahā'ī Faiths*, ed. M. Sharon (Leiden: Brill, 2004), 47.

research of mystical practices and techniques that appear in the hasidic literary corpus.

Idel himself has dedicated many studies to the topic of kabbalistic and hasidic mystical practices, among them one may find practices such as *qol* (voice) and music,[12] weeping,[13] *hitbodedut* (contemplative isolation),[14] oneiric techniques,[15] combination of letters of the divine name,[16] placing of one's head between one's knees,[17] shutting one's eyes,[18] and many more. Many of his studies explore linguistic praxes connected to the divine name, combination of letters, liturgical texts, and Torah.

This new definition and focus on praxis made possible the conditions for my research in kabbalah and hasidism. This book methodologically engages with one type of praxis—the imagery technique or waking dream. I will focus primarily on the beginning of the twentieth century in which this technique, in my opinion, reached new heights. I will demonstrate that this zenith is clearly linked to kabbalistic literature, the beginning of hasidism, and the developments within them, as well as to non-Jewish developments.

---

12 Idem, "The Magical and Theurgic Interpretation of Music in Jewish Sources from the Renaissance to Hassidism," *Yuval* 4 (1982): 33–62; idem, "Kabbalah and Music," in *Judaism and Art*, ed. D. Cassuto (Ramat Gan: Bar Ilan University, 1989), 275–289; idem, *The Mystical Experience in Abraham Abulafia*, trans. Jonathan Chipman (Albany: State University of New York Press, 1988), 53–71; idem, *Nocturnal Kabbalists* (Jerusalem: Carmel, 2006), 64, 67–68; idem, *Enchanted Chains*, 26–30, 208–212; idem, "Conceptualizations of Music in Jewish Mysticism," in *Enchanting Powers: Music in the World's Religion*, ed. L. E. Sullivan (Cambridge: Harvard University Press, 1997), 159–188.

13 Idem, *Kabbalah: New Perspective*, 75–88.

14 Idem, "'Hitbodedut' qua 'Concentration' in Ecstatic Kabbalah," *Da'at* 14 (Winter 1985): 31–81; idem, "Hitbodedut as Concentration in Jewish Philosophy," *Jerusalem Studies in Jewish Thought* 7 (1988): 39–60; idem, "Hitbodedut: On Solitude in Jewish Mysticism," in *Einsamkeit: Archäologie der literarischen Kommunikation VI*, ed. A. Assmann and J. Assmann (Munich: Fink, 2000), 189–212.

15 Idem, *Nocturnal Kabbalists*, 15–35, 45–74, 95–108.

16 Idem, *Kabbalah: New Perspectives*, 97–103; idem, *Mystical Experience*, 13–30; idem, *Language, Torah, and Hermeneutics in Abraham Abulafia*, trans. Menahem Kallus (Albany: State University of New York Press, 1989), 1–11, 101–109; idem, *Enchanted Chains*, 76–121.

17 Idem, *Kabbalah: New Perspectives*, 78–79, 90. Often the practice of placing one's head between one's knees is combined with the technique of weeping. For more regarding this technique see Jonathan Garb, "Trance Techniques in the Kabbalah of Jerusalem," *Pe'amim* 70 (1997): 52, regarding *hitbodedut* ibid., 51, "dream question" ibid., 53, imagery ibid., 52,57, shutting one's eyes ibid., 57, music ibid., 57, combination of letters ibid., 51, 62–64. Garb serves as an example of the next generation that researches praxis.

18 Moshe Idel, *Studies in Ecstatic Kabbalah* (Albany: State University of New York Press, 1988), 134–136.

B The Study of Imagery Techniques

As has been well documented, the modern field of Jewish mysticism was founded by Gershom Scholem,[19] who structured it in such a manner as to privilege certain forms and understandings of Jewish mysticism, specifically theosophic kabbalah and its textual analysis, and thereby denying other forms and understandings, specifically ecstatic-mystical kabbalah and phenomenological research. Therefore, Scholem negated the imaginative and visual component in theosophic kabbalah:

> The concentration on the world of Sefirot is not bound up with visions, but is solely a matter for the intellect prepared to ascend from level to level and to meditate on the qualities unique to each level. If meditation activates at first the faculty of imagination, it continues by activating the faculty of the intellect.[20]

Elliot Wolfson argues with Scholem and claims that the state of *devequt* is actually enabled through the faculty of imagination and not that of the intellect,[21] and stresses that the central concern of theosophic kabbalah, alongside older forms of Jewish esotericism, is "the visualization of the divine in the form of an *anthropos*."[22] Likewise, as opposed to Scholem, Wolfson brings multiple examples from the *Zohar* that demonstrate the ecstatic and mystical nature of the gnostic theosophy in the zoharic corpus.[23]

I will briefly survey the existent scholarship regarding imagination in Jewish mysticism and I will elaborate on how my research adds and innovates: Elliot Wolfson, who in my opinion is the most important and significant researcher on the subject of imagination in the field of Jewish mysticism, has extensively researched the visualization of the divine in the medieval kabbalistic and zoharic literature.[24] Haviva Pedaya has studied revelatory mysticism which seeks to

---

19 See Daniel Abrams, "Defining Modern Academic Scholarship: Gershom Scholem and the Establishment of a New (?) Discipline," *The Journal of Jewish Thought and Philosophy* 9 (2000): 267–302.
20 Gershom Scholem, *Kabbalah* (Jerusalem: Keter, 1974), 370.
21 Wolfson, *Luminal Darkness*, 116; idem, *Through a Speculum that Shines: Vision and Imagination in Medieval Jewish Mysticism* (Princeton: Princeton University Press, 1994), 279–325.
22 Wolfson, *Luminal Darkness*, 116–117.
23 Ibid., 119–130.
24 A non-comprehensive selection of his work: Wolfson, *Through a Speculum that Shines*; idem, *Luminal Darkness*; idem, *Language, Eros, Being: Kabbalistic Hermeneutics and Poetic Imagination* (New York: Fordham University Press, 2005); idem, *A Dream Interpreted Within a Dream: Oneiropoiesis and the Prism of Imagination* (New York: Zone Books, 2011); idem, "Images of

see images and receive visions, primarily in her work *Vision and Speech: Models of Revelatory Experience in Jewish Mysticism.*[25] Moshe Idel has researched color-visualization techniques in kabbalistic thought,[26] visualizing the tetragrammaton,[27] and viewing the form of the *anthropos* and letters in the thought of Abraham Abulafia' and others.[28]

With this being said, in this work I am primarily interested in presenting a different imagery technique. Not the visualization of letters or a certain object, rather imagery exercises comprised of entire imaginal plots, known as waking-dreams. Not the viewing of imaginary static images, rather dynamic images which together construct a multi-scenic storyline.[29]

God's Feet: Some Observations on the Divine body in Judaism," in *People of the Body: Jews and Judaism from an Embodied Perspective*, ed. H. Eilberg-Schwartz (Albany: State University of New York Press, 1992), 143–181; idem, "Iconic Visualization and the Imaginal Body of God: The Role of Intention in the Rabbinic Conception of Prayer." *Modern Theology* 12 (1996): 137–162; idem, "Phantasmagoria: The Image of the Image in Jewish Magic from Late Antiquity to the Early Middle Ages," *Review of Rabbinic Judaism: Ancient, Medieval and Modern* 4 (2001): 78–120.

25 Haviva Pedaya, *Vision and Speech: Models of Revelatory Experience in Jewish Mysticism* (Los Angeles: Cherub Press, 2002(; idem, "Sight, Fall, Song: The Longing for a Vision of God and the Spiritual Element in Early Jewish Mysticism," *Asufot* 9 (1995): 237–277.

26 Idel, *Kabbalah: New Perspectives*, 103–111; idem, *Enchanted Chains*, 228–232; idem, "Intention and Colors: A Forgotten Kabbalistic Responsum," in *Tribute to Sarah: Studies in Jewish Philosophy and Mysticism Presented to Sara O. Heller Wilensky*, ed. M. Idel, D. Diamond, and S. Rosenberg (Jerusalem: Magnes Press, 1994), 1–14; idem, *Golem: Jewish Magical and Mystical Traditions on the Artificial Anthropoid* (Albany: State University of New York Press, 1990), 121–124.

27 Idem, *Mystical Experience*, 30–37.

28 Ibid., 95–105. Abulafia mostly engaged in receiving visions and not in imagery, and although vision is an imaginal picture—the distinction is great between them. Imaginal visualization is an active endeavor whereas the "vision," which Idel discusses, appears to man in revelation, without necessarily a purposeful imaginal act, but rather a product of inspiration. Regarding imagination as an active human endeavor in Abulafia's thought see below, n. 34. On non-visual active imagination, see ibid., 104, an extraordinary excerpt from *Sefer ha-Ḥesheq* attesting to the suggestive act of the mystics in which they configure the letters of the tetragrammaton as if they are independent entities, "and think as if they are speaking." Regarding imagery techniques in the thought of R. Joseph b. Shalom Ashkenazi (a German kabbalist of the late thirteenth century who was expelled to Barcelona) see, Idel, *Kabbalah: New Perspectives*, 105. On imagery techniques in a short anonymous commentary on the prayer *shema yisrael* that recommends visualizing the divine names in the prayer, see ibid., 108. More about the visualization of the tetragrammaton in kabbalah and hasidism see idem, *Enchanted Chains*, 97–102.

29 Indeed, in the visualization of the *ṣaddiq*'s form and the tetragrammaton (below in chap. 4 and 5) I will present imagery of static images; however, these imaginal exercises are exceptions to the rule. The overwhelming majority of imaginal exercises, which the figures that I will discuss developed, are types of waking-dreams or complete lengthy complex plotlines.

Wolfson's research focuses on the tension between the visualization of the divine and its anthropomorphic materialization. His work primarily deals with the visualization of the divine and is not concerned with the practitioner's imaginal multi-scenic storyline visualized in a conscious and awake (and not in a dream) manner. Likewise, most of his research regarding imagination focuses on medieval mysticism and not on the thought and mysticism of later hasidism.[30]

Most of Idel's research of imagery techniques discusses linguistic techniques: the divine name, canonical texts, combination of letters, Torah study, and prayer.[31] Overall the common quality shared by most of these imagery techniques is the connection between the imagination to a letter, text, or language.[32]

Pedaya's studies in the field of imagery mainly discuss images that appear in revelation and not imagery techniques initiated by the mystic or practioner (at times—to receive revelation). Pedaya imparts an important discussion about the tension between the desire to visualize the divine and the prohibition of materializing the divine, which has served me in my discussions regarding attempts at justifying imagery techniques in light of the halakhic prohibition of corporealizing the divine. Likewise, her research on the subject of religious emotional ecstasy facilitated by the imagination is very important; however, it should be repeated, that these cases engaging with visionary revelation are products of inspiration from above and not human initiative.[33] Pedaya, like Idel, has focused

---

30 However, see his recent essay discussing the visualization of the divine in the modern period, Elliot R. Wolfson, "Imagination and the Theolatrous Impulse: Configuring God in Modern Jewish Thought," in *The Cambridge History of Jewish Philosophy: The Modern Era*, ed. M. Kavka, Z. Braiterman, and D. Novak (Cambridge: Cambridge University Press, 2012), 663–703, which was later incorporated into his book *Giving Beyond the Gift: Apophasis and Overcoming Theomania* (New York: Fordham University Press, 2014), which delves extensively into the conception of the imagination in modern Jewish thinkers. In this extensive and illuminating study Wolfson focuses on Jewish thinkers from the twentieth century like Hermann Cohen, Franz Rosenzweig, Martin Buber, and Emmanuel Levinas. However, in this study the focus is on the divine figure and not on the imaginal multi-scenic storyline which I will be discussing.

31 Regarding Torah study, see Idel, *Enchanted Chains*, 125–144; on prayer, see ibid., 168–172.

32 It is important to note that Idel also explores non-linguistic imaginal exercises, see for example regarding active and guided visualization in Abulafia's thought, ibid., 98, "Prepare your true thought to imagine God... and the supernal angels, and imagine them... as though they are man standing or sitting around you," yet it is appropriate to generally state that most imaginal techniques studied by Idel are linguistic.

33 On the distinction between products of inspiration and initiative, see below, chap. 1, at the conclusion of the subchapter, "R. Judah Halevi." Certainly, celestial inspiration as well, is sometimes a product of human effort, yet this effort is made with non-imagery techniques, like oaths of silence, fasts, and the like, and the vision appears from above due to these techniques, which are not imagery. Human initiative in the context of imagery techniques is a conscious and willful

mostly on imagery techniques appearing primarily in nomian rituals, meaning within behavioral frameworks which have undergone a canonization process in rabbinic literature,[34] such as religious commandments, prayer, Torah study, and sacred times.[35]

Jonathan Garb has stated the necessity of describing Jewish culture as being comprised of multiple systems of representation: visual, auditory, and sensory. Regarding the visual system, he wrote:

> Until the last decade the prevalent conception in scholarship stressed the linguistic and auditory elements in Jewish culture as compared to the visual element, preferred in the West… indeed in recent years a few studies have been published in the fields of rabbinic literature and kabbalah which have placed much more importance on the visual conceptions of the Jewish religious experience.[36]

In light of this and Garb's other statement that "In the late nineteenth and twentieth centuries, by contrast, the influence of anomian thinkers (who circumvented or disregarded Halakha) and antinomian thinkers (who sanctioned the violation of Halakha under certain circumstances) rose sharply,"[37] it is no wonder that

---

exercise of imagination. In contrast, inspiration is the appearance of a vision to a person (that sometimes follows certain practices), but is not a conscious entry into imaginal activities.

34 On the definition of rituals see Idel, *Enchanted Chains*, 202.

35 See Haviva Pedaya, *Vision and Speech*, 21–22: "The mystics' conscious or imagined objects of focus during the mystical training process in most kabbalistic methods are: letters, words, names, ritual instruments, and commandments… a visual description of the revealed dimension of the divine is in the figure of commandments, figure of Torah, or in the figure of names."

36 Jonathan Garb, *Manifestations of Power in Jewish Mysticism: From Rabbinic Literature to Safedian Kabbalah* (Jerusalem: Magnes Press, 2005), 166–167. In this book Garb presents the visual element as marginal in hasidic thought and prefers the power of language and signs as primary representatives of hasidic techniques. However, in his later work, idem, *Shamanic Trance in Modern Kabbalah* (Chicago: University of Chicago Press, 2011), he returns the visual element to its central place in mystical and hasidic literature.

37 Garb, *The Chosen Will Become Herds*, 76. Also, ibid., 76–77, "circumvention of halakha" is not opposition to halakha, rather it is the creation of channels that are not bound to the habitual performance of the commandments and learning of halakha. The categorization of mystical techniques as nomian or anomian has been accepted in light of Idel's classification, idem, *Kabbalah: New Perspectives*, 74–75. Nomian techniques are practices relating to halakhic performance, like the kabbalistic "intentions" in prayer or in the system of commandments. Anomian techniques are unrelated to the halakhic framework, like *nigun* (hasidic melody), dance, uttering a voice, etc. According to this distinction, imagery techniques are in the anomian category, for they are practices which are not utilized within the halakhic framework and are not bound by halakhic performance. Through this distinction Idel wishes to reconfigure the Jewish religion, as representative of tensions between two poles, between the theocentric spirituality centered around the *nomos* and the anthropocentric spirituality which is concerned with the development

imagery techniques reached new heights, as I will demonstrate, for it is precisely the twentieth century in which there is a certain disconnect between halakhah and kabbalah.[38]

The visual-optical system of the later hasidic teachings, specifically in the late nineteenth and early twentieth century, is not marginal in relation to the power of language and linguistic techniques, but at times it is even quite dominant. Twentieth century hasidic literature barely engages in linguistic techniques, including visualizing letters, combinations, and the like. In contrast, the visual component, which is non-linguistic, appears significantly more often, as we will see.

A study of hasidism from its beginning until the twentieth century shows that the component of combinations of the divine name, such as in liturgical intentions (*kavvanot*), gradually weakened.[39] There is a linguistic component in

---

of the soul and searching for experiences obtained through anomian practices, see Moshe Idel, *The Mystical Experience in Abraham Abulafia* (Jerusalem: Magnes Press, 2002), 186–187. For an objection to this distinction and a bold binding of the nomian halakha with personal experience and mysticism, see Garb, *Shamanic Trance*, 136–139. Also, see Elliot R. Wolfson, *Venturing Beyond: Law and Morality in Kabbalistic Mysticism* (Oxford: Oxford University Press, 2006), 186–285, reagarding his proposal of the hypernomian category, which transcends the distinctions of nomian, anomian, and antinomian. Also, idem, *Abraham Abulafia—Kabbalist and Prophet: Hermeneutics, Theosophy, and Theurgy* (Los Angeles: Cherub Press, 2000), subchapter, "Hypernomianism and the Prophetic Kabbalah."

38 Garb, *The Chosen Will Become Herds*, 78–83, 118–119. I have adopted Garb's claim that it is necessary to discern this phenomenon in a global context, and that there are modern and postmodern influences on kabbalah and hasidism, as will be discussed in the end of the book.

39 See the guidance of Kalonymus Kalman Epstein, *Ma'or ve-Shemesh* (Breslau: s.n., 1842), "Parashat Neṣavim," s.v., "ki," that one should not deal with "intentions" (*kavvanot*), meaning combinations of the holy names, *gematria*, and more, "In our time one should not practice the liturgical intentions passed down to us in R. Isaac Luria's prayer book, whether [recited] from a written text or studied to be recited from memory , and so I heard from R. Elimelekh Weisblum [of Lyzhansk] that one should not contemplate thoughts and calculations of the intentions of the [divine] names, but should rather connect his revealed [aspect] and his concealed [aspect], which are his *nefesh*, *ru'aḥ*, and *neshamah* (three lower aspects of the human soul) in the Infinite, blessed be he, and through this he connects all of the revealed worlds and internal worlds in him, may He be blessed. And his thought will be so cleaved to God's pleasantness that he will not have free time, even a moment to perform intentions. And for who prays in this manner, the intentions and the unifications are effected on their own through his prayer." Also see ibid., "Parashat Eqev," s.v., "hen," "Indeed the matter is that there are many people who pray with the intentions of the names, however in these generations we do not need this." Also see there a more detailed explanation as to why they are not dependent on intentions. It should be noted that Epstein was the great grandfather of Kalonymous Kalman Shapira, whom I will discuss at length, and that the latter was named after the former. As a testimony to the direct influence of these words on Shapira, they were quoted by him in his book *Mevo ha-She'arim*,

hasidic literature, which we will discuss. However, it is largely theoretical and theological, used for the purpose of homilies and commentaries. Instruction in divine names and combining letters techniques significantly weakened, including the visualization of letters and their combinations; while in contrast, the practice of visualizing multi-scenic storylines rose.[40] In the hasidic literature that I will review in this work, unlike kabbalistic literature, imagery-linguistic practices are reduced to solely visualizing the tetragrammaton and the basic unification of the divine names of YHWH (tetragrammaton) and ADNH (lord, the customary pronunciation of YHWH), and no more. In contrast, in the twentieth century the free-style dramatic imagery techniques reach an unprecedented height: an imaginary "cinematic film" in a waking-dream, and sometimes the plot is no less detailed and complex than a modern screenplay.[41]

23a. On the decline of Lurianic intentions in hasidic prayer from its inception see Rivka Schatz Uffenheimer, *Hasidism as Mysticism: Quietistic Elements in Eighteeth-Century Hasidic Thought*, trans. Jonathan Chipman (Princeton: Princeton University Press, 1993), 215–241; on the abandonment of kabbalistic intentions in hasidism and their being exchanged with *devequt* see Louis Jacobs, "The Uplifting of Sparks in Later Jewish Mysticism," in *Jewish Spirituality: From the Sixteenth-Century Revival to the Present*, ed. A. Green (New York: Crossroad, 1987), 122–123; Also see Idel, *Hasidism*, 149–152, also, see ibid., 334 n. 19, many early hasidic sources attesting to the distancing from Lurianic intentions, and intentions in general, in different ways. For more on the weakening of intentions in the twentieth century, in oral traditions of Bratslav hasidism it is told that R. Gedaliah Aharon Koenig (1921–1980) prayed with a group of kabbalists, who prayed the eighteen benedictions for a very long time due to the many intentions. When they asked him if he prays with "intentions," he answered, "No! I do not pray with "intentions," (*kavvanot*) I try to pray with intention (*kavvanah*)." His students stated that he would lengthen his prayer to fit the pace of the kabbalists' prayer, but without kabbalistic intentions. It is of no consequence whether this story is authentic or not, the attitude towards Lurianic intentions and the message are in any case clear.

40 I have collected tens of imagery exercises from hasidic literature of the nineteenth and twentieth centuries. This is not the place to enumerate them, also see below some of them in section II, additionally see Meir Bernstein of Radom, *Sefer Orakḥ Mishor* (Warsaw, 1900), 18; R. Joseph David Rubin son of the Grand Rabbi Eliezer of Sasów, *Atzei HaLevanon* (s.l.: s.n., 1899), 26, 222; R. Benjamin Friedman of Miszkolc (murdered in the Holocaust), *Tif'eret Avot* (Tel Aviv: 1966), 92; R. Elijah of Wiskitki, *Ezor Eliyahu* (Warsaw, 1885), 116; Barukh Kasber (b. Abraham), *Na'im ve-Neḥmad: Yesod ha-Emunah* (Józefów, 1884), 164. It may be said that there is also a development within this technique: from imagining a short scenario to a complete multi-scenic storyline. In the nineteenth century, one finds brief imagery exercises comprised of one scenario while in the twentieth century they develop into scripts of multiple scenes. Also see below chap. 4, subchapter "R. Kalonymous Kalman Shapira's Imagery Techniques and His Imaginal-Literary Style."

41 For example, see in Shapira's book, *Hakhsharat ha-Avrekhim*, that all of chap. 7 is dedicated to the imagery exercise of the exodus. Likewise, the majority of chap. 8 is the visualization of the day of one's death. It is of interest to note that specifically Aryeh Kaplan was wary of free-story visualization and preferred to return and focus on static linguistic-imagery, "In deeper forms of

Kabbalistic and hasidic literature until the nineteenth century, as has been studied, indeed has a special place for imagery techniques. However, generally speaking, it focuses on a vision of letters or a static object: a letter, number of letters, combinations of divine names, light, fire, and so forth.[42] This is correct, whether the image is a product of inspiration or human initiative. To my knowledge, it is only in twentieth century hasidic literature that we find, for the first time, imagery exercises that are in essence waking-dreams. The guidee seeks to visualize an entire plot, lengthy and complex, almost without the use of words or text.[43]

These later imagery techniques which developed at the end of the nineteenth century and primarily in the twentieth, although anomian, possess a clear religious character and their purpose is the intensification of religious worship: stimulating an emotional "worry" in order to experience absolute dependence upon God; subduing one's evil inclination; assisting the recognition of the essential, "uniquely-Jewish" value; a means to improve one's character traits

meditation, one often sees visions. As I discussed earlier, these visions should not be taken too seriously... Some sources recommend that visions, when they occur, should be banished from the mind and replaced with the Tetragrammaton." Aryeh Kaplan, *Jewish Meditation: A Practical Guide* (New York: Schocken Books, 1995), 82. Also, ibid., 77–82 is dedicated solely to the visualization of letters.

42 Regarding light see Idel, *Mystical Experience*, 77–83; idem, *Enchanted Chains*, 125–133; for more on light and fire see Garb, *Manifestations of Power*, 170; idem, *Shamanic Trance*, 29, 36–38, 45, 82–89. For the intensive engagement with letters in kabbalistic literature understood through Elliot Wolfson's work, discussed within the kabbalistic conception of the Torah as a hyper-text and the letters as the foundation and representation of being, see Elliot R. Wolfson. "The Body in the Text: Kabbalistic Theory of Embodiment," *JQR* 95 (2005): 485–486: "In the Jewish context, the metaphor is not to be understood metaphorically but hyperliterally, that is, Torah, the prototype of all books, the hyper-text, if you will , informs us about the semantic character of nature; alternatively expressed, Torah was thought to impart cosmological and anthropological knowledge because the substance of the world and the human self consists of the letters that constitute the building blocks of the revealed word. Medieval kabbalistic authors understood the rabbinic idealization of Torah in this manner, and there is at least enough ambiguity in dicta attributed to rabbis of the early period to entertain seriously the possibility that kabbalistic sources open a way to ascertain older forms of a mystical specularity predicated on viewing the book as a speculum of nature and nature as a speculum of the book."

43 Also in the nineteenth century one may find non-linguistic imagery exercises which are also story-like, but they are much shorter and are incomparable to the imagery exercises of the twentieth century, which are rich in story and imagery. Also see below chap. 4. On the concept of a "waking-dream" see Wolfson, *A Dream Interpreted Within a Dream*, 187. Wolfson demonstrates that the imagination acts like a dream, and therefore one may treat it as a waking-dream. Similar to a dream, the imagination is able to coalesce logical contradictions, it is possible to dream of a squared circle, and the like.

(*avodat middot*); preparation to attain a state of equanimity (*hishtavvut*); arouse repentance; means to achieve a state of *devequt* (communion/union); to enliven and reenergize one's service of God; and as a part of one's study. These are a few examples, and in the main portion of this study we will demonstrate and examine more and in greater detail.

Lastly, it must be noted that the development of imagery techniques, which reached the point of lengthy, imageristically rich, and multi-scenic plots, has a clear European cultural context. This development of imagery techniques in the Jewish world parallels the evolution of a number of spiritual and psychiatric doctrines in Europe. I will mention several of them now, and a larger discussion will take place in section four. The centrality of the visual-imaginal component appears together and in parallel to spiritual movements that began to rise at the end of the nineteenth century, like the theosophic and anthroposophic movements, which are full of imagery exercises; medicinal-psychological methods which developed in Western Europe like hypnosis, and its roots in mesmerism; relaxation therapies like autogenic training, a method developed by the German psychiatrist Johannes Heinrich Schultz (1884–1970) which was first publicized in 1932;[44] the entry of Sufism into Europe, through the influence of academic studies, for example the research of the French philosopher and Islam scholar Henry Corbin (1903–1978) who saw in Sufism a "creative imagination." This concept was developed in his research and is largely elucidated in his book *Creative Imagination in the Sūfism of Ibn ʿArabī*;[45] furthermore, due to colonialism, the

44 This technique generally involved three daily imagery exercises, including states of calm and relaxation.

45 Corbin introduced the term *imaginaire* to the modern discourse of the second half of the twentieth century. He studied religion and mysticism from within this concept of *imaginaire*, viewing the human imagination as a system possessing internal rules which must be revealed. This conception, which already began to be influentual in the forties, caused a philosophical shift in France and the entire world. This trend utilized Corbin's teachings not only for understanding religion, but also in a variety of academic disciplines, like literature and history. Corbin also wrote about the *mundus imaginalis* or imaginal world that appeared in Sufi teachings as an intermediary between the material and spiritual realms, see Henry Corbin, "*Mundus Imaginalis*, or the Imaginary and the Imaginal," in *Swedenborg and Esoteric Islam*, trans. L. Fox (West Chester: Swedenborg Foundation, 1995), 1–33 (for parallels between the *mundus imaginalis* in sufism and kabbalah see Idel, *Studies in Ecstatic Kabbalah*, 73–89, as well as Elliot Wolfson's extensive use of this concept in *Through a Speculum that Shines* as well as his subsequent work). Although Corbin's influence was primarily in the second half of the twentieth century and our study focuses on the first half, Sufism had made inroads into Europe before Corbin, and his research is a result of that, also see below chap. 9.

East also came to the West, and with it Eastern techniques.[46] Lastly, romantic philosophical concepts, like the "creative imagination," appeared in Hebrew literature and in translated studies of the first half of the twentieth century, for example the French psychologist Théodule Armand Ribot's (1839 – 1916) *Essay on the Creative Imagination*.[47] These translations into Hebrew were able to have a direct influence on Jewish thought and create a fertile environment between general European developments and particular Jewish developments.[48]

This information, upon which I will expand in the fourth section of this book, is important in order to understand that the development of imagery techniques in the later hasidic movement of the late nineteenth and twentieth centuries, as well as in the Musar movement, did not occur in a vacuum, and that this development may be identified as part of a more encompassing and universal structure.

The bulk of the book deals with imagery techniques as means of "empowerment" and "prophecy," and in the second section I expand on these two terms and their influence on the format of imagery techniques. This research, which focuses on praxis, will hopefully contribute to a greater understanding of central issues in the field of twentieth century Jewish mysticism.

---

46 This access contributed to the study of religion, specifically the research of Mircea Eliade, who already in the late twenties and early thirties visited India and experimented with mystical techniques, which were presented in Europe not only as objects of academic study, but also with the distinct purpose of significantly disseminating their influence.

47 Published in New York-Warsaw-Moscow in 1921. The original, *Essai Sur l'imagination Créatrice*, was published in 1900.

48 It should also be noted that many hasidic leaders spoke and read the European languages of their home country. For example, see below chap. 6 on Menaḥem Ekstein and his family.

Section I: **Imaginative Models**

Chapter One
Models of Imagination

Contemporary thinkers have noted the philosophical transformation of the imagination that occurred between classic and medieval philosophy and modern philosophy in the Western tradition. As Richard Kearney has stated:

> There is of course a fundamental difference between the image of today and the former times: now the image precedes the reality it is supposed to represent. Or to put it in another way, reality has become a plane reflection of the image.... The real and the imaginary have become almost impossible to distinguish.[1]

I shall depict different models of imagination in Western philosophy as they have been primarily presented by Kearney and Meyer Abrams.[2] These models will mostly allow us to understand what lies at the foundation of different imagery techniques that I will introduce throughout this book, and will assist us in distinguishing between them.[3] Additionally, through the utilization of these differ-

---

1 Richard Kearney, *The Wake of Imagination: Toward a Postmodern Culture* (Minneapolis: University of Minnesota Press, 1988), 2.

2 Meyer Howard Abrams, *The Mirror and the Lamp: Romantic Theory and the Critical Tradition* (New York: Oxford University Press, 1953).

3 A clarification: the development which occurred in Western philosophy was that of one elite among many. A specific European elite which may be insignificant for other European elites, even more so for Eastern groups like Hindus, Indians, and Chinese who were not heavily influenced by Western philosophical trends in any case. Therefore, I am not arguing for the application of processes from a particular culture on another. Kearney's and Abrams's work tend to present each era as a paradigm, however their work cannot be fully applied to mystics and religious figures who had an intimate connection to their traditions. It is incorrect to limit these figures to meta-processes of which they were unaware (if in fact they were not). Nonetheless, it is important to present these processes, for there are certain patterns of thought which occur parallelly in different places at the same time, a type of global mindset (as I will discuss below). Likewise, I will not reject possible influences, especially when they are demonstrable and feasible. As a rule, I am uninterested in forcing models developed in Western philosophy on Jewish mystics, especially when the mystic generally did not know this philosophy or the models presented by it. I will adopt Johann Gottfried Herder's critique of the Enlightenment, in which people believe that reality is determined according to eternal rules and principles. In contrast, Herder argued that "each sphere has its own center of gravity" (*Auch 509*), each culture has its own character and therefore it is impossible to compare different historical and cultural phenomena according to uniform principles, in contrast to the natural sciences (see Samuel Hugo Bergman, *A History of Modern Philosophy from the Enlightenment to Kant* (Jerusalem: Mosad Bialik, 1978), 57–58). At the same time, it is clear to me that comparison

https://doi.org/10.1515/9783110535884-004

ent models I will clarify and categorize the different developments in relation to the imagination and thus attempt to provide an answer to the question of why these imagery techniques developed precisely in the twentieth century. Presently, I will briefly outline different models of imagination that developed in Western philosophy, from the Hellenistic period until the twentieth century; afterwards, I will concentrate on the conceptions of imagination embraced by a number of Jewish thinkers in light of these models.

A Models of Imagination in Western Philosophy

Imagination in Hellenistic conceptions was never understood as an internal process of subjective autonomous forces within man. The imagination was always considered in relation to something external: man's relation to cosmic potencies or to a sublime celestial power of the imagination itself. Imagination is an aliorelative concept, which acts through the imitation of external matters.[4] This understanding is founded upon Plato's theorization of the imagination. Plato viewed the imagination as possessing a mimetic function, which binds man to a lower order of existence and also separates him from supernal reality. In his opinion, the utilization of the imagination leads man upon an erroneous path, since the imagination is merely an imitation of material existence, which is itself only an imitation of the world of Forms, of true being, and thereby it is an imitation of an imitation.[5] Another negative attitude towards the imagination in Plato's thought is linked to the Greek preference of the universal over the particular, and politics over art. The creations of the imagination are deemed unproductive and are therefore rejected, for they do not contribute in a practical man-

is quite important for the understanding of different religious and spiritual phenomena; concerning this importance see Joseph Dan, "Research in Jewish Mysticism and Corresponding Phenomena in Other Religions," in *Studies in Judaica: Collected Papers of the Symposium in Honour of the Sixtieth Anniversary of the Institute of Jewish Studies*, ed. Moshe Bar-Asher (Jerusalem: Hebrew University of Jerusalem, 1986), 137–143; Idel, *Kabbalah: New Perspectives*, 41–42. Comparative methodology is also interested in difference, the decisive differences which establish the special quality of each elite, without forcing one's cultural processes on the other. It is worthwhile to quote Elliot Wolfson on the matter, "Consistent with all my work, in this study I delve deeply into one tradition out of the conviction that the particular is indexical of what we are still compelled to call the universal… My upholding of the universal is certainly not meant to efface the particular; indeed, the universal I envision is one continuously shaped by the particular, the *universal singularity*" (idem, *Giving Beyond the Gift*, xiii).

4 Kearney, *The Wake of Imagination*, 88.

5 Abrams, *The Mirror and the Lamp*, 8.

ner to the functioning of the polis or serve the public.[6] The artist's imagination imitates God's creation by turning a mirror towards the surrounding world, "If you should choose to take a mirror and carry it about everywhere. You will speedily produce the sun and all the things in the sky, and speedily the earth and yourself and the other animals and implements and plants."[7] This metaphorical use of a "mirror" to characterize the imaginative function would become a standard motif in the classic aesthetic doctrines and will serve us as well in this book as a model of conceiving the imagination in classic and modern Western philosophy.

In contrast to Plato's disposition to present the imagination as a mimetic act of exterior reality, Aristotle tends to focus on the psychological status of the image as a mental representation. According to Aristotle the imagination constitutes an intermediary stage which mediates between sensorial and rational experience, "The thinking faculty thinks the forms in mental images... for mental images are similar to objects perceived except that they are without matter."[8] As Yohanan Gliker wrote regarding Aristotle's philosophy, "When a man contemplates he must do so through certain images. Thus, there is no thinking in pure, imageless, concepts, since the concepts exist in actual reality, which is grasped through senses (and not in the world of ideas)."[9]

In *On Memory and Recollection*, Aristotle emphasizes that in order to think of theoretical mathematical concepts, like "magnitude," man must imagine something with magnitude:

> It is impossible even to think without a mental picture. The same affection is involved in thinking as in drawing a diagram; for in this case although we make no use of the fact that the magnitude of a triangle is a finite quantity, yet we draw it as having a finite magnitude. In the same way the man who is thinking, though he may not be thinking of a finite magnitude, still puts a finite magnitude before his eyes, though he does not think of it as

---

6 Kearney, *The Wake of Imagination*, 93.

7 Plato, *The Republic*, 10.596.4§§423 (Shorey LCL).

8 Aristotle, *De an.*, 7.431.a-8.431b§§177–181 (Hett LCL). Regarding the intermediary nature of the imagination in Aristotle's thought see Kearney, *The Wake of Imagination*, 106–108. There is a disagreement among scholars concerning Aristotle's "images." One side argues that they are pictorial depictions, whereas the other side claims that it is only an appearance without any type of analogous image. See Richard Sorabji, *Aristotle on Memory* (Chicago: University of Chicago Press, 2006), xi-xix. Sorabji himself maintains that the Aristotelean image in this context is pictorial in every sense. Also, see ibid., his distinction between *phantasia* and *phantasma*, in which the former is appearance and the latter is an "image like a picture."

9 Yohanan Gliker, "Imagination in Aristotle's Soul Doctrine" (PhD diss., Hebrew University, 1948), 9.

> such. And even if the nature of the object is quantitative, but indeterminate, he still puts before him a finite magnitude, although he thinks of it as merely quantitative.[10]

Ultimately, in Aristotle's opinion as well, the imagination serves as an imitation of the original and not the original item itself. While according to Plato it is an imitation of an imitation and therefore has illusionary elements; according to Aristotle the imitation is more faithful, for it constitutes a precondition for rationality. Whether like the former or the latter, the imagination remains an action of reproduction rather than original creation, a servant rather than a master, imitation and not invention.[11]

Kant's Copernican revolution in philosophy brought about a turning point regarding the imagination as well. The mimetic paradigm of the imagination was exchanged with an inventive paradigm—the *creative imagination.* According to Kant, reality is not able to be known ontologically, but only epistemologically. Therefore, the imagination is not an imitation of the original, since the original in itself cannot be known. Indeed, the imagination is not a reproduction of reality; rather it is an original production of human consciousness! In other words, the imagination, according to Kant, acts as the main component in human consciousness. Following Kant, and the German Idealism of the late eighteenth and early nineteenth century, the creative imagination was officially recognized in mainstream Western philosophy.[12] Henceforth in modern philosophy a new path has been paved, in which the imagination is understood as an autonomous human potency which creates a world of values and genuine truths.[13]

This Copernican revolution also influenced the conception of art in general and poetry in particular, as expressed by the poet William Yeats (1865–1939), "It must go further still: that soul must become its own betrayer, its own deliverer, the one activity, the mirror turn lamp."[14] While in the pre-Kantian paradigm, the imagination was presented through the metaphor of a "mirror," thus constituting an imitation and copy of true external existence—the Kantian paradigm's metaphor is that of a "lamp," a creator and disseminator of inner light towards the exterior, a creator of existence.[15]

10 Aristotle, *Mem. rem.*, 1.449b-450a§§291 (Hett LCL).

11 Kearney, *The Wake of Imagination*, 112–113.

12 Ibid., 156.

13 Ibid.

14 Abrams, *The Mirror and the Lamp*, quoted on the inner cover flap.

15 This metaphor was first expressed by the English romantic literary critic and philosopher William Hazlitt (1778–1830), see Abrams, *The Mirror and the Lamp*, 52. Also see ibid., 58–60, concerning this conception's pre-Kantian roots in English poetics of the seventeenth century

German Idealism (Fichte and Schelling) and Romanticism advanced further. Johann Gottlieb Fichte (1762–1814) claimed that all of reality is formed only and solely through the imagination.[16] In fact all objects are representations, or in Fichte's words—images (*bilder*).[17] Kant claimed that we cannot know nature in and of itself, but rather only through images, whereas Fichte pushes the envelope further—nature itself is fashioned through the imagination. In Friedrich Wilhelm Joseph Schelling's (1775–1854) thought this claim is intensified. He maintains that the external object is nothing other than a product of the creative imagination. Through imaginal contemplation actual reality is produced. There is no world unless the spirit (*geist*) knows it.[18]

The theme of the creative imagination of German Idealism was warmly accepted and adopted by the Romantics. The absolute power that was given to the imagination, human freedom, liberty, and the like was apposite to the aspirations and perspectives of Romanticism.[19]

Postmodern philosophy conceived the imagination in a different manner than what has been presented so far and offered a third model. While classic philosophy saw the imagination as an imitation of the *original* and modern philosophy saw it as the creator of the *original*, postmodern philosophy denies the entire idea of *originality.* The "textual revolution" of postmodernism heralded the deconstruction of the category of *original.* "Language" is already not understood as relating to "true" external meaning, rather as an infinitely open process of meanings.[20]

This understanding of imitation lacking the original reached its sharpest formulation in Jacques Derrida's (1930–2000) thought. Through deconstructionist thought Derrida refutes the dichotomy between imagination and originality (truth), existent from Plato until Sartre, whether truth is external (as in the

---

and even in Hobbs's and Locke's philosophy; however it did not become a full fleshed out philosophical theory until Kant.

16 Samuel Hugo Bergman, *A History of Philosophy: Jacobi, Fichte, Schelling* (Jerusalem: Bialik Institute, 1984), 52–53; Wolfson, *Giving Beyond the Gift*, 2–3, quotes Fichte statement, "All reality... is brought forth solely by imagination... this act of imagination forms the basis for the possibility of our consciousness, our life, our existence for ourselves, that is, our existence as selves."

17 Bergman, *Jacobi, Fichte, Schelling*, 53; Frederick Charles Copleston, *History of Philosophy*, vol. 7, *Fichte to Nietzsche* (Mahwah: Paulist Press, 1963), 83–84.

18 Kearney, *The Wake of Imagination*, 110–111.

19 Ibid., 181–185. Also see ibid., 196–229 concerning the development of the conception of the imagination in the nineteenth and twentieth century (Nietzsche, Kierkegaard, Heidegger, and Sartre).

20 Ibid., 252–253.

Greek conception that places reality before the imagination, in which reality is the original and the imagination is the imitation) or internal (as in the Romantic conception imagination is placed before reality, in which reality is a product of the imagination). Ultimately, Western metaphysics constantly preferred truth over the imaginative. This preference is based on the presumption that there is something true and original. Derrida's deconstructionism, which neutralizes the term *original*, in fact neutralizes the mimetic and imitative as well.

The image, according to Derrida, is a type of writing which does not imagine something preceding it. This is a writing that composes a parody of itself. In actuality, there is neither imagination, nor an imaginer. It is no longer possible to ask, "what is imagination?" for the question is constructed through the presupposition that there is something differentiating the true world from the imagined. In Derrida's opinion, the distinction between imagination and existence (truth, original) dissolves within the mimetic textual process. The world becomes text without a beginning and without end, in which everything is reflected in the text. Just like the text has no author, so too there is no imaginer.[21]

> There is no imitation. The Mime imitates nothing. And to begin with, he doesn't imitate. There is nothing prior to the writing of his gestures. Nothing is prescribed for him. No present has preceded or supervised the tracing of his writing. His movements form a figure that no speech anticipates or accompanies. They are not linked with logos in any order of consequence.... We here enter a textual labyrinth panelled with mirrors.[22]

Hence, three primary models regarding the imagination may be found in Western philosophy from the classic until postmodern periods.

1. The "Mirror" Model:
Variations of the Platonic and Aristotelean model, in which the imagination is conceived as serving or imitating the original, and is itself not original. The original is external to the imagination and the imagination's function is to mimic the external original.

2. The "Lamp" Model:

21 Ibid., 285, 290. Also, see Elliot R. Wolfson, "From Sealed Book to Open Text: Time, Memory, and Narrativity in Kabbalistic Hermenutics," in *Interpreting Judaism in a Postmodern Age*, ed. Steven Kepnes (New York: New York University Press, 1996), 145–178, for a discussion of this Derridean hermeneutic and Jewish mysticism, specifically that of Elijah ben Solomon Zalman, the Gaon of Vilna.

22 Jacques Derrida, *Dissemination*, trans. Barbara Johnson (London: The Athlone Press, 1981), 194–195.

This model reflects the conception which views the imagination as a productive one, as man's internal creator of original matter (Romanticism), or in the more modern variation, a form of thinking that does not imitate, but rather originates. This model emphasizes inner originality without appealing to anything external. It is generally referred to as the "creative imagination" or "productive imagination," where the imagination is understood as an autonomous human potency creating a world of values and original truths.

3. The "Mirroring Mirrors" Model:
Following postmodern philosophy's objection to the concepts of *original* and *imitation*, a third model of imagination was presented: a multitude of mirrors mirroring one another in an infinite mirroring, thus widening the infinite infinitely. In this maze of mirrors, the distinction between imagination and reality dissolves, as the categories blend into one another.

B Models of Imagination in Jewish Thought

Unfortunately, there is not sufficient space to explore the subject of the imagination in Jewish thought throughout its history, a subject that could fill several volumes. I will briefly elucidate the conception of the imagination of three thinkers: R. Judah Halevi, Maimonides, and R. Naḥman of Bratslav, before I begin discussing the imagery techniques found in hasidism. Here I will reiterate that it is impossible to fully apply the Western philosophical models of imagination to religious culture in all its varieties. For instance, the "mirror" model is not entirely applicable for religious reality where frequently the *image* precedes existence,[23] for no one saw an angel and afterwards imagined them in a mimetic fashion. The imagination does not serve, in most cases, as an imitation of external reality in religious life, rather it is prior to reality, similar to the "lamp" model found in modern philosophy. Kabbalists have a certain image of day and a certain image of night, images that produce practices and techniques, so that the image is anterior to the practice, and not the reverse.[24] This fundamental matter is a cornerstone of religious experience, found in every historical period and traversing all cultural, religious, and ethnic borders. The model of the creative imagination found in religious and mystical thought greatly precedes its appear-

---

23 See Elimelekh Weisblum of Lizhensk, *No'am Elimelekh*, "*Ki Teṣe*": "For in the imagination it is possible to depict even something that he has never seen."
24 See Idel, *Nocturnal Kabbalists*, 1–9, 45–74, 95–109.

ance in Western philosophy. It is already prevalent in the thought of the Sufi mystic Ibn ʿArabī of the thirteenth century,[25] as well as in Jewish philosophical and kabbalistic thought as we will see below. Furthermore, in many kabbalistic and hasidic texts, it is not easy to identify the conception of imagination with one of the aforementioned models, for example the Beshṭ's (R. Israel b. Eliezer) parable of the palace, in which he presents *aḥizat einayim* (a state of delusion or illusion; lit. a holding of the eyes), or in other word–the imagination:

> I heard from my teacher, may his memory be for the world to come, a parable which he said before the blowing of the shofar, that there was a wise and great king, who through an illusion (aḥizat einayim) [erected] walls, towers, and gates, and commanded that [people] shall come to him through the gates and towers, and he commanded to disperse at every gate treasures of the king, and there are those who walked until the first gate and took the money and returned [from whence they came], and there are those etc.... until his beloved son greatly exerted [himself] to go to his father the king, then he saw there is no barrier separating him and his father, for all was an illusion (aḥizat einayim).[26]

In truth "there is no barrier separating him and his father," all the walls, towers, and gates were only imagined. If we analyze this conception of imagination well, we will see that it is difficult to correlate it with the Western philosophical models. There is no mimetic activity of external reality, for the parable insists that the external reality is illusory, for the primary conclusion of this conception is that "there is no barrier separating man from God."[27] In other words, the external reality is itself imagined, and therefore here the imagination is not an imitation of something original. Likewise, this imagination is not completely identifiable

---

25 See, Henry Corbin, *Creative Imagination in the Sufism of Ibn 'Arabi*, trans. R. Manheim (Princeton: Princeton University Press, 1969); idem, "Mundus Imaginalis: or the Imaginary and the Imaginal," trans. R. Horine, *Spring Journal* (1972): 1–13 (A different translation may be found in idem, *Swedenborg and Esoteric Islam*, trans. L. Fox [West Chester: Swedenborg Foundation, 1995], 1–33).

26 See Jacob Joseph ben Ẓevi Ha-Kohen Katz of Polonnoye, *Ben Porat Yosef*, 70c. Also, see a similar formulation in *Keter Shem Ṭov* (Lemberg: s.n., 1851), 7b. Concerning this parable see Netanel Lederberg, *Sod HaDa'at: Rabbi Israel Ba'al Shem Tov, His Spiritual Character and Social Leadership* (Jerusalem: Rubin Mass, 2007), 32–34, also, ibid., 219–220 n. 36 for the bibliographic note on this parable. Also, see Moshe Idel, "The Parable of the Son of the King and the Imaginary Walls in Early Hasidism," in *Judaism: Topics, Fragments, Faces, Identities: Jubilee Volume in Honor of Rivka Horwitz*, eds. H. Pedaya and E. Meir (Beer Sheva: Ben Gurion University of the Negev Press, 2007), 87–116; idem, "Prayer, Ecstasy, and 'Alien Thoughts' in the Religious Experience of the Besht," in *Let the Old Make Way for the New: Studies in the Social and Cultural History of Eastern European Jewry*, eds. D. Assaf and A. Rapoport-Alpert (Jerusalem: Zalman Shazar Center, 2009), 102–103.

27 *Keter Shem Tov* (Lemberg: s.n., 1851), 7b.

with the "lamp" model. Indeed, in this parable there appears the motif of the "creative imagination," for the imagination is what forms and creates the screens, the separation barriers between man and God. Nevertheless, despite its proximity to the "lamp" model, it is not identical, since it is unclear if the imagined reality in this parable has an ontological status.[28] This parable is characterized by a different view of imagination inconsistent with the Western philosophical models. Here there is a configuration of imagination in which there are certain mimetic features and creative features, a type of admixture of what we have presented thus far together with certain unique aspects which do not characterize the Western philosophical elite. In addition, this parable reflects a common phenomenon in kabbalistic and hasidic thought and practice, in which the border between the imagination and reality is blurred. In the aforementioned parable it is unclear what is imaginal and what is real, is the son seeking his father also an illusion or does he have a separate and distinct existence from God. Does the Beshṭ, like Kant, presume that the self, which conceives of the object, exists itself? Can the "transcendental unity of apperception" be found in the Beshtian tradition? Or perhaps the imagining self is itself illusionary and the acosmism is absolute, and if so, is this acosmism ontological or epistemological? A final answer does not exist. In this case, the question is more important than the answer, for the question highlights the very blurred boundaries between the real and imaginal, a feature found only in postmodern philosophy.[29]

In summary, in Jewish thought and mysticism (as well as in other religions and different cultural elites, Eastern and Western, which developed, parallel to Western philosophy, independent discourses and terminology) we may encounter alternative conceptions of imagination. There are and will be correlative points between them and Western philosophical variations, and there will be configurations which will be incompatible with the Western models and categories, where we must present a different model, if that is at all possible.

28 See the scholarly disagreement on this topic between, on one side, Rivka Schatz-Uffenheimer and Rachel Elior and on the other side, Yoram Jacobson, Jacobson, "The Rectification of the Heart: Studies in the Psychic Teachings of R. Shneur Zalman of Liadi," *Teudah* 10 (1996): 359–363, specifically, n. 4.

29 See Kearney, *The Wake of the Imagination*, 2, regarding the postmodern condition, "The real and the imaginary have become almost impossible to distinguish."

R. Judah Halevi

According to Halevi, since man is a material creature, meaning he is formed out of matter, his epistemological knowledge always relies on his sensory awareness and is not entirely based on his intellect, like the non-material angels.[30] Man is dependent upon his senses (including the imaginative sense, which is the prophetic sense), as utilities for his intellect. His intellect interprets that which his senses perceive, and without the intellect the senses may err and stumble:

> The senses detect in the objects which are perceived only their accidents, not their essence. They detect in the king, for example, only his appearance, form, and proportions. This, however, is not the essence of the king, whom you acknowledge and exalt.[31]
>
> For there is no disagreement between my optic view and your optic view, for the flat disc, which illuminates and warms, is the sun. And even though these qualities (*alṣfa'at*) are distant from the intellect, the knowledge [gained by the senses] will not harm it, rather it will be beneficial, since we take from them a proof for what we desire. For an intelligent clear-sighted person who searched for his camel may benefit from a person with blurred vision who sees two [instead of] one: [when he states] "I see in some place two *girniq*,"[32] and the clear-eyed person knows that he [in fact] saw the camel, and in his poor vision it appeared to him as a *gir* and due to his poor vision, it appears to him as two, and the clear-eyed person benefits from his testimony, and judges him favorably regarding his bad advice due to his bad vision, and so it is for the intellect regarding the senses and the imaginative faculty.[33]

Halevi demonstrates his conception through two parables, that of the king and that of the sun. In both cases man only grasps the external aspects (the king's garments; the two-dimensional area of the sun) and the intellect arrives at the truth (the king himself; the three-dimensional volume of the sun). That is to say, the inexact facts gathered by the senses are interpreted by the intellect in order to attain real knowledge, and the senses are reliable only to the extent that they act under the critical auspices of the intellect.[34] This relation between the external senses and the intellect also exists, according to Halevi, in regards to prophetic vision, "The prophets contemplate the incorporeal divine world

30 Warren Zev Harvey, "Judah Halevi's Synthetic Theory of Prophecy and a Note on the Zohar," *Jerusalem Studies in Jewish Thought* 13 (1996): 142.
31 Judah Halevi, *Sefer ha-Kuzari*, ed. A. Tzifroni (Tel Aviv: Mahbarot Lesifrut,1989), IV:3§§225. Translation from Howard Kreisel, "Halevi' s Influence on Maimonides: A Preliminary Appraisal," *Maimonidean Studies* 2 (1991): 108.
32 Type of bird.
33 Halevi, *Sefer ha-Kuzari*, 227–228.
34 Harvey, "Judah Halevi's Synthetic Theory of Prophecy," 143.

through the inner eye (which is similar to the imaginative faculty), but they do not see the incorporeal entities in their essence, rather they see them as material forms, suitable to their mortal material nature and they depict the divine world as they saw it (like a corporeal world) and not as it is in its essence (incorporeal world)."[35] Imagination is the prophetic sense, which is a higher attainment than philosophical truth. "One for whom this [inner] eye has been created is a clear-sighted person in truth":[36]

> Just as the creator established with precision this relation between the external sense and the corporeal entity that is perceived, so he established with precision the relation between the internal sense and the incorporeal entity. Upon the noblest of his creatures God bestowed an "inner eye" that sees all things in their unchanging reality. The intellect learns by means of it the essence of these things. One who was created with this "eye" is the one who has true vision. He sees the whole of humanity as blind, and directs and guides them. This "eye" is possibly the imaginative faculty when it serves the intellectual faculty. It sees great, awesome forms that teach unmistakable truths. The best proof of their truth is that this entire species agrees upon these forms—that is, all of the prophets witness things that affirm one another, just as we do with our sensory objects. We affirm the sweetness of honey and bitterness of colocynth. If one contradicts us we say that he deviates from what is natural. They [the prophets] without doubt saw the divine world with an "inner eye." They saw forms that were appropriate to their nature and to which they were accustomed. They described in corporeal terms what they saw. These descriptions are true in regard to what estimation, imagination, and the senses grasp, but they are not true regarding the essence that the intellect grasps.[37] As we saw regarding the image of the king. For one who states that he is tall, clothed in white silk, has a crown on his head and the like, is not lying, and one who states that he is none other than the intelligent [person], the knower, who commands and prohibits in some land at some time over some people, is also not lying. And when the prophet sees with his "inner eye" the perfect form of forms, he saw it in the image of a king or a judge sitting on his seat of judgment, in the matter of commanding and prohibiting, establishing, and removing [people of the court], he knows that this is a suitable form for a king who is served and obeyed. And if he sees a figure carrying instruments [of war] or writing instruments, or girdled to work, he knows that it is a form suitable for an obedient servant.[38]

---

35 Ibid., 144. Also see idem, "Three Theories of the Imagination in 12th-Century Jewish Philosophy," in *Intellect et Imagination dans la Philosophie Médiévale*, eds. M.C. Pacheco and J. F. Meirinhos (Turnhout: Brepols Publishers, 2002), 292–293.
36 Translation from Diana Lobel, *Between Mysticism and Philosophy: Sufi Language of Religious Experience in Judah Ha-Levi's Kuzari* (Albany: State University of New York Press, 2000), 113. Also see her discussion of prophecy and the inner eye, ibid., 103–145, spec. 108–111.
37 Translation from Howard Kreisel, *Prophecy: The History of an Idea in Medieval Jewish Philosophy* (Dordrecht: Kluwer Academic Publishers, 2001), 127. Also, for his discussion of Halevi's conception of prophecy from this section of the *Kuzari*, see ibid., 125–135.
38 Halevi, *Sefer ha-Kuzari*, 227–229.

In contrast to Maimonides, as we will see below, according to Halevi the prophet sees through the imagination an ontic entity, "They [the prophets] without doubt saw the divine world... They described in corporeal terms what they saw." The imagination is a vision of real entities, but is a prophetic vision. In other words, these entities are controlled by the intellect which ascertains the meaning behind them; nonetheless, these entities are ontic, as sensory entities are ontic, and are inspected by the supervising intellect.

The inner eye is the ability to directly see the divine realm. Halevi identifies the inner eye with the internal sense in general and the imaginative faculty in particular.[39] The prophets corporeally see incorporeal entities and therefore depict them as corporeal. An incorporeal object is grasped through corporeal images. The prophet's visions faithfully depict the divine world, just as the external senses depict the physical world.[40]

Halevi, in contradistinction to neo-Platonic philosophy, does not view the imagination as an imitation of the truth. Meaning, the imaginal ascertainment only reflects the truth in a symbolic fashion. Halevi presents a conception in which the imagination is not a secondary means of ascertainment, but rather is the primary and unique means for understanding. The imagination is the medium for the direct perception of the divine realm. Therefore, the prophet, in Halevi's teachings, is found on a higher level than the philosopher. According to the neo-Platonic theory the philosopher knows God through the intellectual faculty, and is greater than those who conceptualize him through the imagination, whereas according to Halevi the seer possessing the inner eye is found at a higher level.[41] Halevi's conception of prophetic imagination approximates the "lamp" model of "creative imagination," in which the imagination is the sole medium to acquire original truths and insights. It is important to note that Halevi's understanding of prophecy is founded upon Alfarabi's conceptualization of the matter, as shown in previous studies. That is to say, this is not an idiosyncratic view of one person within the development of the imagination in Western philosophy, which only conceived of the imagination in this manner in modernity, but rather

---

39 Regarding internal senses in Islamic philosophy and their influence on Halevi, see Harry Austryn Wolfson, "The Internal Senses in Latin, Arabic, and Hebrew Philosophic Texts," *Harvard Theological Review* 28, no. 2 (1935): 104–106. Regarding the identification of the inner eye with the imagination, see Harvey, "Three Theories of the Imagination in 12th-Century Jewish Philosophy," 292–293. Harvey demonstrates that Halevi produced an original synthesis between the Aristotelean "inner sense" and the Sufi and Islamic "inner eye."

40 Harvey, "Judah Halevi's Synthetic Theory of Prophecy," 146–147.

41 Ibid., 150.

was a commonly held view in a much wider circle, in this case, Islamic philosophy.[42]

Nonetheless, the mimetic conception of the imagination is also rightfully found in Halevi's thought. Halevi does not suffice with the necessity of the imaginative faculty for the prophet and prophecy; rather he wishes to expand the imaginative expanse to all men, "Halevi offers us, those who have not been granted prophecy, a substitute, and it is piety (*ha-ḥasidut*). What is the instrument of the pious one (*ḥasid*)—again the imagination."[43] In order to merit the religious experience of *devequt* (communion), the *ḥasid* recreates sublime religious events, through the imagination, such as the binding of Isaac and the Sinaitic theophany:

> And he commands his willing faculty (*al-quwa al-aradi*) to accept and keep that which will be commanded, and to do it timely... And he commands his imagination to produce the elegant forms that may be found through the aid of [his] memory, to imagine the desired divine aspect (*al-amr al-ilahi*), such as "standing at Mount Sinai," "Abraham's and Isaac's standing at Mount Moriah" [i.e. the binding of Isaac], etc.[44]

The imagination utilized for the recreation of these clearly religious events is of a mimetic nature and is not employed in order to directly perceive the divine world. The imagination grants religious fervor, even to those who have not prophesized, "These visual images give the *ḥasid*['s] (pious person's)... religious world tangibility and color... the imagination straightens out the path for emotions of belief, joy of [fulfilling] commandments, and *devequt*."[45]

---

42 A number of scholars have demonstrated that Halevi's understanding of the imaginative faculty is based on Alfarabi's thought see Herbert Davidson, "The Active Intellect in the Cuzari," *Revue des études juives* 131 (1972): 367–368; Lobel, *Between Mysticism and Philosophy*, 108–109; Kreisel, *Prophecy*, 129–130.

43 Shimon Gershon Rosenberg, *We Walk in Fervor* (Efrat: Yeshivat Siach Yitzhak, 2008), 255. Also see Ron Margolin, *Inner Religion: The Phenomenology of Inner Religious Life and Its Manifestation in Jewish Sources (from the Bible to Hasidic Texts)* (Ramat Gan/Jerusalem: Bar-Ilan University Press and Shalom Hartman Institute, 2011), 398–402. Margolin characterizes this imaginal activity as "active cognitive interiorization," also ibid., 400, "This imagination is not unbridled, rather it is employed to imitate the divine entity (*ha-inyan ha-elohi*) to enable the inner consciousness to draw near to the unimaginable God by means of cultural imagery related to divine revelation." Also see Elliot R. Wolfson, "Merkavah Traditions in Philosophical Garb: Judah Halevi Reconsidered," *Proceedings of the American Academy for Jewish Research* 57 (1990–1991): 203–235.

44 Halevi, *Sefer ha-Kuzari*, III:5§§143–144.

45 Rosenberg, *We Walk in Fervor*, 255.

Both Warren Zev Harvey and Shimon Gershon Rosenberg, regarding the two aforementioned passages from the *Kuzari*, asserted that there are two types of imagination. Harvey viewed the prophetic imagination as *superimaginatio*, an imagination that is not an imitation, rather an epistemological mode,[46] and the pietistic imagination as mimetic imagination.[47] Rosenberg portrays in a similar, but different, manner, the types of imagination—imagination as a product of inspiration and imagination as a product of human initiative and effort. The prophetic imagination is the former, a product of inspiration and *ru'aḥ ha-qodesh* (the holy spirit), in contrast to the latter imagination, which originates in and is a product of human initiative, a result of practice and training.[48] Inspired-prophetic imagination approximates the creative imagination–as mentioned, a conception that only developed in eighteenth century Western philosophy, around six hundred and fifty years after Halevi and almost eight hundred years after Alfarabi,[49] whereas the imagination that is a product of human effort approximates the mimetic imagination. Inspired-prophetic imagination is characterized by spontaneity, uninhibitedness, and suddenness, while imagination produced by human effort is characterized by structure, order, and gradualness. This distinction serves our categorization of "guided imagery,"[50] as imagination produced by

46 See Harvey, "Judah Halevi's Synthetic Theory of Prophecy," 146–147, where he states that this conception contradicts the Aristotelean theory of epistemology, which states that the internal senses, including the imaginative faculty, are dependent on the external senses and without them the internal senses cannot be epistemologically aware of anything.

47 Ibid., 150, "In *Kuzari* III:5, Halevi explicitly presents a mimetic conception of imaginal activity."

48 Rosenberg, *We Walk in Fervor*, 131, 255.

49 This is one example among many of how Kearney's and Abram's theory of the imagination's development is not entirely applicable regarding circles outside of their field of research, and even within their field of research I suspect that there is not such a stark distinction between period to period (regarding the imagination) as they have presented it. It is probable that their analyses are influenced by the philosophies of Hegel, Marx, and specifically Foucault, who saw each period as a paradigm in and of itself. Kearney and Abrams demonstrate a progression from period to period regarding the imagination; even if they are correct, it should be solely viewed within the narrow framework of Western philosophy, one elite among many. With that being said, even within this elite a more tempered analysis is possible, in which the distinction between "change" and "continuity" exists, such as in Herder's philosophy (see Bergman, *A History of Modern Philosophy from the Enlightenment to Kant*, 59). Also see Abrams, *The Mirror and the Lamp*, 58–60, where he incidentally states that one may find pre-Kantian roots for the *creative imagination* in the English poetics of the seventeenth century and in Hobbs's and Locke's thought. What Abrams saw as marginal, I see as central. This current work does not purport to find these roots, but it is clear that it demonstrates a type of continuity and asserts an alternative conception than that of Abrams and specifically Kearney.

50 See below chap. 5, subchapter "Categorization of Imagery Techniques."

human effort, and as such—it is a ready field for the flowering of different techniques.

Maimonides

Two primary sources from the *Guide of the Perplexed*, which appear to contradict each other, serve as the foundation for the analysis of Maimonides's attitude towards the imagination. The first source is Maimonides's direct treatment of the matter, in which the imagination is less revered than the intellect and is even treated negatively, as in Plato's conception in which the imagination distances man from the truth and creates an illusory reality:

> You already know that imagination exists in most living beings... Accordingly, man is not distinguished by having imagination; and the act of imagination is not the act of the intellect but rather its contrary. For the intellect divides the composite things and differentiates their parts and makes abstractions of them, represents them to itself in their true reality and with their causes, and apprehends from one thing very many notions, which differ for the intellect just as two human individuals differ in regard to their existence for the imagination. It is by means of the intellect that the universal is differentiated from the individual, and no demonstration is true except by means of universals. It is also through the intellect that essential predicates are discerned from accidental ones. None of these acts belongs to the imagination. For the imagination apprehends only that which is individual and composite as a whole, as it is apprehended by the senses; or compounds things that in their existence are separate, combining one with another; the whole being a body or a force of the body. Thus, someone using his imagination imagines a human individual having a horse's head and wings and so on. This is what is called a thing invented and false, for nothing existent corresponds to it at all. In its apprehension, imagination is in no way able to hold itself aloof from matter, even if it turns a form into the extreme of abstraction. For this reason, there can be no critical examination in the imagination.[51]

According to Maimonides, the act of the intellect is differentiation and abstraction, thus allowing for a uniform law of physics, which encompasses and unifies many different phenomena. In contrast, the imagination cannot free itself from sensory images and in fact constitutes only one component of the sensory depiction, "For the intellect, sensory reality is only a means for abstraction, material for future experimentation. The intellect strives to produce a general formula, for the study of a mathematical equation... Maimonides views this factual distinction as the sole means for realizing the truth. It is only through this distinction

---

51 Moses Maimonides, *Guide of the Perplexed*, trans. Shlomo Pines (Chicago: University of Chicago Press, 1963), I:75§§I:209–210.

that the principle behind sensory presentation may be known—a principle which is distant from the imagination."[52] Furthermore, in this passage it emerges that the imagination can only depict corporeally and not abstractly, "for according to the imagination, there are no existents except bodies or things in bodies."[53]

The second primary source in which Maimonides discusses the imagination is in his theory of prophecy. Here the imagination is not an insignificant factor, on the contrary–the imagination is an indispensable component of the prophetic process, and therefore is viewed as an important and essential element in the process of man's perfection:

> Know that the true reality and quiddity of prophecy consist in its being an overflow overflowing from God, may He be cherished and honored, through the intermediation of the Active Intellect, toward the rational faculty,[54] in the first place and thereafter toward the imaginative faculty. This is the highest degree of man and the ultimate term of perfection that can exist for his species; and this state is the ultimate term of perfection for the imaginative faculty. This is something that cannot by any means exist in every man. And it is not something that may be attained solely through perfection in the speculative sciences and through improvement of moral habits, even if all of them have become as fine and good as can be. There still is needed in addition the highest possible degree of perfection of the imaginative faculty in respect of its original natural disposition. Now you know that the perfection of the bodily faculties, to which the imaginative faculty belongs, is consequent upon the best possible temperament, the best possible size, and the purest possible matter, of the part of the body that is the substratum for the faculty in question... You know that [the Sages] have said time and again: A dream is the sixtieth part of prophecy...[55] Similarly, the action of the imaginative faculty in the state of sleep is also its action in the state of prophecy; there is, however, a deficiency in it and it does not reach its ultimate term. Why should we teach you by means of the dicta of [the Sages], may their memory be blessed, and leave aside the texts of the Torah? If there be a prophet among you, I the Lord do make Myself known unto him in a vision, I do speak with him in a dream. Thus He, may He be exalted, has informed us of the true reality and quiddity of prophecy and has let us know that it is a perfection that comes in a dream or in a vision [mar'eh]. The word mar'eh [vision] derives from the verb ra'oh [to see]. This signifies that the imaginative faculty achieves so great a perfection of action that it sees the thing as if it were outside.[56]

52 Rosenberg, *We Walk in Fervor*, 129.
53 Maimonides, *Guide of the Perplexed*, 211. Also see, José Faur, "Maimonides on Imagination: Towards a Theory of Jewish Aesthetics," *The Solomon Goldman Lectures* 6 (1994): 93.
54 Meaning, the intellectual faculty, see Kapah's translation and Moses Maimonides, *Guide of the Perplexed* (ed. Schwarz), 126 n. 15.
55 *b. Berakhot* 57b.
56 Maimonides, *Guide*, II:36§§2:369–379. Concerning the imagination as a central component in Alfarabi's theory of prophecy, see Fazlur Rahman, *Prophecy in Islam* (London: Allen & Unwin, 1958), 36–45.

Indeed, regarding Moses's prophecy Maimonides stated in several places in the *Guide* that Moses's prophecy is without imagination, and is unique for it is founded solely upon intellectual apprehension.[57] Nevertheless, Maimonides scattered hints throughout his writings that Moses's prophecy also entailed and utilized the imaginative faculty.[58] In fact, according to Dov Schwartz the uniqueness of Moses's prophecy may be that the dominating force is the imagination and not the intellect, and that Moses is differentiated from the other prophets precisely due to his imaginative faculty. Schwartz has demonstrated that Moses's prophecy in medieval Jewish philosophy, including that of Maimonides's disciples, is characterized as possessing strong imaginative qualities, and that Moses was unparalleled regarding his imaginative prowess, which the other prophets lacked.[59] Accordingly, the imaginative faculty was a key factor in Moses's prophecy and is the measure of prophecy in general. Regardless, it is clear that the imaginative faculty is a major factor in prophecy, at least for the other prophets, in contrast to Maimonides's negative approach discussed above, in which the imaginative faculty is presented as inferior.

This contradiction in Maimonides's thought is interpreted by scholars in two different manners: if the first source is understood as denying the act of imagination and the second source as requiring the imaginative faculty as part of man's perfection, then one approach views the first source as Maimonides's authentic opinion and the other approach views the second source as his authentic opinion.

Shimon Gershon Rosenberg was a contemporary religious thinker who identified the discussion regarding the imaginative faculty as possessing much importance and dedicated a number of discourses and essays, which have been published postmortem. He held the former approach, in which the imagination is utilized solely as a technical instrument for delivering the prophetic message to the populace:

---

57 See Alvin Reines "Maimonides' concept of Mosaic Prophecy," *Hebrew Union College Annual* 40–41 (1969): 325–361; Menachem Kellner, "Maimonides and Gersonides on Mosaic prophecy," *Speculum* 52, no. 1 (1977): 62–79.

58 Jacob S. Levinger, *Maimonides as Philosopher and Codifier* (Jerusalem: Bialik Institute, 1989), 32–33.

59 Dov Schwartz, "Psychological Dimensions of Mosaic Prophecy—Imagination and Intellect," in *Moses the Man–Master of the Prophets: In the Light of Interpretation throughout the Ages*, eds. M. Hallamish et al (Ramat-Gan: Bar-Ilan University Press, 2010), 251–283; idem, "On the Conception of Prophecy of R. Isaac Polcar, R. Solomon Alconstantin and Spinoza," *Asufot* 4 (1990): 57–72; idem, "The Fourteenth Century Jewish Neoplatonic Circle on Mosaic Prophecy," *Journal of Jewish Thought and Philosophy* 2 (1992): 97–110.

> Prophecy, according to Maimonides, is inspiration in which illuminated truth and understandings are garbed in sensory images and are expressed through them. Maimonides sees rationality (be-havanah) as a superior instrument than imagination for the attainment of truth. The prophet is the philosopher with imaginative capability, a required capability for the prophet solely due to the social function imposed on him. The effect of the sensory depictions on the populace is much greater than the effects of intellectual claims.[60]

Rosenberg stressed Maimonides's negative attitude towards the imagination as a fundamental attitude and discussed this in relation to the original sin, eating of the fruit of knowledge, a sin caused by the imagination. The serpent which caused man to sin is symbolized by the imagination. The imagination is the source of evil and is immoral, "All this follows imagination, which is also in true reality the evil impulse. For every deficiency of reason or character is due to the action of the imagination or consequent upon its action."[61] The sole positive function of the imagination, according to Rosenberg, is the technical use of it by the prophet in order to influence the masses, who are not receptive to intellectual messages.[62]

In contradistinction, José Faur viewed the second source as representing Maimonides's primary opinion and therefore had to interpret the other. Faur developed his position from within his conception that many pre-Kantian Jewish thinkers anticipated Kantian and Romantic thought, specifically regarding the "modern" idea of the "creative imagination." It is in this light that he understood Maimonides's attitude towards the imagination:

> The idea of creative imagination was an early concern in Jewish intellectual history. It forced the attention of such thinkers as Abraham bar Hiyya (d. ca. 1136), Isaac Israeli (14th century), Joseph Albo (15th century) and Isaac Abarbanel (1437–1508)—to mention just a few. Yet explorations of the idea of creative imagination uncritically assume that it was a development of mainly the eighteenth century.... Jewish authors from the twelfth to the seventeenth century are hardly mentioned.[63]

60 Rosenberg, *We Walk in Fervor*, 130. Emphasis mine.

61 Maimonides, *Guide*, II:12§§2:280. Also see Rosenberg, *We Walk in Fervor*, 130, 252.

62 Regarding the imagination's role as a medium of transmission for the masses, due to its use of imagery and parables, see Schwartz's articles in the above note. Nevertheless, Schwartz demonstrates that simultaneously the imagination also has an independent stature, which allows the prophet to prophesize, and that a distinction should be made between its essential and functional nature.

63 José Faur, "Imagination and Religious Pluralism: Maimonides, Ibn Verga, and Vico," *New Vico Studies* 10 (1992): 36–37.

> Imagination for Maimonides is an independent mental process standing at the basis of the political, social, religious, and artistic activities of humankind.[64]

The internal contradiction regarding the imagination in the *Guide*, according to Faur, demonstrates that Maimonides sophisticatedly weaved a revolutionary theory asserting a novel and refreshing approach regarding the imagination and the place of the imagination in humanity's development.[65] The imaginative faculty in Maimonides's thought is portrayed by Faur as that in the model of Romantic philosophy:

> Imagination is a key concept in Maimonides' philosophical apparatus. Whereas in traditional philosophy, imagination is at best a tool of reason,[66] Maimonides conceived of imagination as an independent faculty conditioning the perception, mental associations, and institutions regulating human activities at the religious, social and political levels.[67]

However, there are many difficulties with Faur's statement. First of all, he ignores the Muslim philosophers upon whom Maimonides's based his theory of prophecy and presents Maimonides as an unparalleled pioneer.[68] Furthermore, this conception of imagination as Faur presents it, which is similar to the Romantic model and even Sartre's conception,[69] is entirely inconsistent with the Maimonidean understanding of the imagination as an imitation, a mirror and not a lamp, "You know, too, the actions of the imaginative faculty that are in its nature, such as retaining things perceived by the senses, combining these things, and imitating them."[70] In any case, the fact that there is a debate among Maimonidean

---

64 Ibid., 38. Also, see Faur, "Maimonides on Imagination," 89.
65 Faur, "Maimonides on Imagination," 89; idem, "Imagination and Religious Pluralism," 39.
66 This is the Aristotelean view. It is very interesting to see the broad spectrum of interpretation in Maimonidean scholarship. Rosenberg presents Maimonides as a Platonist, whereas Faur relates Maimonides to Aristotle and presents him as a Romantic.
67 Faur, "Maimonides on Imagination," 89–90.
68 Regarding the development of Maimonides's theory of prophecy and its roots in Alfarabi's works, see Kreisel, *Prophecy*, 241–246. Furthermore, concerning the gradations of prophecy according to the empowerment of the imaginative faculty, ibid., 279–284. Regarding the connection between the intellect and prophecy in Alfarabi's thought and its influence on Maimonides, see Wolfson, *A Dream Interpreted within a Dream*, 115–116.
69 See Faur's claim that the Maimonidean imagination is a function of a unique thought process in which humanity and civilization are embodied, Faur, "Maimonides on Imagination," 90.
70 Maimonides, *Guide of the Perplexed* II:36§§2:370. Maimonides ascribed three functions to the imaginative faculty: memory of sensory presentations, a partial sensory agent, and an imitator of objects already perceived by the senses. These functions are not suitable for the modern theory of the creative imagination.

scholars demonstrates that it is not simple to categorize and classify Maimonides according to Western philosophical metrics; even though Maimonides was familiar with Greek philosophy and was influenced by it, nevertheless one cannot ignore the fact that he was a religious person with an intimate relationship with Jewish tradition and God.[71] Faur's scholarly contribution is very important, even though I remain unconvinced by his analysis and conclusions. This importance lies in his emphasis on the creative and potent abilities of the imaginative faculty, and not just its instrumental value for the masses. The imaginative faculty is vital for prophecy itself and not just its popularization. According to the *Guide* II:36, prophetic awareness is superior and loftier than intellectual awareness. Prophetic awareness is the epitome of human perfection, and is distinguished from intellectual awareness in that the emanation (*shefa*) flows from the intellectual faculty into the imaginative faculty and they are then united in a single awareness.[72] Even if we omit the "creative imagination" part of Faur's claim, we still possess an important principle; the imagination plays a primary role in the process of perfection, on the condition that it is controlled by the intellect:

> Imagination is creative and beneficial only when guided by reason. Left uncontrolled, imagination becomes an instrument of perdition and destruction... This is why Maimonides was careful to stipulate that the creative imagination of the prophet is realized after the development of the intellectual faculty.... An essential trait of the prophet is to know how to project one's imagination beyond the boundaries of ordinary rationality—penetrating a different world, and transcending in this fashion the strict boundaries of pure rationality limiting the philosopher.[73]

Through this principle Faur explains Maimonides's negative attitude towards imagination found in the first source presented. This negative attitude is only when the imagination is not controlled by the intellect. In fact, this was stated

---

71 See Abraham Joshua Heschel, "Did Maimonides Believe That He Attained the Rank of a Prophet?," in *Louis Ginsberg Jubilee Volume* (New York: American Academy for Jewish Research, 1945), 1:159–188. Also regarding the chapters on *devequt* (communion) in the *Guide* III, see Adam Afterman, *Devequt: Mystical Intimacy in Medieval Jewish Thought* (Los Angeles: Cherub Press, 2011), 134–168. For more on mystical union in Maimonides's thought see idem, *"And They Shall Be One Flesh": On The Language of Mystical Union in Judaism* (Leiden: Brill, 2016), 109–126.

72 See Moses Maimonides, *Guide of the Perplexed*, annot. Judah Even Shemuel (Jerusalem: Mossad Harav Kook, 2005), 4:123.

73 Faur, "Maimonides on Imagination," 96.

by Maimonides himself in his parable of the rider, which, according to Maimonidean interpreters, is about the imaginative faculty, a parable that surprisingly is not mentioned by the aforementioned scholars:[74]

> Among the things you ought to know is the following explanation, which they give in the Midrash. They mention that the serpent had a rider, that it was of the size of a camel, that it was the rider who led Eve astray, and that the rider was Samael. They apply this name to Satan. Thus, you will find that they say in a number of passages that Satan wanted to tempt Abraham our Father not to agree to offer Isaac as a sacrifice, and that he also wanted to tempt Isaac not to obey his father. And with reference to that story, I mean to say the binding [of Isaac], they say likewise: Samael came to our Father Abraham and told him: What, old man! have you lost your senses, and so on. Thus, it has become clear to you that Samael is Satan. This name is used with a view to a certain signification, just as the name serpent (naḥash) is used with a view to a certain signification. When they speak of its coming to deceive Eve, they say: Samael was riding upon it; and the Holy One, blessed be He, was laughing at both the camel and its rider.[75]

Samael and the serpent signify the desiring faculty and the imaginative faculty. The desiring angel is Samael, riding the imagination–the serpent.[76] That is to say, man's desiring faculty utilizes the imaginative faculty, which envisions the transgressions filled with sin. Man's desire, or evil inclination, utilizes the imaginative faculty to depict the pleasure and delight found in sin and only God, the intellect in man, can laugh at both of these forces simultaneously. It should also be noted that the serpent's influence on man is not on man's intellect, but his material being. The imaginative faculty does not have direct influence on the in-

74 However, this has been noted by Harvey to settle this contradiction in Maimonides's thought, see Harvey, "Three Theories of the Imagination in 12th-Century Jewish Philosophy," 300–301.

75 Maimonides, *Guide* II:30§2:356.

76 See Maimonides, *Guide*, annot. by Judah Even Shemuel, 4:84–85. There are interpreters who saw Samael as the imaginative faculty and the serpent the desiring faculty. See Maimonides, *Guide* (ed. Schwarz), 368 n. 64, where Schwarz brings the comment of Adolf Weiss, relying on several interpreters, in which he writes that according to Maimonides Adam symbolizes the form of mankind—the intellect; Eve symbolizes matter; the serpent is the imaginative faculty; Samael is Satan—the evil inclination. This is Levinger's opinion as well, idem, *Maimonides as Philosopher and Codifier*, 26. In contradistinction, Sara Klein-Braslavy, *Maimonides' Interpretation of the Adam Stories in Genesis: A Study in Maimonides' Anthropology* (Jerusalem: Magnes Press, 1986), 193–208, agrees regarding the identification of Adam and Eve, but she asserts that the interpreters did not agree regarding what Samael and the serpent symbolize, ibid., 215. She concludes that the serpent symbolizes the inclination, and Samael the imagination, ibid., 209–233. Furthermore, see Sara Klein-Braslavy, "Identification of Nahash and Samael in the Guide of the Perplexed," *Da'at* 10 (1983): 9–18. A summary of this argument may be found in Harvey, "Three Theories of the Imagination in 12th-Century Jewish Philosophy," 301.

tellect, symbolized by Adam, who is the human form, but rather on the material, the vital soul (*ha-nefesh ha-ḥiyunit*), which wants to be pleasant and helpful—a soul symbolized by Eve. Through the imaginative faculty, desires are in fact awoken within Eve, the vital soul:

> Among the things you ought to know and have your attention aroused to is the fact that the Serpent had in no respect direct relations with Adam and that it did not speak to him, and that such a conversation and relation only took place between him and Eve; it was through the intermediation of Eve that Adam was harmed and that the Serpent destroyed him. Extreme enmity only comes to be realized between the Serpent and Eve and its seed and hers. On the other hand her seed is indubitably the seed of Adam. Even more strange is the tie between the Serpent and Eve, I mean between its seed and hers, a tie that is in the head and the heel; she being victorious over it through the head I and it over her through the heel. This also is clear.[77]

Adam is harmed through Eve and indirectly by the serpent. The vital soul has a connection to the intellectual soul and ultimately the imagination overpowers the intellect as well. Nevertheless, Eve's seed will fight the serpent's seed and will defeat him, "I will put enmity between you and the woman, and between your offspring and hers; they shall strike at your head, and you shall strike at their heel" (Gen. 3:15). The connection between the serpent's seed (the imaginative faculty) and Eve's seed (the vital soul) is through the "*the head and the heel.*" Eve's seed will defeat the imaginative faculty through the assistance of the head, that is, through the intellectual faculty controlling the imaginative faculty! Recall, the serpent is a vehicle, meaning a catalyst of energy and power, but nevertheless it is a neutral power, which is related to differently depending on the nature of the rider. If Samael rides upon it then it is negative, but if the intellect rides upon it, then the intellectual faculty gains a powerful burst of energy.

This conception presents the imaginative faculty as a neutral force thereby multiplying its features. Maimonides's treatment of it alternates according to the circumstance and context, for the central question is who is controlling this faculty. If the evil inclination rides it then Maimonides denounces this faculty, whereas if the prophet controls it with his intellect ("It is then that a certain overflow overflows to [the intellectual] faculty according to its disposition... This same overflow is the cause of the prophecy") then this faculty is transformed into a medium for prophecy, full of energy and power, just as a passerby riding an animal cannot be compared to one on foot.

In summary, it is difficult to neatly categorize Maimonides's view of the imagination's function according to the Western philosophical models, a fact

77 Maimonides, *Guide*, II:30§§ 2:356.

which demonstrates the complexity and dissimilarity of his view. However, regarding the nature of imagination clear stances may be argued: Maimonides sees it as a neutral force. On the one hand, the imagination may constitute a danger as it does in Plato's philosophy, on the other hand when it is controlled by the intellect then the prophetic flow streams through it. Then the imagination may be a vital force for the empowerment of prophecy.[78] This conception is able to explain an additional matter. The imagination does not appear in Aristotle's thought as one of the faculties of the soul, while Maimonides does register it as one of the five parts of the soul, in contrast to Aristotle.[79] Gliker writes:

> Maimonides views the imagination as one of the five parts of the soul. In contradistinction to Aristotle, according to Maimonides the imagination is a psychic force, which does not only preserve the senses, but acts through them as well, by its very essence, acts of conjoining and separating.... According to Aristotle the imagination is not free, it is a movement within sense perception (ha-teḥushah), which is caused by sense perception in actuality.[80]
>
> The imagination does not appear in Aristotle's list of the faculties of the soul. It is not, according to Aristotle, an independent faculty of the soul. It is a particular manifestation of sense perception, and its place is in the *sensus communis*.[81]

The conception of the imaginative faculty as a vital force for prophecy is an explanation for why Maimonides grants this faculty independent stature. The imaginative faculty is not just a manifestation of sense perception, but rather it is also a medium through which prophecy is given to man and intensified, and therefore Maimonides counts it as an independent faculty of the soul.[82]

At this juncture, I must discuss Elliot Wolfson's analysis of dreams and his highly original study of Maimonides's conception of prophecy and imagination.[83] Wolfson approaches the Maimonidean conception of prophecy by comparing Mosaic prophecy with common prophecy in Maimonides's teaching. In Maimonides's *Mishneh Torah* a distinction is made between these two types:

---

78 On empowerment as a mystical action see the following chapter.

79 Moses Maimonides, *Eight Chapters* (Introduction to Commentary on Mishnah Avot), chap. 1. Also see Maimonides, *The Eight Chapters of Maimonides on Ethics*, ed. and trans. Joseph I. Gorfinkle (New York: Columbia University Press, 1912), 39 n. 1.

80 Gliker, "Imagination in Aristotle's Soul Doctrine," 27.

81 Ibid., 22.

82 Regarding the classification of the imaginative faculty as an independent psychic force and its roots in Alfarabi's thought, see Harry Austryn Wolfson, "Maimonides on the Internal Senses," *Jewish Quarterly Review* 25 (1935): 441–467.

83 Wolfson, *A Dream Interpreted within a Dream*, 115–136.

> What is the difference between Moses' prophecy and that of all the other prophets? All the prophets [prophesized] in a dream or vision. Moses, our teacher, would prophesy while awake and standing, as stated: "When Moses went into the Tent of Meeting to speak with Him, he would hear the Voice addressing him" (Num. 7:89). All the prophets [prophesized] through an angel [intermediary], therefore, they perceive that which they perceive through parable and riddle. Moses, our teacher, [prophesized] without an angel [intermediary], as stated: "With him I speak mouth to mouth," (Num. 12:8) and as stated: "The Lord would speak to Moses face to face," (Ex. 33:11) and as stated: "and he beholds the likeness (temunat) of the Lord," (Num. 12:8) meaning, there was no parable. Rather, he would perceive the matter in its entirety, without riddle or parable. The Torah testifies concerning him, "[With him I speak...] plainly and not in riddles" (Num. 12:8). He does not prophesize through riddles, but through a vision which perceives the matter in its entirety.[84]

The meaning of the intermediary angel is the imaginative faculty. This is made clear from Maimonides's words in the *Guide*, "Accordingly, *Midrash Qoheleth* has the following text: *When man sleeps, his soul speaks to the angel, and the angel to the cherub.* Thereby they have stated plainly to him who understands and cognizes intellectually that the imaginative faculty is likewise called an *angel* and that the intellect is called a *cherub.*"[85] Consequently, all prophets prophesy through the imaginative faculty. According to Maimonides, prophecy is a speculative event in which, "they perceive that which they perceive." They do not see God directly, rather they see through images of "parable and riddle." In contrast, Wolfson stresses that Moses saw "the likeness of the Lord." Moses's prophecy is visionary as well, however, "Ironically, to behold the divine image is to have an intellectual vision without recourse to images, a mode of sight that is completely untethered to the imagination, a seeing that is, in effect, unseeing, seeing that there is nothing to be seen,"[86] an "envisioning [of] what is not."[87] Moses constitutes the paradigm for the prophet who sees through a "speculum that shines," for he sees only his own unseeing.[88]

Similar to Sartre,[89] Michel Foucault also viewed the imagination as the presence of something's absence.[90] Wolfson compares Foucault's conception of the

---

84 Moses Maimonides, "Laws of the Foundations of the Torah," 7:6.
85 Maimonides, *Guide*, II:86§§II:264 – 265.
86 Wolfson, *A Dream Interpreted within a Dream*, 123.
87 Ibid., 115.
88 On "seeing the unseen" see ibid., 129, and furthermore ibid., 129 – 136. The source of the midrash is in *b. Yevamot* 49b, "All the prophets saw through a speculum (*aspaqlaria*) that does not shine, but Moses looked through a speculum that shines."
89 See Jean Paul Sartre, *The Psychology of Imagination*, trans. Bernard Frechtman (New York: Washington Square Press, 1966), 16; Kearney, *The Wake of Imagination*, 224 – 248; as well as my discussion in *Vision as a Mirror* (Los Angeles: Cherub Press), 38 – 42.

imagination with that of Maimonides's conception of Mosaic prophecy, and claims that they are in agreement regarding human imagination, which is "directed towards the fullness of a presence that is beyond images, a fullness that can be ascertained only through the attenuation of its own abundance... The imagination dissolves in the collapse of its own power to sustain anything but the imagining of images that cannot be imagined."[91] Wolfson's words, comparing the old with the new, Maimonides and Foucault, are quite important and demonstrate the impossibility of correlating Maimonides's view to the Western philosophical models of his age.

R. Naḥman of Bratslav

Similar to Maimonides, one may find an ambivalent relation to the imagination in Naḥman's teachings as well. On the one hand he states, "all sins come through the imagination" and wholly identifies the imaginative faculty with the evil inclination,[92] and on the other hand, he claims, "that the primary [aspect] of faith is dependent upon the imaginative faculty."[93] This contradiction is even more pronounced in Naḥman's thought since it is connected to the common man's faith, whereas according to Maimonides the positive aspect of the imagination is only relevant to the inner world of the prophets. Naḥman, like Halevi, broadened the intended audience of the imagination and believes that the masses are also able to and even must utilize the imagination. Similar to Halevi, it appears that Naḥman conceived of the imagination in two primary manners, each multifaceted: the imaginative faculty in its prophetic context and the imaginative faculty in its faith context, but in Naḥman's thought the differences, to a certain degree, between these contexts are blurred. I shall begin with his critical attitude towards the imaginative faculty:

90 Wolfson, *A Dream Interpreted within a Dream*, 136 – 142.

91 Ibid., 142.

92 Naḥman of Bratslav, *Liqquṭei MoHaRaN*, I 25:5.

93 Naḥman, *Liqquṭei MoHaRaN*, II 8:7. Concerning Naḥman's conception of the imagination see Eliezer Shore, "Letters of Desire: Language, Mysticism, and Sexuality in the Writings of Rabbi Nahman of Bratzlav" (PhD diss., Bar-Ilan University, 2005), 286 – 297, regarding the two aspects of the imagination, ibid., 288 – 291, furthermore ibid., 349 – 352 for Maimonides's and Naḥman's conception of the imagination in regard to prophecy. Also see Yaara Levitas-Bivas, "Imagination in the Thought of R. Nahman of Bratslav" (master's thesis, Bar-Ilan University, 2007). On the connection between faith and the imaginative faculty see ibid., 57 – 59.

> "True sacrifice to God is a contrite spirit (ru'aḥ nishbarah)" (Ps. 51:19), that the breaking of the imagination (she-shevirat ha-dimyon) are the sacrifices... And when man follows the imagination (ha-medameh) that is in his heart, that is after his desires, God forbid, which occur due to the imaginative faculty, this is an actual animal act, for the animal, too, has an imaginative faculty, and therefore when a man sins, God forbid, and all sins come through the imaginative faculty, for from there all the desires are drawn, he needs to bring a sacrifice of animals, and he needs to place his hands on it (lismokh alav), and confess his sins... And immediately afterwards he places his hands [on the animal for] slaughter. And they slaughter the animal as a sacrifice, and through this the imagination is subdued and broken.... After the aforementioned statement was stated, and there all desires are referred to and called the evil inclination because of the imaginative faculty. Then he said: we need to call it and refer to it with a different name... that is it should not be called the evil inclination anymore, only the imaginative faculty. And he said this jokingly, but I understood that he had a complete intention in this, and I did not merit to understand his intention in this.[94]

In a different place Naḥman explains that the breaking of the imagination is accomplished through *da'at* (knowledge), which distinguishes between the evil spirit and good spirit, between the divine spirit and a spirit of folly (*ru'aḥ sheṭut*). This act of distinguishing is termed by Naḥman as "subduing the imagination." Naḥman explicates the relation between *da'at* and the imagination in *Liqquṭei MoHaRaN*, I, 54:5 stating:

> The imaginative faculty is the animalistic potency... and when knowledge (da'at) is withdrawn from him, and he falls from the love of God blessed be he, and falls to [the level] of animalistic love. In the aspect of, "Because you have rejected knowledge (da'at), I reject you as My priest" (Hos. 4:6)... And then the imaginative faculty, which is the animalistic potency, overpowers him. In the aspect of, "My people is destroyed (nidmu) because of lack of knowledge" (ibid.), nidmu (destroyed), that is the ko'aḥ ha-midameh (imaginative faculty).

The imagination is in control when man lacks knowledge. At that point, man's animality is empowered and his religious worship is rejected by God, in a reciprocal fashion, since man rejects knowledge. How can the imaginative faculty be subdued? Naḥman proposes an answer, namely, through the use of melody:

> When the prophet hears a tune from a person who knows melody, he receives a spirit of prophecy from him... and this is [the meaning of the verse], "he will play it and you will

---

94 *Liqquṭei MoHaRaN*, I, 25:5. Also see Zvi Mark, *Mysticism and Madness in the Work of R. Nahman of Bratslav* (Tel Aviv: Am Oved; Jerusalem: Shalom Hartman Institute, 2004), 100 – 101. Mark demonstrates the parallels between Maimonides and Naḥman also in regard to the identification of the evil inclination with the imaginative faculty.

> feel better (ve-ṭov lakh)" (I Sam. 16:16). "Good for you (ve-ṭov lakh), specifically, for he purifies the good from the evil... From this, we learn that when a person plays upon a musical instrument with his hand, he separates the good spirit from the evil spirit. This corresponds to the spirit of prophecy mentioned earlier, and all of this corresponds to the "subduing of the imagination"—that it is the quality of the evil spirit, the spirit of folly, which desires to damage and confuse the good spirit, the spirit of prophecy. And it is subdued and nullified, through the joy caused by the playing of the instrument with his hand mentioned earlier. And this instrument player, must know how to play as previously mentioned... So that he may properly separate and direct (u-le-khaven) the melody in perfection, which is in the aspect of that which separates the good spirit... the aspect of the spirit of prophecy, from... the evil spirit as previously mentioned... When he has the aspect of the hand (yad), as previously mentioned, which gathers and separates the good spirit form the evil spirit, then he subdues the imagination, in the aspect of, "I will be imagined by (u-bi-yad) the prophets," as mentioned earlier.[95]

The knowledgeable musician in this context is the one who is able to prophetically create distinctions and order in the imaginal realm.[96] The subduing of the imaginative faculty is not its annihilation; rather it is the removing of its sole control over man and the transferring of the reigns to the intellectual faculty. It is through the imaginative faculty that man is granted prophecy. The issue is that the evil spirit passes through it as well, and only consciousness (*da'at*) is able to subdue the imaginative faculty and separate the good spirit from it.[97]

Zvi Mark demonstrates that the imagination has two aspects in Naḥman's thought concerning dreams as well: on the one hand the dream is a lower gradation of prophecy, while on the other hand the oneiric realm may give expression to man's animalistic and impure aspects. The dream is an admixture of two simultaneous streams of inspiration: the angelic and the demonic.[98] As regarding prophecy, here as well man, through the purification of his consciousness,

---

95 *Liqquṭei MoHaRaN*, I, 54. Translation partly based on Zvi Mark, *Mysticism and Madness: The Religious Thought of Rabbi Nachman of Bratslav* (London: Continuum, 2009), 4. All references unrelated to translation of Naḥman's work will refer to the Hebrew edition, unless otherwise noted.

96 Mark, *Mysticism and Madness*, 89.

97 Ibid., 90–91. See Levitas-Bivas, "Imagination in the Thought of R. Nahman of Bratslav," 28–72, regarding the dual- facetedness of Naḥman's conception of the imagination in connection to the immanent dual-facetedness of reality due to Naḥman's conception of "the empty void" (*ḥalal ha-penui*). The empty void according to Naḥman is the location in which "opposites are integrated." Accordingly, just as one is to skip over the empty void, so too one is to skip over the negative facet of the imagination and simultaneously to cling to the positive facet and through it ascend from height to height.

98 Mark, *Mysticism and Madness*, 91.

is able to distill the proper channel from which he receives the dream,[99] "And when the consciousness (*ve-ke-she-ha-moḥin*) becomes translucent (*zakhim*) then also the remaining imaginative faculty is in the aspect of an angel."[100] Indeed, this refinement of consciousness (*da'at*) is neither the development of the intellectual faculties nor cognitive-scholastic abilities as found in Maimonides's thought, rather it is correlated to the field of character traits (*middot*): refinement and purification of character traits and the suppression of desires.[101] The same is true regarding *da'at* (knowledge): *da'at* is a term which incorporates more than just man's intellect. *Da'at* is one of the *sefirot* found in the central pillar and parallels the *sefirah* of *Yesod* (Foundation) and a blemish in *Da'at*, similar to a blemish in *Yesod*, also referred to as a blemish of the covenant (*pegam ha-berit*), constitutes an imperfection in man's character traits:

> For through the blemishing of da'at, he descends from the sacred love (me-ahavot di-qidushah)... and then the imaginative faculty overcomes him... and this is why he finishes there at this verse, "And you have forgotten your God's Torah" (Hos. 4:6), and you have certainly forgotten, for through the blemish of the mind (pegam ha-da'at), through which the imaginative faculty is empowered, through which the memory (ha-zikaron) is blemished and he comes to forgetfulness, as mentioned previously. And this is "I will forget your children" (ibid.). For through the blemishing of the memory and the falling into forgetfulness, through this he will not have a male (zakhar) child."[102]

---

99 Ibid., 92.

100 *Liqqutei MoHaRaN*, II, 5:9. However, the primary means which Naḥman offers to engage the imaginative faculty is joy, see Mark, *Mysticism and Madness*, 92–95.

101 Ibid., 105, 10 n. 109.

102 *Liqquṭei MoHaRaN*, I, 54:6. *Da'at* is identified with holy love (*ahavah de-qedushah*), that is love of God, see ibid., 4:4. Also "primary fear" (*iqar ha-yirah*) is found in *da'at*, ibid., 15:3. Blemish of the mind (*pegam ha-da'at*) is the forgetting of God, a forgetting that is a result of a lack of fear, and this is *pegam yesod* (blemish of the foundation/covenant). The potency of love, instead of being a force for holiness, is directed towards sexual desires (*ta'avat ha-ni'uf*). Concerning the relation between *da'at* and sexual desires see ibid., 36:2. For more on the imagination as the basis for sexual thoughts in Naḥman's thought see Shore, "Letters of Desire," 297. Regarding these themes of forgetfulness, memory, and sexuality, see Elliot R. Wolfson, "The Cut That Binds: Time, Memory, and the Ascetic Impulse," in *God's Voice from the Void: Old and New Studies in Bratslav Hasidism*, ed. Shaul Magid (Albany: State University of New York Press, 2002), 103–154. Regarding *shemirat ha-berit* in general, see Shilo Pachter, "Shemirat Habrit: The History of the Prohibition of Wasting Seed" (PhD diss., Hebrew University, 2006), concerning Bratslav, ibid., 325–339.

Da'at is the *sefirah* which connects the intellect to the character traits, "*Da'at* is the subsistence of the traits (*middot*) and their vitality."[103] *Da'at* is not solely theoretical knowledge; the intellectual effort detached from character traits is sterile. True knowledge is an act of communion and intimacy with the divine.[104] Through *da'at*, understood in this fashion, man is able to control his imaginative faculty and guide it towards holiness.

The opposing effects of the imagination, the angel and demon, caused an ambivalent attitude towards it. This attitude stems from the apprehension of destructive implications and consequences of the unrestrained imagination on the one hand, and the need for the imagination as a prophetic instrument on the other–common to both Maimonides and Naḥman. The two axes of the imagination are not identical, rather, "the evil in it is greater than the good," as Naḥman wrote.[105] Yet despite this statement, Naḥman radically declared, "that the primary [aspect] of faith is dependent upon the imaginative faculty."[106] Bratslavic faith is supported by and relies on the prophetic spirit,[107] and since prophecy traverses through the imaginative dimension—so too does faith. Faith cannot appear as an abstraction, for its revelation is dependent upon a different medium, the imagination.[108] Faith is not philosophical knowledge; rather it is a situation in which the believer sees that which he has faith in.[109] This is not a vision of a picture, but rather it is a feeling of the undeniable presence of God, so clear that "the matter is revealed for the believer, as if he optically sees the matter that he believes in, due to the magnitude of his complete faith."[110] Faith is an experience in which there is a mystical inspiration similar to prophecy,[111] and therefore it

---

103 Shneur Zalman of Liadi, *Liqquṭei Amarim: Tanya* (Jerusalem: Heiḥal Menaḥem, 1997), part 1, chap. 3, p. 14.
104 Jacobson, "Rectification of the Heart," 404–405.
105 *Liqquṭei MoHaRaN*, I, 54:6.
106 Ibid., II, 8:7.
107 Mark, *Mysticism and Madness*, 95.
108 Rosenberg, *We Walk in Fervor*, 132.
109 Mark, *Mysticism and Madness*, 96.
110 *Liqquṭei MoHaRaN*, I, 62. Mark, *Mysticism and Madness*, 96. Also see Levitas-Bivas, "Imagination in the Thought of R. Nahman of Bratslav," 59 n. 279, that the meaning of the word "as if" (*ke-ilu*) should be understood as "actually" (*mammash*). For an analysis of the figurative and literal in kabbalistic thought, see Elliot R. Wolfson, "Suffering Eros and Textual Incarnation: A Kristevan Reading of Kabbalistic Poetics," in *Towards a Theology of Eros: Transfiguring Passion at the Limits of Discipline*, eds. Virginia Burrus and Catherine Keller (New York: Fordham University Press, 2006), 2–10, also see idem "Exchange: Open Secret in the Rearview Mirror," *AJS Review* 35, no. 2 (2011): 403–405, regarding the word *mammash*.
111 Mark, *Mysticism and Madness*, 114.

requires the purified and refined imaginative faculty, for if not, "the imagination is likely to blur (*le-arev*) [his faith] and confuse man with false beliefs."[112]

In contrast to Maimonides's philosophy, in which the imaginative faculty is only relevant for select individuals destined for prophecy, in Naḥman's thought, similar to that of Halevi, the imaginative faculty is relevant for all; however, they differ regarding its relevancy. For Halevi the imagination is utilized as an instrument for feelings of faith and religious passion, whereas for Naḥman the need for the imagination is much broader and foundational—the very essence of faith is dependent upon the imaginative faculty. Thus, this potency is transformed into a central and vital force for the believer's religious life.[113]

An additional feature of the imagination, which allows it to be a precondition for faith, is its liberty.[114] It is precisely its freewheeling nature,[115] unconstrained by rigid guidelines, which allows for faith. According to Naḥman faith is in contradiction to philosophy, in contrast to Maimonides and Halevi, since faith relies on the awareness of God's infinite ability, which is bound neither by any guidelines in general, nor by human intellectual categories in particular.[116]

I have noted that a blemish of the mind leads to a blemish of the covenant (*pegam ha-yesod*) and that this occurs through the imaginative faculty; however, this is not inevitable and "you must believe that you are able to rectify (*le-taqen*)." *Tiqqun ha-yesod* (the rectification of the covenant), which is the transformation of sexual energy, leads to the spirit of prophecy upon which faith is dependent. The mystically inspired Bratslavic faith, in which man visualizes

---

112 *Liqquṭei MoHaRaN*, I, 8. For a recent exploration of Bratslavic faith, see Roni Bar Lev, *The Avant-garde Faith of Rabbi Nachman of Breslov* (Ramat Gan: Bar-Ilan University Press, 2017).
113 Mark, *Mysticism and Madness*, 96–97.
114 Regarding the uninhibited and freewheeling nature of the imagination in Naḥman's thought see Shaul Magid, "Associative Midrash: Reflections on a Hermeneutical Theory in *Likkutei MoHaRan*," in *God's Voice from the Void: Old and New Studies in Bratslav Hasidism*, ed. Shaul Magid (Albany: State University of New York Press, 2002), 43–48. Magid demonstrates that the concept of *beḥinah* (aspect) in Naḥman's thought, is utilized as a literary tool for reconstruction, rather than interpretation. Naḥman does not interpret classic rabbinic texts, rather he employs them as he pleases for new creations, for the reconstruction of the tradition. According to Naḥman this construction is done by the *ṣaddiq* who gathers classic rabbinic texts and filters them through his associative imagination. Magid demonstrates that Naḥman widens the elasticity of the traditional texts in order to absorb the freewheeling nature of the human imagination.
115 Magid argues that Naḥman is interested in the unbound nature of the imagination and that his reading of traditional material is through an associative imagination, ibid., 45–46. Furthermore, Magid shows that Naḥman is interested in perfecting the imagination.
116 Rosenberg, *We Walk in Fervor*, 132–133. Also see Abraham Joshua Heschel, *God in Search of Man: A Philosophy of Judaism* (New York: Farrar, Straus and Giroux, 1955), 18–20, 101–103.

God—a visualization through the imagination—is a conversion of the evil inclination which is rectified through the guarding of the covenant (*shemirat ha-berit*).[117] This rectification (*tiqqun*) restores the imaginative faculty, which was utilized for man's destruction through sexual stimulation, and with its rectification he receives prophetic inspiration.[118]

C Conclusion

According to Halevi the imaginative faculty has two functions:

1. The prophetic ability to directly see the divine realm. This imagination approximates the "creative imagination," in which the imagination may arrive at original truths.
2. The granting of religious fervor and *devequt* to the pious person (*ḥasid*). This imagination approaches the mimetic conception. In this category, the imagination is employed as a means by which religio-historic events are recreated. The recreation enlivens the events and grants them contemporary significance and experiential actuality.

Maimonides gave the imagination its primary potency in his theory of prophecy. According to Maimonides, the imaginative faculty is a neutral force—when it is utilized uncritically it can be disastrous and lead man towards his dark passions, whereas when it is utilized critically (with the intellect), it is a medium for the empowerment of prophecy. Similar to a riding animal, the imagination grants its rider a burst of energy and allows him to reach distances and discoveries that he would be unable to grasp without it. Without the imagination, prophecy would remain unattainable, an inaccessible far off land.

Naḥman, similar to Maimonides, portrayed the imagination in a dialectical manner, but added an existential and foundational element to it. For him the imagination is not only a component in prophecy—it is the very foundation of faith. According to Naḥman, faith is a type of experiential prophecy, a situation in which the believer sees that which he believes in. Just as Maimonides under-

117 Rosenberg, *We Walk in Fervor*, 133–1334.

118 Concerning the transformation of sexual thoughts into scholarly innovations—a transformation based in the imagination—see Magid, "Associative Midrash," 47–48. Magid demonstrates that the imagination is the root of both sexual thoughts and Torah innovations. The transformation of the former into the latter constitutes a rectification of the imagination. Also see regarding the rectification of the imagination ibid., 65 n. 155. Lastly, see Levitas-Bivas, "Imagination in the Thought of R. Nahman of Bratslav," 81–93.

stood the imaginative faculty as a key to prophecy, Naḥman viewed it as a key to faith. Since faith is relevant for all humanity the audience is much greater than those elite capable of prophecy, and thereby the imaginative faculty becomes immeasurably relevant and gains existential significance for all people.

These three thinkers: Halevi, Maimonides, and Naḥman, would be able to constitute a conceptual foundation for the innovative thought of two figures about whom I shall discuss at length in this book, R. Kalonymous Kalman Shapira (The Piaseczno Rebbe) and R. Menaḥem Mendel Ekstein, who developed the practical aspect of the imagination more than the theoretical aspect. On the one hand, Halevi and Naḥman saw a need for the imagination's general accessibility for all and not solely for select individuals—a motif which appears in both Ekstein's and Shapira's thought. On the other hand, Maimonides granted the imagination a central place in his theory of prophecy—a motif which frequently appears in Shapira's prophetic and practice-based thought (in which the concept of prophecy is expanded, thus allowing for more people to be included and thereby making the imagination relevant for all and not just an elite). At the same time, the rise of the creative imagination in Western philosophy and its realization in art, literature, and psychological practices, as will be shown in section four, gave rise to a certain mindset in Europe and its modes of thought, which allowed for Jewish thinkers as well to explore the imagination in general and its practical side in particular.

I do not accept Faur's claim that Maimonides and other Jewish thinkers were before their time regarding their conception of the imagination, even though it is an interesting claim. In my opinion, thinkers from diverse circles should not be situated along a linear timeline, thus creating an anachronistic view, since this conception places these Jewish thinkers together with Western philosophers within the same linear development. In contrast to this conception, a different perspective may be presumed, namely, models developed in Western philosophy cannot be applied towards those from different circles, all the more so regarding figures with an intimate connection to religious traditions. To state this in mathematical terms, I am arguing that there are multiple fields, each field or algebraic structure is an enclosed entity with specific features. I am not stating that as individual fields they cannot be compared or that they do not share commonalities. For instance, all integers are rational numbers (while not all rational numbers are integers) and all rational numbers are included within the field of real numbers (while not all real numbers are rational). Nevertheless, each field is comprised by its own unique system which characterizes it. That is to say, each philosophical circle constitutes a field with its own terminology and unique features, features which scholars attempt to define. A circle characterized by a quality of religious thinking cannot be forced to adapt itself to the very specific circle which we term "Western philosophy." With this being stated, this incompatibility does not mean that there is no overlap or incomparability. This is surely not the case—as I stated, mathematical fields overlap and include one another, while each field remains separate and to itself. The Western philosophical models presented in this chapter may surely be utilized in order to clarify imaginal techniques in Jewish-religious thought, as I will do later in this book. At the same time, I am not claiming that the Jewish thinkers who I will present are beholden to these models. In this work, I will attempt to walk a tightrope: on the one hand, I will maintain the Jewish "field," the autonomous thought of the thinkers who were not bound by Western philosophy, and on the other hand, I will demonstrate that modern Western philosophy, and in its wake the modern psychological and psychiatric development that swept Europe, also influenced mystical religious Jewish thinkers. I will show that the comparison in and of itself is important, and that it has the ability to clarify, even if only slightly, the teachings which constituted the foundation for the techniques developed by these Jewish thinkers.

To conclude this chapter, I will elucidate its connection to the main portion of the book. The bulk of this book explores the development of unique imagery techniques, and specifically (but not only) Jewish mystical practices of early twentieth century Europe. Already in the Middle Ages (and even classic rabbinic thought to a certain extent), Jewish thought presented models of imagination which were not only mimetic or ways of recreating past events, but were a way of gaining epistemological knowledge of reality as well as an autonomous human ability to create original values and truths. Separately, in the twilight of the nineteenth century, Western philosophy empowered the "productive" and "creative imagination," enlarging their practical role as psychological and psychiatric techniques. Combined, these two corpora formed a possible foundation for the understanding of imagery technique development in twentieth century Jewish mysticism.

Section II: **Parameters for Mystical Praxis**

Chapter Two
Empowerment

Man is mystical by nature.[1]
—Abraham Isaac ha-Kohen Kook

A Defining the Concept "Mysticism"

The definition of mysticism is problematic to say the least. Gershom Scholem famously quipped, "Far be it for me to bother you with definitions, for no one knows what mysticism is, except for the mystics themselves, and they have different opinions, everyone according to his comprehension and apparently his spirit's comprehension. There are as many writers on this subject as there are definitions."[2] Yet, just as Scholem could not exempt himself from a precise definition, I as well must clarify the meaning of this term and how I use it in this book. Within this framework I am unable to enter the extensive discussion and interesting arguments between the essentialist-universalist schools of William James and Evelyn Underhill (established in the beginning of the twentieth century) and currently promoted by Robert K. C. Forman, and the contextualist or constructivist schools, primarily of Steven Katz, of what characterizes mysticism.[3] In brief, the essentialist school views mystical experience as a universal

---

1 Alexander Ziskind Rabinowitz (Azar), "Keter Torah," in *Ha-Maḥshavah ha-Yisra'elit*, ed. E Kalmanson (Jerusalem: s.n., 1920), 26.
2 Scholem, *Explications and Implications*, 72. Also see idem, *Major Trends in Jewish Mysticism* (New York: Schocken Books, 1961), 3–4: "There are almost as many definitions of the term as there are writers on the subject."
3 For the essentialist conception see William James, *The Varieties of Religious Experience* (New York: Longmans, Green, and Co., 1902), 379–429; Evelyn Underhill, *Mysticism: A Study in the Nature and Development of Spiritual Consciousness* (1911; repri., Mineola: Dover Publications, 2002), 3–25, 70–94. On the contextualist view see Steven T. Katz, "Language, Epistemology and Mysticism," in *Mysticism and Philosophical Analysis*, ed. S. Katz (New York: Oxford University Press, 1978), 26; idem, "The Conservative Character of Mysticism," in *Mysticism and Religious Tradition*, ed. S. Katz (Oxford: Oxford University Press, 1983), 4–6; idem, "General Editor's Introduction," in *Comparative Mysticism: An Anthology of Original Sources*, ed. S. Katz (New York: Oxford University Press, 2013), 3–22. For an extensive overview of the argument between these two schools, see Jess Byron Hollenback, *Mysticism: Experience, Response, and Empowerment* (University Park: Pennsylvania State University Press, 2000), 1–27; Wolfson, *Through a Speculum*, 52–58. For an overview in Hebrew see Garb, *Manifestations of Power*, 289; Boaz Huss, "The Mystification of the Kabbalah and the Myth of Jewish Mysticism," *Pe'amim* 110 (2007): 9–11, 15–19;

https://doi.org/10.1515/9783110535884-005

foundation common to all mystics, while the experience's description and interpretation change in accordance with the mystic's religious, cultural, and social context. Therefore, this school claims that mystical experience constitutes a common essential foundation that is independent of context as well as cultural and religious changes. In contradistinction, the contextualist (or constructivist) approach perceives the mystical experience as a specific cultural-linguistic construct, and thereby denies the possible extraction of "essential" universal components from mystical phenomenon.

There are a number of intermediate approaches claiming that the contextualist position is correct—yet, in their opinion, it is possible to identify a different external element, which allows the researcher to compare different mysticisms. Elliot Wolfson presents an adjusted contextualism, in which people in different eras experience ancient texts through their interpretation. These texts, through the hermeneutical act, shape their consciousness, language, and mystical experience. Wolfson offers a model of interdependence between the mystic's experience and the text which he interprets and through his interpretation—experiences:

> A dialectical relationship ensues between past visions recorded in literary texts and the present visionary experience, making a new experience, in effect, the reenvisioning of an original event. Furthermore, insofar as the visionary experience is hermeneutically related to the text, it may be said that the way of seeing is simultaneously a way of reading.[4]

According to Wolfson, different mystics may be compared to the extent that they engage in each other's texts. As long as the mystic's experience is linked to the experiences of those who preceded him (and wrote about their experience), although each mystic's experience is contextually dependent on his life and background–the mystic's very own life and cultural background are already always interwoven with the lives of those who preceded him! Moshe Idel, as well, produced a middle position, which identifies a shared quality of very different mysticisms, namely intensification (or empowerment). This common characteristic

---

Melila Hellner-Eshed, *A River Flows from Eden: The Language of Mystical Experience in the Zohar* (Tel Aviv: Am Oved, 2005), 29–30; Margolin, *Inner Religion*, 180–182, Margolin objects to Katz's position and attests to an unstructured experience, which according to the contextualist position cannot exist. Margolin asserts that there is a universal phenomenon of "religious internalization," and thus tends to be closer to the essentialist position, see ibid. 51–57. For more on these positions, Scholem's, and intermediate approaches, see Daniel Reiser, "'To Fly like Angels': Imagery or Waking Dream Techniques in Hasidic Mysticism in the First Half of the Twentieth Century" (PhD diss., Hebrew University, 2011), 32–44.

4 Wolfson, *Through a Speculum*, 53.

allows and necessitates the study of each mysticism in its context since it empowers and intensifies the foundations of its particular religion, while also granting a shared commonality, called intensification:

> I think the two approaches can work together. Let me propose a scheme for understanding a tentative convergence between the two scholarly approaches. I suggest that religious mysticism has two major components that are found, in various ways and degrees, in many of its manifestations. They are the intensification of religious life on the one hand, and the attempt to and eventually the feeling that a contact was established with a more sublime realm, widely understood as more spiritual than what happens in the religious experience of what is conceived of as being normal in a certain religion. Thus, we may speak about more general characteristics of mysticism, which differ from R[obert] Forman's assumption as to the existence of a special cognitive level that is specifically representative of the mystical experience. On the other hand, the sort of the intensification and the nature of the contact, vary from one sort of mysticism to another, even within the same religion, and should be understood against the background of themes and ideals found in the specific religion within which the mystic operated. I assume that most of the ideals shared by the specific mystics are also shared by the specific religious structures, which host the much more limited religious events described by scholars as mystical. Thus, a performative religion will intensify the religious acts, a religion based on faith will intensify faith, a more philosophical oriented religion will emphasize the importance of intensified acts of cognition.[5]

According to Idel, common to different mysticisms is the empowerment of religious life, and the feeling of a connection with a more sublime dimension. Therefore, in his opinion, it is possible to bridge the different schools through more general characteristics of mysticism, that differ from the presuppositions of Forman, who claims that there is an essential cognitive level at the base of all mysticisms. The commonality, according to Idel, is the experience of the connection with the transcendent and the empowerment of religious life in the specific context of each religion.[6]

In light of these matters, I would like to relate to mysticism in a complex manner, allowing for a discussion of it as an essential-shared experience from within a specific religio-cultural context. Thus, in this work, primarily analyzing twentieth century hasidism, the meaning of mysticism will be within the Jewish religious hasidic context. Privileging the context leads me to use the term mysticism in a restricted manner, appropriate for the context of this work and not in the general (universal) manner of transcending into a paranormal state of con-

5 Moshe Idel, "Performance, Intensification and Experience in Jewish Mysticism," *ARCHÆVS* 13 (2009): 96–97.
6 Ibid., 98–99.

sciousness,[7] or a radical change of consciousness occurring in a state of wakefulness, or experiments with paranormality, and the like; rather I will confine myself to the definition of mysticism as the empowerment of the experience of the divine presence, a connection with divinity (in kabbalistic and hasidic terminology: *devequt* [communion] or *hitqashrut* [binding]); the experience of, "contact with the Divine, differing from the common religious experiences cultivated in a certain religion both in its intensity and in its spiritual impact."[8] This definition corresponds to that of many scholars of mysticism (from both the contextualist and essentialist schools) like Evelyn Underhill, Rufus Jones,[9] Gershom Scholem,[10] Steven Katz,[11] Moshe Idel,[12] and Elliot Wolfson.[13]

I will relate to mysticism in this manner, in addition to the understanding that I presented in the introduction, namely that mystical experience is often a product of techniques designed to make the divine present. This remark is significant, for the assumption in the beginning of Jewish mysticism scholarship, which germinated in Gershom Scholem's research, was that mystical experience preceded the techniques and that the techniques are the fruits of such experience, causing the research field of mystical techniques to lay fallow.[14] Viewing the technique as prior to mysticism does not only create a new field of research, rather it allows for a deeper understanding of mysticism itself:

> The term 'mysticism' in Jewish texts refers to spiritual and corporeal phenomena resulting from certain practices designed to ensure and sometimes to attain, a unitive experience. By 'unitive' I mean being in the immediate presence of God... My basic assumption is that Jewish mysticism has more to do, though certainly not exclusively, with the search for and the

7 On mysticism as quieting one's consciousness and passing to a new consciousness, in kabbalah (Ḥayyim Vital, Judah Albotini, Joseph ibn Sayyah, Moses Ḥayyim Luzzatto) and in hasidism see Garb, *Shamanic Trance*, 51–74, 99–118.

8 Idel, *Kabbalah: New Perspectives*, xviii.

9 Rufus Matthew Jones, *Studies in Mystical Religion* (London: Macmillan, 1909), xv: "I shall use the word mysticism to express the type of religion which puts the emphasis on immediate awareness of relation with God, on direct and intimate consciousness of the Divine Presence. It is the religion in its most acute, intense and living stage."

10 Scholem, *Major Trends*, 3–4; Also see there Scholem's appreciation of Underhill and Jones and his attitude towards their books as "brilliant" even though they utilize the essentialist method.

11 Katz, "Language, Epistemology, and Mysticism," 27.

12 Idel, *Enchanted Chains*, 3.

13 Wolfson, *Through a Speculum*, 55: "The immediate experience of the divine presence that is characteristic of mysticism as an historical phenomenon."

14 See above in the introduction.

experience of contact with the divine realms rather than with obscure so called mystical theologies, symbolic knowledge or meditation upon their structure.[15]

The understanding of mysticism as both the structuring and product of techniques, expands the possibility of mystical experiences to a greater audience. It is not specifically a spontaneous, traumatic, and unexpected experience that descends on unique individuals alone, as William James preferred to describe it. A person is able, through technique, to consciously "enter" a mystical experience. Mystical experience, by means of technique, becomes available to wider circles. Advanced preparation, often lengthy and difficult, but accessible and possible, allows a person to encounter the divine.

Lastly, every use of the concept of mysticism in research must respond to Boaz Huss's critique of the term itself and the very study of mysticism itself. Huss has critiqued the universalist approach and claims that the term mysticism is a discursive construct of a Christian theological concept, which has been applied to different cultures, dissimilar to one another, through the colonialist framework of the West,[16] as well as the structuring of the national identities of different cultures within the European discourse of terms.[17] This application caused an erroneous claim that all phenomenon referred to as mysticism in different cultures, belong to the same category, and through this identification the methodological approach of comparing them was derived.[18] Huss has challenged the presumption that all of these phenomena are of the same category and has called for the research of these subjects, not as expressions of universal religion, but rather as cultural products anchored in the historical, social, and political

---

15 Idel, *Enchanted Chains*, 4.

16 For Huss's further critique against Christian theological terms that have entered academia, see Boaz Huss, "Religionization of Non-Christian Cultures and the Formation of New Secularities" (Paper presented at the the final symposium of the ANR-DFG Neoreligitur Research Program: (De-)secularization and New Religiosities through the prism of the Turkish Case, Paris, France, October 2017), https://www.academia.edu /35249861/ Religionization_ of_ Non-Christian_Cultures_and_the_Formation_of_New_Secularities

17 Huss, "The Mystification of Kabbalah," 12, 20–27. Also see his critique of the contextualist approach, which does not offer a sufficient alternative definition for mysticism, nor does it provide criteria for the inclusion of different cultural phenomenon within the category of mysticism, ibid., 16–19. Huss claims there that the contextualist approach actually continues to affirm the essentialist approach, whether it is aware of it or not.

18 Ibid., 12–13. Also idem, *The Question About the Existence of Jewish Mysticism: The Genealogy of Jewish Mysticism and the Theologies of Kabbalah Research* (Tel Aviv: Van Leer Institute and Hakibbutz Hameuchad, 2016), 17–19.

contexts that formed them.[19] In his opinion, the term mysticism should be discarded when attempting to characterize specific practices, and the theological explanation for these phenomena forsaken.[20] At the foundation of the definition of mysticism is a theological assumption that people are able to experience an encounter with a divine or metaphysical entity. Huss does not discredit this theological conception, rather its use as a component of academic research:

> I do not disparage this theological stance; however, I think that academic research should not be based on theological postulations and categories. Inasmuch as theological explanations of physical and biological phenomena based on the will of God (or "Intelligent design") are unacceptable in the academic study of the natural sciences, a theological explanation according to which the cause for historic, social and cultural phenomena is an experience of meeting God or a "transcendent reality."[21]

Additionally, he criticizes many scholars in the fields of religion and mysticism for their theological foundation, in which a metaphysical reality, divinity, transcendent entity, sublime power, or the like, underlies their research. This is because, according to his claim, this type of methodology confuses academic scholarship with religious practice, Huss writes, "The prevalent theological assumption accepted in the scholarship of Jewish mysticism, according to which Kabbalistic theories and literary productions were created following their unmediated encounter with the divine or metaphysical reality, blurs the distinction between academic research and religious and spiritual practice."[22]

---

19 Idem, "The Mystification of Kabbalah," 12–13, 27.

20 Ibid., 15.

21 Boaz Huss, "The Mystification of the Kabbalah and the Modern Construction of Jewish Mysticism," *BGU Review* (Summer 2008), accessed August 8, 2016, http://in.bgu.ac.il/en/heksherim/2008/Boaz-Huss.pdf. Also see his statement in idem, "Jewish Mysticism in the University, Academic Study or Theological Practice," *Zeek* (December 2007), assessed August 8, 2016, http://www.zeek.net/712academy: "I shall make two related arguments. The first is that the term "mysticism" is a theological concept, and the second is that theological concepts have no place in academic studies... I would like to emphasize that I do not oppose theological praxis.... I argue that theology can not be the basis of academic research of historical, social, and cultural phenomena." As he has also emphasized in his essay, idem, "The Theologies of Kabbalah Research," in *Jewish Thought and Jewish Belief*, ed. Daniel J. Lasker (Be'er Sheva: Ben-Gurion University Press, 2012). Also see Magid's reaction to Huss, Shaul Magid, "Is Kabbala Mysticism? Another View," *Zeek* (March 2008), assessed August 8, 2016, http://www.zeek.net/803huss/, and Huss's reply, idem, "'Paying Extra': A Response to Shaul Magid," *Zeek* (March 2008), assessed August 8, 2016, http://www.zeek.net/803huss/. Also, see Huss, *The Question About the Existence of Jewish Mysticism*, 24–27.

22 Idem, "Theologies of Kabbalah Research," *Modern Judaism* 34, no. 1 (2014):13.

I understand Huss's desire to contrast between "religious studies" and the exact sciences and to demand scientific objectivity, however I disagree with him on this matter. The natural sciences operate in line with causality, whereas the humanities operate outside of this category of thought (like the question: how did causality come to be?). The natural sciences discuss the "how" question, while the humanities are engaged with the "why." These are two different types of questions: the first explores data and processes in being, i.e. nature, and therefore something of this type may be "objective," or "pure," whereas the humanities discuss the very essence of being. The social sciences and psychology (psychiatry, psychotherapy, etc.) use many assumptions regarding the psyche, while the natural sciences are barely able to offer a satisfying description of matters that are on the border of psyche activity! The demand to compare social sciences and humanities to the natural sciences would in the end lead to their annulment, for often the premises which enable these fields are unable to be integrated within a worldview entirely based on objective facts and data. For example: the psycho-somatic connection, in which the psyche affects the body, is a common presupposition in psychology, yet scientifically-logically impossible. A matter which in of itself causes an acute philosophical problem: perhaps our instruments of thinking cannot coincide with reality at all.[23] There are parallel assumptions in sociological studies, which are also scientifically impossible. In the social sciences, in complete contrast to the natural sciences, many thinkers recognize a psychic reality that exists unto itself and operates on the physical plane and they do not see any need or reason to prove it: they simply posit it.[24]

Furthermore, even the term "theology," which Huss uses as a rejection of "mysticism"—is an academic construction, whose source is a Greek term,[25] found in certain manuscripts of the New Testament and used by Christians in the Middle Ages, which was then used in academic research for different cultures and religions. The invalidation of the experience of divine presence due to its theological nature, is itself an invalidation based on academic enforcement of this foreign term into religion. The kabbalist does not know the term theology and for him, as well as the religious person, God is real, like life itself is real. Just like a person is conscious of himself without any scientific proof, and just as he recognizes that his desires influence his actions—a recognition which is not accepted in the natural sciences (but is accepted in the humanities and so-

23 Yeshayahu Leibowitz devoted his book, *Body and Mind: The Psycho-Physical Problem* (Tel Aviv: The Ministry of Defense, 1989), to this issue.

24 Regarding the distinction between recognition and understanding see ibid., 57–60.

25 See Huss, "The Theologies of Kabbalah Research," 35 n. 5.

cial sciences), so too his recognition of the divine or his encounter with it is admissible.[26]

Finally, none of the researchers, as I recall, truly base their arguments on what Huss calls theological definitions. For example, Idel and Wolfson do not state in any of their writings, to the best of my knowledge, that people are able to experience an encounter with the divine, nor do they assume or state the existence of God. They describe and research figures throughout history who claimed such connection, but it is impossible for the reader to know their own opinion. Moreover, I do not understand what alternative Huss leaves us. He does not sufficiently demonstrate how his criticism contributes to the study of kabbalistic texts and how these texts can be analyzed differently in light of his criticism.

Now that I have explained the manner in which I will utilize the term mysticism, I will present two primary parameters that I will use for analyzing imagery techniques and their characterization as mystical: the concept of "empowerment" and "intensification," which we have briefly discussed in this preface, and the concept of "prophecy."

26 Huss in his essay, "The Theologies of Kabbalah Research," has also expanded on his demand for "religious studies" to be not only like the natural sciences, but also like the social sciences and historical studies by claiming that they have rid themselves of theological assumptions for quite some time already. Ibid., 18: "Theology, queen of the Middle Age sciences, was pushed aside in modern academia and in modern theological claims, and the claim that God is a causal factor that explains physical, biological, historical, or social phenomena, is not accepted in academic disciplines today." On the contrary! Social sciences, and even historical studies, have indeed ridden themselves of theological assumptions, yet they have adopted other non-scientific assumptions in their stead (like the existence of the soul in social sciences). These disciplines are the furthest possible from Huss's demand for "objective" research. Historical research is oriented without a doubt from the personal inclinations of the researcher, as Huss himself has demonstrated regarding Gershom Scholem, in his article, "Ask No Questions: Gershom Scholem and the Study of Contemporary Jewish Mysticism," *Pe'amim* 94–95 (2003): 57–72, specifically 64–65 (translated and published in *Modern Judaism* 25, no. 2 (2005): 141–158). The countless disagreements in the field of historical research form and reinforce the impression that the researcher brings her own world and ideas and with them analyzes history. Academic research in the humanities is naturally contextual, dependent on her personal *weltanschauung* and it is dissimilar to natural sciences due to its different and distinct nature. A worldview which negates God is able to influence the researcher to invalidate theological concepts just like a worldview which requires it may influence her to adopt theological terms.

B Empowerment

The scholar of mysticism Jess Byron Hollenback has asserted that the concept of "empowerment" is one of the primary features of mysticism and mystical experience.[27] Hollenback has discussed the importance, in the research of mysticism, of *enthymesis*, as he writes:

> My third objective–and this is one of the most unusual aspects of this study—is to draw attention to the importance of *enthymesis* or what I have termed the empowerment of thought, will, and imagination as a significant process that shapes visionary landscapes, ensures that a mystic's experiences will seem to confirm empirically the truths that his religious tradition proclaims in its myths or scriptures, and transforms the imagination and will into "organs" of supernormal perception. (Empowerment… refers to that peculiar simultaneity between thinking and being that often operates during mystical experiences).[28]

Hollenback's conception of empowerment is always magical empowerment—as I have termed it. That is to say, the empowerment of thought or imagination allows the empowerer to make actual changes in being. This is a unique state of simultaneity of imagining (or thinking) and being. This simultaneous state plays an important and central role in the concept of empowerment that Hollenback presents in which the empowered thought is translated into the plane of reality.[29] The Sufi master Al-Hujwiri, when writing about the miracles of the Sufi masters, brings an example of how living in proximity to the sacred causes the empowerment of thought in a significant fashion. His personal spiritual mentor told him that a true spiritual master has no need of actually visiting his students, it is enough that he think of them and through this he will appear before them.[30] Franz Boas, a researcher of Inuit people, has described how Inuit shamans are able to kill people through thought alone.[31] Hollenback describes mystics, who by empowering their imagination, are able to move certain objects. They visualize its movement and through this action of visualization—it indeed moves,[32] meaning that imagination is concretely materialized. Hollenback characterizes the mystic as a person who has magical-empowering ability, in other words, the ability to actualize the imagination and transform it into reality.

---

27 Hollenback, *Mysticism.*
28 Ibid., 25.
29 See also Garb, *Manifestations of Power*, 288–289.
30 Hollenback, *Mysticism*, 150.
31 Ibid., 151.
32 Ibid., 168.

The actualization of imagination is described in detail in the mystical and astral experiences of Sylvan Muldoon (1903–1969) and Robert Allan Monroe (1915–1995), and is termed in their writings as *exteriorization*, meaning "to become exterior", that is to actualize or to be actualized. One of the recommended techniques for acquiring a state of exteriorization is the waking dream. Muldoon, an American writer who engaged in astral experiences, suggested the following technique for exteriorization: a person must enter a state of sleep; however before he enters into a deep sleep, one moment before loss of consciousness, in a state of somnolence—if he will succeed at remaining in this state and dream in it —then he will have an astral projection in which the soul exits the body and is able to stroll about the world.[33] Monroe stated that in the state of a waking dream all a person must do is visualize the person or local he wants to arrive at and the journey begins.[34]

Muldoon and Monroe explained that the astral experience is not a subjective interpretation and that it entails exteriorization, meaning the simultaneity of imagination and reality. A clear example of this can be found in the experiential attempt which Monroe conducted in the afternoon on Saturday, August 15, 1963. In a waking dream Monroe had an astral projection that reached his friend, R. W.:

> This afternoon, I lay down to renew experimentation, and decided I would make a strong effort to 'visit' R.W. wherever she was.... I lay down in the bedroom about three in the afternoon, went into a relaxation pattern, felt the warmth (high order vibrations), then thought heavily of the desire to 'go' to R.W. There was the familiar sensation of movement through a light blue blurred area, then I was in what seemed to be a kitchen. R.W. was seated in a

33 Ibid., 174–176. Regarding astral journeys in the *Zohar* see Wolfson, *Luminal Darkness*, 120–121. Wolfson cites *Zohar* 2:250a: "It is written ["My beloved is like a gazelle or like a young stag; there he stands behind our wall] gazing through the windows" (Song of Songs 2:9). These exist so that he might see all those worshippers who come first to the Synagogue and are counted amongst the first ten. Then they ascend and are written above for they are called comrades (*ḥaverim*) in relation to Him, as it is written. "Lovers (*ḥaverim*) are listening; let me hear your voice" (ibid., 8:13). Happy are the righteous who know how to set their prayer as is appropriate, for when that prayer began to ascend they ascend by means of that prayer, and they enter all the heavens and all the palaces until the gate of the upper opening [i.e., the *Shekhinah*] and that prayer enters before the King to be crowned." Wolfson treats the soul's journey like an astral projection, which through prayer man ascends to the heavens until the highest gate. Furthermore, he asserts that the *Zohar* creates a link between the journey and sacred times, like the Sabbath, New Moon, and Festivals. However, it should be noted, that in the *Zohar* astral projection with an exteriorization component, as we will discuss in the following paragraph, does not appear.

34 Hollenback, *Mysticism*, 151–155.

> chair to the right. She had a glass in her hand. She was looking to my left, where two girls... were sitting, each with glasses in their hands, drinking something. The three of them were in conversation, but I could not hear what they were saying... I then turned to R.W... I reached over and... I pinched her in the side, just above the hips and below the rib cage. She let out a good loud 'Ow,' and I backed up, because I was somewhat surprised. I really hadn't expected to be able actually to pinch her... I turned and left. It is Tuesday after the Saturday of the experiment. R.W. returned to work yesterday, and I asked her what she had been doing Saturday afternoon... she reported... she was alone with her niece and the niece's friend. They were in the kitchen-dining area of the cottage... and she was having a drink... They were doing nothing but sitting and talking. I asked R.W. if she remembered anything else, and she said no.... I asked her if she remembered the pinch. A look of complete astonishment crossed her face. "Was that you?" She stared at me for a moment... I never had any idea it was you! It hurt![35]

According to Monroe it is within the capability of the imagination, in a waking dream, to act in an objective manner and affect the visualized object and thereby items are moved and people pinched. Hollenback treats ecstasy in the same fashion and emphasizes that it is not subjective, and that via ecstasy one may reach objective truth.[36]

"Empowerment," as Hollenback presents it, is essentially the empowering of thought, will, and imagination to leave their trace in reality. This definition is narrow, since it only relates to situations in which thought or imagination leave a concrete mark.[37] I will utilize this term in a more expansive manner to include circumstances in which the effect of empowerment is not felt in the material world. The primary meaning of the term "empowerment" is strengthening, enhancement, or intensification. If so, "mystical empowerment" would be the intensification of experience, and even religious experience, into a mystical one. An experience, like dancing or singing, is able to function as an emotional, even religious, experience to the extent that it constitutes a religious ritual and is not necessarily a mystical experience. Participation in a religious experience does not require an immediate or even an indirect experience of divinity or divine presence. Nonetheless, it is possible for an act of transformation to occur in which the emotional or religious experience is intensified into a mystical experience. This transformation is a process of mystical empowerment and inten-

---

35 Robert A. Monroe, *Journeys Out of the Body* (New York: Doubleday, 1977), 33–34.

36 Hollenback, *Mysticism*, 156. On the external effect of ecstatic prophecy see the following chapter and Daniel Reiser, "'To Rend the Entire Veil': Prophecy in the Teachings of Rabbi Kalonymous Kalamish Shapira of Piazecna and its Renewal in the Twentieth Century," *Modern Judaism* 34, no. 3 (2014): 334–352.

37 For this variety of empowerment and its use in hasidism see Garb, *Shamanic Trance*, 6, 22, 41, 109. On empowerment via trance see ibid., 47–74.

sification, and the techniques which make this transition possible are mystical techniques, for they facilitate the shift from normal experience to one in which divinity is encountered.

The primary difference between Hollenback's conception of empowerment and my own is that Hollenback's understanding has an external focus—an effect on the world, and may be termed "cosmocentric empowerment," whereas my formulation, which I identify with hasidic mysticism, as we will see, is primarily "anthropocentric empowerment." This is empowerment which affects man's internal world. The transformation of a religious experience into a mystical experience empowers the essence of the experience. However, I will not pass over Hollenback's conception, particularly regarding the phenomenon of the *ṣaddiq*'s empowerment via imagination and the external effect of ecstatic prophecy on the *ṣaddiq*'s or prophet's surroundings and their ability to cause physical changes.[38] Both models of empowerment, the cosmocentric and anthropocentric, constitute a common foundation which explain how mystical experience functions and is formed. The essence of mystical experiences and techniques, like the imagery techniques to be presented throughout this work, is the concentration of consciousness,[39] which enhances the religious experience into a mystical experience.

Moshe Idel writes, "The intensification of religious life on the one hand, and the contact with what is conceived of as a spiritual sphere on the other, are two main general features of mysticism that distinguish mystical literatures from other religious ones."[40] Accordingly, although one must research each form of

---

38 See the following chapter.

39 However, see Garb's critique of Hollenback: Garb, *Manifestations of Power*, 290: "The presentation of concentration as a central technique leading to an empowered consciousness is overemphasized. As I have shown, in mystical literature there is a more decentralized model, including for example possibilities like... states of consciousness relaxation, the exact opposite of concentration." Due to this work's focus on imagery techniques, which is usually done through concentration and not relaxation of consciousness, I have used Hollenback's model. However, in the discussion of "silencing techniques" of the Piazeczno Rebbe I will need to engage with states of relaxation.

40 Idel, "Performance, Intensification and Experience in Jewish Mysticism," 98–99. On the intensification of religious life as a characteristic of most forms of mysticism, idem, *Kabbalah: New Perspectives*, 35. It should be noted that in English Idel uses the term *intensification* and in Hebrew *hagbarah* (enhancement). See idem, *Enchanted Chains*, 75. Also regarding the lack of this motif in Yoga, see ibid. Furthermore, see idem, *Ascension on High in Jewish Mysticism: Pillars, Lines, Ladders* (Budapest: Central European University Press, 2005), 23; idem, *Abraham Abulafia: An Ecstatic Kabbalist* (Lancaster: Labyrinthos, 2002), 161; idem, *Ben: Sonship and Jewish Mysticism* (London: Continuum, 2007), 67; idem, *Kabbalah and Eros* (New Haven: Yale University Press, 2005), 7; idem, *Absorbing Perfections: Kabbalah and Interpretation* (New Haven: Yale Uni-

mysticism in its cultural, religious, and social context, the concept of empowerment should be viewed as a common universal factor of different configurations of mysticism:

> Though traditional mystics belong to their respective religious frameworks, and should be studied as such, they intensified their religious activity in order to reach stronger experiences than the regular religious ones in their religion. This intensification is a more universal characteristic, which is nevertheless applied to particularistic ways of religious behaviour.[41]

In regard to hasidism he has stated that, "We witness an intensification of mystical phenomena in comparison to all the other phases of Jewish mysticism."[42] Below, I will demonstrate that imagination was used as an empowerment instrument by several hasidic masters, who added it to many different experiences and thereby intensified emotional-religious experiences into mystical ones. Jonathan Garb has stated that in hasidism the highest mystical experience is not serenity, but rather sensory intensification, hence the preference for the visual over the abstract *histaklut ha-da'at* (contemplative knowledge).[43] Prophecy is a manner of visual intensification, transforming simple visual sensory into a mystical vision, in which the prophet *sees* the divine. Additionally, the quest for individual experiences of empowerment engendered new forms of practices and anomian

versity Press, 2002), 170; idem *Hasidism: Between Ecstasy and Magic* (Albany: State University of New York Press, 1995), 212; idem, *Messianic Mystics* (New Haven: Yale University Press, 1998), 234; idem, *Studies in Ecstatic Kabbalah*, 7.

41 Idem, "Performance, Intensification and Experience in Jewish Mysticism," 99. In respect to Judaism, which stressed the obligation of deeds, Idel present three forms of mysticism (ibid., 100–133) and concludes that "In the three different versions of Jewish mysticism... there is an interesting common denominator: performance, even when it has to do with spiritual processes, emotional, or mental, have strong corporeal stating points. The performance of the commandments in theosophical-theurgical Kabbalah, the loud recitations of letters, acts of rhythmic breathing, movements of hands and head in ecstatic Kabbalah, and what is called worship by corporeality in Hasidism and the relative greater importance of feelings related to limbs in this literature, are reflecting this intensification."

42 Idem, *Hasidism: Between Ecstasy and Magic*, 212.

43 *Histaklut ha-da'at* is a concept from Naḥmanides teachings which means a direct cognitive comprehension, inferior to actual vision, see Moshe Halbertal, *By Way of Truth: Nahmanides and the Creation of Tradition* (Jerusalem: Shalom Hartman Institute, 2006), 203. The preference of vision over knowledge in Naḥmanides teachings is central for understanding his mystical conception, ibid., 203–209. Also regarding the influence of the Naḥmanidean conception of prophecy on hasidism, see Jonathan Garb, "In Honor of Moshe Halbertal's book *By Way of Truth: Nahmanides and the Creation of Tradition*" (lecture, Van Leer Institute, Jerusalem, Israel, May 27, 2007). https://www.academia.edu/8016459/In_honor_of_Moshe_Halbertal_By_Way_of_Truth_-Nahmanides_and_the_Creation_of_Tradition.

activities.[44] One of these forms was *derekh ha-nevu'ah* (the path of prophecy) that yielded different techniques, which do not quiet one's thoughts, but rather empowers and invigorates them. Both in prophetic kabbalah and theosophic kabbalah the path of prophecy requires combining the letters of the divine names. This activity is not the silencing of the mind, which appears in different forms of linguistic mysticism, but rather triggers and accelerates mental processes.[45] The centrality of hasidism lies in the attempted empowerment and intensification of religious life, through different mystical techniques characterized by mental effort and not consciousness relaxation.[46] The path of prophecy, as I will discuss in the following chapter, is an activity of empowerment—in which a person merits to see the divine and "fly like angels."

44 Idel, "Performance, Intensification and Experience in Jewish Mysticism," 116–117.
45 Ibid., 119.
46 However, see Garb's study of passive trance states and relaxation of the mind. Garb proves that these states are central to sixteenth century kabbalah and onwards, including hasidism. Idem, *Shamanic Trance*, 7–12, 51–74, 105–118.

Chapter Three
Prophecy, Ecstasy, and Mysticism

A Two Models of Prophecy

Scholars of the Bible and mysticism have developed two distinct conceptualizations of biblical prophecy: the ecstatic model and the emissarial model. Ecstatic prophecy is characterized as a subjective individual event, in which man experiences the effacement of his corporeality and selfhood. The ecstatic prophet experiences only God's presence with great intensity. The emissarial model, however, describes prophecy as a phenomenon concerned with the public. The prophet functions as a messenger from God, sent to reprove the community and improve their ethical and moral behavior. In the first model, the prophet is interested only in the individual, and sometimes displays outright hostility to and alienation from the physical world—the prophet wishes to isolate himself from the world and transcend it. In the second model, the prophet is deeply invested in the material realm and the community, exhibiting a positive, even sympathetic, outlook upon the world and is involved in societal affairs and problems.[1]

Rudolf Otto (1869–1937) was among the twentieth-century scholars of religion who considered mysticism to be a universal phenomenon.[2] His studies examine the nature of religious experience, including that of biblical prophecy.[3] Otto drew heavily upon the romantic theology of Friedrich Schleiermacher (1768–1834), who argued that religious consciousness is grounded in one's feeling of total dependency upon God.[4] Another of Otto's fundamental assumption reflects the philosophy of Jakob Friedrich Fries (1773–1843), a Kantian thinker who maintained that religious experience is *a priori*; not derived from any other phenomenon. Otto claimed that people have an innate aptitude for the un-

1 For a recent survey of the different scholarly approaches to biblical prophecy, see: Margolin, *Inner Religion*, 154–160. For an alternative model describing the relationship between God and man in the Bible as an encounter, ibid., 154–155.
2 Therefore, he subscribes to the essentialist school of mysticism, see above chap. 2, concerning definitions of mysticism.
3 Otto's remarks on prophecy are found in his works: *The Idea of the Holy*; idem, *Religious Essays: A Supplement to 'The Idea of the Holy'*, trans. Brian Lunn (Oxford: Oxford University Press, 1931); idem, Mysticism East and West (New York: Macmillan, 1932).
4 Binyamin Uffenheimer, "Rudolf Otto's Approach and the Prophetic Consciousness," *Beit Mikra* 38, no. 1 (1983): 1–2. This article was reprinted in his book *Classical Prophecy: The Prophetic Consciousness* (Jerusalem: Magnes Press, 2001), 50–61.

https://doi.org/10.1515/9783110535884-006

prompted experience of the presence of the "wholly other" (*ganz andere*), namely divine power. This, he claimed, is the feeling of "holiness," an inarticulable and uncategorizable mystery, since the absolute experience of God lies outside of human conceptualization, utterly beyond the spatiotemporal realm.[5] Otto identified the uniqueness of prophetic experience in its distinction between flesh and spirit. Spirit is eternal, and therefore true, while the body is only transient, and subsequently false. The prophetic experience opens up the path to mystical experience, since it is a sensation of the power of spirit, in contrast to the nothingness of physicality. Otto identified this experience with biblical prophecy, and particularly, the figure of Isaiah.[6]

Benjamin Uffenheimer has described the different approaches to biblical prophecy at great length. He argued that scholars' personal feelings regarding ecstatic experiences often influenced their research, "on one side are the romantic scholars who wax poetic in praise of ecstasy as an undying fountain of creativity. Against them stands the rationalist and Marxist school, which claims that [ecstasy] is a state of drunkenness and confusion of the senses that destroys the creative faculties."[7] In a phenomenological analysis of four types of ecstasy, Uffenheimer attempted to soften the disagreement by demonstrating that their argument is purely semantic.[8] However, he sharply criticized Otto's ecstatic characterization of biblical prophecy. Uffenheimer considered the ecstatic revelations recorded in Scripture, in which the prophet exits his body and his personal identity is momentarily erased,[9] to be marginal, temporary phenomena

5 Uffenheimer, "Otto's Approach," 2. On the "wholly other" and the notion of holiness in Jewish thought, see: Moshe Idel, "*Ganz Andere:* On Rudolf Otto and Concepts of Holiness in Jewish Mysticism," *Da'at* 57–59 (2006): v-xliv. Idel demonstrates that Jewish mystics use the term "holiness" to describe an ontological state of intimacy and encounter between God and man, in many cases accomplished by means of theurgy. This is to be distinguished from Otto's portrayal of holiness (as well as those of Mircea Eliade and Gershom Scholem), who saw God as the "wholly other" unaffected by the deeds of man, and "holiness" as a concept that distinguishes between man and God.

6 Uffenheimer, "Otto's Approach," 2.

7 Idem, "Prolegomena to the Problem of Prophetic Ecstasy," *Sefer Bar-Ilan* 22–23 (1988): 61. For a literature review, see ibid., 45–52. Also see idem, *Early Prophecy in Israel* (Jerusalem: Magnes Press, 1973), 278–281.

8 Idem, "Prolegomenon," 53–54, 61–52; idem, *Early Prophecy*, 80–91.

9 The term "ecstasy" employed here is according to its limited definition delineating a temporary erasure of personhood, or the advent of a passive state in which God is the active agent and the person is but a divine vessel. This usage is accepted by many prominent scholars of Jewish mysticism, such as Moshe Idel, Haviva Pedaya, and Elliot Wolfson.

found only rarely and in extenuating circumstances.[10] He viewed prophecy as an institution of messengers through whom God spoke, and as a neutralization of the magical and ecstatic elements that were associated with it in the ancient Near East.[11] Uffenheimer's critique of Otto reveals his unambiguous belief that the Bible contains no elements of ecstatic or mystical experience in regards to the religious life in general, or prophetic experience in particular:

> The ethos that arises from Otto's words is one of individualism and social passivity. Individualism–because he describes the incessant striving of an individual for his own happiness and the redemption of his soul; yet in the Bible a social and communal ethos predominates, one in which the lives of individuals are bound up with the fate of the community and the history of the nation. Indeed, every once in a while the question of theodicy (*ṣiduq ha-din*) comes up, yet even in that case the central concern is not the happiness of the individual but repairing the world, which is the essence of the prophet's mission. In Otto's writings religiosity is socially passive. The believer stands with equanimity before the entire world, since everything is utter vanity... yet the singular faith of the bible is based in social activism, upon a feeling of responsibility for others and society, expressed in "you shall surely reprove your kinsman" (Lev. 19:17).[12]

> The religious experience in the Bible in general... and the experience of prophecy in particular... are essentially different from mysticism. Prophecy and mysticism are two distinct forms of religious experiences that encompass two religious archetypes with very different goals, as Friedrich Heiler (1892–1967) argued in his time... the prophet sees himself as an agent of God... the essence of his actions... is reproof and social action... This is not true of the mystic... he is closed off to the world and sequestered within himself... in order to enable his soul to turn to higher worlds and devote himself to matters of the spirit alone.[13]

This conception is based on the work of Yehezkel Kaufmann, who argued that the *raison d'être* of an Israelite prophet was to be God's emissary in order to re-

---

10 Idem, *Early Prophecy*, 51; idem, *Classical Prophecy: The Prophetic Consciousness* (Jerusalem: Magnes Press, 2001), 110, 115.

11 Idem, *Early Prophecy*, 51. Uffenheimer suggests that the story of Balaam, which began with magic and ended in prophecy, symbolizes the historical development of Israelite prophecy that "sought to become disentangled from the flickering sparks of magic and mantic powers." On the ecstatic elements of Balaam's prophecy, see ibid., 51–52. Elsewhere he describes the transition from the "spirit of God," a source of ecstasy that alights upon the prophet and overtakes him, to the "word of God," a more institutionalized (and non-ecstatic) phenomenon that characterized prophecy from the establishment of Israelite kingdom until the destruction of the Temple; see idem, *Classical Prophecy*, 109–116.

12 Idem, "Otto's Approach," 7.

13 Ibid., 10–11. For more on the distinction between the prophet and the mystic, see idem, *Classical Prophecy*, 59–61.

pair society, and promote justice and righteousness.[14] On the other hand, the mystic's "goal is substantial unity with the divine, entailing a forsaking of physicality and an attitude of equanimity, alienation from the world and society and sequestering himself within the four ells of his personhood.[15] Indeed, Uffenheimer saw the prophet qua agent as an integral part of Israelite culture.[16]

Abraham Joshua Heschel also downplayed the ecstatic component of biblical prophecy for a number of reasons.[17] Heschel believed that biblical prophecy lacked many of the important elements characteristic of ecstasy and mysticism, such as union with God, nullification of personhood, incommunicable experience, individualism, and yearning for the world beyond:

> The root of ecstatic experiences in ancient religions lies in a thirst to become possessed with a god, or to become one with a god... Such a thirst to become one with God–the supreme aspiration of many mystics—is alien to the biblical man. To him the term "union with God" would be a blasphemy... Prophetic consciousness is marked by a shuddering sense of the unapproachable holiness of God.[18]

> To attain enthusiasm a person must lose his identity... Self-extinction is the price of mystical receptivity... The prophetic personality, far from being dissolved, is intensely present and fervently involved in what he perceives.[19]

> Ecstasy is an experience which is incommunicable... It is a moment of speechless communication, transcending words, images, and worldly affairs... Prophecy, on the other hand, is meaningless without expression. Its very substance is a word to be conveyed, a messege to

---

14 Yehezkel Kaufmann, *The History of Israelite Religion* (Jerusalem: Bialik Institute, 1972), 3:720–730.
15 Uffenheimer, "Otto's Approach," 13; idem, *Classical Prophecy*, 60. Kaufman's conception of prophecy forms the basis of that of Uffenheimer; see Uffenheimer, *Early Prophecy*, 18–36.
16 Idem, *Classical Prophecy*, 13.
17 Abraham Joshua Heschel, *The Prophets* (New York: Harper and Row, 1962), 351–366. See also: Dov Rafel, *Prophecy Through the Lens of Jewish Thought* (Jerusalem: Amanah, 1971), 197–205. Rafel assembled passages about prophecy from throughout Heschel's writings and arranged them by subject.
18 Heschel, *The Prophets*, 355–357. For similar remarks on Jewish mysticism in general, see Scholem, *Explications and Implications*, 72: "If we speak of mysticism as direct unification with God, without any intermediary, then Jewish mysticism simply does not exist. There is nothing of the sort within the framework of the Jewish tradition, for this kind of unification is too daring to be possible within the concepts of the tradition for anyone who considers themselves Jewish. But if we define mysticism as the recognition or lived experience of something divine, then certainly Jewish mysticism exists." Also, see Gershom Scholem, *The Messianic Idea in Judaism* (New York: Schocken Press, 1971), 203–227.
19 Heschel, *The Prophets*, 357.

> be imparted to others. The habit of the mystic is to conceal; the mission of the prophet is to reveal.[20]
>
> The mystic is driven into trance by a personal impulse... In contrast... prophecy is not a private affair of the experient. The prophet is not concerned with his personal salvation, and the background of his experience is the life of the people.[21]
>
> Mysticism, born in a longing for a world beyond this world, strives for a perception of timeless reality... In contrast, the prophet's field of concern is not the mysteries of heaven, but the affairs of the market place; not the spiritual realities of the Beyond, but the life of the people.[22]

Heschel generally maintained that the uniqueness of the prophet was in his being sent on a divine mission. Thus, he could not associate any ecstatic elements with prophecy, since, "The state of ecstasy is its own end; the prophetic act is a means to an end."[23] In place of ecstasy Heschel emphasized a feature of prophetic experience that he referred to as "sympathy" or *pathos*. God is concerned with and takes part in the destiny of mankind and the world, mirrored by the prophet who represents human participation in the fate of God. For Heschel *pathos* refers to a phenomenon that is constant and stable, and therefore far greater than the temporary and transient experience of ecstasy.[24] Gershom Scho-

---

20 Ibid., 360–361.

21 Ibid., 361–362.

22 Ibid., 363–364.

23 Ibid., 362. A thought-provoking discussion of Heschel's approach may be found in Uffenheimer, *Classical Prophecy*, 61–71.

24 Heschel, *The Prophets*, 308–315. However, there is a rather strange contradiction between Heschel's writings and his personal deeds. Heschel himself was fascinated with the writings of Abraham Abulafia, whom he described in terms of grandiose admiration unusual for even his rather effusive style. In 1944 Heschel published a critical edition of the work "Commentary on Prayer" (*Perush al ha-Tefillah*), published as Abraham Joshua Heschel, "A Cabbalistic Commentary on the Prayerbook," in *Studies in Memory of Moses Schorr*, eds. Louis Ginzberg and Abraham Weiss (New York: The Professor Moses Schorr Memorial Committee, 1944), 113–126, which originated in Abulafia's circle, based on extensive comparisons between different manuscripts. This monumental effort has no other parallel in Heschel's career. See: Moshe Idel, "Abraham J. Heschel on Mysticism and Hasidism," *Modern Judaism* 29, no. 1 (2009): 96. Heschel was interested in the concept of Holy Spirit (*ru'aḥ ha-qodesh*) and wrote a number of articles on this subject, all of which express his belief that the longing for prophetic, even paranormal, experiences never disappeared from Jewish thought. Heschel's emphasis and the central place he awards mystical experiences in Judaism, together with his outspoken admiration for Abulafia and his prophetic experiences, do not seem to fit with his depiction of prophecy as totally devoid of any mystical elements. See ibid., 97. Also, regarding this "Commentary on Prayer", see Adam Afterman, *The Intentions of Prayers in Early Ecstatic Kabbalah: A Study and Critical Edition of an Anonymous Commentary to the Prayers* (Los Angeles: Cherub Press, 2004). For a critique of He-

lem similarly denied the existence of any ecstatic elements in prophecy, severing the connection between biblical prophecy and later Jewish mysticism.[25]

Not all scholars agree with Uffenheimer's and Heschel's rejection of the ecstatic component of biblical prophecy. Indeed, Henry Wheeler-Robinson, and later Haviva Pedaya, claimed that it is impossible to deny clear examples of ecstasy in Scripture, even though they may not be central.[26] Biblical portrayals of prophecy often connect clairvoyance with ecstatic states, characterized by madness, fainting, or falling asleep. These include the story of Balaam, the group of prophets met by Saul, Elisha and the "disciples (*benei*) of the prophets," and others.[27] Pedaya analyzed a number of ecstatic revelations in the Bible from a phenomenological perspective, with a particular focus on the prophet experience of Ezekiel during his vision of the chariot. She identifies the urge to see God with the ecstatic element of prophecy, and claims that when the normal mode of revelation is auditory, a revelation by means of an unusual vision forces one into ecstasy.[28] Ezekiel nearly loses his mind and faints in response to the vision of God, and after that experiences an aural revelation.[29] He is so shocked by the vision that he becomes unconscious, and feels the divine spirit filling him and raising him; he is like a passive vessel in God's hands. In other words, Ezekiel is utterly emptied of self during his vision, which is an example of an intensely ecstatic mode of prophecy.[30] These types continued to appear later, both in apocalyptic and Hekhalot literature.[31]

We should note that Uffenheimer's critique of Rudolf Otto makes a number of assumptions that do not necessarily fall in line with Otto's conception of prophecy. Uffenheimer did not take into account the characterization of mysticism in Otto's own thought, and in a paradoxical way this created a situation in which Uffenheimer criticizes Otto's identification of prophecy with mysticism by using the concept "mysticism," which is foreign to Otto. Ron Margolin has demonstrated that for Otto the point of departure of the mystic is not the total

---

schel's portrayal of prophetic consciousness and the problematic aspects of his theory of *Sympathy*, see: Uffenheimer, *Classical Prophecy*, 71–79.

25 Gershom Scholem, *Major Trends in Jewish Mysticism* (New York: Schocken Press, 1961), 7–14.

26 Henry Wheeler Robinson, "Hebrew Psychology," in *The People and the Book: Essays on the Old Testament*, ed. A. S. Peake (Oxford: Clarendon Press, 1925), 353–375. Wheeler argued that paranormal elements cannot be removed from biblical prophecy.

27 Haviva Pedaya, "Sight, Fall, Song: The Longing for a Vision of God and the Spiritual Element in Early Jewish Mysticism" *Asufot* 9 (1995): 239.

28 Ibid., 242.

29 Ibid., 245–246.

30 Ibid., 246–247.

31 For apocalyptic literature, see ibid., 250–259. For Hekhalot literature, see ibid., 259–274.

dependence on the "wholly other," meaning God, but rather the awareness that God fills the entire world. A mystic who emerges from a religious culture in which God is identified with concept of justice cannot be indifferent to ethics and morality. Just the opposite is true: an experience of divine presence strengthens his resolve to fulfill the ethical commands of the same God who is present, and the mystic takes active steps in order to realize this. According to Margolin, Otto describes a type of mystic who is involved in the world and has a positive attitude toward the physical realm.[32]

This is radically different than the portrait of mysticism drawn by Uffenheimer, who claimed that mystics reject the world and seek to escape it. Uffenheimer's ideas are based on the research of his wife Rivka Schatz-Uffenheimer, who argued that mysticism has two primary goals. The first is withdrawal from the world and a perspective of detached indifference regarding the events of the world, called the "attribute of equanimity" (*midat ha-hishta'avut*) in hasidic literature. The second goal of mysticism is entering the world of the spirit by means of fleeing from all that is not essential and enduring, referred to as "casting off corporeality" (*hitpashṭut ha-gashmiyut*) in hasidic thought. Shatz-Uffenheimer derived both of these goals from her own interpretation of hasidic texts.[33] By relying on these definitions Uffenheimer concluded that mystical religiosity is characterized by absolute individualism, which creates a rift between mankind and the world, and between one person and another.[34] In addition, Uffenheimer adopted the conception of history voiced by Gershom Scholem and

---

32 Ron Margolin, *The Human Temple: Religious Interiorization and the Structuring of Inner Life in Early Hasidism* (Jerusalem: Magnes Press, 2005), 36.

33 Uffenheimer, "Otto's Approach," 11–12.

34 Ibid., 12. In Rivka Schatz-Uffenheimer, *Hasidism as Mysticism: Quietistic Elements in Eighteenth-Century Hasidic Thought*, trans. Jonathan Chipman (Princeton: Princeton University Press 1993), Schatz-Uffenheimer identified Jewish mysticism with Christian Quietism. Through this comparison she emphasizes that the concept of self-annihilation found in hasidism is based in a rejection the world. Schatz-Uffenheimer identified nihilistic and antinomian elements in the basic teachings of hasidism, and argued that devotion to the world beyond requires a total break with this world, or, at the very least, an attempt to leave it completely behind; see Margolin, *The Human Temple*, 45–46, 51. Schatz-Uffenheimer thus criticizes the reading of hasidism put forward by Martin Buber, who argued that Hasidism embraces a theology in which God dwells within the world and has a markedly positive relationship to physical reality. Buber's interpretation had been criticized with great frequency and vehemence by Gershom Scholem and his students, including Schatz-Uffenheimer, and since then has been marginalized by most scholars (ibid., 27–32, 46, 52). For a full list of scholarship written on this debate, see Sam Berrin Shonkoff, "Sacramental Existence and Embodied Theology in Buber's Representation of Ḥasidism," *Journal of Jewish Thought and Philosophy* 25 (2017): 142 n. 34.

argued that the mystical trend is a later stage in the classical history of religion.[35] He added that the circumstances that lead to the emergence of mysticism are "dissatisfaction with the external reality, discomfort and depression of the soul, disgust with the world and cultural exhaustion."[36] Identifying mysticism with a rejection of the world and withdrawal from society resulting from frustration, depression, despondency, and disgust with the world, and prophecy with an ethical message to society, forced Uffenheimer to disavow any connection between prophecy and mysticism.

Recent studies have challenged these assumptions. Eliezer Schweid has reexamined the historical scheme outlined by Scholem,[37] and Ron Margolin and Israel Koren have reappraised the conclusions of Rivka Schatz-Uffenheimer adopted by Benjamin Uffenheimer. There is now a great need for a new discussion about the nature of biblical prophecy. In their research regarding the phenomenon of mysticism in general, Margolin and Koren revealed a clear distinction between two types of mysticism with different attitudes toward the physical world. They have demonstrated that alongside those who reject the world, many mystics view physical reality in positive terms. Even concepts such as "casting off corporeality" and "equanimity" may also be interpreted in a way that appreciates the world and does not preclude mystic's involvement in society.[38] Similar-

---

35 Although Uffenheimer does not refer to Scholem explicitly, it is clear that he is drawing upon Scholem's first lecture at the beginning of *Major Trends*. Scholem described a historical scheme in which mysticism is a necessary later stage in the development of all religions. The first stage is characterized by a naïve religiosity in which people had certain and spontaneous experiences of the divine. This is followed by a period of institutionalized religion in which spontaneity disappears. Mysticism then appears after the stage of institutionalization, a reawakening characterized by the desire to return to lived experiences of God together with an acceptance of the institutions; mysticism seeks to split asunder the "husk" and find a window back into direct experience of the divine presence. This is not the same as the simple, spontaneous religion of the first stage, which can never fully return. Mysticism acknowledges the institutional framework, although it constantly prioritizes direct experience even within the order and law. On Scholem's understanding of the history of religion, see Eliezer Schweid, "Mysticism and Judaism According to Gershom Scholem," *Jerusalem Studies in Jewish Thought* 2 (1983): 8.

36 Uffenheimer, "Otto's Approach," 12. Although Uffenheimer himself argued that the personal proclivities of other scholars influenced their research regarding the connection between ecstasy and prophecy, it seems that his analysis was similarly guided by his own inclinations.

37 See above, n. 35.

38 See the entire second part of Margolin, *Human Temple*; Israel Koren, "Martin Buber—From Ecstasy to the Mysticism of Life," *Kabbalah* 5 (2000): 371–410; expanded upon in idem, *The Mystery of the Earth: Mysticism and Hasidism in the Thought of Martin Buber* (Leiden: Brill, 2010), 31–183. For more on differing relationships to the physical world in mysticism, see Zohar

ly, Yoram Jacobson has argued that the concept of "the negation of existence" (*biṭṭul ha-yesh*) in Ḥabad thought does not imply rejection of the world and does not necessarily adduce an acosmic worldview, as was argued by Schatz-Uffenheimer and Rachel Elior.[39] The world exists as an ontological reality, and only within it can the ultimate goal of Ḥabad, namely creating a "dwelling place [for God] in the lower realms," be realized. "Nullifying existence" is an internal paradigm shift in which the hasid is called to look beyond the perceived multiplicity and reveal the divine unity as expressed *within* the physical world.[40]

New studies, such as those of Koren and Margolin, present a more complicated picture of mysticism. Their work demands a renewed examination of the mystical elements of prophecy, and raises the question of whether a single monochromatic description of a prophet—whether as ecstatic or messenger—may preclude more subtle models. Indeed, can prophecy accurately be described in general, one-dimensional terms, or might there be a number of different types of prophecy and a diverse array of prophetic experiences?

The Notion of Biblical Prophecy in Rabbinic Literature

A nuanced examination of the phenomenon of prophecy is already found in rabbinic literature. The sages' offer a multi-faceted description of prophecy, and they identify at least two types of prophets, each with their own discrete characteristics:

> The sages taught: forty-eight prophets and seven prophetesses prophesied for Israel, and they did not diminish or add on to what is written in the Torah, except for reciting the scroll [of Esther]... And no more? But it is written, "and there was a man from Ramatayim Ṣofim" (1 Samuel 1)—one of the two hundred (*matayim*) seers (*ṣofim*) who prophesied for Israel. There were many! As it is taught, "there were many prophets in Israel, twice as many as those who left Egypt. But only prophecy needed for later generations was written down; if it was not needed, it was not written down.[41]

Maor, *A New Secret Doctrine: Spirituality, Creativity and Nationalism in the Prague Circle* (Jerusalem: Zalman Shazar Center, 2010), 68–100, 241–246.

39 Also, see Elliot R. Wolfson, *Open Secret: Postmessianic Messianism and the Mystical Revision of Menaḥem Mendel Schneerson* (New York: Columbia University Press, 2009), 66–160, for a more nuanced and non-dichotomous understanding of Ḥabad's conceptualization of this world and the somatic body.

40 Yoram Jacobson, "The Rectification of the Heart: Studies in the Psychic Teachings of R. Shneur Zalman of Liadi," *Te'udah: Studies in Judaica* 10 (1996): 359–363, and n. 4.

41 *b. Megillah* 14a.

This suggests that the sages had a tradition that many more prophets were active in biblical times than are counted in the twenty-four books of Scripture.[42] According to this passage individuals such as Elkanah, the husband of Hannah and father of Samuel, and many others like them were among these two hundred prophets.[43] These figures are not referred to as prophets in the Bible, and their prophecies were not written down for posterity because they were of no relevance for later generations. This distinction allows for the understanding of two types of prophecy, which differ in both their content as well as in their very nature.[44]

A distinction between different types of prophecy may already be found in the plain-sense meaning of Scripture. This notion has served as the source for many later interpretations of prophecy, from the rabbinic traditions to the medieval commentators, and even to the present day. Scripture contrasts the prophecy of Moses with that of all the other prophets: "He said, 'Hear these My words: When a prophet of the Lord arises among you, I make Myself known to him in a vision, I speak with him in a dream. Not so with My servant Moses; he is trusted throughout My household. With him I speak mouth to mouth, plainly and not in riddles, and he beholds the likeness of the Lord'" (Num. 12:6–8).

The sages make a distinction between the different biblical books of the Torah, the Prophets and the Writings: "Come and hear: one may place... a Pentateuch on top of [copies of the] Prophets and Writings. But Prophets and Writings may not be put on top of a Pentateuch."[45] This ruling was understood by one medieval commentator as distinguishing between three different levels of biblical prophecy:

> "He put the breastpiece on him, and put into the breastpiece the Urim and Thummim" (Lev. 8:8). This was an inscription of the tetragrammaton... It was the level of the holy spirit, which is below the rung of prophecy but above that of the divine voice (*bat kol*). Know that

---

42 The classical commentators on the Talmud debated the identity of these forty-eight prophets. See Rashi ad loc, and the beginning of Menaḥem Meiri's commentary on *m. Avot.*

43 In order to make this number agree with the *barayta* citing that there were twice as many prophets as those who left Egypt (i.e. 120,000 prophets), R. Samuel Eidels (1555–1631) explains that the two hundred prophets were only those in the generation of Elkanah, whereas the total number was much greater.

44 See below, subchapter, "Kalonymous Kalman Shapira's Conception of Prophecy: A Third Model," that this text is the source for Shapira's distinction between ecstatic prophecy and emissarial prophecy. In Rashi's commentary on *b. Megillah* 14a, he explains that prophecy recorded for generations to come has a socio-ethical message, "Prophecy needed for later generations: giving instruction and teaching repentance. All of the forty-eight were necessary."

45 *b. Megillah* 27a. This statement was accepted into normative halakhah: Maimonides, *Mishneh Torah*, "Laws concerning Phylacteries," 10:5; Joseph Karo, *Shulḥan Arukh*, Yoreh De'ah, §282:12

> this is the distinction between prophecy and the holy spirit: when prophecy comes upon the person, all of his faculties and senses are totally negated, and he is disconnected from the ways of the world and utterly removed from material; he meditates with the intellect alone. All of this happens while he is awake. This was the sublime level of the eight prophets. None of his senses are nullified during the holy spirit, and he speaks like any other person. Yet the supernal spirit arouses him and the words appear on his tongue, and he foretells the future with divine assistance. This is the level of the Writings. However, the level of the Torah that Moses enjoined upon us is higher than all of this, since Moses's prophecy was above any other prophet. For this reason you will find that the sages always mention the Torah, the Prophets and the Writings in the order of the level of their prophecy. So they have said explicitly, "one may place... a Pentateuch on top of [copies of the] Prophets and Writings. But Prophets and Writings may not but put on top of a Pentateuch." The sages employed this in order to describe the levels of prophecy, so that people will pay attention to the source of prophecy. They are ordered according to their level, and Moses's prophecy is different than all others.[46]

Rabbenu Baḥya characterizes prophecy as an ecstatic moment, resulting in the total erasure of a prophet's personal identity, "All of his faculties and senses are totally negated, he is disconnected from the ways of the world and utterly removed from material." In contradistinction to this, the "prophecy" or holy spirit of the Writings is not ecstatic, "None of his senses are nullified and he speaks like any other person." Mosaic prophecy, which is the source of the Torah's authority, is understood as prophecy of the highest order. It should be noted that Rabbenu Baḥya does not characterize Moses's level on its own, but rather compares it to all other forms of prophecy. His ranking of prophecy from the most intense to the least, or from the Pentateuch to the Writings, is an interpretation of the rabbinic law mentioned above. It is forbidden to place scrolls of the Prophetic books or Writing on top of the Torah, because the latter's authority flows from a higher source, and it is similarly forbidden to place the Writings on top of the Prophets. The opposite, however, is permitted. In other words, this law ordaining which books may be physically placed on one another is directly rooted in the book's source and type of prophetic inspiration. Therefore, ecstatic prophecy is clearly above that of the Writings. Rabbenu Baḥya characterizes the latter as the work of the prophet who is first and foremost a messenger, "He foretells the future with divine assistance. This is the level of the Writings."[47]

---

46 Rabbenu Baḥya, *Commentary on the Torah*, ed. Hayyim Dov Chavel (Jerusalem: Mossad HaRav Kook, 1972), 2:437–438.

47 Foretelling the future is generally a reflection of the prophet's role as an emissary, either to implore the nation to repent and become just and upright in the face of the impending tragedy, or to impart words of comport and strength.

We have seen that according to the sages, biblical prophecy is not monolithic, rather there are many types; there is no biblical *prophecy*, but *prophecies*.

Biblical Prophecy through the Prism of Prophetic Kabbalah

Ecstatic *devequt* in Abulafia's doctrine, acquired through the utilization of mental concentration techniques and letter-combination, is termed by Abulafia as prophecy. This is due to the *devequt* process entailing the unification of man's intellect with the active intellect, a phenomenon depicted as mystical union.[48] Abulafian prophetic kabbalah identified prophecy as an ecstatic process in which there is a shift of consciousness as a result of mystical combination techniques, allowing for the descent of the divine spirit within man.[49] The author of *Sha'arei Ṣedeq* discusses ecstatic experience as a result of combination techniques.[50] One of the central motifs of Isaac of Acre's *Oṣar Ḥayyim* is the drawing down of divine radiance into the soul, which is the foundation of prophecy.[51] Isaac of Acre identifies this motif with Mosaic prophecy,[52] and claims that the kabbalistic tradition was passed down by Moses and Elijah the prophet,[53] and that the prophecy learned from them is characterized by sensory nullification, "The meaning of 'you shall prophesy' is that... they would try to nullify the physical senses, to negate from the thought of the soul every physical sensation, and to garb it in the spirituality of the intellect... Indeed, the pure thought of the soul of Elijah, of blessed memory, was attached to *YH YHVH*, the God of Israel, alone.[54] In the book *Ketem Paz*, R. Shimon Ibn Lavi (16th c.) characterizes biblical prophecy as ecstatic, "This matter was found in the prophets when the holy spirit (*ru'aḥ ha-qodesh*) rested upon them, their feelings would be nullified

---

48 Idel, *Kabbalah: New Perspectives*, 61–62.
49 Idem, *The Mystical Experience*, 22–24; Margolin, *The Human Temple*, 102.
50 Ibid., 308.
51 Ephraim Gottlieb, *Studies in Kabbalistic Literature*, ed. Joseph Hacker (Tel Aviv: Tel Aviv University, 1976), 245; Margolin, *The Human Temple*, 309. Also, see Isaac of Acre's depiction of ecstatic practice in *Oṣar Ḥayyim*, "A person will not acquire completeness (or perfection) until he breaks and subjugates these two souls... By emptying
his body of them... And after he does this, his soul will attach itself to the supernal dew. After all this, the light of the *Shekhinah* will shine onto him," as quoted in Eitan P. Fishbane, *As Light Before Dawn: The Inner World of a Medieval Kabbalist* (Stanford: Stanford University Press, 2009), 270–271.
52 Gottlieb, *Studies in Kabbalistic Literature*, 245.
53 Regarding the portrayal of Binayahu ben Yehoyada, see Fishbane, *As Light Before Dawn*, 170.
54 Ibid., 262–263.

until they would not feel their selves, if they had bodies or not, for their souls cleaved on high."[55] In the work *Sulam ha-Aliyah* of R. Judah Albotini, prophecy is considered as the cleaving of the soul to the active intellect, an activity that entails the separation of the soul from the body.[56] This cleaving allows for the garbing of the soul through the imaginative faculty, which is thereby able to engage with prophecy and esoteric teachings.[57] According to R. Moses of Kiev, the author of *Shoshan Sodat*, prophecy is a spontaneous state, which comes through forgetting of one's self or the disappearance of one's self.[58] Ron Margolin has argued that these conceptions of prophecy, which base themselves on biblical forms of prophecy, stand in stark contrast to the positions of the biblical scholars who have denied the identification of the biblical prophecy with ecstatic prophecy.[59]

Prophecy in the New Testament and Medieval Christian Theology

Ecstatic prophecy is found in the New Testament as well. Paul experienced a spontaneous revelation that weakened him. He fell to the ground during the revelation and lost his sight. His loss of vision lasted for three days, together with the loss of his ability to eat and drink. Ecstatic characteristics, such as anxiety and dread are to be found in his account:

> Now as he was going along and approaching Damascus, suddenly a light from heaven flashed around him. He fell to the ground and heard a voice saying to him, "Saul, Saul, why do you persecute me?" He asked, "Who are you, Lord?" The reply came, "I am Jesus, whom you are persecuting. But get up and enter the city, and you will be told what you are to do." The men who were travelling with him stood speechless because they heard the voice but saw no one. Saul got up from the ground, and though his eyes were open, he could see nothing; so they led him by the hand and brought him into Damascus. For three days he was without sight, and neither ate nor drank (Acts. 9:3–9).

As a reaction to the vision of heavenly light, Paul's spirit departs, he falls, and afterwards receives an auditory revelation. This reaction matched the principle that Haviva Pedaya has identified, namely, the norm is auditory revelation,

55 Within: Boaz Huss, *Sockets of Fine Gold: The Kabbalah of R. Shimo'n Ibn Lavi* (Jerusalem: Magnes Press, 2000), 180.
56 Margolin, *The Human Temple*, 310.
57 Ibid.
58 Ibid., 316–317
59 Ibid., 311.

while the exception is aural revelation, in which there is an ecstatic event.[60] In the wake of this revelation, Paul loses his physical bearings, in a sense, discarding his corporeality and bodily needs, thereby transforming him into a passive vessel capable of receiving the divine spirit. Nevertheless, the purpose of his prophecy was to fulfill an emissarial function; therefore, his prophecy represents a more complex picture, integrating aspects of both the ecstatic and emissarial models. In general, prophecy in the New Testament, similar to biblical prophecy, consists of a message for the individual and society, "Those who prophesy speak to other people for their building up and encouragement and consolation" (I Cor. 14:3). Furthermore, Paul did not conceive of prophecy as being for the select individuals and promoted its expansion by instilling the idea that all are able to be prophets. In his opinion, prophecy is not meant for only God's chosen few, rather it is attainable by all, thus broadening the scope of religious authority from the Church to the general congregation. This action was based on the Christian focus on love. According to Paul, Jesus elevated love above the yoke of the commandments. Love can transform man into being capable of prophecy through love as the body become a divine vessel. This conception transferred the weight of religious authority to the people and encouraged them to prophesy, "For you can all prophesy one by one, so that all may learn and all be encouraged. And the spirits of prophets are subject to the prophets... So, my friends, be eager to prophesy, and do not forbid speaking in tongues" (Ibid., 31–32, 39).

Prophecy in the New Testament differs from prophecy in the Hebrew Bible, primarily regarding its apocalyptic content. Subsequently, there is a dominant strain of otherworldliness in Christian prophecy, which stands in contrast to its emissarial features. Paul's Epistles to the Thessalonians convey a sense of the immanent apocalypse, thus, there is no need to engage with "the times and the seasons," i.e. things of this world:

> Now concerning the times and the seasons, brothers and sisters, you do not need to have anything written to you. For you yourselves know very well that the day of the Lord will come like a thief in the night. When they say, 'There is peace and security,' then sudden destruction will come upon them, as labour pains come upon a pregnant woman, and there will be no escape! But you, beloved, are not in darkness, for that day to surprise you like a thief; for you are all children of light and children of the day; we are not of the night or of darkness (I Th. 5:1–5)

Later, at the end of the Medieval and during the Renaissance periods, prophecy was once again identified with the apocalyptic age, due to the predictions of the

60 Pedaya, "Sight, Fall, Song," 242.

end of the world that arose between the fourteenth and sixteenth centuries, primarily owing to the Roman "apocalyptic preachers."[61] Some, such as Egidio da Viterbo (1469 – 1532), Bernardino Lopez de Carvajal (1456 – 1523), Paulus Angelus (c. 1490 – 1568), and others, were thought of, or even thought of themselves, as prophets.[62] Medieval Christian prophetic figures saw their time as the end of days.[63] An abundance of new prophetic literature was written in these centuries and, surprisingly, were accepted by the Church, in the event that it was accompanied by the old prophecies.[64] There were even some figures who were influenced by kabbalistic literature and based their teachings on it.[65] In these cases as well, the ecstatic and emissarial elements of prophecy are intertwined, a fact that raises the question regarding this dichotomy of prophetic types.

The Limitation and Expansion of Prophecy in Medieval Jewish Rationalist Thought

The study of medieval prophecy is a massive field and here is not the place to explore it in its entirety.[66] I will briefly discuss one aspect of it, namely, the recipient of prophecy. There are two key trends in medieval Jewish philosophy concerning prophecy: those who limit it to the select few and those who expand it to the masses. An analysis of these trends will serve us in understanding different characteristics of mysticism. Similar to prophecy, a question exists regarding mysticism of whether esoteric knowledge and mystical experience are reserved

---

61 There was great confusion in the Christian world regarding this apocalypse, whether nature would continue to exist or not, whether there would there be a great war between good and evil that would bring about the end of history, or whether, in a more positive conception, the end of days might occur within the historical process. See Marjorie Reeves, *The Influence of Prophecy in the Later Middle Ages* (Oxford: Clarendon Press, 2000), 506 – 507.

62 Concerning these figures, see the collected essays in idem, ed., *Prophetic Rome in the High Renaissance Period* (Oxford: Oxford University Press, 1992), 89 – 199.

63 Ibid., 19, 21, 25, 101. 150 – 151, 204 – 213, 389.

64 Ibid., 23.

65 For example, see Egidio da Viterbo's thought, ibid., 91 – 110, esp. 97 – 99. Regarding the Abulafian works available to Egidio da Viterbo, see Moshe Idel, "Agideo da Viterbo and the Writings of Abraham Abulafia," *Italia* 2 (1981): 48 – 50. Also, see Egidio da Viterbo's *Libellus de litteris hebraicist* (*Book on Hebrew Letters*), which was recently translated into Hebrew by Yehuda Liebes (Ægidius Viterbensis, *Libellus de Litteris Hebraicis*, trans. Yehuda Liebes (Jerusalem: Carmel, 2013). Furthermore, see Brian Copenhaver and Daniel Stein Kokin, "Egidio da Viterbo's Book on Hebrew Letters: Christian Kabbalah in Papal Rome," *Renaissance Quarterly* 67, no. 1 (2014): 1 – 42.

66 See above, chap. 1 n. 42, 68.

for ascetics and isolated select individuals, or available to and meant for society at large?

Prophecy in Halevi's thought is conceived as not only the prophetic content, namely, God's will, but also as an experience of divine presence, which is the climax of prophecy.[67] Prophecy is the ultimate completion of the Jewish person (and not the non-Jew, who, according to Halevi, cannot attain prophecy) and it is what exceeds the *inyan ha-sikhli* (intellectual matter), which consequently exceeds man's natural capabilities.[68] Similarly, Maimonides understood prophecy as the completion of man's personhood (Jew and non-Jew alike), occurring as a result of his human traits and characteristics.[69] The foundation of both Halevi's and Maimonides's conceptions, despite their differences, is found in the Neo-Aristotelean Islamic understanding of prophecy as the perfection of man.[70] This understanding limits prophecy to select individuals, whether it be due to ethnic or intellectual concerns. In contrast, one may find in the writings of Abraham Maimuni, Maimonides's son, an expansion of prophecy.

Paul Fenton and Dov Maimon have each argued that Maimuni followed in his father's footsteps and restricted prophecy to the select few.[71] In contradistinction, Hannah Kasher and Mordechai A. Friedman maintain that his teachings do entail a desire to instruct people in the ways of prophecy.[72] Shahar Rubenstein holds an inclusive opinion and argues that according to Maimuni prophecy is at-

---

67 Eliezer Schweid, *The Classic Jewish Philosophers: From Saadia through the Renaissance*, trans. Leonard Levin (Leiden: Brill, 2008), 132.

68 Halevi, *Sefer ha-Kuzari*, 1:41–43.

69 Concerning the differences between Halevi's and Maimonides's conceptions of prophecy, see Yitzhak Sheilat, "The Uniqueness of Israel: Comparing the Kuzari and Maimonides," *Ma'aliyot* 20 (1999): 275–288.

70 See Maimonides, *Guide of the Perplexed*, 2:32§2:361, "The third opinion is the opinion of our Law and the foundation of our doctrine. It is identical with the philosophic opinion except in one thing." Also, see Herbert A. Davidson, *Alfarabi, Avicenna, and Averroes, on Intellect: Their Cosmologies, Theories of the Active Intellect, and Theories of Human Intellect* (Oxford: Oxford University Press, 1992), 181–207, 218–219.

71 Paul Fenton, "The Literary Legacy of the Descendants of Maimonides," *Pe'amim* 97 (2003): 10; Dov Maimon, "Rabbinical Judaism and Islamic Mysticism: The Limits of a Relationship," *Akdamot* 8 (1999): 61–66. Also, see Elisha Russ-Fishbane, *Judaism, Sufism, and the Pietists of Medieval Egypt: A Study of Abraham Maimonides and His Times* (Oxford: Oxford University Press, 2015), regarding Maimuni in general and regarding prophecy, see ibid., 187–243.

72 See Hannah Kasher, "Students of the Philosophers as Disciples of the Prophets: Written Directives for Prophecy among the Successors of Maimonides," in *Joseph Baruch Sermoneta Memorial Volume* (Jerusalem: Hebrew University of Jerusalem, 1998), 73–85.

tainable for everyone.[73] Rubenstein concludes on the basis of a number of polemics that Maimuni wrote that he viewed himself as the head of the community, who leads his congregation towards the attainment of prophecy.[74] Maimuni's insertion of prophetic techniques in his halakhic decision as obligatory upon everyone, demonstrates the expansion of the prophetic goal.[75] Additionally, the messianic atmosphere of this time period created the expectation of prophetic renewal.[76]

Maimuni's conception of prophecy does not coincide with the two models that we have presented thus far. Prophecy as the completion and perfection of man is not essentially ecstatic or of an emissarial nature. This conception attests to an alternative possibility.

B Kalonymous Kalman Shapira's Conception of Prophecy: A Third Model

Eliezer Schweid has surveyed the renewed interest in prophecy in the twentieth century, with a particular emphasis on the conception of a prophet as an emissary to society.[77] He argued that among contemporaneous elites and intellectuals, such as Jewish authors writing in Hebrew, Yiddish and German, as well as poets, philosophers, a certain "prophetic" consciousness may be found, which manifested as a striving for the historical renewal of prophecy.[78] The unwavering belief of the champions of modernity in the inevitability of ethical progress, built upon rationality, was shaken by the wave of racial anti-Semitism that overtook "enlightened" leaders such as intellectuals, academics, writers and men of spirit at the end of the nineteenth century. This secular form of anti-Semitism was worse than the classic religious persecutions by Christianity throughout the middle ages. The rise of anti-Semitism shattered expectations that rationality and progress alone would bring about a just and ethical society, peace between nations and religions, and the full acceptance of the Jewish people in equal terms.[79]

73 Shahar Rubenstein, "Prophecy in the Teachings of R. Abraham ben ha-RaMBaM" (master's thesis, Hebrew University, 2009), 69–84.
74 Ibid., 72–84.
75 Ibid., 73, 76, 79.
76 Ibid., 83; Russ-Fishbane, *Judaism, Sufism, and the Pietists of Medieval Egypt*, 187–243.
77 Eliezer Schweid, *Prophets for Their People and Humanity: Prophecy and Prophets in 20th Century Jewish Thought* (Jerusalem: Magnes Press, 1999).
78 Ibid., 9.
79 Ibid., 11–12.

However, concomitant with this emissarial model, the twentieth century saw the rise of a very different kind of renewed involvement in prophecy, together with its related technical and contemplative practices. Schweid left out several twentieth-century thinkers who explicitly, and in some cases, exhaustively, dealt with prophecy, whose notions did not conform the concept of prophet as emissary. Those omitted include R. Shem Tov Gefen (1856–1927);[80] R. David Kohen (1887–1972), known as "the Nazir";[81] and Kalonymous Kalman Shapira (1889–1943).[82]

Shapira, one of the foremost hasidic thinkers of the twentieth century, immersed himself in the study of prophecy.[83] His teachings on this subject are woven throughout his five books: *Benei Maḥshavah Ṭovah*; *Ḥovat ha-Talmidim*; *Hakhsharat ha-Avrekhim*; *Mevo ha-She'arim*; and his mystical diary *Ṣav ve-Zeruz*. In fact, his work *Mevo ha-She'arim* is devoted to in-depth and comprehensive description of the phenomenon of prophecy.[84]

It should be noted that Shapira did not distinguish between biblical prophecy and its later developments. Indeed, much of his attitude towards prophecy was shaped by his interpretation of scriptural stories. However, his uniqueness lies in his desire to restore prophecy, as well as his development of new contemplative techniques to achieve this goal.[85]

---

80 Shem Tov Gefen, *Dimensions, Prophecy, and Geology* (Jerusalem: Mosad Harav Kook, 1974). See ibid., 17–18, 27, for his own account of ecstatic and mystical experiences. Gefen was a bold and original thinker who integrated kabbalah with philosophy, psychology, and especially physical sciences and mathematics. He has yet to receive serious scholarly attention. For the only article about Gefen's thought I have been able to locate, see Aharon Shear-Yashuv, "The Harmony between Maimonides, Kabbalah and Kant According to Rabbi Shem Tov Gefen," *Da'at* 64–66 (2009): 343–350. Also, see Dov Schwartz's brief discussion idem, *Faith at the Crossroads: A Theological Profile of Religious Zionism*, trans. Batya Stein (Leiden: Brill, 2002), 101–105. Gefen's teachings on prophecy appear in his book, *Prophecy and Purity, or Mathematical Philosophy of Infinity* (Cairo: Ḥayyim Vidal, 1923).

81 David Kohen, *The Voice of Prophecy* (Jerusalem: Mossad Harav Kook, 1970). On the connection between the Nazir's longing for prophecy and the writings of Abulafia, see Moshe Idel, "Rabbi Abraham Abulafia, Gershom Scholem and Rabbi David Ha-Kohen (ha-Nazir)," *Jerusalem Studies in Jewish Thought* 19 (2005): 819–834.

82 Schweid was certainly acquainted with the mystical thought of "the Nazir" and Shapira, for in his book *From Ruin to Salvation* (Tel Aviv: Hakibbutz Hameuchad, 1994), 111–113, he describes Shapira's theological response to the Holocaust.

83 For Shapira's biographic details, see below, chap. 4 n. 1.

84 Regarding his writings, see below, chap. 4., subchapter, "R. Kalonymous Kalman Shapira's Books."

85 See Ron Wacks, "Nevu'ah ve-Ḥasidut be-Torato shel ha-Rebi me-Pi'asechnah," in *Prophesy, O Son of Man: On the Possibility of Prophecy*, ed. Odeya Tzurieli (Jerusalem: Rubin Mass, 2006),

Many of the elements described by Schweid are lacking in Shapira's works, such as certain knowledge of an impending historical disaster of international proportions, an encompassing national and societal vision, improvement of daily life, and the historical realization expressed through physical actions.[86] These aspects are characteristic of the socio-ethical emissarial model of prophecy. Given that this model played a secondary role in Shapira's thought, it is unsurprising that they are missing. Instead, we will see that his understanding of prophecy emphasizes its ecstatic and mystical elements.

Shapira interpreted the sages' distinction between transcribed prophecy for posterity, and other non-recorded prophecies, as referring to two different archetypes of prophecy that existed in biblical times: ethical prophecy and mystical prophecy. Ethical prophecy is societally focused, and its message is relevant for generations to come, whereas mystical-ecstatic prophecy is unconcerned with the future. Its influence is felt in the present, by those in immediate proximity of the prophet who intensely experience the divine presence.

Shapira saw the emissarial model of prophecy, as well as the miracle-magical model, as corruptions, "An erroneous conception of what a prophet is has formed in our mind. We see him in terms of our own needs, as one who foretells the future to Israel when they need to find their donkeys,[87] or any increase of blessing in the flour jar and the oil flask,[88] or to teach them the ways of war... and if it seems from our holy Bible that the words of the prophet are to teach repentance and [give other] instruction, one could err by thinking that he was only an admonisher."[89] However, if prophecy is solely a mission of ethical rebuke and a call for repentance, Shapira asks, "What makes the instruction and [call] for repentance of a prophet any greater than that of a teacher... why is the prophet any greater than an admonisher who is not a prophet?"[90]

Indeed, although Shapira accepts the notion that biblical prophets were ethical emissaries, he sees this model of prophecy as only partially accurate. It describes the actions of the prophet but glosses over the true nature of prophecy; it is a model that describes what he does, but not his essence. Not distinguishing between the actions of the prophet and his essence leads to the mistaken belief

45–51; idem, "The Technique of Guided Imagination in the Thought of R. Kalonymos Kalman Shapira of Piasecno," *Kabbalah* 17 (2008): 247–249; idem, *Flame of the Holy Fire*, 221–223; Reiser, "To Fly Like Angels," 179–218.

86 Schweid, *Prophets for Their People*, 9.

87 See I Sam. 9.

88 See II Kings 4.

89 Shapira, *Mevo ha-She'arim*, 1b.

90 Ibid., 1a.

that prophecy is just a socio-ethical message. A distinction between the essence of prophecy and the actions of the prophet allows for a more complex way of reading of the prophetic corpus and understanding the different forms of prophecy:

> The people referred to them [the prophets] according to their needs, and changed their names according to the ways in which prophets acted. When there were prophets whose primary service was instructing them and [calling for] repentance, they called him a prophet (*navi*), from the phrase "utterance" (*niv sefatayim*). If it his job was to foretell the future, and his other functions were extraneous, he was referred to as a seer (*ro'eh*). But even though we refer to an angel (*malakh*) as such because it is a messenger (*malakh*), and the soul (*neshamah*) because of breath (*neshimah*), we know that the angel is not only a messenger and the soul is not just a breath. They have a spiritual essence that we cannot apprehend, and we see only its actions… The same is true with them: if [they used] the name prophet, seer or visionary (*ḥozeh*), they were referring to him by his actions which he carried out for them, but these are not his total essence and were performed only for their benefit. This was at the time when the prophet stood before their eyes… [but] now it is not so, for only their names and actions [recorded] in the holy writings remain for us. Therefore, the erroneous conception mentioned above has come about in the mind of some people… they consider them to be only as speakers of the future or admonishers, who reprove in the name of God, and that only these were his actions, and nothing more.[91]

It is certainly possible to understand the biblical prophet as a messenger who calls for repentance at the gate of the city and seeks to improve society's ethical standards. However, Shapira claims that this description captures only the prophet's actions and not his essence, since the true nature of the prophet is more than someone who reproves the people. For him, the belief that a prophet is just an ethical emissary and admonisher detracts from the prophet's value. The names prophet, seer and visionary are three ways of describing deeds that all flow forth from a single source–the essence of prophecy.

Jess Hollenback has argued that one of the central elements of mysticism is "empowerment," referring to the mystic's ability to exert influence upon things outside of himself, either on nature or on the people surrounding him.[92] In light of this, we may characterize Shapira's prophet as a mystic who possesses this

91 Ibid., 2a.

92 Hollenback, *Mysticism*, 150–176. Hollenback's idea of mystical empowerment is deeply intertwined with the power of magic, namely that thought and contemplation can alter the world in very real ways. Here we see a unique phenomenon in which the mystic's mind and reality are simultaneous aligned; according to Hollenback's description of empowerment, his contemplative thoughts are translated directly into reality. Also, see Garb, *Manifestations of Power*, 288–299. Also, see my discussion above, chap. 2.

quality of empowerment. He is a mystic, because his very essence is defined by a mystical attachment with God; and empowered, since this personal, even individual, connection to God has a direct influence on society:

> The essence [for the prophets] was their constant attachment to God. This connection brought about the holy spirit, which rested upon them not only in order to predict the future, but to guide and instruct them, meaning themselves[!] regarding the path of God. This means that performing miracles and predicting the future are not the true nature of the prophet–rather, it is his intimacy with God... [and] the clarification of his body until it becomes as the soul. Through this he becomes worthy of an absolute connection with God, since he has broken down the iron wall and it no longer separates between him and the holy.[93]

The prophet at his essence is characterized as one blessed with ecstatic powers who has refined his body "until it becomes as the soul"; he is the exemplar of a human being totally connected to God. This is mystical ecstasy, a nullification that leads him to being filled with God, and a process of refinement that leads to the holy spirit resting upon him. However, this mystical connection has an impact on far more than the prophet. Although Shapira writes that the prophet's "guidance" or "instruction" is highly personal ("to guide and instruct them, meaning themselves"),[94] we must not ignore the mystical prophet's "empowerment" that allows him to affect society. Shapira repeatedly emphasizes that the prophet's essence leads him to influence and illuminate those around him:[95]

> The prophet was for all Israel, for his path in the service of God was to clarify his body into a soul, and to cleave to God always, not separating between physical matter and the holy. He became the place in which the earth and the firmament kiss. The prophet was like one of floodgates of the heavens. Through him the light of God spread out to Israel, filling their hearts and even their bodies. And so it was at the moment God spoke to the prophet— not only did he acquire knowledge and information, simply knowing what God wanted or did not want, but light, awareness and the will of God filled him so intensely that he said: "But [His word] was like a raging fire in my heart, shut up in my bones; I could

---

93 Shapira, *Mevo ha-She'arim*, 3a.
94 Following R. Ḥayyim Vital; see ibid.
95 The theme of light, which according to Hollenback is an essential part of the mystical experience (Hollenback, *Mysticism*, 56–74), appears in connection to nearly every subject in Shapira's thought. For a critique of Hollenback's claim regarding the importance of light, see: Garb, *Manifestations of Power*, 291. Garb argues that his characterization is only partial, since he seeks out only those aspects of mysticism that belong to a certain tradition but fit within the universal model. However, there is no doubt that the motif of light is an integral part of Shapira's mystical teachings; see: Reiser, "To Fly Like Angels," 68, 165–171, 191–193. For more on the theme of light, see: Elliot R. Wolfson, "The Body in the Text," 492.

> not hold it in, I was helpless" (Jer. 20:9). So too with Israel, to whom the prophet spoke. Not only with words did he instruct them… and reprove them… but through the prophets the light of God flowed out to Israel, filling them until they realized their low level. Then by means of the spirit of God that was given to them, they strengthened and sanctified themselves.[96]

For Shapira the role of the prophets is to bring the spirit of God to the people. The content of their prophecies, such as visions of the future and ethical rebuke, was simply a garment surrounding the light of God that passed through them into the community. The prophet functioned as a channel, a pipeline through with divine light rushes into the hearts and bodies of the Jewish people. This light flows automatically to those around the prophet because of his mystical empowerment:

> The world[97] is sanctified through the prophets, and the Jewish people who lived in the world could spark into prophecy. This is what transpired with Saul, before he came to Samuel. Even as he drew near to [Samuel's city], "the spirit of God came upon him too; and he walked on and prophesied," (I Sam. 19:23) for the prophet Samuel sanctified the world as well, and so much holiness and prophecy dwelt in his city that when Saul approached he too began to prophesize.[98]

The mystic-ecstatic prophet is not cut off from society, and his connection to the people is a strong one indeed. In fact, the prophet's bond with society, or the divine effluence that flows from him to the society, is reciprocal rather than one-sided. The prophet transmits divine light, the spirit of God, to those around him, but at the same time the presence of those around him inspires a great light within the prophet, like the kindling near a bonfire that feeds and increases the fire itself:[99]

> With the other prophets as well [i.e. those not numbered amongst the forty-eight biblical prophets], we see that whether or not they needed to prophesize, tell the future or give ethical rebuke to Israel at that moment, the prophet would stand with his students and perform the service of God, a sublime and prophetic service. He would reveal the light that came upon him, and they were illuminated by his light, and because of them his own light increased, as the verse says, "He saw a band of prophets prophesizing, with Samuel

96 Shapira, *Mevo ha-She'arim*, 4a.

97 In hasidic Hebrew the word *olam* can mean both "the world" and "the people," from the Yiddish *oylem*. Shapira uses it with both of these connotations.

98 Ibid., 5a.

99 Ibid., 37b. For more on the relationship of the *ṣaddiq* and his community as a parallel to the prophet and those who surround him, see also Reiser, "To Fly Like Angels," 166–169; Leshem, "Between Messianism and Prophecy," 76–88. This parallel proves that Shapira saw the Hasidic leader as a prophet.

standing over them; and the spirit of God came upon Saul's messengers and they too began to prophesize" (I Sam. 19:20)... The prophet's light from on high was felt by all of them. Even Saul's servants prophesized when they came under his holy shadow. But is it really possible for much of the prophet's light to reach those people who throughout the year are occupied with their vineyards and olive groves, coming to him only infrequently? Can the prophet be built just by this? Will this be the extent of his great ascent, influencing those who are busy with this world and its needs? Therefore, the prophet needed his disciples. They were with him always, and they constantly praised and served God's blessed name together with him.[100]

The prophet is primarily concerned neither with "the world and its needs," whether the personal needs of individuals or the socio-ethical needs of the society, nor with foretelling the future or reproving the people. The chief goal of the prophet is revealing the divine light to those who surround him, "The prophet is the revelation of divine essence down below. His uniqueness is found not in his words, but in his very being, in his existence, and his words are important because of the presence of his essence within them... the divine essence manifest in him."[101] Like those who conceive of the prophet as a mystic within whom the divine essence surges, "the place in which the earth and the firmament kiss,"[102] Shapira defines prophecy itself as a deeply mystical phenomenon, "it is gazing upon the supernal glory."[103]

We have seen that Shapira outlined a third model of biblical prophecy, an alternative model that is both complex and nuanced. The two models commonly found in academic scholarship, namely the ecstatic model and the emissarial model, represent extreme formulations. One model describes the prophet as an individual who is entirely cut off from reality and society, while in the other he is totally immersed in the needs of society without any personal interest in mystical experience whatsoever. To briefly employ the words of Heschel, one is concerned with the mysteries of heaven, and the other is concerned with the affairs of the market place. The teachings of Shapira offer a model that is more complex. In his understanding, the prophet's personal mystical experience has a direct influence and impact upon the world and society. Shapira's prophet is

100 Shapira, *Mevo ha-She'arim*, 44a. This passage should be understood within its broader context. It appears in a chapter in which Shapira compares the *ṣaddiq* to a prophet, and criticizes the Hasidim who rarely journey to see their leader. The excerpt above alludes to the diminished influence the *ṣaddiq* can have on those who do not visit him often.

101 Schweid, *From Ruin to Salvation*, 112.

102 Shapira, *Mevo ha-She'arim*, 4a.

103 Ibid., 2a. Cf. *Zohar* 1:238a.

concerned with both the individual and the collective; he is an ecstatic emissary, and, in the words of Hollenback, a model of "mystical empowerment."

Margolin has demonstrated that there are indeed types of mysticism that are not alienated from the world, but are profoundly involved with it and have a positive attitude toward physicality. His argument is strengthened by the teachings of Shapira, who claims that a prophet's own ecstasy in no way estranges him from the world. The divine light that fills the prophet bursts forth and extends beyond the boundaries of his self, spilling over into the society. Prophecy is an individual experience that influences the public. This understanding fuses together the two extreme models. A private experience does not necessarily negate one's connection with the world and society, and in many cases it influences society, "The prophet was like one of floodgates of the heavens. Through him the light of God spread out to Israel, filling their hearts and even their bodies with light."[104] Furthermore, Shapira suggests that prophets had many different functions, which encompass both of the extreme models: sometimes the prophet called for the community to repent, gazed into the future, saw what took place in another location, and cried out in castigation and reprimand. But these represent the prophet's deeds, and do not fully describe his essence. His true nature is that of an ecstatic messenger; his personal ecstasy is indelibly bound to the reality and effects a change upon society. Shapira's innovative mystical conception of prophecy is a model in which the prophet is not removed from other people or the world. The prophet qua mystic strives to influence those around him, imbuing them with his own powers on their behalf.

The Twentieth-Century Quest to Renew Prophecy in the Teachings of Shapira

Shapira was not satisfied with a theoretical interpretation of biblical prophecy alone. His analysis of the Bible was a springboard from which to jump to the twentieth century. Gershom Scholem was ready to recognize the existence of mystics in the twentieth century, but only those for whom mysticism was an entirely private affair. He identified the early Hasidic movement of the eighteenth century as the "last phase" of Jewish mysticism with any meaning for the masses, one whose goal was "to influence the generation, to give instruction not only for the enlightened... but to pass this knowledge on to others."[105] Shapira clearly

104 See above, n. 102.
105 Gershom Scholem, *Explications and Implications*, 72–73.

represents an anti-thesis to Scholem's claim, or, at the very least, an exception to his sweeping conclusions.

Shapira's description of the prophet as a mystical emissary, one who was not cloistered within his private space and actively sought to influence those around him, represents a spiritual type to be emulated and resurrected. Shapira, a twentieth-century thinker, sought to endow all of Israel with the capacity for mystical prophecy. His mystical conception of prophecy aimed, in the twentieth-century no less, "to influence the generation, to give instruction to the masses." Expanding the boundaries of prophecy and making it relevant to each and every Jew is a theme found throughout all of Shapira's writings. His was a unique attempt to form a modern and communal mystical movement:

> *Tanna de-Bei Eliyahu* teaches the following on the verse "Deborah was a prophetess" (Judges 4:4): Behold I call heaven and earth to witness, that a man or a woman, Cuthite or a Jew, servant or a maidservant, all according to their deeds—the holy spirit may dwell upon him. Thus far are the words of the holy midrash. Surely a Jew of our own time is no worse than a Cuthite of those times. *Even now each Jewish person can earn the holy spirit according to his deeds.*[106]

According to Shapira, the actualization of each and every person's capability to become worthy of prophecy is God's will: "God longs and desires to connect with complete attachment to all of Israel, His beloved nation, not with the prophets alone *but with all of them. The ultimate goal of God's wish for the Jewish people is that all of them become prophets.*"[107] Drawing a distinction between prophecy and the "service of prophecy" (*avodat ha-nevu'ah*) makes it applicable to everyone, thereby extending the potential to attain prophecy to all: "This is the matter discussed by R. Ḥayyim Vital... the *service* of prophecy continues now as well, even though prophecy has ceased";[108] "in the present moment, even though one may not be worthy of having God speak to him by means of prophecy, the service of prophecy may be done by everyone. His [God's] blessed light and holiness are united within their innermost hearts, and even the cavities of their bodies."[109] Despite this distinction, Shapira repeatedly reiterates his claim that every Jewish person has the capacity to attain prophecy,[110] at all times.

---

106 Shapira, *Mevo ha-She'arim*, 13a.
107 Ibid., 3b.
108 Ibid., 3a–3b. The emphasis appears in the original. On the difference between prophecy and the service of prophecy, see Wacks, *Flame of the Holy Fire*, 211–213, 217–219.
109 Shapira, *Mevo ha-She'arim*, 3b. See also ibid., 13a.
110 Idem, *Benei Maḥshavah Ṭovah*, 32–33. On this book, see below, chap. 4., subchapter, "R. Kalonymous Kalman Shapira's Books."

The prophet himself desires to expand the sphere of prophecy to include the public, for his entire being is devoted to illuminating the community with the light of God, and there is no illumination equal to that of prophecy:

> In general, the prophets, the mouths of God on earth, were not satisfied to correct the nation so that they would not steal and rob, or do other abominable things. Instead, they longed to make them into God's people, into a *nation of prophets.* Moses our teacher said, "Would that all the Lord's people were prophets" (Num. 11:29), and his generation was known as the generation of knowledge... none of them were satisfied with their individual greatness alone. They yearned to raise up *all* of their generation to its messianic goal, and through their holiness bring about the cosmic repair of the end of times... not just the individuals, but *everyone*... If Rabbi Pinhas ben Yair illuminated even his donkey, to such a degree that [the beast] himself kept the Torah and was stringent beyond the letter of the law, knowing with holy spirit that his food had not been properly tithed,[111] we can extrapolate from this how great the prophet's yearning to make the Jewish people into God's chosen treasure, a kingdom of priests and a holy nation.[112]

If a Cuthite or donkey can become worth of the holy spirit, then so can everyone. For Shapira, this capability is equally relevant in the modern period. His identification of the *Ṣaddiq* with the biblical prophet[113] allows him to apply his teachings regarding prophecy to the twentieth century. The proximity of an ordinary person to the *Ṣaddiq* brings him to the level of prophecy, just as the biblical man achieved this state through being near a prophet:

> In this we can see the affinity between hasidism and prophecy more clearly: regarding prophecy, if even a simple person who is not in the presence of the prophets wishes to approach them, then their light will shine upon him as well—he too becomes a different person and prophesizes with them. Even if he himself was not a prophet, and his prophecy dwindles when he becomes distanced from them physically and in spirit, like Saul and his people, nevertheless they prophesized as well when they came before Samuel the prophet. So it is in hasidism: simple people, if only they fear God, keep the commandments with honesty and have faith, are transformed into hasidim according to their station when they cleave to their *rebbe*, even if [the spiritual path of] hasidism is a very high level.[114]
>
> The Sephardic prayer liturgy is a very great and illuminated rite, which is so great that the general populace is unworthy of using it... If you object that some people who are not on such a high rung pray with this liturgy, connecting themselves with the very pious (*hasidim elyonim*) and they too are called pious. The holy verse says, "and they believed in the Lord

111 The passage refers to R. Pinḥas ben Yair's donkey, which refused to eat untithed food; see *b. Ḥullin* 7a–7b; cf. *Bereshit Rabbah* 60:8.
112 Shapira, *Mevo ha-She'arim*, 4b.
113 On the relationship between hasidism and prophecy, see Leshem, "Between Messianism and Prophecy," 76–88; and see above, n. 99.
114 Shapira, *Mevo ha-She'arim*, 36b.

and in Moses His servant" (Ex. 14:31). Moses our teacher sanctified himself until he attained the level of prophecy, ascending on high and bringing down the Torah to Israel. Not all of Israel was able to arrive at the rung of Moses our teacher, [directly] receiving the Torah by means of prophecy. But because they believed in Moses and connected themselves with him, he influenced them with his spirit of holiness. It was as if they themselves achieved his level, and were able to receive the Torah through their unity and connection with Moses… The hasidim may be equated with this… not all of whom are worthy of prophecy.[115]

In addition to this, Shapira claims that the longer that the Jewish people continue to live in exile and the process of the decline of the generations continues, the easier it is to attain the holy spirit. The opportunity to become worthy of the holy spirit in the twentieth century is paradoxically even greater than it was in the time of the biblical prophets themselves: "Why is it more possible to be worthy of the holy spirit than in the days of the prophets? Because after the destruction [of the Temple], the light was drawn even further down, into exile as well."[116]

Shapira's Attempts to Actualize Prophecy in the Twentieth Century

Shapira sought to fulfill his own words. The idea of expanding the sphere of prophecy from a few unique individuals to encompass broader circles did not remain a theoretical idea in Shapira's writings.[117] He attempted to actualize his dream through two different strategies: establishing elite fellowships, and developing contemplative techniques as training for prophecy.

Shapira established a society of comrades called the *benei maḥshavah ṭovah*.[118] The goal of this group was similar to that of the biblical circle known as the "disciples of the prophets" (*benei ha-nevi'im*)—attaining prophecy: "Look upon each member of the fellowship as one of the elite, and honor him and treat him with respect, for he is indeed one of the disciples of the prophets. He too has already devoted himself fully to the holiness that God will bestow

---

115 Ibid., 37a, quoted in the name of Elimelekh Weisblum of Lizhensk.
116 Ibid., 58b. Regarding the idea that it is easier to achieve prophecy outside of the land of Israel, see ibid., 58a (cited from the book *No'am Elimelekh* by Elimelekh Weisblum of Lizhensk). For a similar belief found in the teachings of Abulafia, see Reiser, "To Fly Like Angels," 191–192; see also Wacks, "Nevu'ah ve-Ḥasidut," 46–49.
117 See above, "The Limitation and Expansion of Prophecy in Medieval Jewish Rationalist Thought."
118 Regarding the meaning of this name, and the connection between it and the preparation for attaining prophecy by means of contemplative techniques, see Reiser, "To Fly Like Angels," 176–177, and esp. n. 960.

upon him."[119] The goal of this fellowship was to see God "eye to eye": "Not only in prayer and divine service will we feel our closeness to God... but our senses... will know the holiness of God... and eye to eye one will see that he is in God's garden in Eden before the blessed One's Throne of Glory. This is the goal of our fellowship."[120] In this internal pamphlet, of which, according to one report, only six copies were published in the 1920s until it was republished after the Holocaust, Shapira outlined the terms of acceptance to the fellowship,[121] and he promised that whoever keeps these terms would become worthy of prophecy. This assurance relies upon the distinction between prophets and disciples of the prophets, according to which prophecy includes a rather wide spectrum of different levels and is not a single monochromatic phenomenon. This broad definition of prophecy assures each person a place on the spectrum:

> Do not object once more by asking if we want to transform you into a prophet, [an institution] nullified by our numerous sins. Hillel the Elder already taught that although the Jewish people are not prophets, they are descendants (or disciples) of the prophets. Even among the prophets we see that God answered Moses our teacher, "no man can see me [and live]" (Ex. 33:20). But Isaiah and Ezekiel both said, "And I have seen the Lord." There are many different levels. That which Moses wanted to glimpse cannot be seen by any living person. Yet Isaiah and Ezekiel saw a lower level than this, and there remains a much lower rung for you, as a Jew and descendent of the prophets, to see. Do not let your heart fall by saying, "I am a sinner and a lowly person. How can I see You, who are King of the World?" Even on the lowest of all the levels, for we have surely known your state, and even in this we rely upon God and the holiness of Israel that lies within you–you will see! But you must be one of the people we have described in the chapter regarding the content of the fellowship (terms one through five). Even if you do not always behold this sight, you will very often have such a vision.[122]

The establishment of this fellowship, intended as an example to be emulated by other such societies,[123] and whose explicit goal was to prepare its members to

---

119 Shapira, *Benei Maḥshavah Ṭovah*, 58.

120 Ibid., 7. On the relationship between a vision of God and prophecy in Shapira's teachings, see Reiser, "To Fly Like Angels," 195–206.

121 See the publisher's introduction to the book; for more on the terms of acceptance to the fellowship, see ibid., 10.

122 Ibid., 32–33.

123 On the possibility of establishing other fellowships such as this, see ibid., 58 (#13); see also *Hakhsharat ha-Avrekhim*, 60b: "If the students from different Hasidic groups in a single city wish to come together as one–this too can be, as long as their Hasidic paths are compatible with one another." On the question of pluralism within the Hasidic world in Shapira's teachings, see Reiser, "To Fly Like Angels," 167.

attain prophecy, demonstrates Shapira's attempt to renew prophecy amongst the people. This concrete attempt grew out of Shapira's longing for prophecy to become the prerogative of all, and, as we saw at the end of the previous section, to transform the entire Jewish people into God's nation by endowing all of them with prophecy.

Shapira's second strategy for reviving prophecy, and perhaps the more significant of the two, was to develop new contemplative techniques,[124] which were intended to prepare people for prophecy: "We are not speaking to you of deliriums, or of things beyond the world and nature that only elite can attain, [but rather] tried and true things that *each Jewish person can achieve* with only a little, albeit consistent, effort."[125] The pamphlet *Benei Maḥshavah Ṭovah* was not intended for wide publication. However, the books *Hakhsharat ha-Avrekhim* and *Mevo ha-Sha'arim* were delivered for print in 1939. These two works present the reader with many practical contemplative techniques, and make unabashedly clear that their goal was to make prophecy accessible the masses. Their publication was tragically interrupted by the invasion of Poland by Germany in early September 1939.[126] Shapira even alludes already in his first book, *Ḥovat ha-Talmidim*, to the need to prepare the hearts of the people for prophecy: "We must train ourselves so that the holy spirit of the disciples of the prophets can enter and dwell within us."[127] This preparation was to be accomplished by developing a range of contemplative techniques, which will be discussed in the fifth chapter.

C Conclusion

The call to renew mystical prophecy, both amongst rarefied individuals and the public, returned in the twentieth century after having been long hidden. Moshe Idel has shown that the attacks upon early Hasidic movement include the claim that the Ba'al Shem Tov considered himself a prophet. This accusation, Idel argues, led to a subsequent deemphasis of prophecy in later Hasidic circles.[128] It is reasonable to assume that initial fears of prophecy voiced by the opponents of

124 On the uniqueness of Shapira's techniques, see ibid., 78–84.
125 Shapira, *Benei Maḥshavah Ṭovah*, 26.
126 See below, chap. 4., subchapter, "R. Kalonymous Kalman Shapira's Books."
127 Shapira, *Ḥovat ha-Talmidim*, 67b.
128 Moshe Idel, "The *Besht* as a Prophet and Talismanic Magician," in *Studies in Jewish Narrative: Presented to Yoav Elstein*, ed. Avidov Lipsker and Rella Kushelevsky (Ramat Gan: Bar Ilan University Press, 2006), 124, 132–133.

hasidism continued to decline, and that by early the twentieth century they had largely disappeared. Thus, new mystical and prophetic elements were able to break free once more, including Shapira's teachings and his attempts to actualize them.

Shapira offered a nuanced and complex model of prophecy. In his eyes, the nature of a prophet need not be understood in a dichotomous manner, as either an emissary concerned with the ethical wellbeing of society, or an ecstatic mystic utterly cut off from the world. Shapira describes a third model, which emerged from his own interpretation of Scripture and rabbinic teachings. His prophet is a mystic who attains ecstatic states, thereby influencing the people and world around him. Mysticism does not necessarily engender alienation from the world and humanity. On the contrary, for Shapira mysticism and ecstasy sanctify the world. This conception of prophecy, which looks favorably on a connection to the physical world and society, inspired Shapira to attempt to renew prophecy. He expressed this both by founding the elite fellowship *benei maḥshavah ṭovah* and by developing practical contemplative and meditative exercises intended to prepare people for attaining prophecy.[129]

As we have seen, much of the research regarding different forms of prophecy in the twentieth century has downplayed the ecstatic element, thereby marginalizing mystical forms of prophecy. Modern thinkers who emphasized the mystical prophecy have not yet received the attention they deserve.[130] In order to study those modern figures who focused on the mystical dimensions of prophecy, we must employ a more nuanced understanding of the phenomenon of prophecy itself, one in which different elements such as the prophet's mission, ethical message, ecstasy and mysticism are treated as coterminous instead of contradictory.

Both intensification and prophecy—the intensification of religious ritual and experience, transforming them into mystical experiences, in which one senses the divine presence or even comes into contact with the divine, as well as the striving to develop ecstatic-mystical prophecy for all—are dependent upon certain techniques in order to materialize them. In the next section, I will demonstrate that these trends of intensification and prophecy in Jewish mysticism in the twentieth century may be found primarily in imagery techniques meant to actualize these mystical elements.

129 On the features that unite Shapira's various contemplative exercises, see Reiser, "To Fly Like Angels," 26–29.

130 For example, see the teachings of Shem Tov Gefen and "the Nazir;" see above, n. 80.

Section III: **Imagery Techniques**

Chapter Four
Imagination as an Empowering Factor in R. Kalonymous Kalman Shapira's Thought

A Introduction: Imagination in R. Kalonymous Kalman Shapira's Thought

Biographical Introduction

R. Kalonymous Kalman Shapira (The Piaseczner Rebbe),[1] was born on July 13 1889,[2] to R. Elimelekh Shapira (The Grodzisker Rebbe) (1824–1892) and Ḥannah Berakhah, the daughter of R. Ḥayyim Shemu'el Horowicz of Chęciny (Chentshin).[3] Before the age of three his father passed away and he was taken in by his father's grandson through his first marriage–R. Yeraḥmi'el Mosheh Hopstein (The Kozienicer Rebbe) (1860–1909), who later became his father-in-law as well, when Shapira, at age sixteen, married his daughter Ḥayyah Raḥel Miriyam (the

1 For biographic details, see Aharon Soroski, ed., "Me-Toldot ha-ADMO"R ha-Qadosh Maran Rabi Kalonimus Kalmish Shapira ZȘ"L me-Pi'aschenah," in Kalonymous Kalman Shapira, *Esh Qodesh* (Jerusalem: Sifra Press, 1960), i–xxviii; Nehemia Polen, *The Holy Fire: The Teachings of Rabbi Kalonymus Kalman Shapira, the Rebbe of the Warsaw Ghetto* (Northvale: Jason Aronson, 1994), 1–14; Mendel Piekarz, *The Literature of Testimony as a Historical Source of the Holocaust and Three Hasidic Reflections to the Holocaust* (Jerusalem: Bialik Institute, 2003), 89–100; Isaac Hershkowitz, "Rabbi Kalonymus Kalmish Shapira, The Piasechner Rebbe His Holocaust and Pre-Holocaust Thought, Continuity or Discontinuity?" (master's thesis, Bar-Ilan University, 2004), 17–18; Zvi Leshem, "Between Messianism and Prophecy: Hasidism According to the Piaseczner Rebbe" (PhD diss., Bar-Ilan University, 2007), 1–5; Ron Wacks, *The Flame of the Holy Fire: Perspectives on the Teachings of Rabbi Kalonymous Kalmish Shapiro of Piaczena* (Alon Shevut: Tevunot, 2010), 21–33; Daniel Reiser, *R. Kalonymus Kalman Shapira: Sermons from the Years of Rage* (Jerusalem: Herzog College, World Union of Jewish Studies and Yad Vashem, 2017), 1:13–24. Also, see the recent extensive work, David Biale, et al., *Hasidism: A New History* (Princeton: Princeton University Press, 2018), 614–616, 660–662. Since this book was only published as this translation was in its final stages I have been unable to adequately refer to it in my references.

2 According to Grodzisk Mazowiecki Birth registry book of 1889, registration no. 53. I thank Mr. Matan Shefi, Head of The Emanuel Ringelblum Jewish Historical Institute Jewish Genealogy & Family Heritage Center, for helping me find this birth certificate.

3 R. Elimelekh's marriage to Ḥannah Berakhah was his second and therefore Kalonymous Kalman Shapira had many siblings from both sides. We have a number of letters written by Ḥannah Berkahah in Yiddish and Hebrew demonstrating her uniqueness, which I wish to discuss in future studies.

https://doi.org/10.1515/9783110535884-007

engagement lasted for three years and began when he was thirteen).[4] His wife, Ḥayyah, was learned and took an active role in the composing of his books.[5] In 1913, at the age of twenty four, he was appointed as the rabbi of the city Piaseczno, close to Warsaw. After World War I, in 1917, he moved to Warsaw and continued to briefly visit Piaseczno. In 1923, he founded the yeshiva *Da'at Mosheh*, named in memory of his father-in-law, and it was one of the largest hasidic yeshivot in Warsaw with three hundred students enrolled.[6] His hasidim said he was pleasant looking, elegant, and projected an air of *gravitas* and nobility.[7]

At a young age, he had already learned to play the violin like his father-in-law,[8] and he also became a *mohel* (one who ritually circumcises male Jewish children).[9] He composed *nigunim* (melodies) and played them on his violin after the Sabbath;[10] he only stopped this custom after the death of his wife in

4 Consequently, Shapira's father R. Elimelekh was also the grandfather of Ḥayyah Raḥel Miriyam.

5 See Uziel Fuchs, "Miriam the Prophetess and the Rebbe's Wife: The Piaseczner Rebbe's Sermons on Miriam the Prophetess," *Masekhet* 3 (2005): 65–76. See the letter that Shapira wrote about her after her death, in 1937, at the end of his book, Shapira, *Derekh ha-Melekh*, 445, which describes her as knowledgeable and educated in hasidism and kabbalah, "Almost no day passed in which she did not study Torah… And for its own sake (*lishmah*) she studied in order to [spiritually] bind with the Torah and holiness… her studies were Bible, midrash, *Zohar*, as well as kabbalistic and hasidic books, and she had a broad knowledge of kabbalah and hasidism, and I was amazed many times by her knowledge and the breadth of her knowledge of these matters." Likewise, she would review his books, proofread them, and comment upon them, see the annotation on idem, *Hakhsharat ha-Avreikhim*, 21b.

6 Reiser, *Sermons from the Years of Rage*, I:14, 337.

7 Polen, *The Holy Fire*, 6. I have only included this due to my interviews with Shapira's disciple Ya'aqov Qorman (1913–2011) who constantly repeated, "He was a very handsome man (*er iz geven zeyer a sheyner man*)," Ya'aqov Qorman (Shapira's disciple), in discussion with the author, May 2010.

8 Concerning Yeraḥmi'el Mosheh Hopstein's violin (as well as flute) playing, see Malkah Shapiro, *The Rebbe's Daughter: Memoir of a Hasidic Childhood*, trans. Nehemia Polen (Philadelphia: The Jewish Publication Society, 2002), xxii, 27, 51–52, 152. Regarding Shapira's violin playing, see Leibel Bein, *From the Notebook of a Hassidic Journalist* (Jerusalem: s.n., 1967), 30. It should be noted that from the age of three until the age of twenty Shapira was in Hopstein's home and saw him play every Saturday night, and perhaps learned how to play from him.

9 Ibid.

10 Ibid., 31. For Zvi Leshem's reconstructed version of Shapira's "quieting melody," Zvi Leshem, "Piaseczna Rebbe's Quieting Tune," YouTube video, 2:44, from 2007 by Rav Zvi Leshem and his students at Yeshivat Bat Ayin, November 16, 2016, https://www.youtube.com/watch?v=zoDCpYHaoxE.

1937.[11] He taught himself medical knowledge as well as other general and worldly knowledge.[12]

Shapira was a member of the Agudath Israel and encouraged others to join this movement, which was known in Poland as *Agudas Shlumei Emunei Yisro'el* (Union of Faithful Jewry).[13] Nevertheless, he also belonged to the faction within Agudath Israel that had a positive view of the settlement of the Land of Israel and due to the influence of his brother, R. Yeshayahu Shapira (the "Pioneer" Rabbi) who was a member of Mizrachi, the religious Zionist movement, he bought land in Kefar Ata (currently Kiryat Ata) with other members of *Avodat Yisra'el–Varshah* (Workers of Israel–Warsaw),[14] which was later named *Avodat Yisra'el Varshah–Kefar Ata Ereṣ Yisra'el* (Warsaw Workers of Israel–Kfar Ata, Land of Israel).[15] Today there is a synagogue in his memory in that area.[16]

At the outbreak of World War II, Germany began bombing Poland and within a matter of days Shapira lost his only son, daughter-in-law, and his sister-in-law in the bombings. Around the same time his elderly mother passed away as well, and he recited *qaddish* (a prayer traditionally said after the burial).[17] During the

---

11 Polen, *the Holy Fire*, 6. Ya'el Levin, "Ha-ADMO"R she-Nigen be-Kinor ve-Ḥadal I'm Histalqut Ra'aiyato," *Daf le-Tarbut Yehudit* 273 (2007): 39.

12 See Bein, *From the Notebook of a Hassidic Journalist*, 31–32. Concerning his clinical attempts, see Polen, *The Holy Fire*, 160 n. 17. Also see a copy of a kind of prescription in Ḥayyim Frankel and David Ḥayyim Zilbershlag, eds., *Zikharon Qodesh le-Ba'al Esh Qodesh* (Jerusalem: Va'ad Ḥasidei Pi'asechna—Grodzhisq, 1994), 28. However, see Reiser, *Sermons from the Years of Rage*, 15–16, who undermines their thesis.

13 See *Ha-Derekh*, Zurich, volume 6–7, (February-March 1920): 1–3 (Shapira's signature to be found ibid., 3). He appeared again in *Qoveṣ Histadruti shel Agudat Yisra'el, 5672–5683* (Vienna: Lishkat ha-Merkaz shel Agudat Yisra'el ha-Olamit, 1923), 24–32 (Shapira's signature appears, ibid., 29).

14 Frankel and Zilbershlag, *Zikharon Qodesh*, 15–17, 34.

15 The settler group *Avodat Yisrael* was established in 1924 by Yeraḥmi'el Mosheh Hopstein's son R. Yisra'el El'azar Hopstein, Shapira's brother-in-law. This group established Kefar Hasidim in 1925. Following, the group *Avodat Yisra'el–Varshah* was established by R. Yeshayahu Shapira and they founded Kiryat Ata.

16 Beit Keneset Pi'asechna, Ha-Atsma'ut St. 100, Kiryat Ata.

17 Polen, *The Holy Fire*, 12. His sister-in-law Ḥannah Hopstein, the daughter of Yeraḥmi'el Mosheh Hopstein, immigrated to Mandatory Palestine in the 1920's and was one of the founders of Kefar Hasidim. She was a religious-Zionist pioneer and took part in the guarding of the village, rode horses, and fought against Arab rioters during the 1936–1939 Arab revolt. To my knowledge, she was not married, and she arrived in Warsaw for a family visit a short time before the outbreak of World War II and the German invasion of Poland, and stayed in Shapira's house (and perhaps married him, following his two-year widowerhood, an accepted practice among hasidic dynasties; I would like to thank Zvi Leshem for making this suggestion to me). This woman pioneer, whose life came to a tragic end, has not received historical attention, and

Holocaust he resided in his home on 5 Dzielna St. in the Warsaw Ghetto. There he delivered sermons from 1940 until 1942, sermons that were afterwards hidden in the underground archive of Emanuel Ringelblum. Following the war and the subsequent discovery of this archive, they were published under the name *Esh Qodesh* (Holy Fire).[18] He had a number of opportunities to leave the ghetto, however he refused for, "he declared that it was unthinkable that he should save himself and leave his brothers to moan."[19] The American Joint Distribution Committee wanted to procure for him an exit visa from Poland, yet it was reported that he said, "I will not abandon my hasidim at such a difficult time."[20] It appears that on November 2, 1943, Shapira was murdered in the Holocaust and scholars are in disagreement regarding his place of death.[21]

R. Kalonymous Kalman Shapira's Books

During his lifetime Shapira produced one book, *Ḥovat ha-Talmidim* (*The Students' Responsibility*), in 1932, and one booklet, *Qunṭres Benei Maḥshavah Ṭovah* (*A Tract on Disciples of Proper Thought*),[22] which was printed in a few journals, and was privately distributed to a select group of students.[23] Likewise, his students published a sermon that was delivered on the Sabbath before Yom Kippur (The Day of Atonement), September 18 – 19, 1936, in Piaseczno—in Yiddish.[24] The rest of his works: *Hakhsharat ha-Avreikhim* (*The Young Men's Preparation*),

her fascinating journal and letters, which contain enough material for an excellent historical biography, currently reside in a corner of the Kefar Hasidim archive under the direction of Ms. Shulah Bamberger, open to the public.

18 See my recently published critical edition of this work, Reiser, *Sermons from the Years of Rage*.

19 Bein, *From the Notebook of a Hassidic Journalist*, 34.

20 Polen, *The Holy Fire*, 7; According to the Yiddish newspaper *Forverts* (New York), March 30, 1940.

21 See the scholarship cited in Leshem, "Between Messianism and Prophecy," 4 n. 11.

22 Zvi Leshem has dated it to be between 1920 and 1928, ibid., 5 n. 15.

23 One copy of *Benei Maḥshavah Ṭovah* is found in New York Ḥabad Library, MS 1192:27. I would like to thank Zvi Leshem who pointed out this manuscript to me. This manuscript is a printed copy with handwritten notes in the marginalia and text, some of these notes are written in block letters, while others are in cursive letters. Another printed copy, signed by Shapira, which is forbidden to be copied from, is in the property of R. Avraham Hamer in Bnei Brak. This copy was given to his father R. Eliyahu Hamer, who was one of Shapira's main disciples and one of the first copiers of his sermons.

24 Kalonymous Kalman Shapira, *Derashah* (Warsaw: Ḥevrei ha-Qehilah ha-Ivrit de-Pi'acesna, 1936).

Mevo ha-She'arim (*The Entrance to the Gates*), his personal journal *Ṣav ve-Ziruz* (*Command and Urging*) and his sermons delivered during the Holocaust, as aforementioned—were discovered in 1950 with the second section of Ringelblum's archive and were subsequently published from the 1960's and onwards.[25] The original manuscripts may be found in the Jewish historical archives of Warsaw and I can state, after examining each of them, that they are in impeccable condition.[26] Additionally, after the Holocaust, his students published his sermons from the 1920's and 1930's in two books: *Shelosh Derashot* (*Three Sermons*) and *Derekh ha-Melekh* (*The Way of the King*).[27]

Shapira's books should be categorized into two groupings. Sermons—*Derekh ha-Melekh* and *Esh Qodesh*; and guidance and instruction—*Benei Maḥshavah Ṭovah*, *Ḥovat ha-Talmidim*, *Hakhsharat ha-Avreikhim*, *Mevo ha-She'arim*, *Ṣav ve-Ziruz*, and *Shelosh Derashot.*[28] It should be noted that most of the imagery techniques appear in his instructional and guidance works, but rarely appear in his sermons at all.

Maḥshavah (Thought), Imagination, and Visualization in R. Kalonymous Kalman Shapira's Teaching

An examination of Shapira's writings reveals that the term *maḥshavah* (thought) does not connote the analytical investigation of an idea or object. On the contrary, he uses the term in the same context of such expressions as "feeling" and

25 My quotations from the published editions have been contrasted with the extent manuscripts. I have noted all relevant variations.

26 The book *Hakhsharat ha-Avreikhim* was sent to the publishers in 1939, according to the letter written to R. Avraham Mosheh Gribstein (Kalonymous Kalman Shapira, *Kalonymous Kalman Shapira to Avraham Mosheh Gribstein.* MS Ring. II/432. Mf. ZIH-806, p. 4; Jewish Historical Institute, Warsaw, *Ringelblum Archive*), and perhaps the German invasion of Poland derailed it. It should be noted that in that manuscript *Hakhsharat ha-Avreikhim* and *Mevo ha-She'arim* were bound together and seemingly he sent them both to be printed.

27 Kalonymous Kalman Shapira, *Shelosh Derashot* (Tel Aviv: Merkaz Hasidei Koźnic, 1985); idem, *Derekh ha-Melekh.* Not all of the sermons are of the same nature. Some are copies of sermons he wrote, while others are summaries by his students. see my examination on the editing process of these sermons Reiser, *Sermons from the Years of Rage*, 26–53.

28 Regarding this distinction and depiction of his books, see Leshem, "Between Messianism and Prophecy," 5–14. The book *Shelosh Derashot* includes a Hebrew translation of Shapira, *Derashah*, which was published in his lifetime. Despite being a book of sermons, I have catalogued it as an instructional work, since these sermons are in fact lengthy *musar* discussions delivered at the Agudath Israel World Congress, and their literary character is full of pathos and imagery.

imagination (*dimyon*; *ṣiyur*),[29] and opposes it to such terms as "wisdom" and "intellect;" he even writes, "Indeed, thought (*maḥshavah*) is not intellect."[30] One may find numerous references to explicit imaginal states in his writings, when he uses the term *maḥshavah* in the sense of imagination, "A man must raise *in his thought* at all time the annihilation of the self (*mesirat nefesh*) as it is in *Tsetil Katan* (A Small Pamphlet) of R. Elimelekh [Weisblum of Lizhensk] of the holy elders (*me-ziqnei ha-qadosh*), blessed be the memory of the righteous for the world to come."[31] Indeed, what does it state in Weisblum's *Tsetil Katan*? "And he will imagine (*ve-yedameh*) in his soul and visualize (*ve-yeṣayair*) in his thought as if a great and terrible fire burns in front of him until the heart of heaven, and he, for [the sake of] the sanctification of the God, blessed be he, breaks his nature and lowers himself into the fire for the sanctification of the God, blessed be he."[32] Clearly Weisblum's teaching concerns the imagination and visualization, and this is definitely how Shapira understood it as well,[33] however he translates Weisblum's words into concepts of thought. This rendering is already present later in Weisblum's teaching itself, "And the Holy one blessed be He adjoins a good thought to the deed (*b. Qiddushin* 40a)." The roots of this identification between thought and imagination largely appears in kabbalistic-hasidic literature, in which the imaginal function is frequently depicted through different amalgamations of the word *ṣiyur*, which in contemporary Hebrew is generally translated as drawing or depiction, but in this context, due to its imag-

---

29 For example, see Shapira, *Hakhsharat ha-Avreikhim*, 14a, "The feeling does not disseminate within you, and is not garbed by some thought or form, and due to this it is not assimilated into your body and limbs, and something you are not quite aware of your feeling... give it a thought and image (*ṣiyur*)." Meaning, thought is an instrument that internalizes emotions, it is the framework (garb) that informs and grants the emotions a place.

30 Idem, *Benei Maḥshavah Ṭovah*, 13. Also see his explanation in idem, *Ḥovat ha-Talmidim*, 62a, "It will be easier for man to stir himself when he will begin to stir his soul and spirit (*ha-nefesh ve-ha-ru'aḥ*) [the two lowest gradations of the soul], than if he would begin to arouse his soul (*nishmato*) [a higher gradation of the soul] with an intellectual (*sekhel*) matter. We specifically say with 'intellect' (*sekhel*), which is difficult to stir oneself through it, unlike with imagination and thought, for imagination and thought sometimes arise from the spirit and soul (*ha-ru'aḥ ve-ha-nefesh*), from traits (*middot*), desires (*ve-reṣonot*), and even senses, and through them it is not very difficult to become aroused, as it is with his intellect and wisdom." Imagination and thought, according to Shapira, are not products of the soul (*neshamah*), i.e. man's intellect (the *sefirot* of *Ḥokhmah* and *Binah*), rather they are products of man's *ru'aḥ* and *nefesh*, which are mental traits and senses.

31 Idem, *Derekh ha-Melekh*, 150.

32 Elimelekh Weisblum of Lizhensk, *Sefer Tsetil Katan* (Kisvárda: s.n., 1925), 1 (§1).

33 Shapira quotes this passage as well in idem, *Hakhsharat ha-Avreikhim*, 15b, in a clearly imaginal context.

inal connotation, I have consistently translated (and will be translating as) visualization, an imaginal depiction. This identification is also expressed through the conjunction of the words *maḥshavah* (thought) and *ṣiyur* (depiction), such as the command, "he shall visualize in his thought (*yeṣayair be-maḥshavto*)."[34] A number of definitions have emerged in the scholarship regarding the term *maḥshavah* and its relation to the imagination in Shapira's thought.[35] In fact, the best and clearest definition appears in Shapira's own writings in an intriguing comment that he made in his work *Ḥovat ha-Talmidim:*

> Do not err and say that the *maḥshavah* which we spoke of as arising from the spirit and soul (*ha-ru'aḥ ve-ha-nefesh*) [in the aspect of] *Binah* (understanding), which is within man, for *Binah* is the expansion of *Ḥokhmah* (wisdom) and its understanding, and only the words of wisdom are expanded. However, *maḥshavah* is here, matters that even the words of wisdom do not think. The *maḥshavah* of man, of which we are discussing, *is a type of imagination*, things of form (*ṣurah*) *which are able to be visualized in the imagination*, forms such as a man, a house, etc.—*he sees in the imagination, and things which are formless*, such as "if he will help his friend", and "words spoken by his friend," etc.—*are in thought* (*ḥoshvam*). Even in his dream, in which it would seem that most of his thought (*ḥakhmato*) is resting and sleeping, nevertheless, the *maḥshavah* and the imagination are active within him… and for the most part, just as a man's character traits (*midotav*), so are his dreams, and particularly the dreams which are from the representations of the mind (*hirhurei halev*), and when he has no traits aroused in him these days, then his dreams are also weak or entirely absent. The character traits arouse the *maḥshavah*, and the *maḥshavah* arouses the character traits at their roots until the soul (*nefesh*).[36]

---

34 See Ḥayyim Vital, *Peri Eṣ Ḥayyim*, Sha'ar ha-Shabbat, chap. 3: "If he cannot direct (*le-khaven*) the winds, he should visualize (*yeṣayer*) in his thought four winds and bow westwards"; Menaḥem Azariah da Fano, *Ma'amar Tiqqunei Teshuvah*, chap. 3: "In this manner he will visualize there in his thought"; Isaiah Horowitz, *Shnei Luḥot ha-Berit: Asarah Ma'amarot*, Ma'amar ha-Asiri: "This is the advice advised to him, he shall place God beside him, he shall visualize in his thought that the *Shekhinah* is in front of him"; Kalonymus Kalman Halevi Epstein, *Sefer Ma'or ve-Shemesh ha-Shalem* (Jerusalem: Or ha-Sefer, 1994), 1:384; Parashat Miqeṣ, s.v. "od": "He will visualize in his thought the form of the same righteous person (*ṣaddiq*)."
35 Zvi Leshem has defined *maḥshavah ḥazaqah* (intense thought) as follows, "Thought is a type of intense and clear contemplation of something that is found in a Jew's nature—faith in God" (idem, "Between Messianism and Prophecy," 177). Wacks defined it as, "an act of thinking done consciously" and added, "thought is not intellect, meaning, the thinking that is demanded for acquiring excitement is not a discursive activity, rather an activity of deep contemplation. 'Intense thought' (*maḥshavah ḥazaqah*) means a focused mental effort for a lengthy period of time" (Wacks, "Emotion and Enthusiasm," 81; idem, *The Flame of the Holy Fire*, 111, 227). Also see my discussion of their definitions in "To Fly Like Angels," 86–87.
36 Shapira, *Ḥovat ha-Talmidim*, 62a.

Maḥshavah, or *maḥshavah ha-ḥazaqah* (intense thought),[37] does not functions in a conscious manner,[38] on the contrary, *maḥshavah* functions at its best when "most of his thought (*ḥakhmato*) is resting and sleeping," in unconscious moments. The roots of consciousness are in wisdom (*Ḥokhmah*) and understanding (*Binah*); in contrast, the roots of *maḥshavah* are the character traits. Therefore, the definition of *maḥshavah* is different, "*maḥshavah* is a type of imagination." *Maḥshavah* and imagination are two sides of a coin, where the difference between them is the imaginal content, "things of form (*ṣurah*) *are able to be visualized in the imagination... he sees in the imagination, and things which are formless... are in thought* (*ḥoshvam*)." That is to say, the only matter separating and distinguishing *maḥshavah* and imagination is their respective content. The imagination is imaginal figural representation (man; house), whereas *maḥshavah* is imaginal visualization of a plot-scene ("words spoken by his friend"). In other words, the plot-scene, *maḥshavah*, is the content of the imaginal visualization, of the waking dream. This definition clearly and explicitly appears a second time in Shapira's writings in *Hakhsharat ha-Avreikhim*, referencing the previously cited passage:

> *However, maḥshavah ḥazaqah* (intense thought) *is impossible without depictions* (*ṣiyurim*)... And this is what we stated there in a footnote in *Ḥovat ha-Talmidim:* "When a man thinks with a weak thought about someone who hates him and cursed him, the form of the hater is not depicted (*miṣṭayeret*) in front of him. However, when he thinks with an intense thought, his form [the haters form] is also depicted in front of him. And then not only is the form of the hater, which is depicted in front of him, called a visualization (*ṣiyur*), the words that were spoken to him and all the events that he thinks of now are also referred to as visualizations (*ṣiyur*). And as we stated there, *that ha-maḥshavah ha-ḥazaqah* (the intense thought) *and the imagination, they are of the same kind, only the matters that may be visualized in the imagination, such as a form of a house, man, etc. he sees in his imagination, and the matters that are formless, such as speech, are only thought be-maḥshavah ḥazaqah* (in an intense thought), see there.[39]

Maḥshavah is not a concept distinguishable from imagination for "it is impossible to broaden his thought, lengthen it, and indefinitely strengthen it, if he also fills it with many private images (*ṣiyurim*) which he shall visualize them in it, and especially different images;[40] "And to strengthen your thoughts it is impossible that you will only think a simple thought (*maḥshavah peshuṭah*), for the holiday

37 On the distinction between thought and intense thought and concerning the meaning of intense thought, see Reiser, "To Fly Like Angels," 85–92.
38 As defined by Wacks, see above n. 35.
39 Shapira, *Hakhsharat ha-Avreikhim*, 15b-16a.
40 Ibid., 16a.

and Sabbath are sacred... you rather need to fill them with visualizations (*ṣiyurim*) and images (*ve-dimyonot*)."[41] The imagination is the pictorial component and *maḥshavah* is the dramatic-theatrical element linking these images, spoken words, and occurred events: "The words that were spoken to him and all the events that he thinks of now are also referred to as visualizations (*ṣiyur*)."[42]

We have seen that to a degree in Shapira's thought the imagination and *maḥshavah* are two aspects of the same phenomenon and are intertwined with one another. The *maḥshavah ha-ḥazaqah* and the imagination together are as a waking dream, a dream full of images and scenes. The images with form are in the imagination, while the formless images, meaning the theatrical and thematic, are in *maḥshavah*. This is the conception at the foundation of the imagery techniques which Shapira developed for both the empowerment and intensification of religious life and the development of prophetic thought for the express purpose of starting a spiritual revolution in the Jewish world and renewal of prophecy.[43]

R. Kalonymous Kalman Shapira's Imagery Techniques and His Imaginal-Literary Style

Shapira developed numerous imagery techniques, unique in the hasidic literary corpus due to their quantity and quality, which have been the subject of a number of studies.[44] Although his imagery techniques are based on existing visual techniques found in hasidic literature,[45] they are far more advanced and developed in multiple ways. A digital database search through multiple databases of general hasidic literature, consisting of thousands of works,[46] shows approximately ten visual techniques with numerous variations. In contrast, in Shapira's few writings I have discovered more than one hundred different and variegated

---

41 Ibid., 16b.

42 To be more precise, Shapira employs the term thought in a number of manners, see Reiser, "To Fly Like Angels," 89–90.

43 For a different understanding of *maḥshavah* in Shapira's doctrine, see Tomer Persico, *The Jewish Meditative Tradition* (Tel Aviv: Tel Aviv University Press, 2016), 175–192.

44 Concerning Shapira's imagery techniques see Leshem, "Between Messianism and Prophecy," 223–238; Wacks, *The Flame of the Holy Fire*, 123–166.

45 Regarding the hasidic literature mentioned in his writings see Leshem, "Between Messianism and Prophecy," 56, 58–61; Wacks, "Emotion and Enthusiasm," 72 n. 4.

46 DBS TORAH CD-ROM LIBRARY; Otzar HaHokhmah, https://www.otzar.org/; Bar Ilan Responsa Project, https://www.responsa.co.il; Chabad—Lubavitch Library, http://www.chabadlibrary.org/.

imagery techniques.[47] An examination of the content of these techniques and exercises reveals that they are qualitatively distinct from and more complex than the techniques found in zoharic and prophetic-kabbalistic, thus demonstrating a gradual development of these types of exercises.

Visual exercises, generally linguistic in nature have been a part of prophetic kabbalah since the twelfth century. The name of God, in all of its forms and permutations, became a focal point for visual exercises.[48] Linguistic imagery exercises are also found in Safedian kabbalah of the sixteenth century in both Lurianic and Cordoverian schools.[49] In Hasidic literature of the late eighteenth and early nineteenth centuries, in addition to linguistic-visual techniques, we find imagery techniques in which a particular scene, such as leaping into a fire, imagining God, visualizing one's death, and gazing upon the *ṣaddiq*, is envisioned, as exemplified by the following quotations:

> In every moment when one is free from Torah [study], specifically when one is sitting idly by himself in his room or laying on his bed and is unable to sleep, he should reflect on this positive commandment of "that I may be sanctified in the midst of the Israelite people" (Lev. 22:32), and he shall imagine (*ve-yedameh*) in his soul and visualize (*ve-yeṣayair*) in his mind as if a great and terrible fire burns in front of him until the heart of heaven and he, for [the sake of] the holiness of the Name blessed be he [God], breaks his nature and casts himself into the fire for the sanctification of the Name blessed be he [God].[50]

47 Concerning the centrality of imagery techniques in his thought in contrast to his predecessors, see Wacks, "The Technique of Guided Imagination," 242: "It appears that for R. Kalonymous the engagement with imagination takes up more space than it does for other hasidic thinkers. This conclusion is not based solely on the number of mentions in his writings, in contrast to writings of other thinkers, rather upon the centrality that R. Kalonymous gives this subject in his thought."

48 For divine name combination techniques in prophetic-kabbalistic literature, see below chap. 5, subchapter "Visualizing God's Name as a Technique for the Acquisition of Prophecy." Furthermore, see Elliot Wolfson's conception regarding the anthropomorphic form of the letters, idem, *Language, Eros, Being*, 122, 246, 249, 339.

49 See Ḥayyim Vital, *Sha'ar ha-Kavvanot*, Derushei Seder Shabbat, "Behold, there are four blessings in Grace after Meals, against the four letters of sovereignty (*adanut*), and each blessing is against one letter... In the first blessing, from its beginning until its end, he shall visualize in front of his eyes *AL"F, LM"D, P"'* [*alef*]... In the second blessing he shall visualize in front of his eyes *DL"T, LM"D, T"V* [*dalet*], and if it is the day of the New Moon he shall visualize *TY"V* [*tav*] filled with a *yod*." Also see idem, *Ṭa'amei ha-Miṣvot*, Parashat Eqev, Kavvanat ha-Akhilah le-Talmidei ha-Rav ZLLH"H, "At first he shall visualize in his consciousness four sides of the table sealed with the seventy-two letters [divine] name..., which is the Tetragrammaton in a square and the name *BeN* (52) with them, which is numerologically "animal" (*BeHeMaH*)." Regarding the visualization of divine names with colors during prayer in Cordovero's and Vital's thought, see Idel, *Kabbalah: New Perspectives*, 110.

50 Weisblum, *Sefer Tsetil Katan* (Kisvárda: s.n. 1925), 1 (§1).

> And if man will visualize in his soul that a great king blessed be he and his blessed, glorified, and terrible name stands above him and sees his actions and commands him saying, "My son, do this matter for me so that I shall delight from it and receive satisfaction," [then he] surely [will], as a lion roars and as a lion cub makes it sound, which is not like the sound of a man at all, say, "I will go and act as God, my God, has commanded with the yielding (*be-mesirat*) of my body, soul (*ve-nafshi*), spirit (*ve-ruḥi*), and soul (*ve-nishmati*).[51]

> He must visualize in front of his face and heart, and imagine in his soul, as if he is already dead and his flesh is buried, and his bones are dispersed and buried, and when he will visualize this in front of him when a desire or honor comes to him then certainly everything will be nullified from him.[52]

> About this I heard advice from *ṣaddiqim* (righteous people), that if a man will visualize in his thought the form of the *ṣaddiq* who enabled his desires—then through this he will always remember the wonders of the creator as mentioned above, in his remembrance of the good matter that the [*ṣaddiq*] caused (*she-hishpi'a*) for him.[53]

> There are *ṣaddiqim* who before prayer would visualize that they are lying in suffering in the grave and one would come and say to him, "Rise, stand, and pray."[54]

Indeed, most of these techniques have precedents in zoharic and kabbalistic literature,[55] I also will not argue that there are no linguistic-visual exercises in hasi-

---

51 Ḥayyim ben Solomon Tyrer of Czernowitz, *Sefer Be'ar Mayyim Ḥayyim ha-Shalem* (Jerusalem: s.n., 1992), 2:409.

52 David Solomon Eibenschütz, *Sefer Arvei Naḥal ha-Shalem* (Jerusalem: Maḥon Giv'ot Olam, 2004), Parashat Ki Teṣe, 966. The content of this visualization is based on *Zohar* 1:201b. Eibenschütz, in the beginning of this teaching, references Elijah de Vidas, one of Cordovero's students, who quotes this same zoharic passage, *Re'shit Ḥokhmah ha-Shalem*, ed. Ḥayyim Yosef Waldman (Jerusalem: Or ha-Musar, 2000), 2:769–770. However, Eibenschütz's call for visualization is more direct and clear, "He must visualize... and he will imagine... and when he will visualize like so..." For more imagery techniques based on the *Zohar*, see below subchapter, "Torah."

53 Kalonymus Kalman Halevi Epstein, *Sefer Ma'or ve-Shemesh ha-Shalem*, 1:384.

54 Aaron Ben Asher of Karlin, *Beit Aharon* (Jerusalem: A. Schwortz, 1965), 4b. Also see later that this passage is understood by Shapira as a call for visualization, Shapira, *Ḥovat ha-Talmidim*, 28b, "It is easy for the perceptive to understand, how man is awakened in his prayer if only he would visualize this with an intense thought (*maḥshavah ḥazaqah*)." On the concept of "intense thought" as imagination, see above, "*Maḥshavah* (Thought), Imagination, and Visualization in R. Kalonymous Kalman Shapira's Teaching."

55 For example, see that the *ṣaddiq* visualization that appears in the book *Ma'or ve-Shemesh* already appears in the thought of the kabbalist Abraham Azulai (1570–1643), see his *Ḥesed le-Avraham*, Ma'ayan 2, Ein ha-Qore, Nahar 33, "The matter is understood through what they interpreted in the *Zohar* on the verse, "And Joseph's hand shall close your eyes" (Gen. 46:4) [*Zohar* 1:226a, 3:169a], for the eyes are the gateway to imagined forms (*ha-ṣurot ha-medumot*) to the intellect, he will first visualize in his intellect the matter that is in his consciousness and intellect, and behold the form is visualized there... Behold, when man will visualize in his consciousness a

dic literature; however I am proposing that in hasidism we see a transition from a period in which linguistic imagery was dominant (alongside a few other techniques), to an emphasis upon visualization as the primary meditative technique.

Despite the kabbalistic and hasidic characterizations, Shapira's imagery techniques are comprised of many different scenes patched together into an extended and complex visualization, akin to a dream or a film, a phenomenon that has no prominent precedent in Jewish literature in general, and hasidic literature in particular, before his time.[56] It may further be argued that Shapira created an independent, original, and unique literary genre. His pre-holocaust writings are admixed with numerous images in an original style.[57] Ideas which are also personal experiences are translated in his rich language into an imaginal vision.[58]

---

holy form, behold the same holy form that he imagines in his consciousness will complete his intellect, and this is what R. Abba in [*Zohar*] Parashat Mishpaṭim said when the form of R. Shimon [bar Yoḥai] was depicted in front of him and he would comprehend through this great comprehensions, and this is the meaning of 'Your Teacher will not hide himself any more' (Is. 30:20)." Azulai's great-grandson, the kabbalist Ḥayyim Yosef David Azulai, commonly referred to as the Ḥida (1724–1806), quoted this passage and added, "And so our teacher R. Isaac Luria [Ha-AR"I], blessed be the memory of the righteous, wrote that when one will struggle with a Torah matter, one should visualize the form of his teacher—and it is good for him to understand this issue," Ḥayyim Yosef David Azulai, *Midbar Qedemot* (Modi'in Illit: Ahavat Shalom, 2008), 147. The zoharic source that serves as inspiration for this technique is *Zohar* 2:123b. Also, see Avraham Azulai, *Or ha-Ḥamah* (Bnei Brak: Yahadut, 1972) 2:154b. Furthermore, see further evidence of *ṣaddiq* imagery techniques in Safedian kabbalah, Tsevi Hirsch Koidanover, *Qav ha-Yashar* (Frankfurt am Main: s.n., 1705), consulted on DBS TORAH CD-ROM LIBRARY database, "Behold the maggid of the Beit Yosef [Joseph Karo], blessed be the memory of the righteous, gave sound advice to the rabbi, blessed be his memory, so that man should not come unto sin—he shall visualize the icon of his father standing before him. And he brought a proof from Joseph the righteous, who was asked to lie with Potiphar's wife, and the icon of his father came to his eyes, and Joseph retreated from sin."

56 Concerning this, see Reiser, "To Fly Like Angels," 28–29, 127–128.

57 Ibid., 78–81. His sermons during the Holocaust are quite extraordinary. On the stylistic gap between his pre-holocaust and post-holocaust writings, see Don Seeman, "Ritual Efficacy, Hassidic Mysticism and 'Useless Suffering' in the Warsaw Ghetto," *Harvard Theological Review* 101 (2008): 465–505.

58 See Wacks, "Emotion and Enthusiasm," 86, "R. Kalonymous's writing style is sometimes characterized by pathos, sublime language, and typically flowery, with imaginal depictions." We will add and state that there is a clear connection between Shapira's writings and the *Zohar*. His style imitates the zoharic style and sometimes certain parts of his books are a type of experimental "zoharic writing." Shapira treated the *Zohar* as the central kabbalistic text and even began to write a commentary on the *Zohar* entitled *Reshimat Zohar*. From this commentary we have one passage and an introduction entitled *Mesirat Hoda'ah*, see Shapira, *Derekh ha-Melekh*, 426–434. Regarding the *Zohar*'s centrality in Shapira's thought see Leshem, "Between

What caused Shapira to heavily utilize imagery, both in literary form and religious practice, as techniques for the reader? Due to the combination of his own advanced imaginal talent, which influenced his style, and his being an author with poetic sentiment, he was unable to stop the overflow of imagery. As he himself states in his personal journal *Ṣav ve-Ziruz*, "Also all the teachings (*ha-ma'amarim*) in this tract which have words that appear like poetic flourish (*ke-meliṣot*), I am merely describing my bursting emotions and not extoling poetics."[59] However, these matters alone are not enough to explain his poetic-imaginal style and the many imagery techniques in his writings.

I presume that Shapira was aware of his literary and imaginative powers, and he utilized them self-consciously and deliberately, just as he called upon others to do: "to bring all of one's emotional warmth, ecstasy, and even the human *imagination* to the house of God and transform them into wings and fly with them like the supernal angels";[60] "Each person has *maḥshavah*, imagination, and excitement... only that he should use them for permitted matters... And is such *mesirut nefesh* (self-sacrifice) necessary for you *baḥur* and *avreikh* (yeshiva student) that you should use them for holiness?! The merchant and artist are able to develop within themselves commercial and artistic *maḥshavah* and imagination... their *maḥshavah*, imagination, and excitement for merchandise and art are stimulated, and you find it difficult to discover in your soul *maḥshavah*, imagination, and excitement for holiness?!"[61] This demonstrates a conscious process of utilizing and developing different skills, including the imagination, as a praxis towards a religious aim. Shapira's call reinforces my assumption that his heavy use of the imagination in his writings is intentional. If so, the primary research question is, "why was the utilization of the imagination so necessary for Shapira and in which way did he utilize it." This question has been discussed recently by a number of scholars. I will present their findings, following which I will add a new layer based on the phenomenological analysis of mystical experience.

Nehemia Polen, Zvi Leshem, and Ron Wacks have explored the historical context in which Shapira was active, as well as the significance of secularization

---

Messianism and Prophecy," 132–134. I hope to discuss Shapira's and his contemporaries' attempts to mimic the zoharic style in a separate study.

59 Shapira, *Ṣav ve-Ziruz*, 38. Also see ibid., 42, regarding his personal outbreaks of spontaneous imagination in times of trauma, when his son was sick, "Images of such horror and terror of our frightening future, God forbid, project towards my eyes, like they are being visualized by themselves."

60 Idem, *Mevo ha-She'arim*, 59a.

61 Idem, *Hakhsharat ha-Avreikhim*, 43a.

in his writings.[62] Indeed, the effects and threat of secularization are clearly depicted in Shapira's writings: "Regarding this may our hearts become faint and the hairs of our heads stiffen, how, heaven forfend, in our sight the young generation has become heretical and blasphemous, it has no faith, no awe, and no Torah. They hate God and his servants Israel... Study halls that were filled with Torah learners are emptied, and in their place organizations and fellowships whose purposes, heaven forfend, are heresy and detestment of Torah";[63] "And upon our sons and daughters Satan rose in the figure of [political] parties to poison their souls and pollute their bodies with heresy and other foul and variegated transgressions, heaven forfend."[64] Nonetheless, we must ask if trends of secularization are indeed the primary cause for the development of Shapira's imagery techniques. The aforementioned scholarship answers this question in the positive; however, they do hesitate to attribute developments to his historical context alone.[65]

---

62 See Polen, *The Holy Fire*, 2; Zvi Blobstein (Leshem), "Iyunim be-Shiṭato ha-Ruḥanit shel ha-ADMO"R me-Pi'asechne" (master's thesis, Touro College, 2002), 5–18; idem, "Between Messianism and Prophecy," 15–32; Wacks, "Emotion and Enthusiasm," 75–78; idem, "The Technique of Guided Imagination," 237–240; idem, *The Flame of the Holy Fire*, 53–63.

63 Shapira, *Ḥovat ha-Talmidim*, 4a-b.

64 Idem, *Mevo ha-She'arim*, 41a. Also see ibid., 46a.

65 See the second chapter of Leshem, "*Iyunim be-Shiṭato*," regarding the historical context of secularization, esp. ibid., 18, "It is undoubtedly clear that in such a difficult circumstance a new hasidic social-educational program was required. And that, in essence, is what the Rebbe devoted his life and writings to." This chapter serves as an introduction to Leshem's thesis, which surveys Shapira's new educational program, beginning with the definition of hasidism and concluding with hasidic practices, including guided imagery and mediation. Leshem expanded and deepened this line of thought in his dissertation, and devoted his third chapter to the historical context, and thereby researched Shapira's theoretical hasidic teachings (idem, "Between Messianism and Prophecy," 58–150) and the practical application of it, including guided imagery techniques (ibid., 151–261). Ron Wacks discussed the process of secularization and the educational-religious crisis left in its wake, concluded that "according to R. Kalonymous , the primary cause that led to the crisis of Torah-education was the feeling of alienation towards sacred matters and lack of motivation, and these stemmed from a lack of emotional satisfaction and spiritual desiccation... The solution lies in creating an array of means that will give a person a deep emotional experience, which will assist him to internalize the values of Torah and the commandments" (Wacks, "Emotion and Enthusiasm," 77). According to Wacks the religious crisis required Shapira to create a system of techniques that generate an alternative religious-emotional experience, which he terms "Self-awareness, intense thought (*maḥshavah ḥazaqah*), imagery techniques (*targilei dimyun*), Torah study methods, drinking wine, melody (*nigun*), dance, and binding to a *ṣaddiq* (ibid., 81–86). Wacks repeats this remark in a different article and emphasizes that imagery techniques are one of the means designed to grapple with the crisis of secularization, "A crisis occurred in Torah-education... The solution lies in creating an

According to these scholars, secularization is crucial for understanding the imaginative style in both of its aspects—imagery techniques and exercises and the poetic-imaginal writing style. The culture of the twentieth century—theater, arts, music, film, and coffee houses—all exhilarated the youth. Youth movements, centered on political action, were widespread among the younger generation, as they were also a place of refuge from traditional Jewish education. These incentives stationed outside the four walls of the study hall required Shapira to develop a new education approach for the yeshiva world. It is no longer sufficient to give a student extensive knowledge and in-depth learning; the yeshiva must initiate experiences of the sacred, so as to serve as an alternative to "shepherding in strange fields":

> For even if we penetrate to the very essence of the youth's intellect by enlightening him... nevertheless... his fiery passions will prematurely leave—[he will] become excited and impassioned by the imagined beauty of the vanities of the world, such as theater houses and all sorts of frivolities and lawlessness of the world. If we do not preempt [this by] arousing his soul to be excited by each commandment and become ecstatic from the Torah and the light of God, then we will have done nothing, God forbid, for even if he intellectually understands that he must educate himself, nevertheless his emotions and desires will veer him to the path that even he himself understands is bad.[66]

---

array of means... One of the central methods for affecting the enthusiasm (*ha-hitlahavut*) and motivation in the worship of God is the imagination" (idem, "The Technique of Guided Imagination," 240). In Wacks's book, *The Flame of the Holy Fire*, the phenomenon of secularization is described as an "introductory gate" (ibid., 53–63), since this phenomenon constitutes a central foundation for the book's trajectory, "The depiction of the crisis is very severe... According to R. Kalonymous an array of means must be created to stir within man a deep emotional experience of worshiping God... We will engage this topic in "Gate Four–The Gate of Hasidism," "Gate Five–The Gate of Hasidic Worship," and "Gate Six–The Gate of Prayer." Likewise, the youth and adults' awareness that they are "sons of prophets" must be strengthened and they must be taught to discover this potential. We will deal with this in "Gate Seven–The Gate of Prophecy" (ibid., 61–63). Nevertheless, Wacks concludes his book by mitigating the historical connection between the development of imagery techniques and the crisis of secularization; he notes that this connection is not the sole one and the development of imagery techniques should be viewed from a larger spectrum (ibid., 96.) The crisis of secularization was also briefly discussed by Mendel Piekarz, *Ideological Trends of Hasidim in Poland During the Interwar Period and the Holocaust* (Jerusalem: Bialik Institute, 1990), 17–23; Nehemia Polen, "Sensitization to Holiness: The Life and Works of Rabbi Kalonymos Kalmish Shapiro," *Jewish Action* (Winter 1989–1990): 30–31. Furthermore, it should be noted that Polen did not relate imagery techniques to the phenomenon of secularization. He discussed the phenomenon and the difficult challenge thrusted upon Shapira. However, Polen is careful to not create a closer connection between the phenomenon of secularization and Shapira's teachings, nor does he argue for the development of his thought from a historical context.

66 Shapira, *Ḥovat ha-Talmidim*, 6b.

Wacks has eloquently stated that, "A culture of leisure persists, and if, for example, the youth is more excited by the theater than Torah study, it is a sign that he had not found excitement from what he finds in the study hall, and therefore the educators must administer the cure before the onset of the disease."[67] The creation of a new, original, and sweeping genre served Shapira for this very purpose. Imagery (and non-imagery) techniques were meant to grant access to an experience which could act as an alternative for the secular culture and its entailed experiences. Alongside imagery techniques, Wacks presented many others methods and various sources of inspiration found in Shapira's work united, in his opinion, by the common purpose of "the formation of an experience and development of religious feeling, which are able to fill the large experiential void found in the Polish hasidic study hall and thereby prevent the ever-growing secularization."[68] He concludes, "The lack of inner satisfaction with the life of Torah and commandments as the primary cause for the abandonment of religion was to be contended with by developing emotional faculties through different approaches."[69]

Nevertheless, it must be stated that while the historical circumstances should be considered, they are not the central component. The ever-growing trend in scholarship towards historicization has seemingly not allowed for a broad phenomenological analysis. In a different mode, but instructive for our purposes, Yehuda Liebes and Moshe Idel have both challenged, in their own ways, the Hegelian structure which Scholem presented for the understanding of the dynamic history of kabbalah, in which each stage stands in dialectical tension of thesis and antithesis with that which precedes and proceeds it. According to Scholem, the Spanish expulsion brought forth Lurianic kabbalah, which led to Sabbateanism, which caused the rise of hasidism. Scholem presented a circular historicism in which grand events formed grand symbols, which in turn produce historical movements, which create symbols of their own, and so on. In contradistinction, Liebes has demonstrates that a kabbalist's creativity is not confined solely to his historical context and that his creative capabilities are not restrained by the bounds of time and space.[70] Idel has shown that the kabbalists' writings

---

67 Wacks, "Emotion and Enthusiasm," 76. Also see idem, "The Technique of Guided Imagination," 237–240.

68 Idem, "Emotion and Enthusiasm," 80–88; idem, "The Technique of Guided Imagination," 240.

69 Wacks, "Emotion and Enthusiasm," 88.

70 Yehuda Liebes, *Studies in the Zohar*, trans. Arnold Schwartz, Stephanie Nakache, and Penina Peli (Albany: State University of New York Press, 1993), 1–84. According to Liebes, kabbalah tends to understand itself through its internal logic.

are not defined by their period, but rather that influences from multiple literatures transform them into transperiodic literature.[71]

Likewise, Shapira's grappling with secularization should be analyzed using both historical and phenomenological tools. It is impossible to examine the development and evolution of imagery techniques—which reached new heights in Shapira's writings, becoming detailed dramatic-theatrical scenes of great length —with the terminology of cause and effect alone. Phenomenological research, which is freer than historical studies, allows the analysis of these techniques through their own internal logic, the emotional awareness of their creator, and the mystic's internal freeness. To be clear, I am not claiming that Shapira was unaware of secularization or that he did not try to intentionally combat it. Furthermore, I am not claiming that the historical and cultural contexts should not be explored; rather I am only proposing that an additional stratum of phenomenological analysis must and should be executed. Indeed, the development of imagery techniques occurred within specific historical, as well as political, parameters; nevertheless, its study should not be constrained to these material manifestations. I have no doubt that beyond historical and sociological considerations there is an additional element in Shapira's imagery techniques—empowerment.[72] This concept of empowerment, or intensification, is quite significant in that its ability to bridge the gap between the essentialist and contextualist approaches to mysticism.[73] I propose that the concept of empowerment is at the heart of many of Shapira's imagery techniques and offers a phenomenological answer to the question of why the utilization of the imagination was so necessary for Shapira and how he utilized it.

---

71 From Moshe Halbertal, "Opening Remarks" (presented at Studies in Kabbalah Research: An International Conference in Honor of Prof. Moshe Idel and Prof. Yehuda Liebes at the Van Leer Institute, Jerusalem, Israel, July 10, 2012). While Gershom Scholem never explicitly presented defined periods or specific schematic developments, his different descriptions of the relation between Jewish mysticism and messianism nonetheless presuppose a three-stage development. See Moshe Idel, "History of Kabbalah and History of the Jews," *Theory and Criticism* 6 (1995): 137–148. In this article, Idel objects to Scholem's tripartite division and shows that the two presuppositions of his research, that Jewish mysticism is formed by external historical factors and that Jewish mysticism was understood as a blue print for general Jewish history, were unfounded.

72 See above, chap. 2.

73 Ibid.

B Imagination as an Empowering Factor of Anomian Experiences

Shapira developed techniques in multiples and variegated arenas, including song (*nigun*),[74] creative writing,[75] meditation (*hitbodedut*),[76] individual prayer,[77] dance,[78] rhythmic stomping,[79] self-reproach,[80] automatic speech,[81] consumption of hard alcohol,[82] asceticism,[83] self-denial,[84] and imagery. Besides the spiritual experience that these techniques are able to produce in their contention with secularization, their independent significance and anomian features[85] must not be ignored. Indeed, their anomian characteristics demonstrate that Shapira's hasidic teachings should be understood as mystical-philosophical in nature, as we will expound upon below.

An analysis of Shapira's writings reveals that his imagery techniques were apparently only one type among a lengthy list of others. However, the employment of imagery techniques serves as an empowering factor for all the other techniques. The imagination does not only evoke fresh experiences but also empowers the pre-existing array of experiences within the religious sphere. Unlike the other techniques, imagery techniques function as an enhancement; when joined to other techniques it empowers and intensifies them, thus transforming normative religious experiences into mystical experiences. Meaning, imagery techniques are utilized as empowering instruments for religious-emotional-ritualistic experiences,[86] changing them into experiences in which divine intimacy

---

74 Shapira, *Hakhsharat ha-Avreikhim* 47a-b; idem, *Benei Maḥshavah Ṭovah*, 41–43, 56; idem, *Mevo ha-She'arim*, 43a; idem, *Ṣav ve-Ziruz*, 47.
75 Idem, *Ḥovat ha-Talmidim*, 18a, 30a.
76 Idem, *Mevo ha-She'arim*, 41a; idem, *Hakhsharat ha-Avreikhim*, 17b; idem, *Ṣav ve-Ziruz*, 13.
77 Idem, *Hakhsharat ha-Avreikhim*, 46a, 48a-b, 62b; idem, *Ḥovat ha-Talmidim*, 31b.
78 Idem, *Benei Maḥshavah Ṭovah*, 57; idem, *Ṣav ve-Ziruz*, 22–26; idem, *Hakhsharat ha-Avreikhim*, 61b. For a thorough investigation of Hasidic dance, see Feigue Berman, "Hasidic Dance: An Historical and Theological Analysis" (PhD diss., New York University, 1999).
79 Shapira, *Hakhsharat ha-Avreikhim*, 42b.
80 Ibid., 50b; idem, *Ḥovat ha-Talmidim*, 46b, 28b.
81 Idem, *Hakhsharat ha-Avreikhim*, 68b-69b; idem, *Ḥovat ha-Talmidim*, 29b.
82 Idem, *Hakhsharat ha-Avreikhim*, 46b; idem, *Benei Maḥshavah Ṭovah*, 56.
83 Idem, *Hakhsharat ha-Avreikhim*, 50a-b.
84 Ibid., 51b; idem, *Ḥovat ha-Talmidim*, 47a; idem, *Benei Maḥshavah Ṭovah*, 46–47.
85 For the distinction between nomian and anomian techniques see above, intro., n. 39.
86 Nomian rituals are patterns of behavior that have undergone a canonization process in rabbinic literature, see Idel, *Enchanted Chains*, 202.

or presence occurs. The imagination adds a mystical layer to normative religious emotion and passion.

Shapira reiterates in numerous locations the claim that analytical thought and dry knowledge are unable to inspire and arouse man's soul without *maḥshavah* and imagination: "only *ha-maḥshavah ha-ḥazaqah* (intense thought) can aid the performance of worship and prayer, and not intellectual inquiry (*ha-iyun be-sekhel*)."[87] He also expands this notion as to include anomian practices such as dance and song. The purpose of visualization is to empower these activities and transform them into mystical experiences, from ritualistic (emotional or religious) experiences into intimate experiences in which man encounters the divine presence. The goal of joining imagery techniques to such experiences as song and dance is to enact a transformation of these experiences themselves into mystical ones. I will now examine different techniques in Shapira's teachings and show how the imagery techniques (or *maḥshavah*) which accompany them are designed "to raise them" from normative religious actions to explicit religious-mystical actions.

Dance and Imagery

Exceptional, empowered, and ecstatic dance is mentioned in the Bible, Mishnah, and Talmud. It is written that David danced wildly with all his strength, "David whirled with all his might before the Lord; David was girt with a linen ephod" (II Sam. 6:14). This dancing is not of a conservative or standard dance, but rather a very powerful embodied movement,[88] which was not acceptable or normal. Michal was therefore embarrassed by him, mocking him saying, "Didn't the king of Israel do himself honor today-exposing himself today in the sight of the slave-girls of his subjects, as one of the riffraff might expose himself! (ibid., 6:20). It may be presumed that this dance was ecstatic in nature since it occurred during a time of mystical-religious passion, in which David experienced being present "before the Lord." In addition, David justified his "inappropriate" behavior with a religious reason, "I will dance before the Lord" (ibid., 6:21).[89] The dancing accompanying the joyous water-drawing ceremony (*simḥat beit ha-sho'evah*) dur-

87 Shapira, *Ḥovat ha-Talmidim*, 63b. Concerning the concept of "intense thought" as an expression of imagination, see above in the introduction of this chapter. This sentence, which contrasts intense thought with intellectual thought, demonstrates that intense thought is not discursive.
88 See David Kimhi's commentary on this verse.
89 For more on dance in biblical times see Amos Hakham, "Maḥol ve-Riqud be-TaNa"KH," *Mahanayim* 48 (1960): 30–32.

ing the festival of Sukkot is specifically referenced in the Mishnah, "Men of piety and good deeds used to dance before them with lighted torches in their hands" (*m. Sukkah* 5:4). Rabban Simeon b. Gamaliel is mentioned in the Talmud as rejoicing in an extravagant manner—it is written that "at the Rejoicing at the place of the Water-Drawing, he used to take eight lighted torches and throw them in the air] and catch one and throw one and they did not touch one another." Furthermore, it is reported that he, when prostrating himself, would, "dig his two thumbs in the ground, bend down, kiss the ground, and draw himself up again, a feat which no other man could do" (*b. Sukkah* 53a).

In other classic rabbinic sources, one may find additional references, such as special dancing at weddings, "They tell of R. Judah b. Ila'i that he used to take a myrtle twig and dance before the bride and say: 'Beautiful and graceful bride'... R. Aha took her on his shoulder and danced [with her]. The Rabbis said to him: May we [also] do it? He said to them: If they are on you like a beam, [then it is] all right. and if not, [you may] not" (*b. Ketubot* 17a).[90] Nonetheless, it appears that dancing at this time was reserved for special occasions, like festivals and weddings, and that it was not a routine occurrence. Dance was expanded initially by kabbalists and more so by hasidim:

> The performance of holy dance was one of many ritualistic innovations that kabbalah inserted into spiritual life. The Sabbath Queen was received with the setting of the sun with songs and circular dancing (*u-be-haqafot*) by the kabbalists dressed in white, and her exit was accompanied as well by song and dance. Dance was again inserted into festivals, specifically the festival of Simḥat Torah—a symbol of the higher unity. It is told that on this day, the exemplary kabbalist R. Isaac Luria (1534–1572) would dance and sing with all his ability with a Torah scroll and would traverse from one synagogue to the next in order to join the line of dancers.[91]

An additional stage of the infiltration of dance into everyday routine spiritual life is found in hasidism. No longer solely at moments of joy or holiness, but also before and after prayer and learning, during hasidic gatherings, or whenever a fellowship of hasidim desired to do so, "The dancing [which occurred] by the Beshṭ and his students deviated from the singular framework of *riqud ha-miṣvah* (ritually commanded dancing) and took a prominent place as a technique

90 For more on dance in the classic rabbinic period see Mordechai Piron, "Ha-Riqud ve-ha-Zemer be-Tequfat ha-Talmud," *Mahanayim* 48 (1960): 34–38.

91 Paul Fenton, "Some Remarks on Dance in Hassidism," in *Judaism, Topics, Fragments, Faces, Identities: Jubilee Volume in Honor of Rivka*, ed. Haviva Pedaya and Ephraim Meir (Beer-Sheva: Ben Gurion University Press, 2007), 279.

aimed at a mystical experience."[92] Nevertheless, dancing during holy times was considered to be a higher level, specifically those done on Shemini Aṣeret and Simḥat Torah, which, due to kabbalistic influences, were conceived as dances of the highest mystical significance. The moment of the "giving of the Torah" is the moment of conjunction between the congregation of Israel and the *Shekhinah*, a moment of absolute union and the undeniable presence of *Shekhinah*, "On Simḥat Torah there were members of the holy fellowship of the students of the Besht who were joyful and dancing in a circle and the *Shekhinah* stirring around them."[93]

In hasidism, dance was considered to have mystical significance not only during sacred times, but also in day-to-day life. Circular dance teaches an equanimous unity and grants this experience: "in a circle there is no front or back, no beginning or end."[94] Dance is not arbitrary, but has deep significance. Different groupings and types of dancing symbolize relationships between man and the divine. Different hasidic dance bear these meanings in their names, such as the *broygez tants* (dance of anger), *tehiyas ha-mesim tants* (resurrection dance), *mitsve tants* (commandment dance), and more.[95] Dance expresses (through its rhythm and bodily movements) the separation of *Shekhinah* and the assembly of Israel and the exile of the *Shekhinah*, as well as reconciliation and bringing together of *Shekhinah* and the assembly of Israel.[96] Already in the beginning of hasidism different teachings explore and analyze dance, finding kabbalistic symbolic values in it. R. Phineas of Korzec (1726–1791) saw the wedding dance, in which at first two are one and afterwards one faces the other, as an expression of the lurianic *sod ha-nesirah* (cosmic bifurcation).[97]

---

92 Ibid., 279.

93 Ibid., 280. From *Shivḥei ha-Besht.*

94 Attributed to the Besht, see ibid., 280. Also, see a similar statement in Bezalel Landau, "Ha-Maḥol ve-ha-Riqud be-Tenu'at ha-Ḥasidut," *Mahanayim* 48 (1960): 62, brought in the name of R. Tsevi Elimelekh of Dinov, the author of *Benei Yissakhar.*

95 Concerning the *Mitsve Tants* (mitzvah dance, a dance that is customarily performed at hasidic weddings), see Zvi Friedhaber, "Riqudei ha-Miṣvah: Toldoteihem ve-Ṣuroteihem," *Dukhan* 7 (1966): 75–85; Yaakov Mazor and Moshe Taube, "A Hassidic Ritual Dance: The *Mitsve Tants* in Jerusalemite Weddings," *Yuval* 5 (1994): 164–224.

96 Fenton, "Some Remarks on Dance in Hassidism." Also see Leshem, "Between Messianism and Prophecy," 192–193 n. 655; Elliot R. Wolfson, *Along the Path: Studies in Kabalistic Myth, Symbolism, and Hermeneutics* (Albany: State University of New York Press, 1995), 88–109; idem, "Afterword: To Pray after Praying/To Dance with No Feet," in Aubrey L. Glazer, *Mystical Vertigo: Contemporary Hebrew Poetry Dancing Over the Divide* (Boston: Academic Studies Press, 2013), 267–273.

97 Fenton, "Some Remarks on Dance in Hassidism," 281, from Phineas of Korzec, *Midrash Pinḥas* (Biłgoraj: N. Kronberg, 1930), 14b.

His student, R. Aryeh Judah Leib (1725–1812), the Grandfather of Szpola, saw in each step of his dance an act of *yiḥud* (unification [with God]). The combination of steps in his opinion would enact, "tremendously wondrous unifications."[98] It was said about Aryeh Judah Leib himself that he was "light on his feet like a four year old child and in the heart of all who would look upon him thought of repentance would be aroused."[99] In the Beshṭ's elucidation of the Mishnah regarding how one dances for the bride, he explained that the Mishnah denotes the obligation for man to lift the holy sparks from the lower realm to the supernal realm. Hasidism, in connection to kabbalistic texts that precede it, granted dance, melody, and clapping "a holy significance, in their being both a theurgic language and fruits of ecstatic revelation."[100]

In Hasidic tradition, one finds complex dances entailing creative acrobatics termed *hithapkhuyot* (reversals), or in Yiddish, *kulien zikh*; meaning, cartwheels, somersaults, and handstands.[101] *Hithapkhuyot* have profound significance, and allow one to experience the hasidic ideal of self-nullification (*biṭṭul ha-yesh*).[102] R. Avraham Yehoshua Heschel of Apt, a disciple of the Seer of Lublin, would perform *hithapkhuyot*,[103] as well as the contemporary R. Yoḥanan Twersky of Tolna-Bayit Vegan (1906–1999) who would often do so prior to any holy act, such as reciting the blessing over wine on Friday night (*Qiddush*) or lighting candles for the festival of Hanukkah, as a means for attaining the nullification of the self.[104] *Hithapkhuyot* also serve as an embodied technique symbolizing the inver-

98 Fenton, "Some Remarks on Dance in Hassidism," 281, for more on the Grandfather of Szpola, see Yom Tov Levinsky, "Riqud, Ma'ase'ah, Zemer be-Torat ha-Ḥasidut," *Mahanayim* 46 (1960): 98. Also, there are those who claim that this quote belongs to R. Avraham the Angel, son of the Dov Ber of Międzyrzecz, Landau, "Ha-Maḥol ve-ha-Riqud," 58. Either way Avraham the Angel attributed these words to the Grandfather of Szpola.

99 Ibid. Also see ibid., regarding the utilization of dance for repentance.

100 Haviva Pedaya, "Two Types of Ecstatic Experience in Hasidism," *Da'at* 55 (2005): 90.

101 Regarding *hithapkhuyot*, see Levinsky, "Riqud, Ma'ase'ah, Zemer," 99.

102 Avraham Avishai Shor, "Maran Rebi Aharon ha-Gadol, Zekhuto Yagen Aleinu Amen, ve-Ḥavurat ha-Ḥasidim be-Qarlin," *Beit Aharon ve-Yisrael* 51 (1994): 153–160. Shor suggest that a distinction should be made between the custom of *hithapkhuyot*, which only existed in Russian hasidism (Ḥabad and Kalisk), and whose purpose was the nullification of existence, and the custom of being boisterous (*hishtovevut*), which was widely accepted in Polish hasidism (Karlin, Kosnitz, Amdur), and whose purpose was to enhance joy.

103 David Assaf, "'A Girl! He Ought to be Whipped': The Hasid as *Homo Ludens*," in *Let the Old Make Way for the New: Studies in the Social and Cultural History of Eastern European Jewry Presented to Immanuel Etkes*, ed. David Assaf and Ada Rapoport-Albert (Jerusalem: Zalman Shazar Center, 2009), 1:136.

104 Ibid., 138–139 and ibid. n. 62–63.

sion of poles. The feet represent the lowest *sefirah* of *malkhut*,[105] and the head represents the upper *sefirot* of *ḥokhmah, binah*, and *da'at*. *Hithapkhuyot* raises one's feet upwards, just as *malkhut* returns to its roots (in the aspect of *teshuvah* [repentance]—*teshuv ha-H"E* [return of the letter *he*]).[106] Naḥman of Bratslav granted dance a theurgic function, "When there are, heaven forbid, judgments upon Israel, through dances and the clapping of palms the judgments will be sweetened";[107] "through [the movement of] dance, which is a consequence of drinking merrying wine, which are the roots of *gevurot* (judgments; lit. strengths) that are in *binah*, and they are drawn to the bottom within the feet, meaning that the one who dances—through this excites the externalities (*ḥiṣonim*) through them, and this is the excitement of the dancing, and it is 'an offering by fire of pleasing odor to the Lord.'"[108] As Naḥman interprets, so he fulfills. R. Natan Sternhartz testifies regarding his master that he would dance ecstatic dance of an explicitly mystical aim whose impact and power influenced his surroundings. Naḥman who generally did not dance, saw it fitting in the year 1803 to dance at a number of occasions, due to harsh judgments that were sentenced against the Jewish people at those time. Naḥman, who saw dance as a theurgic and magical technique with the ability to sweeten judgments and change reality danced ecstatically with all his might:

> After he finished saying [a teaching of] Torah, he would dance a great deal with his daughter the bride etc. and one who had not seen his dances had not ever seen good, for even though, blessed be God, we have merited to observe a number of *ṣaddiqim* who have danced before the bride, his dances did not appear as such, and all who stood there certainly had thoughts of true repentance for all his sins, and the stirring and excitement of all the people present at the time of dancing grew is impossible to elucidate and depict whatsoever in writing. And a few very lofty teachings have already been revealed regarding dance and clapping hands… however, he did not dance frequently, rather very infrequently, but in that same year he danced (*meraqed*) numerous times, on Simḥat Torah and after-

---

105 Fenton, "Some Remarks on Dance in Hassidism," 284.

106 Regarding dance as a technique that can reverse poles in Naḥman's thought see Naḥman of Bratslav, *Siḥot Moharan*, §86. For more on dance in Naḥman's thought see Michael A. Fishbane, "To Jump for Joy: The Rites of Dance According to R. Nahman of Bratzlav," *Journal of Jewish Thought & Philosophy* 6 (1997): 371–387. Also, regarding the raising of one's feet, see ibid., 378–380, and regarding the significance of dance for each commandment, see ibid., 383–384. Furthermore, see Shore, "Letters of Desire," 103–108. Lastly, see Wolfson, "Afterword."

107 Naḥman of Bratslav, *Liqquṭei Moharan* I:10.

108 Ibid., 41. Regarding the theurgic dimension of dance, see Fishbane, "To Jump for Joy," 378. Fishbane demonstrates (ibid., 373) that, according to Naḥman, through joy man can strive towards God, and that the pleasure of dancing expresses the yearning for the divine, as well as his ability to draw down the supernal forces into man.

> wards on the sabbath of Hanukkah... and afterwards on Purim and afterwards on the wedding as aforementioned. And he himself said, "This year I danced a lot, and this was due to the decrees called *punktin* heard this year, which they then wanted to sentence upon Israel, God forbid, and because of this he danced a number of times, for through dance the judgments are sweetened, and the decrees nullified.[109]

In classic rabbinic language the term *meraqed* refers to sifting, one of the thirty-nine categories of prohibited work on sabbath, specifically within the group of activities of separating, "The primary labors are forty less one, sowing, ploughing... selecting, grinding, sifting."[110] The Talmud states regarding these activities that "winnowing, selecting, and sifting are identical."[111] The activity of sifting does not arbitrarily share the same root as that for dance, for when man separates the wheat from the shaft his whole body moves as if he is dancing. The material appearance of the dance movements and the body swaying from side to side are frequently mystically interpreted. The activity of sifting is not solely termed *meraqed* due to the bodily movements associated with it, but also due to the act of dancing being a theurgic act of supernal sifting: "For it is known from books, that *riqud* (dance, sift) is an expression of separation, and the separation is accomplished through the joy of the feet (i.e. dance) through which Israel gladden themselves with the creator."[112] Corporeal dance is transformed into a spiritual process occurring on the cosmic plane.[113] The *ṣaddiq*'s purposeful

---

109 Naḥman of Bratslav, *Ḥayyei Moharan*, (Jerusalem and Tel Aviv: Yisroel Ber Odesser Fund, s.a.), 1:188 – 190§116. Also, see ibid., 191§117, 15§4, 335 – 336§263. The last passage that discusses his dancing on Shemini Aṣeret in 1802 parallels our passage here. Also, see Fenton, "Some Remarks on Dance in Hassidism," 283. Lastly, regarding *punktin*, see Arthur Green, *Tormented Master: A Life of Rabbi Nahman of Bratslav* (Tuscaloosa: The University of Alabama Press, 1979), 140 – 141, "This series of threatened measures, known in Bratslav literature as *gezerat ha-punktin (punktin* here probably means" clauses," of which there were many in the Constitution), was a matter of tremendous concern to Nahman."

110 *m. Shabbat*, 7:2. Maimonides comments that the labor of sifting is differentiating the wheat from the unfit parts.

111 *b. Shabbat* 73b.

112 David Twersky of Tolna, *Birkhat David* (Zhytomyr: Shapira Brothers, 1862), 48b-49b. Appearing in Fenton, "Some Remarks on Dance in Hassidism," 286. Also see Twersky's remarks as cited in Landau, "Ha-Maḥol ve-ha-Riqud," 58.

113 For more see Fenton, "Some Remarks on Dance in Hassidism," 286 – 287, primarily from the writings of Dov Baer Schneersohn. In his opinion the corporeal dance reflects the supernal unifications.

dancing intentionally forms an outline of God's name or the sefirotic realm with each step.[114]

Shapira's attitude towards dance is a direct continuation of the kabbalistic and hasidic conception of the subject, although he adapted dance for secular life as well. Shapira instructed his students to not only dance at religious moments, such as during weddings or holidays, but also "from time to time," as they felt: "It is good to drink alcohol together from time to time ... after they drink they will sing a song of stirring (*zemer shel hit'orrerut*)... and if their souls shall become enflamed and they should want to dance together–[then] they should dance!"[115] Similar to the kabbalists, Shapira granted the dancing of Shemini Aṣeret and Simḥat Torah foremost mystical significance. In his opinion, these dances have the ability to illuminate "The Garden of Eden" and unify supernal unifications.[116] Akin to *hithapkhuyot*, in dance as well there is an ecstatic element of self-nullification, "All is nullified now, there is no world and no worries, no body and no form, with Him, blessed be he, with all of my strength I whirl and before his glory I dance";[117] according to Shapira, in dance the component of self-sacrifice (*mesirat ha-nefesh*) may appear as well, "Master of the world, you know that I am prepared at every moment to give my life for you. Though it is true that with all my worship, according to the magnitude of your greatness and holiness, I have not given you anything, but I always give my neck to you, and I spread it out before your glory. With all of my strength I am gladdened by you my God, and for your glory I dance."[118] The joy of dancing on Simḥat Torah creates unifications and constitutes a part of the process of uniting the assembly of Israel with *Shekhinah*, "It is possible that this joy is an aspect of unification, at the time in which the iron wall falls, and all barriers of any kind for a moment are annihilated."[119] In a moving personal testimony, Shapira shares his desire to perform *hithapkhuyot* at a celebration of a new Torah scroll, and his uncertainty regarding this action:

> Often a Jew is filled with a powerful yearning which is greater than his usual spiritual level, Torah, and service. He says, "What powerful and intense act can I do for the sake of God... for at least this moment I will uproot my heart from itself, my body from itself, my self from

---

114 See ibid., 290–291, regarding the dance steps of Ḥayyim Elazar Shapira of Munkacz (1872–1937), which formed the divine name *Shaddai* (*shin, daled, yod*).
115 Shapira, *Hakhsharat ha-Avreikhim*, 61b; idem, *Benei Maḥshavah Ṭovah*, 56. Regarding the drinking of wine, see Leshem, "Between Messianism and Prophecy," 167–171.
116 See Shapira, *Ṣav ve-Ziruz*, 23; idem, *Benei Maḥshavah Ṭovah*, 61.
117 Idem, *Ṣav ve-Ziruz*, 22.
118 Ibid., 24.
119 Ibid.; idem, *Benei Maḥshavah Ṭovah*, 62.

> myself, straight towards God." When I began to prepare myself for the commencement and the dedication [of the Torah], my desire kindled within me with great intensity, becoming like a fire within myself. Surely this is a moment of joy, holiness and awe of this type, perhaps the greatest in my life, but what can I actually do with my body for God? I will rejoice in trembling and dance with all my might! Good–but my soul is still not content! Is there no other great and powerful act that is appropriate for this singular, elevated, and holy moment? And I said [to myself], "I will flip (*ethapekh*) like those inferior and loathsome [people] who debase themselves in joy for the glory of their masters." But Satan came to me and berated me [saying], "What is this worship to you? What is the reason for it? What does the blessed Holy One care if you flip or not? Perhaps your health and senses will be injured. And will you not appear to be crazy and a fool in everyone's eyes?" Then my heart roared within me, "'The Lord rebuke you, O Satan' (Zec. 3:2). Now is not the time for calculations! The moment is great, singular, and urgent. To perform some great act of self-sacrifice (*mesirat nefesh*) for my Maker [is what] I want!"[120]

In this notable confession Shapira describes his intense desire to unite with God. The *hithapkhuyot* constitute a radical act of self-nullification and self-sacrifice in order to unite with the Creator. He writes that he wishes to "uproot my heart from itself, my body from itself, myself from my self, straight towards God." It should be noted that entailed in this remarkable experience is an element of intense imaginal activity. I have argued that Shapira systematically employs the imagination for various empowering experiences. In this event as well he admits that he utilized his imagination as a way to intensify his experience of self-sacrifice, and it is solely through his imagination that he was able to ultimately overcome the naysaying of Satan:

> As the thought of my body (*maḥshevet gufi*) had just begun to ensue and contemplate its simple action of *hithapkhuyot*, immediately my soul came before and a thought of self-sacrifice began to burn within me. Not only simple *hithapkhuyot* did I visualize in my imagination, but a kind of altar glistened before my eyes, the very place we would traverse while dedicating the Torah scroll. Everything was sanctified, consumed by fire, and my blood bubbled up, and my eyes welled with tears.[121]

Visualizing the place in which the Torah scroll passed as an altar, as well as the vision of the blazing fire, allowed Shapira to "sacrifice his own blood," as an offering to God. This act, in which he was totally committed to sacrificing himself, body and soul, expressed itself in the form of *hithapkhuyot*. The *hithapkhuyot* are enhanced and empowered through his visualization. His imagination allows for

---

120 Idem, *Ṣav ve-Ziruz*, 19.

121 Ibid. See a broad and comparative analysis of this text, Zvi Leshem, "Flipping into Ecstasy: Towards a Syncopal Understanding of Mystical Hasidic Somersaults," *Studia Judaica* 17 (2014): 157–183.

an intensified experience that has important physiological elements ("and my blood bubbled up and my eyes welled with tears") not found in normative religious experiences. Shapira's imaginal visualization empowers the emotive and fiery passion expressed in the *hithapkhuyot*, transforming them into an ecstatic experience in which Shapira sought to experience total self-nullification and touch the divine realm.

I have not raised the idea that imagery techniques intensify the experiences which they accompany, in this case—dance, just from Shapira's descriptions of his own experiences. Shapira himself conducts a theoretical discussion of the place of imagination in his empowered dancing. He was aware that for all the mystical potency of dancing, as has been described in kabbalistic and hasidic literature,[122] it also may be futile. In a letter that he wrote to his student Elimelekh ben Porat, who was one of the first settlers of Kfar Ata (now Kiryat Ata) he discusses dance, under certain circumstances, as "solely a shock of the nerves" and the imagination as a transformative potency with the ability to raise and empower dance:

> (A day) [If][123] a festival passes and you dance a lot, [and] you think that you have already ascended unto the heavens by shaking from bottom to the top. He who prepares himself before the festival for the festival, and on the festival itself penetrates, according to his state, through the fog and "collects some honey." Then—when his joy bursts forth and dances—his soul is revealed in this excitement. However, to be covered in dust the entire year and also on the festival and dance, who can guarantee me that that not solely a shock of the nerves.[124]

Without the proper preparation, the person's mental condition is one in which the materiality covers the soul like dust, and dancing is nothing other than a movement of corporeal limbs, lacking the spiritual as well as mystical dimension. Due to Shapira's conception of dance as a potency dependent upon other factors, he adds an imaginal empowering component granting religious and mystical significance to dance. In his treatment of Simḥat Torah dancing, Shapira claimed that without the imagination, the dancing may be sterile and amount to nothing: "If he would only dance he would not have done anything.

---

122 Regarding the theurgical dimensions of dance, see Fenton, "Some Remarks on Dance in Hassidism," 279–281. Also, see Pedaya, "Two Types of Ecstatic Experience," 90.
123 On the same page of the transcribed letter, the original handwritten letter appears, and there one can see that the word "if" (*im*) appears, and not "day" (*yom*), which in this context is much more logical.
124 Frankel and Zilbershlag, *Zikharon Qodesh*, Igarot Qodesh, p. 4.

Only when he also thinks with *maḥshavah ḥazaqah* (intense thought) about God and his Torah as aforementioned, and in it be joyous and dance—[then he] stirs his spirit and soul."[125] Without *maḥshavah ḥazaqah*, the other side of the imagination,[126] dance is not a meaningful activity: "If he would only dance he would not have done anything." Only the addition of *maḥshavah ḥazaqah* to dance guarantees the elevation of this act from a routine religious ritual (occurring every year on Simḥat Torah) into a mystical activity. The imagination empowers the dancing potency and makes it possible for dance to become an instrument of revelation: "when his joy bursts forth and [then] his soul dances [and] is revealed in this excitement." This concept of "soul revelation," which we will discuss extensively in the next chapter, is very important since in Shapira's thought it is the first stage on the path to mystical-ecstatic prophecy.[127] We have seen that dancing, which is itself an anomian technique, is dependent upon the imagination in order to empower it from an emotive-religious act into an act of mystical proportions.

Melody and Imagination

Music is inherently connected to man's emotions and feelings. One emotion that music often arouses is that of joy. When Laban complains of Jacob's departure he does so by saying, "Why did you flee in secrecy and mislead me and not tell me? I would have sent you off with festive music, with timbrel and lyre" (Gen. 31:27). Song and instrumental music may be an expression of joy as well as the cause of joy. Music also plays a calming role. The servants of King Saul advise him to search for a professional musician in order to relax him, "Let our lord give the order [and] the courtiers in attendance on you will look for someone who is skilled at playing the lyre; whenever the evil spirit of God comes over you, he will play it and you will feel better" (I Sam. 16:16). This action was successful as well, "Whenever the [evil] spirit of God came upon Saul, David would take the lyre and play it; Saul would find relief and feel better, and the evil spirit would leave him" (ibid., 25). The common element of these two roles, making one joyous or calm, is the arousal of emotions, and since music was identified with the potential of stirring emotions as well as an instrument for the expression of said emotions, it has been utilized for generations for the arousal of

125 Shapira, *Ḥovat ha-Talmidim*, 63b. The topic of discussion are the *haqafot*, ritualistic circle dancing, done on Simḥat Torah.
126 See this chapter's introduction above.
127 See above, chap. 3.

many different emotions. The sages attest to a custom of playing flutes during the eulogy for the dead,[128] since they arouse feelings, "that their sounds arouse weeping."[129]

However, there is another dimension to music—it was not only adopted as a means by which to tap into man's emotions, but also as an instrument for prophetic inspiration. In the prophet Samuel's vision, which depicts Saul's future, it is implied that there is a direct link between music and prophecy, "After that, you are to go on to the Hill of God, where the Philistine prefects reside. There, as you enter the town, you will encounter a band of prophets coming down from the shrine, preceded by lyres, timbrels, flutes, and harps, and they will be speaking in ecstasy. The spirit of the Lord will grip you, and you will speak in ecstasy along with them; you will become another man" (I Sam. 10:5–6). This connection, which is not entirely clear, is illuminated in the command of the prophet Elisha, "'Now then, get me a musician,'" in which the result of this music is depicted in the continuation of the verse, "As the musician played, the hand of the Lord came upon him" (II Kings 3:15). From this verse one may identify the link between music and prophecy as one in which music acts as an inspirational instrument for prophecy. In other words, music was used as a technique for the acquisition of prophetic inspiration. It should be noted that this prophecy was not of the emissarial model, but rather of the ecstatic-mystical model;[130] consequently, this technique is of a mystical nature. The sages, following these verses, identified music as having a key role in prophetic revelation, "'A Psalm of David' intimates that he [first] uttered [that particular] psalm and then the *Shekhinah* rested upon him. This teaches you that the *Shekhinah* rests [upon man] neither in indolence nor in gloom nor in frivolity nor in levity nor in vain pursuits, but only in rejoicing connected with a religious act, for it is said, "'but now bring me a minstrel.' And it came to pass, when the minstrel played, that the hand of the Lord came upon him."[131] This conception was cited in the Middle Ages by Maimonides, who saw music as a technique for acquiring prophecy, which is realized in stages and gradual human exertion, "All

128 *m. Shabbat* 23:4; *m. Ketuvot* 4:4. See the commentary of Ovadiah ben Abraham of Bartenura on the mishnah in *Ketuvot*, and see Solomon Itzhaki's commentary on *b. Ketuvot* 46b.

129 Bartenura commentary on *m. Shabbat* 23:4. There are traditions that this custom continued until the end of the Middle Ages. It is mentioned as well by Karo (16th c.) in *Shulḥan Arukh*, Even ha-Ezer, §89:1. Also, see ibid., Oraḥ Ḥayyim, §325:15. While in his times this custom was already not common, it was nevertheless still practiced by select communities. Karo does decide that those who choose to maintain this custom must use at least two flutes.

130 Regarding these models, see above, chap. 3

131 *b. Pesaḥim* 117a. Also see *b. Shabbat* 30b.

the prophets could not prophesize at any time they wished… Therefore, the prophets' disciples would always have before them a harp, drum, flute, and lyre when they were seeking prophecy, and this is as written, 'they will be prophesying' (I Sam. 10:5), meaning they would go in the way of prophecy until they would prophesy."[132] However, this conception was unpopular among the medieval rationalist circles, which preferred the conception of the rational faculty (*ko'aḥ sikhli*) as the key component enabling prophetic inspiration, such that music would only play a secondary role assisting the rational faculty.[133] In the prophetic-kabbalah several conceptions of music were developed, yet none of them granted it a role unto itself in prophetic revelation.[134] Music was equated with the technique of letter-combination, just as the combination of notes creates a new tune, so too does the combination of letters produces a new creation.[135] Music acts as an analogy for the mystical-prophetic experience, explaining the mechanics of prophetic realization. The human body serves as a medium for the prophetic voice, just as the musical instrument acts as a medium for the produced sound.[136] However, it should be noted that in spite of the numerous musical analogies utilized for the explanation of prophecy, music in and of itself is not a component in the prophetic process, as it certainly is in biblical literature. Although it does have a role in Abulafian thought, generally as being combined with some letter-combination technique, it has no independent role unto itself.[137] One may find in Abulafia's writings detailed instruction regarding the use of music while reciting divine names for the purpose of receiving prophetic inspiration.[138] According to him, the vowels of the letters are kinds of notes for playing the letters: a *ḥolem* (a single dot, which is placed above the Hebrew letter) signifies a high note, a *ḥiriq* (a single dot, which is placed below the Hebrew

---

132 Maimonides, *Mishneh Torah*, Foundations of the Law, 7:-4.

133 See Moshe Idel, "Music and Prophetic Kabbalah," *Yuval* 4 (1982): 156–158. Idel demonstrates that this conception was shared across a broad spectrum of Jewish philosophers, as well as Abulafia's school. For more, see Idel, *The Mystical Experience*, 53–64.

134 Ibid.; idem, "Music and Prophetic Kabbalah," 156.

135 Idem, "Music and Prophetic Kabbalah," 150–153; idem, *The Mystical Experience*, 61–64.

136 Idem, "Music and Prophetic Kabbalah," 153–155; idem, *The Mystical Experience*, 55–57. Also, for variations of this analogy, see idem, "Conceptualization of Music in Jewish Mysticism," in *Enchanting Powers: Music in the World's Religions*, ed. Lawrence E. Sullivan (Cambridge: Harvard University Press, 1997), 177–178.

137 Idem, "Music and Prophetic Kabbalah," 156, 163–169. However, see ibid. that one may find in Abulafia's school sources that point to music's independent role, nevertheless, it is not a primary feature.

138 Idem, *The Mystical Experience*, 61–64.

letter) signifies a low note, and so forth.[139] Although in prophetic kabbalah music has no independent role in the prophetic process, Abulafia's efforts should be noted in returning music as a mystical technique after its lengthy absence.[140] The integration of music into prophetic inspiration was not theoretical, as in Maimonides's thought, but practical.[141]

This conception of music as a mystical technique was echoed by sixteenth century kabbalists as well.[142] Both in sixteenth century philosophy and kabbalah, particularly of Safed and Italy, music as technique gained new momentum, acquiring magical and theurgical components, being conceived as affecting divinity (theurgy) and the external world (magic).[143] In the writings of Isaac ben Moses Arama, Yohanan Alemanno, Don Isaac Abarbanel, one may find magical conceptions of music.[144] The world is constructed according to the same harmonious template as music and therefore music can affect the world.[145] By playing musical instruments or singing, man draws down the efflux (*shefa*) from above. In the thought of Meir Ibn Gabbai, Yehudah Moscatto, Moses Cordovero, and the book *Kaf ha-Qeṭoret*, one may find theurgical aspects of music.[146] In their opinion, music is capable of renewing the connection between the *sefirah* of *Malkhut* and the *sefirot* of *Ḥokhmah* and *Binah*.[147] Kabbalists, as a whole, believed that human action, specifically the fulfilling of commandments, can cause divinity and reality to reach harmonious states; music too, as a human action, has a similar effect.[148] Safedian kabbalists grasped the liturgical singing on the Sabbath

---

139 Ibid., 62.

140 Since the Hekhalot period. See idem, "Kabbalah and Music," in *Judaism and Art*, ed. David Cassuto (Ramat Gan: Bar-Ilan University), 278. As we discussed, music was used as a means by which to attain an ecstatic state, such as the biblical prophetic-ecstatic state. Idel, ibid., demonstrated that music appears as a mystical technique already in the Hekhalot stratum of Jewish mysticism, raising the practitioner to the Throne of Glory. Also, see Alexander Altmann, "Qedushah Hymns in the Ancient Hekhalot Literature," *Melilah* 2 (1946): 2.

141 See Idel, "Kabbalah and Music," 279; idem, *The Mystical Experience*, 61–64.

142 Idem, "Kabbalah and Music," 279.

143 Idem, "The Magical and Theurgic Interpretation of Music in Jewish Sources from the Renaissance to Hassidism," *Yuval: Studies of the Jewish Music Research Centre* 4 (1982): 33, 35, specifically regarding the sixteenth century, ibid., 33–34.

144 Ibid., 37–45. See there that Isaac ben Moses Arama's conception does not truly relate to musical influence on nature.

145 Ibid., 39. Regarding the magical model of music see idem, "Conceptualization of Music," 182–184.

146 Idem, "The Magical and Theurgic Interpretation of Music," 45–57.

147 Idem, "Kabbalah and Music," 279–280. Regarding the theurgic model operative in music see idem, "Conceptualization of Music," 169–172.

148 Idem, "Kabbalah and Music," 280.

Eve as a theurgical action, causing the *Shekhinah* to unite with her husband, the supernal bride and groom.[149] Moshe Idel has demonstrated that both the theurgical and magical conceptions of music affected its appreciation in early hasidism.[150]

In addition to the theurgic and magical models, music is primarily found in the ecstatic model.[151] The biblical depiction of music, with which I began this section, is apposite of both the ecstatic and prophetic-ecstatic models. The divine spirit rested on Saul, and in a different situation upon Elisha, "as the musician played." Similar depictions can be found in the writings of the German Pietists of the thirteenth century.[152] Abulafia and his school primarily regarded music as an instrument for prophetic-ecstatic experiences.[153] This conception of music was not only confined to Abulafian circles and could be found in other circles as well.[154] Perhaps this model influenced Beshtian hasidism, which strived for ecstatic states through music,[155] whether it be through the German pietistic or Abulafian writings. Idel has shown, in his aforementioned studies, that in spite of the different models, music ultimately appears in kabbalah in limited contexts: as a technique accompanying linguistic combination techniques or during unique days, such as holidays.

In contrast to kabbalah, the hasidic movement elevated music to be a primary element in its spiritual worldview. Similar to dance, music was not restricted solely to sacred occasions and religious ceremonies and rituals; it was brought into the full range of normative experiences. Furthermore, hasidic music was not only lyrical music, based upon liturgy or biblical verses, but included numerous non-verbal melodies as well. In many cases, these wordless melodies were even preferred over their verbal counterparts. Isaiah Tishby and Joseph Dan asserted that the centrality of music in hasidic life was due to its capability of causing joy, which is one of the foundations of hasidism.[156] Aaron

---

149 Idem, "The Magical and Theurgic Interpretation of Music," 55.
150 Ibid., 60 – 61; idem, "Conceptualization of Music," 172, 183 – 184.
151 On this model see idem, "Conceptualization of Music," 173 – 181.
152 Ibid., 173 – 175.
153 Ibid., 175 – 179.
154 Ibid., 179 – 181.
155 Idem, "Kabbalah and Music," 279.
156 Isiah Tishby and Joseph Dan, "Hasidism–Doctrine and Literature," *Encyclopaedia Hebraica* (Jerusalem and Tel Aviv: Encyclopaedia Publishing Co., 1965), 17:810 – 811. For more, see Abraham Zebi Idelsohn, *Jewish Music: Its Historical Development*, intro. Arbie Orenstein (New York: Dover Publications, 1992). Also see, idem, "ha-Neginah ha-Ḥasidit," in *Sefer Hashanah: The American Jewish Yearbook* (New York: Histadruth Ivrith, 1931), 77–78; Meir Shimon Geshuri, *La-Ḥasidim Mizmor: A Collection of Literature and Folk Music of Chassidim with Tunes, Pictures,*

Wertheim maintained that its centrality was due to music's capability of realizing hasidic principles, such as "pouring out one's heart," "nullification of self," and "cleaving one's soul to the supernal realms."[157] Yaakov Mazor has noted that the common element to these conceptions is the connection of music and man's soul. However, Mazor argued, following Idel's research, that this conception is partial, for it does not take into account the theurgical and magical elements of melody. Mazor expanded and brought many hasidic sources that attest to these melodic properties.[158] In the writings of the early hasidim, they differentiated between song (*shirah*), which has a lyrical element, and melody (*nigun*).[159] According to Mazor, this conception is connected to the hasidic understanding of "corporeal worship" (*avodah be-gashmiyut*),[160] an understanding which allows the anomian worship of God, "While the earlier ones related theurgic potency to textual song, as the songs of praise (*hallel*), song of the sea [the song sung by the people of Israel at the splitting of the Red Sea], psalms, and prayer—according to the approaches of the kabbalists of the second half of the fifteenth century and of the sixteenth century, here [however], the later ones [i.e. hasidim] see in song and melody in and of themselves... as powerful activities of theurgic potential."[161]

Shapira's conception of music, which has not yet been fully treated by scholars, is composed of three primary elements: the extension of music into the secular realm; its detachment from sacred texts; and an understanding of music as a technique for achieving ecstasy and prophecy.[162] The extension into secular realms is expressed in Shapira's recommendation to his disciples to sing even when unconnected to religious ritual—such as prayer, Torah study, or sacred days—but rather whenever they may wish from time to time, "It is good to

and Facsimilies (Jerusalem: Ha-Teḥiyah, 1936); idem, *Music and Dance in Hassidism: Through All Its Generations, since the Appearance of Rabbi Israel Baal-Shem Tov up to Date*(Tel Aviv: Netsah, 1955); idem, "Ha-Besht̩ Mefu'naḥ ha-Nigun ha-Ḥasidi," *Mahanayim* 46 (1960): 105–108.

157 Aaron Wertheim, *Law and Custom in Hasidism*, trans. Shmuel Himelstein (Hoboken: Ktav, 1992), 158–162.

158 Yaakov Mazor, "Koḥo shel ha-Nigun be-Hagut ha-Ḥasidit ve-Tafkidav be-Havai ha-Dati veha-Ḥevrati," *Yuval* 7 (2002): 25–36.

159 Ibid., 31–32. For more on hasidic musical terms, see Yaakov Mazor and Edwin Seroussi, "Towards a Hasidic Lexicon of Music," *Orbis Musicae* 10 (1990/1991): 118–143.

160 Mazor, "Koḥo shel ha-Nigun," 32.

161 Ibid., 32–33.

162 Concerning the prophetic element in melody in Shapira's thought and the conception of music as a device for prophecy see Leshem, "Between Messianism and Prophecy," 188–192. I have been informed that Nehemia Polen intends to publish extensive scholarship regarding the melody (*nigun*) as a technique for acquiring prophecy in Shapira's thought.

drink [alcohol] from time to time one drink... after they drink they will sing a song of stirring (*zemer shel hit'orrerut*), such as *Yedid Nefesh* (Beloved Soul), *Adon Olam* (Master of the World), *Mizmor le-David Adonai Ro'i Lo Eḥsar* (A Psalm of David, God is My Shepard I Shall Not Lack), etc.[163] The detachment of music from the text, meaning the separation of the lyrics from the melody, is explained in his thought through the classic hasidic reasoning that sees the melody in itself as possessing a higher expression than the verbal expression, a level of expression that bursts forth from the depths of the soul and cannot be constrained and bound by linguistic rules, "A proof has been brought from sacred books, 'When a man's distress is overpowering, God forbid, already it is impossible for him to speak, he only cries and weeps with his voice alone, therefore the *nigun* (melody), that is sounds of joy or bitterness, stirs man's emotions, within which the sparks and limbs of the soul are disclosed."[164] However, Shapira did not simply continue the classic hasidic conception of music. He created something new by adding imaginal elements. As with dance, he believed that visualization intensified and transformed the experience of music:

> Take for yourself some movement of a song, turn your face towards the wall, or just close your eyes and *think again, that you are standing in front of the Throne of Glory*, and with a broken heart you have come to pour out your soul to God in song and melody which come forth from the depths of your heart, and then you yourself will feel that your soul goes out in song. If at the beginning you were the musician (*ha-menagen*) for your soul to stir from its slumber, little by little you will feel that your soul has already begun to play (*le-nagen*) by itself.[165]

The melody stirs the drowsy soul in conjunction with the thought of, "*standing in front of the Throne of Glory*." This thought here is in fact imaginal visualization,[166] as demonstrated by the continuation of the passage:

> Melody was always an enigma for you, what are the sounds, ascending and descending, what are they, and why is it sometimes lengthy and sometimes short, and everything you already *see*.[167] With its voice your soul pierces for you a path to heights, and in the heavens, it is as if they have grasped her sighs and have drawn her tongue. Her heart, bowels, and all of her inside via her melody exit, and through the sounds ascend, and her as-

---

163 Shapira, *Benei Maḥshavah Ṭovah*, 56; idem, *Hakhsharat ha-Avreikhim*, 61b.
164 Idem, *Benei Maḥshavah Ṭovah*, 42.
165 Ibid. My emphasis.
166 Regarding the imaginative aspect of thought in Shapira's teachings see the introduction to this chapter.
167 See a parallel, with minor, but important variants in idem, *Hakhsharat ha-Avreikhim*, 47b, "Now already you see everything."

censions and descensions and all its revolutions (*gilgulei*) are engraved through her voice, and the melody's movement are etched within it, and the melody is formed, your soul is carried by the melody in its bowels to be poured out and come close to God.[168]

The enigma of the soul is solved through imaginal visioning. Ascension and descension of tones, musical oscillation in the melody, is clarified through imaginal visioning by the transcendent soul. The tonal ascensions are parallel to the soul's ascent and the tonal descensions are parallel to the soul's descent. The melody expresses the soul's metamorphic travels in its attempts to acquire mystical proximity to the divine.[169] The sentence, "and everything you already *see*," or its second iteration, "*now* you already see everything," are only understandable through the preceding paragraph. What has occurred "now" or "already" that it is possible to, "see everything"? The consecutive reading of these paragraphs reveals that "now" is regarding the technique, "Think... that you are standing in front of the Throne of Glory." Thereby, rendering the meaning as, "Now that you have (already) seen the Throne of Glory—the melody's enigma is solved for you." The Throne of Glory is reflected as an image, and not a discursive thought of some kind. This being the case, it is clear that the thinking discussed in the second paragraph is visualization. Consequently, Shapira combined song with an imagery exercise to intensify the musical experience. Imagining God (or the Throne of Glory) during the song strengthens the sense of connection with the Divine: "With its penetrating voice your soul pierces for you a path to heights," through melody and imagination—man's soul ascends on high.

Hitbodedut and Imagination

The common meaning of the term *hitbodedut* is austerity and separation from society as found in Christian monks and Islamic Sufis.[170] In the Bible there are cases of *hitbodedut*, in the isolationist sense of the term, performed for religious reasons, such as Moses's solitude on Mt. Sinai, Elijah's in the desert, and the High Priest's in the Holy of Holies. However, the destruction of the second temple

---

168 Idem, *Benei Maḥshavah Ṭovah*, 42–43.
169 Also, see a hint to a theurgical element in Shapira's conception of melody, "When you will be in a company of hasidim when they play [instruments]... You will also sing with them... in order to extract your soul and raise it in the aspect of "As the musician played, the hand of the Lord came upon him" (II Kings 3:15), a type of wedding melody (*nigun ha-ḥupah*), which pairs the groom and bride, and enough for the intelligent" (ibid., 44; idem, *Hakhsharat ha-Avreikhim*, 47b).
170 Idel, "'Hitbodedut' qua 'Concentration' in Ecstatic Kabbalah," 38.

caused a shift in consciousness. The destruction of the temple was also the destruction of the primary socio-religious framework. As a temple alternative, the rabbinic sages strengthened and established a framework based on what remained—the congregation and at its core, prayer. Jewish law cemented the congregation as a part of religious ritual—praying with a quorum, Torah study, circumcision, and marriage were re-designed as congregational events. This type of lifestyle rejected individualistic separation.[171] However, there is a second meaning to this term. *Hitbodedut* can also be an act of mental or intellectual concentration preceding, primarily, prophetic acquisition.[172] This meaning of the term, according to Idel, emerges both from philosophic and kabbalistic literature.[173]

Abulafia is the first known kabbalist who linked *hitbodedut* with a detail systematic practice. This was not done through societal isolation, but rather through the technique of letter combination. *Hitbodedut*, in Abulafia's opinion, is the necessary concentration that allows the kabbalist to combine letter.[174] The development of this understanding may be found in the thought of the anonymous author of *Sha'arei Ṣedeq* (13th-14th c.),[175] Isaac of Acre (13th-14th c.),[176] Shem Tov Ibn Gaon (14th c.), Judah Albotini (early 16th c.), David ben Zimra (16th c.), Cordovero (16th c.) and his students.[177] This technique, which originally was only directed towards select individuals, was later directed towards a wider audience through the printing of Safedian kabbalistic works, such as Cordovero's *Pardes Rimonim*, Elijah de Vidas's *Re'shit Ḥokhmah*, and Elazar Azkiri's *Sefer Ḥare-*

171 Ibid., 35–36. Regarding the oscillation between married family life and asceticism in the Talmud, see Daniel Boyarin, *Carnal Israel: Reading Sex in Talmudic Culture* (Berkeley: University of California Press, 1993), 134–166. This tension reverberates throughout Jewish history, in the ethical literature of the Middle Ages and comes to full fruition in the kabbalistic fellowship of Safed, for example, see Patrick B. Koch, *Human Self-Perfection: A Re-Assessment of Kabbalistic Musar-Literature of Sixteenth-Century Safed* (Los Angeles: Cherub Press, 2015), 165–176.

172 Moshe Idel, "Hitbodedut as Concentration in Jewish Philosophy," *Jerusalem Studies in Jewish Thought* 7 (1988): 40–41.

173 Ibid.

174 Idem, "'Hitbodedut' qua 'Concentration' in Ecstatic Kabbalah," 40.

175 Ibid., 45–46. Regarding the identification of this work's author see Moshe Idel, "Rabbi Nathan ben Sa'adiah Harar, Author of Sha'arei Tzedek and His Influence in the Land of Israel," *Shalem* 7 (2002): 47–58.

176 Idem, "'Hitbodedut' qua 'Concentration' in Ecstatic Kabbalah," 46–58. From Isaac of Acre's writings, it emerges that the purpose of *hitbodedut* is equanimity and detachment from the senses, in order to attain *devequt*. Furthermore, *hitbodedut* serves a means to draw down the efflux into the soul of man. Concerning *hitbodedut* and prophecy in Isaac of Acre's thought see Fishbane, *As Light Before Dawn*, 252–253, 256–257. Also see ibid., 256 n. 18 regarding the levels between *hitbodedut* and prophecy.

177 Idel, "'Hitbodedut' qua 'Concentration' in Ecstatic Kabbalah," 58–74.

dim,[178] a development that contributed to the popularization of *hitbodedut* as a practical technique within Jewish culture.

Hitbodedut in early hasidism appears in both of the aforementioned meanings—solitude and contemplation.[179] In *Ṣava'at ha-Ribash*, §63, *hitbodedut* is referenced in its contemplative, and not ascetic, meaning, "One may contemplate (*le-hitboded*) with a companion, also it is possible to contemplate (*le-hitboded*) even in a house with people."[180] Both of these conducts have precedent in *Re'shit Ḥokhmah* and *Sefer Ḥaredim*, both of Cordovero's school.[181]

Hitbodedut is one of the primary features of Bratslav hasidism, from its beginning until today.[182] Sometimes *hitbodedut* in Naḥman's thought is only meant as a personal conversation between man and his creator,[183] however, Zvi Mark has demonstrated that Naḥman, in continuation of kabbalistic and philosophic traditions, saw this act of private conversation between him and God as preliminary stage, whose central goal was the attainment of communion (*devequt*) and integration with God.[184] Nonetheless, it should be stated that Naḥman changed the concept of *hitbodedut* from the meanings presented here to one of personal prayer, a marginal focus until now, and there is no doubt that the connection between *hitbodedut* and personal prayer has a strong link in Naḥman's thought.[185]

The technique of *hitbodedut* in Shapira's thought is not in the sense of a "conversation with God." While this type of "conversation" may be found in his thought,[186] he does not use the terminology of *hitbodedut* to describe it. Like-

---

178 Ibid., 77–78. Also, see the difference between Cordovero and his students regarding letter combination techniques, ibid. Also, see Koch, *Human Self-Perfection*, 176–195.

179 Zvi Mark, *Mysticism and Madness in the Work of R. Nahman of Bratslav*, 235 n. 52. Also, ibid., regarding the Beshṭ sources.

180 *Ṣava'at ha-Ribash* (New York: Kohet, 1998), 26–27§63, "When he wants to be in solitude (*hitbodedut*) he needs to be with one comrade, since one man alone is in danger, but two will be in one room, and each will seclude (*yitboded*) himself with the creator, blessed be he. Sometimes, when he is cleaving (*davuq*), he is able to seclude himself, even in a house where there are people."

181 See Ze'ev Gries, *Conduct Literature (Regimen Vitae): Its History and Place in the Life of Beshtian Hasidism* (Jerusalem: Bialik Institute, 1990), 222–224. Also, for more sources, see *Ṣava'at ha-Ribash*, 158§82.

182 Mark, *Mysticism and Madness in the Work of R. Nahman of Bratslav*, 235, ibid. n. 53–57.

183 Naḥman of Bratslav, *Liqquṭei Moharan* II:52. Also, see Joseph G. Weiss, *Studies in Braslav Hasidism* (Jerusalem: Bialik Institute, 1974), 93; Green, *Tormented Master*, 32, 145–147.

184 Mark, *Mysticism and Madness*, 131–133.

185 For a variety of sources, see Leshem, "Between Messianism and Prophecy," 254 n. 839

186 See Shapira, *Hakhsharat ha-Avreikhim*, 46a-b, 48a; idem, *Ṣav ve-Ziruz*, 6. Also, for example see Shapira's personal prayer, idem, *Ṣav ve-Ziruz*, 6–7, 38–46.

wise, *hitbodedut* does not appear in his writings in the sense of solitude. Similar to that which was stated in *Ṣava'at ha-Ribash*, Shapira also states that one may contemplate with companions, "You have sat in contemplation (*be-hitbodedut*)... together with your companions."[187] The *hitbodedut* mentioned a few times in his writings,[188] is closer to the meaning of mental focus found in kabbalistic and philosophic literature, "That the main aspect of all worship is to understand and know that there is a God who governs and provides for particulars,[189] and leads all the worlds and 'there is no place devoid of him.' However, this requires great exertion [in order] to truly acquire this, and one must contemplate (*le-hitboded*)... then he can truly arrive at this knowledge of his God, blessed be he."[190] This act of mental concentration is not of a mystical nature, but is rather a religious intellectual act, "Then he can truly arrive at this knowledge of his God, blessed be he." In order to add a mystical dimension to this experience of God's presence, Shapira intensified this religious experience of contemplation through the utilization of imagery techniques, "Conceal yourself in a special room, if you can, and if not face towards the wall and visualize in your thought that you are standing before the Throne of Glory."[191] In a different place Shapira binds *hitbodedut* with prayer, however, there as well its meaning is more approximate to mental contemplation than to personal conversation with God:

> Leave the world and its noise for an hour or two, the cunningness of its wisdom and its desires that are within you, and isolate yourself (*ve-hitboded*), and if you capable, go to a forest, and behold, see yourself as a simple creature among God's creations, and together with the sun and moon, the birds and all the trees of the forest—to sing before God, you came to reveal and fill all the world with his greatness, blessed be he. Begin, please, for example to proclaim for them and all the world the "Master of the World," etc. and "Beloved of the Soul," etc. and see if your soul does not burst forth in splendor towards her king and God, who has, as it were, come closer to you, to harken to the sound of your song.[192]

---

187 Idem, *Hakhshararat ha-Avreikhim*, 17b.
188 Ibid.; idem, *Mevo ha-She'arim*, 41a; idem, *Ṣav ve-Ziruz*, 13.
189 Referencing the philosophic discussion of how God's providence works, if it directed towards individuals or only species as a whole. See Maimonides, *Guide of the Perplexed*, 3:16 – 24. Unsurprisingly, Shapira is of the opinion that it is directed towards individuals.
190 Idem, *Mevo ha-She'arim*, 41a. Shapira quotes from Epstein, *Sefer Ma'or ve-Shemesh*, Parashat Shemot, s.v. "nir'eh."
191 Shapira, *Ṣav ve-Ziruz*, 6. Regarding contemplation in Shapira's thought see Leshem, "Between Messianism and Prophecy," 253 – 260.
192 Shapira, *Ṣav ve-Ziruz*, 13.

On the surface, going out to the forest and proclaiming god's existence to all of the creations of the world, do not imply imaginal activities. However, it appears that, "behold, see yourself as a simple creature among God's creations... Begin, please, for example to proclaim for them and all the world," is not only an intellectual exercise, but rather an imagery exercise as well. This technique is very similar to Shapira's other imagery techniques that engage celestial bodies and facing them.[193] In these techniques man imagines that he is facing the celestial bodies or terrestrial creatures asking them to join in singing proclamation God's eternal being, "When your thought, imagination, and emotion go out and are strengthened within you to the point of seeing them... you will already see that you with all of the world are kneeling before God... And so, when you will say, 'Praise the Lord from the heavens' (Ps. 148:1), etc., with excitement, then all of the lower and upper worlds are actually in front of you, you stand and command, 'Stand and praise together with us a song for God.'"[194] The *hitbodedut* experience is intensified through the addition of imagery techniques, allowing the isolated practitioner to feel God's presence, through the imagination, in solitude. The imagination offers a different experience for the practitioner, which contains, in addition to the mental concentration, an ecstatic-mystical experience, the soul "bursts forth in splendor towards her king and God." The person who practices *hitbodedut* and intensifies his experience through the imagination, merits God's proximity, "[God, who has,] as it were (*kivyakhol*), comes closer to you, to harken to the sound of your song."[195]

Speaking Out Loud and Imagination

In Moses de León's writing and in the *Zohar* an emphasis is placed on the importance of raising one's voice. This is not due to any aesthetic sensibilities, but is rather due to their magical properties.[196] In sixteenth century Musar and halakhic literature, speaking out loud is used as a technique for *kavvanah* (intention),

---

193 See below, chap. 5, subchapter, "Heavenly Imagery Techniques: Imaginal Substitutions."
194 Shapira, *Hakhsharat ha-Avreikhim*, 29b. Also, see below subchapter, "Prayer."
195 *Kivyakhol* in this context may be a Yiddish term for God, see Yitskhok Niborski, *Dictionary of Hebrew and Aramaic Words in Yiddish* (Paris: Medem, 2012), 207. This term for God also entered new Hebrew literature, see Abraham Even-Shoshan, *The New Dictionary–The Combined Version* (Jerusalem: Kiryat-Sefer, 1997), 1182.
196 Idel, "Kabbalah and Music," 283. On pronouncing of letters in Abulafia's thought, see idem, *The Mystical Experience*, 86–95. Regarding the idea that human speech is an expression of attaining prophecy, ibid., 83–86.

primarily in the liturgical realm of benedictions and prayers. Elijah de Vidas employs the locution, "Voice (*Qol*) arouses intention" regarding the saying of blessings, "He shall bless out loud (*be-qol ram*), I wish to say that he should make his voice heard to his household such that he should not bless in a whisper, for the saying of blessings out loud (*be-qol*) arouses intention and brings [about] remembering (*zekhirah*)."[197] Joseph Karo discusses the recitation of the verse "Hear O' Israel" (Deut. 6:4), in prayer, and decides that it should be recited out loud, since, "voice arouses intention."[198] In hasidic literature a number of pieces have been written regarding this locution, especially in Ḥabad literature.[199] In hasidim this technique was expanded beyond its liturgical borders and was utilized as a psychological technique for actualizing emotions. Religious emotion is naturally weak (*qal*), and without actualization in reality it is unable to survive for a lengthy period of time. Actualizing emotions by speaking out loud intensifies the emotions and grants them real existence. Shapira discusses the inherent intensifying potency in speech writing:

> So it is for every Jew (*ish yisra'el*), all types of stirring and fervor (*hitlahavut*), whether in "awe" or "love or ecstasy (*be-hitpa'alut*) and amazement in the aspect of *Tif'eret* (splendor), when he is stirred the matter stays with him in secret (*be-sod*), and if it is not materialized in speech, it remains a secret and a light (*qal*) emotion that will very soon disappear from him, and he needs to bring them to an aspect of speech (*le-beḥinat dibur*). For example, if he has a stirring of awe or love, even if it is only a slight stirring, he will be stirred and say, "Master of the world, I desire you and from the depths of the abyss in which I am found within matter of the body and soul, my heart and flesh desire you that you should exalt me, purify me, and bring me close to you.[200]

In one place Shapira uses the speaking technique in an "opportunistic" manner. He discusses a case in which man is in a spiritual state of soul elevation, a state of being "close to holiness," and for his purposes it does not matter why he is in this state or how he achieved it. According to Shapira, man must take advantage of the spiritually elated state and use it as an instrument for a fundamentally different state. Man is able to exploit his supernal state as an appropriate time to overcome his ignoble traits, the lowly states he finds himself in at other times:

---

197 Vidas, *Re'shit Ḥokhmah*, Gate of Holiness, chap. 15.
198 Karo, *Shulḥan Arukh*, Oraḥ Ḥayyim, §61:4.
199 Shneur Zalman of Liadi, *Torah Or*, Miqeṣ, 31:1; idem, *Liqquṭei Torah*, Shir ha-Shirim, 13:2. Also, in greater detail see Dov Baer Schneersohn, *Torat Ḥayyim*, Bo, 107d; idem, *Peirush ha-Milot*, 17d. Naḥman of Bratslav, *Liqquṭei Moharan*, II:5
200 Shapira, *Derekh ha-Melekh*, 101.

> At this hour of elevation, with a high and pure soul—look upon your [states of] lowliness that you are always fixed in, on laziness, and other bad traits, on your lowly thought and desires that you think and want, and be ashamed of them, *and be angry and enraged at yourself saying*, "Woe, why do I lie every day in a sludge pit, an actual lavatory of childishness and nonsense, I accept upon myself from now on to be a Jew, a servant of God." ... Thoughts, as well as words, like these should be repeated a few times (*tikhpol kamah pa'amim*), and with the help of God will be quite advantageous for you. *For this is the law of the soul, it submits before spoken words (dibburim) that emerge strongly from the heart. Man may also tempt his fellow with words of the heart and soul and all the more so himself.*[201]

The presumption is that the soul is influenced by "spoken words," yet this is not enough. The words must "emerge strongly from the heart"; the strengthening and intensification play a significant role. This strengthening is a mental and physical effort, together with a suggested mantra technique, "words like these should be repeated a few times," these words are of many images: laying in a pit of sludge, lavatory, childishness, nonsense, and being a servant of God.[202]

In a number of places, Shapira explicitly states that the imagination serves as an intensifying force for spoken words. For example, concerning prayer, although he recommended that one should pray out loud,[203] and asserted that one's voice can open the calloused heart and soul of the prayer, he nevertheless remarked that speaking out loud or shouting and the like do not have much significance without thought and imagination. Meaning, man can scream during prayer, cries that reach the heavens, yet this screaming cry is unable to cause a spiritual arousal, "So it is in his prayer—with crying (*ṣa'aqah*) alone he would not be stirred, but if he also previously took care (*da'ag*) of his closed heart and his distance from God, and he thought with an intense thought (*be-maḥshavah ḥazaqah*) how he is now standing before God, then his prayer out loud will stir him."[204] Since we have mentioned that intense thought is a facet of imagination, and this concept is generally used in the context of visualizing God, it would therefore appear that visualizing God during prayer—"he thought with an intense thought (*be-maḥshavah ḥazaqah*) how he is now standing before God, then his prayer out loud will stir him,"—intensifies his cry, his spoken

201 Idem, *Ḥovat ha-Talmidim*, 28b.
202 Seemingly, in this context thought is imagination, in accordance with the motif of vision in the beginning of his remarks.
203 Idem, *Ḥovat ha-Talmidim*, 74b. This type of prayer can be found among contemporary Karlin hasidism and its branches, see Daniel Reiser, "Voicedness and Audio," in *Hasidism: Anthology*, ed. Rela Kushlavsky (Ramat Gan: Bar-Ilan University Press, forthcoming). It should be noted that Piaseczno hasidism branched off from Karlin.
204 Ibid., 63b.

words. The continuation of this passage reinforces this claim that it is not enough to pray out loud, nor is it enough to think about and understand the meaning of the liturgy. The desired result of stirring the heart and soul during prayer is achieved by combining the imagination with the understanding of the liturgy and spoken word. Man must visualize, for example when he says, "Praise the Lord," that he is facing the world and commends all creations to praise. Similarly, when he quotes other verses stated by others, such as King David or the prophets, he must visualize that he himself is the one originally saying these words, that he is the one praising, exalting, crying, commanding:

> Sometimes when man wants to pray with a stirred heart and soul and he is unable since they are blocked, and he begins *to pray out loud* (*be-qol*)... and he intends the words that he speaks in prayer as they are in essence and not their interpretation only, meaning that when he says, "Praise the Lord; call on His name" (Ps. 105:1), he does not interpret each word and its translation, he intends *only as if he is standing now opposite the world, face to face, and out loud he calls out to them and proclaims, "'Praise the Lord,' are you sleeping?, 'call on his name,'* etc."[205]

Essentially, Shapira suggest a double intensification. The spoken word intensifies the *kavvanah*, "voice stirs intention," and the imagination intensifies the spoken word. In his opinion, the power of the spoken word is slight and is dependent on more power, in order to arrive at its full potential. The imagination serves as an intensifying factor that transforms the emotional-religious experience of the spoken word within its ritual context, whether through intensification or its spiritual influence, into an experience of divine presence, namely, a mystical experience.

Writing and Imagination

Elliot Wolfson has written extensively on the connection between imagination and text.[206] Wolfson posits a fascinating understanding and argues that the imagination itself should be treated to a certain extent as text. The connection between the imagination and text is enriched by Wolfson's elucidation of imaginal *experience* and imaginal *interpretation.*[207] In the imaginal process there is the experience, however this experience is only understood through its interpre-

205 Ibid., 83a. For similar statements, see idem, *Benei Maḥshavah Ṭovah*, 49, and a parallel in idem, *Hakhsharat ha-Avreikhim*, 29b. It is clearly referring to an imaginal visualization.
206 Wolfson, *A Dream Interpreted Within a Dream*, 143–177.
207 Ibid., 101–102.

tation, thereby obfuscating the distinction between experience and interpretation. Since this experience is already an interpretation, it may be hermeneutically explored like other texts. Therefore, each narrator visualizes and each visualizer narrates. Wolfson's conception challenges the clear demarcation between the visual and verbal and can be described, using Ralph Waldo Emerson's locution, as *picture-language.*[208]

Interestingly, this synesthesiac dimension of *picture-language* may be found in one of Shapira's imagery techniques. Shapira presents a therapeutic-psychological exercise mixed with images and texts. In order to overcome one's hatred for a disputant Shapira suggests writing a fictive letter to this person in which one pours out all their wrath towards their imaginal friend-disputant.[209] Following, he is to hide this letter and read it once in a while. I am not claiming that Shapira viewed the imagination as a text or vice versa, I am only demonstrating the admixture of the two in this following exercise:

> If you have a suppressed hatred towards one of your companions and you want to remove it and you are unable... you want to cast away your hate from your heart and you are unable. Therefore, do this, *write a letter to him*, do not send it just put it aside (*tiṭmonahu be-ṣalaḥ-tekha*), and in it disrespect him as much as the angry snake in your heart yearns. And some days you should read the letter in your mouth, *and visualize that you are standing opposite him* and insult him with these insults and curses. Then after some days your anger will surely be removed from upon your heart, and if you are a *ba'al nefesh* (master of the soul) you will run to appease him more so.[210]

Shapira suggests an integrative technique of writing, reading out loud, and imagery. This admixture even calls for the employment of all three techniques simultaneously. Man must read the letter he wrote out loud, while he imagines the disputant standing in front of him. Clearly, reading the letter by itself will not help without visualizing the disputant. Its entire worth is that the reading is done towards the imaginal disputant. A mere reading, without imagination, is a feeble external action in need of spiritual experience. Imagination intensifies the identifying experience with what is written (that is, the feeling that it is not a

---

208 Ibid., 101.

209 Regarding "writing-visualization" techniques, see Barukh ben Avraham of Kosov, *Na'im ve-Neḥmad: Yesod ha-Emunah* (Józefów: Barukh Zetzer's Press, 1884), 164, "Behold, when man prays he should visualize in his consciousness that he is sending a letter to the king of kings, the holy one, blessed be he, requesting him to fulfill his wishes, since it is truly a spiritual writing, which is a visualization of the sound of words engraved on the voice." This technique differs from Shapira's technique, being that there is no actual writing, rather only imaginal writing. Here the image and text mix in a way similar to Wolfson's adaption of *picture-language.*

210 Shapira, *Ḥovat ha-Talmidim*, 30a.

random letter from a stranger, but rather my personal letter) and the experience of the desired anger. This integration of different techniques with imagination is a therapeutic key, in this case, for the liberation of stress and anger as a stage before personal internal reconciliation and external reconciliation with the actual friend-disputant.[211] This is not a case of mystical empowerment, since there is no experience of divine presence, but rather the presence of the disputant; nonetheless, this technique is certainly an imitation of mystical intensification, and employs imagery for therapeutic-psychological needs.

Conclusion

I have brought a number of examples of Shapira combining anomian techniques, such as melody, dance, *hitbodedut*, speaking out loud, and writing, with imagery techniques. In these combinations the role of the imagination is to intensify these different techniques, transforming emotional and religious experiences into mystical ones. The combination of anomian and imagery technique allows man to experience the divine presence.

C Imagination as an Empowering Factor in Nomian Experiences

Introduction

Thus far we have examined the intensification of anomian practices. However, Jewish mystical literature transformed many nomian rituals, such as Torah study, prayer, and other commandments, into practices aimed at achieving God's presence and contact with the divine realm. Since Judaism emphasizes

---

211 See Martin Buber, *Hasidism and Modern Man*, trans. Maurice Friedman and intro. David Biale (Princeton: Princeton University Press, 2016), 74–75, "The true origin of conflict between man and man. Manifestations of conflict are usually explained either by the motives of which the quarrelling parties are conscious as the occasion of their quarrel… or, proceeding analytically, we try to explore the unconscious complexes… The practical difference is that in Hasidism man is not treated as an object of examination but is called up to 'straighten himself out.' At first, a man should himself realize that conflict-situations between himself and others are nothing but the effects of conflict-situations in his own soul; then he should try to overcome this inner conflict, so that afterwards he may go out to his fellowmen and enter into new, transformed relationships with them."

the physical performance of the commandments, it invites a type of mysticism that intensifies and empowers these deeds.[212]

In medieval kabbalistic thought these techniques were heavily concentrated in the linguistic aspect of Torah and prayer.[213] The dual meaning of the term *ha-shem* (God; word) contributed to the movement from the signified (God) to the signifier (word).[214] Nahmanides had already stated, "We have in our possession a true *qabalah* (received tradition) that the entire Torah is the names of the Holy One blessed be he, that the words may be divided into names of a different order."[215] Torah study serves as a technique for communion with God (*devequt*) through the letters incarnating his name. This conception continuously and frequently appears in the Beshṭ's teachings, "It is possible to cleave to him, blessed be he, and [the Beshṭ] explains to be cleaved to his virtues, meaning his garments, the letters, meaning, it is possible always in one's thought to think of

212 See Idel, "Performance, Intensification and Experience," 100. Concerning the connection between mysticism and halakhah and commandments, i.e. the nomian dimension of Judaism, see Garb, *Shamanic Trance*, 119–141. Garb relies upon Wolfson's analysis, who claims that the common denominator of all kabbalists is the halakhic framework, see Wolfson, *Venturing Beyond*, 186–187. It should also be noted that Wolfson sees in daily rituals, such as Torah study and prayer, an element of divine visualization, through "intention" (*kavvanah*), which, in his opinion, is focused on the imaginal anthropomorphic form of the divine, see idem, "From My Flesh I Would Behold God: Imaginal Representation and Inscripting Divine Justice, Preliminary Observations," *Journal of Scriptural Reasoning* 2, no. 3 (2002): 8–9.

213 See Pedaya, *Vision and Speech*, 21–22, "The mystics' objects of imaginal or consciousness focus, within the framework of the mystical training process in most Kabbalistic methods, are letters, words, names, ritual instruments and commandments... the visual description of the revealed dimension of the divine is in the image of commandments, Torah, or names."

214 Idel, *Enchanted Chains*, 121.

215 Nahmanides commentary on the Torah, Introduction to Genesis. Concerning the connection between the letters and language, and being, in kabbalah, through the visualization of the letters which are concealed in the Tetragrammton, see Wolfson, "The Body in the Text," 482: "A current that runs through the landscape of Jewish esotericism presumes that Hebrew, the sacred tongue, is the cosmic or natural language in comparison to which all other languages are derivative. Kabbalists uniformly posit an intrinsic connection between language and being, which rests, in turn, on the assumed correlation of letter and substance expressed in detail in the second part of *Sefer Yetsirah*. In the words of the thirteenth-century Catalonian kabbalist Jacob ben Sheshet, 'The matter of the letters comprises the forms of all created beings, and you will not find a form that does not have an image in the letters or in the combination of two, three, or more of them. This is a principle alluded to in the order of the alphabet, and the matters are ancient, deep waters that have no limit.' From the kabbalistic vantage point, what exists in the world, examined sub phenomenally through mystical vision—that is, seeing with the eye of the heart, in the locution frequently employed by kabbalists—are the manifold permutations of the twenty-two Hebrew letters, themselves enfolded in the four-letter name YHWH." Also, see ibid., 486–488.

the letters of the Torah, and the Torah is his garment, blessed be he."[216] Thinking of the letters and studying Torah with its letters serves as a technique of communion.[217]

Elliot Wolfson understands these daily rituals, such as Torah study and prayer, as components of visualizing God. Many agree that these activities of study and learning are two primary modes of worship, through which man may experience God's presence. However, Wolfson adds an additional element of intentionality (*kavvanah*), which is based on the visualization of the semblance of God in the depths of the imagination:

> Based on older sources, including the foregoing, the localities for the two primary acts of devotion, prayer and study, are signaled out as providing the physical context wherein God appears imaginally to the Jewish people. Prayer and study, according to the rabbis, are the essential modes of worship through which God is experienced as a tangible presence. The point has been affirmed by many scholars, but what is less appreciated is that the intentionality required in these two acts of piety is predicated on an iconic visualization of the divine within the imagination. In the physical space circumscribed by words of prayer and study, the imaginal body of God assumes incarnate form. This is the intent of the statement attributed to R. Abbahu, "'Seek the Lord while He can be found' (Isa. 55 6). Where is He found? In the houses of worship and the houses of study" (Palestinian Talmud, *Berakhot* 5:1, 8d). At the heart of this poetic envisioning (a semiopraxis greatly expanded in medieval *kabbalah*) is the imaginary configuration of that which has no image through the semblance of what it appears not to be.[218]

While Shapira's teachings contain no theological treatment of this imaginal topic, that is, the conception of making God present through these nomian rituals is akin to visualizing God, his depictions of prayer and study are nevertheless saturated with this motif of envisioning the divine.[219] Furthermore, imaginal activity serves Shapira again, to even greater effect, for the intensification of these nomian activities, transforming them into mystical experiences. Judaism

216 *Ṣava'at ha-Ribash*, 51.

217 Regarding the studying of Torah as a mystical technique from the classic rabbinic period until hasidism, see Idel, *Enchanted Chains*, 122–164; concerning the use of prayer, both vocally and linguistically, ibid., 165–202. Also, see Idel's revolutionary article regarding letters, Moshe Idel, "Modes of Cleaving to the Letters in the Teachings of Israel Baal Shem Tov: A Sample Analysis," *Jewish History* (2013): 1–19. Idel claims that for the Beshṭ and his students, the significance of the letters was not in their visualization, but rather their vocalization and audibility.

218 Wolfson, "From My Flesh I Would Behold God," 8–9; regarding the visualization of God, see chap. 5.

219 See below, subchapter, "Prayer," and chap. 5, subchapters, "Prophecy and Imagination" and "Visualizing God's Name as a Technique for the Acquisition of Prophecy," that the motif of vision in Shapira's thought is repeated in his conceptions of prayer and Torah study.

is steeped with nomian practices, due to its ritualistic and performative nature, and these practices were employed by Shapira more than any other rituals as objects of intensification.

Torah

Shapira recurrently wrote that the study of Torah is not only an intellectual activity for the sake of accumulating knowledge. Torah study, he argues, should facilitate a living encounter between God and the person absorbed in religious texts.[220] This type of experience, which stresses the importance of the teacher and the place of study, is further intensified by imaginal visualization. This transforms religious study into an encounter of man and God:

> God is the one who teaches you Torah. The voice of God is garbed in the voice and words of your teacher when he speaks words of Torah, worship, or even ethical behavior (*derekh ereṣ*) in accordance with the Torah. Israel's awe and joy, fear and dread when they stood at Mt. Sinai and heard God's voice from the burning fire—you have a portion of this when you sit in yeshiva, and when you imaginally bring to mind (*mazkirim*)[221] that the room in which you are presently sitting is full of angels and seraphim. From amongst them the voice of God emerges, garbed in the voice of your teacher and entering your ears and hearts. Fear and joy, awe and love permeate your bodies and trembles your heart, and the very essence of your being is subdued before the Torah of our God that are heard in your teacher's words.[222]

This passage depicts the teacher not as a mere instructor imparting knowledge, but as a genuine messenger of God whose words are those of the divine. The in-

220 See his remarks regarding Torah study in general, Shapira, *Hakhsharat ha-Avreikhim*, 30b-32a. Also, regarding the study of Psalms, see idem, *Benei Maḥshavah Ṭovah*, 48. Regarding the studying of kabbalah, see idem, *Mevo ha-She'arim*, 17a, "Behold, he who approaches a kabbalistic book as a book of study or research… and mistakenly thinks that kabbalah is scholarship (*limud meḥqari*)… and come to explain theoretical studies, we then call to him with a bitter shrieking voice, 'Have mercy and desist, and do not dare enter and dirty the temple of God, the sanctuary of *aṣilut*, do not step with your impure feet even on the threshold of the holy of holies and with your stained hands do not touch the handle of the lock."

221 The root *z.kh.r*, in its active causative form, in Shapira's thought means an act of imagination. See his interpretation of the rabbinic advice against the evil inclination, "Let him remind himself of the day of death" (*b. Berakhot* 5a), "'Let him remind himself of the day of death' (*b. Berakhot* 5a), however, not merely as a general idea… [rather], he should visualize the matter" (Shapira, *Benei Maḥshavah Ṭovah*, 22), for more, see below, subchapter, "Visualizing the Day of Death.".

222 Idem, *Ḥovat ha-Talmidim*, 19b.

tensification of study is conjoined with an experience of holiness, "the room in which you are presently sitting is full of angels and seraphim. From amongst them the voice of God emerges," an image rooted in the *Zohar*.[223] By dint of the imagination, Torah study is transformed from an acquisition of information into an act effecting contact between the student and the divine, further strengthening the motivation of all involved:

> So it is with the books of the commentators, whether they engage the plain-sense meaning (*peshaṭ*) of Torah, hasidic [teaching], or *musar*—when you come to delve into a certain book and study it, imagine (*laḥshov*; lit. think) an angel of God stretching out his head from heaven and speaking these words to you in the name of God... And will you not embolden your spirit and make your ears like a funnel to hear with all of your power and be precise with every letter spoken to you from the heavens?![224]

The terms "bringing to mind" and "thinking" are employed by Shapira with imaginal connotations and intensify Torah study transforming it from informational study into mystical study, in which one encounters the divine dimension. The learner sees an "angel of God" and hears each and every letter from the heavens. The Torah is not just another intellectual text, but is rather a living discourse between man and God, in which "every letter spoken to you is from the heavens."

Intensification of Biblical Stories

In his book *Mevo ha-She'arim*, Shapira reiterates a number of times the claim that establishing a group, which strives for divine inspiration (*ru'aḥ ha-qodesh*) and prophecy, is in essence, "restoring the crown to its ancient days" (*b. Yoma* 69b), revitalizing and restoring the biblical experiences that have been lost and are no longer, "When I want to find an example of a fellowship (*ha-ḥevraya*) already in the Torah, I find it with the 'disciples of the prophets.'"[225] This conception is not confined to the realm of the fellowship—Shapira projects this conception on all of hasidism, and specifically on imagery techniques.[226] The hasid's trip to the ṣaddiq is interpreted as a reliving of the biblical pilgrimage, "I will travel to my rebbi... like Israel before their path ascending to the house of

---

223 *Zohar* 2:40b.
224 Shapira, *Ḥovat ha-Talmidim*, 41a. Regarding Torah study and mystical experience in hasidism, see Garb, *Shamanic Trance*, 128–131.
225 Shapira, *Mevo ha-She'arim*, 43b.
226 See Leshem, "Between Messianism and Prophecy," 73 n. 223.

God."[227] The relation between the ṣaddiq and his flock is translated as the relation between the disciples of the prophets and King Saul and his men.[228] According to Shapira, hasidism is a revitalization and restoration of biblical life events and patterns, "Hasidism walked in the path of the prophets."[229]

Abraham J. Heschel asserted that there are two kinds of thinking, the first being conceptual and the second situational:

> Conceptual thinking is an act of reasoning; situational thinking involves an inner experience; in uttering judgment about an issue, the person himself is under judgment… The attitude of the conceptual thinker is one of detachment: the subject facing an independent object; the attitude of the situational thinker is one of concern: the subject realizing that he is involved in a situation that is in need of understanding.[230]

Heschel locates situational thinking within biblical thinking.[231] Although Shapira did not know of these concepts, his position nevertheless undoubtedly approximated the content and spirit of this distinction and strived that engagement with Torah in general, and the Hebrew Bible in particular, should be done through situational thinking, "When you will learn the Bible (*tana"kh*), try to participate in all the holy events that passed, as if you were also there. You participate in the walk of Abraham, our father, and Isaac to the *aqedah* [binding of Isaac], and in Jacob's distress when he prayed to God, 'Deliver me, I pray, from the hand of my brother' (Gen. 32:12)."[232] Shapira believed that man is able to prepare himself for situational thinking through imagery techniques. During the preliminary stage man must collect classic rabbinic midrashim, which according to Shapira, fill in the gaps of the biblical story. The biblical story does not extensively delve into the inner emotional world of its characters. The reader must ask, "What impression was made on Israel by the arrival of Moses, our teacher, and Aaron, the priest, with the heralding of redemption in Egypt. How did they speak in the houses of Israel from this, and the children of Israel, bright and innocent, did they not ask anything when they heard that from this

227 Shapira, *Mevo ha-She'arim*, 39b. Regarding the hasid's voyage to the *ṣaddiq*, see Wolfson, *Along the Path*, 89–109. Also see Garb, *Shamanic Trance*, 204 n. 14; furthermore, see Shore, "Letters of Desire," 109–110, regarding this topic in R, Naḥman's thought.
228 Shapira, *Mevo ha-She'arim*, 36b.
229 Idem, *Hakhsharat ha-Avreikhim*, 7b. Also, see Wacks, *The Flame of the Holy Fire*, 68, regarding the classic hasidic claim that the Beshṭ did not innovate, rather renewed biblical values.
230 Heschel, *God in Search of Man*, 5.
231 Ibid., 16–17, 97–99.
232 Shapira, *Hakhsharat ha-Avreikhim*, 33a.

type of slavery they would go out to freedom?"[233] Shapira develops the midrashic approach as a completion of the biblical story. In this approach, it is clear that the plain-sense meaning of the text and the midrashic layer of the text are interconnected and not to be differentiated, "Rather, from everything you shall make one matter, for everything is truly one matter, and also in your thought one matter it shall be."[234] The issue is that even with all of the midrashic scope, much is missing and there is no answer to many questions. Here enters, in Shapira's thought, the imagination as an ultimate filler. Shapira illustrates how the imagination functions as a supplement for the biblical story, through the story of the exodus:

> Then they certainly felt different things, but *since in the Torah* [and] *even in the midrashim it is not written about how they experienced* [such] *matters, you therefore visualize in your thought and imagination*, the thought and imagination of a man of Israel, in accordance with the manner and the way that it is written in the Torah and midrashim and visualize according to your opinion like this, "... they talk with each other, and they converse with each other, and everyone is joyful. And a man comes unto his house and tells his wife and children the great and wondrous [matters] that he heard and that his eyes saw, and they speak and visualize how their departure from this will look and with what they will prepare for themselves on the road. And there is a scared child who will ask, 'Father, mother! How will we leave... and the oppressor will beat us... I am afraid...' and the simple child will cry and continue to ask...".[235]

This visualization of feelings and emotions underlying the exodus from Egypt spans around ten full pages, and is one of the most enlightening examples of an imagery technique being employed in a detailed and multi-scenic manner. This description, an imaginal fiction that could be a short prose work in and of itself, constitutes an incomparably unique phenomenon without precedent in all preceding hasidic literature. While visualizing biblical stories intensifies them and transforms them from informational knowledge into an all-encompassing myth that influences man's very being, this is not all—this intensification is further accompanied by a mystical intensification as well. Shapira recommends that one visualize, "in accordance with the manner and the way that it is written in the Torah and midrashim." In Shapira's thought, midrashic style is not only a platform for visualizing biblical stories, but is rather one of the instruments for developing one's imaginal abilities and imaginative faculty in order to prepare

233 Ibid., 33b
234 Ibid.
235 Ibid., 33b-34a.

for prophecy.[236] Midrash has a dual purpose—it serves as inspiration for the imaginative faculty and provides it with ample material for visualization. Simultaneously, it develops the essence of the imaginative faculty. Consequently, the intensification of informational biblical stories into participatory experiences through the visualization of midrashim is not only a means for the Torah study, but is also able to develop man's imaginative faculty, something that prepares him for prophecy, as we will see in the next chapter.

Prayer

The establishment of fixed prayer raised a multitude of issues commonly associated with institutionalization: rote performance, lack of intention, habitual observance, and modes of religious behviorism. Kabbalistic and hasidic sources often refer to "alien thoughts" (*maḥshavot zarot*), a particular type of difficulty obtructing concentration.[237] Of course, problems with concentrating for a long period of time are not limited to prayer. The mind naturally wanders and drifts, and can even shift immediately from the holy of holies to the most profane realm.[238] Shapira was quite aware of the problem of "alien thoughts" and combatted it with imagery techniques:[239]

> If… it is difficult for you to overcome the many things that confuse you and concentrate in prayer, *then visualize in your imagination* that you wish to spurn the way of the vulgar masses and go to the place in which God is found. It should be thus in actuality as well, like a person who pushes himself, you must strengthen your body, your limbs, and your sinews, and even wrinkle your face and imagine this: "I must go through the crowd to reach God; I [must pass] with strength in order to reach God."

---

236 Ibid., 30b-32a, "Through what is thought intensified (*meḥazqim*)… increase the learning of *Ein Ya'aqov* midrashim, as well as the holy *Zohar*."

237 Regarding "alien thoughts" see Joseph Weiss, "Beginnings of Hasidim," *Zion* 16 (1951): 88–103; Mendel Piekarz, *The Beginning of Hasidism*, 269–277. Weiss restricted this concept to sexual thoughts alone. In contrast, Piekarz demonstrated that this concept applies to all distracting thoughts. Furthermore, see Yoram Jacobson, *The Hasidic Thought* (Tel Aviv: Ministry of Defense Press, 1986), 107–120; Norman Lamm, *The Religious Thought of Hasidism* (Hoboken: Ktav, 1999), 371–375; Idel, "Prayer, Ecstasy and Alien Thoughts," 58–66. Regarding kabbalistic precedents, from Abulafia to Safed, ibid., 105–113. For a summative exploration of "elevating alien thoughts" in hasidism, see Yehuda Yifrach, "The Elevation of Foreign Thoughts in the Tradition of R. Israel Baal Shem Tov" (master's thesis, Bar Ilan University, 2007).

238 Adin Steinsaltz, *The Thirteen Petalled Rose* (Jerusalem: Maggid Books, 1996), 105–106.

239 For a distinction between imagery techniques that prevent alien thoughts and imagery techniques that remove alien thoughts, see Reiser, "To Fly Like Angels," 126–130.

> But if you have been striving to stand up against your profane thoughts and are unable, or if you tried to focus your thoughts on holy things and could not, [then] envision in this moment a part of your soul on high as it runs from the angels of destruction and terrible wild beasts toward the gate to the garden of Eden. It flees and they chase after it, with one biting and another breaking its bones. This one casts it down, and this other one bars its way. Out of great fear and amidst quivering, the soul cries a great and bitter cry, "O God, save us and bring us near." Heaven and earth shake, the gates of the garden of Eden quake, and even the savage masses are frightened by its wail and stand still. It then flees to the garden of Eden. Just as it is with part above, so too is it with the part in you. You should be afraid of the multitude of vicious thoughts, and your soul will let loose a great and hidden cry unto God in the depths of your heart. They will be frozen, and you may then draw near to holy prayer. Understand this.[240]

Shapira does not just employ imagery techniques as a way of dealing with alien thoughts. More importantly, these imagery exercises are elements of empowerment. They intensify prayer and transform it from the simple experience of a religious ritual into a visceral and direct encounter with the divine.[241] Prayer without "alien thoughts" is also a normal religious ritual devoid of the mystical experience of encountering God:

> Great is worship (*ha-avodah*) and prayer and it is not so easy to achieve it... we will not speak now of "dead prayers" that you do not concentrate on what you say... rather your good prayers we wish to speak of... I will depict for you a little of what is done during your prayer... you want to pray like a hasid... to truly pray before God, you yearn for this prayer-conversation, who will allow you to be able to directly converse from the heart with God... but when you came to it [prayer], behold it is as if a stone is on your heart. It might be true that now you just had an hour of good prayer and your thoughts are not streaming so much, since you prepared yourself for it and you completely determined in your consciousness to abolish all your alien thoughts, but there is no real discourse.[242]

---

240 Shapira, *Ḥovat ha-Talmidim*, 51a. Also, see ibid., where he illustrates the alien thoughts as predatory animals. However, there Shapira suggests a more complex technique, in which man visualizes, in addition to the alien thoughts, himself, "Oh, look at the thought and see how this cruel, disgusting, and filthy beast burst forth into your mind, and with its foul feet it defiles and destroys all that is sacred within you, and its terrible mouth opens wide, and all your bodies sinews (*ḥuṭei*) and veins of your body, soul (*nafshekha*), and your soul (*ve-nishmatekha*) are gnawed.

241 Indeed, he had many predecessors in this regard, such as Weisblum and Aharon of Karlin, see above, subchapter, "R. Kalonymous Kalman Shapira's Imagery Techniques and His Imaginal-Literary Style." However, as we already noted, Shapira's imagery techniques are qualitatively different.

242 Shapira, *Hakhsharat ha-Avreikhim*, 23a.

Tefilah be-kavvanah (intentional prayer), meaning understanding that which is being read, may still be disconnected from man's soul, "I mean that his prayer and worship remain in [the realm of] knowledge and comprehension alone, disconnected from him, for he is in this world of actuality and existence (*mamash ve-yesh*), and his prayer is in the world of intellect."[243] Prayer can be intentional, but somehow lacking a dialogue with God, "there is no real discourse".[244] In order to intensify prayer and to feel the presence of God Shapira recommends that one utilize the imagination:

> One who strengthens *his thought and imagination* for holiness and worship... so each word that he utters in prayer is different than its fellow. ... when also your thought, imagination, and emotion, are revealed and are strengthened within you *to the point that you can see them*, then also your worship will concatenate into your being (*el qirbekha*) to be actualized also to the point of seeing it. And when you say, "Since, for you each knee will bend"[245] ... you will see that you together with all of the world are kneeling before God and are nullified before him, blessed be he. And so, when you will say, "Praise the Lord from the heavens" (Ps. 148:1), etc., with excitement, then to all the lower and upper worlds, which are actually in front of you, you stand and command, "Stand and praise together with us a song for God."[246]

The imagination intensifies prayer from a routine religious ritual into an experience of mystical annihilation, "You will see that you together with all of the world are kneeling before God and are nullified before him, blessed be he." This feeling appears together with the motif of envisioning, repeated here numerous times, "*to the point that you can see them*... to the point of seeing it... you will see." Prayer is transformed into a central location of vision and visualization. Many examples of liturgical intensification may be found in Shapira's writings. Sometimes it is an emotional intensification whose purpose is a spiritual awak-

243 Ibid., 29b.
244 Also, see R. Ḥayyim Soloveitchik of Brisk's distinction between two types of intention (*kavvanah*): intending the liturgical words, meaning understanding what is being read, and the conscious intention of standing in front of and speaking with God. See Ḥayyim ha-Levi Soloveitchik, *Ḥiddushei Rabbeinu Ḥayyim ha-Levi: Ḥiddushim ve-Bi'urim al ha-Rambam* (Brest: Yehoshu'a Qlein, 1936), "Hilkhot Tefilah, chap. 4, halakhah 1," 1b-2a, "There are two types of intention in prayer: the first—concentration (*kavvanah*) on the meaning of the words, and it is the foundation of the law of intention (*kavvanah*), the second—he should intend that he is standing in prayer before God, as it is explained in [Maimonides's] words, 'What is intention? That he should turn his heart from all thoughts and see himself as if he stands before the divine presence (*Shekhinah*)."
245 From the *Aleinu* prayer.
246 Shapira, *Hakhsharat ha-Avreikhim*, 29b.

ening, for example the conjunction of imagery techniques with the recitation of psalms in order to say them with passion:

> All that you will say do not say only as one who tells a story about what King David said thousands of years ago, [rather say it] as if David only intentionally composed (*tiqen*) this for you, and when you say, for example, "My God, my God, why have You abandoned me" (Ps. 22:2), *visualize that you are standing before the Throne of Glory* and pour out your soul, "My God, my God, why have you abandoned me and my family and all of Israel, why have you hidden your face and it is so dark for us."[247]

At other times it is a mystical intensification in which man experiences the divine dimension. Through imaginal visualization man, during prayer, can arrive at "an ascent of soul":[248]

> It appears in the holy book *No'am Elimelekh* that... one who wants his prayer to be heard must visualize as if he is praying in the land of Israel and the holy temple is built and the alter is on its premises and its *heikhal* (sanctuary) [as well]. And behold, it is as if he dwells now in the land of Israel, and through this he comes to complete translucency and communion (*le-bihirut u-devequt gamur*), praying with full intention with awe and love as if he is standing in the holy of holies etc. *and it is as if he sees everything with the optical sense.* So must he *visualize in his thought*, at the moment of his prayer, that he is truly in the land of Israel and the holy temple... this thought verily lifts up his soul, which is a type of *soul ascent. His soul ascends to heaven and sees what it sees.*[249]

The man who "visualizes in his thought" the holy temple merits, through this imaginal act, an ascent of the soul and a heavenly vision, "His soul rises up on high and sees what it sees." Indeed, what does he see? Shapira's answer is concealed within the closing verse of his teaching, "'Three times a year all your males shall appear before (*penei*; lit. face) the Lord your God' (Ex. 34:23) —specifically *penei* (face)."[250] Just as man embarks on a pilgrimage to the holy temple in order to see the face of God, so too, analogously, Shapira wishes to

---

247 Idem, *Hakhsharat ha-Avreikhim*, 46a. Also, regarding imagery techniques during prayer, see ibid., 16b, 32a-b; idem, *Mevo ha-She'arim*, 23b, 43a.

248 Regarding the ascension of the Besht's, R. Jechiel Michael from Zloczow's, and his son's soul, see Mor Altshuler, *The Messianic Secret of Hasidism* (Leiden: Brill, 2006), 15–28, 45, 70, 74, 102, 217. Regarding soul-ascent in kabbalah, see Idel, *Kabbalah: New Perspectives*, 88–96. Regarding other forms of ascension in Jewish mysticism, see idem, *Ascensions on High.*

249 Shapira, *Derekh ha-Melekh*, 136. Also see Wacks, *The Flame of the Holy Fire*, 144–145, for the rabbinical background of this technique.

250 Shapira, *Derekh ha-Melekh*, 136. The verse uses the root word *y, r,', h* (to see) in a simple passive conjugation, rendering its meaning to "every man will appear," however, it is interpreted by Shapira and Weisblum in the simple active, rendering its meaning to "every man will see."

say that man can see during prayer—if he would only make use of his imaginative faculty—the face of God. This imagery technique, which is brought in the name of Elimelekh Weisblum of Lizhensk, is heavily expanded in Shapira's praxis-centered thought. As we have stated, Shapira's innovation is in the employment of multiple sequential scenes. Weisblum suggested one simple scene to imagine, "the holy temple is built and the alter is on its premises," whereas Shapira offers a complete multi-scenic visualization, an entire waking-dream. I will now briefly present his remarks:

> Your simple thought begins to be strengthened, for example, when you see that which we previously mentioned... when a man will intend (*she-yekhavein*) as if he is praying in the land of Israel and the holy temple... so he must visualize in his thought during his prayer as if his is actually in the land of Israel and the holy temple and see everything with the optical sense, see there [*No'am Elimelekh*]. Then begin to visualize only that which is written in this. ... and afterwards train yourself to expand your thought, and connect to it all of your knowledge of the holy temple. And think: here is the [re]built holy temple, the place that [my] eye and the eye of God see, and it is a biblical commandment to ascend three times a year there, and why? In order to see the face of God, Lord of Hosts. The flame descends from the heavens [in front of] everyone's eyes, and the priest stands with the *urim ve-tumim*, Israel asks for their needs from the holy one, blessed be he, and God answers them. And one time a year the priest enters the holy of holies as well and there he saw the God of Israel even more, one time the priest exited and recounted, "I saw an old man, full of mercy, wearing white, and it is a good omen (*b. Yoma* 39a), and one time he exited and recounted... . When a man would transgress, God forbid, he would go to the holy temple and receive atonement, also for a possible sin (*safeq ḥeiṭ*), he would sacrifice a guilt-offering, and the daily offerings (*ve-ha-tamidin*) would atone for the other transgressions of the day and night, until man possessed no more sins. And in this holy place of revelation, you stand and pray, praise, and converse with the holy one, blessed be he. O, how your heart will burn and your soul be impassioned in its prayer and song for God. You will aslo visualize like this in your free time, that at the moment of prayer it is as if you are standing in the holy temple etc. and then when you come to pray it will be easier to stir yourself.[251]

In this exercise, which Shapira recommends be practiced, "also, in your free time," there appears a heavy emphasis on sight, particularly seeing God, "the place that [my] *eye and the eye of God see*, and it is a biblical commandment to ascend three times a year there, and why? *In order to see the face of God*, Lord of Hosts. The flame descends from the heavens [in front of] *everyone's eyes*, and the priest stands with the *urim ve-tumim*... And one time a year the priest enters the holy of holies as well and there *he saw the God of Israel even more*, one time the priest exited and recounted, '*I saw an old man*, full of

---

251 Shapira, *Hakhsharat ha-Avreikhim*, 32a-b.

mercy, wearing white, and it is a good omen.'" Here imagination serves as an intensifying factor, transforming the liturgical ritual into a mystical activity, which entails a dimension of divine visualization, or at least the striving for such vision.[252]

Until now I have investigated institutionalized prayer, however, Shapira devoted a considerable amount of energy discussing private, personal, subjective prayer as well, "Man should set times for himself to stir his love for God with longing and yearning for him, may he be blessed, and should pray, 'Please God, please bring me close to you, why have you hidden your face and why have you distanced me from your holiness'";[253] "not only during the obligatory morning, afternoon, and evening prayers, rather during the entire day you shall strive to find some free time as well, in which you shall converse with God in prayer and song... with a conversation of the soul (*be-si'aḥ ha-nefesh*)."[254] Shapira suggested imagery techniques for personal prayer as well, which intensify and utilize man's individual concerns and worries in order to encounter the divine:

> Every person, God forbid, has been worried about himself or another individual, whose concerns are like his own. *Whenever he remembers and intensely visualizes these [worries] in his imagination as if it is in front of his eyes*, his heart is softened and he becomes emotional, even weeping. Visualize them in front of you as well, and when you begin to be stirred and heartbroken, think to yourself: "Why should I break my heart and cry for nothing? After all, God is before me and I stand now before His blessed seat of glory. I will weep before God, Who hears the sound of tears"... and you will see how effective prayer raises you through it.[255]

> When you will feel a kind of broken-heart, even from corporeal needs, go stand to the side towards the wall... recite some psalms evocative of your [current] happening and in accordance with your concern... *and in your thought visualize God's glory*, before which you stand and supplicate, "O Lord, my foes are so many!... many say of me, 'There is no deliverance for him through God.' *Selah*" (Ps. 3:2–3), so they say, "But You, O Lord, are a shield about me" (Ps. 2:4), etc.[256]

252 This motif of wishing to see God is identified by Haviva Pedaya as central in mystical experience, see above, chap. 3, "Two Models of Prophecy."
253 Shapira, *Ḥovat ha-Talmidim*, 31b.
254 Ibid., 27a.
255 Idem, *Benei Maḥshavah Ṭovah*, 21–22.
256 Idem, *Hakhsharat ha-Avreikhim*, 48a. Also, see idem, *Benei Maḥshavah Ṭovah*, 23–24.

Shapira considers prayer to be a gradation of the holy spirit (*ru'aḥ ha-qodesh*). Therefore, it depends on the imaginative faculty, which is the key to attaining holy spirit:[257]

> This is the matter of prayer: song is one level of holy spirit, and prayer and song are one, a smaller and lesser illumination, so that one must work very hard to recite a song, gazing and becoming impassioned by it... Prayer is the service of body and soul, and to make a great effort and awaken the spirit of song, which is a spark of the holy spirit within... when a Jewish person comes to prayer, he must strengthen his consciousness and *visualize in his thought that the world and all its fullness, all is the light of divinity. His glory fills the world, and I stand amidst this blessed divinity.*[258]

This type of visualization—visualization of divinity, which reappears numerous times in a variegated and multiple forms in Shapira's imagery techniques, whether it be God's glory, the divine light, or the Throne of Glory—goes beyond the liturgical realm and constitutes a serious and complex subject in Shapira's thought, which should be treated in depth independently. This topic, which is rife with the tension created by the desire to envision God and the prohibition to corporealize him, a tension that Haviva Pedaya has identified as key to the mystical experience, will be discussed later in detail.[259]

---

257 Concerning the imaginative component in Shapira's conception of prophecy, see below, chap. 5.

258 Idem, *Ḥovat ha-Talmidim*, 73b-74a. Depictions of mystical experience in terms of being enclosed by light are characteristic of ecstatic kabbalah, see Idel, *Hasidism*, 278–279 n. 74. Concerning "light" in kabbalah, see Margaretta Bowers and Shmuel Glasner, "Auto Hypnotic Aspects of the Kabbalistic Concept of Kavana," *Journal of Clinical and Experimental Hypnosis* 6 (1958): 58–61; Idel, *Mystical Experience*, 77–83; idem, *Enchanted Chains*, 125–133; Wolfson, "The Body in the Text," 492. Regarding light and fire imagery in kabbalah, see Garb, *Manifestations of Power*, 170; idem, *Shamanic Trance*, 29, 36–38, 45, 82–89. Also, for a similar light enclosed imagery technique, see Aaron b. Ẓevi Hirsch ha-Kohen of Opatow, *Or ha-Ganuz le-Ṣaddiqim* (Warsaw: J. Unterhendler Press, 1887), 35, "He shall imagine as if he is standing in the Holy Temple and Tabernacle... and you are encompassed by the light of the holy one, blessed be he"; ibid., 10, "As if the light spreads out around him and he is inside the radiant light of the sky (*ha-or zohar ha-raqi'a*) sitting and he trembling rejoices... that he should visualize himself, and through this he will be able to divest himself of corporeality and terrestriality."

259 See below, chap. 5.

D Imagination as Empowering the Experience of Sacred Time: Sabbath and Festivals

Introduction

Shapira's crowning imagery techniques are those that enliven the experiences of sacred times.[260] These exercises are the most complex and lengthy ones in Shapira's writings and are a central focus in his thought. Furthermore, to my knowledge these types of exercises have no substantial precedents in either kabbalistic or hasidic literature. One may find passages vaguely resembling these techniques, however, they do not contain explicit guided instruction for the reader to practice any technique, but rather are merely poetic depictions of the relived temporal experience of the writer.[261]

Nomian rituals, meaning behavioral patterns that have undergone a process of canonization in rabbinic literature, are based on a certain cyclical-time structure. Many biblical and rabbinic commandments are dependent on time cycles: nocturnal-diurnal, seasonal, sabbatical, and jubical. From among all of these rituals, the ones with a direct link to sacred time are the sabbath and festivals.[262] A

---

260 Regarding sacred time and hasidism, see Garb, *Shamanic Trance*, 132–135.

261 For example, see R. Ḥayyim Tyrer, *Sidduro shel Shabbat* (Jerusalem: Makhon Beer Hayim, 1995), 2:45–46. For many of Shapira's imagery techniques, one may find parallels in kabbalistic and hasidic literature. Shapira's uniqueness lies in his development of these techniques from static to dynamic; from an image to a sequence. However, concerning these sacred time techniques, I know of no such precedent or parallel. While this does not mean that they do not exist, , the very fact that I have not found them is a further indiciation of their uniqueness.

262 On conceptions of time from many different Jewish perspectives in comparison with broader philosophical discussions, see Elliot R. Wolfson, *Alef, Mem, Tau: Kabbalistic Musings on Time, Truth, and Death* (Berkeley: University of California Press, 2006). On kabbalistic conceptions of time, see Martel Gavarin, "The Conception of Time in the Works of Rabbi Azriel," *Jerusalem Studies in Jewish Thought* 6, 3–4 (1987): 309–36; Moshe Idel, "Time and History in Kabbalah," in *Jewish History and Jewish Memory: Essays in Honor of Yosef Hayim Yerushalmi*, ed. Elisheva Carlebach, John M. Efron, and David N. Myers (Hanover Brandeis University Press, 1998), 153–188; also, see the collected essays recently published in Brian Ogren, ed., *Time and Eternity in Jewish Mysticism: That Which is Before and That Which is After* (Leiden: Brill, 2015). Regarding different cosmic models that influence the conception of time, see Shalom Rosenberg, "The Return to the Garden of Eden: Remarks for the History of the Idea of the Restorative Redemption in the Medieval Jewish Philosophy," in *The Messianic Idea in Jewish Thought: A Study Conference in Honour of the Eightieth Birthday of Gershom Scholem*, ed. Shmuel Re'em (Jerusalem: Israel Academy of Sciences and Humanities, 1982), 39–41; Rachel Elior, *Heikhalot Literature and Merkavah Tradition: Ancient Jewish Mysticism and its Sources* (Tel Aviv: Yedi'ot Aharonot, 2004), 20–21; Ze'ev Gries, "Jewish Time and Jewish Identity," *Da'at* 68/69 (2010): 311–321.

religious view of history sees divine intervention within temporal events, beginning with creation and culminating in redemption. Generally, historical time is viewed as linear in essence,[263] however, Moshe Idel has demonstrated that this conceptualization is an artificial construct.[264] Consequently, a different model may be employed to conceptualize biblical and rabbinic time—cyclical-spiralic time. This understanding of time grants each period of time an absolute quality that affects reality.

Cyclical time itself may be understood in two manners. In contrast to certain medieval thinkers who saw cosmic cycles within the framework of natural law, the kabbalists emphasized that an absolutely renewed creation occurred in each cycle.[265] Rachel Elior asserted that, "In Jewish tradition, time is conceived as reflecting the divine order in the universe... and as memory patterns that reconstruct the divine intervention in history. The yearly calendar connects the one-time divine intervention in history and the experience of the event that occurs in a cyclical form, repeatedly every year."[266] Similarly, Shimon Gershon Rosenberg writes:

> Jewish time: this time is eternal time, cyclical... history that is frozen in eternity. Enfolded within the word *shanah* (year), is also the meaning of return (*le-shenot*), time that repeats itself—a past that is frozen, but return and is present as the present... R. Ṣevi Hirsch Broida, blessed be the memory of the righteous, from Kelm, said, "For time does not pass over man, rather man passes (*nose'a*) within time. For example, on the first sabbath a "station" was established—Sabbath—and man arrives each week to the same station—really the same effect of holiness of the first sabbath"... The past exists in this time not as linear history... it lives and is disclosed as relevant, each time in a new manner, in present life.[267]

The linear model of time supports historical chronology. For example, in Judaism the month of Nisan (generally, between March and April) represents a time of freedom and liberty, since, historically, the Israelites departed Egypt in this month. This historical-religious event was engrained in historical memory as a

---

263 Mircea Eliade, *Cosmos and History: The Myth of the Eternal Return* (New York: Harper & Row 1959), 105–107, 111, 161–162. Linear temporality places an emphasis on historical events, such as the Sinaitic theophany in Judaism, from which Jewish religious history begins.

264 Idel, "Time and History in Kabbalah," 153. Also, ibid., 153–155 for his three suggested models: microchronic, linear, and macrochronic.

265 Rosenberg, "The Return to the Garden of Eden," 52. Rosenberg discusses Nahmanides as an example of this conception.

266 Elior, *Heikhalot Literature and Merkavah Tradition*, 20–21. Also, see the implications of linear and cyclical conceptions of time in Gries, "Jewish Time and Jewish Identity," 311–321.

267 Rosenberg, *"A Memorial of the First Day": High Holiday Sermons* (Efrat: Yeshivat Siach Yitzhak, 2001), 104.

time of freedom for generations. Similarly, the month of Av (generally, between July and August) is a period of mourning, due to the national tragedies that occurred at that time, such as the destruction of the second temple. In contrast to this conception, the cyclical-spiralic model, primarily found in kabbalah, represents an opposite conception of time: since Nisan is *inherently* characterized by freedom, therefore the Israelites departed Egypt at that time! Since Av is *inherently* characterized by sadness and mourning, therefore these tragedies occurred at that time. Time in the kabbalistic-cyclical time possesses an absolute character that effects reality, and not vice versa.[268] In order to understand the logic behind this conception, it should be noted that this model of time appears in nature. Certain species of flowers reappear and grow every year in exactly the same range of dates, neither before nor after. That is to say, this time has a certain character or feature that is capable (*ha-mesugelet*, in kabbalistic terminology) of growing and maturing a certain species of flower. Correspondingly, the time is capable of having spiritual characteristics. According to this conception, the festivals do not serve as markers for religious events that happened in the past and ceased; rather the characteristic that underlies the historical event is continuously renewed each year. Just as the blooming season of the Gilboa Iris is only in March and each year it blooms anew in this exact month and afterwards withers and the bulb remains in the ground, so too each year the "time of freedom" returns in the month of Nisan and the "time of calamity" returns in the month of Av. The months and festivals that occur in them are not merely memories or reproductions of canonical religious historic events, but are rather rejuvenations of absolute temporal qualities repeated every year. This temporality is spiralic, since it integrates two movements: a circular movement that incorporates progressive movements.[269] There is a repetition of historical patterns and structures, however it is not a pure repetition since, simultaneously, there is also linear movement. The repetition is not of the historical event itself, rather it of the essential feature that underlies that very event.

The roots of this conception may be found in classic rabbinic thought in the remarks of Rav Papa who recommends a Jew to avoid being sued by a non-Jew during Av, since this month is bad luck, and to delay the proceedings until Adar, associated with good luck, "With the beginning of Av rejoicings are curtailed. Rab Judah the son of R. Samuel b. Shilath said in the name of Rav: Just as with the beginning of Av rejoicings are curtailed, so with the beginning of

268 Regarding this conception of time, presented by Judah Loew of Prague, see Wolfson, *Alef, Mem, Tau*, 55–57, 69.
269 Wolfson, *Alef, Mem, Tau*, 59.

Adar rejoicings are increased. R. Papa said: Therefore, a Jew who has any litigation with Gentiles should avoid him in Av because his luck is bad and should make himself available in Adar when his luck is good."[270] This rabbinic conception of time is antithetical to linear temporality. This talmudic passage is an interpretation of the mishnaic text, "On the ninth of Av it was decreed that our fathers should not enter the [promised] land, the temple was destroyed the first and second time, Beitar was captured and the city [Jerusalem] was ploughed up. With the beginning of Av rejoicings are curtailed."[271] It is impossible to derive a specific perception of time based solely on the Mishnah, however Rav Papa presents Av as possessing absolute bad luck. This presentation demonstrates a temporal perception in which each period of time has a specific quality that influences historical events that occur during that period. Since the month of Av has bad luck—bad events happen in it, and not the opposite.[272]

This cyclic-spiralic conception of time also influenced Lurianic[273] and Cordoverean kabbalah,[274] as well as hasidic thought,[275] and constituted a source of in-

270 *b. Ta'anit* 29a-b. Also, it is halakhically decided as well in Karo, *Shulḥan Arukh*, Oraḥ Ḥayyim, §551:1.

271 *m. Ta'anit* 4:6.

272 However, Maimonides omits Rav Papa's comment and only cites the mishnah from, "When Av..." (idem, *Mishneh Torah*, Laws of Fasting, 5:6), nonetheless, this does not prove that Maimonides argues against the cyclical understanding of time, since, ibid., 5:3, Maimonides employs this type of temporal conception regarding the historical events that occurred on the ninth of Av.

273 See Ḥayyim Vital, *Sha'ar ha-Kavvanot*, Derushei Kavvanot Qeri'at Shema, Derush 1, "Know that day and night are twenty four hours and are divided into four times, for the day is divided into two times, which are halves and so is night divided into two halves, and the supernal governing of these four times are not equal, for after midday the potency of the strength of Isaac is aroused." Concerning the Lurianic conception of the infinite as beyond time, see Wolfson, *Alef, Mem, Tau*, 77–78.

274 See Moses Cordovero, *Pardes Rimmonim*, Gate 21, chap. 8, "It turns out that there are twenty-four combinations and twenty-four forms. And although the twelve and twelve appear to be similar, [they differ, for] one is the figure of the male and the other female; receiver and overflower (*mahpi'ah*), and so they are the twelve hours in the day and twelve hours in the night, of the night they receive from the day and of the day they overflow onto the night, in the mystery of the attribute of day and the attribute of night (*be-sod midat yom ve-midat Lailah*)"; Vidas, *Re'shit Ḥokhmah ha-Shalem*, Sha'ar ha-Ahavah, chap. 5, p. 430–431, 443–450. For an in-depth exploration of Cordovero's concept of non-temporal time, see Wolfson, *Alef, Mem, Tau*, 70–74, 78–80; concerning Cordovero's conception of special time unit qualities, see idem, "Fore/givenness On the Way: Nesting in the Womb of Response," *Graven Images: A Journal of Culture, Law and Sacred* 4 (1998): 155.

275 For example, see Shneur Zalman of Liadi, *Tanya*, chap. 41, p. 116, in which he recommends that during Torah study one pause for a minute and think about how they are prepared to sacrifice their life, "When he learns for many consecutive hours he should contemplate this afore-

spiration for Shapira for the creation of fecund imagery techniques designed to sense the absolute qualities in time, especially on the sabbath and festivals, which reflect the quality of holiness. Sacred times are fertile ground for techniques, which strive to intensify the feeling of holiness and divine immanence disclosed within time, thereby allowing for a living encounter between man and God, through the intensification of temporal experience.

Sabbath

Moshe Idel has suggested that the experience of sabbatical plentitude is rooted in the ontological conception relating temporal moments to divine presence, thus facilitating this experience.[276] Primarily in hasidism, but not less in the kabbalistic doctrines of Abulafia and Gikatilla, the sabbath is presented as messianic time—"a type of world to come." The sabbath is depicted by these thinkers as the promise of the possibility and the immediate availability of an experience of perfect beatitude. Messianic time is not apocalyptic period in which an entirely different world will appear, for this experience is already possible in this world,[277] "A type of world to come—day of Sabbath is rest."[278] In my opinion, this identification may be found already in *Sefer ha-Bahir:*

---

mentioned preparation at least once ever each hour, since each hour is a different drawing down from supernal worlds to vitalize the lower [beings] and the drawing down of vitality of the previous hour returns to its source [in the mystery of "running and returning" (*raṣo va-shov*) of *Sefer Yeṣirah*] with all of the Torah [study] and good deeds of the lower [beings], for each hour is dominated by one combination of the twelve combinations of the Tetragrammaton, blessed be he, in the twelve hours of the day and combinations of the name *Adonai* in the night, as is known." Shneur Zalman presents a kabbalistic conception of time in which each diurnal hour has a specific quality and feature. Whether this be derived by letter-combinations or *sefirot* (also, see Ḥayyim Vital, *Eṣ Ḥayyim*, Sha'ar ha-Shemot, chap. 5, that both of these options merge into each other)—the conception is that each hour is a new reality with its own unique quality. For an analysis of the development of cyclical time from the beginning of kabbalah until hasidism see Wolfson, *Alef, Mem, Tau*, 61–98.

276 Moshe Idel, "Sabbath: On Concepts of Time in Jewish Mysticism," in *Sabbath: Idea, History, Reality*, ed. Gerald J. Blidstein (Beer Sheva: Ben Gurion University Press of the Negev, 2004), 88.

277 Ibid., 90. Also see Wolfson, *Open Secret*, 177–178, 194–196 for the eschatological hypernomian ramifications of the connection of Sabbath and messianic temporality.

278 From a *piyut* recited on Sabbath Eve, "*Mah Yedidut.*" Recited by Ashkenazi communities, the author is unknown.

> R. Berekhi'ah sat and expounded, "What is it that we speak every day of the world to come and do not know what we are saying (*qa'amena*)?"[279] The world to come (*olam haba*) is translated [in Aramaic] as the world that came (*alma de-atei*). What is [the meaning of] the world that came? It teaches that before the world was created, it arose in thought to create a great light to illuminate, and a great light was created that no (*ain*) [eye (*ayin*) of a] creature could control. The holy one, blessed be he, saw that they could not tolerate it, he took *a seventh of it and placed it in his place for them*, and the rest he stored [for the righteous] of the world to come. He said, "If *they merit this seventh and safeguard it*, I will give them this in the other world," therefore it is written, "the world to come," for it is already coming from the six days of creation, that which is written, "How abundant is the good that You have in store for those who fear You, that You do in the full view of men for those who take refuge in You" (Ps. 31:20).[280]

Although this passage does not explicitly mention Sabbath, it may nonetheless be read in this manner,[281] such that "*this seventh*" signifies Sabbath. This reading is strengthened by the following words, "*and safeguard it*," the same command regarding Sabbath. God placed a seventh of the light into the day of Sabbath, and one who guards Sabbath will merit the remaining light in the world to come. This reading of the bahiric passage may be found in the writings of R. Shmuel Bornsztain, the Sochatchover *Rebbe*, of the twentieth century. According to him, this passage asserts that a seventh of the light exists in this world—on the Sabbath. Consequently, Bornsztain emphasizes that it is possible to sense this essence in this world as well, and that it is possible to reveal part of the hidden light, from the world to come, in this world on Sabbath:

> For behold, the world to come is a world that is entirely Sabbath, and the Sabbath that is in time is a kind of world to come, and behold Sabbath is constant and subsists. And it should be understood that *the world to come is in reality now as well*, as it said in *Sefer ha-Bahir* (§39), "That which is written, 'The world to come (*ha-ba*),' that it has already came (*ba*), see there, but it is concealed (*ganuz*), and a part of it is found in this world as well, *and in the six days of creation there was a concealment concealing the light, and on the day of Sabbath the concealment disappears*, as it is written, "it shall be opened on the Sabbath

---

279 In Daniel Abrams, ed., *The Book Bahir: An Edition Based on the Earliest Manuscripts*, intro. Moshe Idel (Los Angeles: Cherub Press, 1994), 191§106, this word appears as two distinct words with the order switched (*mana qa'i*; lit. stand.) However, it appears from the context to be *qa'amena.*

280 Abrams, ed., *The Book Bahir*, 191§161.

281 Prof. Yehuda Liebes informed me that this reading was the most straightforward understanding, and he even thinks that the *Bahir* discussed these matters regarding the Sabbath. Wolfson utilizes this passage for a broader philosophical rendering of time, see Wolfson, *Alef, Mem, Tau*, 153–155, however, Wolfson also hints at a possible interpretation that is regarding the Sabbath specifically, ibid., 154.

> day" (Ez. 46:1), and only good remains without waste and concealment and as it is written, "A psalm. A song; for the sabbath day. It is good to praise the Lord" (Ps. 92:1–2), *and on its own the sacred light of Sabbath will be disclosed.* And that is [the meaning] of Sabbath being constant and subsisting forever in one equalization (*be-hashva'ah*), and there is no difference between Sabbath and the six days of creation, but for the cause of concealment found in the six days of creation which disappears on the day of Sabbath as [that which is] closed is opened. Therefore, "From it the six days [of the week] are blessed,"[282] for then Sabbath is also in reality, but it is in concealment. And so it is in the world to come that is all good without any concealment, and as it is written, "Your Teacher will not hide himself any more" (Is. 30:20), therefore it is entirely Sabbath.[283]

This relation to time in general and Sabbath in particular constitutes the broad context and intellectual setting for the development of Shapira's imagery techniques. Shapira did not focus on sacred temporal experiences, and especially sabbatical experiences, in vain. Sabbath allows the experience of the world to come in this world, a divine experience. God's presence disseminates on Sabbath. However, this experience is not undergone by everyone, but only by those who prepare themselves to receive the divine presence.[284] According to this view, there is a hierarchy within time and not all temporalities are equal. Abraham J. Heschel was one of the harbingers of the sacredness of time in the twentieth century, stating that "We must assume that He is not at all times at our disposal. There are times when He goes out to meet us, and there moments when He hides His face from us… Jewish tradition claims that there is a hierarchy of moments within time, that all ages are not alike… God does not speak to man equally at all times."[285] This hierarchy, which gives preference to Sabbath and festivals, together with the need of personal preparation for the experience of encountering the divine presence, served as fertile ground for the blossoming of Shapira's best imagery techniques, which are directed towards the reader as preparation and means for the desired encounter.

Certainly, for Shapira, the halakhic observance of Sabbath was the primary and foundational preparation for the containment and application of the sabbatical divine presence. This halakhic observance was the foundation for the possibility of mystical encounter, "When a Jew keeps the Sabbath, his soul (*nafsho*), his spirit (*ruḥo*) and his soul (*ve-nishmato*) [the three lower aspects of the soul]

---

282 An amalgam of locutions found in *Zohar* II:63b.

283 Shmuel Bornsztain, *Shem me-Shemu'el* (Jerusalem: Eastern Books Press, 1992), Parashat va-Yeḥi, 242–24. My emphasis.

284 Idel, "Sabbath," 82–83.

285 Heschel, *God in Search of Man*, 129. Also, see idem, *The Sabbath: Its Meaning for Modern Man* (New York: Farrar, Straus and Giroux, 1951), 2–24.

enter the garden of Eden, and together with the pure souls on high and with the righteous souls there, the light of the garden of Eden is moderated and with a radiance of supernal love and awe they are delighted (*mita'negot*)."[286] Yet, Shapira is interested in intensifying this basic experience through the imagination, "Now it follows that when you will want to discover your sacred feelings that move within you on some festival or holy Sabbath, strengthen your sacred thoughts concerning the festival and Sabbath, and [in order] to strengthen your thoughts it is impossible that you should think a simple thought alone, that the festival and Sabbath are sacred... rather you must fill them with depictions and images."[287] Shapira taught and created exercises that intensify the experience of sabbatical sacredness, primarily the experience of *se'udah shelishit* (the third meal on Sabbath day), in which he saw "the climax of the Sabbath,"[288] as he wondered, "I wonder why people are not excited when they walk to the third meal in the same way they are excited walking to *Kol Nidrei* [the first prayer of Yom Kippur eve]."[289] Due to their lengthiness, I am unable to quote these imagery techniques in full, nonetheless, a brief citation and analysis are in order:

> For each man needs to gaze, think, visualize, and imagine in accordance with his state, and the simple viewing at the third meal, for example: the Sabbath, a day entirely holy, has passed over you... you did not deal with your merchandise, you did not stroll in the markets and streets, and you did not belittle the Sabbath (*ve-lo hiqalta et ro'shekha*)... you engaged with Torah and conversations of holiness and hasidic teachings. You washed yourself from all dust and stain that ascended upon you during the entire week, and you strived to come unto your soul, and in each hour you felt within yourself that you are rising from one state to another state, and from a level of holiness to a level of greater holiness, until you neared the third meal, the climax of the Sabbath, this hour of grace (*debei ra'ava*).[290] This meal is one of three meals, but you already feel that this is not the place or circumstance to be satisfied with meat and fish, but only to search for God hidden in heaven's vaults (*be-shafrir*

---

286 Shapira, *Ḥovat ha-Talmidim*, 77a.
287 Idem, *Hakhsharat ha-Avreikhim*, 16a-b.
288 Regarding the hierarchal conception of gradations of holiness on the Sabbath in Shapiras writings see, idem, *Ḥovat ha-Talmidim*, 84b-85a. Regarding his devotion to the third meal, see the testimony of R. El'azar Bein in his approbation in Yitzhaq Moshe Erlanger, *Quntresei Ḥasidut: Inyanei Shabbat Qodesh* (Jerusalem: Ha-Makhon le-Iyun be-Ḥasidut, 2007), "Close to my heart are the points of preparatory work on prayer (*avodat ha-tefilah*)... Studying before prayer, and the matter of the third meal that I saw by my teacher and holy master, may God avenge his blood, from Piaseczno, who dedicated himself to these points."
289 Shapira, *Ṣav ve-Ziruz*, §26. Furthermore, see the parallel between the Day of Atonement and the third meal idem, *Hakhsharat ha-Avreikhim*, 61b-62a.
290 From the song *Benei Heikhala* attributed to Isaac Luria, customarily sung by hasidim at the third meal.

> *ḥevyon)*[291] [*sefirah* of *Keter*] and to be satisfied from his radiance. And you sit with comrades, who are also seekers of God's face, and you sit in darkness. The customs of Israel are Torah [law], for they adapt the corporeal activities to the soul's state at that very time, "For there is darkness and there is [another type of] darkness (*Tiqqunei Zohar* 30), concerning God, blessed be he, it is written, "He made darkness His screen" (Ps. 18:12), it is truly light... and since for a whole day (*me-et le-et shalem*) you distance yourself from this world and come near, step after step to the aspect of "this hour of grace," the supernal will [*sefirah* of *Keter*]... your body is also forced in actuality to sit in darkness... God hides in darkness, and following search and inspection during the entirety of Sabbath you have come to the fog, for there is God... the entire room is filled with the supernal family (*me-famili'a shel ma'alah*). And you push yourself through the entire holy family to the holy of holies. Your soul yearns to enter the inner sanctum and to come to the place that God is, "I held him fast, I would not let him go" (Song. 3:4). And if you had known that you can remain permanently in this state, then your soul would have been forever joyous. However, you are reminded that in one moment they will light candles, and you will fall again into the mundane days, and your soul will be bitter, how you will fall from the darkness of heaven, pure fog, unto the darkness of Egypt... within you the three varieties of darkness are now fighting the three meals. A parable, a prince who is sentenced to be distanced from his father and send him to prison, then at the last moment before he is separated from his father he brings himself even closer to his father, he pushes and comes near, delights and longs, and from within her delight and fear the soul cries from the depths, "Though I walk through a valley of deepest darkness, I fear no harm, for You are with me" (Ps. 23:4), the hands are almost trembling and searching, "You are with me," "I held him fast, I would not let him go."[292]

These imagery exercises are designed to intensify the experience of the divine felt during sacred times, beyond the religious-normative experience that already exists in these times, as well as during the rituals that are performed then, as well. The sense of sabbatical sacredness is in fact the feeling of mystical encounter expressed as touching and holding God, "to come to the place that God is, 'I held him fast, I would not let him go' (Song. 3:4)." The departure of the Sabbath is accompanied by a difficult experience of separation from clinging to God, "[you] delight and long... the hands are almost trembling and searching, 'You are with me,' 'I held him fast, I would not let him go.'[293] Shapira's remarks in continuation of this exercise come to remove all doubt that perhaps this exercise

---

291 A popular kabbalistic poem, composed in sixteenth century Safed by Abraham Maymin, disciple of Moses Cordovero. These words refer to *Keter* and were sung commonly by hasidim at the third meal.

292 Ibid., 17a-18a. Also, see a parallel, with slight differences, idem, *Benei Maḥshavah Ṭovah*, 28–30.

293 Shapira adapts the mystical experience of the third meal to the words of the songs associated with it, primarily from Psalms.

is an example of mere mental reflection and not fecund imaginal-visualization, "If you do not think about anything or if you will think, but you will not fill your thoughts with images (*ṣiyurim*)... and do not weave these thoughts with actual events, then the spark and also the thought will be extinguished and soon melt."[294]

The experience of the holiness of the Sabbath according to Shapira transcends normative-religious experience. Each Sabbath allows for the experience of divine encounter. This experience rises and intensifies within the progression of sabbatical temporality, according to the kabbalistic partition which identifies three qualities of sabbatical temporality that fluctuate from meal to meal, in which the climax of divine presence is at the third meal, culminating in mystical union.[295] Imagery techniques serve Shapira as intensifying factors for normative sabbatical experience, transforming the Sabbath into an encounter with God.

Passover

Similar to Sabbath imagery techniques, Shapira developed imagery techniques in order to intensify festival experiences from normative-religious experiences into mystical experiences. The two criteria that I presented above, that of self-preparation for the purpose of intensifying the experience of sacred temporality and that this preparation be done through imagery exercises, can be identified in a letter that Shapira wrote to his followers in 1939:

> Life, peace, and blessing for our honored friends (*anshe shelomeinu*)... to you men I will call and to your souls I will speak. The holy days of Passover are approaching, which in their holiness we will sanctify ourselves—[both] internally and externally, and with their light we will be filled and surrounded, but the verse states, "Light is sown for the righteous, joy for the upright" (Ps. 97:11), the supernal light and joy, in the aspect of sowing, that needs exertion and much engagement in the beginning... also we must prepare ourselves before the festival... and the main aspect is in the festival itself... that when he comes to the [Passover] Seder, he shall visualize now that he is in the garden of Eden, and the meal is of the meal to come... supernal angels densely stand to listen to our gaiety, and

---

294 Ibid.

295 In the evening the feminine aspect of the Sabbath appears, in the day the masculine aspect appears, and in the third meal both are present in a pairing of these aspects. Regarding the hierarchal conception of sacred times within Sabbath, see Heschel, *The Sabbath*, 54–55, also see above n. 288.

> our father our king stand and is happy and delights in receiving our song and praise, as is known from the holy *Zohar*,[296]... I bless you for a kosher and joyous festival.[297]

Shapira was not sufficed by the nomian ritual of the Passover Seder as brought in halakhic literature, but rather demanded previous preparation, primarily based on imaginative faculties, "we must prepare ourselves before the festival... that when [we] come to the [Passover] Seder, [we] will visualize." This imaginative faculty, in Shapira's teachings, is the "spark of prophecy": "If his soul (*nafsho*) and spirit (*ve-ruḥo*) will not be stirred with song, joy, and the spark of the disciples of the prophets within him, he will not know what Passover night is and why there is such a commandment to retell the exodus from Egypt and to enhance so much."[298] The theme of vision is emphasized in his thought regarding Passover, and not in vain. The source of corporeal vision is the eye, whereas the source of mystical vision, experiencing the divine, is in the imaginative faculty, and this is the prophetic spark within man.[299] Shapira contrasts the Passover preceding the destruction of the temple with the Passover following it, a comparison in which vision stands at its epicenter, in the form of divine visualization and the yearning for said visualization in the wake of the destruction, "Eye in eye, we saw the splendor of our father, our king's holiness and together with the Assembly of Israel, "a rose of Sharon" (Song. 2:1), in the heights of song that we sang and praise to the honored king we sang. And now everything has been taken from us... neither mourning nor sadness are stirring now, only yearning for his holy splendor."[300] Haviva Pedaya identified the urge for divine visualization with the ecstatic element and defined the religious mystical experience as the tension between wanting to visualize God and the prohibition of doing so.[301] According to this definition, the longing for divine visualization in Shapira's words constitutes a clear mystic motif.

Shapira dedicated an entire chapter in one of his books to the visualization of the exodus from Egypt.[302] This exercise is one of the longest in his oeuvre, ex-

---

296 It appears that he is referring to *Zohar* 2:40b, "It is a different commandment to recount with praise the exodus from Egypt," etc.

297 Shapira, *Derekh ha-Melekh*, 444.

298 Idem, *Ḥovat ha-Talmidim*, 65b.

299 Regarding the "spark of prophecy" and "the spark of the disciples of the prophets" as imagination in Shapira's thought, see the following chapter.

300 Idem, *Ḥovat ha-Talmidim*, 66b.

301 Pedaya, "Seeing, Falling, Song," 237, 242. See below, chap. 5, subchapter, "Imagination as a Technique for Illustrating God," for a further discussion of this tension.

302 Shapira, *Hakhsharat ha-Avreikhim*, chap. 7.

tending over some ten lengthy pages. Due to its length I will only quote an excerpt from it. This exercise is a striking example of how Passover may be intensified; transforming a normative-religious experience into a visionary encounter with God:

> Visualize according to your knowledge something of this sort: "They made their lives bitter with hard work of bricks and mortar, and all work of the field; all the difficult labors they made them perform" (Ex. 1:14). The cruel Egyptians did not need the buildings, and wanted only to afflict Israel and strove to make their lives bitter... they sought out and searched for all types of difficult work for Israel (*b. Sotah* 11)... Israel were debased, downcast in their eyes, and they decried their pure religion that they had inherited from their holy forefathers (*Zohar* 2:15a) . . . and from amidst these sufferings our teacher Moses and Aaron the Priest came to them, and the voice of God called forth from them, "I have surely remembered you"... Even a person cold of spirit and callous of faith would find it impossible to doubt such holy words, because they truly saw that it was not Moses who spoke, but rather God speaking through him... They talk with each other, and they converse with each other, and everyone is joyful. And a man comes unto his house and tells his wife and children the great and wondrous [matters] that he heard and that his eyes saw, and they speak and visualize how their departure from this will look and with what they will prepare for themselves on the road. And there is a scared child who will ask, "Father, mother! And how will we leave... and the oppressor will beat us... I am afraid... and the simple child will cry and continue to ask... [But] all see the wonders of our God . . . and all of them bow, acknowledging and prostrating to God... *He is before us; how can we not see?*[303]

This long exercise weaves together various elements: a direct address to the reader with instructions (to visualize); different textual sources integrated into a single polyphonic fabric (*peshat*, aggadah, Talmud, *Zohar*); the metaphor of seeing and even imagining within the exercise ("and visualize how their departure from this will look"); that is, the imaginal figures are visualized.[304] This lengthy technique is an example of personal preparation for experiencing divine immanence, revealed in times of holiness, and human effort for encountering the divine realm and even seeing God.

Hanukkah

The rabbinically established festivals are not generally counted as sacred days in which the divine light is revealed and God's holiness experienced. Halakhically

---

303 Idem, *Hakhsharat ha-Avreikhim*, 34a-36a.

304 Ibid., 35b. Concerning imagination within imagination, see below chap. 5, subchapter, "'To Visualize the Holy Name': Outflanking Imagination—Imagination within Imagination."

one does not refrain from labor and in the times of the temple they were not characterized by a specific sacrificial order, namely the festival sacrifice. Nonetheless, many kabbalistic and hasidic teachings discuss the uniqueness of these times and their unique potency as well as the light "sparkling" within them.[305] The hierarchal conception of temporality allows for the exploration of these days and their unique qualities. Shapira shares this view and maintains that the soul ascends on rabbinic festivals as well, an ascension that may be experienced through imagery techniques, "Every Jew lights Hanukkah candles for the miracle that God did for us then, but if he does not have a conception or mental visual (*ve-ṣiyur shel maḥshavah*) in his thought, then it will be difficult for him to feel what the soul ascensions are, and he merely lights a simple candle remembering the miracle, as is sometimes done for his own celebration as well."[306] It is impossible to deny the negative attitude that Shapira expresses towards routine ritual, as well as his desire to infuse this ritual experience with intensity through an experience of soul ascension. In an extreme manner he compares the activity of lighting Hanukkah candles, a rabbinic commandment, to the mundane action of lighting candles for no apparent reason. While Shapira indeed recognized that routine is a natural trait, he demanded that it be overcome and strived to supplement it with mystical experience through the use of imagery techniques:

> When a man begins to stir and visualize an impression of a "simple thought" (*maḥshavah peshuṭah*), such as how he and all of Israel during the entire year are troubled by making a living and other bodily needs, and are forced to strive with all their power for them, and each deed is followed by a deed... and when he adds to his exertion... he adds to his profit. Then little by little he thinks that everything is dependent upon his own effort... but through the power of his faith in his heart, he must remember and teach himself that all his actions too are dependent upon God... and after he has had many thoughts like this reminding that everything is dependent upon God... that he should always know and be in awe that clearly he and all his deeds, even his individual (*ha-praṭi'im*) ones, are solely dependent upon God alone, and in general due to Greece's [old culture], which was immersed in materialism, therefore he and all of the world descend further into the darkening of the soul and body, God save us... And as it was in the days of the Greeks, who blemished and damaged Israel's opinions and beliefs to the point that they dared to say to Israel, "Write on the horn of an ox that you have no portion in the God of Israel" (Gen. Rabbah 2:4), heaven forfend, as it is known. And then, from within the vastness of this darkness that appears, heaven forfend, to have no gateway from which to leave all the darkness and troubles of the

---

305 For example, see Epstein, *Sefer Ma'or ve-Shemesh*, Remezei Ḥanukah, s.v. "ve-hinei"; Tsevi Elimelekh of Dinov, *Benei Yissakhar* (Jerusalem: s.n., 2005), 59b. Also see the sources cited by Wolfson, *Open Secret*, 41–42, 85–86, 151–152, 216, and regarding Purim and its pivotal role in Ḥabad thought ibid., 40, 55–58, 147–149, 167–168, 249, 288–289.
306 Shapira, *Derekh ha-Melekh*, 52.

> body and soul, God, blessed be he, reveals himself to them in his holy light with unnatural salvation, the mighty [fall] into the hands of the weak, the many [fall] into the hands of the few, saying, "See, I am God and everything is dependent upon me." And by God rending all the concealing veils... Israel's souls ascended again and were sanctified in the supernal light... and since you see now that this world is not of concealment, or an independent entity, heaven forfend, rather everything from the world of emanation (*olam ha-aṣilut*) until the lower [world of] doing is of one holiness... you now see that these candles of Hanukkah are not only a hint and remembrance, but are a contraction of the supernal light, and Hanukkah with these candles that we light is a kind of revelation and sanctification of his essence and entire world. Supernal light is revealed in these candles, in these days when God's light is revealed to this world and Israel's hearts, as is brought by R. Isaac Luria, blessed be his memory, that the light in the Hanukkah candles is drawn downwards even to the lowly places, and corporeal and spiritual salvation also comes to us.[307]

Simple thought is not a discursive action but rather an imaginal one. This term is well defined in Shapira's thought: "He shall intensely think (*yaḥshov be-ḥazaqah*) of the matter that he hears and sees. When he visualizes it without any additions—this is called *simple thought.*"[308] That is to say, this exercise presents a waking dream in which man sees himself, "troubled by making a living and bodily needs." Through this imagery technique, man senses how material attraction overpowers him and how he loses the sense of divine immanence, until he overrides this attraction and returns to this feeling. This action is analogously compared to the overcoming of the Greeks, who symbolize and represent material potency. This overcoming will always be "unnatural... the many [fall] into the hands of the few." Sacred potency is weak, nevertheless, man must overcome the evil, the many, and the mighty, "saying, 'See, I am God.'" Also in this exercise, Shapira finds it appropriate to emphasize that his intention is not that man should engage in analytical thought, but rather in multi-scenic imagery and plot, "Then with an image (*ṣiyur*) of this thought he is able to feel... and so too for other images (*ṣiyurei he-maḥshavah*) that arise within a Jew on Hanukkah and with other commandments, as in the matter of the three meals that I wrote about in the tract *Benei Maḥshavah Ṭovah.*"[309] Imagery techniques intensify the banal religious ritual of Hanukkah candle lighting, transforming it into an experience of the divine within the candles. The candles in essence are a "contraction of the supernal light." "Supernal light is revealed in these candles" and like biblical sacred times, Hanukkah as well is "a kind of revelation and sanctification of

---

307 Ibid., 52–53.

308 Idem, *Hakhsharat ha-Avreikhim*, 32a. Concerning the difference between "simple thought", "widening thought", and "renewing thought", see Reiser, "To Fly Like Angels," 132–133.

309 Shapira, *Derekh ha-Melekh*, 53. The contrast with a parallel imagery technique in idem, *Benei Maḥshavah Ṭovah*, 28–30, shows that this is clearly an imagery technique.

[God's] essence." On Hanukkah, God's "light is revealed to this world and to Israel's hearts." Nonetheless, the initiative to receive this light is upon man, and if not, the lighting of these candles remains just that and nothing more. He who does desire the supernal light of Hanukkah must prepare himself, according to Shapira, through imagery techniques and exercises.

In this subchapter I have demonstrated that Shapira mystically utilizes nomian-religious practices, such as Torah study, prayer, and the observance of the Sabbath and festivals. By adding the imagery exercises to these nomian rituals, they are intensified and are brought to a living encounter between the practitioner and God. This living encounter is not able to come to fruition without man's preparation and effort. Receiving the light that is disclosed in sacred temporalities, or in other words, the mystical encounter with the divine dimension within time,[310] happens and is made possible through man's use of imagery techniques.

Shapira did not only employ these intensifying techniques for nomian and anomian Jewish practices, but rather extended them to psychological channels: self-empowerment, increase of emotions, and others. Also, frequently in these cases, this intensification strives to establish contact with God and experience his presence. In these instances, as well, imagery techniques are a key component for mystical intensification.

E Imagination as Empowering Emotions

The Imagination as a Self-Empowering Factor

Self-visualization is an instance when man sees himself in an imaginal vision. There are many precedents for this self-encounter.[311] Most of these sources concern a subject who sees one's body in extracorporeal space (as a "double"). I would like to limit myself to cases of self-visualization and not include every kind of autoscopic phenomena in this sub-chapter. I will not be discussing self-imaginings that occur without imaginal preparation, as in a dream or spontaneous prophetic inspiration. I am solely interested in intentional acts of visualization, in which man consciously strives to see himself. This type of self-visual-

310 For more on the intensification of sacred temporal experiences, whether for biblical or rabbinic holidays, see above, "Dance and Imagination."

311 For more, see below, chap. 6, subchapter, "Autoscopy and Self-Visualization in Menaḥem Mendel Ekstein's Teachings."

ization appears numerous times in kabbalistic and hasidic sources as a technique for acquiring prophecy and as a key for entering the world of esotericism and ecstasy.[312] In contradistinction, Shapira did not engage in self-visualization for prophetic purposes, rather as a psychological component of self-empowerment, in the sense of striving for self-perfection.

Shapira recommends man to visualize his personal religious worship, how he will look and what his aspirations are through self-visualization. This is not an abstract thought in which man sets his goals and ambitions, rather through a clear multi-scenic visualization. In *Ḥovat ha-Talmidim* he remarks in passing that the enfeebled man, who suffers in his worship of God due to his feebleness, "He does not have a *visual or image* (*ṣiyur ve-demut*) of his worship as well, not even delight nor joy,"[313] implying that man should have such a visual and image of his worship. One may learn about the character of this visual in his work *Ṣav ve-Ziruz*. The visualization of religious worship is not abstract thought, but rather a script full of figures and visuals in which self-visualization stands at their center:

> If you want to serve God and raise yourself upwards, and not stand at your seventieth year of life like the day of your Bar Mitzvah [thirteen years old], then do this: every year set a goal for yourself, visualize yourself, for example, if your name is Re'uven, which Re'uven will you be next year, what will be his accomplishments, worship, traits (*midotav*), and character. And the imaginal Re'ueven will be a scale for you to measure yourself, how much more are you lacking [compared] to the imaginal Re'uven... And if the following year arrives and you measure yourself and you did not even reach the ankles of the new year's Re'uven, you will consider it as, God forbid, heaven forefend, you did not grow up (*lo he-erakhta yamim*). For, only the Re'uven of yesteryear or from ten years ago is living, and not the Re'uven of this year.[314]

In this multi-scenic imaginal visualization, the practitioner goes "back to the future" and sees his "future self" in a vision that is similar to a waking-dream; a visualization may be very short or quite lengthy, depending upon the imaginer. This imagery translates the abstract concept of religious worship into images and visuals. The imagined religious worship is not yet possessed by the imaginer, but rather remains solely an aspiration. The purpose of this exercise, which offers a role model to imitate and even compete against, is twofold: the intensification of man's religious activities and measurement of their progress. Both aspects are for the same goal—the striving for perfection. Shapira's attitude towards imagi-

312 Ibid.
313 Shapira, *Ḥovat ha-Talmidim*, 15a.
314 Idem, *Ṣav ve-Ziruz*, §2.

nal perfection is clarified when contrasted with that of the Danish philosopher Søren Kierkegaard. Kierkegaard describes the aspiring youth who is led astray by his imagination. The youth falls in love with his fictional perfected self-image, inspiring him and robbing him of sleep. According to Kierkegaard this image is deceiving. There is an unbridgeable gap between reality and imagination, which reflect complete opposites; since the youth wants to materialize this image in a reality antithetical to the imagination, failure, and the accompanying agony, is guaranteed.

> The imagination has deceived the youth, has by means of that image of perfection made him forget that he is, after all, in actuality… Since the image he wants to resemble is the image of perfection and since the actuality in which he is and wants to express the resemblance is anything but perfection, suffering is in store and is not to be avoided.[315]

Similar to Kierkegaard, Shapira identifies the gap between imagination and reality, admits that reality does not even reach the "ankles" of the imagined vision, and it may also be presumed that he was aware of the accompanying sufferings caused by the feeling of disappointment triggered by the gap between reality and imagination. However, in contrast to Kierkegaard, Shapira is interested in these sufferings, "you will consider it as, God forbid, heaven forefend, you did not grow up." Shapira does not see this existential gap between imaginal self-perfection and distant reality as a deceitful aspect of imagination; on the contrary, Shapira is interested in this gap and utilizes it as an instrument to "raise yourself upwards." Shapira's presumption is that man is unable to avoid this gap and one day he will have to meet and confront it. Shapira is interested in the existential conflict and the agony that follows. These sufferings constitute the key to a spiritual ascension and experience, and seemingly, in his opinion, themselves have an aspect of sacredness, in the sense of coming closer to God. I will present a similar imagery technique, in which Shapira presents a competitive spiritual challenge through visualizing, "one's lifespan." This technique, in opposition to the preceding one, is directed at the world to come:

> When he will contemplate himself that the days of his life are short and when his short days will pass and eternal days will come, then in the same world and same state that he chose in this world he will remain for eternity—whether, God forbid, [he is in a state of] lowliness of a dog or rat, or a thousand times different, in [a state of] supernal purity at the heights and holiness between the holy and pure souls, angels, and seraphim. When he will contemplate this, even the worst [man], all of his body will tremble and his heart

315 Kierkegaard, *Practice in Christianity*, 190.

> within his being will be terrified. However, it is dependent on man's thought and imagination, if they are strong or not.[316]

Similar to the previous technique, this technique also places a challenge of perfection before man—to reach the level of "holy and pure souls, angels, and seraphim," before his death and not that of a "dog or rat." This technique is only effective if man succeeds in seeing actual images and multiple scenes: "However, it is dependent on man's thought and imagination, if they are strong or not." Common to all of these various techniques is the use of imagery techniques for the purpose of intensifying man's personal ambitions. In this sense it is possible to use the term "empowerment" or "intensification" (*ha'aṣamah*) as it is used in contemporary psychological treatments and spiritual-therapy—as empowering one's personality by setting goals and striving to materialize them,[317] and therefore self-visualization has a vital role in this process. Indeed, psychological empowerment is not mystical intensification. Nonetheless, the aspiration for empowerment is part of the apparatus for the intensification of emotions, which is certainly meant to enable the encounter with divinity and make it present in the individual's life, as I will demonstrate.

Visualizing Distress and Worry as Intensifying Factors for Seeking God

"Seeking God" implies the mystical impulse and yearning of the soul for an unmediated experience of divinity, termed in the hasidic corpus as *devequt* (communion), *hitkallelut* (integration), *hitqashrut* (spiritual bonding), and so on.[318] According to Shapira, the experience of *devequt* occurs through preparatory work. In his teachings, this preparation is termed *avodah* (work). In order to understand this concept, we must examine the distinction Shapira offers between

---

316 Shapira, *Hakhsharat ha-Avreikhim*, 29a. This conception of what man acquires in this world as his spiritual property for the world to come, relies upon a Maimonidean conception of the world to come, see Maimonides, *Mishneh Torah*, Laws of Repentance," chap. 8–9.

317 There are hundreds of workshops today devoted to "self-empowerment" in Israel, and websites that use the term *ha-aṣamah* (empowerment) in the sense of self-preparation, training, and realization, for example, see the website *Haatzama*; www.haatzama.com.

318 For a study of this term in its hasidic context, see Gershom Scholem, *The Messianic Idea in Judaism: And Other Essays on Jewish Spirituality* (New York: Schocken Books, 1971, 203–27); Schatz-Uffenheimer, *Hasidism as Mysticism*, 144–67; Idel, *Hasidism*, 86–89. For a summary, see Yoram Jacobson, *From Lurianic Kabbalism to the Psychological Theosophy of Hasidism* (Tel Aviv: Ministry of Defense, 1984), 89–97; idem, *Hasidic Thought* (Tel Aviv: Ministry of Defense, 1986), 44–53, 95–106. Also, albeit not in its hasidic context, see Afterman, *Devequt*.

the two terms, *shimush* (utilization) and *avodah* (preparatory work). *Shimush* is the performance of commandments, such as prayer and Torah study,[319] whereas *avodah* is the intensification of said performance, "*Shimush* is only when he utilizes and performs these matters without *avodah* and he does not give his power to it, and with this alone it is impossible to know God."[320] *Avodah* intensifies the routine religious ritual, transforming it into an experience in which man comes "to know God." Preparatory work supports the seeking of God, while the opposite is true as well—seeking God supports preparatory work. The powerful desire to integrate with God serves as motivation for the preparatory work. It is impossible to arrive at a state of mystical communion without preparatory work and it is impossible to continue preparatory work without experiencing mystical communion, "It is impossible for man to [spiritually] bind (*le-hitqasher*) with persistent preparatory work, if he does not constantly seek it. Note that King David sought God, 'Show me Your way, O Lord' (Ps. 86:11)... And obviously we should go in his path"[321]

In order to stir man to seek God, Shapira sought to create a state of experiential dependency upon God. This experience of dependency is acquired through an imagery technique scattered throughout his works, in which the verse "Show me Your way, O Lord" (Ps. 86:11) appears. This meditative technique makes use of situations of crisis and distress. For example, imagery of murderers and predatory animals brings the imaginer to a feeling of great distress from which there is no escape except with God's help. This distressing experience—which situates man between life and death—together with the knowledge that the only escape is by the help of God, serves as an intensifying factor for the feeling of divine dependency. The constant seeking and turning towards God, as depicted in the verse, constitute a returning theme in the development of this technique:

> Visualize a son of a king wandering in the mountains in the desolate wilderness among predatory animals and lurking murderers, and he knows that there is a path leading to his father the king, but the path has disappeared and is unknown, and how very great and constant is his seeking and searching for the path, and how great are his cries to his father, "Show me your way, O father." Only if like the king's wandering son you will *see* yourself [as] distant from the king your father in heaven, wandering the desolation of this world, physicality and nonsense wrecking the body and killing the soul. Only then will you persistently seek the way to God and in the depth of your heart constantly cry out, "*Show me your way, O Lord*" (Ps. 86:11). And to the extent that you will constantly

319 See Shapira, *Ḥovat ha-Talmidim*, 67b.
320 Ibid.
321 Ibid., 34a.

> seek, you will constantly serve (*la-a'vod*) him, and if you will not constantly seek from the depth of your heart, it will be impossible to constantly serve him as well.[322]

> The man should visualize himself as if he is wandering in a wilderness, an unformed (*tohu*) place among untamed animals and bandits, murders and robbers, and he does not know where he will turn, and with every step and stride he may wander even more and come closer to the animals' lairs and robbers' cave, and his heart will ache more in knowing that his father can save him immediately from all his oppressions that are very close to him, but he does not know the way to him. How he will wail, the poor wrench, for his father, "Father, father show me your way." "*Show me your way, O Lord*" (Ps. 86:11), I desire to walk unto you, therefore you show me this [way].[323]

The call, "*Show me your way, O Lord*," is in fact an expression of yearning for a direct connection to God and the experience of his immanent presence in all of man's deeds, including eating, drinking, and even business, "This is the meaning of 'Show me your way, O Lord,' that I will see in all [aspects] of my life only a path [to God], and I will behave as one who walks on the path to you, creator of the great world! In the hour that I am eating, drinking, engaging in trade or labor."[324] At times, the intensification of man's distress and worries though imagery techniques are for explicitly mystical purposes. Shapira makes a distinction between *hitragshut* (excitement) and *hitlahavut* (fervor, ecstasy),[325] in which the latter is characterized by ecstatic experience in which man experiences his own annihilation, "If you will grow until you will rise with passion (*belahav*) like coal of fire that have been enflamed (*she-nitlahavu*), then his entire self will be nullified, and this is ecstasy (*hitlahavut*)."[326] Shapira intensifies man's worries through imagery techniques in order to arouse ecstatic fervor:

> We shall search for advice and tricks how to arouse fervor (*hitlahavut*) of the heart... Behold, if we begin at first with an arousal of holiness, it is not in man's capability... We already have with what to begin and with what to knock on the openings of our hearts... For

322 Ibid.

323 Idem, *Derekh ha-Melekh*, 312.

324 Ibid., 470, Derash 1. This explains why after the silencing technique (*hashqaṭah*) (see below, chap. 5, "Silencing Techniques"), Shapira said that they should recite the verse, "Show me your way, O Lord" (Ps. 86:11), "After the silencing, which necessitates a kind of inspiration from on high, he is commanded to recite the verse, 'Show me your way, O Lord' (Ps. 86:11), in the special tune of the Rebbe." (ibid., 451). The recitation of this verse with Shapira's special melody, together with its utilization in Shapira's thought, brings man to fill his consciousness, which was emptied, with a divine consciousness.

325 See idem, *Hakhsharat ha-Avreikhim*, chap. 2

326 Ibid., 7a-b. Also, see Wacks, "Emotion and Enthusiasm," regarding the meaning of *hitlahavut* in Shapira's thought.

> example, every person, God forbid, has already been *worried* about himself or another individual, whose concerns are like his own. Whenever he remembers and intensely visualizes it in his imagination as if it is in front of his eyes, his heart is softened and he becomes emotional, even weeping. Visualize them in front of you as well, and when you begin to be stirred and heartbroken, think to yourself: "Why should I break my heart and cry for nothing? After all, God is before me and I stand now before His blessed throne of glory. I will weep before God, who hears the sound of tears."[327]

The visualization of concern arouses man's fervor, which is not just an emotional experience of excitement, but rather an intensified experience of excitement to the point of self-annihilation and disconnection from earthly aspirations, "When your feelings are burning so much, that in any case at this time the whole world and its aspirations are disgusting to you, and you have but one desire and one longing—God... then in accordance with our evaluation, it is already the beginning of fervor (*hitlahavut*)."[328] Furthermore, according to Shapira, the feeling of worry is itself a "revelation of holiness," meaning the immanent presence of the divine within man. Yet there is a tragic aspect to this revelation, due to the worrier not recognizing the sacred component within his worry whatsoever, in the sense of, "the miracle maker does not recognize his miracles," "Since for the most part he had a kind of worry about his lowly state, and does not think that *this worry is a kind of revelation of holiness*."[329] Shapira presents a conception of worry, or other similar emotions, as a kind of internal arousal of holiness, in the sense of an internal encounter with God. In contradistinction to Kierkegaard, Shapira is interested in using imagery techinques as a means of preserving and reproducing the sense of worry and unease as a dimension of encounter with holiness, namely, the internal experience of God's presence within man. The imagination has the capability of intensifying the feeling of naturally occurring worry, transforming it from an existential-emotional feeling into a sacred experience, a living experience of the divine.

Visualizing the Day of Death

The motif of worry appears numerous times in Shapira's thought, disproportionately so when contrasted to joy. Seemingly there are two reasons for this: first, Shapira believed that it was easier to utilize worriedness for holiness than joy-

---

327 Shapira, *Benei Maḥshavah Ṭovah*, 21–22.
328 See above n. 326.
329 Idem, *Derekh ha-Melekh*, 61a.

ousness;[330] second, Shapira argued that realistically people naturally worry more frequently, "For the most part, thoughts of worry are within the man";[331] "And generally it is natural that everything that is feared by him always comes to him in his thought."[332] Accordingly, when one wishes to intensify his feelings, he generally will first find his sense of worry. An intriguing mixture of intensified worry and self-visualization may be found in his writings about the day of death,[333] one of the lengthier and detailed exercises in his writings:

330 See idem, *Benei Maḥshavah Ṭovah*, 23 – 24, the lengeth at which he describes how to use this feeling of heartbrokenness and worry for the purpose of prayer and recitation of psalms, in contrast to joy, which he briefly discusses and only mentions offhand, and even notes that psalms should not be recited at length, "He should stand at an angle and say a few chapters of psalms (it is good to not [say] many psalms now [!]), such as chap. 18. Also, see a parallel to these remarks in idem, *Hakhsharat ha-Avreikhim*, 48a-b. It is of interest to compare Shapira with his contemporary Hillel Zeitlin, who also identified sadness with sacredness, see Zeitlin, *Al Gevul Shenei Olamot*, 38 – 39.

331 Shapira, *Derekh ha-Melekh*, 358.

332 Ibid., 449.

333 The visualization of the day of death can be found in de Vidas, *Re'shit Ḥokhmah*, Sha'ar ha-Teshuvah, chap. 5, "One who transgresses with one sin, acquires one prosecutor (*m. Avot* 4:11), and when he will visualize the ascent of his soul upwards as a few prosecutors are prosecuting it and are pushing it out, it is appropriate that he should weep and mourn and be embarrassed by his sins." Also, for a different treatment of this passage, and others from sixteenth century Safed, see Elliot R. Wolfson, "Weeping, Death, and Spiritual Ascent in Sixteenth-Century Jewish Mysticism," in *Death, Ecstasy, and Other Worldly Journeys*, eds. Daniel Collins and Michael Fishbane (Albany: State University of New York Press, 1995), 229. This visualization can be found as well in David Solomon Eibenschütz, *Sefer Arvei Naḥal ha-Shalem*, Parashat Ki Teṣe, 966, "He must visualize opposite his face and heart, and he shall imagine in his soul, as if he is already dead and his flesh is buried and his bones are scattered and buried." Also of interest is Avraham Elimelekh Shapira (a contemporary and relative of Shapira, his grand-nephew from his father's first marriage, as well as his brother-in-law through marriage, for Avraham Elimelekh was married to Shapira's wife's sister), *Mishnat Ḥakhamim* (Jerusalem: Shneur Zalman Grossman, 1934), 24:103, in which he connects the visualization of the day of death to the *Zohar*, "It is a fundamental principle (*kelal gadol*) to remember that which is written in the holy *Zohar*, [Parashat] va-Yeḥi, 'Righteous pious ones (*zaka'ei ḥasidei*) every day look (*mistaklei*) in their hearts [i.e. imagine] as if this day they will depart (*mistalqei*) from this world, and they do a complete repentance before their master [God].' And only in love and joy, without sadness, God forbid." Also see Shmuel Bornsztain, *Shem me-Shemu'el*, Parashat Ṣav (Parah), Year 5679. Nevertheless, the death-day visualizations in these works should not be compared to those of Shapira. His predecessors did not give practical examples, or only brief ones. The only comparable work, which has a very similar style to that of Shapira, both in length and content of the technique is R. Ḥayyim Berish b. R. Ya'aqov ha-Kohen, *Sefer Ṭov Me'od* (Jerusalem: Gushtzineni Press, 1889), 15a-16a. This book is mentioned in Shoshana Halevy, *The First Hebrew Books Printed in Jerusalem in the Second Half of the Nineteenth Century (1841 – 1890)* (Jerusalem: Ben-Zvi Institute, 1975), 226§662, however I have been unable to identify this author, although it appears that he was

> He shall visualize what happens to every person after the length of his days and years. How in his last moment he will look upon the entire world and his children, which he is forced to separate from them and go with his body under "dust, worms, and maggots" (*m. Avot* 3:1)... his children will surround him and they will weep for him and cry out, "Oy, father, father." His loved ones and his family will call for him, and he hears and understands everything, but it is impossible for him to help at all. He desires and pleads to live, but his heart is pressed to the point of bursting, and his throat shrinks to the point of chocking, and his soul is being forcefully torn from his throat and heart. And afterwards, when they [his children] accompany him to his eternal home, one slams his head into the wall and cries and weeps, "Father, father, how have you left us, forever torn from us," and this one lays herself down on the ground and with a bitter voice shrieks, yells, and howls, "It is impossible for me to live without you father, may I have died instead of you." Tears and shouts flow from her until it appears that, God forbid, her entire being will burst with lament and pain bursting from within her. Their voices terrify the living as well the dead. The masses, too, out of pity issue a bellowing cry for him and them. Tumultuous screaming and confusion appear all around.[334]

The goal of this exercise is to intensify the natural worry that each person bears concerning death.[335] In Shapira's opinion, the intensification of this concern brings one to spiritual arousal, "If it is impossible for you to stir from past worry, do as advised by the Talmud, 'Let him remind himself of the day of death' (*b. Berakhot* 5a)."[336] Freud denied the possibility of visualizing one's own day of death, claiming that, "whenever we attempt to do so we can perceive that we are in fact still present as spectators... in the unconscious every one of us is convinced of his own immortality."[337] Freud feared that the consciousness of

part of the "Hungarian Kollel" of Jerusalem. His book discusses the day of death and includes lengthy and complex imagery techniques with a similar dramatic style to Shapira's techniques. I doubt that there was any influence from one book on another, and it is more likely that at the end of the nineteenth and beginning of the twentieth century similar literary styles were developed in a parallel manner. Regarding this "universal" phenomenon, I will discuss in Section IV.

334 Shapira, *Benei Maḥshavah Ṭovah*, 22.

335 An impressive depiction of anxiety caused by death appears in Franz Rosenzweig, *The Star of Redemption*, trans. Barabra E. Galli (Madison: The University of Wisconsin Press, 2005), 9–10. In this framework we will not engage with the meaning of death, but rather only the imagery techniques associated with it. Concerning the meaning of death in Jewish mysticism in connection with western philosophy, in an original and extensive manner, see Wolfson, *Alef, Mem, Tau*, 156–174.

336 Shapira, *Benei Maḥshavah Ṭovah*, 22.

337 Sigmund Freud, "Thoughts for the Times on War and Death," in *The Standard Edition of the Complete Psychological Works of Sigmund Freud*, Vol 14. Translated and edited by James Strachey (London: Hogarth Press, 1955), 289. Also, see Avriel Bar-Levav, "Story, Ritual and Metaphor: Comprehending the Day of Death as a Spiritual Exercise and the Internal War in Jewish Ethical

death would cause passivity, depression, or despair. However, the very same fear can be an impetus for personal and spiritual development,[338] and even mystical development, as utilized by. The rememberance of the future overcomes the forgetfulness of the present. Sometimes the memory of death grants an intensity to life in the present and highlights the need for living an ethical life. The depiction of death in Ecclesiastes comes to rouse man to live a religious life, "So appreciate your vigor in the days of your youth... But man sets out for his eternal abode, with mourners all around in the street before the silver cord snaps and the golden bowl crashes, the jar is shattered at the spring, And the jug is smashed at the cistern. And the dust returns to the ground as it was, And the lifebreath returns to God Who bestowed it."[339] The purpose of this allegorical detailed depiction of death in these verses is to stir man and grant his life ethical meaning, and one should therefore remember the day of death even in one's youth. The sages in the Babylonian Talmud present the day of death as an internal ethical process endowing life with a higher value. This conception is presented in the context of interpretations offered regarding the verse, "So tremble, and sin no more; ponder it on your bed, and sigh, Selah."[340] Man must remember day of his death in order to control his inclinations. The awareness of death becomes a stimulus for personal and ethical development:

> R. Levi b. Hama says in the name of R. Simeon b. Lakish: A man should always incite the good impulse [in his soul] to fight against the evil impulse. For it is written: "So tremble, and sin no more." If he subdues it, well and good. If not, let him study the Torah. For it is written: "ponder it." If he subdues it, well and good. If not, let him recite the *Shema'*. For it is written: "on your bed." If he subdues it, well and good. If not, let him remind himself of the day of death. For it is written: "and sigh, Selah."[341]

In kabbalistic literature multiple techniques and different rituals were suggested to be performed near the time of death,[342] primarily consisting of different confessions and rituals simulating the four death penalties sentenced by Jewish

---

Literature," in *Peace and War in Jewish Culture*, ed. Avriel Bar-Levav (Jerusalem: Zalman Shazar Center, 2006), 152.

338 Ibid.

339 Ecclesiastes 12: 1, 5–7. Also, see Bar-Levav, "Story, Ritual and Metaphor," 149.

340 Psalms 4:5. Also, see Bar-Levav, "Story, Ritual and Metaphor," 150.

341 *b. Berakhot* 5a.

342 For example, see Avriel Bar-Levav, "Death in the Thought of the Kabbalist Rabbi Naftali Hakohen Katz" (master's thesis, Hebrew University, 1990), 114–120, 137–151. Concerning the spiritual and physical treatment of the sick and deceased through prayers and rituals, see idem, "The Concept of Death in *Sefer ha-Ḥayyim* (*The Book of Life*) by Rabbi Shimon Frankfurt" (PhD thesis, Hebrew University, 1997).

courts.[343] Less frequently, one finds death-day imagery techniques that are not executed near the time of death, or as part of the dying process. For example, see the suggestion of R. Shabtai Sheftel Horowitz of Prague (1590 – 1660), son of R. Isaiah Horowitz, and the spiritual disciple of Cordovero, concerning the visualization of one's day of death at least once a month:

> While being in a healthy stage—a man should choose a time to seclude himself (*she-yitboded*), and should confess this great confession, and he shall think in his consciousness (*she-yaḥshov be-da'ato*) that it is as if he is dying. And here I will teach you the ritual of confession (*seder ha-vidui*), which is practiced while he is in health when he remembers (*ke-she-yizkor*) the day of death... In any case, he should behave like this on each eve of the New Moon, which is a minor day of atonement (*yom kippur qatan*), and he should fast an entire day, as the law of the ninth of Av and with all of the stringencies [associated with that day], and he should thoroughly check (*va-yifashfesh be-me'od*) his deeds, and in any case he will cleave himself to the *Shekhinah* for one moment, and he will be closed off, his eyes downwards and his heart upwards, and he will remember the day of death.[344]

Here is the first formalized ritual visualizing the day of death, at least once every month, and it is quite plausible that, "he shall think in his consciousness (*she-yaḥshov be-da'ato*)" and "when he will remember (*ke-she-yizkor*)," are references to the act of imagining. In early hasidic literature one may find sources, derived from this kabbalistic literature. the development of rituals carried out with great frequency, such as every day during the recitation of the *shema* prayer.[345] It should be noted that Shapira's death-day visualization that I presented above,

---

343 For example, see the spiritual will of the kabbalist R. Yiṣḥaq Aiziq Ḥaver (1778 – 1853) in Seraya Deblitzki, *Beino Shenot Dor ve-Dor* (Bnei Brak: s.n., 2006), 54 – 58.

344 *Ṣava'at R. Shabtai Sheftel*, 43b, as quoted in Bar-Levav, "Death in the Thought of the Kabbalist Rabbi Naftali Hakohen Katz," 145.

345 For example, see Ḥayyim ben Solomon Tyrer of Czernowitz, *Sefer Be'ar Mayyim Ḥayyim ha-Shalem*, Parashat Lekh Lekha, chap. 12, "With the intention of the recitation of *shema*, when man cleaves his soul to his creator and accepts upon himself the four methods of judicial execution (*arba mitot beit din*) for the sanctification of his name, blessed be he [martyrdom], he will so deepen in his thought the image (*ṣiyur*) as if they are actually truly performing all four methods of judicial execution to him, in order that 'his mouth and heart will be equal' (*m. Terumot* 3:8)"; Avraham Weinberg, *Yesod ha-Avodah*, part 2, chap. 8, "The holy AR"I (Isaac Luria) wrote and later wise man as well, that when man reads the *shema*... he is commanded to accept [God's] oneness and the yoke of his kingship... and he shall visualize in his heart, as if they now want to put him to death... and he feels in his consciousness the magnitude of the pain of death, and even though he accepts it upon himself with love... and he who intends this with a complete heart and a true acceptance... he that sacrificed his soul *in posse*, is as if he sacrificed his soul *in esse*."

is a condensed version of his description in *Hakhsharat ha-Avreikhim*,[346] a multi-scenic detailed description that covers many pages.[347]

At the foundation of this type of imagery exercise is Shapira's interesting interpretation of the talmudic statement, "If not, let him remind himself of the day of death. For it is written: 'and sigh, Selah.'" Shapira identifies the act of remembering with that of visualizing, "If it is impossible for you to stir from past worry, do as advised by the Talmud, 'Let him remind himself of the day of death.' (*b. Berakhot* 5a) But, not merely as a general idea, as the Talmud states, 'The wicked know etc.,' and this is the disadvantage, that they only know, a general knowledge that does not break the heart into tiny pieces (*be-paroṭeroṭ*). He should *visualize* the matter."[348] This conception is supported by the distinction made between knowledge and thought, and its parallel, visualization, in Shapira's thought. According to Shapira, informational knowledge does not entail internal experience, and therefore cannot cause man to deter from sin. In contrast, thought bound to imagination brings about existential involvement and spiritual awakening, "I Know that I stand before God, knowledge that is without thought, and without thought it is impossible to be aroused";[349] "Only intense thought can aide action during worship and prayer, not analytical investigation."[350]

346 Shapira, *Hakhsharat ha-Avreikhim*, 38a-41a. The shorter version in idem, *Benei Maḥshavah Ṭovah*, is the original, whereas the variant found in *Hakhsharat ha-Avreikhim* is an expansion of this original version. On the dating of Shapira's books see Leshem, "Between Messianism and Prophecy," 5–7.

347 Similar to the imagery technique of the Exodus from Egypt. The visualization of the day of death constitutes the majority of the eighth chapter of *Hakhsharat ha-Avreikhim*. In the lengthier version, Shapira adds the sickly days prior to the final heart attack, and the soul-reckoning done in those days. Following, he cites from *Zohar* 3:126b-127a, which describes at length the meeting with the angel of death holding a sword, and after man fails at hiding from him, he delivers himself to death.

348 Idem, *Benei Maḥshavah Ṭovah*, 22

349 Idem, *Benei Maḥshavah Ṭovah*, 18. Also, see idem, *Ḥovat ha-Talmidim*, 28b. Interestingly, the term "knowledge" in Shapira's writings is opposed to "feeling", whereas "thought" goes hand in hand with "feeling". More on this opposition, see idem, *Benei Maḥshavah Ṭovah*, 10. "Only these will be able to bring closer and enter into the holy company—he who truly feels the aforementioned pain and sorrow within himself , concerning his distance from God, and not that he merely knows his lowly condition, for intellectual knowledge (*yedi'ah be-sekhel*), everyone knows." The opposition between thought and knowledge and the identification of thought with feeling, indicates the direct connection between thought and imagination.

350 Idem, *Ḥovat ha-Talmidim*, 63b. This distinction between knowledge and thought appears in numerous places and different variations in hasidic literature. It is of interest to contrast Shapira's understanding of *da'at* (knowledge) as external analytical knowledge and that of Shneur Zalman of Liadi, who conceives it as internal experiential knowledge. For Shneur Zalman *da'at* is connected to the *sefirah* of *da'at*, which mediates between the intellect (*sefirot* of *Ḥokh-*

This dichotomy obligated Shapira to identify the memory of the day of death with imaginative activity, in other words "the visualization of the day of death."[351] Only the imagination that arouses internal experience can affect man and become a significant technique for controlling the evil inclination.[352] In practice, Shapira wants man, through fear and worry, to experience a tremendous tension that will bring about a different state of being and create a consciousness of constant repentance, namely, the experience of return to and intimacy with God.[353] If it is difficult for man, "to think of himself and visualize each thing that is unpleasant to him,"[354] Shapira suggests that he imagine a tragedy that actually occurred to someone dear to him, so that the he might experience the heartbreak himself, "In any case, visualize someone close to you or beloved to you who died (*she-halakh le-olamo*). His appearance when he was with you, [when he] spoke and played with you... and his current appearance in the grave, blackened, torn flesh, bones revealed, etc. You are in your spacious

---

mah and *Binah*) and the emotions (*sefirot* of *Ḥesed* and *Gevurah*). See idem, *Tanya*, chap. 3, "*Da'at* is the substance of the *middot* [traits, specifically, love and fear] and their vitality." This act of binding and union that is in *da'at* is bound "in the feeling of the soul" (ibid., chap. 46). That is to say, in Shneur Zalman's thought *da'at* is an intense experience of the realness and presence of the object of contemplation, rather than discursive knowledge. See Yoram Jacobson, "The Rectification of the Heart: Studies in the Psychic Teachings of R. Shneur Zalman of Liadi." *Teudah* 10 (1996): 359–409.

351 The end of the verse *ve-domu selah* may be interpreted by the sages in two ways: 1. Silence (*dimamah*), meaning that remembering the day of death causes the evil inclination to be silenced; 2. Imagination (*dimyon*), meaning that man is meant to use his imagination against his evil inclination.

352 I must note that these terms are not entirely consistent in Shapira's writings and at times he switches between them, or uses others (for example, see idem, *Ḥovat ha-Talmidim*, 34b, "Nevertheless, he only knows in his thought, and his heart does not hurt him." In this example thought is being used in a discursive manner and not an emotional one. Also, see idem, *Benei Maḥshavah Ṭovah*, 49§4, "There are those who only render (*metargeim*) it in thought," in which thought once more is not being used as to mean emotion or personal experience). Nevertheless, this distinction holds for almost every instance. Ultimately, the tension between these two terms is repeated in Shapira's writings, in which he demands an experiential knowledge to be added to analytical knowledge. Regarding "thought" see above in this chapter's introduction.

353 For more on the visualization of the day of death, see idem, *Benei Maḥshavah Ṭovah*, 53. There Shapira uses this for one purpose, the total utilization of one's time for good deeds. Furthermore, contrast to Maimonides, *Mishneh Torah*, Laws of Repentance, chap. 3. Regarding this see Shimon Gershon Rosenberg, *Return, O My Soul: Divine Grace or Human Free Will* (Efrat: Yeshivat Siach Yitzhak), 70–72, also see Adiel Kadari, "Thought and Halakhah in Maimonides' Laws of Repentance" (PhD thesis, Ben Gurion University of the Negev, 2000), 97–101, 107–109, 112.

354 Shapira, *Hakhsharat ha-Avreikhim*, 41a.

home, sitting, standing, and speaking as you wish... And this loved one is in the constrained, dark, and wet ground."[355] The purpose of causing fear is only to bring man spiritual happiness, "How happy you would have been if only you were capable of subduing your desires as they begin to go mad and wild"[356] Through man's imaginative faculty he is able to create a fearful experience and thereby acquire happiness, "Why is this happiness really not in your hands?... rather everything is dependent upon the level of the extending of thought (*hitpashṭut ha-maḥshavah*) within you."[357] Concern and anxiety, which are significantly intensified through imagery techniques, establish a mental state of turning towards God, through a repentive consciousness or feeling of dependence. This connection can ensure man absolute self-control, thus allowing him worldly happiness. Man encountering the divine is not tempted by his desires, but is free.[358]

Spiritual and Theurgical Worry

Shapira was interested, beyond man's natural worry or anxiety concerning death, in intensifying spiritual worry. The anxiety and worry concerning sin and falling from spiritual heights, for Shapira, ensure an encounter with the divine. These actions parallel the sefirotic interactions of *Gevurah* and *Ḥesed*. *Gevurah she-be-ḥesed* (strength within grace) or *yir'ah she-be-ahavah* (fear within love) are not pure strength or fear, for they contain a component of grace-love,[359] namely, the anxiety (fear) about losing love. The constant worry of love lost, as well as the tension created in its wake, stirs man to take existential actions, such as developing techniques to safeguard and maintain this love. Shapira presents the anxiety of sinning as this type of concern, whose meaning, at its core, is the worry concerning separation and distance from God, "He worries and feels bitter in his heart, saying, 'O, I see that I am distant, God forbid, from

355 Ibid.
356 Ibid., 37b.
357 Ibid., 38a. *Hitpashṭut ha-maḥshavah* is imagination, see ibid., "Remember the day of death... please try to expand it... and extend it until you are entirely excited from it."
358 Regarding self-control as a mystical fundamental, see below chap. 6, subchapter, "*Raṣo va-Shov* (Running and Returning): Numerous Scenes and Their Successive Progression."
359 See Shneur Zalman of Liadi, *Tanya*, chap. 19, "This is called 'the fear contained in love.'" *Gevurah* and *Yir'ah* are common designations for the upper left *sefirah* of the lower seven *sefirot*. This *sefirah* is synonymous with the judgmental and harsh forces of the Godhead. When they are contained by *Ḥesed* and *ahavah*, respectively, their harshness is mitigated.

God,' and what will be my life's end in this [world] and the next. Will I, God forbid, remain cast away from the sacred and immersed in filth, God forbid, forever... between donkeys, jackals, and dogs.'"[360] It appears that Shapira is again hinting at his own feelings and aspirations![361] This is demonstrable from his personal prayer made on the occasion of his fortieth birthday, in which the zoharic motif, "between donkeys, jackals, and dogs," returns, expressing his distance from God. In this prayer, he supplicates, "Master of the world, observer and perceiver of all that is concealed, before you I will confess and before you I will plea, I am cast away and distant from you and from all of your palaces (*heikhalekha*) I am very distant, I simply want from now on to convert [!], and from now on be a Jew. Master of the world, save me, so that I will not waste the rest of my years between donkeys, jackals, and dogs, bring me closer to you and have me enter the internal palace (*heikhal le-fanim me-heikhal*), bind me to you forever and ever."[362] The engagement with fear and punishment, similar to the teachings of R. Israel Lipkin and the Novardok school of the Musar movement, is designed to stir religious emotion, which in Shapira's thought is intensified through imagery techniques:

> Furthermore, you are able to expand this holy thought, if you have been, God forbid, in distress or you saw your friend in distress, may God save us, *visualize* this past worry (*ha-da'agah shel az*), and how many [religious stringencies] you would accept upon yourself or your friend in order to get out of it. And why should you be unafraid now that God will not come upon you, God forbid, in such manners.[363]

> To the extent that man will constantly *visualize in his consciousness* the evil of sin and the fear of it, even fear of the punishment caused by sin, nevertheless the continuation of these fearful thought establishes within him fear and infuriation of sin itself... And all the more that he adds fear and anger for sin, even if in its beginning it is only from punishment, nevertheless, he will be distanced from evil through this, and come closer to God.[364]

---

360 Shapira, *Hakhsharat ha-Avreikhim*, 39b. Also, see idem, *Benei Maḥshavah Ṭovah*, 8–9.
361 Concerning worldviews stemming from personal-mystical experience and shared with the public, as found in Kook's and Ashlag's circles, see Garb, *The Chosen Will Become Herds*, 24–25, 28, 42. Shapira easily fits the description offered by Garb.
362 Shapira, *Ṣav ve-Ziruz*, 14§79. The locution "donkeys, jackals, and dogs" is borrowed from *Zohar* 3:107b; 3:207a. To the best of my knowledge, this locution is not utilized anywhere else in either kabbalistic or hasidic literature, except by Shapira. The employment of this locution in his personal prayer at the age of forty and at the same time in the description of the person worthy of joining the company in *Benei Maḥshavah Ṭovah*, demonstrate the effect of Shapira's personal feelings on his thought. This is an instructive example, one of many, of a mystic's personal experience and experimentation acting as a constructive factor in their overall thought.
363 Shapira, *Hakhsharat ha-Avreikhim*, 32b.
364 Idem, *Derekh ha-Melekh*, 99–100.

However, it does not appear that his intention is to concentrate on sin and fear alone, but rather to make God present in the individual's life through the fear of sin:

> In your imagination, which we will raise and sanctify, you will take a peek into the upper worlds, the world of formation (*olam ha-yeṣirah*) with its angels, the world of creation (*olam ha-beri'ah*) and its thrones, and until the world of emanation (*olam ha-aṣilut*) and its holy *sefirot*, souls of the patriarchs, prophets, tannaim, amoraim, kabbalists, hasidim, and all the righteous men, and everyone nullifies and are nullified to the great and holy God, exalted above all blessing and praise, who encompasses all worlds and surrounds all world, infinite and without end. They worship him and sing him song and praise his great name. And only I, the least of the least, the awful, and nothing, I dared, God forbid, to free myself of his commandments (*liferoq o'lo me-a'lai*) and rebel with my sins against him blessed be he, and how could I truly dare to be against him… how could I have such gall.[365]

This imagery exercise intensifies the experience of brokenness that accompanies sin, the feeling of embarrassment when facing God, and the feeling of embarrassment at having been so bold, "how could I have such gall." Shame serves as a motivating force for the yearning and longing of the soul to become nullified before "the great and holy God," and experience the divine presence of he "who encompasses all worlds and surrounds all world."[366]

These feelings of anxiety and worry appear in Shapira's writings as "supernal," and even theurgic, worries, that through man's failure the divine structure is blemished. As Shapira employed imagery technique for earthly worry, so too does he employ it for the intensification of theurgic-heavenly worry:

> Man should contemplate [a scenario] as if they have situated him before a mountain [volcano], in which in its belly are fire and sulfur, which are about to break forth and destroy many forests and villages, and even the king's courtyard is within this area, which when the fire will break forth will be destroyed [it as well]. And they placed this man in front of the mountain so that he might fix it so that the fire of hell will not burst forth, and he stands confused in front of the mountain, without knowing what he will do, since some miniscule (*daqah min ha-daqah*) incorrect action may, God forbid, destroy worlds, and if he has [the requisite knowledge] and does not utilize it, then also they will be destroyed, for surely the fire will burst forth. O how has this man's fear and trembling grown, his limbs will knock against each other, he will be covered in sweat, and horror will seize him, he will not remember anything concerning his self, neither his eating nor his drinking, for the fear nullifies his self. So the man stands and the will of God is in his hand to do and to fix it, and not specifically in deed, but even in thought, and even in the slightest thought (*be-maḥsha-*

---

365 Idem, *Hakhsharat ha-Avreikhim*, 67a.

366 See further Jonathan Garb, "Shame as an Existential Emotion in Modern Kabbalah," *Jewish Social Studies: History, Culture, Society* 21, no. 1 (2015): 89–122.

> *vah daqah min ha-daqah*), which he himself does not sense—everything needs to be aligned with God's will and if not, God forbid, he blemishes the divine will, God forbid.[367]

This imagery exercise of a volcanic eruption and the fearful experience that follows in its wake are meant to bring man to an ecstatic experience through a temporary erasure of his personhood, "for the fear nullifies his self"; "he will not remember anything concerning his self, neither his eating nor his drinking." In practice, this exercise serves as an instrument for experiencing the divine presence. The volcanic imagery intensifies the anxiety and fear of destroying and injuring the divine structure, a blemish that can wreak destruction upon the supernal worlds, "since some miniscule (*daqah min ha-daqah*) incorrect action may, God forbid, destroy worlds... everything needs to be aligned with God's will." It appears that Shapira is interested in the experience of tension between self-nullification and empowered individuality and autonomy. Man must sense the nullification of his worth due to his dependence upon God, together with a grave sense of personal autonomic responsibility for God's work. Through imagery techniques, Shapira intensifies this tension and brings man to new heights of experiential states.

The Imagination as an Intensifying Factor of Self-Sacrifice Experiences

For Shapira, Elimelekh Weisblum of Lizhensk sketched the path for the development of self-sacrificial (*mesirat ha-nefesh*) imagery. Weisblum began his *Tsetil Katan* (A Small Pamphlet) with the following two paragraphs:

> A. In every moment that he is free from Torah [study] and specifically when he is sitting idly by himself in his room or he is laying in his bed and he is unable to sleep he should reflect on this positive commandment of "That I may be sanctified in the midst of the Israel" (Lev. 22:32), and he shall imagine (*ve-yedameh*) in his soul and visualize (*ve-yeṣayair*) in his thought as if a great and terrible fire burns in front of him until the heart of heaven and he, for [the sake of] the holiness of the Name blessed be he [God], breaks his nature and lowers himself into the fire for the sanctification of the Name blessed be he [God]. And God attaches a good thought (*ve-maḥshavah ṭovah*) to the deed, and it is found that he is not lying or idly sitting, rather he is fulfilling a biblical positive commandment.
> B. In the first verse of the *shema* prayer, and in the first blessing of the eighteen benedictions, he should think about the aforementioned. Furthermore, he shall visualize (*ye-khaven*) as if the nations of the world [non-Jews] are torturing him with all the severe tortures, and they strip his skin from his flesh, [in order to have him] deny, God forbid, [God's] one-

367 Idem, *Derekh ha-Melekh*, 245.

> ness, and he suffers all the agonies and does not concede to them, God forbid. And he shall visualize in his consciousness and thought as if they are doing such to him, and with this he fulfills his obligation of reciting *shema* and *tefilah* (prayer) [eighteen benedictions] properly.[368]

This passage and its vivid depictions of self-sacrifice certainly served as sources of inspiration for Shapira in regard to imagery techniques in general and self-sacrifice imagery in particular.[369] This is demonstrated through the numerous repetitions of "jumping into the fire" imagery in Shapira's writings in different contexts, cited in Weisblum's name. Shapira repeatedly emphasizes that this is not merely a thought, but rather an imaginal vision made of clear and distinct images which affects man's entire being, from his cognitive abilities to his physiological reactions, "The thought of self-sacrifice (*mesirut nefesh*) in the recitation of *shema* will not be merely a thought, but rather actual imagination and vision. The pyre (*ha-moqed esh*) is in front of you, and you jump into it to sanctify his blessed name... A thought of actuality, which all of your body feels because of it, to the point that, at times, your body really shakes in actuality from the jump into the pyre that is in your thought."[370]

The goal of this technique is none other than mystical union;[371] martyrdomic self-sacrificial imagery is meant to stir a longing for union with the divine, "to transform into a limb of the king's limbs"; "When you come to the recitation

368 Elimelekh Weisblum of Lizhensk, *No'am Elimelekh* (Jerusalem: Yarid Hasfarim, 1995), opening pages. *Tsetil Katan* was printed numerous times and amended to many prayerbooks, specifically those of *nusaḥ sefarad* liturgy, which is widespread among hasidim. Also, see Avraham Elimelekh Shapira, *Mishnat Ḥakhamim*, 24§101, "[In the name of R. Aharon of Karlin] Blessed, our God, who created us (*barukh eloheinu she-bara'nu*) etc., the acronym is *b'sh* (*be-esh* in fire); and he shall visualize as if a fire is prepared etc., and even if he is, God forbid, immersed in desire, it does not impede him, since self-sacrifice is obligatory upon each Jew (*ish me-yisra'el*)."
369 Regarding self-sacrifice through the visualization of jumping into a fire in the thought of Dov Baer Schneersohn, see Garb, *Shamanic Trance*, 80–81.
370 Shapira, *Hakhsharat ha-Avreikhim*, 30a. Here the term "thought" should be understood in its discursive meaning. As I have noted previously, Shapira was not always consistent with his terminology, see above n. 352. In contrast, "a thought of actuality," is already a facet of imagination.
371 Concerning mystical union in Jewish mysticism, see Idel, *Kabbalah: New Perspectives*, 59–73; Shatz-Uffenheimer, *Hasidism as Mysticism*, 212–216; on *mesirat ha-nefesh* (self-sacrifice) and mystical union, see Rachel Elior, *The Paradoxical Ascent to God: The Kabbalistic Theosophy of Habad Hasidism*, trans. Jeffrey Green (Albany: State University of New York Press, 1993), 186–188, esp. the quotation of Shneur Zalman of Liadi, ibid., 186, "One should intend to prepare one's heart to fall into fire to sanctify the Name... and one should imagine that one must truly and actually sacrifice one's soul." Also, for the most recent an extensive treatment of mystical union in Jewish mysticism, see Afterman, *"And They Shall Be One Flesh"*.

of the *shema* and you shall visualize in your thought as if you came to a trial (*nisayon*), and you were forced to sacrifice your soul for God—you would sacrifice your soul; the constant desire stirs within you again… [to], as it were, transform into a limb of the king's limbs."[372]

The last chapter of *Hakhsharat ha-Avreikhim*, the climax of the book, Shapira dedicates to the topic of self-sacrifice. This topic, following Weisblum's teachings, reflects Shapira's attitude towards the imagination in general as a peak experience in the worship of God. The imaginal act, despite its abstract nature, is regarded in Shapira's thought as an actual deed in every sense, "It is brought by our saint the Beshṭ, blessed be the memory of the righteous and holy, that 'where a man thinks, there he is completely.' Therefore, when he visualizes with an intense thought (*be-maḥshavah ḥazaqah*), as if he really saw with his eyes, a fire in front of him and he is cast within it, then it will be considered as if he is doing this in actuality now as well."[373]

Self-sacrificial imagery techniques are equivalent to actual martyrdom, granting their practitioner a mystical experience, a prophetic experience in which man *sees* the divine immanence concealed within the world, "In any

372 Shapira, *Benei Maḥshavah Ṭovah*, 35.
373 Idem, *Hakhsharat ha-Avreikhim*, 68b. Also, see Naḥman of Bratslav, *Liqquṭei Moharan*, 2:193, "The thought is so strong, until it is possible to actually sacrifice his soul in his thought, meaning that he will feel the actual pain of death, by accepting upon himself in his consciousness that he wants to sacrifice his soul for the sanctification of the name, by whichever death it will be." Undoubtedly, the thought referenced here is one of imagination. I wish to suggest, parenthetically, that this conception is the source of the name of Shapira's mystical fraternity, *Benei Maḥshavah Ṭovah* (Men of Proper Thought), as well as the handbook of this fraternity (see idem, *Benei Maḥshavah Ṭovah*, 56), in which the meaning of this name is "sons of imagination" (*benei ha-dimyon*), meaning, masters of imagination. There are three classic rabbinic sources that use the locution "God considers *maḥshavah ṭovah* (good thought) to be as an actual action", or similar locutions (*t. Pe'ah*, ed. Lieberman, 1:4; *b. Qiddushin* 40a; *y. Pe'ah* 16b) as well as zoharic sources (*Zohar* 1:28b, 2:159a, 3:29b; *Zohar Hashmaṭot* 1:267a, 3:307a, *Zohar Ḥadash*, *Tiqqunim* 2:98a), seemingly, these sources act as sources of inspiration for Shapira's usage of this locution as referring to imagination. (See Shapira, *Derekh ha-Melekh*, 135, for this type of usage). According to his approach, imaginative action transforms the imaginal object from imaginary to real. Imaginative activity considers its object as actual, not in an ontological sense, but rather in a "value" sense—the visualization of self-sacrifice is of equal value to the actual act of self-sacrifice. In this conception, imagination is considered as action, Shapira interprets the rabbinic terminology of *maḥshavah ṭovah* as imagination, for this good thought (*maḥshavah ṭovah*) in rabbinic thought is equivalent to action, since "the holy one, blessed be he, links a good thought to an action" (*b. Qiddushin* 40a), similar to imagination. In other words, analogously to the rabbinic maxim, which understands a "good thought" as adding value to a deed, Shapira identifies this "good thought" with the imagination, and uses this rabbinic terminology for his creativity.

case you will merit a little towards self-sacrifice in the recitation of *shema*... and with this already you will ascend a little toward [being] a man of spirit (*le-ish ru'aḥ*), and then also a supernal vision will begin to spark within you, seeing a holiness of the 'majestic, beautiful, radiance of the world'[374] in all matters... And you will ultimately not remain a man of the field (*ish sadeh*), but rather be a son of the world to come, also while you are in this world."[375] This ascension, which comes to expression in the mystical ability of identifying divine immanence in the world, is connected to the plane of prophetic ability, developed through man's imaginative faculty, a topic that we will expand upon in the following chapter.

F Conclusion

The second chapter began with a description of two academic schools that fundamentally disagree regarding the understanding of mysticism: the essentialist and the constructivist approaches. I have argued that the notion of empowerment, or intensification, as developed in the research of Hollenback, can serve as a bridge between these two opposing camps. The prism of empowerment has allowed scholars, such as Moshe Idel, to reassess mystical techniques as intensifying methods transforming normative religious life into an encounter with God.

With this element in mind, I have offered a new perspective on Shapira's imagery techniques. I have demonstrated that Shapira employed imagery techniques as methods of intensification and empowerment. This included anomian practices like dance, song, and *hitbodedut*, as well as legal rituals like prayer, Torah study, Sabbath, and festivals. Through the addition of imagery techniques, Shapira intensified and transformed normative religious experiences into living encounters with God.

Shapira utilized the imagination to intensify basic feelings, such as worry and anxiety, as instruments for experiencing the divine presence and the constant seeking of it. The feeling of dependency, stemming from these intensified emotions, bring man to seek God and for stirrings of holiness. The intensification of these feelings through imagery techniques ensure that the yearning for a divine encounter will not fade away within the monochromatic nature of everyday

374 A citation from the poem "Yedid Nefesh", a popular kabbalistic poem, composed in sixteenth century Safed by Rabbi Elazar ben Moshe Azikri (1533–1600).
375 Shapira, *Benei Maḥshavah Ṭovah*, 59.

life. Through the development of these emotions, Shapira sought to combat the pitfalls of routine, the greatest enemy of mystical experience, as Heschel proclaimed, "Life is routine, and routine is resistance to the wonder";[376] "There is neither worship nor ritual without a sense of mystery... all worship and ritual are essentially attempts to remove our callousness to the mystery of our own existence and pursuits."[377] In Shapira's teachings, worry, as well as its intensification, constitutes an important element in mystical experience, to the extent that Shapira made it a precondition for those who wished to join his mystical fraternity, "We are aware that for our fraternity only worried men will be accepted."[378] Indeed, the concern of routine religious ritual can be seen in a wider spectrum and explained in terms that do not exclusively belong to the realm of mysticism, but rather to the entire internal religious life. However, since we have dealt with the concept of empowerment, a concept that defines mysticism and constitutes a phenomenon that bridges the various research schools in relation to the study of mysticism, I see no reason to refrain from examining Shapira's teachings with the research tools of mysticism. Shapira utilized imagery techniques in order to intensify all aspects of internal life, not only nomian and anomian rituals, but religious experiences and emotions as well, transforming them into mystical experience and living internal encounters with the divine.

Now we are prepared to answer our central question: in what way did Shapira use imagery techniques, and why were they so essential to his spiritual path? Regarding the former, I argue that Shapira employed imagery as a catalyst for empowerment. The practice of imagery exercises intensifies a variety of religious activities and transforms them into mystical experiences. Why? The use of imagery techniques originates in a deeply internal, even personal need for mystical spirituality that extends forth across history. In Judaism, this tendency has been embodied in a great many spiritual thinkers, including Shapira. His imagery techniques should be appreciated from a broad perspective. In addition to taking note of his historical, social, and political context, we must consider internal factors as well. I do not mean to negate the role of secularism as a factor in his

376 Heschel, *God in Search of Man*, 85.

377 Ibid., 62–63.

378 Shapira, *Benei Maḥshavah Ṭovah*, 9. Also, see idem, *Hakhsharat ha-Avreikhim*, 79a, "We are directing our words only towards the youth (*ha-baḥurim ve-el ha-avreikhim*), who are concerned about themselves and their worship." It is clear that this concern is the key to maintaining religious enthusiasm and fervor and therefore the intensification of worry is so important and foundational. According to Shapira, without worry there is no foundation for mysticism. Also, see idem, *Benei Maḥshavah Ṭovah*, 10.

development of imagery practices. However, I seek to nuance our understanding of his thought by recognizing the importance of the internal longing for contact with the divine. The academic preference for historicization, in terms of both direct continuity and reaction, leaves little room for phenomenological study. The attempt to explain the centrality of imagery techniques in Shapira's writings simply as a response to the rise of secularism in the later nineteenth and early twentieth centuries does not fully address the question at hand, and it prevents us from seeing the relationship between imagery techniques and the other practices which appear in his writings.[379] For Shapira, imagery is not simply one technique among many that function as alternatives to the experiences made possible by secularism, as has been claimed in studies based on historical readings of his works. Imagery techniques are, in addition, a powerful tool that intensifies all other practices. They are unique precisely because they may be combined with other techniques in order to strengthen and transform them into mystical experiences.

In this chapter I have analyzed Shapira's imagery techniques from a wide perspective. The historical, social, and political contexts, must be complimented by processes of internalization. For, while the phenomenon of secularization and the need to combat it were important incentives for the development of imagery techniques, it nevertheless seems that the internal consideration for the development of imagery techniques is the mystical need and human need for certain spiritual images, for contact with the divine, as it is written, "Yet I was always with You, You held my right hand... As for me, nearness to God is good" (Ps. 73:23, 28).

G Addendum—*Ṣaddiq* Imagery Techniques: "One Longing to Seek God's Face"

The *Ṣaddiq*'s Status in Shapira's Thought

The conception of the *ṣaddiq* has been extensively researched,[380] and I will not elaborate on this subject here.[381] Isaac Hershkowitz has made two claims regard-

---

379 See Daniel Reiser, "Historicism and/or Phenomenology in The Study of Jewish Mysticism: Imagery Techniques in the Teachings of Rabbi Kalonymus Kalman Shapira as a Case Study," *Modern Judaism* 36, no. 1 (2016): 1–16.

380 See the list of scholarship cited in Idel, *Hasidism*, 365 n. 1. A summary of these studies appears in Leshem, "Between Messianism and Prophecy," 118–128. Regarding the conception of the *ṣaddiq* as a shaman see Garb, *Shamanic Trance*, 75–76, 83; concerning the significance of the *ṣaddiq* and psychoanalysis, ibid., 91–93.

ing the status of the *ṣaddiq* in Shapira's thought: one radical and the other moderate. According to the former claim, there is no place for the *ṣaddiq* figure in Shapira's thought, "In his understanding, no actual room is given to the classic hasidic-mystical *ṣaddiq* figure."[382] Although the context of these remarks were in regards to suffering and the act of "mitigating decrees," nonetheless, it seems that Hershkowitz had decided this matter in accordance with this context and expresses his reservations about the perception of the *ṣaddiq* and his status in the entirety of Shapira's teachings. Furthermore, even if he did not intend to relate the *ṣaddiq* phenomenon as a whole in Shapira's writings, it is impossible to deny the status of the *ṣaddiq* in the matter of "mitigating decrees" (*hamtaqat hadinim*) in Shapira's thought.[383] His more moderate opinion does not negate the *ṣaddiq*, but it diminishes him, denying his mystical and magical abilities, and presents him as a pedagogue and guide only, as he explains, "Clearly, the classic hasidic *ṣaddiq* does not take his place in Shapira's hasidic thought. The *ṣaddiq*'s role that we have surveyed until now, is limited to imparting the awareness of constant divine proximity to every Jew and guiding towards the correct path to disclose this proximity and to live within its light. We did not find any *ṣaddiq*-mystical conduct in [his thought], and certainly he did not bear the burden of suffering on his own back."[384] In truth, from Shapira's writings, it is difficult to identify *ṣaddiq*-mystical activity. However, this does not demonstrate that he rejected this classic hasidic paradigm,[385]but rather merely points to the fact that he did not view himself in this light.[386]

---

381 Concerning the conception of the *ṣaddiq* in Shapira's thought see Leshem, "Between Messianism and Prophecy," 54, 118–128; Hershkowitz, "Rabbi Kalonymus Kalmish Shapira," 16, 43, 128; Wacks, *The Flame of the Holy Fire*, 74–76; idem, "Emotion and Enthusiasm," 87–88; Reiser, "To Fly Like Angels," 163–174.

382 Hershkowitz, "Rabbi Kalonymus Kalmish Shapira," 128.

383 See Resier, "To Fly Like Angels," 171–172.

384 Hershkowitz, "Rabbi Kalonymus Kalmish Shapira," 43, also, ibid., 16.

385 Nonetheless, Shapira does discuss the weakness of the *ṣaddiq*'s stature in his generation, see idem, *Mevo ha-She'arim*, 57a, "The holy efflux (*shefa*) of the rebbe and the company… it was in their [the *ṣaddiqim*] power to nullify [the hasid's] corporeal potency… the rebbe purified him with a holy efflux… it is not so now, since the rebbe is not like the rebbe R. Baer [seemingly, Dov Baer, the Maggid of Międzyrzecz], blessed be the memory of the righteous and holy for the world to come, and there is almost no company." Also, see the interesting argument of Wacks, *The Flame of the Holy Fire*, 74–76. Wacks argues that alongside the acceptance of the *ṣaddiq* doctrine, Shapira recognized the decline of the *ṣaddiq*'s stature in the twentieth century, and that Shapira's own writings are meant to be a partial substitute for this lacking (ibid., 74). Furthermore, Wacks argues that Shapira believed that due to the weakness of the *ṣaddiq*'s stature, man must be responsible for himself, more than in past generations, in which the *ṣaddiq*'s efflux

A perusal of the components of the hasidic-*ṣaddiq* paradigm, as have emerged from the relevant scholarship, and the examination of Shapira’s thought in light of these findings, demonstrates that a majority of these components are present in his thought and even serve as the foundation for his conception of hasidism and the *ṣaddiq*’s place therein.[387] The *ṣaddiq*, in Shapira’s thought, does not only constitute a personal role model to imitate or a spiritual guide—the *ṣaddiq* is clearly a mystical influence as well,[388] “Their attraction to their rabbi is not only for the sake of hearing in their ears the words that he speaks from his mouth to them alone, but rather for conjoining lights and cleaving now in actuality, the overflower with the receivers (*ha-mashpi’a im ha-meqablim*), like the kind of unifications that are in the *sefirot*... and with this they rectify themselves, the world, and also the supernal worlds.”[389] According to Shapira, the *ṣaddiq*-flock relationship has a theurgic significance. The mutual communion of souls between them, the master and his followers, and the followers and their master, rectifies supernal worlds. Furthermore, this mutual cleaving affects the drawing down of divine light from on high into this world, “[The has-

was more common. With that being said, Wacks brings Shapira’s remark, that “also now” the *ṣaddiq*’s efflux is active for those who journey to him (ibid., 81).

386 However, see Leshem, “Between Messianism and Prophecy,” 125–126, where he brings testimony that Shapira would receive *kvitlech* (note slips asking the rebbe for a blessing) as well as charms. Even if we do not accept this testimony, Shapira never invalidated such practices or *ṣaddiq*’s abilities. The opposite is just the case, see Shapira, *Mevo ha-She’arim*, 44b. Also, in the documentary *In the Warmth of the Holy Fire*, directed by Ze’ev Har’el (2008; Yad Binyamin, Israel: Torat ha-Ḥayyim), digital media, https://www.youtube.com/watch?v=i0a2Mh8UFkk, which won the category of short film and documentary at the 2008 Jerusalem Film Festival, Chaim Kenner (blessed be his memory), a student of Shapira, was interviewed and he described how Shapira was the only rebbe to write prescriptions that were honored by the pharmacy, this is a very similar description to that of a *ba’al shem*, master of the name, who as considered a kind of doctor of sorts, as well as a miracle worker. Also, see above n. 12, as well as Polen, *The Holy Fire*, 5, 160 n. 17, in which many testimonies have been collected regarding Shapira’s *ṣaddiq* behavior. Also, Ya’aqov Qorman (Shapira’s disciple), in discussion with the author, May 2010, where Qorman described Shapira’s *ṣaddiq*-like behavior, accepting *kvitlech*, hosting *tishes*, and signing prescriptions. These testimonies unanimously indicate a certain kind of *ṣaddiq* behavior. However, this does not attest to any mystical behavior, nonetheless, he does act as more than just a spiritual guide.

387 For more, see Reiser, “To Fly Like Angels,” 164–171. The components being the *ṣaddiq* as a vessel for the *Shekhinah*, a talismanic conception of the *ṣaddiq*, the *ṣaddiq* as a reflection of divinity, the soul’s root being common to both the *ṣaddiq* and his flock, the *ṣaddiq* as *axis mundi*, and the *ṣaddiq*’s responsibility for the spiritual and material needs of his congregation.

388 Also, see Leshem’s critique of Hershkowitz, Leshem, “Between Messianism and Prophecy,” 54.

389 Shapira, *Mevo ha-She’arim*, 39a.

idim] together with their rabbi... will be ignited and from everyone together a torch will be made that will even light and illuminate the entire world with God's light and supernal fire."[390]

Visualizing the Ṣaddiq

The face of the *ṣaddiq* as an object of visualization appears in kabbalistic, and primarily, hasidic literature.[391] Shapira sees it fit to emphasize that the visualization is of a clear figure and not a vague thought:

> It is brought in the holy book *Or ha-Ḥamah* (great-grandfather) of the Ḥida (R. Ḥayyim Yosef David Azulai), blessed be the memory of the righteous, on *Parashat Va-Yeshev* of the holy

390 Ibid., 37b.

391 Regarding the visualization of the *ṣaddiq*'s face, see Abraham Azulai, *Ḥesed le-Avraham*, Ma'ayan 2, Ein ha-Qore, Nahar 33, "This is what R. Abba in [*Zohar*] Parashat Mishpaṭim said when the form of R. Shimon [bar Yoḥai] was depicted in front of him and he would comprehend through this great comprehensions." Also, see Yehuda Liebes, "Zohar and Eros," *Alpayim* 9 (1994): 79–80; regarding group *ṣaddiq* visualization in the study house of R. Jechiel Michael, see Altshuler, *The Messianic Secret of Hasidism*, 70, "The righteous ones of the generation, whose likenesses he is familiar with and whom he then envisions in his thoughts." Also, see ibid., 75–77. Furthermore, see the "Ṣava'at Rebi Yeḥiel me-Aleksander," in *Ṣava'at ve-Hanhagot me-ha-Beshṭ ve-Talmidav* (Bnei Brak: Maḥshevet, 1987), 203, which recommends that one "visualize the form of his master." Also, Epstein, *Sefer Ma'or ve-Shemesh ha-Shalem*, 1:384, "About this I heard advice from *ṣaddiqim* (righteous people), that a man will visualize in his thought the form of the *ṣaddiq* who enabled him to do as he desires and through this he will always remember the wonders of the creator as mentioned above, in his remembrance of the good matter that influenced him." On the utilization of this technique in order to affect one's offspring during intercourse, see ibid., Liqquṭim, s.v. "ba-mesekhet", "For it known that it is a very great *segulah* (merit) to have good sons, during copulation he should visualize in his thought the form of *ṣaddiqim*." Also, see the holy letter of Weisblum's son (quoted in Zeitlin, *Be-Pardes ha-Ḥasidut ve-ha-Qabbalah*, 38 n. 11), in which there is a description of an imagery technique that has the *ṣaddiq* learning Talmud, "When [the *ṣaddiqim*] study Talmud they encloth themselves in fear and trembling, and great awe from God, blessed be he, and Torah illuminates their faces. When they reference a tanna's name... they visualize [him] in their intellect, as if the tanna is alive standing before them." On the visualization of Sabbatei Ṣevi's face in Nathan of Gaza's writings see Avraham Elqayam, "Eretz ha-Zevi: Portrayal of the Land of Israel in the Thought of Nathan of Gaza," in *The Land of Israel in Modern Jewish Thought*, ed. Aviezer Ravitsky (Jerusalem: Yad Ben-Zvi Institute, 1998), 175. Lastly, regarding Azulai's technique mentioned above, see Ada Rapaport-Albert, "God and the Zaddik as the Two Focal Points of Hasidic Worship," 321 n. 71; Miles Krassen, *Uniter of Heaven and Earth: Rabbi Meshullam Feibush Heller of Zbarazh and the Rise of Hasidism in Eastern Galicia* (Albany: State University of New York Press, 1998), 131–135, 261 n. 48.

> *Zohar*, folio 192a, in the name of R. Moses Cordovero, blessed be the memory of the righteous. And this is his holy language, "He shall study the wisdom that he learned from his teacher, *and visualize his form*, and cleave his soul to [his] soul, etc. As R. Abba explained in *Parashat Mishpaṭim*, that when he thought and imagined the form of R. Shimon [bar Yoḥai] the *halakhah* would become illuminated for him, and this is the topic of cleaving soul in soul..." see there.[392] Through thought, *and specifically with imagination, and specifically when in form* [!] he will merit to cleave in holiness to the visualized and through it holiness, as well as Torah and comprehension from on high, will be drawn down to him.[393]

Note well: according to Shapira, the mere figural visualization of the *ṣaddiq*, "specifically when in form," is able to create a magical effect of drawing down supernal comprehensions. This figural image is not presented as temporary or as a compromise.[394] In addition to the figural visualization of the *ṣaddiq*, more advanced imagery techniques appear in Shapira's writings. As I mentioned, visual techniques of static imagery appear in early hasidic literature; in contrast, Shapira's imagery techniques incorporate elaborate plots and multiple scenes.[395] This development parallels the philosophical development regarding the conceptualization of the imagination, progressing from a mirror model, mimetic imagination, to a lamp model, creative imagination, producing entirely new items. Similarly, Shapira is not satisfied with the static imagery of the *ṣaddiq*'s face, but rather expands this imagery to weave an entire multi-scenic plot, and suggests the visualization of the *ṣaddiq*'s lifestyle and behaviors, "the path of a *ṣaddiq*":

> The advice is, go out, on the tracks of the sheep (Song. 1:8), if it is difficult for you to walk on an unforged path, follow the path which was already paved, and you shall take in your thought *the path of the ṣaddiq*. For example, the Rebbe R. Elimelekh, blessed be the memory of the righteous and holy... the truth is that I do not have any comprehension of any of Rebbe Elimelekh's greatness or holiness, but nevertheless, according to my comprehension... *I visualize in my consciousness* a kind of holiness and this path... in his path I want to walk... and not specifically one *ṣaddiq*, rather you can visualize in your consciousness, according to your comprehension, this path of the Rebbe R. Elimelekh or this path of the Maggid (Yisrael Hopstein) of Kozhnitz (Kozienice), blessed be the memory of the righteous, seeing the entire chariot (*merkavah*) and supernal holiness in this world as well, and to worship God with joy and fervor (*ve-be-hitlahavut*) from the holiness that is in front of

---

392 The rest of the passage is Shapira's remarks.
393 Shapira, *Hakhsharat ha-Avreikhim*, 16b.
394 On this tension in Shapira's thought see below, chap. 5.
395 See above, "R. Kalonymous Kalman Shapira's Imagery Techniques and His Imaginal-Literary Style."

> you, and prepare the path to worship God with awe, joy, and fervor from the holiness before you (*asher le-einekha*).[396]

Not every person can become a *ṣaddiq*, a magical-mystical figure, nor may every person even comprehend the essence of a *ṣaddiq*, "the truth is that I do not have any comprehension of any of Rebbe Elimelekh's greatness or holiness." Nonetheless, Shapira believed that man can visualize the *ṣaddiq*'s lifestyle and strive towards the manifestation of this visualization in order to acquire the joy, fervor, and holiness for himself.

Shapira further expanded the technique of *ṣaddiq* visualization by offering advice for a person who attempts to make the divine present in his life again and again, but fails, a person who attempts to awaken mystical fervor, "desire and longing," but to no avail. Surprisingly, Shapira advises this person to think of themselves as a *ṣaddiq*. This combination of self-visualization and *ṣaddiq* visualization is presented by Shapira as the ultimate guarantee for a person attaining passion to the point of "*yearning of the soul* (*klot ha-nefesh*)":

> If you have already tried everything, and have been unsuccessful. If you have already stirred yourself by all means, but your soul has not been stirred... to actually desire the desires and longings that need to be desired; you should therefore do this: *visualize yourself as a ṣaddiq*, and see in your imagination the size of your soul in its root and its glory at the hour that God comes, escorted with his angels, to delight and travel with it [your soul] in God's garden in Eden.[397] Invest and persist with this thought and imagination in front of your eyes, and then it is impossible that greater caution will not be aroused within you, so that the preciousness of its glory not be spoiled when she is in the arms of the king of the universe, *and the desire* to achieve this, *to the point of "yearning of the soul"* (*klot ha-nefesh*), *will be stirred within you.*[398]

---

396 Shapira, *Derekh ha-Melekh*, 255–256.

397 On self-visualization in the Garden of Eden, see Dov Baer of Międzyrzecz, *Liqquṭei Amarim*, 262, "When man studies or prays he should think of himself as if he is in the Garden of Eden, where there is no jealousy, desire, or pride"; Levi Yiṣḥaq of Berditchev, *Qedushat Levi*, Remezei Shir ha-Shirim, "In the moment of Torah and prayer he will raise in his consciousness that he is in the Garden of Eden and all of the patriarchs and holy souls that are in the Garden of Eden are listening to his voice and are delighting in it."

398 Shapira, *Ṣav ve-Ziruz*, 16§24. There is an opposite technique in which the *ṣaddiq* visualizes his hasidim, "Sometimes when [the *ṣaddiq*] wants to give advice... to people in different states, then people of his hasidim will rise in his imagination with their different circumstance and they awaken his consciousness to find a cure and remedy for their situations, and a fire [inspiration] rises in his being, which derives [pieces of] advice and paths for them, and he writes them [the advice] in a book" (idem, *Mevo ha-She'arim*,29b).

Ṣaddiq visualization techniques intensify man's experience, transforming it into an extreme mystical experience of "*desire to the point of klot ha-nefesh.*" In the imaginal encounter with the *ṣaddiq*, there is to some extent an encounter with God, the mystic's desire. The encounter with the *ṣaddiq* is depicted numerous times in Shapira's writings as a divine encounter.[399] The *ṣaddiq* reflects God's presence in the world, "I will travel to my Rebbe, there at the Temple Mount the evil inclination does not have such dominion... the walking path [of the hasid] was an immediate path of repentance, for where he walks is to witness (*laḥzot*) God's grace and visit his sanctuary. If so, it is to God that he returns... for the most part on the path he met other hasidim... and the convoy went... with one heart and one desire to seek the face of God."[400]

399 Regarding this idea, see Rapoport-Albert, "God and the Zaddik," 296–325.
400 Ibid., 39b-40a. In a dramatic-literary fashion, Shapira describes the encounter with the *ṣaddiq* as an encounter with God, through parallel idioms between the *ṣaddiq* and God. Shapira generally tends to intensify the *ṣaddiq* figure and grant it empowerment abilities, similar to Hollenback's discussion of externalizing. Meaning, according to Shapira, the *ṣaddiq*, similar to the prophet, is able to change reality through his thought, see Shapira, *Mevo ha-She'arim*, 5a, 36b-37a. Furthermore, the *ṣaddiq* is able to influence the hearts of his hasidim without saying anything, ibid., 42a, "The light and holiness with which the rebbe directly affects their hearts, without speaking and without words." This is an example of the *ṣaddiq*'s external influence, towards his hasidim, an influence which according to Hollenback characterizes mysticism.

Chapter Five
Imagination as a Prophetic Factor: The Yearning for Prophecy in the Twentieth Century

> Hellenistic culture... viewed Jews as devoid of creative imagination. This accusation is based on Judaism's disinclination towards making statues and images, on the rationality of the study hall, and the deficient Jewish artistic creativity in the plastics arts... Hasidism, in principle, accepted this description of Judaism, but did not see it as an ideal state, but rather as a product of the deterioration of the Jewish people. According to it, the state in which the intellect is transformed into the central, and almost only, means by which to cling to the holy one, blessed is he, is not an ideal state. It involves the nullification of prophecy, which in general is the nullification of the imagination.[1]

A Preface

Eliezer Schweid has examined one of the more surprising phenomena of the late nineteenth century and first half of the twentieth century—the renewal of prophecy:

> At the end of the nineteenth century and in the first half of the twentieth century, a new surprising phenomenon stood out in the modern denominations of the Jewish nation: the rise of spiritual leadership possessing a renewal-missionary awareness, which adopted the biblical prophetic figure of Moses and the later prophets... as a model. This phenomenon characterized a large, one may even say the more influential and distinguished, part of Jewish literature in Yiddish and German of that era, and specifically in the fields of philosophy and poetry.[2]

Schweid analyzed and demonstrated the phenomenon of the renewal of prophecy as a national and societal mission through figures from the beginning of the twentieth century such as A. D. Gordon, A. I. Kook, Martin Buber, Leo Baeck, A. J. Heschel and others—who lived with prophetic consciousness and spoke in its name. They spoke in the name of God, based on the unmediated revelation of his will and commandments for the individual and especially for the nation, and from the certain knowledge that a historic event of global proportions embedded within a spiritual cataclysm would soon occur. Schweid identified this phenomenon with catastrophic historic events such as the crisis of humanism

1 Rosenberg, *We Walk in Fervor*, 128. This statement is based on Zadok's thought.
2 Schweid, *Prophets for their People and Humanity*, 9.

https://doi.org/10.1515/9783110535884-008

in the first half of the twentieth century, the threat of destruction emenating from Germany, and the pan-European rise of antisemitism. These manifestations necessitated a new thinking about the future of mankind and the Jewish people, its place, culture, and purpose.[3] Likewise, momentous historical events, like the return of the Jewish people to its ancestral homeland and the founding of the Zionist movement (linked directly to the previous phenomena), intensified the intuitive sense of a number of prophet-thinkers that the Jewish people were on the threshold of a new era and that the murmurings of redemption might be heard.[4]

Scholars of the Bible and mysticism have generally presented two parallel competing models for the characterization of biblical prophecy: the ecstatic model and the emissarial model. Prophecy in the ecstatic model is typified as a subjective experience in which the person experiences the effacement of his corporeality and internally senses the divine presence and potency. In contradistinction, prophecy in the emissarial model is characterized as belonging to the public domain, in which the prophet serves as God's messenger in order to reproach the public and improve its moral character.[5] Schweid described the phenomenon of the modern prophetic awakening in a similar fashion to the biblical emissarial model in which prophecy is conceived of as a calling striving for a concrete redemption upon the stage of the Jewish people's national history. Yet the arrival of the phenomenon of prophecy at its zenith precisely in the twen-

---

3 Ibid., 9–11.

4 A clear connection can be located between the revival of the Zionist movement and the revival of prophetic consciousness in the thought of *Ha-Nazir* (R. David Kohen, 1887–1972), a student of Kook. See his words in *Mishnat ha-Nazir* (Jerusalem: Nezer David, 2005), 71: "But prophecy shall surely come, the renewal has begun, the return to Zion has begun, and God has returned his captured people." Also see ibid., 42–43, as well as his book *Qol ha-Nevu'ah* (Jerusalem: Nezer David, 2002), 5, §7; 318. See the words of a different student of Kook, R. Jacob Moses ben Zebulun Ḥarlap, who identified the twentieth century as the era of "the footsteps of the Messiah" and said that "in the footsteps of the Messiah a powerful demand for the disclosure of prophecy is awakened" (*Mei Marom: On Maimonides' Eight Chapters* (Jerusalem: Bet Zevul, 1982), VI:208).

5 On different models of prophecy and bibliographic material for research on this subject see above chap. 3 and see Daniel Reiser, "'To Rend the Entire Veil': Prophecy in the Teachings of Rabbi Kalonymous Kalman Shapira of Piazecna and its Renewal in the Twentieth Century," *Modern Judaism: A Journal of Jewish Ideas and Experience* 34, no. 3 (2014): 334–352. This differentiation starts with Friedrich Heiler's distinction between "Mystical" and "Prophetic" prayer and continues with the works of Yehezkel Kaufmann, Henry Wheeler-Robinson, Binyamin Uffenheimer, Abraham Joshua Heschel, Haviva Pedaya and more. For a survey of the different scholarly approaches to biblical prophecy, see Ron Margolin, *Inner Religion: The Phenomenology of Inner Religious Life and its Manifestation in Jewish Sources (from the Bible to the Hasidic texts)* (Ramat Gan: Bar-Ilan University Press, 2011), 154–160.

tieth century is not fully accounted for. Even Schweid does not purport to explain this phenomenon in its entirety, and, despite his excellent historical explanations, more remains hidden than revealed. For the time being, the appearance of prophecy in the twentieth century remains an enigma without a comprehensive solution.

One, however must still ask: is this model of prophecy in the twentieth century entirely unique?? The answer is—no. Alongside the revival of emissarial prophetic consciousness, there also arose a renewed striving for ecstatic prophecy in the twentieth century. This awakening, whose scope is no less than that of the other phenomenon discussed until now, has not been properly accounted for. This lack of clarity does not exempt us from attempting a description of this resurgence, nor from suggesting different hypotheses for this renaissance, even if we are unable to reach a complete summarization.

Ecstatic prophecy, as opposed to emissarial prophecy, makes extensive use of the imagination as a central and key instrument, whether in the process of developing skills for acquiring prophecy, or prophesizing itself. It may be stated that this component lies at the difference between the two types of prophecy. While in emissarial prophecy the individual obviously has a vision as well, which may be viewed as imagination, this is not imagination in the concentrated sense of seeing a picture, a full script with figures, and a plot, but rather a general picture not requiring clear visualization. Aditionally, the vision in emissarial prophecy is not a technique intended to be used by the individual in a particular fashion, like an instrument. On the other hand, in ecstatic prophecy the imagination plays a central role as a guided tool which serves as a medium in the prophetic process itself, and is not merely a target placed before the prophet.

B Prophetic Imagination in the Teachings of R. Zadok ha-Kohen of Lublin and R. Abraham Isaac ha-Kohen Kook

According to the sages, prophetic inspiration ceased at the dawn of the second temple era.[6] At that same time, the men of the Great Assembly abolished the de-

6 *b. Sanhedrin* 11a. See at length Ephraim E. Urbach, *The World of the Sages: Collected Studies* (Jerusalem: Magnes press, 2002), 9–49. For an overview of studies devoted to the cessation of prophecy see Nehemia Polen, "The Spirit Among the Sages: *Seder Olam*, the End of Prophecy, and Sagely Illumination," in *"It's Better to Hear the Rebuke of the Wise than the Song of Fools" (Qoh 7:5): Proceedings of the Midrash Section, Society of Biblical Literature*, vol. 6, eds. W. David Nelson and Rivka Ulmer (Piscataway, N.J.: Gorgias Press, 2015), 83–85. For more see below n. 13.

sire for idolatry.[7] The author of *Sefer Ḥasidim* links these two phenomena, and in his opinion, the temporal proximity of these events is not incidental, "And there is no holy spirit in the world [in order] to be prophets in the second temple period, for during the [time of the] second temple, the desire for idolatry was destroyed."[8] R. Elijah b. Solomon Zalman, the Vilna Gaon (1720–1797), saw a clear connection between the cessation of prophecy and the destruction of the evil inclination, "since they killed the evil inclination, prophecy was nullified."[9] A number of reasons have been suggested for the simultaneous decline of prophecy and obliteration of idolatrous desire from the midst of the Jewish people,[10] and it seems that the most profound reason is that offered in the hasidic teachings of R. Zadok ha-Kohen Rabinowitz of Lublin (1823–1900), \a member of Izbica-Radzhin hasidic group who came to lead the group later in his life. His works were widely read by various hasidic groups in the twentieth century.[11] Zadok argued that the end of prophecy did not occur spontaneously; rather, it was a product of a crisis and mental transformation which necessitated its disappearance. The rise of rationality displaced prophecy and in its stead there arose the study of the Oral Torah, characterized by intellectuality and rationality:

> According to Zadok Ha-Kohen of Lublin, the rise of the intellect, the emphasizing of the intellectual facet, and the transformation of Torah study into a central force in Judaism, instead of prophecy, are products of crisis and decline. The rise of the intellect is inherent in the disappearance of idolatry, which brings about the cessation of prophecy, as well. According to *Ḥaza"l*'s famous words, the men of the Great Assembly nullified the desire for idolatry… However, the disappearance of this desire, says Zadok, occurs at the same time in which prophecy ceases and the Oral Torah ascends. Furthermore, the rise of Oral Torah occurs alongside the ascent of Greek philosophy and rationality in the wider world.[12]

Religious worship in biblical times was expressed both temporally and spatially. The temporal dimension was manifested by the prophet who foresaw the future. The spatial dimension was exhibited by the priests who served God in his place

---

7 *b. Sanhedrin* 64a; *b. Yoma* 69a.

8 Judah ben Samuel he-Ḥasid, *Sefer Ḥasidim*, eds. Judah Wistinetzki and Jacob Freimann (Berlin: H. Itzkowski, 1891), §544, from the Hebrew section of Bezalel Naor, *Lights of Prophecy* (New York: Union of Orthodox Jewish Congregations of America, 1990), 2. Naor collected many sources which engage in this dialectical process.

9 Ibid. Elijah ben Solomon Zalman, *Seder Olam im Perush ha-GR"A* (Warsaw: Israel Alapin Press, 1876), chap. 30.

10 See Urbach, above.

11 Concerning Zadok's influence on the *musar* movement in general and this topic specifically see Elijah Eliezer Dessler, *Mikhtav me-Eliyahu*, vol. 3 (Jerusalem: Sifriyati, 1992), 277–278.

12 Rosenberg, *We Walk in Fervor*, 252–253.

—the temple in Jerusalem. The Bible contains no paradigm of a study hall or religious worship via in-depth interpretation of texts. In contrast, in the post-biblical era, and especially after the destruction of the second temple, a third model of religious worship developed, centered not around the prophet nor priest, but the sage. The development of the Oral Torah intensified in the first millennium of the Common Era, and the study of it was transformed into the primary component of religious worship. Zadok notes that this mental shift did not only occur in the Jewish sphere, but rather was an axial shift across the Western world. The rise of Greek philosophy and intellectuality in the world demystified the religious landscape of magic and sorcery, together with prophecy. Not only did prophets disappear, but Egyptian sorcerers and magicians as well, as rationality and reason henceforth became the primary instruments for the development of Western culture.

According to Zadok magic, sorcery, ecstasy, and prophecy disappeared together, for they are all structured upon the same element—the *imagination*. In contrast, rationality is based on causality and systematic logic:

> In the Greek [period] the principle of in-depth study (*pilpul*) of the Oral Torah was spread by Shimon the Pious, who was a remnant of the Great Assembly. Alexander of Macedonia lived in his time, and Greek wisdom emerged as well, for in Babylon there were still prophets. So too in Egypt, there existed at the time of the revelation of the Written Torah a symmetrical opposition (*le-umat zeh*), namely, the husk of Egyptian wisdom, which was primarily sorcery and the like; these are not directed by the intellect [and], but are rather from the potencies of impurity. And so in Babylon when there were still later prophets among the men of the Great Assembly, there existed in symmetrical opposition to them (*le-umat zeh*) magicians, exorcists, and dream interpreters, who [act] not according to the intellect but the potencies of impurity. But later, when the Oral Torah began to spread forth from the intellect of the sages which graced them, the intellectual Greek wisdom emerged in symmetrical opposition (*le-umat zeh*).[13]

Elsewhere we read:

> Just as the Torah directs Israel, so too does God direct all the worlds; even the nations are directed according to the principle of symmetrical opposition (*zeh le-umat zeh*). All increas-

---

13 Zadok ha-Kohen Rabinowitz, *Peri Ṣaddiq, Devarim*, 12; idem, *Peri Ṣaddiq le-Ḥanukah*, 1. See Polen, "The Spirit Among the Sages," 85–94 where, from a passage in *Seder Olam* which discusses Alexander of Macedonia, he demonstrates in an original, fascinating, and compelling manner, in contrast to all other studies, that according to *Seder Olam* prophecy is continuous, and that there is no clear line of demarcation between the period of prophecy and rationality. According to Polen, the rabbinic sages of the tannaitic period did not only decide matters with the use of logic, but also with the use of divine inspiration. Either way, ultimately, Polen admits that this change did occur, however at a later period.

> es of idolatry, as well as of magicians and sorcerers, took place when there was a revelation of the divine Presence (*gilui shekhinah*) and prophecy in Israel. Once it (i.e. prophecy) departed, the Oral Torah emerged and for them, Greek wisdom—that is, human wisdom—began. For the era of the men of the Great Assembly began at the dawn of the Greek empire, which was the end of prophecy.[14]

The ascension of Greek wisdom, contemporaneous with the rise of the Oral Torah and the concurrent abstention of prophecy, was not an arbitrary process. The principles of rationality, whether they are of Greek wisdom or Jewish Oral Torah, are diametrically opposed to the principles of prophecy and the relation between them is symmetrical (*zeh le-umat zeh*). The rise of one presupposes the descent of the other and vice versa.[15] One of the foundations of prophecy is vision, "to optically see visions of God." The rise of rationality necessitates the disappearance of this vision:

> In accordance with man's virtue and perfection, so does he have an equal symmetric deficiency. From the days of Adam's sin, everything is symmetrically mixed with good and evil, for God made them be in confusion... and since the desire of idolatry was dominant, so the light of prophecy was revealed *to see visions of God with the eye, from this the evil inclination was drawn to make other gods that are visible to the eye.* And therefore, [the sages] stated in [*b.*] *Yoma* [69b] that when the men of the Great Assembly nullified [the evil inclination], they said, "We want neither him, nor reward through him"—the meaning of reward is the perfection drawn from it, for prophecy left Israel from the time that the desire for idolatry was uprooted. When there is no deficiency, there is no perfection to recognize the presence of God through visual truth, but only through concealment.[16]

The foundation of idolatry and prophecy are the same—vision. The desire for prophecy, which is the yearning for a vision of the divine, flows from the same desire and yearning "to make other gods visible to the eye." When the desire for idolatry was nullified the element of vision disappeared and prophecy was no longer accessible.

This "vision" is understood by R. Abraham Isaac ha-Kohen Kook (1865–1935) as the imaginative faculty. Kook did not directly engage with Zadok's re-

---

14 Zadok ha-Kohen Rabinowitz, *Resisei Lailah*, 56.

15 For more on the symmetrical evaluation of history in Zadok's teachings see Yaakov Elman, "The History of Gentile Wisdom According to Zadok Hakohen of Lublin," *Journal of Jewish Thought and Philosophy* 3, no. 1 (1993): 153–187; Alan Brill, *Thinking God: The Mysticism of Rabbi Zadok of Lublin* (New York: Yeshiva University Press, 2002), 348–349. [My translation of *zeh le-umat zeh* as the "symmetrical principle" follows Elman.]

16 Ibid., 13. Also see idem, *Divrei Sofrim*, 38.

marks. However, Kook did know of Zadok and referenced his works.[17] Yeshayahu Hadari discussed Kook's relation to Zadok and the philosophical proximity of these two thinkers, primarily regarding their view of Israel's holiness, and especially their analysis of traditional sources through a historiosophic lens.[18] Similar to Zadok, Kook identified the decline of prophecy, and the imaginal elements within it, as a necessary dialectical reaction for the ascent of rational, scientific, and objective thought, which deny the place of the subjective imagination. Likewise, he identified the foundation of prophecy and the foundation of idolatry with the same faculty—the imagination.[19] However, Kook also heralded the opposite progression. He identified in his era the return of the imaginative faculty, and announced the consequent possibility of a prophetic revival:

> The imaginative faculty had to be somewhat repressed and eclipsed by the influx of the spirit of the higher knowledge (*ha-da'at elyon*)... Nevertheless, the basic foundation of the imagination remained in Israel; its inner ingredient is truly the source of all beauty and is revealed through prophetic vision, in which the light of holiness is garbed: *By means of the prophets I have spoken in images...* until the imagination was disempowered in Israel. The drive for idolatry was captured in a "lead pot"' and "slaughtered." By the same token, *there is no more any prophet...* Until at the End of Days, the traces of power of imagination are revealed and the love of the Land is aroused. The thing appears with its dregs, but it is destined to be purified. *The smallest will become a thousand, and the youngest, a powerful nation, I am the Lord, in its time I will hasten it.*[20]

---

17 See, for example, Abraham Isaac ha-Kohen Kook, *Olat Re'iyah* (Jerusalem, Mosad Harav Kook, 1996) 2:494, Kook references Zadok's work *Resisei Lailah.*

18 Yeshayahu Hadari, "*Sheni Kohanim Gedolim,*" in *Me'at latzadik: Anthology on Rabbi Tzadok Hacohen*, ed. Gershon Kitsis (Jerusalem: Bayit, 2000), 77–95.

19 See Abraham Isaac ha-Kohen Kook, *Orot ha-Emunah* (Jerusalem: Mossad Harav Kook, 1945), 60, "In the world of secular knowledge, until the advent of Aristotle, inner vision dominated external rationality... Israelite prophecy was still vital... The inclination for idolatry derived sustenance therefrom; while on the side of holiness, inner greatness of soul and sublime faith coupled with the substance of life prevailed. The cessation of prophetic inspiration in Israel, established in the secular sphere the superiority of rationality... Subsequent Greek Philosophy was unable to encompass the realm of the spirit." Translation from Naor, *Lights of Prophecy*, 27–28. Also see idem, *Ma'amarei ha-Ra'ayah: Qoveṣ Ma'amarim* (Jerusalem: Mossad Harav Kook, 1984), 492, in which Kook identifies the evil inclination with the natural desire for belief, concerning this motif see Mordechai Pachter, "The Kabbalistic Foundation of the Faith-Heresy Issue in Rav Kook's," *Da'at* 47 (2001): 69–100. Lastly, see Abraham Isaac ha-Kohen Kook, *Orot ha-Qodesh*, vol. 1 (Jerusalem: Mossad Harav Kook, 1994), 262, regarding the use of the imagination as a preparation for divine inspiration.

20 Idem, *Orot* (Jerusalem: Mossad Harav Kook, 1985), 35–36. Translation from Rabbi Abraham Isaac Hakohen Kook, *Orot*, trans. Bezalel Naor (Spring Valley, NY: Orot; New Milford, CT: Maggid Books, 2014), 205–207.

The "end of days,"—in which the imaginative faculty will be revealed in a refined manner without the evils of idolatry, and prophecy will be able to manifest in utter purity—are preceded by the return of the imaginative faculty in an imperfect and unrefined manner. Kook identified this period with the twentieth century. This century is characterized in his writings as one of revolution, in which the imagination overtakes rationalism. From Zadok's symmetrical principle of *zeh le-umat zeh*, Kook identified this process, even with the antithesis phase in it, as a process heralding the revival of prophecy. According to Kook, twentieth century culture was characterized by imaginal spirit, specifically in art, poetry, and drama.[21] With the ascent and flourishing of these disciplines, analytical philosophy lost its standing. Men of imagination influenced society, whereas the voices of analytic and rational thinkers went unheard. The loss of rationality and rise of the imaginative faculty had disastrous consequences specifically in the field of morality:

> All of contemporary culture is built on the foundation of the imaginative faculty. This is the pagan legacy of the civilized nations caught up in the imaginative faculty, from which developed physical beauty, both in action and in representation. The imaginative faculty progresses, and with it, the applied and empirical sciences, and in proportion to the ascendance of the imaginative faculty and its hold upon life, the light of intellect recedes, because the entire world supposes that all happiness depends on the development of the imaginative faculty. So things continue gradually, until the remains of reason in the spirit of secular wisdom are also converted to the imaginative faculty. The speakers and raconteurs, the dramaturges and all engaged in *les beaux arts*, assume prominence in society, while philosophy hobbles and totters because pure reason disappears. As much as reason recedes, so "impudence increases, and the wisdom of sages rots, the sin-fearing are reviled and truth is absent, and the face of the generation is as the face of a dog." That inner gentleness, which comes from the spirit of wisdom, disappears. The longing for spirituality and transcendence, for divine communion, for the higher world, for the clarity of ethics in the apex of its purity, for the concepts of intellect in and of their eternal selves, becomes a rare spectacle. This global phenomenon is reflected proportionately in Israel *vis-à-vis* divine inspiration and love of Torah with an inner spirit and essential freshness of faithful Judaism. There rules in the world a material spirit. *Woe unto you, O land, when your king is a lad and your princes eat in the morning!*[22]

---

21 On the zeitgeist surrounding Kook and his reaction to it see Yehudah Mirsky, *Rav Kook: Mystic in a Time of Revolution* (New Haven and London: Yale University Press, 2014), especially, 92–120.

22 Ibid., 34–35. Translation from Kook, *Orot*, trans. Naor, 203. Cf. Joseph B. Soloveitchik, *Halakhic Man*, trans. Lawrence Kaplan (Philadelphia: The Jewish Publication Society, 1983), 139–143 n. 4, where he identifies the tragedy of the Holocaust with the loss of rationality and the rise of Romantic philosophy in the years preceding the Holocaust, "First, the entire Romantic aspiration to escape from the domain of knowledge, the rebellion against the authority of objec-

Indeed, Kook in his unique way identified here as well a process, which even with its negative aspects, would produce positive and necessary results. The return of the imaginative faculty heralds the return of prophecy. The departure of the imaginative faculty from the nation was an expression of the *Shekhinah*'s departure, and the reinstitution of the imaginative faculty allows for the renewed manifestation of the holy spirit. The imaginative faculty prepares the heart to receive God's spirit:

> But all of this is a far-reaching plan, the Lord's plan to perfect the imaginative faculty, for imagination is the healthy basis for the supernal spirit that will descend on it. As a result of the ascendancy of the spiritual perception that came early in Israel, the imaginative faculty was forced to collapse, weakening the position of the supreme divine spirit destined to come through King Messiah. Therefore, now the imaginative faculty is being firmly established. When it is completely finished, the seat will be ready and perfect for the supernal spirit of the Lord, fit to receive the light of the divine spirit, which is the spirit of the Lord, *a spirit of wisdom and understanding, a spirit of counsel and strength, a spirit of knowledge and awe of the Lord.*[23]

The understanding of the imaginative faculty as constituting the foundation of prophecy has precedence,[24] yet the presentation of it as able to be presently actualized and achieved was silenced for years, as we will see below. This is perhaps the reason for the flourishing of prophetic techniques in the twentieth century: conceptions of prophecy which view it as presently attainable are liable to lead to practical activity for the purpose of its achievement. In the thirteenth century, there was a practical, and not theoretical, engagement with the imaginative faculty and prophecy within Abulafia's thought, and indeed, the central topics of his works are the mystical techniques through which one may attain prophecy. Abulafia was primarily interested in the experiential-practical aspect of prophecy and less in the theoretical-essential aspect.[25] While he inherited the prophetic

tive, scientific cognition... and from the midst of which there arose in various forms the sanctification of vitality and intuition, the veneration of instinct, the desire for power, the glorification of the emotional-affective life and the flowing, surging stream of subjectivity... have brought complete chaos and human depravity to the world. And let the events of the present era be proof! The individual who fress himself from the rational principle and who casts off the yoke of objective thought will in the end turn destructive and lay waste the entire created order." Ibid., 141 n. 4.

23 Kook, *Orot*, 34–35. Translation from Kook, *Orot*, trans. Naor, 203–205.

24 The conception of the imagination as a central potency in prophetic inspiration appears in the thought of Judah Halevi and is further developed in Maimonides's thought. See above, chap. 1.

25 Moshe Idel, "Definitions of Prophecy—Maimonides and Abulafia," *Da'at* 64–66 (2009): 1–2.

ideal from Maimonides, the mechanism by which to achieve it were quite different.[26] At the end of the nineteenth and course of the twentieth century, one may find once more after years of relative silence, an expediated engagement with and development of techniques for the attainment of ecstatic prophecy.

One example of a personality who utilized techniques in order to acquire divine inspiration at the end of the nineteenth century is Mordekhai Ze'ev Feierberg (1874–1899), a young author, lover of Zion (*ḥovev ṣi'on*), and a maskil, who published a number of short stories in the journals *Ha-Sefirah* and *Ha-Shilo'aḥ* with the encouragement of its editor, Ahad Ha-Am.[27] Feierberg studied in a *bet midrash* of Chernobyl hasidim and was exposed there to Haskalah literature! Nevertheless, "in contrast to most of the maskilim of that time, Mordekhai Ze'ev did not exit the *bet midrash* with fury onto the old world, but rather the opposite: he paid tribute to the generations of Jews who were pious (*yir'im*) and faithful, and his heart broke within him at the sight of the ruins of the old *bet midrash*."[28] Until his death (prematurely at the age of twenty-five) of tuberculosis, Feierberg refined his primary literary creation, his novel *Le'an?* (Whither?), which was published shortly after his death in the leading Hebrew-language literary journal *Ha-Shilo'aḥ*.[29] Feierberg, in this composition, depicts the experimentations of a youth named Naḥman, a self-referential figure, with divine inspiration. These experimentations included different techniques, such as immersing in a ritual bath, reading the Book of Psalms, reciting *kavvanot* while the cantor extends the tune "Where is His Glory" during the High Holidays, and lastly, through the imagination.[30] Imagery techniques serve him primarily as instruments for the development of personal-religious fervor. The imagination, in his writings, appears in the simple model of recreating a past critical historical events, alongside the principle of "The place of which a man thinks—there his spirit lies": "Thousands of images pass before his eyes, his spirit roams in each of these wondrous places, in which there were these great heroes."[31] Naḥman visualizes,

26 Ibid. On techniques for the acquisition of prophecy see ibid., n. 2.

27 See Hamutal Bar-Yosef, "Feierberg, Mordekhai Ze'ev," *YIVO Encyclopedia of Jews in Eastern Europe*, http://www.yivoencyclopedia.org/article.aspx/Feierberg_Mordekhai_Zeev (accessed November 1, 2017). Concerning this author and the parallels to Shapira regarding the development of self-awareness, the imaginative faculty, and the emotions in order to achieve prophetic ability see Don Seeman, "Ritual Efficacy, Hassidic Mysticism and Useless Suffering," 475.

28 From the introduction to Mordekhai Ze'ev Feierberg, *Le'an* (Tel Aviv: Kneset, [n.d]).

29 See about this journal Avner Holtzman, "Shiloaḥ, Ha", *The YIVO Encyclopedia of Jews in Eastern Europe*, http://www.yivoencyclopedia.org/article.aspx/Shiloah_Ha- (accessed November 1, 2017).

30 See Reiser, "To Fly like Angels," 185–186.

31 Feierberg, *Le'an*, 30.

in the form of stationary images, classic figures from Jewish history who forfeited "their world" for the sake of heaven:

> He now envies "soldiers," heroes, who, "forgot everything and forfeited everything," for the sanctification of the heavenly name and the salvation of Israel, and cautionary images pass before him in a vision, images of lofty soldiers: an image of R. Aqiva, whose flesh they combed with combs of iron, and R. Yosi, whose flesh they made like a sieve on account of his ordaining five sages, the slain of Betar, R. Judah Halevi, Abarbanel, Menasseh Ben Israel, Ar"i [Isaac Luria], Besht̩ [Israel Baal Shem Tov], the author of *Or ha-Ḥayyim* [Ḥayyim ben Moshe ibn Attar], the Rabbi of Berdychiv [Levi Yitzchok of Berditchev], the Maggid of Mezhirichi [Dov Ber of Mezeritch]... And more heroes that were in Israel in each generation and generation, who truly forfeited everything and forgot everything.[32]

This forfeiture "of everything" to the point of self-sacrifice (*mesirat ha-nefesh*), as in the tragic story of R. Aqiva, is nothing other than the annihilation of one's personality for the purpose of following God's command, a clear feature of ecstasy. Feierberg constitutes one example of yearning for divine inspiration and the utilization of the imaginative faculty,[33] not for an emissarial-prophetic conception, rather for human self-perfection and mystical ecstasy.

R. Kalonymous Kalman Shapira, the Piaseczno Rebbe, was definitely acquainted with Zadok's books, which were widespread in Warsaw in the twenties and thirties, and he also knew Kook.[34] On this subject, Shapira refers neither to Kook or Zadok. However, he did not disregard the resurfacing of the imagination in the twentieth century and the attempts to develop prophetic ability. Moreover, he instigated an organized prophetic teaching and far-reaching techniques, which utilized the imagination in order to prepare and advance the prophetic ability in man.[35]

32 Ibid., 47.

33 See ibid., 42, the use of the imagination during the study of Torah, "He stands leaning on his lecturn and supports, with both hands, his head immersed in Gemara. Many colors, dots, and dark images run and fly in front of him; the letters rise within the Gemara and dance in front of his eyes in an image of a thousand reddish dots."

34 See Reiser, *Sermons from the Years of Rage*, 1:19.

35 Regarding the nature of prophecy in Shapira's thought and his desire to make it manifest in the twentieth century see above, chap. 4; idem, "To Rend the Entire Veil." However, here we will discuss the connection between imagination and prophecy in his teachings.

C Imagination and Prophecy in R. Kalonymous Kalman Shapira's Thought

Nefesh Geluyah (A Revealed Soul)

In order to understand the connection between the imagination and prophecy in Shapira's thought, we must first discuss the concept he termed *gilui ha-nefesh* (revelation of the soul) or *nefesh geluyah* (a revealed soul). This concept served as a foundational notion in his practical-prophetic thought—in which the imagination plays a central role—appearing multiple times in his writings. Ostensibly, it is an original idea and I have not found precedents in kabbalistic or hasidic literature. That being said, it is reasonable to assume that it is a borrowed term from kabbalistic literature, albeit with an altered meaning.[36] Although this combination of words is similar to the locution *hitgalut ha-nefesh* (revelation of the soul), this term itself is sparingly mentioned in hasidic literature.[37] *Gilui ha-nefesh* is, to a certain extent, an experience of the divine presence, "When you will adapt yourself to the hasidic ways, *your souls* will be aroused *and will be revealed*, the sparks of the Garden of Eden within you will shine, *you*

36 In Ḥayyim Vital, *Sefer Sha'arei Qedushah ha-Shalem* (Tel Aviv: Amnon Gross, 2005), 3:7, there are five levels of holy spirit. The lowest level is the dream, "he will see in his dreams matters of the future," the second level is a revelation of Elijah, the third level is the revelation of a *magid*, the fourth level is the revelation of the souls of righteous men, "when some soul of a righteous man will reveal itself to him," and the highest level is the revelation of his own soul (*gilui nafsho*), "When he will draw down onto his soul a supernal light from the root of his supernal soul, as aforementioned in the fifth gate [of this book] and it will reveal itself (*ve-titgaleh*) unto him, and that is complete holy spirit." Vital does not use the exact locution of *gilui nefesh*, and it is unclear why the revelation relates to a supernal light or the soul. At the opening of the fourth gate of *Sha'arei Qedushah*, he repeats the five levels of the holy spirit from the highest to the lowest, and the highest is referred to solely as "the divine spirit," without any reference to the soul, "Five types of acquisition are the divine spirit, souls of the righteous, angels called *maggidim*, Elijah, may he be remembered for good, and a dream." Even if Vital's intention is in fact Shapira's conception of *gilui ha-nefesh*, it does not appear as the highest level of the holy spirit. It therefore appears that Vital is most likely a source of inspiration for Shapira's locution, especially since Shapira quotes from *Sha'arei Qedushah*, 3:7, "And behold we heard with our ears and saw with our eyes special individuals who acquired the level of the holy spirit in our times," in *Mevo ha-She'arim*, 38a. Nonetheless, the concept of *nefesh geluyah* is Shapira's original conception and its meaning is different than that of Vital's. Also see Ron Wacks, *The Flame of the Holy Fire*, 100–102.

37 It appears once in Naḥman of Bratslav, *Liqquṭei MoHaRaN*, II:98. Natan of Nemirov uses this term twice in *Liqquṭei Halakhot*, "*Halakhot birkhat ha-perot*," 3 and "*Halakhot erev*," 3. Furthermore, this term appears one time in Yehudah Leib Alter of Ger, *Sefat Emet*, *Liqquṭim le-berit milah*. However, Shapira does not mention these works in his writings.

will feel the Jewish holiness that is in the Torah, and *you will enjoy* the splendor of its presence."[38] However, in its most basic sense *gilui ha-nefesh* is any feeling of emotion, even non-religious, "All excitement from mundane matters opens a spark of one's soul, in any case *the soul is revealed* a little... physical excitement also opens and reveals our souls a little";[39] "In all types of feeling even of commerce and other physical matters whether they be of a broken heart or joy, there is an aspect of *gilui ha-nefesh* (soul disclosure)."[40] Feeling, in and of itself, is a disclosure of the soul no matter the relation to the content of the feeling itself; from this vantage point, feeling itself is neutral. Indeed, according to Shapira, it is upon man to utilize this opportunity of neutral soul disclosure and transform it into holiness.[41] This action, according to Shapira, is carried out through the imagination:

> Since physical feeling also opens and *reveals a bit of our souls*, we already possess what we need to begin, to knock upon the doors of our hearts, calling it to come out from the iron gates in which it is imprisoned, [saying] "Let me in, my own, My darling" (Song. 5:2)—come forth and serve God... For example, every person, God forbid, has been worried about himself or another individual, whose concerns are like his own. Whenever he remembers and intensely visualizes it in his imagination as if it is in front of his eyes, his heart is softened and he becomes emotional, even weeping. Visualize them in front of you as well, and when you begin to be stirred and heartbroken, think to yourself: "Why should I break my heart and cry for nothing? After all, God is before me and I stand now before His blessed seat of glory. I will weep before God, Who hears the sound of tears"... and you will see how effective prayer will elevate you.[42]

The soul is revealed because of the tangible feeling of concern, and the imagination uses this opportunity as a means to uplift this concern for the purposes of prayer. In a deeper sense, Shapira reasons that the emotions of the soul are not neutral. They are at their core sacred, and sin only constitutes a husk which leads these emotions down corrupt paths. The soul itself sees a holy vision, "For your soul is truly itself—it sees a holy vision,"[43] but when there is something dividing it from the sacred, it is upon man to remove this matter, "and only the body stops [it], and since you control the body, your soul may exit and see."[44]

38 Kalonymous Kalman Shapira, *Hovat ha-Talmidim*, 38b-39a.
39 Idem, *Benei Maḥshavah Ṭovah*, 21.
40 Ibid., 23. Paralleling this principle that in all emotion there is an aspect of soul disclosure see idem, *Hakhsharat ha-Avreikhim*, 48a.
41 See ibid., 47a; idem, *Hovat ha-Talmidim*, 26a.
42 Idem, *Benei Maḥshavah Ṭovah*, 21–22.
43 Ibid., 34.
44 Ibid.

This conception distinguishes between the soul's essence and its psychic state, a foundational conception in hasidism. The soul is engrained with holiness, whereas its actual condition may change with man's actions, which, if sinful, create husks around his soul.[45] The meaning of *gilui ha-nefesh* is the peeling away of the husks surrounding the soul and disclosing it anew, "a part of your soul was garbed in a polluted garment of evil excitement and you stripped it, and in this you gained this part of your *soul, disclosed* without the evil garment remaining."[46] That is to say, at its most basic level *gilui ha-nefesh* is the uplifting of feelings and their being channeled towards sanctity; at a deeper level, *gilui ha-nefesh* is a reversion to man's natural state of holiness. It should be noted that this experience of holiness, in Shapira's thought, is none other than an experience of prophecy, an emanated vision and a glimpse of the divine dimension hidden within the world, "And when we shall merit... *to disclose* a little of *our soul*... at times we will see both the essence and the emanator. Afterwards, due to our human knowledge, we will not be able to intellectualize what we have seen and what flashed before our eyes... but in our souls we will know and we will be sure that we glimpsed the illumination of the master of the world in the splendor of the world!"[47]

Gilui ha-Nefesh (Revelation of the Soul) and Prophecy

The revelation of the soul in Shapira's thought has two purposes. The first is that of the intensification and empowerment of religious-emotional experiences, transforming them into mystical experiences.[48] The second is preparation for prophecy, a preparation for theophany, "Behold, the beginning of revelation

---

45 See for example Shneur Zalman of Liadi, *Liqquṭei Amarim: Tanya*, part I, chap. 2, that the essence of the soul is, "really a part of god above," also see ibid., chap. 29. Lastly see Shapira, *Hakhsharat ha-Avreikhim*, 2b.

46 Ibid., 52b.

47 Ibid., 58a. While *gilui ha-nefesh* may be a new term, it seems that it is based on Shneur Zalman of Liady's notion of *neshamah* and *qelippah*—a sense that there is a pure essential self that needs to emerge from the qelippot surrounding it. This world-picture is developed especially in Shneur Zalman's book Tanya, see Ariel Evan Mayse, "The Sacred Writ of Hasidism: Tanya and the Spiritual Vision of Rabbi Shneur Zalman of Liady," in *Books of the People: Revisiting Classic Works of Jewish Thought*, ed. Stuart W. Halpern (New York: Straus Center and Yeshiva University Press, 2017), 109–156.

48 See Daniel Reiser, "Historicism and/or Phenomenology in the Study of Jewish Mysticism: Contemplative Meditation in the Teachings of R. Kalonymous Kalman Shapira as a Case Study," *Modern Judaism: A Journal of Jewish Ideas and Experience* 36, no. 1 (2016): 1–16.

within God's holy people was their Israelite soul, which is a portion of God that is above, which is in their inner being—which was revealed to them, and then in their revealed soul they were prepared to be made into a vehicle (*merkavah*) for a great and sublime revelation, which they merited in their holiness."[49]

The conception of divine immanence in hasidism maintains that divinity dwells within man's soul such that, consequently, the soul is "a portion of God from on high."[50] If so, divine revelation does not have to be supernal or transcendent, but rather may come from within man, in the immanent aspect of "from my flesh I shall see God" (Job 19:26). The soul in and of itself is "a part of God," however it is hidden and concealed. The disclosure of the soul is thereby a disclosure of the divine within man. By shedding his husks man is able to uncover his soul from its concealment and stir it from its slumber. According to Shapira, this disclosure is a "vehicle of revelation," (*merkavah le-hitgalut*) a locution which creates an association with the classic locution "a vehicle for the *Shekhinah*," and implies, in other words, a means for prophecy. The issue is that *gilui ha-nefesh* also has the meaning of psychic emotion or feeling, without any connection to prophecy—so how does Shapira vehemently attach a distinctly prophetic aspect to the term? He answers this question by stating that each dimension of "soul disclosure" is a specific level of revelation, of a process leading to God, "And in the introduction to *Sha'arei Qedushah* of R. Ḥayyim Vital it is [written] 'when his soul is very refined it will disclose itself to man and will lead him in all his ways,' until here his holy words. Meaning, a righteous person who did not merit more than *the revelation of his soul*, neither prophecy nor the divine spirit, *this is also a gradation* [of prophecy] and it also leads him in the way of God."[51] A *ba'al nefesh* (master of the soul) is one who has revealed his soul and uncovered the divine within him from its concealment and *qelippot* (husks). This act of disclosure is a central action on the path to acquire divine inspiration and angelification:

> *Ba'al nefesh—ḥasid* (a master of the soul—a pious person), meaning that his soul is not hidden and concealed so much in his body, but is rather in the aspect of *ḥesed* (grace), *ḥad arikh* (referring to the large influx from the right column of *sefirot: Ḥokhmah, Ḥesed*, and *Neṣaḥ*; lit., one long), until his soul is disclosed within him, and for that he is called a *ba'al nefesh*, and his revealed soul yearns for God until he himself does not desire sin,

---

49 Shapira, *Hakhsharat ha-Avreikhim*, 2b.
50 See Yoram Jacobson, *The Hasidic Thought* (Tel Aviv: Ministry of Defense Press, 1986), 9–19. Also see above n. 45.
51 Shapira, *Hakhsharat ha-Avreikhim*, 3a.

> but only [the performance of] commandments and to do more variegated good deeds… until he comes to divine spirit… until he is made into an angel of the Lord of Hosts.[52]

We have seen that the disclosure of the soul itself is a level of divine revelation, for the soul itself "sees a holy vision" and is in its nature a "portion of God above." The disclosure of the soul is a function of shedding the husks which surround it it; at the moment that they are separated, the soul's essence is exposed and ascends. The practical means for this revelation in Shapira's thought is through the use of imagery, "The one who strengthens his thought and imagination (*maḥshavto ve-dimyono*) for holiness and worship, then all his worship in general, from the beginning of each level to the end of each level in it, is different… he is more able to feel the emotions of his soul, he is more able to become more excited, [thereby] *revealing his soul*."[53]

A comparison thereby emerges between the imagination as a means for the disclosure of the soul, and the disclosure of the soul as a means for prophetic inspiration. In any case, the imaginative faculty is a central component of prophetic inspiration. Indeed, this conception has precedent and is quite developed in Maimonides's theory of prophecy,[54] but Shapira adds a practical facet to it in his essentially practical, and not theoretical, interest.

Prophecy and Imagination

Prophecy in Shapira's thought is closer to that of the ecstatic model rather than the emissarial model. Despite the subjective character of the ecstatic model and its individualistic emphasis, Shapira saw fit to spread prophecy among everyone and thought that all Jews were fit for prophetic inspiration.[55] As a consequence of this conception, preparatory techniques were created for the acquisition of prophecy, "And we must train ourselves as to allow this holy spirit, which is in the aspect of *disciples of the prophets* (*benei ha-nevi'im*), to enter and serve

52 Idem, *Mevo ha-She'arim*, 36b.
53 Idem, *Hakhsharat ha-Avreikhim*, 29a-b. It should be noted that "intense thought" (*maḥshavah ḥazaqah*) in Shapira's thought is actually a facet of imagination. See above, chap. 4, subchapters, "R. Kalonymous Kalman Shapira's Books," and "Maḥshavah (Thought), Imagination, and Visualization in R. Kalonymous Kalman Shapira's Teaching."
54 See above n. 24.
55 Concerning Shapira's original and complex model of prophecy, and his attempt to disseminate it see Reiser, "To Rend the Entire Veil." And see above, chap. 3, the last three subchapters.

our beings."[56] Similar to Maimonides's theory of prophecy, which connects the imaginative faculty and prophetic capability, Shapira declares, "We wish to merit revealing the spark of vision of the *disciples of the prophets* in our being, and for this purpose we must discover and extract an intense thought (*maḥshavah ḥazaqah*) and holy imagination."[57] In other words, prophetic preparation is accomplished through imaginal development.[58]

Joseph Weiss claimed that a pneumatic group associated with early hasidism renounced prophetic activities, since prophecy was understood as characterizing Sabbateanism.[59] This is in contradistinction to Gershom Scholem, who maintained that there were prophetic elements in early hasidism.[60] Moshe Idel has suggested, in contrast to both of them, that the term "prophecy" may not refer to one explicit concept, but rather to a number of concepts and meanings, and he demonstrated that the Beshṭ intertwined different elements into his conception of prophecy.[61]

The attacks against leveled against the hasidism, which claimed that the Beshṭ viewed himself as a prophet, may have led them to minimize their discus-

56 Shapira, *Ḥovat ha-Talmidim*, 67b.

57 Idem, *Hakhsharat ha-Avreikhim*, 30a.

58 Shapira's resembles Abulafia in his primary engagement of developing prophetic techniques, who was also primarily interested in the practical-experimental side of prophecy. Regarding Abulafia's practical aspect of prophecy and the role of the imaginative faculty in this process see Moshe Idel, "Definitions of Prophecy," 19. Another similarity between Shapira and Abulafia is regarding prophecy occurring outside the land of Israel. Judah Halevi stated, according to his interpretation of classic rabbinic texts, e.g. *b. Mo'ed Qatan*, 25a, that prophecy can only occur within the borders of the land of Israel, Judah Halevi, *Sefer Kuzari* I:95, II: 9–14. In contradistinction, both Abulafia and Shapira did not accept this restriction and believed that prophecy could occur in all locations. Regarding Abulafia's opinion of prophecy being able to occur outside of Israel, see Moshe Idel, "On the Land of Israel in Medieval Jewish Mystical Thought," in *The Land of Israel in Medieval Jewish Thought*, ed. Moshe Hallamish and Aviezer Ravitzky (Jerusalem: Yad Izhak Ben-Zvi, 1991), 200–210. For Shapira's opinion see Wacks, "Nevu'ah ve-Ḥasidut," 46–49; concerning the connection between R. David Kohen's striving for prophecy and Abulafia's writings see Moshe Idel, "Abraham Abulafia, Gershom Scholem, and R. David ha-Kohen [*ha-Nazir*]," *Jerusalem Studies in Jewish Thought* 19 (2005): 819–834.

59 Joseph Weiss, *Studies in Eastern European Jewish Mysticism*, ed. David Goldstein with intro. Joseph Dan (Oxford: Littman Library of Jewish Civilization, 1985), 27–42.

60 Gershom Scholem, *Major Trends in Jewish Mysticism* (New York: Schocken Books, 1967), 334; for an overview of Scholem's and Weiss's opinions see Idel, "On Prophecy and Early Hasidism," 43–45.

61 Moshe Idel, "The Besht as Prophet and Talismanic Magician," in *Studies in Jewish Narrative (Ma'aseh Sippur) Presented to Yoav Elstein*, ed. Avidov Lipsker and Rella Kushelevsky (Ramat Gan: Bar-Ilan University Press, 2006), 124–126.

sions of prophetic phenomenon.[62] Nonetheless, one may find a continuum of certain circles which strived for prophecy, even utilizing Abulafian techniques for this purpose. R. Aaron ben Ẓevi Hirsch ha-Kohen of Opatow (Apta), widely known for his work *Keter Shem Ṭov* (a compilation of the Beshṭ's statements from his disciples), testifies in his book *Or ha-Ganuz le-Ṣaddiqim*, printed in 1800, about a company of disciples who strived for prophecy and practiced prophetic techniques like celibacy and solitude (*hitbodedut*). At a certain stage "their master, the prophet" taught the suitable students the technique of "combining names"—a clear transformation of Abulafian conceptions of prophecy:

> The matter of prophecy is [as follows]: it is impossible, by and large, to prophesy suddenly, without a certain preparation and holiness. But if the person who wants to prepare himself to prophecy sanctifies and purifies himself, and he concentrates mentally and utterly separates himself from the delights of this world, and he serves the sages, (including) his Rabbi, the prophet, and the disciples that follow the path of prophecy who are called "the sons of the prophets," and when his Rabbi, (who is) the prophet, understands that this disciple is already prepared to (the state of) prophecy then his Rabbi imparts to him the notion of the recitations of the holy names, which are keys for the supernal gate.[63]

Prophecy is conceived as accessible through the use of these techniques transmitted from teacher-prophet to disciple—a conception which parallels that of Abulafia, primarily in its use of "combining holy names."[64] The concern about publishing this passage is apparent in the later editions. After eighty-seven years the book was republished in Warsaw (1887) and this passage was censored; in its place there appeared an asterisk demonstrating its omission, "And so he will do when he wants to cling in divine communion (*be-devequt elohut*), he shall sit at rest with holy thoughts, reverence, and *devequt*. This is secretly interpreted in the verse, "When the Ark was to set out" (Num. 10:35) etc. "And when it halted" etc. (Num. 10:37) wonders of wisdom*."[65] An additional omission which attests to concerns about prophetic practices may be found in a passage written about *Parashat Beḥuqotai*. In the 1800 edition it is written, "And according to the [level of] *devequt* man merits the achieving of the holy spirit and

62 Ibid., 132–133.

63 Aaron b. Ẓevi Hirsch ha-Kohen of Opatow, *Or ha-Ganuz le-Ṣaddiqim* (Zhovkva: Rabin-Stein Press, 1800) quoted in Moshe Idel, "On Prophecy and Early Hasidism," 68.

64 Idem, *Hasidism: Between Ecstasy and Magic* (Albany: State University of New York Press, 1995), 59. Concerning *Or ha-Ganuz le-Ṣaddiqim* and its linguistic-mystical techniques in it see Jonathan Garb, *Shamanic Trance in Modern Kabbalah* (Chicago: The University of Chicago, 2011), 87–88, 101, 122.

65 Aaron b. Ẓevi Hirsch ha-Kohen of Opatow, *Or ha-Ganuz le-Ṣaddiqim* (Warsaw: J. Unterhendler Press, 1887), 72.

prophecy," whereas in the 1887 edition, on page 68, it appears as "And according to the [level of] *devequt* man merits achieving etc."—the focus on prophecy and the divine spirit are omitted. Despite the omissions, many imagery techniques appear in this book, even in the later edition published in Warsaw.[66] These techniques primarily consist of visualizations of being covered in light, incorporating self-visualization. Man must visualize himself as surrounded by light:

> In the Sinai desert... and what are the ramifications of this command to be guides for the worship of God? This is its explanation: "In the Sinai desert"—when you will speak words of Torah that were given at Sinai; "In the Tent of Meeting"—*you will imagine* as if you were standing in the Holy Temple and Tabernacle, which is called the Tent of Meeting. "In one"—*and you are surrounded by the light of the blessed Holy One*, who is called the one God.[67]

> In the beginning (*be-re'shit*) [God] created etc.—it should be noted... and for the fear of God, as is written in the holy *Zohar* and the *Tiqqunim* for fear, which is called, "the beginning of wisdom is fear of God." Therefore, "God (*Elohim*)[68] created the heavens and the earth," according to this design (*ṣiyur*). For the heavens appear in several places as a half sphere above the earth, and it is as if at the edges, "heaven and earth kiss one another" (*b. Bava Batra* 74a) and this is what was said, "God created the heavens and the earth," specifically for [the] beginning (*re'shit*). Meaning, for fear, as it was taught, "and let the fear of heaven be upon you" (*m. Avot* 1:3), as if the heavens and light of *Shekhinah*, which is called "fear of heaven," that are upon them, are actually upon them, *and it as if the light is spread around him and he is inside the radiating light of the sky, he sits and rejoices in trembling, and this is what is said "for fear," so that man will visualize [it] for himself.* Through this, he may come to divest his corporeality and terrestriality. And this is what is written, "and the earth was,"—you can acquire being when you will be "formless and empty" (*tohu ve-vohu*), meaning when you will purify the terrestriality and become formless and empty, emptied and freed of corporeality. And he shall do so by sanctifying for himself four cubits of prayer [and] four cubits of halakhah, and it is as if the light blazes around him.[69]

---

66 Perhaps this later edition was available to Shapira.

67 Aaron b. Ẓevi Hirsch ha-Kohen of Opatow, *Or ha-Ganuz le-Ṣaddiqim* (Warsaw: J. Unterhendler Press, 1887), 35.

68 According to the kabbalistic cosmic structure the name *Elohim* represents the *sefirah* of *Gevurah* associated with fear.

69 Ibid., 10. Also see ibid., 22. Other imagery techniques appear in this work, such as visualizing the Holy Temple, ibid., 35; visualizing the Tetragrammaton, ibid., 5, 62; visualizations connected to the Sabbath, ibid., 66, "He will imagine in his consciousness as if he is sitting here and he is eating in the world of delight, which is called Sabbath"; visualizing a commandment, ibid., 24, 25, "And so you should do for all commandments, visualize the beginning of the commandment before you do them, a true visualization in thought, and afterwards spiritually garb the commanded deed with the conscious (*ha-maḥshevi*) visualization." Also see ibid., 22, for a linguistic imagery technique, "When he will have an impure thought (*hirhur*) for example, coveting someone's objecy, he shall visualize opposite him the prohibition of coveting, as if it is written before

The depiction of mystical experience as a surrounding light is a characteristic of ecstatic kabbalah,[70] the imagery techniques transmitted to Aaron b. Ẓevi Hirsch ha-Kohen, and are also found in Shapira's imagery techniques, "And when a Jewish man (*ha-ish yisra'el*) comes to pray, he needs to strengthen his consciousness (*le-ameṣ et da'ato*) and visualize in his thought how all the world is filled with divine light, he and his glory fill the world and I stand within his divinity, may he be blessed."[71]

Aaron b. Ẓevi Hirsch ha-Kohen's imagery techniques strive to achieve prophecy. He writes that through imagery techniques, the surrounding light may allow man to, "divest his corporeality and terrestriality." In his teachings, corporeal divestment is a stage in the acquisition of prophecy, "And this is as stated regarding Jacob, "He had a dream; a stairway was set on the ground and its top reached to the sky" (Gen. 28:12), meaning, see the heaven and the earth as if they are close to one another and behold God is above them and so even in a waking dream; *when man is divested of corporeality he is able through this to come to a gradation of prophecy*, since he can see the far as if it is actually near."[72]

The omissions made in the book *Or ha-Ganuz le-Ṣaddiqim* demonstrate the tendency to downplay prophecy in hasidic circles. Nonetheless, it is reasonable to presume that the anxiety spurred by the opposition to engagement with prophecy weakened and declined over the years, paralleling the larger decline in opposition to the hasidic movement. With the general opposition to hasidism no longer a threat at the beginning of the twentieth century, Shapira was able to raise the issue of prophecy and revitalize it in his writings—specifically in *Mevo ha-She'arim* where he primarily engages with this topic and calls for a renewal of prophecy—without the slightest concern or apologetics. In Shapira's thought, this process of prophetic renewal is furthered through the development of a new sense:

> This is the purpose of our holy company: that you may become transformed into a person of spirit and thought, and not only thought, but pure intense thought (*ha-maḥshavah ṭehorah ha-ḥazaqah*). You shall overcome your senses *and a new, holy sense will be revealed within*

---

him." Many of Shapira's imagery techniques are similar to these techniques, a fact that supports my hypothesis that he may have used this work.

70 Idel, *Hasidism*, 278 n.74.

71 Shapira, *Ḥovat ha-Talmidim*, 73b-74a.

72 Aaron b. Ẓevi Hirsch ha-Kohen of Opatow, *Or ha-Ganuz le-Ṣaddiqim* (Zhovkva: Rabin-Stein Press, 1800), Parashat va-Yeḥi; (Warsaw: J. Unterhendler Press, 1887), 14. It is interesting that the connection between the divestment of corporeality and prophecy was not omitted in the later edition.

> *you*, so that when you recite, "Blessed be you (*atah*) Lord our God, King of the world (*melekh ha-olam*)," *you will see* the You (*atah*) and King of the world (*melekh ha-olam*), your eyes by themselves will open to the spirit to see the King of the world, Who surrounds the world and yourself... Do not make it difficult once more by asking if we are trying to make a prophet out of you... Hillel the Elder already stated regarding every man of Israel, "although they are not prophets, they are sons of prophets"... there are levels and levels... and the lowest level, after many rungs of diminishment, *remains for you as well man of Israel, a son of prophets, to see!*"[73]

This "new sense" is in fact the prophetic sense characterized by vision, and is acquired through intense thought (*maḥshavah ḥazaqah*).[74] Indeed, Shapira saw the imagination as a new instrument of "intellectual" development, "Therefore he visualizes... only in general, *a new intellect*, wisdom, and his illuminated extended soul he extracts."[75] A new intellect or sense is a term for prophetic capability inherent in man, which is actualized through the utilization of the imaginative faculty.

This prophetic ability belongs to every man, on the condition that he actualizes it and prepares himself to acquire prophetic consciousness, "Every man of Israel is able to come to them with slight, but persistent, effort";[76] "When we will have begun to be hasidim [who are] *ba'alei nefesh* (masters of the soul), our eyes and hearts will open, and they will perceive in the world that which until now they have not seen... new heavens will be revealed before us; who now will stop you from rising, when the floodgates of heaven are opened before you?"[77] This preparation, which is designed to open the floodgates of heaven and yield new visions, is based on variegated imagery techniques that Shapira developed for the wider public, whose common denominator is the visualization of God, in this form or another. The visualization of God, in conjunction with the halakhic prohibition of visualizing God, oscillated Shapira's religious experience, while the recognizable difficulty with the metaphorical anthropomorphic representation of God guided the variegated and intriguing imagery techniques found in Shapira's thought.

---

73 Shapira, *Benei Maḥshavah Ṭovah*, 32–33.
74 Regarding "intense thought" see above.
75 Shapira, *Mevo ha-She'arim*, 16b
76 Idem, *Benei Maḥshavah Ṭovah*, 26.
77 Idem, *Hakhsharat ha-Avreikhim*, 40b.

Imagination as a Technique for Illustrating God

Haviva Pedaya defined religious mystical experience as a tension within the visual spectrum, "The urge to see God linked to the prohibition of seeing God are the two potencies between which religious experience oscillates... the structure of religious experience is bound by a 'urge to' and 'flight from.'"[78] In the religious world, God is approachable for conversation and dialogue; however, in contrast to human conversation, when conversing with God the visual barrier remains prominent, "The primary expression of God's holiness within the framework of revelation is his invisibility."[79] Alongside this tension, one may find in the Bible extraordinary prophetic visions in which God is visualized without any conflict. One such instance is the Sinaitic theophany, "And they *saw* the God of Israel: under His feet there was the likeness of a pavement of sapphire, like the very sky for purity. Yet He did not raise His hand against the leaders of the Israelites; they *beheld* God, and they ate and drank."[80] Still, for the majority of classic prophecy the deep tension between the visualization of God and the prohibition to do so is found, "But, He said, 'you cannot see My face, for man may not see Me and live'";[81] "The Lord said to Moses, 'Go down, warn the people not to break through to the Lord to gaze, lest many of them perish.'"[82] The terror caused by seeing God and the expectant death which accompanies such an event, is described a number of times, "And Manoah said to his wife, 'We shall surely die, for we have seen a divine being.'"[83] One may identify a fascination and aversion to seeing God in Moses's first, visually oriented, revelation.[84] The sight of the burning bush was a source of fascination, however, following the revelation, this same bush becomes a source of aversion, "Moses said, 'I must turn aside *to look at this marvelous sight*; why doesn't the bush burn up?' When the Lord saw that he had turned aside to look, God called to him out of the bush: 'Moses! Moses!' He answered, 'Here I am'... 'I am,' He said, 'the God of your father, the God of Abraham, the God of Isaac, and the God of Jacob.' *And Moses hid his face, for he was afraid to look at God.*"[85] After a

78 Pedaya, "Seeing, Falling, Song," 237.
79 Ibid., 238.
80 Exodus 24:10–11.
81 Ibid., 33:20.
82 Ibid., 19:21.
83 Judges 13:22. Also ibid., 6:22–23.
84 Pedaya, "Seeing, Falling, Song," 240.
85 Ex. 3:3–6.

while Moses wishes to behold God's face and is answered in the negative, or at least partial negative, "He said, 'Oh, let me behold Your Presence... He said, 'you cannot see My face, for man may not see Me and live'... 'Then I will take My hand away and you will see My back; but My face must not be seen.'"[86] The aversion towards this sight returns numerous times in the descriptions of the prophets. For example, Isaiah cries out, "Woe is me; I am lost! For I am a man of unclean lips and I live among a people of unclean lips; yet my own eyes have beheld The King Lord of Hosts."[87]

One of the mystic's goals is to transform God, within the mystic's field of consciousness, from an entity which appears in the "third person," into an entity which appears and is revealed in the "second person." The significance of this appearance is in the experience of God as present and the perpetual yearning for the experience of "placing God before me always." Different techniques have been suggested over the years to make this experience of divine presence possible. In hasidism, the techniques of contemplation (*hitbonenut*), amongst Ḥabad Hasidism, as well as techniques of solitude (*hitbodedut*), amongst Bratslav Hasidism, are well known. These two techniques are meant to make God present in the life of man, although neither one has an explicit visual element. In contemplation, the divine is made present through intellectual concentration, while in *hitbodedut*, a non-visual dialogue exists between man and God. Shapira's uniqueness is his broad use of imagery techniques, which serve as means for allowing God to appear in a person's consciousness as "You," "When you speak to God in the second person, for example, 'You our god' or 'Blessed are you, etc.'... *visualize in your mind* that opposite you is God [to whom] you are saying 'You.'"[88] The imagination makes God manifest and thereby transforms him into a presence situated before the imaginer.

Visualization of God is a highly contested subject, and one may locate the roots of the disagreement around it in the different conceptions of the imagination.[89] The approach that conceives of the imagination according to the "mirror" model, as a mere imitation of material reality, views the visualization of God as an anthropomorphic act and corporealization of God. Medieval rational Jewish philosophy tended to forbid any attribution of form or figure to God. Maimonides counts those who claim that God has an image among his list of heretics, "These are those who lose their portion in the world to come, rather they are cut off and

86 Ibid., 33:18–23. Also see Pedaya, "Seeing, Falling, Song," 241 on the connection between the Glory and Face.
87 Is. 6:5.
88 Shapira, *Ḥovat ha-Talmidim*, 28a.
89 Regarding different models of imagination see above chap. 1.

our lost and they are judged for their great wickedness and their sin forever and ever.... the *minim* (heretics)... Five are called *minim*... one who says that there is one master (God), but that he has a body and image."[90] The attempt to visualize God also raised the ire and opposition of hasidic thinkers. For instance, Zadok viewed every attempt to visualize God as an act of corporealization, which should be judged as no less than idolatry! He interprets Maimonides's ruling as including those who visualize:

> A third commandment is that of unifying the Name, blessed be he: It is a positive commandment to unite him, as written, "Listen O Israel etc. the Lord is one" (Deut. 6:4)... And Maimonides included under the rubric of this commandment the convinction that God does not have a body or corporeality, and that corporeal events do not happen to him.... And in the third chapter of [*Mishneh Torah*] "Laws of Repentance" Maimonides writes: "Five are called *minim*, one who says that the world has no guiding diety, or that there are two [such dieties], or that there is one, but he has a body and image"... And the believer in [God's] corporeality, even though it is from his simple faith in the Torah and rabbinic statements according to their straightforward meaning, should be referred to as serving idols in pure innocence,[91] for [the statement of] in scripture, "[For your own sake, therefore,] be most careful [since you saw no shape when the Lord your God spoke to you at Horeb out of the fire]" (Deut. 4:15) is said regarding idolatry, that this is a kind of idol worship.... *And so, whoever visualizes, God forbid, in his imagination any image* (*ṣurah*) [of God is an idol worshiper]. *And therefore, one must be very weary of the imaginative faculty, that he should only visualize corporeal entities like himself.*[92]

This conception is obviously based on a specific conception of imagination, which maintains the "mirror" model, claiming that, "according to the imagination, there are no existents except bodies or things in bodies."[93] Yet, in contradisction to this conception, a different approach developed in modern philosophy. Jean-Paul Sartre asserted that we use spatiotemporally derived concepts

90 Maimonides, *Mishneh Torah*, "Laws of Repentance," 3:6–7.
91 The origin of the locution "serving idols in pure innocence" is in *b. Avodah Zarah* 8a. Its meaning according to Zadok is an action or conception done with a pure heart, but whose external appearance is a perversion. See his remarks in *Maḥshavot Ḥaruṣ*, §17, §19 that serving idols in pure innocence is a "kind of idolatry" and not "actual idolatry," which has implications regarding the punishment, "Although the Talmud refers to him as one who serves idols in pure innocence, seemingly it is not considered as an accessory to idolatry such that he should 'be killed and not transgress'" (ibid., §20).
92 Zadok ha-Kohen Rabinowitz, *Quntres Sefer ha-Zikhronot*, *Miṣvah* 3. See a similar opposition towards visualization in the kabbalah of the late thirteenth century in the thought of Menaḥem Recanti, Moshe Idel, *Rabbi Menahem Recanati the Kabbalist* (Jerusalem: Schocken, 1998), 168–171.
93 Maimonides, *Guide of the Perplexed*, 1:73§§1:211.

to depict the act of being conscious of imaginal objects. For example: vision (I see the imaginal object), and this is despite my eyes being closed (the straightforward meaning of "vision" is spatial vision) and no spatial vision has occurred. The same goes for hearing and the other senses. There is no doubt that concepts are borrowed from the perceptual consciousness and applied towards the imaginative consciousness. However, Sartre maintained this this application has an unintended error. The sight, sound, smell, taste, and touch which appear in the imaginative consciousness are not the same as perceptual consciousness. Sartre cites psychological studies which asked people to imagine the Pantheon of Rome. Most of them were able to do so with no difficulty, yet when asked to count the number of columns therein, all of them failed. This failure was not due to miscounting, but was located in an earlier stage, in the very the attempt at counting itself. This failure is explained by Sartre as due to the nature of imagination as "presence in absence":

> Let us suppose that my imagination consciousness envisions the Pantheon... "this object before me, I *know* that it has columns, a facade, a gray color.... hat I *sense* there is a Pantheon"... But the Pantheon exists *elsewhere* and it presents itself as existing elsewhere: what is present is, in some way, its absence.[94]

The absence of the imaginal object is the reason for its elusiveness. There is no possibility of counting the columns, no possibility of truly depicting, deciphering, counting, or categorizing imaginal objects:

> I *can do nothing* with this object which I believe able to describe, decipher, enumerate. The visible object is there, but I cannot see it—it is tangible and I cannot touch it—audible and I cannot hear it.[95]

Sartre demonstrates the paradoxical nature of: the columns of the Pantheon constitute objects in man's consciousness, yet he is unable to count them. The imaginative consciousness is different in nature from perceptual consciousness. Sight, sound, and other senses found in imaginative consciousness are only borrowed concepts and do not function in their full sense. If we continue Sartre's line of thought, we may conclude that in the visualization of God as a sensory object, there is no actual image, rather only an ethereal and elusive image that cannot be truly seen or accurately depicted, as was the case with the columns of the Pantheon. It can be concluded, then, that the visualization of

94 Sartre, *The Psychology of Imagination*, 112–113.
95 Ibid., 114.

God should not be equated with his corporealization. Envisioning God is solely a borrowing of perceptual concepts, and these concepts in their imaginative form are not the same as in their perceptual one. In this instance, unlike a statue or drawing, there is no actual corporealization of God. The imagined images are never actually corporealized. Corporealization of God can only occur in the physical plane, such as in the making of a statue or drawing, but not on the plane of imaginative consciousness.

Elliot Wolfson presents a similar conception, which in his opinion represents that of the sages.[96] Wolfson challenges the accepted scholarly consensus that Judaism, unlike Christianity, rejected any idea of the incarnation of God in the form of a human body.[97] While the sages indeed rejected the conception of divine embodiment as flesh and blood, one may nevertheless find forms of embodiment in their thought, as in the sense of metaphorical representation of the divine in human form.[98] While rejecting the Christian doctrine of incarnation, the sages attempted, in their own way, to revive experiences of the divine. The effort to mediate between the aniconic and iconic trends culminated in the creation of the "imagined body."[99] Wolfson demonstrates different aspects of embodiment in Judaism in which the divine is embodied in the image of an imagined anthropoid.[100] For example, Wolfson discusses divine embodiment in prayer, in which he explores the role of the imagination in *kavvanah* (intention) during prayer, and shows the use of anthropomorphic visualization of the divine as an object for prayer in rabbinic literature.[101] According to this claim, the sages believed that the divine may be visually and discernibly revealed through the act of prayer. In contrast to medieval Jewish philosophy, which rejected *in toto* all anthropomorphic representations, one may find these very conceptions in

---

96 Wolfson, "Iconic Visualization and the Imaginal Body of God," 137–162.
97 Ibid., 135.
98 Ibid., 139.
99 Ibid., 149. See, as well, according to Wolfson, that the anthropomorphic imaginal representation of the divine is a central component of kabbalistic teachings, idem, "The Body in the Text," 479: "An essential component of the kabbalistic worldview is the anthropomorphic representation of the divine to the point that the priestly notion of the image of God by means of which Adam was created is applied by kabbalists to limbs of the supernal human form configured in the imagination."
100 Primarily in his book, Wolfson, *Through a Speculum*; Wolfson demonstrates that this theme begins in the Hekhalot literature, continues in a variety of kabbalistic literature, and is prominent in the *Zohar.* Also see Elliot. R. Wolfson, "Judaism and Incarnation: The Imaginal Body of God," in *Christianity in Jewish Terms*, ed. T. Frymer-Kensky et. al. (Boulder: Westview Press, 2000), 239–253.
101 Idem, "Iconic Visualization and the Imaginal Body of God," 139–149.

classic rabbinic thought, alongside a refutation of corporeal conceptions of the divine. While the sages rejected the conception of God as corporeal in the physical realm, an incarnational body in the imaginal realm was permissible in their thought.[102] A similar position may be found in the halakhic works of Abraham Isaac ha-Kohen Kook, who, in contrast to Zadok ha-Kohen Rabinowitz, did not find an explicit halakhic prohibition against visualizing the divine, but rather saw himself as approximating the objections of Abraham ben David of Posquières against Maimonides:

> Even though an error in divine matters is very damaging, nevertheless, the primary aspect of the damage, which is drawn from the flawed concepts, is not actualized, to the point that one who has [these flawed conceptions] is to have a soul-death (*mitat ha-neshamah*), only when he actualizes [them] in deed, or at the very least when he descends into these type of thoughts and feelings, whose ends necessarily are revealed in deed. However, as long as the matter is in an abstract form, this is not a fundamental heresy (*aqirah*). And in this we are close to R. Abraham ben David's reasoning, in which he objected to Maimonides' calling someone who believes in God's corporeality a heretic (*min*). We can agree that as long as the man who corporealizes does not make an idol or [a physical] image, behold, he has not completed his thought, and it still remains in the company of the spirit, which is not able to be considered heresy and a departure from religion.[103]

The corporealization of God, according to Kook, is restricted to "deeds," while thought (and even more so, imagination), which is found in the spiritual realm and not among concreate actions, cannot constitute corporealization. However, the reader who does not readily accept this position and prefers to view the visualization of God as an act of corporealization, despite all that has been said, would do well to pay heed to Haviva Pedaya's positioning of the tension between the imaginal content and the warnings against corporealization as characterizing the mystic's state of consciousness and as forming the awareness of some kabbalists.[104] According to Pedaya, the charge and effort of the kabbalist is to refine the images, "A man found in a state in which he actualizes his imaginative faculty while also undergoing a process of refinement, cleansing, and purification of images, and defines them in a refined and abstract manner—here we have come closer to understanding the state of consciousness of some of the kabbalists."[105] Implied here is that if we treat the visualization of

102 Ibid., 152.
103 Abraham Isaac ha-Kohen Kook, *Shemonah Qevaṣim* (Jerusalem: Mossad Harav Kook, 2004), 1:8–9.
104 Pedaya, *Vision and Speech*, 20, 81.
105 Ibid., 22–23.

God as an act of corporealization, we must remember that the mystic's purpose is to purify this image to the point of renunciation or destruction:

> The kabbalist's self-consciousness... is a specific and very elusive state of consciousness that allows for the maintaining in his mind of a number of figurative elements which do not together form a specific image... the tension between the contents and warnings [against them] form a particlar state of mind in which the image exists alongside its destruction.[106]

> The state of perception through visions may lead to a vision-less state. Apophatic mysticism (negation of images and words) and kataphatic mysticism (achieving visions and leading to words) are not always different paths... sometimes they are two subsequent stages. Quite dialectically, the acute awareness of the unknown and the impediment of human consciousness as it seeks to transcend towards the divine, often appear in the mystical type who obtains visions and subsequently senses that he abandons them.[107]

Pedaya's formative distinctions attest to a phenomenon of providing images and abandoning them, while the phenomenon of maintaining several figurative elements in one's thought that do not form a particular discernable image resembles Sartre's characterization of imagination. The understanding of the imagination's evasiveness, as well as its accompanying lack of clarity, is extremely important for any discussion of visualization and corporealization, allowing for broader insights. Henceforth, discussions of visualizing God cannot be limited to the two opposing axes of envisioning or not envisioning, visualization or lack of visualization. There is a wider range of intermediate positions allowing for states that are not entirely distinct, elusive states in which the workings of the imagination are more blurred and complex. These two critical insights, which Pedaya identified in her work, will accompany us in the following exploration of the link between the visualization of the divine and corporealization. The first is that the mystic himself oscillates between the imaginal content and the warning against corporealization, and is thus situated in a perpetual tension which both forms and characterizes his state of consciousness. It should not be understood in static terms such as "corporealizing" or "non-corporealizing," but rather as fluctuating in a state of "running and returning" (*raṣo va-shov*) between corporealization and incorporealization. This understanding changes our attitude towards the mystic and our perception of the mystical personality. The second insight, which may offer a solution to the question of divine corporealization, is the assertion that a grouping of figurative elements or images do not constitute a precise and exact image and therefore they do not constitute an in-

106 Ibid., 20.
107 Ibid., 23.

stance of corporealization, "The relation between the 'image of images' [God] and individual images does not in its essence allow for any kind of corporealization of or signifying of God's countenace, for one would must have to hold many images in one's thought at once";[108] "The massive overflow of images and figures does not allow for [one's] consciousness to form a single image which is, as it were, the image of God."[109]

The Visualization of God and Corporealization in Shapira's Thought

The great tension between the need to permit corporealization and the halakhic prohibition against doing so, is fully expressed in Shapira's work *Benei Maḥshavah Ṭovah*, which was primarily intended for a small "fraternity" (*ḥavurah*), not to be disseminated among the masses.[110] Due to the rarity of such a text, which a penetrating discussion is conducted regarding the visualization of God—granting a qualified legitimacy to the practice—, I will cite it in full. I will also note that to my knowledge no such texts are to be found in the annals of Jewish thought in general, and in modern times in particular! Despite his qualifications and concerns, Shapira permits imaginal corporealization, and even uses halakhic terminology in order to grant halakhic justification to the practice, itself a rarity in his writings:

> A young man (*avreikh*) has already apologized before me and stated, "*If only I could visualize before me some image* when I stand [to pray] before God, may he be blessed, I would become stirred in every facet just as one who requests and pleads before an omnipotent one who is able to save me, or I would be shaken and trembling from the thought and the image itself of standing before the Throne of Glory. *However, since it is forbidden to visualize any image or depiction (ve-ṣiyur) and I only have the knowledge* that I stand before God, knowledge bereft of the imaginal realm (*maḥshavah*). Without the imaginal realm it is impossible for me to become stirred, and all the more so to maintain a constant state of excitement—that is entirely impossible for me. And who knows if this was not also the basis and reason for the sin of the mixed multitude, who said, "Come, make us a god who shall go before us" (Ex. 32:1), that we will see him; only they went too far and did not merely request a mental depiction (*ṣiyur maḥshavah*), but an actual figure as well, even, in their foolishness, desiring the figure of an Egyptian god, heaven save us. And since the foundation of our fraternity is not to berate and arbitrarily decree that a

---

108 Ibid., 13.
109 Ibid., 21. For more on the simultaneous observation of multiple images see idem, "Sabbath, Sabbatai, and the Diminution of Moon—The Holy Conjunction: Sign and Image," *Eshel Beer-Sheva* 4 (1996):161–169.
110 See the introduction to chap. 4

> man do such and such—for he will not listen to us, or he will present himself as though he has a good thought (*maḥshavah ṭovah*) and stirring, while [in fact] he does not, for, truth be told, everyone wishes to be of pure heart and "sons of heaven" (*b. Sukkah* 45b), only it is impossible for them to transcend their slime, as aforementioned, and the entire foundation of our fraternity is to bend down to the lowered place of [our] members, until the very end of their soul and body, and from there to raise them through suitable means—therefore we shall offer them a solution and advice for how to acclimate them, each according to his state. Therefore, this person, who is in such a situation at the beginning of his growth and expansion of his thought, will rely on the Raba"d (Abraham ben David of Posquières), may his memory be blessed, who comments on Maimonides, may his memory be blessed, Chapter Three, from "The Laws of Repentance," Halakhah Seven [who declared all who believe in God's corporeality to be heretics], and these are his words, "Abraham said, "And why did he call this heresy? Several men greater and better, etc. maintained this belief." It is difficult to understand the words of the Raba"d, may his memory be blessed, according to their simple meaning, for there is an explicit biblical verse [stating]: "You saw no image" (Deut. 4:15), and so forth. Refer to the question of the *Kesef Mishnah*—according to him, the Raba"d, may his memory be blessed, did not mean to mislead one to say, God forbid, that there is any image in heaven, may it not be mentioned. Rather, what it really means to say is that while one knows that God is without any image, God forbid, he who is made of matter (*qaruṣ me-ḥomer*), a physical being who utilizes images, may visualize this so that his thought may grasp, grow, and expand, and when God helps him and strengthens his thought and he will be able to think of God with an intense and pure thought (*maḥshavah ḥazaqah*), and the imagination, the spark of prophecy, will be revealed to him—then this corporeal visualization be nullified of its own accord, and he will be able to visualize during his prayer that he stands before God and before the Throne of Glory. [All of this is] in order that he might better comprehend and understand what he is able to think and imagine. As for you, a member of the fraternity, in a time of distress you should visualize yourself standing before the Throne of Glory, praying and beseeching from God like a son who cries and pleads before his father, "Please, have mercy on me, my father, I can no longer tolerate the temptations of the body and the dearth of spirit, and from the time that you threw me away from you and hid your face from me, I am surrounded by fear." Who is the person, even with a heart of stone, who does not melt away in the hour that he visualizes this image in his mind, how he stands before the Throne of Glory, a consuming fire, and pleads for himself, his household, and all of Israel.[111]

An analysis of this text demonstrates a sharp dialectic between on the one hand, the disguised identification with the questioner, and, on the other hand, a concern that this act of visualization may constitute idolatry, one of the most severe sins in Judaism, a sin for which one is meant is to let themselves die rather transgress. This passage, the desire to see God, "If only I could visualize before me some image," appears in conjunction with the prohibition of visualizing him, "since it is forbidden to visualize any image or depiction." As we mentioned,

---

111 Shapira, *Benei Maḥshavah Ṭovah*, 18–20.

these are the two forces between which mystical experience fluctuates. It appears that the anonymous young man's reqiest, "to visualize before me some image," is merely a personal request, and if Shapira is lenient in allowing this young man and those like him to visualize an image, this is seemingly only an *ex post facto* dispensation granted for solely in response to an emergency situation. It further appears that this dispensation derives from a pedogical approach which recognizes the need to meet the questioner at their level,[112] "and the entire foundation of our fraternity is to bend down to the lowered place of [our] members, until the very end of their soul and body, and from there to raise them through suitable means." The descent to the spiritual state of the questioner, and the ensuing attempts to incrementally elevate him, necessitate a temporary dispensation to materialize God in a visualized image. This allowance is solely intended for the most basic stage, prior to any subsequent elevation to a more advanced level, "Therefore, this person, who is in such a situation at the beginning of his growth and expansion of his thought, will rely on the Raba"d." With this said, I believe that this question is a fundamental and existential question for Shapira himself, and that he himself identifies deeply with the questioner. He does not merely identity out of empathy, but also with the content of the problem that the questioner raises. Do not forget that in formulating the young man's question, the question becomes Shapira's as well.[113] We shall delve into it a little, "If only I could visualize before me some image when I stand [to pray] before God, may he be blessed, I would become stirred... however, since it is forbidden to visualize any image or depiction and I only have knowledge... knowledge bereft of the imaginal realm. Without the imaginal realm *it is impossible for me to become stirred... and all the more so to maintain a feeling of excitement—that is entirely impossible for me.*" A sensitive reading of this text indicates that Shapira himself feels that it is impossible to maintain constant stimulation or ecstatic excitement without a visual image.[114] This is demonstrated by the last section of

112 This resembles Naḥman of Bratslav's story of the "Rooster-Prince," see S. M. Zinqover, "*Ben ha-melekh ve-ha-ḥakham,*" *Qoveṣ le-Torah ve-Ḥasidut: Mevo'ei ha-Naḥal* 37 (1981): 35–37.

113 This text is somewhat unclear regarding where the questions end and the answers begin. The answer to the question may begin with the words, "And who knows if this was not also the foundation and reason for the sin of the mixed multitude." However, this may be the continuation of the young man's question, while the answer actually begins with, "And since the foundation of our fraternity is not to berate." Furthermore, this ambiguous phrasing of question and answer may in fact reflect the fact that they are being uttered by the same person. I do not doubt that this question was posed to Shapira, but it is clear that the phrasing here, both of the question and answer, is that of Shapira.

114 On the quality of *hitlahavut* (ecstasy; passion) in his thought see Shapira, *Hakhsharat ha-Avreikhim*, chap. 2.

the text, which clearly expresses both sides of this dialectic, "As for you, a member of the fraternity, in a time of distress you should visualize yourself standing before the Throne of Glory, praying and beseeching from God like a son who cries and pleads before his father, "Please, have mercy on me, my father.'" It would have sufficed for Shapira to conclude his statement with an expression of reservations regarding his permissive stance, as well as his concerns regarding idolatry, thereby cementing the practice for emergency situations and the specific lowly people who are, "at the very end of their soul and body." However, Shapira's furthering of the discussion demands an explanation. Shapira continues at length to describe his suffering from the temptations of body and the lack of spirit, on the one hand, and God's hiddenness, on the other hand, "I can no longer tolerate the temptations of the body and the dearth of spirit, and from the time that you threw me away from you and hid your face from me, I am surrounded by fear." If Shapira's only related to this corporealizing imagery technique as a concession, then his continuation here would be superfluous. It seems to me that Shapira did not perceive this imagery technique as a necessary evil, but rather found in it something rousing, something legitimate, that might revitalize passionate emotions and strong yearnings, as he describes in an unambiguously positive manner, "*Who is the person, even with a heart of stone, who does not melt away in the hour that he visualizes this image in his mind, how he stands before the Throne of Glory,* a consuming fire, and pleads for himself, his household, and all of Israel." He appears to identify with this particular imagery technique, which contains a specific divine image, namely, "the Throne of Glory." It is difficult to assert that this identification is a compromise, given that in many situations Shapira requests of the practitioner to perform this exercise without any hint or distinction between a *a priori* a *ex post facto* circumstances, "Take hold [in your mind] of a certain movement of a melody, turn your face towards the wall, or just close your eyes, *and think once more that you are standing before the Throne of Glory*";[115] "Hide yourself in a special room if you can, and if not, turn your face towards the wall *and visualize in your thoughts that you are standing before the Throne of Glory, may he be blessed*";[116] "The person in possession of intense imagination (*maḥshavah ḥazaqah*), may, in the hour of stirring and excitement when his thought is strengthened and cleansed, *see in his thought and imagination*—[through his prophetic] imagination of Israel, sons of prophets—*God, may he be blessed and his Throne of Glory.*"[117]

---

115 Shapira, *Benei Maḥshavah Ṭovah*, 42. Also see Leshem, "Between Messianism and Prophecy," 180–181.
116 Shapira, *Ṣav ve-Ziruz*, 6.
117 Idem, *Benei Maḥshavah Ṭovah*, 13.

The anonymous young man presumes that an imaginal object is corporeal. The primary implication of this question concerns the corporealization of God, yet Shapira fashions a different model of imagination. This model is similar to the modern post-Kantian conception, which does not conceive of imagination as mimicking material existence, but is rather an independent creation, a type of original independent consciousness or thinking, which does not mimic, but is rather itself the original. The imagination that does not copy material existence is referred to in Shapira's thought as "supernal imagination" (*dimyon ila'ah*) or "an imagination of Israel, sons of prophets," which is identified with prophetic imagination, "the spark of prophecy." Shapira distinguishes between these two types of imagination, and claims that the imagination of the latter kind is independent of matter and its imitations:

> However, as mentioned, this question is only suitable for one who is now beginning to worship through thought (*be-avodat ha-maḥshavah*), who has not yet perfected it nor tasted the taste the of purified thought. Since he is immersed solely in physical labors and activities, and his thought too is only utilized for his physical needs—how will he eat and drink, depictions and images of his merchandise, and the like—and most of his thoughts are still self-centered as he not yet looked out from himself, he therefore believes that the revelation of thought and imagination, which is really a spark of prophecy... is only an expansion of these types of thoughts. He therefore asks [for permission to visualize God]. ...You can see that *thought* is not in itself sensory or corporeal, but only seemingly bears a corporeal depiction. When we will use our intelligence to try to separate this from that, namely, the imagination with thought, from the form (*ṣurah*) and form an image of them informed exclusively by the senses... then there will remain a spiritual imagination, which we cannot see or sense to the point that we might know and describe it.[118]

If so, Shapira's answer to the problem of corporealization entails a fine distinction between *thought* and *imagination*. The imagination indeed bears corporeal "forms." In contrast, the abstract dimension of imagination—*thought*, i.e. theme and story (which coincide with the imagination)—is removed of all components of form (*ṣurah*), "Intense thought and imagination, are of the same type, rather that matters that are may be visualized, such as the form of a house, man, etc., are seen in the imagination, while matters that are formless, such as words, are thought solely in intense thought."[119] Ezekiel saw a "spiritual anthropoid" and not a "corporeal anthropoid":

> One must first divest as much corporeality as possible from an idea and to delve into spiritual ideas without corporeality and without a corporeal conception. Even when during

118 Ibid., 15–16.
119 Idem, *Hakhsharat ha-Avreikhim*, 15b-16a.

> study we discuss worldly terms, such as, land, throne, virtues (*midot*), etc., the intention is that in thought and comprehension we will divest their corporeality and examine the [remaining] spiritual abstraction.[120]

> "And on top, upon this semblance of a throne, there was the semblance of a human form" (Ez. 1:26). We are not attemping to explain or understand what Ezekiel the prophet saw... For our purposes, the prophet hints that you should not think that he saw God, may he be blessed, in his absolute selfhood, for it was already stated, "For man may not see Me" (Ex. 33:20). It is rather the *divine revelation*, which was revealed in all the worlds, from the first level until the last level, through the vessel, man, in his image, is an icon of a *spiritual man*—this is what he beheld![121]

On the one hand, Shapira demanded the visualization of corporeal figures and sensory forms, "Through thought, and specifically with imagination, *and specifically when it is in form* (*ba-ṣurah*) he will merit to conjoin (*le-hitdaveq*) with holiness";[122] "It is impossible for intense thought to be without images in it... and when he thinks with intense thought, its *form* is visualized in front of him as well."[123] On the other hand, he demanded that this form be divested, "He is to divest as much corporeality as possible." These two extremes semingly constitute the margins within which Shapira oscillates, in a movement of "running and returning." The demand to visualize an image and then divest it is the movement that Pedaya identified as characteristic of the kabbalistic consciousness, which strives to perceive an image and then afterwards forsake it. These two demands, visualization and abandonment, should not be seen as contradictory, but rather as characteristic of mystical consciousness. This state of awareness accounts for the sharp dialectic in Shapira's thought, which, as I previously mentioned, is on many occasions the result of his personal experiences.[124]

---

120 Idem, *Mevo ha-She'arim*, 16a.
121 Idem, *Ḥovat ha-Talmidim*, 75a.
122 Idem, *Hakhsharat ha-Avreikhim*, 16b. Also, see above, chap. 4, subchapter, "Visualizing the *Ṣaddiq*." Although this statement does not refer to the corporealization of God, but rather the materialization of the Ṣaddiq, one may nevertheless see the importance of figuration in Shapira's imaginal process.
123 Idem, *Hakhsharat ha-Avreikhim*, 15b.
124 Concerning Shapira's deep desire to see God in conjugation with his failure to see, idem, *Ṣav ve-Ziruz*, 20, "And it is possible that I have fooled myself.... for the vision that I hoped for I did not merit, and the spirit that I was almost certain would be revealed to me... was not revealed."

Heavenly Imagery Techniques: Imaginal Substitutions

Although Shapira allowed the visualization of a corporealized God, he often preferred, to visualize something else as a substitute or as a means of visualizing God, perhaps in order to distance himself from the problem of corporealization. For example, he suggested contemplating the heavens and similar entities as a barrier seperating prayer from God. By doing so, one can indirectly turn to God and stand before him, without needing to directly engage with the problem of corporealization:

> If you are still having difficulty *visualizing yourself standing before God*... since you are found in a corporeal world, your eyes only see corporeality and your hands feel matter. Please look heavenwards and contemplate, strengthen your thought and think, "I am standing here on this side, however, beyond heaven an entirely different world exists, angels, seraphs, and all the souls of the patriarchs, prophets, and *ṣaddiqim*, and within them the Throne of Glory is found, and God, the great, holy, and awesome, dwells upon it" ... strengthen this gaze and think, "I stand here on this side and say to God, 'Blessed are you God'... *I strengthen my eyes and I look and bless and speak to you, God.*"[125]

While substituting the visualization of God with the contemplation of the heavens solves the problem of divine corporealization, it arouses an earlier theological dispute, intensified in the Middle Ages,[126] regarding engaging "intermediaries" in religious worship. Shapira reveals his sources:

---

125 Idem, *Ḥovat ha-Talmidim*, 27b. Also see Elimelekh Weisblum of Lizhensk, *No'am Elimelekh*, Parashat Lekh Lekha, "A person is especially able to see the glory of God by gazing at the heavens and the stars in their paths on their shifts as they radiate with their radiating light. From this, man will come to awe, understanding God's loftiness... and this is an example of what we wrote above, that a man needs to look on high with a vision of stars and constellations, "Who created these" (Is. 40:26), as if he sees everything with the optical sense, so he must visualize in his thought at the time of his praying as if he is actually in the Land of Israel and in the Holy Temple and sees everything with the optical sense." The comparison of these two parts of this text, "seeing and understanding of God's loftiness," and the visualization of the Holy Temple, a comparison made by the author himself through the conjunction word "so" (*ken*), demonstrates that the understanding and seeing here is in fact imaginal seeing, "as if he sees everything with optical sense." If so, Weisblum anticipated Shapira with this technique. We see from Shapira, *Derekh ha-Melekh*, 136; idem, *Mevo ha-She'arim*, 23b, 43a, that Shapira was aware of this, however he did not cite Weisblum as the source of his technique.

126 See Maimonides on intermediaries, idem, *Guide of the Perplexed*, 1:36; idem, *Mishneh Torah*, "Laws Concerning Idolatry," 1:1. See the discussion in the glosses on this work and their halakhic implications R. Ḥayyim Palaggi, *She'elot u-Teshuvot Ḥayyim be-Yad*, §34, s.v. "me-aḥer alot."

> It is taught in the Hekhalot literature… "When God said, 'Blessed are you to the God of heaven and descenders of the chariot (*yordei ha-merkavah*)… and taught them to lift up their eyes to the firmament corresponding to their house of prayer" (meaning, to the heavens, and this is the gate of heaven) and bear themselves on high, [telling them] "There is nothing as fine to me in the world as that hour when your eyes are lifted up to My eyes and My eyes are in your eyes. In that hour I grasp the throne of My glory in the visage of Jacob and embrace them and kiss them (meaning each person of Israel) and remind them of their redemption and quicken their redemption,'"[127] until here is its holy language. These words are outstanding! Envisage therefore: our eyes looking upon the firmament, in His eyes, as if it was possible (*kiveyakhol*), and God, blessed be he, looks into ours, and his Glory delights from this looking.[128]

---

127 It appears that the Hekhalot literature cited is based on *Hekhalot Rabbati* §163–164. I have used James R. Davila, *Hekhalot Literature in Translation: Major Texts of Merkavah Mysticism* (Leiden: Brill, 2013), 85–86, for the translation of this passage, with modifications for the parts that did not match the text as translated there.

128 Shapira, *Ḥovat ha-Talmidim*, 27b. It is very interesting to note that this ancient source influenced the development of the halakhah regarding looking at the heavens during prayer. Joseph Karo, the great halakhic decisor and authority of the sixteenth century, made no mention of looking up at the heavens, but in fact the opposite—he decided that one must look towards the ground during their recitation of the eighteen benedictions, "He must bend his head a little, so that his eyes will be downwards towards the earth, and he shall think that it as if he is standing in the Holy Temple, and in his heart he will concentrate (*ye-khaven*) skywards" (*Shulḥan Arukh*, Oraḥ Ḥayyim, §95:2). Indeed, this was already discussed by R. Joel Sirkis (Poland, 1561–1640) in his work *Bayit Ḥadash*, "Before he begins to pray he should look at the windows towards the heavens so that his heart will be subdued" (from *Mishneh Berurah*, §95:4). R. Moses Isserles (Krakow, c. 1525–1572) anticipated this as well, however his remarks are more succinct and only reference the *qedushah* (Trisagion liturgy) said during the cantor's repetition of the eighteen benedictions, "A gloss: 'One should lift his eyes on high when the *qedushah* is said'" (*Shulḥan Arukh*, Oraḥ Ḥayyim, §125:2). Israel Meir Kagan emphasized these remarks in his *Mishneh Berurah*, §125:5, "And one should lift etc.—For they, blessed be their memory, wrote in *Sefer Hekhalot*, 'Blessed to God of heaven be the descenders to the chariot, if you say and tell my sons what I do in the hour that they sanctify and say, "Holy, holy, holy" (Is. 6:3), and teach them that their eyes should be lifted on high to their house of prayer and they themselves are lifted on high, for I have no benefit in the world like the hour in which their eyes are lifted and my eyes are in their eyes in that very hour, I grasp the throne of My glory the visage of Jacob and embrace it and kiss it and remind their merit and quicken their redemption.'" He adds, as well, that it is not only during *qedushah* that the one praying should look heavenwards, but every time he loses his concentration, ibid., §90:8, "For as it is brought in the Talmud that a person should only pray in a house with windows, even though he must direct his eyes downwards… nevertheless, when he loses his concentration he should lift his eyes heavenward to stir [his] concentration." R. Jacob b. Asher, known as *Ba'al ha-Ṭurim* (1269-c. 1343), already referenced this source (and Kagan seemingly quotes it from him), "And after concluding the second blessing he will say, "we will revere and sanctify you" [the first words of the *qedushah*]… and Sephardim have a custom to direct their eyes downward when they say, "Holy, holy, holy," and Ashkenazim and French Jews direct their eyes upward and lift their bodies upwards;

Similar to A.J. Heschel, Shapira notes the reciprocal relation between man and God. This indirect materialization of God creates a sense of relation and an intimate experience of connection between God and man, "Our eyes look out upon the firmament at his eyes, as it were (*kiveyakhol*), and God, blessed be he, looks into ours, and his Glory delights from this looking. The father and son gaze at each other, as it were, and through love and a growing affection the father is unable to restrain himself, and grasps and embraces and kisses *me*, the son. The heart rejoices, and the soul bursts forth in rapture and calls out, 'To my father, to my Holy one, I arise, I fly.'"[129] These words give a sense of the potency of the imagination to generate excitement, ecstasy, and relation, and most of all, the urge to see God and experience his presence. However, this technique is not widely agreed upon as a solution for the problem of corporealizing God, as the theological attitude towards the use of divine hypostases is itself disputed. As such, the tension between the urge to see God and the prohibition against doing so continues, a tension that characterizes the mystic's consciousness.

"To Visualize the Holy Name": Outflanking Imagination—Imagination within Imagination

The technique of divine name combination appears already already in the Hekhalot literature. A more detailed and systematic technique of letter combination was developed in the medieval ages in the teachings of Eleazar of Worms and, through his influence, the Spanish kabbalists, particularly Abraham Abulafia, who developed these traditions in an extremely detailed manner.[130] However,

a support for their custom is found in *Sefer Hekhalot*, "Blessed to God of heaven be the descenders to the chariot, if you say and tell my sons what I do in the hour that they sanctify and say, "Holy, holy, holy" (Is. 6:3), and taught them that their eyes should be lifted on high to their house of prayer and they themselves are lifted on high, for I have no benefit in the world like the hour in which their eyes are lifted and my eyes are in their eyes" (*Ṭur*, Oraḥ Ḥayyim, §125). In summary, the Hekhalot literature deals with the contemplation of the heavens during the *qedushah* of the cantor's repetition of the eighteen benedictions. Sirkis expanded this technique as an activity preceding the praying of the eighteen benedictions, designed to cause a spiritual awakening for the one praying. Kagan expanded it further, locating it during the prayer service itself—every time that man loses his concentration he may use this technique. Shapira advanced this technique one step further, intending for its use outside of prayer. According to Shapira, this technique instills God's presence in all areas of man's daily life.

129 Shapira, *Ḥovat ha-Talmidim*, 27b-28a.

130 Idel, *Kabbalah: New Perspectives*, 97–103. Regarding *Sefer ha-Shem* by Eleazar of Worms, which expands upon the understanding of the Tetragrammaton, see Joseph Dan, *On Sanctity:*

these techniques focus on the pronunciation of combined divine names, as well as the active production of letter combinations, and do not generally engage with the imaginal realm. While we have found appearances of the divine name within prophetic visions in Abulafian and German pietistic circles, these appear in a spontaneous, inspired manner, without active human effort, such as the mystic visualizing the letters in his imagination.[131] The first trace of the visualization of the letters of the divine name may be found in the writings of Joseph ben Shalom Ashkenazi, a German kabbalist who was active at the end of the thirteenth century and moved to Barcelona, "It is not improbable that there will be a person to whom matters will appear in his imaginative faculty to that which appears to the imaginative faculty in a dream. All this [could take place] while someone is awake, and all his senses are obliterated, as the letters of the divine name [stand] in front of his eyes, in the gathered colors."[132] A short anonymous commentary on the *shema* prayer advises the visualization of the divine names in the prayer, "Don't pronounce the word *Israel* until one visualizes the divine name, which is *YHWH*, with its vowels."[133] Already in this period imagery techniques regarding the name of God were connected to the verse, "I have set the Lord always before me" (Ps. 16:8),[134] which was refined in Lurianic kabbalah, as I will

Religion, Ethics, and Mysticism in Judaism and Other Religions (Jerusalem: Magnes Press, 1997), 123–126.

131 Idem, *The Mystical Experience*, 100–105. The exceptional introduction of *Sefer ha-Ḥesheq* records an activity suggested for the mystic in which he is to visualize the letters of God's name as individual entities, "And the visualizer will think of them as though they are speaking to him," ibid., 104. Also concerning the revelation of the letters as "speaking" and fighting against God's enemies, idem, "*Milhemet ha-Yetzarim:* Psychomachia in Abraham Abulafia's Ecstatic Kabbalah," in *Peace and War in Jewish Culture*, ed. A. Bar Levav (Jerusalem: Zalman Shazar Center, 2006), 114–115.

132 Translation from idem, *Kabbalah: New Perspectives*, 105; Idel focused on the visualization of colors, whereas I have used the same text to emphasize the visualization of God's name, since Shapira omitted the component concerning the visualization of colors. Regarding the influence of colors (colorful clothing) on man's soul Shapira quotes Moses Cordovero, *Pardes Rimonim*, 10:1, see Shapira, *Ḥovat ha-Talmidim*, 7b; idem, *Mevo ha-She'arim*, 25a. Concerning the visualization of God's name, as well as an imagery technique, in the thought of Isaac of Acre, see Fishbane, *As Light Before Dawn*, 242–245.

133 Idel, *Kabbalah: New Perspectives*, 108.

134 See Ibid., which quotes the rest of the anonymous commentary presented here. Regarding Wolfson's conception, which understands the visualization of the divine name as concurrently a visualization of the divine anthropoid, idem, *Language, Eros, Being*, 122, 249, 246, 339; according to Wolfson the letters of the Tetragrammaton constitute the "divine body" and therefore their visualization is a corporealization of the divine, ibid., 125, 128, 240, 246. However, Isaac of Acre, in *Oṣar ha-Ḥayyim*, interprets the divine name in the verse, "I have set the Lord (*yy*) always

discuss below. Linguistic imaginal techniques are to be found in the sixteenth century as well, both in Lurianic and Cordoverian kabbalah.[135] This conception was carried over into later halakhic literature, and from there into halakhic decisions issued in the twentieth century. Joseph Karo (1488–1575) wrote in his comprehensive work *Shulḥan Arukh*, "During the blessings he should focus (*yekhaven*) on the meaning of the words. When he mentions the name, he should focus on the meaning of its reading as mastery (*be-adonut*) that he is the master of all, and he should focus on its being written of the *yod*, *he*, that he was, is and will be, and when he mentions *Elohim* (God), he should focus on his omnipotence and all-powerfulness.[136] Ḥayyim Joseph David Azulai (1724–1806) commented on this, "'When he mentions the name, etc.' Luria's students (*gurei ha-AR"Y*) wrote (*Sha'ar ha-Kavvanot* 4, 3b) "When he visualizes the tetragrammaton, and within the last *he*, he shall visualize the name Adonai, and also he shall integrate the two names together."[137] Israel Meir Kagan (1839–1933), the author of the *Mishneh Berurah*, most accepted contemporary ashkenazic-halakhic composition, which elucidates the *Shulḥan Arukh* (set table) and the *Mappah* (tablecloth) (Moses Isserless), comments on the opening remarks of Isserless on the *Shulḥan Arukh*—"A gloss: 'I have set the Lord always before me' (Ps. 16:8), is a major rule in the Torah and of the virtues of righteous people who walk before God,"[138]—with the following remark, "And they wrote in the name of Luria (*ha-AR"Y*), blessed be his memory, *that one should always visualize the tetragrammaton* before his eyes with the diacritization (*be-niqud*) of the word *yir'ah* (fear/awe) like this *YiHeVaH*,[139] and this is the mystery of 'I have set the Lord always before me' (Ps. 16:8), and this is greatly beneficial for the matter of awe."[140] For Shapira, the need to visualize the name of God further developed and sharpened

before me" (Ps. 16:8), as visualizing the ten *sefirot*, and not the name of God, see Fishbane, *As Light Before Dawn*, 245.

135 See above chap. 4, n. 49.

136 Joseph Karo, *Shulḥan Arukh*, Oraḥ Ḥayyim, §5.

137 Ḥayyim Joseph David Azulai, *Birkei Yosef*, Oraḥ Ḥayyim, §5. Azulai was a prolific author, brilliant halakhist, eminent kabbalist, important emissary, and bibliographer.

138 Moses Isserles gloss on Joseph Karo, *Shulḥan Arukh*, Oraḥ Ḥayyim, §1:1. His remarks are based on Maimonides, *Guide of the Perplexed*, 3:52.

139 Since in Hebrew the vowels are not part of the word, but rather are above or below the word, one can envision words of the same number of letters with different vowelization, without changing the word's form. Generally, the Tetragrammaton is written as *Yehovah*, but Kagan is suggesting that it should be envisioned (not pronounced, as it is never pronounced) as *Yihevah*.

140 Israel Meir Kagan, *Mishneh Berurah*, 1:4. For more on the visualization of the Tetragrammaton see Wacks, *The Flame of the Holy Fire*, 158–162.

the question of the link between the imagination and the intellect. I will begin with his depiction of man's failure to visualize the name of God:

> Behold, the greatness and holiness of visualization (*ṣiyur*) is known from the sacred books, that man should visualize the tetragrammaton before his eyes in accordance with the aspect of, "I have set the Lord always before me," and it is a bad sign for him if he will not be able to visualize it. What shall this helpless man do, who wants to visualize it and is unable to do? Like anger, the more he seeks to exert himself in order to visualize the holy name, the more difficult it is for him, even an image of a letter will be difficult for him to see.[141]

The helpless man fails due to his very efforts to envision. This is a concentrated intellectual effort, a nearly obsessive act of thought. It is this cognitive act which undermine the visualization:

> Moreover, the dearest image of your father, brother, son, that are now and always present in your imagination, when you will only begin to think, "What is now in my imagination, an image of my father, I want to properly envision his image, if his image truly in my imagination;" then his image is darkened in your imagination and entirely brought to an end, and the more you seek to try to visualize them in your imagination, the more their images will be removed from you at this hour.[142]

Shapira attempts to explain this psychological phenomenon by presenting the imagination and the intellect as two conflicting entities, "When his knowledge (*da'ato*) and ipseitic intellect are emboldened through this, then the imaginative faculty is weakened, even entirely evanescent… and the more that he wants to overcome and visualize, and the more that his knowledge and human intellect exert [themselves] and emerge (*ve-yoṣe*)—the more his imaginative potency is weakened and the harder it is for him to visualize the holy name."[143] The intellect, as a conscious action, represents more than anything else man's ipseity, the experience of self, the nullification of which—*biṭṭul ha-yesh*, the nullification of substance—is a foremost hasidic principle.[144] The imagination, in contrast to the intellect but similar to a dream, is active when one's consciousness is in a state of relaxation, when man is at a certain level of "nullification." It is difficult for someone to pinpoint the exact moment that they fall asleep; likewise it is challenging for one to note the exact moment that their thoughts drift during prayer

141 Shapira, *Mevo ha-She'arim*, 56b.
142 Ibid. Emphasis in original.
143 Ibid., 56b-57a.
144 See Jacobson, *Hasidic Thought*, 36–43, 54–64. Also see the subchapter, "Silencing Techniques," that intellectual activity is identified with the sense of self.

and begin to entertain "strange thoughts," for at that precise moment his self-awareness is enfeebled and ceases, and the imagination begins to take effect. In order to enable the imagination, one must silence the intellect, one's self-consciousness.

The silencing of consciousness occurs within a "person whose soul and body are holy."[145] A holy man of this sort, who has annihilated his ego, "has no natural or corporeal obstacle interfering with his visualization in his imagining the tetragrammaton, blessed be he, as it is written, at anytime that he wants."[146] However, this possibility is only for extraordinary saintly individuals, and cannot be a realistic solution for the broader, who are unable to arrive at this level of self-nullification, and the corresponding visualization devoid of self-awareness. Shapira suggests for them a technique of "imagery within imagery", whose purpose is to distract one's *da'at* (consciousness). I will term Shapira's suggested solution, "outflanking imagination," which I have borrowed from its militaristic sense of of bypassing and utilizing the element of surprise.[147] Shapira advises one to outflank the visualization of God and to surprise it from the rear, using entirely different imagery:

> He must use tips... for example he should think of the Torah reader, who read from the Torah, as he was standing or sitting and listening, and then suddenly he was called to the Torah, and he shall exert his consciousness (*da'ato*) to visualize in his imagination the details of the words. At first, he is a little discomfited, for had he not already had an *aliyah* (gone up to the podium to say a blessing on the Torah)... and he did not know if he should go to the Torah [podium] on the side where the Rebbi stands, or the other side, and he opened the Torah scroll and the Torah reader read, and he looks at each verse, "And God spoke to Moses saying," and contracts his thought to remember if it is "And God (*Elohim*) spoke, or "And God (*YHVH*) spoke," which he sees in the *parashah* (Torah portion) that they read in front of him, and in this fashion he shall visualize the entire verse and also the tetragrammaton in his imagination, without anything disturbing his visualization.[148]

The visualization of "Going up to the Torah" is a tetragrammaton imagery technique which distracts one's consciousness. The outflanking imagination, in its very essence as imagination, weakens the intellectual-consciousness power,

---

145 Shapira, *Mevo ha-She'arim*, 56b.
146 Ibid.
147 Its source is from Ezekiel 38:9, "You shall advance, coming like a storm; you shall be like a cloud covering the earth, you and all your cohorts (*agapekha*), and the many peoples with you." In this original context it appears in a militaristic imagery as well. The meaning of *agaf* in this verse is the two sides of the army encampment, see R. David Kimhi's explanation in situ.
148 Shapira, *Mevo ha-She'arim*, 56b.

thereby neutralizing the dominating obsessiveness that flows from man's egoism and allowing the desired imagery—the visualization of the divine name—to appear. This technique uniqueness's lies in its utilization of imagination within imagination. There is an imaginal plot (the story of going up to the Torah) which strives to reach a static visual (seeing the letters of the divine name). I have noted that Shapira is distinct in comparison to his predecessors is his development of multi-scenic imagery techniques, such as "waking dream" techniques, in contrast to kabbalistic static imagery techniques, such as visualizing letters, which have no story element. Here, surprisingly, Shapira develops multi-scenic imagery exercises for the purpose of performing a static imagery exercise, a phenemenon which attests to two things: the importance, for Shapira, of visualizing God's name despite its static nature, and his originality in creating a technique of imagination within imagination.

The significance of visualizing God's name in Shapira's thought does not culminate with the increase of awe or the arousal of religious passion. Unlike Kagan, who sees the purpose of this visualization as a medium for the acquisition of the "fear of heaven," as "this is the great purpose of the matter of awe," Shapira views the visualization of God's name as the central component of the preparatory work required to become a prophet.

Visualizing God's Name as a Technique for the Acquisition of Prophecy

Mentioning God's name as a means of acheiving ecstasy appears already in the Hekhalot literature, and afterwards in the geonic era as well. Similar testimonies appear also in German Pietistic circles.[149] The sacred names are also used as a means for receiving prophetic influx.[150] Joseph ben Shalom Ashkenazi focused

149 Idel, *The Mystical Experience*, 14–22.

150 Ibid., 19. For more on "the path of Names for prophecy," see idem, *Language, Torah, and Hermeneutics in Abraham Abulafia*, trans. Menahem Kallus (Albany: State University of New York Press, 1989), 101–109. For more regarding the conceptualization of the letters, ibid., 3–7 and on letter combinations, 8–11. Concerning Shapira's conception of divine names and letters as revelations of holy concatenations, idem, *Esh Qodesh*, 98, "In the forms of the holy names the ink is only a means by which to depict these letter-forms, and what are the forms themselves which necessitate specifically these forms? The concatenation of the illumination of the supernal holy lights are revealed through them. If so, they are, as it were, an icon of the king. And it is known from the holy book *Sha'arei Orah* concerning the verse, "The precepts (*pequdei*) of the Lord are just, rejoicing the heart" (Ps. 19:9), that in all of the Torah God's name, blessed be he, is deposited (*nifqad*), and all of it is weaved of holy names, through acronyms of initial let-

on seeing the tetragrammaton[151] for the purpose of prophecy, "Sometimes he will hear a voice, a wind, a speech, a thunder and a noise with all the organs of his hearing sense, and he will see with his imaginative faculty with all the organs of sight... All this while the holy letters are in front of his eyes, and its colors are covering it; this is the sleep of prophecy."[152] It is possible that Shapira saw the visualization of the divine name as a technique leading to prophecy as well:

> This is the purpose of our holy company, that you will be transformed into a man of spirit and thought—and not only thought, but pure and intense thought (*ha-maḥshavah ṭehorah ha-ḥazaqah*). Overcome your senses *and a new holy sense will be revealed within you*, so that when you say, "Blessed be you (*atah*) Lord our God, king of the world (*melekh ha-olam*)," *you will see* the you (*atah*) and king of the world (*melekh ha-olam*), your eyes by themselves will be open to the spirit to see the king of the world who surrounds the entire world and yourself. They [your eyes] will pierce and perceive through the entire exterior world the *you* and *the king*, which surround it. Your eyes will be empowered, and they will scour and see God who fills the world while he is in front of you, "*you*, king of the world."[153]

It is difficult to ascertain the author's intentions in this passage: is he teaching one how to visualize the divine name—"king of the world," or perhaps it is automatically disclosed to man in a prophetic vision, without human effort. Perhaps the intention is not about seeing the name at all, but rather perceiving divine immanence in the world.[154] Either way, Shapira recommends visualizing God's name, "Man shall visualize the tetragrammaton in front of his eyes,"[155] as part of a cohesive system of human-initiated attempts to acquire prophecy.[156]

---

ters, ending letters, or numerology (*gematria*), etc." Regarding this tradition of the Torah being comprised of holy names see Moshe Idel, *Absorbing Perfections*, 314–351.

151 See above the subchapter, "'To Visualize the Holy Name.'"

152 Idel, *Mystical Experience*, 32.

153 Shapira, *Benei Maḥshavah Ṭovah*, 33. Above we discussed this text in the subchapter, "Prophecy and Imagination," regarding the development of the prophetic sense.

154 The second person *Atah* (you) expresses a sense of divine intimacy and imminence, in contrast to the third-person *Hu* (he), which expresses an aspect of concealment and transcendence. *Melekh ha-Olam*, like *Atah*, constitutes an explicit sense of immanence. Also see idem, *Ḥovat ha-Talmidim*, 28a, "When you speak to God in the second person, for example, 'You are God,' or 'Blessed are you etc.' [... Say] the 'You' precisely and visualize in your consciousness that God is opposite you [when] you say, 'You.'" (Emphasis in original).

155 Idem, *Mevo ha-She'arim*, 56b.

156 His remarks concerning the visualization of the divine name were stated in the broader context of developing prophetic abilities. See ibid., 59a, that the development of the imagination together with other potencies constitute a stage of the process of "bringing all of one's emotional warmth, ecstasy, and even the human imagination to the house of God to transform them into wings and fly with them like the supernal angels."

D The Silencing Technique

The silencing technique is a remarkable exercise[157] within the ensemble of techniques that Shapira offered. Silencing is the polar opposite of imagery. The entire point of imagery techniques is to fill one's thought with numerous visualizations and items, whereas the silencing technique is meant to empty one's thoughts, similar to Eastern meditative techniques.[158] Robert Forman has distinguished between two types of mysticism: apophatic and kataphatic. The former is emptying one's consciousness, while the latter is the filling of one's consciousness with perceptions or images together an absolute focus on these objects.

> What is generally known as mysticism is often said to have two strands, which are traditionally distinguished as *apophatic* and *kataphatic* mysticism, oriented respectively towards emptying or the imagistically filling. These two are generally described in terms that are *without* or *with* sensory language. The psychologist Roland Fischer has distinguished a similar pairing as *trophotropic* and *ergotropic*, experiences that phenomenologically involve inactivity or activity. *Kataphatic* or imagistic mysticism involves hallucinations, visions, auditions or even a sensory-like smell or taste; it thus involves activity and is *ergotropic*. *Apophatic* mystical experiences are devoid of such sensory-like content, and are thus *trophotropic.*[159]

Generally, Shapira's imagery techniques do not include those of a thought-emptying character, like those found in Max (Eli'ezer Mordekhai) Théon's writings,[160]

157 Concerning this technique see, Leshem, "Between Messianism and Prophecy," 247–252; Natan Ophir, *Quieting the Mind: The Admor of Piaseczno* (Jerusalem: Jewish Meditation Institute Jerusalem, 1999); Wacks, *The Flame of the Holy Fire*, 170–180. Wacks associates this technique primarily with the realm of strange thoughts during prayer, in which, according to him, the goal of this technique is to silence them. Yet in the source itself, Shapira does not relate this technique to prayer at all and it is entirely designed for the reception of prophetic inspiration. In my opinion, this technique should be assigned to the realm of prophecy, and not prayer.

158 Regarding trance techniques of silencing and emptying the mind, and at times achieving a new state of consciousness, see Garb, *Shamanic Trance*, 11, 105–118. Concerning the imagination in this and similar states in Tantric Buddhism, see ibid., 99.

159 Robert K.C. Forman, "What Does Mysticism Have To Teach Us About Consciousness?," *Journal of Consciousness Studies* 5, no. 2 (1998): 188.

160 An unknown figure who has hardly been researched. Eli'ezer Mordekhai Théon, born in Warsaw in 1848 (moved to the Tlemcen Province in Algeria in 1887 two years after he married in England) died in Algeria in 1927. He and his wife were spiritual teachers in certain circles, which are still active today in the form of "Argaman Circle" in Jerusalem. About his wife see Boaz Huss, "Madame Théon, Alta Una, Mother Superior: The Life and Personas of Mary Ware (1839–1908)," *ARIES: Journal for the Study of Western Esotericism* 15 (2015): 210–246. Concerning his apophatic conception see the collection of his statements that his students published,

and as are found in Far Eastern meditation—the one exception being this "silencing technique." "The matter of silencing," is depicted by his student El'azar Bein,[161] who wrote this testimony during World War II after fleeing from Poland to Japan, still during Shapira's lifetime.[162] The testimony relates to remarks made by Shapira in c. 1936–1937:

> In the year 1936 or 1937... Our master, teacher and rabbi (*admo"r*), may the memory of the righteous be a blessing for the life of the world to come, began then with the statement of the rabbis blessed be their memory (*b. Berakhot*57b), "A dream is one-sixtieth of prophecy." As is known from his tract *Ḥovat ha-Talmidim*,[163] the approach of the *Admo"r* is that the ego of man stands in opposition to inspiration from above. And if his consciousness (*da'ato*) and his thought are awakened, then it is difficult for him to be inspired by the inspiration from above. And at the time man sleeps, his consciousness and thought are quiet; it is precisely then, since then he does not have self-consciousness, that it is possible for him to become inspired from above, and this is the matter of "a dream is one, etc."... Therefore, the main aim is to attain a state of sleep while he is awake, whenever he desires, by silencing his thoughts and wishes that flow through man without end... And he [Shapiro] then remarked, "when a person will begin to perceive his thoughts for several moments every hour, thinking 'what I am thinking,' then he will slowly feel that his head is emptying and that the regular tide of his thought has been halted. He should then begin to say a verse, for example, 'The Lord is truly God' (Jer. 10:10), in order to now bind his empty mind (*ro'sho*), emptied of all other thoughts, to one holy thought." ... It is also possible to silence [the mind] by staring at a clock [at the small hand that almost does not move (i.e., the hour hand)] for a duration of some time,[164] for this also silences his desires and thoughts. Following the silencing, which must bring some kind of inspiration from

Eliezer Mordekhai Theon, *The Gate to the Secrets of Contemplation* (Jerusalem: Argaman Circle, 1995), esp. 20–21, 26–27. Theon presents a passive meditative method that advocates emptying/silencing one's consciousness and abandoning images, "A sensory person sometimes needs to deepen his passive state, in order to add and progress... sensory people need to undergo a lengthy period of relaxation without vision or imagination" (ibid., 20); "It is forbidden to mix ideas of the imagination in authentic passive visions" (ibid., 21). Theon emphasized the meditative methods he developed: relaxation, contemplation, tranquility, and silence, "Relaxation of the physical senses and of the active intellect allows for the stirring of spiritual senses" (ibid., 20), and focused on passivity, "The importance of spiritual passivity... will be common knowledge at the dawn of the period of redemption" (ibid., 25).

161 The son of Leibel Bein, the author of *From the Notebook of a Hassidic Journalist.*

162 See Leshem, "Between Messianism and Prophecy," 247 n. 818.

163 According to the manuscript. In print, "in his books," appears (however, at this time he had only published *Ḥovat ha-Talmidim*). I would like to thank my colleagues and teachers Dr. Zvi Leshem and Prof. Nehemia Polen, who gave me copies of the manuscript.

164 The words, "on the small hand that almost does not move," do not appear in the manuscript. It is probable that this addition was written in as to clarify the matter at hand by the editors of *Derekh ha-Melekh.* Regarding the implications of this addition see below chap. 8, subchapter, "The Unconscious and the Occult."

> above, he is commanded to say the verse, "O Lord, lead me along Your righteous [path]" (Ps. 5:9), in the special tune of the *Admo"r*… The *Admo"r* stressed this matter greatly at the time, and he said that he is certain that it is very advantageous. For example, regarding faith, he said that after practicing this silencing technique for a few weeks, when the person will say, "This is my God and I will enshrine Him" (Ex. 15:2), it will be in the aspect of "pointing with a finger" as is taught in the midrash.[165]

Those imagery techniques in Shapira's thought, which are not based on emptying one's thoughts from all content and arriving at a state of nothingness and emptiness but are rather rooted in filling one's thoughts with "many detailed visualizations,"[166] are constitutive of the kataphatic mystical model. In contrast, the silencing technique is constitutive of the apophatic mystical model. However, the emptying of one's mind using the silencing technique is not the goal, but is rather solely a means or intermediate stage preceding the filling of one's consciousness with one thought, "in order to now bind his empty mind (*ro'sho*), emptied of all other thoughts, to one holy thought."

Both the imagery techniques and silencing technique share the common goal of prophecy. Similar to imagery techniques, silencing aims attain inspiration from above. This teaching is based upon the rabbinic statement, "a dream is one-sixtieth of prophecy," and concludes with a direct reference to the outcome of optical prophecy, as Shapira writes, "[After practicing this silencing technique for several weeks] when the person will say, 'This is my God and I will enshrine Him' (Ex. 15:2), it will be in the aspect of 'pointing with a finger.'" This last clause referes to the rabbinic midrash that claims that at the time of the splitting of the sea, all of the Israelites reached a higher gradation of prophecy than that of Ezekiel. The sages use the motif of sight to characterize this level of collective prophecy:

> "This is my God and I will enshrine Him" (Ex. 15:2)—R. Eliezer says, "From where do you know that the handmaiden at the sea saw that which Isaiah and Ezekiel did not see? For it is written, 'This is my God and I will enshrine him.' And it is written, 'And spoke parables through the prophets' (Hos. 12:11), and it is written, 'The heavens opened and I saw visions of God' (Ez. 1:1), but at the sea everyone saw and said, 'This is my God and I will enshrine Him.'"[167]

---

165 Shapira, *Derekh ha-Melekh*, 450–451, with changes made according to the manuscript.
166 Idem, *Hakhsharat ha-Avreikhim*, 16b.
167 *Pesiqta Zuṭrata* (*Leqaḥ Ṭov*), Exodus 15, s.v. "azi ve-zimrat." For more detail, see also in the later midrash *Yalqut Shim'oni*, Parashat be-Shalaḥ §244, "'This is my God': R. Eliezer says, 'From where do you know that the handmaiden at the sea saw that which Isaiah and Ezekiel did not see? For it is written, "This is my God and I will enshrine him." And it is written, "And spoke parables through the prophets" (Hos. 12:11), and it is written, "The heavens opened" (Ez. 1:1).

The silencing of thought appears in a additional sermon of Shapira in the midst of a theoretical discussion. While not engaging with the praxis of the technique, nevertheless, he adds an analytical dimension to the matter of silencing, unmistakably demonstrating that its goal is prophecy, "This may also be guidence for how people may come to be stirred and reveal the divine portion within their being, without stirring regarding his own needs... and if man would steady [himself] and cease for one hour *his entire stream of thoughts and wants*, a divine portion would appear to him without a garment (*levush*)... and then a pure '*HV"Y* [one of the highest combinations of the divine name] of his *aṣilut* aspect will reveal itself to him."[168] According to this remark, the divine immanence that is within man might be revealed to him "without a garment" (again the motif of sight) through the silencing technique of emptying one's mind. As I demonstrated above, the disclosure of man's soul (*hitgalut ha-nefesh*) to himself (and in this case, "his *aṣilut* aspect will reveal itself to him"), is a level of prophecy.[169]

E Categorization of Imagery Techniques

Comparing silencing and imagery techniques sharpens their specific definition, as well as the attempts to categorize the use of the imagination as a praxis. The silencing technique is seemingly apophatic in nature, as the silencing of consciousness is meant to bring about spontaneous prophetic inspiration. In contrast, imagery techniques are kataphatic in nature, encouraging human effort and action to fill and stimulate the consciousness. This distinction is similar to that between imagination as a product of human effort and imagination as a product of spontaneous inspiration.[170] That said, the picture is more complex. These two different aspects led Shapria to treat these techniques in ambivalent and different, even paradoxical, fashions. Sometimes he would stress the human facet, the analytical and intentional effort, while at other times he would negate

A parable—to what is the matter similar? To a king of flesh and blood who entered a country and a on his behalf a horn [is blown] around him and his warriors are to the right and left of him and soldiers in front of him and behind him and everyone would be asking, 'Is that the king?' since he is flesh and blood like them, but when the holy one, blessed be he, was revealed by the sea, no one needed to ask, 'Is that the king,' for when when they saw him they recognized him and everyone began by saying, 'This is my God and I will enshrine Him.'"

168 Shapira, *Derekh ha-Melekh*, 5. Emphasis in original.

169 See above subchapters, "*Nefesh Geluyah* (A Revealed Soul)" and "*Gilui ha-Nefesh* (Revelation of the Soul) and Prophecy."

170 See above, intro., n. 35, and for more on this distinction see above chap. 1, at the end of subchapter, "R. Judah Halevi."

this facet and emphasize the spontaneous and "non-awareness" needed for the development of an "imagination of holiness." Consequently, the categorization of imagination as a technical instrument wavers between its characterization as a deliberate human initiative and its characterization as spontaneous prophetic inspiration. However, these different characteristics should not be viewed as contradictory; rather, they sometimes act as two succeeding stages. At times, Shapira advocates for the practice of sophisticated and intentional imagery techniques in order to acquire the capability for spontaneous prophecy, abandoning the previous images and allowing for the influx of divine images. One example of this is found in his discussion of the third meal eaten on the Sabbath. Shapira distinguishes between the imagination intent on *visualizing visualizations* (*le-ṣayer ṣiyurim*) and the development of the *visualizing soul* (*nefesh ha-meṣayeret*), which allows for spontaneous-prophetic inspiration:

> You should surely know and [let it be] engraved in your mind that you should not mistakenly think that it is our intention that when the hour of third meal comes that you should direct your consciousness (*da'atekha*) to seek thoughts and visualize visualizations, certainly not. For the main aspect of the third meal is to become bound to God and to pour out one's heart in front of him—in this you should be immersed. Our general intention is not to disclose visualizations alone, but to rather [disclose] your visualizing soul... and it is not our demand that our visualizing soul will disclose from itself secular matters (*devarim hedyoṭim*). Rather, it should only visualize sacred matters and sacred images will be disclosed from within us, and from within ourselves it will reveal them without our needing to seek thoughts and images.[171]

At times, the aim of human initiative is to arrive at the nullification of said initiative. Man visualizes images in order to develop a visualizing soul in order that he no longer has to visualize images; rather, they will be presented to him spontaneously. There are three topics addressed in this text: first—the trend to disclose the visualizing soul and not the visualizations. Second—the need to direct this soul energy towards the prophetic-mystic terrain with the goal of revealing sacred images. Third—the imaginal activity is to be done in a spontaneous fashion, "and from within ourselves it will reveal them," without intention or awareness, "without our needing to seek thoughts and images." The guiding of this mental energy towards the goal of prophecy is accomplished in two primary ways. The first is through use of imagery techniques, through which Shapira intended to develop of man's natural imaginative faculty and prepare the imagination to receive prophetic inspiration, "At the time that you will feel some holy excitement, *do not search for images* and parables, but rather wait and contem-

171 Shapira, *Hakhsharat ha-Avreikhim*, 18b.

plate your holy feeling and add to its stirring, *and thoughts with sacred images upon them will ascend of their own accord, if you will only strengthen and broaden your thoughts with your holy imagination.*[172] The strengthening of thought and imagination, autonomous human actions, allows for the ascension of holy images of their own accord.

An additional path suggested by Shapira for the preparation of the imagination for spontaneous-prophetic inspiration is the engagement with the mystical-midrashic aspect of Torah. In his opinion, the mystical aspect of the Torah has a feature, a unique quality (*segulah*), of empowering the sense of holiness in one's life and endowing this quality of holiness to the one who engages with it.[173] The quality of a man's life determines the objects of his imagination, and therefore, he who experiences the mystical as an essential and integral aspect of his life will subsequently have his imagination shaped accordingly:[174]

---

172 Ibid. His guidance to "not search for images" appears additionally within the following statement, "Pay attention and listen, and do not err. You have already been warned above that it is not our intention that upon feeling some feeling within your being, that you should begin to roam intellectually and search for this or that image that will suit your feeling—nothing of the sort. For your feeling will be exchanged by this, and furthermore the depictions that come about through searching are only acts of the intellect, and we want through this that God will help us to see the soul that is higher than the intellect" (ibid., 30a). In contrast, and almost paradoxically, Shapira tends to present a certain aspect of the imagery technique as a result of calculated and intentional human effort, "The person who has intense thought (*maḥshavah ḥazaqah*), at the time that he is stirred and impassioned his thought is intensified and cleansed and he sees in his thought and imagination... God, blessed be he, and his throne of glory... to the extent that even afterwards, after his ecstasy, he is able to grasp his earlier thought without losing it [and] visualize also now his glory, blessed be he, in front of him, and this intense thought is able to stir his fervor again at any and every time when he prepares himself" (idem, *Benei Maḥshavah Ṭovah*, 13). A person who practices with intense thought is able, through the imagination, to stir his ecstatic fervor at any time. The ability to grasp something and use it in the present, "also now," is a skill of deep consciousness and intentionality, "at any and every time when he prepares himself." This activity is nothing other than a function of consciousness and intention.

173 See also ibid., 52–53, "Study hasidic books... and even if there are matters that you do not understand... the words themselves and the holy spirit within them will cling to you and you will be purified."

174 And similarly concerning his dreams, see idem, *Hakhsharat ha-Avreikhim*, 13a, "Since at the time that he feels, his will, his consciousness, and thoughts are given over to the mire of worldly matters, the murmur of his soul and its voice are heard to whimper. This may be compared to a sleeping man who is bitten by a fly on his forehead. If he is a merchant, he sees in his dream that a package of merchandise fell on his forehead and is damaged, and if he is tailor he sees a needle stab his forehead etc. Each person perceives his dreams through the garb of his ideas."

> And with what does one strengthen *maḥshavah* (thought)—also with Torah... increase your learning of the midrashim of *Ein Ya'aqov,* and of the holy *Zohar* as well... and besides the precious [ability] of the midrashim and aggadot to draw holiness onto a man, they also have a unique quality (*segulah*) of revealing his thought in order to intensify (*le-ḥazaqah*) and sanctify it... You should also increase the study of holy hasidic books... you should increasingly think of matters written there, not only in order that you should remember to fulfill that which is written there, but also in order to sanctify and strengthen your thought.[175]

Shapira highlights and emphasizes that every person imagines in a sub-conscious and spontaneous fashion, "For it is simple and a well-known rule that one's mind thinks small thoughts even without their awareness."[176] The more one lives a mystical-religious life of "excitement and fervor" (*hitragshut ve-hitlahavut*),[177] the more he prepares his soul for prophetic imagination. The conception of spontaneous imagination, which appears when man's consciousness is at rest, and intentional, human-initiated, imagination, are not paradoxical, but rather form a continuous process leading towards prophetic inspiration. This may be clarified through the following image: when a man is interested in sleeping, he undertakes a number of activities in order to materialize his goal, activities which are undertaken consciously. However, the moment of "falling" asleep is when man loses awareness of his surroundings and drifts into unconsciousness. Without this occurring, man would not be able to fall asleep. This explains why one is unable to pinpoint the moment that he falls asleep, for if he would know, that would means that he would be conscious of it, yet this is a moment of unconsciousness. In this regard, imagery techniques resemble falling asleep: the conscious activities undertaken by the person lead him towards an unconscious state, and from that state onwards he is in a dream state in which matters occur spontaneously, without calculation or intention. Consciousness leads to its own

175 Ibid., 30b-32a.

176 Idem, *Ḥovat ha-Talmidim*, 43b. Regarding the imagination as a natural component see Adir Cohen, *To Dream with Open Eyes (Guide): Bibliotherapy, Guided Imagery, Creative Writing* (Tel Aviv: Mishkal, 1995), 78, "Each person has imaginal pictures in his mind, without any connection to thought processes or his expectations. It is enough for him to calm down and close his eyes, and imaginal pictures will be created in his psyche. It is not for nothing that the imagination is called, "the eye of the soul."

177 The concept of excitement in Shapira's thought is clarified and elucidated in *Hakhsharat ha-Avreikhim*, 5b-6b, as a spiritual, and not ecstatic, experience, "For you also want the world and its matters at this hour, only that your soul is excited for God your soul as well." In contrast to excitement, fervor or impassionment (*hitlahavut*) has an ecstatic dimension, "At this hour, all of the world and its aspirations are loathsome for you and you have but one desire and yearning —for God... [this] is already the beginning of fervor and not excitement" (ibid., 7a-7b).

undoing. Concerning daydreams as well, it is difficult to identify the precise time in which they occurr. At that point he has ceased paying attention to what he was consciously doing and spontaneously began to imagine. Shapira aimed to design imagery techniques, carried out in an intentional manner, in order to develop one's spontaneous-prophetic ability—in which revelation occurs unconsciously.

We have defined imagery techniques as visualizations that are a byproduct of human initiative and effort. This endeavor is done as a preparation for different goals, as we have seen thus far. Among these goals is prophecy—or more specifically, the acquisition of prophecy. This field is irrigated by these two different categorizations of imagination: imagination as a byproduct of calculated intentional human endeavor and imagination as a moment of spontaneous inspiration in which effort is used to acquire this inspiration, despite the implied paradox.

F Conclusion

I have discussed the relation between imagination and prophecy in the thought of Zadok ha-Kohen Rabinowitz and Abraham Isaac ha-Kohen Kook, and the aspiration for ecstatic prophecy in the twentieth century. The rest of the chapter was dedicated to the discussion of Shapira's longing for such prophecy. This yearning, which is foundational for his thought, led him to devise imagery techniques for the development of the prophetic sense and prophetic inspiration. I analyzed the imagination in his thought as an instrument for corporealizing God (with different variations: God, heavens, divine names, etc.), and the tension within the imaginal spectrum, in which Shapira oscillated, between the urge to see God and the prohibition to do so, a tension in which the mystical experience fluctuates.

Imagery techniques are characterized by effort and human endeavors designed to develop a prophetic sense within man, a sense in which the imagination's characterization is altered from an intentional and calculated to a prophetically inspired imagination, from "intense thought (*maḥshavah ḥazaqah*) and the imagination of holiness" to "sacred thought and the imagination of disciples of the prophets (*benei ha-nevi'im*)":

> We wish to become worthy of revealing the visionary spark from the disciples of the prophets that is within us. To this end, we must reveal and actualize [our capacity for] intense thought (*maḥashavah ḥazaqah*) and holy imagination within ourselves. We have earlier cited from the holy books how he must imagine holy visions as if they were before his eyes. [We mean] intense thought, not seductive imaginings, or empty hallucinations (phantasms) that are nothing... you should raise up contemplations of the soul and holy visions

> within yourself. When you have been moved and the soul hidden within you starts to be revealed, little by little reaching out to your mind and heart, you will find the intense thought and holy imagination of the disciples of the prophets; you will even have visions of your excitement and your passionate enthusiasm.[178]

Shapira's conception of prophecy, a mystical conception, in contradistinctions to A.J. Heschel's, views the ecstatic-experiential components as central, without diminishing or negating the emissarial aspects. Shapira believed that the ecstatic component of prophecy is what grants the prophet his emissarial abilities. The experiential encounter with the divine, which shakes man's being, grants him the power, passion, and ability to change reality.[179]

---

178 Ibid., 30a.

179 See above chap. 3. However, see now Eugene Matanky's claim that Heschel's understanding of prophecy may well be ecstatic as well as emissarial, idem, "The Mystical Element in Abraham Joshua Heschel's Theological-Political Thought," *Shofar: An Interdisciplinary Journal of Jewish Studies* 35, no. 3 (2017): 33–55.

Chapter Six
A War of Imaginations: Imagery Techniques in R. Menaḥem Ekstein's Teachings

> Incidentally, I will not withhold the good from the pleasant reader, I shall write what I heard from my friend, the rabbi, the hasid, a packed treasure trove (*oṣar balum*) R. Menaḥem Ekstein from Rzeszów (Rayshe), may his light shine, who said in the name of the holy genius, the rabbi, and *ṣaddiq* of Dzików, blessed be the memory of the righteous for the world to come, that the art of musical notes in several songs are similar in their images to the sacred *sefirot*, and the matter is like this: in the notes there are long lines and short lines and medium lines and through the mixture of the types of instrumental playing a pleasant melody emerges from them. So too with the sacred *sefirot*—one is long and one short and one medium, and the long one is *ḥesed* (grace) which comes from the virtue of *erekh appayim* (long suffering), therefore the *sefirah* of *ḥesed* in the books of true scholars is called *gedulah* (greatness), as is known to those who know the esoteric wisdom (i.e. kabbalah).
> —Alter Ḥayyim Levenson, *Sefer Tiqqun Olam* (Warsaw: Feder Brothers Publishing, 1932), 69.

A Biographical Introduction

R. Menaḥem Mendel (Menye, Munye) Ekstein was born on December 21, 1884 in the city of Rzeszów (Rayshe) in the center of Western Galicia (Poland after World War I).[1] Although born into a prominent family about which much has been written, very little has been written about Menaḥem Mendel himself. His father R. Mordekhei Ekstein, a senior Dzików hasid,[2] nown warmly as Reb Motish, was an esteemed Jew who owned a flour and saw mill (and bakery).[3] Ita, Mordekhei's wife, managed the businesses and Mordekhei dedicated most of his time to pub-

1 Mendel Ekstein's birth certificate, The Polish National Archive of Rzeszów, Mic. no. 553/62, 332–333. I am grateful to Dr. Grzegorz Zamoyski, the archive's director, who assisted me in locating genealogical details about the Ekstein family and with their translation from Polish. Two pages of testimony in Yad Vashem place the birth year as 1881, however the birth certificates show that this was the birth year of his brother Re'uven Ekstein (idem, Mic. no. 533/62, 110–11).
2 On Dzików Hasidism, see Yitzhak Alfasi, *The Kingdom of Wisdom: The Court of Ropczyce-Dzików* (Jerusalem: Carmel, 1994).
3 Berish Weinstein, *Reyshe: Poeme* (New York: Ignatov Fund, 1947), 17: "The mill, the saw, the bakery." In many sources the Ekstein family appears as an esteemed family owning a flour and saw mill; it is only in this source that they also have a bakery.

https://doi.org/10.1515/9783110535884-009

lic concerns.[4] Mordekhei held prayer services in his home for the Sabbath and festivals; his home also hosted many Dzików ḥasidim on different occasions and was nicknamed the *Dzikover Kloyz*,[5] and the *Shtibl* (an informal house of prayer and gathering).[6] Mordekhei's home, which was famous for its generosity and warmth, was open to all: "Reb Motish's hasidic home was renowned far and wide."[7] When the Rebbe, R. Joshua of Dzików would come to Rzeszów, he would only stay in Mordekhei's house.[8] Reb Motish founded an "Agudath Israel" branch in Rzeszów and his household was active in the "Agudah" and in the activities of "Agudath Israel Youth."[9]

Reb Motish and Ita had five children: Me'ir, Re'uven, Menaḥem Mendel, Yehudis (Ida), and Tehilla (Tila).[10] The three sons are recorded as rabbinic scholars and erudite learners.[11] Besides Me'ir's studiousness,[12] he is described as possessing general and extensive knowledge, as well as fluency in languages, including German and Polish, an uncommon trait among ḥasidim of Rzeszów.[13] Expertise in these languages was acquired due to Reb Motish, a detail that testifies to a certain atmosphere of openness in his home.[14] Me'ir's openness to modernity cost him greatly, prompting slander and libel about his wife's dress and mannerisms.[15] Alongside his learning, like his father, he was a public figure, a member

---

4 Moshe Yari-Wold, ed., *Rzeszow Community: Memorial Book* (Tel Aviv: Former Residents of Rzeszow in Israel and the USA, 1967), 280; Weinstein, *Reyshe*, 17.

5 Yari-Wold, *Rzeszow Community*, 158.

6 Weinstein, *Reyshe*, 17, 58.

7 Ibid., 18. Also ibid., 58.

8 Ibid., "When the Rebbe R. Joshua would come to Rzeszów... he would always stay in R. Motish's house" (*az der rebbe yehoshuele kumt keyn reyshe... shteyt er tomid bay reb motishn in hoyz*).

9 Yari-Wold, *Rzeszow Community*, 158, 164.

10 According to birth certificates they had an additional child, Shemu'el (1887–1888), but he passed away before the age of one.

11 Yari-Wold, *Rzeszow Community*, 280. Weinstein, *Reyshe*, 18. Re'uven wrote a commentary on *seliḥot* (penitential poems) entitled *Ma'amar Mordekhei*, and halakhic and talmudic essays in Torah journals, see *Tel Talpios* 6 (1898); *Apiryon* 1 (1924): 139; *Ohel Mo'ed* 1 (1898): 46 and see Me'ir's article, ibid, 58–59. Also see the halakhic response of the Rebbe of Dzików to Reb Motish Ekstein in Meir Horowitz, *Responsa Imre No'am* (Krakow: Josef Fisher Publishing, 1888), 287–289§§6, s.v. "teshuvah le-motish eqshtein be-qehilah qedosha reyshe." I am grateful to Netanel Yechieli for these references.

12 Weinstein, *Reyshe*, 18.

13 Yari-Wold, *Rzeszow Community*, 280; Weinstein, *Reyshe*, 18. Me'ir is also described as reading general newspapers, "And he even reads newspapers from the greater world."

14 Ibid.

15 Ibid., 19. His wife is described as following Western European fashion, walking in the streets, and enjoying coffee shops.

of the municipal senate and active on the rabbinic committee.[16] Following World War I, he engaged in rebuilding the Jewish essentials of the city, like fixing the ritual bathhouses, synagogues, and *eruvim* (ritual enclosures).[17] Alter Ḥayyim Levenson, who taught Me'ir's children described the Ekstein family as follows:

> I then traveled to Dzików to the rebbe to ask his advice about one town in his area which wanted me to be a teacher (*melamed*) and he said to me in these words: "My mind is inclined that you should travel to Rzeszów for the simple reason that you are a native of Poland, for in our land [Polish natives] are considered foreigners, therefore you need to choose men of a rare disposition and good heart, for this you shall go to the city of Rzeszów and you will find there men of a rare disposition and good heart and I will also give you a letter for friends (*anshe shelomeinu*) who will take you in." Immediately, I heeded his advice and I traveled to the city of Rzeszów and I went to one of our friends, the rabbi, genius, lord, famous R. M. Ekstein,[18] may his light shine, and he graciously welcomed me and he gave me his sons together with the sons of our lord and generous, teacher and Rabbi Elḥanan Nussbaum, may his light shine, and since they observed that I was diligent in my learning with their sons, I was loved by them as a family member, with a strong love, and so I was with them for the duration of the war. And when the tidings of the terrible war came then due to the greatness of noise, all the city's inhabitants panicked and rushed to escape, one this way and one that way in order to find shelter for themselves (*nafsham*).[19]

Me'ir died in his prime on January 4, 1928 in Dzików during a tragedy that occurred on the *yortsayt* (anniversary of the day of death) of the Rebbe R. Joshua of Dzików.[20] Re'uven and his family were killed in the Holocaust. The only survivor of R. Motish's family was Yehudis, who studied medicine in Vienna and after-

---

16 Ibid., 18.

17 Alter Ḥayyim Levenson, *Sefer Tiqqun Olam* (Warsaw: Feder Brothers Publishing, 1932), 23: "And may the name of my friend, the esteemed and kind rabbi and ḥasid R. Me'ir Ekstein, may he merit long and good days, amen, be remembered for good, for he repaired and built *eruvim* (ritual enclosures) throughout the entire city with the permission of the government, according to [the prescriptions of] law and halakhah and also prompted Torah scholars and god fearers to make a society of Sabbath observers."

18 This abbreviation "R. M." is difficult for it may stand for three different individuals simultaneously: Mordekhai Ekstein, Me'ir Ekstein, and Menaḥem Ekstein. In light of the dating, Mordekhai's sons are not being referred to in this passage, for they were in their thirties during World War I. Me'ir's sons apparently became famous and excelled scholastically: Eliyahu and Yosef Ekstein, see Weinstein, *Reyshe*, 17: "The grandchildren Yosef and Elia learned day and night in their grandfathers *shtibl.*"

19 Levenson, *Sefer Tiqqun Olam*, 21.

20 Yari-Wold, *Rzeszow Community*, 280. The innkeeper forgot to open the chimney and Reb Me'ir choked on the poisonous vapors in his sleep. He was buried next to the grave of R. Joshua of Dzików.

wards in Tel Aviv.[21] Chavah Yoles, daughter of Tehilla (who also perished in the Holocaust), was a partisan fighter and a central pillar in the Kraków Jewish underground. After a lengthy period of brave acts—such as attacking a train station, shooting at Gestapo detectives, attacking officers clubs, shelling senior officers, changing her identity, and fleeing—she was caught in March, 1943. Even more, during the execution march of the underground companies she decided to die with honor, and was shot in the back while attempting escape.[22]

Unlike most of the Ekstein family members, I have not found much documentation about Menaḥem Mendel, possibly because he did not devote himself, like his father and brother, to public matters. He studied in 1897 at the talmudic academy of the famous R. Jekuthiel Aryeh ben Gershon Kamelhar (1871–1937),[23] with his brother Re'uven.[24] He and Kamelhar and were very close, and even during the great dispute in Rzeszów between Motish Ekstein and Kamelhar,[25] Menaḥem Mendel remained loyal to his teacher (and not his father). This relationship continued for many years. Later Kamelhar would refer to Ekstein,[26] in his books and letters, with words of love and friendship, like "my love" and "friend of my soul", and the like.[27] At a certain stage, after he married, he moved from Rzeszów to Sanok, which is found in the same region (Rzeszów County). There he fathered twin sons, Moshe and Barukh, in 1908. However, he returned to Rzeszów no later than 1910.[28]

In the wake of World War I, he settled in Hungary between 1916 and 1917, and exchanged letters with Kamelhar, who was then travelling between Austria, Hungary, and Poland.[29] This period was not easy, consisting of spiritual difficulties and physical dangers, as Ekstein wrote in one of these letters:

---

21 Ibid.

22 Ibid., 336–338. Chavah was one of the organizers of the escape and thanks to her four fighters succeeded and survived.

23 Concerning him see Yehoshua Mondshine, *Ha'Tsofeh Le'Doro: Rabbi Yekuthiel Aryeh Kamelhar, His Life and Works* (Jerusalem: Rubin Mass, 1987).

24 Ibid., 28.

25 Regarding this turbulent disagreement in Rzeszów, see ibid., 47–50.

26 From this point Ekstein solely refers to Menaḥem Mendel Ekstein.

27 See the end of the introduction in Jekuthiel Aryeh Kamelhar, *Ḥasidim Rishonim: Dor Dorim* (Vác: s.n., 1917), ii; Mondshine, *Ha'Tsofeh Le'Doro*, 158.

28 According to Yad Vashem archives, his daughter Chaya was born in 1910 in Rzeszów.

29 These are nine lengthy and fascinating letters, each one a few pages. The letters are found in the archives of Jekuthiel Aryeh b. Gershon Kamelhar, in the archive department of the National Library in Jerusalem, ARC. 4°1517; I am grateful to Netanel Yechieli who informed me of these letters. Also see their mention in Mondshine, *Ha'Tsofeh Le'Doro*, 147–149. The fact that he was in Hungary and moved throughout Hungary is demonstrated in his letters: Wednesday, Sep-

> I am also living in a village by Pest, home to hundreds of families from the capital city in the summer, while in the winter there is neither a quorum nor anyone with whom to speak. A journalist correctly compared our lives with those of soldiers lying in defensive trenches in wait. Every one of us has also dug a trench and cave to shelter himself, live in, and wait until the fury will pass. This waiting is indeed a very difficult matter... However, a man who is at some spiritual level... has a greater power to be strengthened without being totally broken by the suffering of this burden. Specifically, the devotees of God (*ḥasidei ha-shem*), [for] he [God] will not leave them... so God will help us and soon may we merit and see the end of the war and soon may we merit to rejoice in the pleasantness of peace.[30]

These letters reveal the broad world of Ekstein and his thirst for general knowledge: "I feel a soul-hunger to read in [my] spare time, *Ha-Tsefirah* does not satisfy my soul and I only find a little in it here and there."[31] These letters contain the initial inklings, of what later became his mature thought in his book. Nonetheless, most of these letters revolve around finding an acceptable solution for the exiled Jewish people following World War I, attitudes towards nationalism, and collaboration with the secular Zionist movement.[32] It appears that following the

---

tember 20, 1916: "I am also in a village adjacent to Pest;" Wednesday December 27, 1916: "My dear brother Re'uven, may his light shine, perhaps can be found on Stefánia St. 8/8 where I lived with him last year." Indeed, this fact emerges as well from Kamelhar's letters: "On Passover eve 1918 (27th of March) I was in the village of Nagymaros near Vác, in the house of my beloved friend R. Menaḥem Ekstein, may his light shine, for Passover." Ibid., 158. Pest is the Eastern part of Budapest (which is comprised of Pest, Buda, and Óbuda); Vác (*Vacz*) is 34 kilometers north of Budapest on the Eastern shore of the Danube River. In Vác, from the beginning of the twentieth century until the Holocaust, there was a flourishing Jewish community, see *Ha-Maor: Rabbinical Bi-Monthly Journal* 35, no. 2 (December/January 1982–1983): 38; Chaim Bloch, *Heikhal le-Divrei Ḥaza"l U-Pitgameihem* (New York: Pardes, 1948), 11 (like Ekstein, Bloch also settled in Vienna in the wake of World War I: "Meanwhile World War I broke out. I was forced to flee my city of birth Deliatyn [in Galicia], adjacent to the Hungarian border... For some time, I was in the holy congregation of Vác by Budapest... from Vác I went with my family to Vienna"). In 1917 Kamelhar's book *Ḥasidim Rishonim* was published with the financial assistance and support of Ekstein (see above, n. 27) it appears that the place of printing was not arbitrary, but rather was due to Ekstein's living in that area during those years.

30 Wednesday, September 20, 1916.

31 Wednesday, December 20, 1916 (the first day of Hanukkah). *Ha-Tsefirah* began (in 1862) as a Hebrew newspaper which promoted Haskalah (Jewish Enlightenment) ideas in the Jewish intellectual sphere. At the end of the nineteenth century, after Nahum Sokolow became the editor in 1894, the newspaper changed its orientation to Zionism and from the year 1917 the paper received financial support from the Zionist Organization. Ekstein's reading of this newspaper, as well as his disappointment with it, reveal his cultural leanings.

32 See Ekstein's attitude towards the settlement of Palestine in a letter written on October 4, 1917: "The fact that a great benefit sprouted in our land [Palestine] because of the war, and that the deserts and the desolate areas there are beginning to be built up from the destruction

war he moved to Vienna,[33] together with 77,000 other Jewish refugees, most of them from Galicia and Bucovina.[34] The Jewish refugees from Galicia, Hungary, and Czech Republic brought with them an Eastern European Jewish spirit to a Western Vienna. Many hasidic rabbis, such as the Rebbe of Czortków, the Rebbe of Husiatyn, the Rebbe of Sadigura (all three grandsons of the Rebbe of Ruzhin, Yisroel Friedman, the Rebbe of Kopyczyńce, the Rebbe of Storozhynets, the Rebbe of Stanislaw, and the Rebbe of Skolye (Skole), and their courts were among them. Each one of them had thousands of followers who continued their lifestyles and traditions almost without any change and "brought a new bloodstream of Judaism... into the arteries of the Viennese community."[35] This concentration of hasidic courts led to the introduction of the first major convention (*Kenessi'ah Gedolah*) of the Ḥaredi movement "Agudath Israel" in Vienna in 1923, and a center was established there along with the movement's magazine "*Ha-Derekh.*"

Ekstein published his Hebrew book *Tena'ei ha-Nefesh le-Hasagat ha-Ḥassidut* (*Mental Conditions for Achieving Hasidism*) in Vienna in 1921. The work was enthusiastically praised by *Ha-Derekh* in the same year.[36] Ekstein even published two articles in this magazine in 1924, however his articles were not new

of the world—in this fact one is to see the beginning of the redemption and one may found there strength and hope that also here, outside of the Land of Israel, God will save us in some way through other messengers." However, Ekstein was against collaborating with the Zionist movement until it would forsake the notion of a Jewish national collective without any religious or traditional identity, see his letter written on September 24, 1916: "There is no doubt that many of the statements and decrees that are going around due to the nationalistic idea greatly upset the religious soul, and the religious spirit cannot tolerate them."

33 Yari-Wold, *Rzeszow Community*, 280. Also see his father's letter, included as a *haskamah* (approbation) to Ekstein's book *Tena'ei ha-Nefesh le-Hasagat ha-Ḥassidut* [*Mental Conditions for Achieving Hasidism*] (Vienna: Union Press-Appel Brothers, 1921): "My dearest son, my soul's delight, our master and teacher Menaḥem, may his light shine, who at this moment is in Vienna." In the second half of the nineteenth century Rzeszów was connected to Vienna via the train route Lviv-Vienna, in which Rzeszów was a main stop.

34 Regarding Jewish refugees during World War I in Vienna see Moshe Ungerfeld (Agaf), *Vienna* (Tel Aviv: Naḥum Dreemer Publishing, 1946), 120–124.

35 Ibid., 129–130. Also see Harriet Pass Freidenreich, *Jewish Politics in Vienna 1918-1938* (Bloomington: Indiana University Press, 1991), 138–146.

36 *Ha-Derekh*, Vienna, third year, volume 6, (February-March 1921): 17. Furthermore, see Avraham Ḥomet, ed., *Ṭorne: Kiym un Khurbn fun a Yiddisher Shtot* [*Tarnów: The Establishment and Destruction of a Jewish City*] (Tel Aviv: Landsmanshafṭn fun Torne Yiddn, 1954), 221. Also see ibid., that Ekstein is described as a Dzików ḥasid who frequently visited Tarnów for holidays.

and are taken practically word for word from his aforementioned book.[37] Parts of this book, which dealt with observing the Sabbath, were cited in 1936 in *Sefer ha-Shabbat*[38] by the folklorist Jacob Nacht,[39] the author Zalman Epstein,[40] and the poet Yitzchak Leib Baruch,[41] thus demonstrating the wide popularity of the work. At a certain point, 1932 at the latest, Ekstein returned to Poland.[42] Apparently, he had some type of connection to *Beys Yankev*, the women's division of Agudath Israel. This presumption is based on two facts: the firstly, he is mentioned many times by *Beys Yankev* teachers and educators;[43] the secondly, his book was partially translated into Yiddish and was published by the *Benos Agudas Yisro'el* leaflet, which was distributed in Poland through *Beys Yankev*.[44] The translations appeared in a fragmentary fashion for three years and ceased midway due to the disbanding of the publication with the outbreak of World War II.[45]

---

37 *Ha-Derekh*, Vienna, sixth year, volume 2 (April-May 1924): 6–8; *Ha-Derekh*, Vienna, sixth year, volume 3 (May-June 1924): 9–11. These articles correspond to the first eleven pages, which are chapters 1–6, of his book. After the first article the words "to be continued" appeared and after the second article no continuation was mentioned, and as such the publication ceased.

38 Jacob Nacht, Zalman Epstein, and Yitzchak Leib Baruch, *Sefer ha-Shabbat* (Tel Aviv: Dvir, 1936; repr., Dvir, 1971), 187. The quotation from Ekstein, *Tena'ei ha-Nefesh*, 52.

39 See Natan Mark, "*Daqṭor Ya'aqov Na'kht: Le-Milo'at Ḥeṣi Yovel le-Avodato ha-Sifrutit*," *Ha-Tsefirah* (March 1928): 3.

40 See his essay "*Ḥazon ha-Shabbat*" in *Sefer ha-Shabbat* available at http://benyehuda.org/epstein/008.html (his autobiographical writings are to be found at Project Ben-Yehuda). About his life see *Encyclopaedia Hebraica*, 5:431–432.

41 About him see Moshe Ungerfeld, "Y. L. Barukh: 50 Years of his Literary Activity," *Moznaim* 6 (1947): 135–136.

42 In the town's census for Jews between the years 1932 and 1939 Ekstein appears each year (from the government archives in Rzeszów, Poland). Furthermore, he is mentioned as resident in 1932 in Levenson, *Sefer Tiqqun Olam*, (unpaginated) at the end of the book, where there is a list of donors and their place of residence, most of them from Kraków. The last entry in the Rzeszów list is Ekstein (and on the page before his brother Me'ir is mentioned).

43 See Ze'ev Zohar, *Sefer ha-Yovel ha-Esrim ve-Ḥamishah shel Beit ha-Sefer ha-Tikhon ve-ha-Seminar le-Gananot ve-le-Morot "Beit Ya'aqov" be-Tel Aviv 1936–1961* (Tel Aviv: Beth Yaakov Publishing, 1961), 86; Binyamin Chernetzky, *Midot u-Ma'asim: Si'aḥ Ḥinukhi* (Tel Aviv: Beth Yaakov Publishing, 1992), 369.

44 A.G. Freidnazen ed., *Beys Yankev: Literarishe Shrift far Shul un Heym, Dint di Enyonim fun Beys Yankev Shuln un Organizatzies Bnos Agudas Yisroel in Poyln 1924–1939.* In the twenties the journal appeared under the title *Beys Yankev: Ortodoksisher Familien-Zhurnal Argan fun der Tsentrale Bnos Agudas Yisroel in Poyln: Lodzh, Varshe, Kroke.*

45 The publishing began in May 1930, volume 142, and it ended with the termination of the journal (volume 158, July-August 1939) due to the German invasion of Poland on September 1, 1939. Approximately half of the book (1–40) was translated with omissions of pages 21–22, 25–33, 37. In total, thirty pages were translated with the main deletions consisting of topics dealing with romantic relations, see below, n. 54.

The translator, who signed his name with the abbreviation *Yud Ayin*, *Yud Ayin-Ṭeṭ*, and *Ayin-Ṭeṭ*, appears to be the Hebrew poet Israel Emiot, who is also mentioned as one of the writers of this journal.[46]

Ekstein continued his family tradition and viewed himself as an avowed Dzików ḥasid. As was customary for ḥasidim, he traveled to Tarnów for the holidays to be with R. Alṭer Yeḥezqel Eliyahu Horowitz,[47] the last Rebbe of Dzików, who was of a "spiritual" disposition.[48] Ekstein and his wife Ḥanah (of the Sobol family) had three children,[49] Moshe (Yisra'el Moshe), Barukh (Ḥayyim Barukh),[50] and Ḥayyah (Hella). Moshe worked as a merchant and lived in Tarnów, close to Rzeszów, with his wife Sarah Reizel (of the Parnass family) and their two daughters Sabina and Gizlah. Barukh lived with his wife Ita and their daughter Sheindel in Łódź and, like his brother, was a merchant. Ḥayyah moved to Katowice with her husband and their son Mordekhai. According to family testimo-

---

46 Zohar, *Sefer ha-Yovel*, 86. I have perused numerous volumes of the journal and Israel Emiot published in it abundantly.

47 Ḥomet, *Tarnów*, 221; Meir Wunder, *Me'orei Galiṣiyah: Encyclopedia of Galician Rabbis and Scholars* (Jerusalem: Institute for the Commemoration of Galician Jewry, 1978–2005), 1:169.

48 On this rebbe see Alfasi, *The Kingdom of Wisdom*, 349–364. Horowitz moved from Dzików to *Tarnów* after World War I and appointed his son in his stead in Dzików, ibid., 351. He was a member of Agudath Israel and supported the settlement of the Land of Israel, even establishing a preparatory farm (*hakhsharah*) for immigration to Palestine in Niżniów with the Dzików ḥasid, Kopel Bigleisen. Furthermore, he publicly announced in 1910 that he would immigrate to Palestine, but was prevented from doing so due to the staunch disapproval of his father-in-law the Rebbe of Vizhnitz, ibid., 352. Horowitz was described as a spiritual personality who was likened to early hasidic masters and as a fervent prayer leader who would pray with wild frenzy to the point of ecstasy, ibid., 352–354. This rebbe was also depicted as being quite worldly and open-minded. He called upon his followers to leave Poland and immigrate to Palestine, America (told to me by his grandson Rabbi Yisra'el Shlisel, who immigrated to America with the encouragement of Horowitz), and England, where his followers established a branch already in 1900, ibid., 354. His analysis of the political situation of late 1930's Europe led him to the conclusion that a great war was about to erupt and that Jews would be the primary victims. He called upon hasidic court leaders to leave Poland immediately, which caused much disagreement with other hasidic masters who, following their interpretation of the *Zohar*, believed that nothing would happen, ibid., 356. During the Holocaust, he was in the Tarnów ghetto and was killed by gunfire in the Kraków-Płaszów concentration camp in 1942. We have brought these materials in order to better understand Ekstein's intellectual and religious background.

49 All the facts regarding his children have been taken from the Yad Vashem testimonials and have been compared with the birth certificates found in the government archive of Rzeszów, Poland.

50 Twin boys born in 1908 in Sanok.

nies,[51] during the war Ekstein and his wife stayed at Moshe's house and Barukh and his family were there as well. Almost all of Ekstein's family was killed in the *Aktion* of 1942 in Tarnów, an *Aktion* in which thousands were killed in the center of Tarnów and those who survived were brought to the Bełżec extermination camp. There were almost no survivors from Ekstein's family,[52] the sole survivor being Moshe Ekstein's daughter Gizlah, who was hidden by local Poles.[53]

The interest in Ekstein's teachings and his book *Tena'ei ha-Nefesh le-Hasagat ha-Ḥassidut* (*Mental Conditions for Achieving Hasidism*) at the end of the twentieth and beginning of the twenty-first century has been rejuvenated primarily by neo-hasidic *Dati Le'umi* groups and *ba'alei teshuva* (newly observant). The book was translated to English in 2001 and has had its third reprinting in Hebrew with modifications implemented by the Bratslav institute, *Even ha-Shetiya"h.*[54] The institute *Dimyon Nove'a*, led by Amit Qedem, produced a disk in 2009 called *Laḥshov Ein Sof: Targilim le-Pitu'aḥ ha-Maḥshavah.* The imagery exercises located on this disc are based on Ekstein's imagery techniques.[55] The Torah Culture Department of the Ministry of Education and Culture released a pamphlet on hasidism that attempts to offer a general and comprehensive picture of the movement. Within this enormous corpus they saw fit to dedicate a portion to Ekstein,

51 From the testimonies at Yad Vashem.

52 His daughter Ḥayyah, her son Mordekhai and Shemu'el her husband, who lived in Katowice, perished in Stanisławów (according Yad Vashem testimonials).

53 Gizlah Ekstein (daughter of Moshe Ekstein), in discussion with the author, March 11, 2011.

54 The book was reprinted with omissions and changes entitled *Mavoh le-Torat ha-Ḥasidut* (Tel Aviv: Neṣaḥ Publishing, 1960). Likewise, this edition was reedited with new chapter and paragraph divisions, diverging from the original edition. The omissions are by and large anything that can be even slightly related to Zionism or sexuality. The book was reprinted again in 2006 by newly observant Bratslav ḥasidim according to the restructuring of the 1960 edition (i.e., the censorship continued), entitled *Tena'ei ha-Nefesh le-Hasagat ha-Ḥassidut* (Beitar Ilit: Makhon Even ha-Shetiya"h, 2006) and was translated into English as Menachem Ekstein, *Visions of a Compassionate World: Guided Imagery for Spiritual Growth and Social Transformation*, trans. Y. Starett (New York: Urim Publications, 2001). Notice that both later editions add the element of "Jewish meditation" or "guided imagery" to the book's title, both evidencing New Age influence within the religious community. The 2006 publication also includes a disc with guided imagery exercises led by Amit Qedem with background music.

55 Regarding this institute and disc see the website http://www.dimyonovea.com. On the back of this disc the following text appears: "Through these processes you will be capable of experiencing how the encounter with the richness and multifacetedness of creation and the vastness and powerfulness of the universe pour new light onto the reality of your lives. The processes are based on Rabbi Menaḥem Ekstein's, may God avenge his blood, book... it appears according to this book that this form of worship was accepted and common in hasidic courts of that period."

under the heading of "Contemporary Ḥasidim,"[56] thereby demonstrating the resurgence that this figure is currently experiencing.[57] This resurgence is further evinced by the quotations of his book in the writings of contemporary spiritual teachers and Neo-Kabbalists.[58]

B The Book and Its Sources

On January 27, 1937, Ekstein wrote a preface on the occasion of his book's initial translation into Yiddish in the journal *Beys Yankev*. This preface testifies to his bold presumptuousness to define the principles of hasidism: "In my book, I have made *a preliminary effort* to find suitable definitions and a correct style as to express the principles of hasidism."[59] A comparison with Hillel Zeitlin—who also attempted to define the fundamentals of hasidism a decade earlier in 1910, such as the concepts of "*yesh* and *ayin*" (being and nothingness), "*ṣimṣum*" (divine contraction), "*ha'alat niṣoṣot*" (uplifting of sparks), "*ha'alat maḥshavot zarot*" (uplifting of foreign thoughts), and "*ha'alat ha-midot*" (uplifting of character traits),[60]—demonstrates that Ekstein's project was quite different. Zeitlin gathered concepts from students of R. Israel ben Eliezer (Beshṭ) and attempted to present them in a systematic fashion as principles of hasidic thought. In contrast, Ekstein extolled modern psychological concepts such as "self-awareness", "self-control", "integration", "war of imaginations", "ecstasy", and "astonishment", and presented them as fundamentals of hasidism, consequently, universalizing hasidism, as we will see below. Furthermore, Ekstein's

56 Aryeh Strikovsky, ed., *Daf le-Tarbut Yehudit* 278 (December 2009): 73.

57 I felt an obligation to dwell on the historical-biographical section of Ekstein's life, for at least, to my knowledge, this is the first one written. The preface to the 2006 edition does not contain significant biographical material on Ekstein. Likewise, in the English translation of the book there is only a slight amount of biographical material due to the ignorance of the translators (the translation itself is lacking as well, but this is not the place to expand on this matter). For example, they wrote that Ekstein was in his late twenties when he published his book, when in fact he was thirty-seven, Ekstein, *Visions of a Compassionate World*, 16.

58 E.g. Yiṣḥaq Me'ir Morgenstern, *Yam ha-Ḥokhmah* (Jerusalem: Makhon Yam ha-Ḥokhmah, 2008), 832.

59 Emphasis in the original. Brought as a forward to the Hebrew edition, Ekstein, *Mavoh le-Torat ha-Ḥasidut*, 16. Presumably this preface, being written for the Yiddish translation of his book and published within a Yiddish journal, was written in Yiddish as well. I have been unsuccessful in obtaining the original likely published in *Beys Yankev* 141 or 142 (March-June, 1937).

60 Hillel Zeitlin, *Ḥasidut le-Shiṭotehah u-Zeramehah* (Warsaw: Sifrut, 1910)

presentation of imagery exercises together with guided instruction,[61] constitutes a formative example of a genre of modern literature paralleling popular instruction and self-help books of the early twentieth century, which advised readers on how to improve their lives through their own efforts.[62] Moses is even presented as the penultimate spiritual teacher and the most remarkable psychologist of humanity, possessing the ability to disclose the deepest strata of the soul and discern the unconscious: "Moses our teacher, the greatest teacher in the world and of all-time, beyond compare to those who preceded and followed him, who intimately knew the depths of each man's soul as well as its relation to all known things in the world and their effects on it."[63] Ekstein begins his work with the following words: "The first principle that hasidism espouses to all who knock on its gates and wish to enter its inner sanctuaries is 'Know thyself'… to raise all the natural inclinations of your soul and know them well."[64] To the reader's surprise according to Ekstein the foundation of hasidism is not knowledge of God, observing the commandments, or classic hasidic concepts like "the nullification of existence" (*biṭṭul ha-yesh*), cleaving to God (*devequt*), etc. The foundation of hasidism is a universal concept—self-awareness, an awareness which allows for an innate understanding of one's tendencies and full command of them: "to raise all the natural inclinations of your soul and know them well."

It must be noted that Ekstein does not reference one hasidic source in his entire book. He mentions the Beshṭ three times in the entire work,[65] and he is the sole hasidic figure referenced. Despite this fact, he claims that his sources are entirely founded upon hasidic literature: "In my book, I have made *a preliminary effort* to find suitable definitions and a correct style as to express the principles of hasidism, so that it may be understood by all readers; everything is taken from primary sources."[66] Ekstein describes his book in its opening pages as a guide for contemplation as compiled from hasidic works, "In which ways and in which manners will it be possible for us to learn the way of contemplation and arrive at it? We shall attempt and strive to supply an answer to this question. An answer compiled from different sources of hasidic books, organized here in a

---

61 See Ekstein, *Tena'ei ha-Nefesh*, 3–5, 13. Henceforth all references to Ekstein's work are to the Vienna 1921 edition, unless otherwise stated.
62 See Tomer Persico, "Jewish Meditation: The Development of a Modern Form of Spiritual Practice in Contemporary Judaism" (PhD diss., Tel Aviv University, 2012), 293.
63 Ekstein, *Tena'ei ha-Nefesh*, 48.
64 Ibid., 1.
65 Each mention is found in the same paragraph, ibid., 28–29.
66 Ekstein, *Mavoh le-Torat ha-Ḥasidut*, 16 (see above n. 59).

systematic fashion."[67] Processes of self-work, such as self-awareness, are portrayed by Ekstein as obvious hasidic principles without any need for explicit references. In the last third of the book, he mentions hasidism and hasidim numerous times, however without precise citations or specific names.

Even though he claims that his sources are solely from within the hasidic tradition, Ekstein valued openness to non-Jewish knowledge. He described hasidic sages as spiritual people conversant with general philosophy: "Spiritual giants, possessing an all-pervasive view, rich in the wisdom of life, whose comprehension shined like the sun, they weaved in their minds all philosophical theories, not only from our treasury of wisdom, but also the wisdom of the nations of the world."[68] Ekstein himself was of the opinion that one should teach and instill "new wisdoms" to one's students in a manner that does not contradict traditional teachings: "*H"D* is very necessary in order that we may be well strengthened before the new spirit and movements in the world, in order that we may taste of the new wisdoms essential for living today, without causing some form of damage to our tradition, which is the primary component for our nationhood and lives."[69]

It is plausible to postulate that Ekstein was influenced by non-hasidic sources. As a disciple of Kamelhar, who educated towards a broadening of knowledge, and even was criticized for it,[70] coming from a family which had a certain openness towards worldliness and fluency in languages,[71] and lastly as a follower of a rebbe, who projected openness to culture and secular studies—he was presumably acquainted with and absorbed sources of information, methods of self-work, and life experiences beyond hasidic literature. Furthermore, it should not be forgotten that Ekstein himself was well learned and interested in general

67 Ekstein, *Tena'ei ha-Nefesh*, 1.
68 Ekstein, *Mavoh le-Torat ha-Ḥasidut*, 16.
69 From a letter to Kamelhar on December 23, 1917. It is unclear what the acronym *H"D* means. It is repeated numerous times in this letter, and from the context it may be ascertained that Kamelhar coined it in his previous letter to Ekstein, which is not in our possession. They are exchanging words regarding the establishment of a yeshiva for youth, which would incorporate secular studies. For more see the following footnote.
70 Mondshine, *Ha'Tsofeh Le'Doro*, 48. Also see in Kamelhar's archives at the National Library in Jerusalem, ARC. 4º1517, folder 4, letter no. 38, from the organization *Shelomei Emunei Yisra'el* (Agudath Israel of Poland) from 1919, in which they request Kamelhar to be the head of the yeshiva which will be established in Warsaw for adolescents (aged 14–17). In the yeshiva's curriculum fifteen weekly hours are designated for secular studies.
71 See the biographical introduction above.

thought,[72] had a critical disposition towards the current events of his day,[73] a desire to be aware of new happenings,[74] and wanted to adapt the religious curriculum to the modern condition.[75] The use of terminology not found in hasidism, but rather hypnosis,[76] and certain sentences translated into German (and *not* Yiddish) found in his text, demonstrate his broad knowledge, the character of the intended audience, and the broader reserve of sources available to him which facilitated the development of his mystical doctrine.

In this chapter I will present a few principles which Ekstein viewed as foundational to hasidism, as well as imagery techniques which, according to him, are ways of acquiring these principles. I shall outline his imagery techniques and demonstrate their mystical character. I will compare and contrast Ekstein's imagery techniques and those of Kalonymous Kalman Shapira, in regard to content and practice. These contrasts will sharpen and clarify Ekstein's uniqueness as both an original thinker and practitioner of imagery techniques in twentieth century hasidism.

C The Bifurcated Soul and Self-Awareness

The conception of the divided soul, the belief in the existence of a part of the soul in the supernal realm paralleling the soul found in the corporeal body, appears in numerous sources over many periods. I will concisely present a sample of them with a specific focus on kabbalistic literature. Already in the classical age, in Plotinus's teachings, there is a view that a portion of man's soul is situ-

---

72 For example, see his letter with Kamelhar from Monday in the week of Parashat va-Yeshev (no year written, so either in November or December) in which he quotes the English proverb, "Everyone mourns their material state, but is satisfied by their intelligence."

73 For instance, he is aware of many "enlightened" (*maskilim*) claims and argues against them, see Ekstein, *Tena'ei Ha-Nefesh*, 29–40, for his knowledge of general European culture and his attitude and treatment of political realia, see ibid., 59–60, this was censored in later editions.

74 See for example the biographical introduction above and n. 31.

75 In his letters to Kalmehar, Ekstein commented about Kalmehar's future education plans and stated that they need to be adapted for modernity and warns him that if they are not then they will not be accepted by a wider audience. For example, see his letter from Monday in the week of Parashat va-Yeshev (no year written, so either in November or December): "[Kamelhar's] desire and idea of organizing the manner of learning and education in order to strengthen a person's religious self-awareness so that the entire nation will accept this manner of learning... the possibility of its realization, {?} one {?} it will be very difficult if it is not adapted for our state of affairs, if it is not brought closer to life and reality."

76 See below, section D.

ated on high.[77] In this view, the soul is split into two parts, one found in the physical realm and the other found in the non-corporeal realm, while a possible correlation exists between the two parts. It should be emphasized that the subject of discussion is not a general collective soul, like the Active Intellect, but rather individual souls.[78] Appearing in the Greek magical papyri and early medieval esoteric traditions, which were preserved in Arabic texts, was the notion of *principium individuationis*. This essence is a part of the individual soul found in the supernal realm. This part of the soul is treated numerous times as the "perfected nature."[79] In the Hekhalot literature, great importance is placed on the "double presence," meaning the ability for man's essence to be in two places simultaneously. R. Neḥunya ben ha-Kanah is described as being surrounded by students in a trembling state, while concomitantly having a vision of the chariot.[80] Isaiah Tishby asserted that there is a similarity between the kabbalistic perception of a bifurcated soul and the conception of the astral body found in ancient religions, and which also appears in neo-Platonic philosophy.[81] Indeed, the doctrine of the bifurcated soul appears many times in kabbalistic and other Jewish literature. The author of the kabbalistic work *Torat ha-Nefesh* defines this phenomenon as follows "the body is split into two parts—the body which is seen sensorially… and a different body which is sensorially hidden, which is also referred to as *eṣem gufani* (essence of corporeality)."[82] A similar conception of the individual soul may be found in the *Zohar* in the concept of *ṣelem* (image). *Ṣelem* is described in zoharic literature as an ethereal body corresponding to the viewable corporeal body;[83] the *Zohar* thereby, identifies *ṣelem* with the astral body, an external spiritual duplicate of the carnal individual.[84] Eleazar of Worms (late twelfth and early thirteenth century) identified the *ṣelem elohim* (image of God) with the *ṣelem* of an angel in the individual's likeness, an image, which

77 Isaiah Tishby, *The Wisdom of the Zohar: An Anthology of Texts*, trans. David Goldstein (London: Littman Library, 1991), 2:770.
78 Gershom Scholem, *On the Mystical Shape of the Godhead: Basic Concepts in the Kabbalah*, trans. Joachim Neugroschel (New York: Schocken Books, 1991), 257. Regarding the connection between this conception of the soul and self-visualization, see the end of this chapter.
79 Scholem, *Godhead*, 254–255.
80 Idel, *Golem*, 285.
81 Tishby, *Wisdom of the Zohar*, 771.
82 Pseudo-Baḥya, *Sefer Torat ha-Nefesh*, ed. D. Broyde (Paris: Levinsohn-Kilemnik, 1896), 26. (a pre-zoharic work), mistakenly attributed to Baḥya ibn Paquda, cited in Scholem, *Godhead*, 262.
83 Tishby, *Wisdom of the Zohar*, 770.
84 Scholem, *Godhead*, 267; Tishby, *Wisdom of the Zohar*, 771. Furthermore, see ibid., n. 104 regarding Hillel Zeitlin's assertion regarding the connection between the astral body and the zoharic *ṣelem* in Hillel Zeitlin, "Mafte'aḥ le-Sefer ha-Zohar," *Ha-Tequfah* 9 (1921): 290, 296–297.

is imprinted on the person from the moment of his birth, and even conception, for his entire life, that acts as his personal angel.[85] In the *Zohar*, a more developed understanding of the soul appears. In place of the angelic figure is a pre-existent heavenly garment, which the soul wore in its paradisiac form before its entrance into the physical body. This garment was also conceived of as a spiritual body.[86]

One may find the psychologization of the divided soul doctrine in Ekstein's teachings. Ekstein developed an interesting theory similar to that of the divided soul, with the addition of the subject of "self-awareness." The division of the soul into two parts facilitates, according to Ekstein, the possibility of man "knowing himself." This self-awareness, which is made possible through the divided soul and imagery exercises, is presented by Ekstein as the key to the innermost aspects of hasidism. Anyone who lies on "the doorstep which leads towards the inner chambers of hasidism," needs this key.[87]

> The first principle that hasidism espouses to all who knock on its gates and wish to enter its inner sanctuaries is 'Know thyself'... to raise all the natural inclinations of your soul and know them well. To bifurcate yourself, the natural man who dwells below and lives a daily existence and is acted upon by all temporal events... and a supernal man who is not drawn by temporary occurrences and is not affected by them, for he sits on high in his palace within a high tower and constantly gazes down on the lower man, on all the many things that happened to him and how they affect his soul, he observes them and knows them, he examines them and is able to orientate them and use them as he desires.[88]

The foundation of hasidism, "the first principle," according to Ekstein is not a theological conception or a classic hasidic notion, but rather self-awareness. This awareness allows its possessor full command over his soul, to the extent that he is able "to orientate [his natural inclinations] and use them as he desires."[89] This control is not only during defined contemplative times, like in the morning before leaving for work or at night as a type of introspection before

---

85 Scholem, *Godhead*, 260 – 261.

86 For more on the connection between the doctrine of the bifurcated soul, self-visualization, and prophecy see the end of this chapter.

87 Ekstein, *Tena'ei ha-Nefesh*, 22.

88 Ibid.

89 The principle of self-control already appears in a preliminary and less-developed fashion in his letters to Kalmehar. See his letter from September 16, 1906: "There are many psychological points here... one of them is from the foundations of faith, training a child to place upon himself a yoke from his youth so that he should not accustom his soul to liberation and profligacy and placing a fence around his natural inclinations within himself to lead them towards the commandments of the religion and its fences."

sleep, as adherents of the Musar movement practiced, but rather encompasses all of man's being and accompanies him in all of his activities. It is absolute and constant self-awareness. This type of self-awareness, according to Ekstein, is made possible through the conception of the bifurcated soul, in which man observes himself from on high at each and every moment and fully oversees and inspects his deeds and feeling:

> Now we may thoroughly understand the division of the soul into two... we see before us a new [form of] worship, even while we exert ourselves in our work during the day as well as when different events will injure us, even then our soul is still on high... also then it will command and the actions will be in its hands... this is the worship of the bifurcated soul.[90]

The conception of the divided soul is the theological position at the foundation of this understanding of constant self-awareness and the individual's ability to be in total command of himself. Indeed, Ekstein did not suffice with the theological dimension, nor did he cease there; his primary interest was in the practical realm. Ekstein mainly engaged with the question of how one acquires self-awareness and complete control of one's soul. His answer to this question was through the imagination:

> If a man is able to critique himself so that he may know at all times what state his soul is in... then he will easily know the correct nutrition to give to his soul at that time. If his emotions will be inclined towards sadness and melancholy, then he shall intentionally raise to his consciousness (*maḥshavato*) the *images* (*ṣiyurim*) of his smallness, how he is annihilated and lost in the grand existence (*beriyah*) and is unimportant... he will then also think about the order of his being, the putrid drop from which his body was fashioned and what will come of his body in the end.[91] Indeed all of these matters are known to everyone, however only superficially. The more that one contemplates them, *the more accurately will he see them* and the more they will stimulate his soul,[92]... and one who is unable to tolerate the truth of sensorially viewing his insignificance will also be unable to become very ecstat-

90 Ekstein, *Tena'ei ha-Nefesh*, 16–17.

91 The source for this exercise, *m. Avot* 3:1: "Akaviah b. Mahalaleel said: perceive (*histakel*) three things and you will not come into the power of sin: know where you come from, and where you are going, and before whom you are destined to give an account and reckoning. Where you come from?—from a fetid drop. Where you are going?—to a place of dust, of worm, and of maggot. Before whom you are destined to give an account and reckoning?—before the King of the Kings of Kings, the Holy one, blessed be He." This "perception" is interpreted by Ekstein as visualization. Visualization, as a technique for the achieving of self-awareness in Ekstein's thought, will be a main discussion of this chapter.

92 On the distinction between knowing and imagination and regarding the consequential differences see, in a very similar manner, Shapira's thought, chap. 4, subchapter "Visualizing the Day of Death."

ic (*le-hitpa'el harbeh*) from the general life that fills the entire existence (*min ha-ḥayyim ha-kelalim ha-memala'im et ha-beriyah kulah*).[93]

D Self-Awareness and Imagination

Ekstein presents two psychological barriers preventing total self-awareness. The conception of the self (*ani*) at the center of the individual's conscious and his "experience of the moment:"

> There are two large and primary obstructions on the path and they do not allow us to arrive at these characteristics. The first is a deceiving imagination (*dimyon shav*) that blinds the eyes so that they are unable to see our place and true value in the world, and the second is the sphere of shortsightedness... the first comes from our sense of selfness (*anokhiyut*), from the natural egoism within us, so that each one of us feels that he is a very important creature, as if he was the center of the world, and by no means can he see himself through the same lens that he sees his fellow, and because of this it is very difficult for him to properly understand and feel the clear truth, that he is a tiny and lowly creature among millions of creatures like him. The second occurs due to every one of us being totally drawn with all of his senses after the activity of the moment... if, for instance, we are sad at this moment, then we entirely forget how we were previously and how we will be later... all of our lives our only sadness as if there is nothing else in the world.[94]

It is interesting that Ekstein not only presents self-centeredness and egoism as false consciousness (*dimyon shav*, lit. deceptive imagination), but momentary experiences as well: "Both of these shortcomings are [types of] false consciousness, which occur due to our aforementioned natural inclination, and this is ipseity, our self-love and sense of solipsism (*ve-ha-hargashat aṣmeinu bilvad*) ."[95] It is important to note that Ekstein's use of the word *dimyon* (imagination) lacks a pictorial-visual component and its use appears closer to the concept of false consciousness as translated here. Nevertheless, his proposed solution to this issue does utilize imaginal visualization. However, imagination is to be understood in the preceding paragraph, Ekstein's mode of dealing with this false consciousness is through devising imagery exercises with a clear opposing image. These

93 Ekstein, *Tena'ei ha-Nefesh*, 42, also see further there that the subject of discussion is clearly visualization, seeing imaginal images. Regarding the feeling of ecstasy caused by viewing all of creation in Ekstein's thought, see below, subchapter, "The Sublime and the Imagination in Ekstein's Teachings."

94 Ibid., 1–2.

95 Ibid.

simulations are his creation and are presented as exercises directed towards the reader, namely, guided imagery exercises:

> How may one be cured from these distracting images? Hasidism provides a very simple answer for this question as well, and states: through different true images. It is appropriate for us to begin immediately from our youth exercises that stimulate the imaginative faculty within us, to develop it, and perfect it, so that we will be able to construct in our minds different true images and in this manner slowly weaken in our midst the false and misleading imagination (*dimyon shav*) and be cured of them.[96]

The setting of image against image is presented in Ekstein's thought through militaristic terminology: "Here we see a war between imaginations."[97] The false imagination is characterized as natural and spontaneous without the need for practice and preparation, and is termed "the natural imagination." On the other side of the trench stands the opponent referred to as "the artificial imagination" (*dimyon ha-mal'akhuti*).[98] It is precisely the artificial imagination which Ekstein claims is the true imagination, "that show the individual his true value and condition."[99] The necessary effort, in contrast to spontaneity, and the lengthy acclimation process, earn it the term "artificial."[100] The result of this war of imaginations is full self-awareness, which is formed precisely through the battle ("As light is superior to darkness" [Ecc. 2:13], a phrase used to convey that it is precisely the contrasting of light and darkness which gives light its superiority), where the central weapons are imagery exercises derived from the conception of the bifurcated soul.

E War of Imaginations

The idea of the evil inclination (*yeṣer ha-ra*) as the opposite of the good inclination (*yeṣer ha-ṭov*) is an innovation of the rabbinic sages. The *yeṣer* indicates both the power of thought and power of the heart, meaning man's desires.[101] The

---

96 Ibid., 2.
97 Ibid., 4.
98 See ibid., 12: "There the imaginative faculty is natural… it works by itself without any action from our side… without our will and even without our knowledge, however here the imaginative faculty is 'artificial' for we force it to work in our minds."
99 Ibid.
100 Ibid.
101 Ephraim E. Urbach, *The Sages: Their Concepts and Beliefs* (Jerusalem: Magnes Press, 1975), 1: 471–472.

struggle against the evil inclination is a central aspect of the ethical teachings of the sages, and many different devices were proposed against it.[102] Still, there is no identification, at least directly, of the evil inclination with the "faculty of imagination" in rabbinic literature. Rather, such an identification appears in the work of Plato. Plato viewed the imaginative faculty as an inferior force which reflects false opinions—*doxa*, and even as immoral, since it allows for emotions and imagination to influence and control the intellect.[103] Plato described this struggle with militaristic images, which continued in Aristotle's writings as well. This opposition between the intellect and imagination became a traditional Jewish concept in Maimonides' thought, particularly *Guide for the Perplexed*, and Abulafia's thought. In their thought, these concepts were transformed into a hermeneutical foundation for the understanding of religious processes like prophecy.[104] Abulafia used many different methods to subdue the corporeal body and imagination, so that the intellect might develop and achieve spiritual feats and prophecy. This subduing is often described through warlike imagery.[105] This battle is primarily waged between the man's intellectual faculty and his inferior spiritual faculties. According to Abulafia, the imaginative faculty is the most dangerous. When it is empowered the intellectual faculty is weakened, and the imagination proceeds to deploy its schemes and sabotage the intellect:

> Your mind will be confused, your thoughts confounded, and you will not find any way to escape the reveries of your mind. The power of your imagination will overwhelm you, making you imagine many utterly useless fantasies. Your imaginative faculty will grow stronger, weakening your intellect, until your reveries cast you into a great sea. You will not have the wisdom ever to escape from it, and will therefore drown.[106]

The struggle with foreign thoughts, which appears frequently in Abulafia's corpus, is the fight against the imaginative faculty:

---

102 Ibid., 472–483.

103 See Abrams, *The Mirror and the Lamp*, 8–9; Kearney, *The Wake of the Imagination*, 87–105, esp. 93–94.

104 Regarding Abulafia see Moshe Idel, "*Milhemet ha-Yetzarim:* Psychomachia in Abraham Abulafia's Ecstatic Kabbalah," in *Peace and War in Jewish Culture,* ed. A. Bar Levav (Jerusalem: Zalman Shazar Center, 2006), 103, 106–107 and for a more concise English version see "Inner Peace through Inner Struggle in Abraham Abulafia's Ecstatic Kabbalah," *The Journal for the Study of Sephardic & Mizrahi Jewry* (March 2009): 63–97. For Maimonides see above chap. 1, subchapter, "Maimonides."

105 Idel, "*Milhemet ha-Yetzarim,*" 101.

106 *Sefer ha-Ṣiruf*, 1b, as translated by Aryeh Kaplan, *Meditation and Kabbalah* (Boston: Weiser-Books, 1985), 80.

> And the way that you should hold and cling to it, all the days of your life, is the way of reversing (*hipukh*) letters and conjunctions... just like the flaming sword which turns (*she-mehapekh*) every way, in order to wage war with the surrounding enemies, for the images and the portrayal (*ṣiyur*) of the otiose thoughts born from the spirit of the evil inclination, they are the ones that go out against the intellect (*ha-ḥeshbon*) and encompass it like murderers and confuse the intellect (*da'at*) of man who is degraded due to the sin of Adam and Eve.[107]

According to Abulafia, the primary adversary of the mystic attempting to focus is the imagination, which portrays false and vain images.[108] Abulafia identifies the evil inclination with the imaginative faculty which interferes with the necessary concentration needed to achieve prophetic experiences.[109] This identification appears previously in Maimonides' writings.[110] Even though he did not use combative terminology, his portrayal of the struggle between the two faculties is nevertheless not far from this depiction.

Moshe Idel has demonstrated that in contrast to biblical times, and even after the unsuccessful Bar Kokhba revolt, when the Israelites waged physical wars, the sages preferred to emphasize and heighten the value of peace. In the Middle Ages Jews did not actively serve in wars, but rather suffered from them, and there consequently evolved a lack of religious interest in wars.[111] The importance of militaries and warfare gradually decreased and was transformed into an inner battle within the soul. In early ascetic Christianity a conception developed, according to which the inner-spiritual struggle, and not the external militaristic warfare, is most important. Likewise, in rabbinic literature and thereafter, a similar transformation occurred in which an emphasis was placed on this internal battle. This development became central in an array of mystical literature.[112]

Abulafia mentions the locution "war of the inclinations" (*milḥemet ha-yeṣerim*) numerous times. This locution appears in a similar variation in Baḥya ibn Paquda's work and in many other places referencing to either man's struggle

107 Abraham Abulafia, *Sefer Ḥayyei ha-Olam ha-Ba*, cited in Idel, "*Milhemet ha-Yetzarim*," 108.
108 Ibid., 109. Also see there that Abulafia is not preoccupied much with the conception of foreign thoughts as sexual desire.
109 Ibid., 106–110.
110 See above chap. 1, subchapter "Maimonides," however, see Idel, "*Milhemet ha-Yetzarim*," 134: "I have not found the subject of *milḥemet ha-yeṣerim* (battle of inclinations/urges) in the philosophical writings of Maimonides." In the above subchapter, I presented a Maimonidean source (*Guide of the Perplexed*, 2:30) which according to some interpreters is referring to this type of battle.
111 Idel, "*Milhemet ha-Yetzarim*," 99–100.
112 Ibid., 100–101.

with his evil inclination or his sexual urges. In contradistinction, in Abulafia's work the battle is between the intellect and imagination.[113] Furthermore, Abulafia sought to situate the concepts of the intellect and imagination at the center of his religious worldview.[114] For a majority of Abulafia's contemporaneous kabbalists and those who followed, particularly Moses Cordovero and Isaac Luria, the primary tension was not within man, but between him and external entities. These kabbalists treated inclinations as marginal in their methods. In contrast, Abulafia enhanced their religious significance and granted them a central place in his teachings.[115] The struggle between the intellect and imagination is of unique and central spiritual importance in his work. The internalization of this inner struggle drastically increases within hasidic literature, particularly Polish hasidic literature,[116] and continues to do so over the entire breadth of the movement's history. Hasidic thought, including that developed in the twentieth century, frequently deals with the internal tension and the struggles within man that must be overcome so that he may reach perfection.[117] Ekstein's book constitutes another link in this chain of the internalization of war. The book itself constitutes an occurrence of internalization; its entirety discusses internal warfare waged between the "natural" imagination and "artificial" imagination within man and it is upon him to practice imagery techniques in order to subdue his false imagination.

I believe that Ekstein's innovation lies in is his use of the imagination as a weapon against itself. I have not found any significant precedent within the kabbalistic literature in general and the hasidic literature in particular. The battle is no longer between the intellect and imagination, as in Maimonides' and Abulafia's teachings, but between the imagination and imagination! No longer a "war *against* the imagination," but rather "a war *of* imaginations." Ekstein portrays this battle as a perpetual process which consumes and absorbs one's life. Ekstein presented numerous attitudes towards the internal battle: the deserter, the negligent warrior, the unwilling warrior, and the war lover—above all, Ekstein prefers the lover of war:

---

113 Ibid., 116.
114 Ibid., 140.
115 Ibid.
116 Nonetheless, in contradistinction to Abulafia, hasidic thinkers engaged in a very wide variety of techniques and emphasized greatly the importance of the commandments and *avodah be-gashmiyut* (corporeal worship). See ibid., 141.
117 Regarding the phenomenon of internalization in hasidism see Margolin, *Inner Religion*, 419–421.

> For they simply feel a delight in their work even when they are defeated. They see in their lives more content and more internality, and they naturalize the obligation that they have taken upon themselves., for they know and always feel that there is something for them to do and that there is some goal in front of them. In particular those lovers of war, for they have come to realize that life in its essence is war. For combat rescues man from the emptiness and it gives his life a frequent yearning to perpetually desire something and do something.[118]

Occasionally, the aim of the artificial imagination in its battle is not to completely annihilate the natural imagination, but rather to acquire absolute command over it: "We must strongly fight them and distance them by force for an hour or two, and afterwards when we will desire, return, and grasp them for ourselves. Indeed, here as well there lies before us a war between the natural imagination and the artificial imagination;"[119] "There is no need to uproot and terminate its existence entirely, it is only necessary that it be dependent on our thought and will, for every time that we will desire, we will be able to arouse and illuminate our artificial imagination and it will be entirely in our hands."[120]

The development of this original doctrine, which presents the imagination as a weapon against the imagination, includes lengthy imagery techniques which are focused on the two psychological obstructions presented earlier: the sense of "self" in the center of the individual's consciousness, and his "experience of the moment." Ekstein's imagery techniques are characterized by a visual richness of broad dazzling universal images, like the cosmos, planet earth, and the known zoological, geological, and botanic world, without any mention of religious topics like the Torah, commandments, or even God. According to Ekstein, these imagery techniques are meant to cause the practitioner to feel the correct proportions of his ego and thereby uproot the previously presented psychological hindrances. Due to the length of the exercises we will present only one and in annotated form:

> Here we will clarify therefore two faculties of the imagination which entirely oppose the first [natural and false] ones, and if we utilize them we will then uproot from our souls our embedded deficiencies, which are the false and mistaken [imaginations]. To begin,

118 Ekstein, *Tena'ei ha-Nefesh*, 18.

119 Ibid., 12.

120 Ibid., 5. Also see ibid., 12–13: "Each battle and attempt from our side to overcome [the natural imaginings] will do their part, and even [though] this time we are defeated and fall, a great impression will nevertheless remain in them. Day after day they will be weakened, day after day they will submit before us, until finally they will hide in holes and cracks and will not dare to raise their heads." This is not an abnegation of the natural imaginings, but rather control of them, so that they "will not dare to raise their heads."

> we will elucidate the imagination which illuminates and opens our eyes to see our true place and value in the world and our awful degeneration. In order to arrive at this, it is proper that we should begin in the following manner: we shall first of all strive to visualize (*le-ṣaiyer*), in our intellects and with the imaginative faculty, planet earth and we shall visualize the entire earth as if we are seeing it from a distance, with all five continents and the oceans surrounding them. We will also visualize all the nations dwelling in all parts of the world, according to their languages and borders, and the number of people of each nation and language. All of this we will visualize (*neṣaiyer*) very well, as if we are actually seeing this dramatization (*ha-maḥazeh*) with our corporeal vision… as if we could touch this vision with our own hands. Not only shall we visualize the people, but also the rest of the known creatures in the world, meaning all the beasts and animals that we know of, where they are found and how they look and what their nature is, the many predatory animals in the deserts and forest, how they consume and eat, the many domesticated animals which are among people, how people use them and benefit from them, the many other types of smaller creatures, like mosquitos, and the larger ones, like elephants, snakes and the other types of crawling and swarming [creatures], how they teem across the land, walk and run, rest, eat, procreate, and die. The many types of thriving birds, the many chirpings and melodies that they chirp and play in the sky, trees, fields, and vineyards. The various types of fish in the seas and rivers, how they swim, consume, give birth, are hunted, and die. The many varieties of countless plants, crops, vegetable, shrubbery, thorns, and flowers. The gardens, orchards, and forests. All of these things to the extent that we know of them and how they appear, how they flourish, develop, grow, dry up, become speckled, collapse, and vanish. All of this we shall very clearly visualize for ourselves… until we become excited by them in our souls and feel with our senses how this beautiful dramatization rouses and enthralls us, similar to a man who is stirred by the beauty of nature when he sees the physical [entity] with his eyes, then we shall progress further and attempt to visualize the location upon which we currently standing, and we shall exhort ourselves to present ourselves among the numerous people and creatures. At first it will be very difficult for us to visualize such an image, for all of our being and all of our imaginative thoughts embedded in our souls will rise against us and they will not let us, in any way whatsoever, to be lost or nullified (*u-le-hibaṭṭel*) among all of those creations, they will not allow us under any circumstances to abandon our imagined pride and see the uncomfortable truth, our degradation and awful diminutiveness.[121]

The aim of this imagery technique is to cause an experience of nullification (*biṭṭul*), which is situated against the experience of the egocentricity of the "self", whose source is also the imagination, in the battle at the center of man's consciousness. According to Ekstein, the experience of being a singular creature within the whole zoological world including humanity, an almost infinite world, is meant to impart a sense of nullification, a classic hasidic concept which is obfuscated here with universally characterized imagery. This imagery technique is a primary example of the war between imaginations.

---

121 Ekstein, *Tena'ei ha-Nefesh*, 2–4.

Ekstein knew very well the influential capabilities of the imagination. It is not for naught that Greek philosophy, Maimonides, and Abulafia fought against it. The imagination was perceived as a stimulant of the evil inclination, specifically the sexual urge: "Thou shalt keep thee from every evil thing—meaning that one should not indulge in such thoughts by day as might lead to uncleanliness by night."[122] Ekstein's original claim is that one may use the power of the imagination against itself. To the same extent that the imagination constitutes an emotional and even psychological stimulant for "desires of the flesh," it is also an impetus for spiritual and even mystical desires such as communion (*devequt*) and integration with the divine:

> Now begins the battle between the "natural imagination" and the "artificial imagination"... We shall begin by slowly visualizing all of creation, the Father in our minds gives birth to the first thought, the Mother receives it, matures and expands it very precisely until it influences the Sons in our heart... who will be stimulated and nourished [by it].[123] That which the visualizations and images (*she-ha-ṣiyurim ve-ha-dimyonot*) of sexual desires, earning money, etc. do, [so too] must the beautiful images of the splendor of nature, of the land, the sun, the moon, and all of the celestial hosts do. *And then when the soul has already freed itself somewhat and this light will thoroughly illuminate for us, then we shall discuss and decide which of these imaginations are false, delusional, and fantastic, and which are true life and the essence of our souls' yearning, if the images are in favor of the [physical] bodies that concern us, or if the images are of all of creation! There is no doubt in this matter that then we will thoroughly, and always with further clarity, recognize that the vision of the entirety of creation is the link of one's soul to all of life, which fills everything and propels everything, and the vision of the particular, which concerns the body, is a separation from the worldly and filled life. The first is the ascent of the soul, its loftiness and liberty, and the second is [its] contraction, shrinkage, and enslavement.*[124]

The link to "life, which fills everything and propels everything" is actually no different than the connection to the divine. It is easy to comprehend within Ekstein's work that his teachings of self-awareness and the divided soul are quite sophisticated. Their meaning is not the New Age "self-actualization" or "self-em-

---

122 *b. Avodah Zarah* 20b.
123 This is an example of kabbalistic language being translated into psychological, internal, and personal language. This case discusses the Lurianic *parṣufim* (countenances) doctrine. For a concise overview of the Lurianic system of *parṣufim* see Shaul Magid, *From Metaphysics to Midrash: Myth, History, and the Interpretation of Scripture in Lurianic Kabbala* (Bloomington: Indiana University Press, 2008), 16–33. See below chap. 8, subchapter "Transformation of Traditional Concepts into Modern Concepts and the Translation of Kabbalah into Psychological Terminology."
124 Ekstein, *Tena'ei ha-Nefesh*, 31. Emphasis in original.

powerment," etc., although they do appear so in the beginning.[125] Not only are hasidic concepts like *biṭṭul* (self-nullification) at the center of his universalistic imagery exercises, but Ekstein's goals are unmistakably religious too. Ekstein saw in the return to oneself, through self-awareness, a tool for divine awareness: "The first principle that hasidism espouses to all who knock on its gates and wish to enter its inner sanctuaries is 'Know thyself' for it is certain *that all who gain a deep and clear self-awareness, are compelled to acquire divine awareness*, a certain and inner awareness, that is the purpose of all hasidism."[126] This opinion is very similar to that of his contemporary's, Abraham Isaac ha-Kohen Kook, who viewed the return to oneself as a return to the divine: "when one forgets the essence of one's own soul, when one distracts his mind from attending to the substantive content of his own inner life, everything becomes confused and uncertain. The primary role of penitence (*teshuvah*)... is for the person to return (*she-yashuv*) to himself, to the root of his soul. Then he will at once return to God, to the Soul of all souls."[127] Both of these thinkers share the opinion that self-awareness leads to divine awareness, in an almost automatic manner: "compelled to acquire" and "then he will at once return."[128] Ekstein's imagery techniques are designed to detach man from his egocentricity, which is an obstacle towards divine awareness, and consequently the recognition of God. These imagery exercises, although possessing universalistic features without specific religious connotations, are directed towards religiosity, awareness of God and even the mystical concept of integration with God.

125 Despite the universalistic characteristics of Ekstein's imagery techniques, they are directed towards religiosity. The adept reader will see that the book has been carefully organized: the first half of the work is entirely universal, without one mention of religion, whereas in the second half he adds the religious dimension, which he applies to all that he had written until that point.
126 Ekatein, *Tena'ei ha-Nefesh*, 46. (My emphasis)
127 Abraham Isaac ha-Kohen Kook, *Orot ha-Teshuvah* (Jerusalem: Mossad HaRav Kook, 1994), chap. 15, sect. 10. Translation from Ben-Zion Bosker, ed. & trans., *Abraham Isaac Kook: The Lights of Penitence, Lights of Holiness, The Moral Principles, Essays, Letters, and Poems* (New York: Paulist Press, 1978), 117.
128 Also see a similar statement by Mordekhai Yosef Lainer of Izbica (1800–1854), *Mei ha-Shilo'aḥ*, Parashat Lekh Lekha: "When Abraham our Father (*a"h*) began to desire and search for the root of his life... about this God (*hashem*), may he be blessed, said to him, 'Go forth' (*lekh lekha*), [which should be rendered as, 'Go forth] to yourself!' For in truth all the matters of this world cannot be referred to as 'life', for the essence of life will be found in yourself, 'And you shall rejoice in the Lord, And glory in the Holy One of Israel.' (Is. 41:16) Here as well one may identify the motif of self-awareness: "Go forth to yourself," as a means by which one becomes aware of the divine "you shall rejoice in the Lord."

F Integration (Hitkallelut)

The concept of integration (*hitkallelut*), or unity, appears prominently in hasidic literature, whereas it is only marginal in Lurianic kabbalah, a fact that proves, according to Idel, the panoramic spectrum of hasidic sources, which were not only confined to Luria, but were also absorbed from other kabbalistic compilations beginning in the thirteenth century.[129] This concept has a number of meanings on several levels.[130] On a social level, it indicates identification with the other or the collective, to the point of the nullification of the sense of "self" as it is exchanged with the experience of the "other". Indeed, the hasidic movement in its beginning was identified with influential charismatic personalities who possessed social-spiritual communicative capabilities, especially among their followers.[131] On the theological level, the meaning of this concept is *unio mystica*.[132] It is this meaning that mainly appears in hasidic literature. As Rachel Elior has written about Ḥabad contemplation, "The precise examination of the processes of creation and meditation on the process of emanation from *Ayin* to *Yesh*... bring one to annihilate the *Yesh* and to lay bare the *Ayin*... These lead to ecstatic unification and enthusiastic inclusion within divinity."[133]

Regarding the social dimension, it is worth citing the Beshṭ's grandson, Moses Ḥayyim Ephraim of Sudylkow: "And there is another aspect for the worshiper of God, that he needs to integrate himself with all the creatures from the little earthworm to the Lebanese oryx...and he must integrate himself with all of

---

129 Idel, *Hasidism*, 10–11.

130 Regarding Buber's conception of unity and the various metamorpheses of his thought regarding it in different stages of his life see Elliot. R. Wolfson, "The Problem of Unity in the Thought of Martin Buber," *Journal of the History of Philosophy* 27, (1989): 423–444, specifically ibid., 423–424: "In his mystical stage Buber maintained that unity was found in the subjective experience of ecstasy whereby the individual transcends the conditional world of space and time. In his existential stage Buber held that unity was not found but rather created by the individual confronting the world with all his uniqueness. In his dialogical stage Buber claimed that unity is realized—continuously and never absolutely—in the "Between," i.e., in the meeting of two beings who nevertheless remain distinct."

131 Rachel Elior, *The Paradoxical Ascent to God: The Kabbalistic Theosophy of Habad Hasidism* trans. Jeffrey M. Green (Albany: SUNY Press, 1993), 3. Furthermore see regarding the integration of the *ṣaddiq* with his ḥasidim, idem, *Freedom on the Tablets: The Mystical Origins and Kabbalistic Foundations of Hasidic Thought* (Tel Aviv: Ministry of Defense, 1999), 168–170, 175–184.

132 For an extensive treatment see Adam Afterman, *"And They Shall Be One Flesh": On the Language of Mystical Union in Judaism* (Leiden: Brill, 2016).

133 Elior, *The Paradoxical Ascent to God*, 138. For more on *unio mystica* in Jewish mysticism see above chap. 4 n. 371.

the souls."[134] Idel terms this integration as "mystical solidarity" and uses it to explain the emergence of hasidic society.[135] Idel claims that the mystic's integration with creation is based on a presupposition, the primal existence of the unifying force of reality through the letters of the Hebrew alphabet and the ten utterances.[136] Indeed, Ekstein does not reference the power of the letters in his writings, yet the imagination plays the same role for him, serving as a substitute for them. Through the faculty of the imagination, the mystic unites reality.

The concept of integration is also found in both medieval philosophic and kabbalistic discourse. In that context, it refers to the unification of the individual soul with an elect general object, as man clings to this object. Sometimes the soul unites with the Neoplatonic world-soul and sometimes with the divine itself.[137] *Hitkallelut* is the integration of man into the "all", the universal.[138] This "all" may be the general soul (Neoplatonism), the Active Intellect (Aristotelianism), society, or God. Common to all of these descriptions is the departure of man from his own particularity unto something greater and totalizing. "Integration" is essentially *devequt* (communion/union), with an emphasis on a general and universal entity. One is not cleaving to all objects, but rather to one general object. Abraham ibn Ezra (1089 – 1164) adopted the concept of *devequt* to refer to the transformation of the individual soul into the universal soul or unification with God.[139] Abulafia depicts the unification of the individual soul and the Active Intellect with universalistic descriptions. In his writings, Abulafia combines Aristotelean elements, such as the union of man's intellect with the Active Intellect, with Neoplatonic elements, like the transformation of the individual particular soul into the universalistic general soul.[140]

---

134 Moses Ḥayyim Ephraim of Sudlikov, *Degel Maḥaneh Efrayim*, 168, cited in Moshe Idel, "'Forever, Lord, Your Word is Firm': Studies in the Early Doctrine of the Baal Shem Tov and Its Development in Hasidism," *Kabbalah* 20 (2009): 249. See ibid., 250 – 251, and specifically n. 137 for more sources.

135 Ibid., 249 – 250. On the feeling of the harmony and unity of reality through the letters of the Hebrew alphabet see ibid.

136 Ibid., 250.

137 Moshe Idel, "Universalization and Integration: Two Conceptions of Mystical Union in Jewish Mysticism," in *Mystical Union in Judaism Christianity and Islam: An Ecumenical Dialogue*, ed. M. Idel and B. McGinn (New York: Continuum, 1996), 28.

138 Ibid., 35, "Integration of some elements into a more comprehensive entity."

139 Ibid., 28 – 29. Also see Afterman, *They Shall Be*, 88 – 90; idem, *Devequt: Mystical Intimacy in Medieval Jewish Thought* (Los Angeles: Cherub Press, 2011), 110 – 115.

140 For more on mystical union in Abulafia see, Afterman, *They Shall Be*, 151 – 170. On Neoplatonic and Aristotelean influences on the concept of *devequt* see Idel, *Kabbalah*, 39 – 46; Afterman, *They Shall Be*, 60 – 101.

Without entering into the debate of whether or not extreme forms of *unio mystica*—in which man and God are completely undifferentiated—exist in Jewish mysticism,[141] there are in any case numerous examples of integration from the beginning of kabbalah until, and primarily, in hasidism.[142] Whether this integration is total or partial, it is enhanced and intensified in hasidism for understandable reasons. Hasidism espoused the concept of *devequt* and acclaimed the importance of liberation from the ego. In order to understand the importance of liberating oneself from the ego's hold, it is necessary to introduce a number of ideological statements, primarily found within Ḥabad thought.[143] At the foundation of the panentheistic hasidic view, in contrast to the acosmic, is the existence of the world in a distinguishable manner. In contradistinction to the acosmic perception, which views the world as an illusion, the panentheistic conception requires the ontic existence of the world. Nevertheless, this approach does not view the world as an independent entity, "a thing unto itself," but rather as an entity within the divine essence. The world exists, but only within the fullness of the infinite divinity.[144] Just as this conception applies towards existence so too, according to hasidism, does it apply to man's personal psychological-consciousness. While in light of the panentheistic perception the "self" exists, it is not "a thing unto itself," but is rather found within the divine nothingness (*ayin ha-elohi*). When the "self" separates and enters into a contracted state, and thereby intensifies its own being and views itself as "a thing unto itself," it distances the divine presence and obstructs the encompassing light (*or maqif*) of divinity from penetrating him.[145]

---

141 See above chap. 3, n. 18. For more about *unio mystica* in Jewish mysticism see above chap. 4 n. 371.

142 See Idel, "Universalization and Integration," 33–50, for more examples, primarily from the hasidic period.

143 See Netanel Yechieli's observation regarding Ḥabad's influence on Ekstein in idem, "On the Book *Tena'ei ha-Nefesh le-Hasagat ha-Ḥassidut* by R. Menaḥem Ekstein, May God Avenge His Blood: Hasidic Psychological Worship Assisted by the Imaginative Faculty" (seminar paper, Hebrew University of Jerusalem, 1998), 25.

144 Yoram Jacobson, *From Lurianic Kabbalism to the Psychological Theosophy of Hasidism* (Tel Aviv: Ministry of Defense, 1984), 90.

145 Ibid., 91. In this conception man actually exists and *biṭṭul ha-yesh* (the nullification of existence) is not ontological. The meaning of *biṭṭul ha-yesh* is that man does not see himself as "a thing unto itself", but rather as an instrument in God's hand. See the disagreement between the understanding of *biṭṭul ha-yesh* between Jacobson and Elior in Yoram Jacobson, "The Rectification of the Heart: Studies in the Psychic Teachings of R. Shneur Zalman of Liadi." *Teudah* 10 (1996): 359–363, and n. 4. For a more recent exposition of the "pantheistic" and "acosmic" views found in Ḥabad see Elliot R. Wolfson, *Open Secret: Postmessianic Messianism and the Mystical Revision of Menaḥem Mendel Schneerson* (New York: Columbia University Press, 2009), 66–

The goal of integrating within the all, in its many variations, is to go beyond the limitations of the "self," which constitute a barrier towards ultimate integration with the divine. This issue at its various stages is emphasized and expanded upon in Ekstein's thought, in which man must liberate himself from the "self," through the proposed use of imagery exercises that precisely envision universalistic images.[146] The aim of these imagery techniques is to shift man's consciousness from his egocentricity to being centered on the universal (the world and mankind). In a gradual manner, he first presents these universalistic imagery techniques and afterwards adds the mystical element—integration with God—such that the first integration is a "means" for ultimate integration. Let us view this stage by stage: the "artificial imagination" is defined in his work as an imagination whose purpose is to bring man to a universal integration and contract his natural focus onto his "self" through the visualization of his proper relative place as an individual within creation and society: "This is what we referred to in chapter four as 'artificial imagination,' which strives to visualize all of creation and our true place in the world;"[147] "We shall feel in our minds a quasi-demand to liberate ourselves from particular minute matters, for there the place will be narrow for us and we will desire to rise above our essence [and] go out to the all—the general world and mankind."[148] One of the most basic hasidic ideas is that the soul's essence is sacred and its bad characteristic traits are merely a removable husk (*qelipah*).[149] Within the human self is the divine nothingness, and the nullification of the self is actually the disclosure of this nothingness. Hasidic communion (*devequt*) stresses the liberation from the self and the mystical connection of man and the divine, or the internal divine

---

129, specifically, 90 – 100, where he argues for a more nuanced view. Also see the fascinating remarks of the famous philosopher Solomon Maimon (1754 – 1800), who brings authentic testimony regarding the Dov Baer, Maggid of Międzyrzecz's court, and portrays the conception of *biṭṭul ha-yesh* as a nullification through one's consciousness of the divide between man and God, such man thereby sees himself as God's instrument, as he learned from the Maggid of Międzyrzecz's circle, "True service of God, in their view, consist in exercises of devotion with exertion of all our powers, and annihilation of self before God; for they maintain that man, in accordance with his destiny, can reach highest perfection only when he regards himself not as a being existing and working in and for itself, but as an organ of the Godhead." Moses Hadas, ed., *Solomon Maimon: An Autobiography* (New York: Schocken Books, 1947), 50.

146 Similarly, albeit slightly differently, Buber during his mystical stage understood integration as the integration between the self and the world, see Wolfson, "The Problem of Unity," 425 – 427.

147 Ekstein, *Tena'ei ha-Nefesh*, 14.

148 Ibid., 15.

149 See above chap. 5, at the beginning of the subchapter "*Gilui ha-Nefesh* (Revelation of the Soul) and Prophecy."

root within him—the nothingness within the self (*ha-ayin she-ba-ani*).[150] Ekstein distinctly continues this hasidic trajectory and sees the liberation from the contracted self to the general expanses as an act of connection to the nothingness in the soul, calling for the liberation from the self and the return to the soul's essence through integrating with creation:[151]

> We are compelled to clearly know that every feeling of pain and anger are not the essence of our souls, [but rather] they come from the exterior. Therefore, it is only possible to free oneself and be healed of them if we know the way to return to ourselves and our souls. Which way is it? Studying to exalt the soul and establish it... this is its departure from its particularity to be integrated into the whole of creation.... the contraction of the soul... is the separation from the universal (*ha-gadol ha-olami*) all, towards the small and passing individual. This is the descent of the soul and she is very saddened by it. However, it has the capability to be integrated into the all... and this is the connection to all of life, which fills the world, this is the return to its self and source.[152]

The imagination serves, according to him, as an instrument for self-nullification within creation: "Through the imaginative faculty man perceives, connects to, ascends towards, and nullifies himself in all of creation (*be-kelal ha-beriyah*)."[153] This allows the soul to return to its essence, which, in accordance with the hasidic idea that identifies the soul with divinity, ("a part of the divine above"), is the universal divine essence.

At times, Ekstein's conception of integration is in the more simplistic context of societal needs: "Even such a small man, if only he would want to act on behalf of everyone, is able to save many souls from sickness and hunger. Do these matters not bring you joy, vigor, and a will to take great pity on the world and work on behalf of all of humanity?"[154] Ekstein also portrays the mystical connotation of integration, namely, union with God. This conception appears only at the end of Ekstein's book. It becomes clear there that the universalistic imagery techniques and the call to integrate into the social collective are in fact instruments for integration with the divine: "Hasidism... teaches man to exalt himself anew each day... beyond the world and creation until he connects with the cre-

150 Jacobson, *From Lurianic Kabbalisim*, 89.
151 Which, as we have seen in both Kook's and Ekstein's teachings, there is a return to the divine root. However, Ekstein still does not clearly present this idea. Nonetheless, he incrementally discloses his true intentions and goals in his book.
152 Ekstein, *Tena'ei ha-Nefesh*, 15–16.
153 Ibid., 16.
154 Ibid., 20.

ator blessed be he."[155] The world and creation are only an intermediary stage leading up to the relation between man and God:

> Men are immersed in an awful egoism, individual and national egoism. Men who never learned how to exit their bodies, to exalt themselves towards the "all" and feel with the "all," to rise *towards the source and feel it*... men who have distanced themselves from faith, who have emptied themselves of the awareness of the creator may he be blessed, which is the only thing that can extract them from their individual bodies and teach them to integrate into the "all" and be nullified in it.[156]

> The primary purpose of our Torah is to exalt man's soul from the individuality of the body [so] that it may know [how] to integrate into the "all" and through this find the way *back to its source,* [*and*] *know its creator blessed be he and connect to him.*[157]

The goals of Ekstein's imagery techniques are to liberate man from the egoistic enslavement of the "self," and from the limitations and restrictions of the ego, through integration with the collective all and its needs. This path, the elimination of enslavement to the "self", ipso facto leads from the "self" to the nothingness (*ha-ani el ha-ayin*), from man through the collective (society) to God. The subject of mystical communion is the liberation from the feeling of independent ontic existence and the transition to the feeling of the self as part of the divine totality. This occurs within the panentheistic conception of reality, in which the self is part of the divine. This type of consciousness allows for man to unite with the divinity within himself.

In the end Ekstein is revealed as a mystic,[158] striving to unite with society and creation as a stage towards ultimate integration with the immanent divine, which sustains creation: "The same perception of all of creation is the soul's link to all of life, which fills everything and propels everything."[159] In Ekstein's teach-

155 Ibid., 35. Similarly, Buber saw integration with the world, as a phase of integrating with the divine. Still, Buber dealt more with the existential-philosophic dimension, whereas Ekstein focuses on the praxis and development of concrete imagery techniques of integration with the world in order to achieve mystical integration with God. This analysis of Buber may be found in Wolfson, "The Problem of Unity," 427: "One who intuitively experiences *(erlebt)* the unity of *I* experiences in turn the unity of *I* and *world*. From the unity of *I* and *world*, moreover, there emerges the unity of God."

156 Ekstein, *Tena'ei ha-Nefesh*, 36.

157 Ibid., 38.

158 Also see Garb, *Shamanic Trance*, 117, "The ultimate aim of such techniques is... self-empowerment.... However, there are also hints at more mystical goals, such as purification of thought, and a sense of being surrounded by divine light."

159 Ekstein, *Tena'ei ha-Nefesh*, 31.

ings, "the life" which propels everything is nothing other than God, and the perception is nothing other than the imagination.[160]

G Ecstasy and Amazement

The Sublime

The sense of the sublime is a central, nearly unique,[161] feature of the Bible, in which the image of God is connected to the sublime, "The Lord is exalted, He dwells on high" (Is. 33:5).[162] Furthermore, this verse creates a link between the sublime and height. The heights in scripture serve as a metaphor, arousing a sense of gravitas, reverence, mystery, astonishment, awe, upheaval, and recoil, and, simultaneously, allure, and excitement.[163] The Greek word for sublime only appears later, in the first century. The first philosophical work on this subject, *On the Sublime*, traditionally attributed to Dionysius of Halicarnassus or Cassius Longinus, was written in the third century.[164] The work's author claimed that man's inner greatness allows him to sense the sublime within nature: "Sublimity is the echo of a noble mind,"[165] and, like the Bible, the author claimed that, "The true sublime naturally elevates us."[166] Nevertheless, Pseudo-Longinus characterizes the sublime primarily as a literary style and ecstatic experience. The link between the sublime and the concealed is absent from classic Greek philosophy.[167]

---

160 On the use of the concept of "the life which fills all" and "the life which drives all" as a substitute for the religious concept of God see below chap. 8.
161 Heschel, *God in Search of Man*, 33, 37–38.
162 Idit Einat-Nov, "The Sublime and the Image of the Divine in Psalms and some Genres of Medieval Spanish Hebrew Liturgical Poetry," *Jerusalem Studies in Hebrew Literature* 21 (2007): 222.
163 Ibid. Her assertions are influenced by the conception that amazement caused by the sublime is translated into a feeling of recoil and attraction simultaneously, however see below, especially in Heschel's thought, that this model is not the sole one.
164 Regarding the identity of the author and his Jewishness see *Longinus: On the Sublime*, trans. Yoram Bronowski (Tel Aviv: Sifriat Poalim, 1982), 7–9.
165 Longinus, *On the Sublime*, Loeb Classical Library, trans. W. H. Fyfe (Cambridge: Harvard University Press, 1995), 9.2 (185).
166 Ibid., 7.2 (179).
167 Heschel, *God in Search of Man*, 37. Nevertheless, Pseudo-Longinus is open to a wide range of interpretations and there are places in his book in which it appears that the sublime is an awakener of the imagination and ecstatic experience, see Longinus, *On the Sublime*, trans. A.O. Prickard (Oxford: Clarendon Press, 1926), 14, 37, 67.

Eighteenth century Western European philosophy, specifically romanticism, adopted this and amplified this concept. The sublime gradually developed into an aesthetic concept, and ever since, it has appeared in literature, visual and musical arts, and in descriptions of nature.[168] The Irish philosopher Edmund Burke (1729–1797) published his book *A Philosophical Enquiry into the Origin of Our Ideas of the Sublime and Beautiful* in 1757; Burke was the first who contrasted the sublime and the beautiful.[169] He identified the beautiful with pleasure and the sublime with pain and anxiety.[170] The concept of "delight" allowed him to link the beautiful and sublime, and between pleasure and anxiety.[171] The sublime, in his opinion, is a feeling of *delightful horror.*[172]

Although Kant disagreed with Burke regarding his contrast of the beautiful and sublime, he did accept his view that the feeling of the sublime is to be identified with anxiety, fear, awe, etc., in contrast to the beautiful: "The beautiful coincides with the sublime in that both please for themselves... But notable differences between the two also strike the eye. The beautiful in nature concerns the form of the object, which consists in limitation; the sublime, by contrast, is to be found in a formless object."[173] Since the sublime is found in the formless, typified by its limitlessness, immeasurableness, and totalization, it does not lie within our judgmental capability, and, as opposed to the beautiful, which corresponds to our judgment and aesthetic sensibilities, "the sublime" is a feeling which contradicts are judgmental capabilities, and therefore, according to Kant, is characterized by strong feelings (*Gemütsbewegung*) and anxiety.

Kant identified Burke's "delightful horror" or "pleasurable fear" as "negative pleasure," writing, "Since the mind is not merely attracted by the object, but is also always reciprocally repelled by it, the satisfaction in the sublime does not so much contain positive pleasure as it does admiration or respect, i.e., it deserves to be called negative pleasure."[174] Friedrich Schiller (1759–1805) heightened the feeling of negative pleasure: "The sublime object may be considered in two lights. We either represent it to our comprehension... or we refer it to our vital

---

168 Regarding Longinus see Samuel Holt Monk, *The Sublime: A Study of Critical Theories in XVIII-Century England* (1935; repr., Ann Arbor: University of Michigan Press, 1960), 10–28.
169 Edmund Burke, *A Philosophical Enquiry into the Origin of Our Ideas of the Sublime and Beautiful* (Oxford: Oxford University Press, 1987) 32–35. For more on Burke see Monk, *The Sublime*, 84100, esp, 87–88.
170 Burke, *A Philosophical Enquiry*, 39–40, 57–58.
171 Ibid., 35–37.
172 Ibid., 73, 136.
173 Immanuel Kant, *Critique of the Power of Judgment*, ed. P. Guyer, trans. P. Guyer and E. Matthews (Cambridge: Cambridge University Press, 2000), 5:244 (128).
174 Ibid., 5:245 (129).

force... But though in both cases we experience in connection with this object the painful feeling of our limits, yet we do not seek to avoid it; on the contrary we are attracted to it by an irresistible force... The sight of a terrible object transports us with enthusiasm."[175] According to Schiller, the sense of shock and recoil caused by the sublime is vital for man and expands his emotional capacity: "The sublime must be joined to the beautiful to complete the aesthetic education, and to enlarge man's heart beyond the sensuous world."[176] The sublime grants man an extra-sensual dimension, in contrast to physical beauty: "Thus the sublime opens to us a road to overstep the limits of the world of sense, in which the feeling of the beautiful would forever imprison us."[177]

Rudolph Otto, relying on Kant's opinion, stated that negative pleasure is the foundation of the sublime experience and the zenith of religious experience. An additional stage is introduced here: until now the attitude towards the sublime, primarily in eighteenth century philosophy, was in the aesthetic domain, yet now Otto adds a religious dimension, specifically, religion in his opinion is founded upon the feeling of the sublime. This assertion is very significant, since it claims that religion's foundation is ultimately mystical. However, Otto's view is not clear enough and even has an internal contradiction.[178] On the one hand, he conceived of the sublime as linked to divinity, referred to in his writings as "the numinous feeling," stating that, "there exists a hidden kinship between the numinous and the sublime which is something more than a merely accidental analogy."[179] There is thus an affinity between the feeling of the sublime and the numinous, as they both constitute something secret that cannot be completely told. On the other hand, Otto denied this view, asserting that, "Religious feelings are not the same as aesthetic feelings, and the sublime is as definitely an aesthetic term as the beautiful, however widely different may be the facts denoted by the words."[180]

---

175 Friedrich Schiller, *On the Sublime*, trans. William F. Wertz, last modified October 29, 2016, https://www.schillerinstitute.org/transl/trans_on_sublime.html.

176 Ibid., 84.

177 Ibid., 81.

178 Joseph Ben-Shlomo wrote about this contradiction in his afterword to Rudolf Otto, *The Idea of the Holy: An Inquiry into the Non-Rational Factor in the Idea of the Divine and Its Relation to the Rational*, trans. Miryam Ron (Jerusalem: Carmel Publishing, 1999), 199–202.

179 Rudolf Otto, *The Idea of the Holy: An Inquiry into the Non-Rational Factor in the Idea of the Divine and Its Relation to the Rational*, trans. J. Harvey (Oxford: Oxford University Press, 1958), 63.

180 Ibid., 41–42.

Abraham Joshua Heschel deepened the link between the sublime and the concealed, negating it as an aesthetic category, as well as its opposition to the beautiful: "The sublime is not opposed to the beautiful, and must not, furthermore, be considered an esthetic category. The sublime may be sensed in things of beauty as well as in acts of goodness and in the search for truth. The perception of beauty may be the beginning of the experience of the sublime. The sublime is that which we see and are unable to convey. It is the silent allusion of things to a meaning greater than themselves;"[181] "The sublime... stands in relation to something beyond itself that the eye can never see."[182]

The Sublime and the Sense of Astonishment

Burke emphasized the sense of astonishment, or wonder, as a reaction to the sublime. Astonishment, according to him, is man's natural and uncontrolled response towards the sublime. Thomas Rice Henn (1901–1974) noted the conflicting characterization of Burke's and Pseudo-Longinus' senses of astonishment. Moreover, Pseudo-Longinus' sense of astonishment is not necessarily connected to fear and terror, while in wake of Burke's thought, within eighteenth century romantic philosophy, the sense of astonishment was identified with terror:

> Burke starts with the assumption that "astonishment is the effect of the sublime in its highest degree:" Longinus would probably have agreed with the conception of "wonder," but not with the idea of terror which is to produce it. Terror, in Burke's view being the most powerful of the passions, is best fitted to produce the sublime; it therefore, in part at least, is a negative emotion, closely allied to pain, whereas Longinus' is positive—the ecstasy.[183]

The identification of the sense of astonishment with terror made a strong impression, and many authors and thinkers of the nineteenth century documented their experiences of astonishment with terms of great terror, turmoil, and fear. William James collected numerous testimonies, including those of Leo Tolstoy, John Bunyan, and Henry Alline.[184] Even Hillel Zeitlin, the hasidic thinker, was influenced by these descriptions, and included some of them from James' work[185] in his an-

181 Heschel, *God in Search of Man*, 39.
182 Ibid., 40.
183 Thomas Rice Henn, *Longinus and English Criticism* (Cambridge: Cambridge University Press, 1934), 119.
184 James, *The Varieties of Religious Experience*, 149–165.
185 Zeitlin, *Al Gevul Shenei Olamot*, 31–32.

thology of experiences of astonishment from the Bible until the first generation of hasidic leaders.[186] The common denominator of all these collections of personal testimonies is a sense of fright and, primarily, terror, as Zeitlin aptly defined, "astonishment also includes a certain sudden bewilderment and a sort of great trembling. The bewilderment passes, but the trembling remains;"[187] "Astonishment also contains a sense of self-negation and submission before that strange and wondrous thing that so causes us to tremble and also bears such awesome beauty;"[188] "Berdyczewski thinks that just as wonder gave birth to inquiry, so too did it bring forth religion. But it was not wonder that gave birth to religion, but *astonishment.*"[189]Zeitlin seemingly viewed mysticism as the foundation of religion: "Wonder asks all sorts of questions. Astonishment asks nothing... It stands confounded, amazed, blown away, transported... Astonishment births religion and its sisters—poetry and music."[190]

---

186 Ibid., 25–35.

187 Ibid., 25; Translation from Arthur Green, *Hasidic Spirituality for a New Era: The Religious Writings of Hillel Zeitlin* (New York: Paulist Press, 2012), 138.

188 Ibid., 18; Green, *Hasidic Spirituality for a New Era*, 138–139.

189 Ibid; Green, *Hasidic Spirituality for a New Era*, 131. Emphasis in original. Also see there regarding the distinction between wonder and astonishment according to Zeitlin.

190 Ibid. The source of Zeitlin's remarks are to be found in the Introduction to the *Zohar* I:1b in R. El'azar's interpretation of the verse "Lift your eyes on high and see: Who created these?" (Is. 40:26). In this passage R. El'azar states that there is a divine dimension of which language is unable to grasp and therefore there is no possibility of asking "*Who*[?] Beyond, there is no question." Also see Zeitlin's translation and interpretation of this zoharic passage in *Pardes ha-Ḥasidut ve-ha-Qabalah*, 231–232. Also see Ludwig Wittgenstein's (1889–1951) similar, but more complex and developed conception regarding linguistically inexpressible matters: "What can be said at all can be said clearly, and what we cannot talk about we must pass over in silence." *Tractatus Logico-Philosophicus*, trans. D. F. Pears and B. F. McGuinness (London: Routledge, 1974), 3; "What we cannot speak about we must pass over in silence." Ibid., 7 (89); "Propositions can express nothing that is higher." Ibid., 6.42 (86). Wittgenstein's conception is determined by his view of language as all-encompassing: "It will therefore only be in language that the limit can be drawn, and what lies on the other side of the limit will simply be nonsense." Ibid., 4. It is possible to understand Wittgenstein as denying all dimensions outside of language, however a careful reading demonstrates that not only does he not negate these dimensions—he in fact demands that they be. This requisite is directly linked to the experience of astonishment, although he does not explicitly write as such. The sentence which shows Wittgenstein's astonishment regarding the world's existence is: "It is not *how* things are in the world that is mystical, but *that* it exists." Ibid., 6.44 (88). The very existence of the world causes the astonishment, which is mystical. The visible world's very existence, proves that there is something beyond the realm of language and therefore lies beyond the limits of thought, which therefore constitutes it as mystical: "There are, indeed, things that cannot be put into words. They *make themselves manifest*. They are what is mystical." Ibid., 6.522 (89). Also see ibid., 4.1212 (31): "What *can* be shown, *cannot* be said." As far as I am aware Zeitlin does not quote or cite Witt-

Althoug Heschel argued against the identification of astonishment with terror, he nonetheless shared Zeitlin's opinion that astonishment derived from the sublime is one of religion's foundations.[191] Consequently, Heschel saw the disappearance of wonder and astonishment from the American landscape of the twentieth century as a terrible tragedy:

---

genstein, however both were influenced by similar sources like Schopenhauer, Nietzsche, Karl Robert Eduard von Hartmann, and Leo Tolstoy. Zeitlin and Wittgenstein are alike regarding their attitudes towards the inexpressible, yet their conceptions of astonishment diverge. The mystical astonishment which Wittgenstein describes is essentially the world's being. This form of astonishment is not necessarily identified with anxiety and fear, and is more akin to Heschel's view. Furthermore, the teaching of Mordekhai Yosef Lainer of Izbica is remarkably similar to Wittgenstein, both in content and concepts: "'Who is like You, O Lord, among the celestials; Who is like You, majestic in holiness:' 'Who is like You, O Lord, among the celestials'—for his essence, blessed be he, is concealed from the eyes of the living, and there is no one who can grasp him as it is stated in the Talmud: "Who is like unto Thee among the silent ones," (Jacob Z. Lauterbach, ed. *Mekhilta de-Rabbi Ishmael, Shirata* 8) and "Majestic in holiness"—for it is obvious that for each thing it will be explicitly recognized that there is a creator, for from all of the creations it will be seen that there is a creator. For on everything that comes into the heart of man, it seeks God, saying, 'Who created these' (Is. 40:26)." Man is silent when confronting the divine essence, man is unable to apply language to that which is higher than language (similar to Wittgenstein's statement, "Propositions can express nothing that is higher"), nonetheless man is certain of the divine reality, since the world (or creations) point towards it and this causes a sense of astonishment when confronted with this entity, for it evokes the sense of amazement of "Who created these?" understood by Lainer as meaning, "For from all of the creations it will be seen that there is a creator," or analogously, in Wittgenstein's words, "They *make themselves manifest.*" Wittgenstein's mysticism is also based on astonishment, for from the very fact that reality exists, our encounter with it causes astonishment, and through this amazement caused by the wonder of the world's existence—our lives are understood as being wondrous, see Shimon Gershon Rosenberg, "Faith and Language According the Admor ha-Zaqen of Habad from the Philosophical Perspective on Language of Wittgenstein," in *On Faith: Studies in the Concept of Faith and Its History in the Jewish Tradition*, eds., Moshe Halbertal, David Kurzweil, and Avi Sagi (Jerusalem: Keter, 2005), 376–377. Also see on Wittgenstein's mystical wonder, Yuval Lurie, *Tracking the Meaning of Life: A Philosophical Journey* (Haifa: Haifa University Press and Maariv, 2001), 147–150, 162–166. I would like to express my gratitude towards my friend Yishai Mevorach who exposed me to the mystical understanding of Wittgenstein. Regarding the comparison between Wittgenstein's silence with hasidic *devequt* see Michal Govrin's comments in "Théatre Sacré: Contemporain: Théories et Pratiques" (PhD diss., Université de Paris III, 1976), 263–264; for a comparison of Wittgenstein's silence with that of Naḥman of Bratslav's, see Yehuda Liebes, "Naḥman of Bratslav and Ludwig Wittgenstein," *Dimmui* 19 (2001): 12–13.

191 According to Heschel, the experience of astonishment stands in direct relation to the mystical sense of the sublime and of the divine presence. Biblical man responded to the sublime with a sense of wonder and amazement. See Heschel, *God in Search of Man*, 41, 48. Regarding his view of "mystery" (*mistorin*) being the foundation of religion, see ibid., 54–60.

> The awareness of grandeur and the sublime is all but gone from the modern mind... The sense for the sublime, the sign of the inward greatness of the human soul and something which is potentially given to all men, is now a rare gift. Yet without it, the world becomes flat and the soul a vacuum.[192]

> This is the tragedy of every man: "to dim all wonder by indifference." Life is routine, and routine is resistance to the wonder. "Replete is the world with a spiritual radiance, replete with sublime and marvelous secrets. But a small hand held against the eye hides it all," said the Baal Shem. "Just as a small coin held over the face can block out the sight of a mountain, so can the vanities of living block out the sight of the infinite light."[193]

Heschel, Zeitlin, and Ekstein, discounting their many differences, were active, to a certain extent, in the same geographical, cultural, and historical contexts. Each of them perceived hasidic thought and its concepts as central foundations of Judaism and Torah, through which man is able to connect with divinity. There is no doubt that their conception of astonishment and wonder—mediated through the contemplation of nature—was neither developed in a vacuum, nor in purely Jewish circles. The preoccupation of eighteenth century philosophy, particularly romantic and neo-romantic, with the sublime, influenced a certain type of European spirit. In the late nineteenth and early twentieth century the sublime progressed and developed from a purely aesthetic category into a religious-*mysterium* concept. The understanding of mysticism as the foundation of religion was very widespread and no doubt played a central role in Zeitlin's, Heschel's, and Ekstein's thought. It is true that their writings are marked by the thought of many hasidic thinkers,[194] regarding the experience of mystery in general and astonishment in particular, as the foundation of religion,[195] yet none of

---

192 Ibid., 36.
193 Ibid., 85.
194 Regarding Heschel's use of kabbalistic and hasidic sources specifically in his *God in Search of Man*, see Michael Marmur, "Heschel's Rhetoric of Citation: The Use of Sources in *God in Search of Man*" (PhD diss., Hebrew University, 2005), 184–259.
195 See Lainer, *Mei ha-Shilo'aḥ*, Parashat Lekh Lekha: "It is stated in the midrash, 'Who is the owner of the palace (*birah*)? [Is it possible that the palace lacks a person to look after it, he wondered] The owner of the palace glanced upon him (*alav*).' (Gen. Rabbah 29:1) (The bracketed portion is the actual midrash which Lainer paraphrases.) Seemingly it should have written 'upon it (*aleha*)' and not 'upon him (*alav*),' however, when Abraham our forefather, may peace be upon him, looked upon the doings of the postdiluvian generation, this is referred to as the burning palace, for it was a great wonder and he was angered in his soul [and asked] 'Who created these?' (Is. 40:26) 'The owner of the palace glanced upon him (*alav*),' meaning, the Holy One blessed be He answered him, 'Surely, see for yourself that the entire world is not troubled and no one has placed upon his heart to say, "Who made this?" but in your eyes it is wondrous, and from the anger of your heart you shall be able to surmise that certainly there is a creator

these hasidic thinkers defined the word "astonishment," nor did they dedicate a concentrated or extensive discussion of the topic.[196] This process of indicating "the mystery" (*mistorin*), or the concealed, as a foundation of Judaism, primarily occurred in the late nineteenth and early twentieth century in the works of neo-romantic scholars of hasidism, some of whom were concomitantly active within certain hasidic circles, like Zeitlin, Heschel, Martin Buber, Fischel Schneerson, and David Kogan. Ekstein should be added to this list, as well. For them, "mystery" was not some light through meant for the elite, but was rather the foundation of religion, and for this reason a number of them wanted to revive mystery in Judaism.[197]

The Sublime and the Imagination in Ekstein's Teachings

According to Kant, man reacts to the sublime by struggling with the absolute,[198] which signifies the imaginal realm of the sublime. Kant viewed the sublime as psychological state that occurs when man's rational understanding takes upon itself an undoable task. Man's reason judges reality according to defined and limited categories, whereas the imagination, through which we attempt to understand the absolute, brings his reasoning beyond the limitations of comprehension towards infinity. The tension created due to the lack of correspondence be-

who encompasses all worlds and fills all worlds and he is the one who aroused your heart and soul about this.' And this is [the meaning of] the language 'upon it' (*alav*), meaning upon his question, for it in itself is a sufficient answer for him." Lainer is saying here that the word *alav* seemingly referring to Abraham is in fact referring to his astonishment, and that God is not looking at Abraham, but rather he appears to Abraham through his astonishment, which in actuality is placed in his heart by God. The astonishment itself precedes the belief in God and actually awakens it.

196 *Tract on Ecstasy* (*Qunṭres ha-Hitpa'alut*) by the Mittler Rebbe of Ḥabad, Dov Baer Schneersohn, is an exception. Nonetheless, its subject is not a type of proto-religious ecstasy or astonishment, an experience which creates religion, but rather a different level of religiosity, namely, that after man accepts the religious idea of divinity, ecstasy comes as an additional experience of the disclosure of divinity in man's soul.

197 As far as I am aware, there has been no extensive research conducted regarding the concepts of the sublime and astonishment in relation to hasidism, a topic which directly relates to the question of whether mysticism is the foundation of religion, or vice versa.

198 Kant connects, like the Bible and Longinus, the sublime with the absolute. This is due to his claim (in his book *Critique of the Power of Judgment*), that it is only possible to state that an object is large in contrast to a smaller object. In contrast, when we relate to something as large in an absolute fashion, we are relating to a largeness that is incomparable. Since the sublime is incomparable it is appropriate to describe it as "the absolute."

tween the external limitless object belonging to the imaginal realm and the rational faculty, which constantly attempts to grasp and comprehend it, arouses in man a supra-sensual feeling, namely, the sublime.[199]

Pseudo-Longinus already perceived the sublime as "the echo of a noble mind," able to awaken the imagination and cause ecstasy.[200] According to the *Zohar*, the restoration of wonder and astonishment are entailed in the restoration of the imagination.[201] The imagination restores wonder to items that have become solely physical in the eyes of man. The repeated Wittgensteinian statement "Not *how* the world is, is the mystical, but *that* it is,"[202] indicates the basic question of existence, why (or how) there is something and not nothing. This question leads to amazement and promotes a consciousness of wonder.[203] This wonder is a state of existence rich with depth and imagination.[204] Heschel called for the return of wonder and amazement to reality, since they instill mystery itself into existence. The restoration of wonder means the return of mystery and sensitivity to a certain meaning beyond physical things into our own lives. Heschel proposes to return the sense of sublimity or majesty to humanity through the contemplation of nature. This, however, is not a scientific contemplation, which sees nature as an instrument of mankind, but rather a contemplation of the mystery: "Nature as a tool box is a world that does not point beyond itself. It is when nature is sensed as mystery and grandeur that it calls upon us to look beyond it."[205] Ekstein intensifies this view regarding the contemplation of nature, and translated it into a guided imagery exercise.[206] Ekstein maintains a connection between astonishment or ecstasy and imagination:

> If we become accustomed to use our imaginative faculty, to develop and greatly perfect it, then we will easily be able to free [ourselves] from any temporary event and we will experience a great delight if we remove for a time the emotion and action which some event arouses within us and stroll in the great world, to go around all the locations that we

---

199 Kant, *Critique of the Power of Judgment*, 5: 250 (134).
200 Longinus, *On the Sublime* (Oxford: Clarendon Press, 1926), 14, 37, 67.
201 Shimon Gershon Rosenberg, *A Time of Freedom: Discourses for Pesach*, ed. Yishai Mevorach (Alon Shevut: The Institute for the Advancement of Rav Shagar's Writings, 2010), 134. Rosenberg relates to the zoharic rendering of "Who created these?" (Is. 40:26; *Zohar* I:1b-2a). It should be noted that this passage in the *Zohar* does not relate to imagination directly, and that this is Rosenberg's interpretation.
202 See above n. 190.
203 See Lurie, *Tracking the Meaning of Life*; above n. 190.
204 Rosenberg, *A Time of Freedom*, 135.
205 Heschel, *God in Search of Man*, 36.
206 See above, subchapter "War of Imaginations," for an example of a lengthy natural imagery technique.

know, to visit in our thoughts the many people, [and] be astonished by their lives and feelings. Afterwards we will return to our concerns and pleasures. If we will do so, then our lives will be elevated on high, and they will be lengthened, full, and rich.[207]

The world is quite large. There are numerous things in each settlement, desert, and seas, which arouse great astonishment, which may nourish man for many years.[208]

According to Ekstein, ecstasy derived from the wandering imagination, "strolling through the world," has the capacity to liberate and remove man from his particularity. Most of his exercises, connected to ecstasy and astonishment, are directed towards the imagery of the world, creation, and existence: "Thereby we will be constantly stimulated [even] more, each day we will marvel anew, and we will experience ecstasy from the same amazing creation. Through this our instruments of ecstasy will progress, develop, and broaden."[209] This ecstasy is not only aesthetic, as may be assumed from the aforementioned quotations. Slowly and gradually, Ekstein reveals the religious purposes of his doctrine. Contemplation or visualization of creation and creatures are part of the process of entering the inner chambers of hasidism:

Until now we have strolled in the corridor before the opening of the threshold which leads to the chambers of hasidism. Before we take the first step of entering inside, we need to know the following three rules: the first rule is about contemplating the whole of creation, how hasidism relates to this very perception. The second rule concerns the contemplation of individuals from a hasidic perspective. The third rule clarifies the relation and connection of these outlooks of the world and people towards the practical commandments (*miṣvot*) and other religious matters.[210]

in Ekstein's teachings, the contemplation of the world and humanity through the imagination is aimed ultimately at experiencing astonishment.[211] Ekstein adds an aspect of mystery to the aesthetic astonishment of romantic philosophy:

207 Ekstein, *Tena'ei ha-Nefesh*, 11–12.
208 Ibid., 31.
209 Ibid., 14.
210 Ibid., 22.
211 Already in his letters to Kamelhar, one may identity the first inklings of this conception of guiding all ecstasies towards God, see his letter from Monday in the week of Parashat va-Yeshev (no year written, so either in November or December): "The truth is that even though many masses are drawn towards hasidism, it is only due to the material promises, or due to their love of themselves and insignificant things such as wanting to be close and sitting first, etc. however, from a different perspective it is difficult to deny that many individuals from among the masses contemplated and penetrated deeper into hasidism and understood that none of these [aforementioned matters] are its purpose. It is difficult to deny that hasidism influenced

> This is the hasidic view of the world and man. However... it does not suffice itself with contemplation alone, but rather elevates everything and is astonished (*u-mitpa'elet*) by the creator, blessed be he, who created and directs all of this. Hasidism elevates man: If the ten powers in his soul have sufficiently developed such that he may receive within himself all of creation and become astonished by it—from this same level will he begin to see that all of creation has a soul which sustains it and constantly directs it... and their soul is the creator, blessed be he![212]

The experience of human astonishment of the divine, in effect, creates an encounter between man and the divine. The hasidic *devequt* is reconfigured here in a new light by Ekstein and becomes a religious communion with God brought about through the contemplation of nature and creation:

> And when the soul is already uplifted from the privation of the body, it begins to become ecstatic due to all of creation (*kelal ha-beriyah*), the sun, the moon, all of the hosts of heaven, all the kings of the lands and nations, all the domesticated and wild animals, and the rest of the creatures. Afterwards it is elevated even higher and is enraptured (*u-mitpa'elet*) by the creator himself, blessed be he, who fills all of creation and "his presence fills all the earth" (Is. 6:3) and "who in his goodness, continually renews the work of creation" and [it] clings to the creator, blessed be he.[213]

The human ecstasy from the creator is the sense of a living encounter characterized by an experience of communion (*devequt*). It is not epistemologically similar to hearing, but rather is an experiential, possibly prophetic, awareness, as though seeing:

> Faith is in the aspect of hearing, however if the ten powers of the soul have already been broadened so that they may be enraptured (*le-hitpa'el*) by the leader of the world (*ha-manhig et olamo*) himself, blessed be he; if the consciousness (*mo'aḥ*) has already been cleansed of bodily corporeality by means of always perceiving all of creation (*be-kelal ha-beriyah*)... then man arrives at faith in the aspect of seeing, this faith... is in his soul and is felt throughout his interiority. Hasidism states about this man that he clings (*davuq*) to life, in contrast to one whose faith is limp [and] is separated from the source of life.[214]

---

and influences many individuals to be more excited and energized about religion and faith and they understand that hasidism primarily requires of them to unite all their emotions and ecstasies of the soul and heart—for [the sake of] heaven."

212 Ekstein, *Tena'ei ha-Nefesh*, 33.

213 Ibid., 50.

214 Ibid., 34.

Ekstein methodologically supports his technique, which seeks the experience of astonishment through imagery techniques, with Maimonides's famous opening words of his code of law, the *Mishneh Torah*. Maimonides portrays nature and humankind as objects of contemplation that are utilized as instruments for the love and fear of God:

> It is a commandment to love and fear this glorious and awesome God, as it states: "And you shall love God, your Lord" (Deut. 6:5) and, as it states: "Fear God, your Lord." (Deut. 6:13) What is the path to love and fear him? When a person contemplates his wondrous and great deeds and creations and is in awe from his incomparable and limitless wisdom—he will immediately love, praise, and glorify, and yearn with tremendous desire to know the great name, as David stated: "My soul thirsts for the Lord, for the living God." (Ps. 42:3) And when he reflect on these same matters, he will immediately recoil and he will fear and he will know that he is a tiny, lowly, and dark creature, standing with his flimsy, limited, wisdom before he who is of perfect knowledge, as David stated: "When I see Your heavens, the work of Your fingers, what is man that You should recall Him" (Psalms 8:4-5).[215]

Maimonides's description contains many facets, such as the contemplation of nature ("his wondrous and great deeds") and living beings ("creations"), which cause him to desire God ("yearn with tremendous desire to know the great name") as well as experience a sense of astonishment tinted by an ecstatic tone associated with feelings of panic and withdrawal ("he will immediately recoil and he will fear.")[216] The imagery techniques that Ekstein presents and develops are portrayed to the reader as "the hasidic path," and "Maimonides's path too!" For according to him, hasidism imitated the Maimonidean path:

> Maimonides began his book, which is the book of all books, with the commandment of knowing God through clear inner awareness, and with the commandment to love and fear God, for without them this knowledge is entirely impossible. Afterwards, he asks, "How does one love him etc." and, "How does one fear him etc." and he demonstrates there the ways [to achieve] this, which is worship through contemplation (*avodat ha-maḥshavah*), which hasidism chose.[217]

215 Translation based on Eliyahu Touger's translation of Moses Maimoniodes, *Mishneh Torah*, "Laws of the Foundations of the Torah," 2:1–2, at "Yesodei haTorah—Chapter Two," last modified May 11, 2016, http://www.chabad.org/library/article_cdo/aid/904962/jewish/Yesodei-haTorah-Chapter-Two.htm

216 On the component of fear in ecstasy see above chap. 3, "Tow Models of Prophecy." According to eighteenth century philosophy, one may describe it as astonishment, for astonishment was identified with fear, terror, and the attraction to this terror.

217 Ekstein, *Tena'ei ha-Nefesh*, 39.

Avodat ha-maḥshavah in Ekstein's thought is interpreted as imagery techniques. It appears to me that Ekstein's originality lies in this interpretation, and more so —in his development of multiple modes of worship. In contradistinction to Maimonides, who in the chapters on prophecy in *Guide of the Perplexed* spoke of and emphasized in a theoretical manner the importance of the imagination in the prophetic process, Ekstein in his work engaged mostly with *praxis* and presented numerous imagery techniques[218] introduced not in the context of prophecy, but rather in the context of the astonishment and ecstasy through which man establishes a living encounter with the divine. Maimonides's statement in his code, "When a person *contemplates* his wondrous and great deeds," can be interpreted in two ways: passive contemplation, meaning entering into nature and contemplating it, or reflective contemplation, which may also be understood in two ways: as deep probing thought or as a spiritual experiential act.[219] Ekstein seemingly interprets Maimonides according to the latter understanding—not optically contemplating in a physical setting in nature, but rather visualizating nature and creatures (people and animals). Ekstein's reliance on the astonishment presented in Maimonides's code explains why he focused on universalistic imagery—in his opinion he is continuing the path of Maimonides, who promulgated universalistic anomian paths intended to achieve the love and fear of God.

---

218 See ibid., 2–15.

219 This division stems from the disagreement regarding the understanding of Maimonides's conception of the commandment to know God (if it is a logical knowing or an experiential awareness). Knowledge of God is the goal of loving God according to Maimonides "He will immediately love… and yearn with tremendous desire to know the great name." This knowledge is generally interpreted as philosophical knowledge, however it is sometimes interpreted as a living-awareness. See the remarks of Josef B. Soloveitchik, *On Repentance: The Thought and Oral Discourses of Rabbi Joseph B. Soloveitchik*, ed. and trans. Pinchas H. Peli. (New York: Paulist Press, 1984), 130–131: "I do not agree with those who interpret 'to know' as meaning 'to understand,' indicating that each and every Jew would have to philosophize and investigate for himself all that is relevant to the existence of God. I do not believe that this is what Maimonides meant. We cannot 'understand' the Almighty; His quality is hidden and unfathomable, and in this Maimonides concurred with the Kabbalists who asserted: 'No intellect can comprehend Him.'… I would say that 'to know' (*lei'da*) means that our conviction of the existence of God should became a constant and continuous awareness… a stte of perpetual affinity, of constant orientation, God should become a living reality that one cannot forget even for a minute… This 'interpretation' actually mirrors an explicit verse of the Bible: 'In all thy ways know Him' (Proverbs 3:6)… Be conscious of God's existence at all times." On Maimonides as a philosopher or mystic see Persico, "Jewish Meditation," 63–77. Also see the work of David R. Blumenthal, *Philosophic Mysticism: Studies in Rational Religion* (Ramat Gan: Bar-Ilan University Press, 2006), 51–154, and especially, v-xiv.

Integration with the "all," together with the sense of astonishment, constitute for Ekstein means through which one may encounter the divine, an encounter that is not acquired solely through adherence to religious law. Ekstein is thereby revealed to not only be a religious person committed to the divine commandments, or a neo-romantic philosopher who is astonished by the aesthetic dimension of nature, but also a mystic in every sense of the word, who seeks, through visualizing creation, a live encounter with the creator:

> Please come and listen to my words. Lay down your work tools, leave your business for one day, distance your thought from corporeal matters, entirely forget them, and please look upon all of creation, how beautiful and magnificent it is! Please see the great world, the very many nations that live in it, with their different languages, clothing, and ways of life. They have built for themselves such beautiful states, such large cities filled with houses and splendid palaces, squares, and markets. Such large seas surround the land, enormous rushing rivers, emerging mountains and boulders... desserts, forest, fields, and vineyards. In the seas are many types of fish... How many kinds of trees in the world, how many types of plants and flowers, how many kinds of fruits... how many types of domesticated and wild animals, and birds. Do you not desire at all to see these creations? Are they not more important in your eyes than these insignificant matters related to your bodily existence? Do you not want to view all of creation, so beautiful and splendid, and do you not want to know the creator, blessed be he, who created it and you, as well as your work and businesses, at all? No my son! Is this not the purpose of your life! Please learn your thoughts and contemplate all of creation, for this is the search for your creator and if you seek him, blessed be he—you will find him![220]

H *Raṣo va-Shov* (Running and Returning): Numerous Scenes and Their Successive Progression

Ekstein developed numerous original imagery techniques which visualized multiple scenes in the original manner of *raṣo va-shov* (running and returning). This imagery operates through transformation and change in which one is required to visualize one thing after another, at times up to ten differing and opposing scenes. This method of imagery exercises is not widespread, neither in kabbalistic nor hasidic literature. A precedent for this technique may be found in the writings of Joseph ben Shalom Ashkenazi, a fourteenth century kabbalist, known for his commentary on *Sefer Yeṣirah*. Ashkenazi wrote a kabbalistic commentary on

220 Ekstein, *Tena'ei ha-Nefesh*, 53. It should be noted that Ekstein addresses the public and does not turn inwards towards himself. This is an example of a modern mystic, who desires to bring mysticism to all of humanity and not let it remain in the private domain, a matter that Scholem did not recognize, see above chap. 3 n. 105.

Genesis based on Genesis Rabbah.[221] In one section, he presents numerous imaginal objects that are possible in a prophetic vision,[222] and after presenting them separately he raises the possibility of visualizing them all together, or paralleling one another, in an intense sequence:

> The image will cause the prophet terror and fear until his senses nullify... and then from within the fear the senses will be nullified from their enrapture and influx will emanate onto the intellectual power and from it, it will emanate upon the [faculty of] imagination and it will appear to him as though he sees a face of man speaking with him by voice, spirit and speech. The visions of that man are sometimes by means of letters [possessing] the color of copper or the color of snow or the color of the [man's] linen or like the color of the fine gold or the color of beryl or the color of lightning or like flaming torches or in the likeness of burnished bronze or in the likeness of the color of the rainbow or in the likeness of blue (*tekhelet*) or in the likeness of fire or in the likeness of water, or *a running admixture of these images.*[223]

The possibility that the subject of discussion is a number of images situated together is well founded from the continuation of his remarks: "It is not improbable that there will be a person to whom matters will appear in a waking dream like those he visualizes in his dreams... as the letters of the divine name [stand] in front of his eyes, in the gathered colors. Sometimes, he will hear a voice... and he will see with his imaginative faculty with all the organs of sight... All this while the holy letters are in front of his eyes, and its colors are covering it; this is the 'sleep of prophecy.' And as the vision of the God's glory soars above, [so too] all the prophetic visions will soar above him."[224] Ashkenazi describes imaginal images concomitantly subsisting with the imaginal letters of the divine name,[225] and when these letter-images are soaring, these images are soaring as well. This imagery technique, visualizing multiple images simultaneously or in quick succession, is not prevalent in kabbalistic literature, not to even mention the imagining of conflicting imagery one after another.

---

221 Regarding him see Moshe Hallamish, *Kabbalistic Commentary of Rabbi Yoseph ben Shalom Ashkenazi on Genesis Rabbah* (Jerusalem: Magnes Press, 1984), 9–14.

222 For scholarship on this passage in the context of visualizing colors see Idel, *Enchanted Chains*, 228–232.

223 Hallamish, *Kabbalistic Commentary*, 223. Translation based on Idel, *Enchanted Chains*, 230. Translation of biblical words based on JPS translation.

224 Hallamish, *Kabbalistic Commentary*, 223. This translation is based on Idel, *Enchanted Chains*, 229.

225 Also see that Idel also understood the visualization of letters and colors, in this text, as visualization, *Enchanted Chains*, 231.

This discussion highlights Ekstein's uniqueness. Ekstein, in his work, utilizes the technique of visualizing numerous images, including opposing ones one after another. He consistantly requires the reader to imagine a scene and immediately afterwards its opposite. When the practitioner is told to visualize a scene that arouses a certain emotion, he is then immediately instructed to visualize a different scene that evokes the opposite emotion. The imagining of the largeness of the world is followed by the visualization of the smallness of the world, and so on, in a manner of *rașo va-shov*, going to and fro. Below are several examples:

1. Opposite Dimensions: Largeness—Smallness

> It is appropriate that the utilization of our imaginative faculty always be in the following manner, that we should begin to visualize (*le-ṣayair*) the world as a small sphere... and little by little enlarge and widen it in our imagination... or we can visualize a place that is well known to us and from there we can lay out the earth and broaden it completely (*le-kol ha-ṣedadim*)... it is fitting to also train [our] minds for contrasts (*ḥilufim*), for after we envision this [the enlarging of the world], we should already enlarge it until its possible limit, then we shall return and reduce it, enlarge it, and reduce it, back and forth.[226]

2. Mourning—Tranquility

> We shall visualize (*neṣayair*)... a feeling of mourning for the dead. For example, we shall visualize the sorrow of a father standing at the bedside of his only son, who is fighting against the pangs of death which overtake him... he sees how those standing around him... have decided that he is already dead, lowering him into the ground, placing him in the coffin... the father accompanies him to his eternal abode, he sees the grave prepared for his son, they lower him into the pit in front of him, cover him with dirt. Afterwards the father returns home... we shall increasingly visualize (*neṣayair*) this in this manner... until it arouses us and we too feel the father's sorrow... afterwards we shall continue to visualize how in the coming days the sorrow begins to digress slightly from the father's heart, the pain begins to be healed and it returns to him only faintly in his daily life... and in the sorrow's departure from the father we will also sensorially feel (*nargish be-ḥush*) in our souls how the sorrow departs from us.[227]

3. Joy—Routine

> We shall also visualize (*neṣayair*)... a wedding... how a certain hall is beautified with splendid flowers... the organization of the tables... the bride and groom (*ha-meḥutanim*) and all the guests gathered and dressed in beautiful garments... until they begin to dance. We can

---

226 Ekstein, *Tena'ei ha-Nefesh*, 6.
227 Ibid.

visualize more details of this sort with our imaginative faculty until we arouse the joy in our souls... we will fully complete the imagery visualization (*haşiyur*), how the bride and groom return to their home and the next day they do not feel anything for they have returned to their daily dealings as before.[228]

4. Happiness—Bitterness

We shall visualize (*neşayair*) a man who makes a great business deal with the hope of being enriched... we shall visualize (*neşayair*) his further happiness... we shall also envision the opposite, if... he will not earn... how the world darkens for him, the bitterness of [his] heart, and [his] despair of life... thus we are able to further weave together the vision with our imaginative faculty.[229]

5. Joy—Sorrow

Let us visualize (*neşayair*) the emotions of a poor person who already without bread in his home... the hungry of his children awaiting his arrival. The happiness of the children if the father brings bread home... the sorrow and wailing if he returns empty-handed. The bitterness of his heart when for the first time he is forced to extend his hand [for charity], the insult to his soul, and his embarrassment (*shefikhat damo*), [and then] his happiness and joy if after the despair he has an opportunity for some business, a source of income and livelihood.[230]

These samples are not only representative of a variety of *raşo va-shov* imagery exercises that Ekstein developed, such as forgetfulness versus memory, love versus hate, anger versus appeasement, despair versus hope, etc,[231] but also demonstrate his preference for exercises that included more than two scenes: exercises possessing tens of scenes, each one arousing different emotions, similar to nocturnal dreams. Ekstein was aware of the difficulty of this method, which demands a very advanced level of proficiency, yet he believed that everyone was capable of gaining said proficiency after practicing:

The switching (*ha-ḥilufim*) [of images] will be very difficult for us, to discard one image and visualize (*leşayair*) another, it will be even more difficult to exchange the emotion in our heart and arouse within us sorrow instead of joy. However, here as well habitual diligence and time will do their part, and in a few days we shall easily be able to have, five, ten, even

228 Ibid., 7–8.
229 Ibid., 9.
230 Ibid.
231 See primarily ibid., 7–11.

> twenty different scenes pass before us, so that scene after scene will pass in front of our spiritual eyes like in a *Kino* (cinema)[232] and each one will be so precise that we will be able to completely live within it and feel the souls that pass through it, and so in our hearts, emotion after emotion will change. A new and wondrous matter appears here, namely, that the emotions in our heart are in our control, we can do with them as we please and we can transpose them and exchange them at any time we wish, and this is the intent and purpose of this worship.[233]

Ekstein presents another lengthy and developed exercise in which there are tens of different scenes of one's life passing before one's eyes:

> We will now pass before our eyes the course of a person's life: from what he is formed, how he is born, nursed... [how he] begins to speak, walk... [how he] begins to learn, the gradual development from level to level... We shall not go over all of this superficially; rather we will tarry on each and every chapter of [his] life, and thoroughly visualize each detail as much as possible: the joyous [occasions], the worries, the delight and the sorrow that are within each chapter.[234]

The demand to dwell on each and every chapter ensures the same feelings of each time period are sensed and re-experienced. Indeed, the transition from one chapter to the next is also an emotional passage that demonstrates an absolute control over one's emotions and inclinations by means of the imagination.

There is a dual aim for this visualization of scenes (and resulting emotional experience): the first—the training of the mind for complex and even dizzying changes for the purpose of making it sharper and more agile: "It is appropriate to condition the mind for changes (*ḥilufim*)... for they are but attempts at quickness and agility of the mind (*Übungen zur Elastizität des Gehirnen*);"[235] the second—the development of complete emotional control. The command of the mind over the emotions, to the point of being able to direct the flow of one emotion after another, even when opposite and contradicting, in an almost immediate manner, allows man utter control over his feelings: "We shall hold the reins

---

232 This was written in German. Ekstein's foreign comments are in German, but written with Hebrew letters. See below n. 235.

233 Ekstein, *Tena'ei ha-Nefesh*, 8.

234 Ibid., 10.

235 Ibid., 6. The fact that Ekstein clarifies his words in German and not Yiddish (for in Yiddish it would not be written "*Übungen zur Elastizität des Gehirnen*," but rather "*Genitungen far der Beygevdikayt fun di Gehirn*") in a book that is considered to be part of the hasidic corpus is very interesting. This clarification in German may indicate who the intended audience of the author was, as he was in Vienna the time of this book's publishing, where German, even among Jews, was the primary spoken language.

strongly in our hands so that we may be able to steer the temporal actions and do with them as we wish."[236]

On a deeper level, Ekstein explains that the goal of the *raṣo va-shov* techniques of switching and reversal is to balance the imagination itself. It is within the imagination's ability to visualize excessive and extreme experiences, expropriating the possibility of a healthy balance. This may ultimately cause the opposite of what is desired, namely, the inability to completely control one's emotions. The creation of a healthy balance is accomplished, according to him, through the visualization of different objects one after another. Regarding the imagery of *qaṭnut ha-adam* (the smallness of man) in contrast to *gadlut ha-boreh* (greatness of the creator), Ekstein attests to man's ability to stumble and feel a sense of self-admiration, or in contrast a sense of depression, following this exercise. As a solution for this risk, he suggests that man practice a technique of switching between images, thus ensuring, in his opinion, that the person will not be totally immersed in any one emotion caused by the imagery, but will rather pass immediately to the opposite emotion and thereby attain complete control of his psyche's functions:

> Two dangers are forseen for these two images (*ha-maḥazot*)... . The essence of these dangers is a type of exaggeration, a sort of excess (*motarot*) and trespassing of limits... in each thought and emotion man tends to trespass the limit and exaggerate it... here too... at the moment of joy and the expansion of virtues (*middot*), a type of excess of trespassing boundaries and exceeding arrogance (*ve-lehitnase yoter midai*) is attached to him. At that time, as well, that he views his smallness, he is likely to stumble (*lipol*) in his heart... The simple advice which hasidism offers to be saved from these dangers is to not always be immersed in one of the two emotions completely, but rather keep his intellect above them, and look upon them at all times. In every mental state that will be, there will remain in him some power that will say to him that he is currently happy... but this state cannot be forever and when some amount of time passes, he will be forced to make room for sadness and bitterness of spirit. These latter ones will also not last forever, for they have only arrived in order to broaden his virtues (*middot*) towards the other side. He will thus constantly know that both mental states are necessary for the emotional instrument of his heart and for the development of his soul. The same power that remains above... is what extracts him from every mental condition so that he will not remain in it more than he must, and so that he will not be greatly delayed on his path of growth and development.[237]

The basis of Ekstein's *raṣo va-shov* imagery techniques is entailed in his conception of the bifurcated soul. The same higher aspect of a man's soul which observes and controls from on high allows man full command of his emotions with-

---

236 Ibid., 19.
237 Ibid., 43.

out unharnessed immersion in any specific emotion or feeling: "The same power that remains above... is what extracts him from every mental condition so that he will not remain in it more than he must." The healthy emotional balance allows man to exist between worlds. Passing between one image after another is meant to rescue man from complete emotional immersion in a single experience, and invite him to live in complex expanses full of emotional variety and color.

I The Technique of "Negative Commandments" (Lav)

In one of the *raṣo va-shov* imagery techniques Ekstein presents an unusual imagery exercise.[238] I will term it the technique of "negative commandments." These imagery exercises that appear in kabbalistic and hasidic literature dealing directly with the commandments, are generally concerned specifically with the positive commandments. It is very rare to find an imagery technique which visualizes halakhic prohibitions. This exercise is consistent with the religious logic that prohibits the imagining and contemplation of prohibitions.[239] An unordinary confrontation with the negative commandments through visualization may be found in the teaching of Aaron b. Ẓevi Hirsch ha-Kohen of Opatow (Apta): "When an evil thought (*hirhur*) comes to him, for instance coveting someone's object, he shall visualize the negative commandment (*lav*) of 'do not covet' as if it is written in front of him."[240] Nevertheless, this is not a direct visualization of the negative precept, for if it was he would remain in the same situation of coveting his fellow's object; rather, it is the imagining of the verse that reminds him to distance himself from said prohibition. Indeed, Moshe Idel has stated that in kabbalistic literature, "the many commandments that consist of prohibition [did not] become techniques."[241] In light of this statement and in contrast to the traditional norm, it is surprising to discover that Ekstein presents an original and rare imagery technique of "desiring a woman." This practice includes many images and details, and it is no wonder that it was entirely censored from the Yiddish trans-

238 This exercise does not appear in the edition translated to Yiddish and was entirely omitted.
239 This prohibition may be found throughout rabbinic Jewish literature. See *b. Avodah Zarah* 20b; *Yoma* 29a; *Keter Shem Tov* (New York: Otzar Hasidim Press, 1987), 33: "In the place that a man thinks in [his] thought, there he is entirely." Therefore, whoever imagines sinning is found in sin. Also see Shneur Zalman of Liadi's interpretation of the verse "And I am ever conscious of my sin." (Ps. 51:5) in *Liqquṭei Amarim: Tanya* III:100 – 101.
240 *Or ha-Ganuz la-Ṣaddiqim* (Warsaw: J. Unterhendler Press, 1887), 22, and in the (Żółkiew: Rabin-Stein Press, 1880) edition—Parashat Yitro, without pagination.
241 Idel, *Enchanted Chains*, 203.

lation.[242] This is an attempt at reconstructing the experience of "loving a woman," wooing her, the experiences of the encounters with her, and even the hating and loathing of her. This technique, like many of Ekstein's imagery techniques, is characterized by an exchanging of the feelings of love and hate:

> We will once more take hold of even more shocking matters, like a man whose heart has been taken by some desire, how it does not allow him any reprieve and he strives with all his strength and by every means to fulfill his desire. We shall visualize (*neṣayair*) how the desire is aroused in him; the first encounter with this woman; her beauty enters his heart and makes a deep impression upon him so that it is difficult for him to remove it; and the image (*mar'eh*) of her face is constantly visualized in his imagination and how he will delight if he shall converse with her and draw near to her. These visualizations increase and his desire constantly burns within him, and he tries different schemes in order to find some opportunity to speak with her; he will not rest or have peace until he accomplishes this matter, he gets angry and bitter if he encounters obstacles and obstructions or if she is unwilling to associate with him, and these obstacles increase even more his desire and efforts to finally fulfill his heart's wishes. We shall visualize his enormous joy if he successfully removes all obstacles, his delight and happiness from each encounter, conversation, and approach. The cooling of his desire after it is fulfilled, the extinguishing of his love-flame or at times its frequent reversal into nausea and hatred. Afterwards his efforts to free himself of this woman and forget her, the emptiness of life that he feels and his unpleasant memories from this event. His endeavor in this condition to immerse himself in other matters in order to remove these memories from his heart, and how eventually this desire is aroused in him once more. And thus, the matter is repeated, God forbid, until the days of his old age.[243]

---

242 In the Yiddish translation of the book, published in the *Beys Yankev* magazine for *Bnos Agudas Yisroel* of Poland, all that pertained to "loving a woman" was omitted, including this entire passage as well as individual words and phrases. For example: "Like a feeling of love." Ekstein, *Tena'ei ha-Nefesh,* 11); "Love." Ibid., 24; "Arousal of love." Ibid., 10; "So it is concerning the desire of the flesh, that the imaginings prior to the action arouse in him delight and pleasure." Ibid., 12. I do not know if these matters were censored because it was decided that they were inappropriate to publish at all, or perhaps only because it was to be published for a magazine targeted at women and perhaps it was decided that the publication of these words in this platform was immodest. Furthermore, it is still unclear whether the censor was the editor Eliezer Gershon Friedenson, or the translator Israel Emiot.

243 Ekstein, *Tena'ei ha-Nefesh,* 9–10. In both later Hebrew editions this passage was shortened, appearing as follows: "Now we will take hold of even more shocking matters, like a man whose heart has been taken by some desire, how it does not allow him any reprieve and he strives with all his strength and by every means to fulfill his desire. A desire that every man fails at, suffers from, and knows well, so that it is superfluous to visualize them here." Ekstein, *Mavoh le-Torat ha-Ḥasidut*, 33–34; *Tena'ei ha-Nefesh* (Beitar Ilit: Makhon Even ha-Shetiya"h, 2006), 31. The shortening of the passage and the addition of the sentence which attempts to justify the omission of this imagery exercise, "A desire that every man fails at, suffers from, and knows well, so

This imagery technique is a type of *rașo va-shov*, setting love against hate, memory against forgetting, and joy against bitterness, and constitutes, as far as I am aware, a unique and singular example of a technique created directly for visualizing a negative commandment.

J Autoscopy and Self-Visualization in Menaḥem Mendel Ekstein's Teachings

Autoscopic Phenomena

The growing and evolving cooperative work between cognitive neuroscientists and scholars of kabbalah has contributed to both the understanding of states of cognitive awareness as well as the research of kabbalah.[244] Phenomena studied in the cognitive sciences, and the divisions between different models of these phenomena, allow for distinctions to be made between an array of types of imagery techniques and for the charting and mapping of self-visualization techniques.[245] Autoscopic phenomena, meaning the seeing of the self, are defined in cognitive sciences as experiences in which the subject observes an identical body outside of his body. That is to say, the person sees his own body in front of him.[246]

Plotinus's conception of the divided soul,[247] was not only theoretical, and his opinion gives rise to practical and mystical implications. Plotinus's description of his intellectual-ecstatic experiences and his entrance into his "self," are

---

that it is superfluous to visualize them here," contradict the author's intentions, who both saw a need for the imaginal visualization of it and did not think it excessive.

244 For the latest examples see Shahar Arzy and Moshe Idel, *Kabbalah: A Neurocognitive Approach to Mystical Experiences* (New Haven: Yale University Press, 2015); Daniel Reiser, "Self-Imagery, Hasidism and Cognition", *BDD: Journal of Torah and Scholarship* 31 (2016): 111–126. For another (and different) utilization of neuroscientific studies for the phenomenological study of oneiric and mystical states, see Wolfson, *A Dream Interpreted within a Dream*, 69–74.

245 On self-visualization techniques and the soul's bifurcation see above, subchapter, "The Bifurcated Soul and Self-Awareness," and chap. 4, "The Imagination as a Self-Empowering Factor."

246 Olaf Blanke, Theodor Landis, Laurent Spinelli and Margitta Seeck, "Out-of-body Experience and Autoscopy of Neurological Origin," *Brain: A Journal of Neurology* 127, no. 2 (2004): 243–244; Olaf Blanke and Shahar Arzy, "The Out-of-Body Experience: Disturbed Self-Processing at the Temporo-Parietal Junction," *The Neuroscientist* 11, no. 1 (2005): 17; Shahar Arzy, Moshe Idel, Theodor Landis and Olaf Blanke, "Speaking With One's Self: Autoscopic Phenomena in Writings from the Ecstatic Kabbalah," *Journal of Consciousness Studies* 12, no. 11 (2005): 4.

247 See above, subchapter "The Bifurcated Soul and Self-Awareness."

interpreted within the framework of "self-visualization."[248] As we previously discussed, the *Zohar* identifies *ṣelem* (image) with man's soul found outside of him.[249] Gershom Scholem connected the zoharic *ṣelem* doctrine to the models of prophecy found in the schools of the German Pietists and Abraham Abulafia in which man sees the "form" of his self. According to Scholem, the self's form, disclosed to the prophet, is itself the *ṣelem.*[250] The book *Shushan Sodot*, edited by Moses b. Jacob of Kiev (in 1509, however the majority of his sources are from the late thirteenth century), presents prophecy as an act of self-visualization and speaking with an imaginal figure: "Know that the complete secret of prophecy to a prophet consists in that he suddenly sees the form of his self standing before him, and he forgets his own self and ignores it… and that form speaks with him and tells him the future."[251] Man's encounter with his self-image appears in *Sefer ha-Ḥayyim*, attributed to Abraham Ibn Ezra, as an encounter that occurs within the imagination: "Image (*temunah*)… and in the manner that a man sees a form within the water… or the form of himself, 'and he shall see the image of God'—he sees his own image in the light of God and His glory, and this is, 'a form against my eyes.'"[252] There is no doubt that *Sefer ha-Ḥayyim* is describing a prophetic process characterized by an autoscopic experience, in which man sees himself. In Abulafia's circle self-visualization was conceived of as part of the prophetic process, since prophecy, in his opinion, is a dialogue between man and his intellect:[253] "Know that he sees nothing other than himself, for he sees himself front and back, as one who sees himself in a mirror."[254] Abulafia writes about himself in his work *Sitrei Torah*, that in the revelatory process he sees the image and likeness of himself: "And I saw an image of his name inscribed in my heart and I looked and I saw there my image and likeness (*ṣalmi u-demuti*, numerically equivalent to 636) moving (*mitno'ei'a* = 636) in two paths (*be-shnei derakhim* = 636) a vision in the form of two Tetragrammata (*terei K"V* = 636), one image one likeness (*ṣelem eḥad demut eḥad* = 636) I saw."[255] Even in

248 Scholem, *Godhead*, 257–258.
249 On the conception of the *ṣelem* in the *Zohar* see above, "The Bifurcated Soul and Self-Awareness."
250 Scholem, *Godhead*, 251–260. Also see Tishby's objection *Wisdom of the Zohar*, 773, where he claims that the connection between prophecy and the *ṣelem* is suitable for non-zoharic conceptions of the astral body, however it is not actually found in the *Zohar.*
251 Scholem, *Godhead*, 253.
252 Idel, *The Mystical Experience*, 90.
253 Ibid., 90–91.
254 Ibid., 91.
255 Cited in Idel, "Definitions of Prophecy—Maimonides and Abulafia," 26; idem, *Ben*, 293. Regarding the significance of these words, see ibid. For more examples of self-visualization in Abu-

a later period, Moses Isserles (Rema), the famous halakhic decisor of the sixteenth century, wrote in his book *Torat ha-Olah*, "the truth concerning the prophetic visions is that they saw the *kavod* (the divine glory) in human shape, *which was the shape of the prophet himself.*"[256]

Descriptions of self-visualization do not only appear as part of the prophetic process, but also, even more extensively, within the ecstatic experience.[257] Self-visualization is the vision in which man sees his likeness within mystical experimentation:[258] "Even the latest Kabbalists maintain the experience of self-encounter as the ultimate initiation experience into the world of esoteric knowledge."[259] Furthermore, we observed above that for Kalonymous Kalman Shapira self-visualization was utilized for ethical-religious purposes and as a spiritual catalyst, in contrast to Kierkegaard's views.[260] We thus see that the autoscopic phenomenon appears in kabbalistic and hasidic literature as a prophetic means, as a key entrance to the world of esoteric knowledge and ecstasy, and as an instrument for ethics.

It must be noted that autoscopic phenomena include all types of self-visualization, whereas this work focuses on *active* imaginal self-visualization, a skill to be acquired through practice and technique. Not every act of self-visualization contains a component of imagination, while not every act of imagining the self involves self-visualization. Self-visualization is broader than active imaginal visualization of the self and may appear in various fashions, such as in a nocturnal dream, in a vision, in prophetic inspiration, and in the imagination. In contrast, the imagining of the self is narrower, and is a product of human effort and not spontaneous inspiration. In imagining the self, man acts in a conscious, purposeful, and premeditated manner.[261] The imagining of the self as a concentrated effort done actively by man reached new heights in Ekstein's mystical teachings. Ekstein broadened the potential audience: he did not only speak of self-visual-

---

lafia's books *Sefer ha-Ḥesheq*, and *Sefer ha-To*, see Arzy, Idel, Landis and Blanke, "Speaking With One's Self," 12. Also for other ecstatic kabbalists see ibid., 13–17.

256 Translation based on Scholem, *Godhead*, 259. (emphasis added)

257 See more examples ibid., 253–254. For more examples of autoscopic phenomena in medieval ecstatic-prophetic kabbalah, see Moshe Idel, "On the Language of Ecstatic Experiences in Jewish Mysticism," in *Religions: The Religious Experience,* ed. M. Riedl and T. Schabert (Würzburg: Königshausen & Neumann, 2008), 64–67.

258 Idel, *Golem*, 290.

259 Scholem, *Godhead*, 272.

260 See above, chap. 4, subchapter, "The Imagination as a Self-Empowering Factor."

261 On the distinction between visualization as a product of spontaneous inspiration and visualization that is a product of specific technique, see above chap. 1, subchapter "R. Judah Halevi."

ization which appears in a spontaneous manner to the prophet or kabbalist, meaning the chosen few, but rather developed techniques which allowed every person, regardless of status, to practice.

I will now present different models of autoscopic phenomena, as they have been presented in cognitive studies. Following this, I will return to the phenomenon of active self-visualization, for these models will allow us to discern the nature of self-visualization in the hasidic teachings of Ekstein and how it is to be distinguished from its predecessors.

Neurocognitive Models of Autoscopic Phenomena

In the cognitive sciences, it is accepted to distinguish between three separate types of autoscopic phenomena: autoscopic hallucination, out-of-body experience, and heautoscopy. These differences may assist the kabbalah researcher in general and the scholar of kabbalistic practice and experience in particular:[262]

1. Autoscopic Hallucination (AH): "is the experience of seeing one's body in extracorporeal space (as a "double"). The self is experienced as localized inside the boundaries of the physical body. The double (right) is seen from the habitual egocentric visuo-spatial perspective."[263] In the case of self-imaginal visualization, man experiences himself in the imagining body and not in the imagined body. To demonstrate look at the figure (right),[264] in which the solid image represents the actual person and the dashed image the imagined double. The beginning of the arrow is the location of consciousness.

This figure (1) demonstrates that man senses his consciousness in his actual physical self and from there he observes the imagined figure. This figure is similar to a man seeing a picture of himself, a reflection of himself, or a movie in which he stars. It is possible to identify with the picture or movie, however ultimately man feels that he is present here and now in material reality, and it is from there that he views the picture or image.

---

262 See Arzy and Idel, *Kabbalah: A Neurocognitive Approach*, 35–84.

263 Ibid., 37.

264 These figures are based on those found in ibid; Blanke, "Out-of-body Experience and Autoscopy of Neurological Origin," 247, 255; Olaf Blanke and Christine Mohr, "Out-Of-Body Experience, Heautoscopy, and Autoscopic Hallucination of Neurological Origin: Implications for Neurocognitive Mechanisms of Corporeal Awareness and Self-Consciousness," *Brain Research Reviews* 50, no. 1 (2005): 184–199; Olaf Blanke and Thomas Metzinger, "Full-Body Illusions and Minimal Phenomenal Selfhood," *Trends in Cognitive Sciences* 13, no. 1 (2009): 7–13.

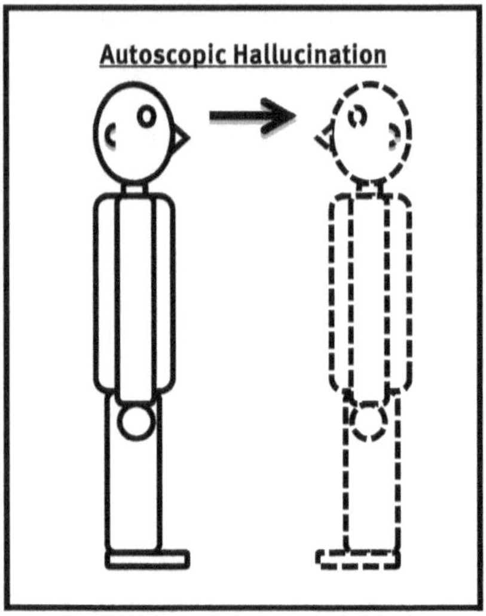

Figure 1

2. Out of Body Experience (OBE): "During an *out-of-body experience* one appears to "see" oneself (top figure) and the world from a location above the physical body (extracorporeal location and visuo-spatial perspective; top figure). The self is localized outside its physical body (disembodiment)." [265]

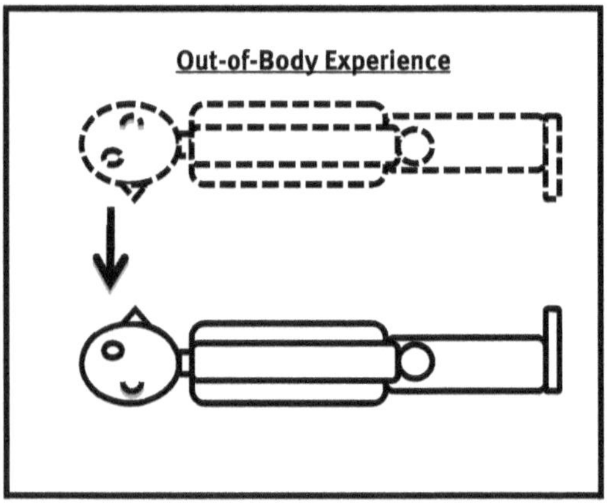

Figure 2

265 Arzy and Idel, *Kabbalah: A Neurocognitive Approach*, 37.

This figure (2) expresses the sense of one's consciousness being located in the imagined double. The imagined doubled feels "real" and it observes the physical person from above. Man (the double) views from above his body and his actions and movements as they actually happen in the material world.

3. HAS (Heautoscopy): "is when one sees one's body and the world in an alternating or simultaneous fashion from both extracorporeal and bodily visuospatial perspectives."[266]

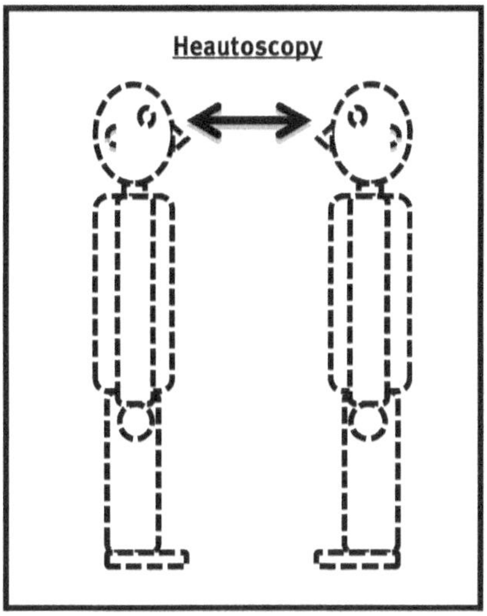

Figure 3

This figure (3) shows the two dashed figures and a two-directional arrow, due to the lack of a fixed position of consciousness, which is nonexistent, alternating, or paradoxically exists in both directions simultaneously. In each of these cases, the inconsistency causes a sense of confusion and uncertainty.

Through the use of these models and the analysis of several ecstatic kabbalists' descriptions of "self-imagining" experiences in light of said models, such as those of Abraham Abulafia, Nathan ben Sa'adyah Har'ar, Isaac ben Samuel of Acre, Yehudah ben Nissim ibn Malka, and the anonymous author of *Sefer ha-Ḥayyim*,[267] Arzy and his colleagues have demonstrated that the description of these kabbalists' self-visualization experiences may be identified as examples of AH and HAS. That is to say, in the many descriptions of self-visualization within the ecstatic kabbalistic literature there were those who experienced the center

266 Ibid.

267 Arzy, Idel, Landis and Blanke, "Speaking with One's Self," 7–19.

of their consciousness in their own bodies and saw the double outside of themselves (AH), and there were those who visualized a double but were unable to identify where their center of consciousness was located—whether in the physical man or in the autoscopic body (HAS). It is of both interest and importan to note that the OBE experience is rarely found in any of these descriptions![268] I am unaware of any kabbalistic document before the sixteenth century that testifies to an autoscopic occurrence in which the kabbalist's sense of consciousness is found in the imagined double, a phenomenon in which man experiences himself in a space external to his body and from above he perceives his physical body and the world in a clear fashion.[269]

Autoscopy in Ekstein's Teachings

In Ekstein's book, a number of imagery techniques similar to autoscopy appear. The reader is asked to visualize himself as one who is outside of his body, and from above, from a bird's eye view, to observe and see the world and its fullness: lands, animals and birds, nations and languages, and finally himself.[270] These characteristics are similar to the three primary phenomenological characteristics of the out-of-body experience—man's consciousness is found outside of his body, he views the world from above, and lastly he sees his physical body from on high:

> In an out-of-body experience (OBE), people seem to be awake and feel that their 'self', or center of experience, is located outside of the physical body... An OBE is defined by the presence of three phenomenological characteristics: disembodiment (location of the self outside one's body), the impression of seeing the world from a distant and elevated visuo-spatial perspective (extracorporeal egocentric perspective), and the impression of seeing one's own body (or autoscopy) from this elevated perspective.[271]

---

268 See ibid., 18 and see Arzy and Idel, *Kabbalah: A Neurocognitive Approach*, 70, that the OBE experience exists mostly in Vital's writings and later on in those of the Besht and the Maggid of Międzyrzecz.
269 I write this following thorough investigation and discussion with Moshe Idel.
270 See above, subchapter "War of Imaginations," for an example of an imagery exercise of this kind.
271 Blanke and Arzy, "The Out-of-Body Experience: Disturbed Self-Processing at the Temporo-Parietal Junction," 16.

While the experience of self-visualization appears and is described by kabbalists primarily through the cognitive models of AH and HAS, surprisingly, Ekstein's techniques are more similar to OBE.[272] Seemingly, Ekstein's conception of the bifurcated soul together with the desire to achieve complete mental control created a preference for the OBE method in which man senses his consciousness within the elevated disembodied image and observes the lower physical man like a flying bird: "To contemplate all of creation, and every man, after you will learn how to be carried on eagle's wings, that were made in his imagination, and be above his contemporaries, and look!"[273] According to Ekstein, in addition to complete self-awareness, the OBE method provides a technique for self-control as well: "our soul will remain above... then too it will govern itself and the actions will be in its hands... this is the [mode of] worship of the soul's bifurcation (*ha-avodah shel hitpalgut ha-nefesh le-shetaiyim*)."[274]

Essentially, Ekstein translated kabbalistic conceptions of absolute control and awareness into practical techniques and developed multiple imagery exercises (and within these techniques of self-visualization) which, as far as I am aware, do not have nearly any precedent in kabbalistic or hasidic literature. They are very lengthy imagery techniques, devoid of the linguistic component commonly found in most kabbalistic literature and have a dynamic plot and many intricate scenes similar to a movie. The self-visualization techniques that Ekstein developed approximate the OBE model, for the human consciousness is located in the imagined figure. Ekstein situates man's consciousness outside of himself: "When we view the earth and the stars from afar *and we are outside of the image*;"[275] "Regarding the contemplation of all of creation we must know... that the space which encompasses the earth and the stars is infinite, and if man towers above all of creation and sees in his imagination the world from this distance, such that it appears small to him like a nut and the sun like an apple, then *he is found in the infinite space!*"[276]

---

272 Note, they are similar, but not identical. In OBE the distance between the physical person and his imaginal body is generally around a meter, whereas Ekstein speaks of a much greater distance.

273 Ekstein, *Tena'ei ha-Nefesh*, 58.

274 Ibid., 16–17.

275 Ibid., 6. My emphasis

276 Ibid., 22. My emphasis. According to this process it appears that self-visualization, in which man visualizes himself and observes himself from above, as in this technique, "We shall attempt to visualize the place that we are now standing upon, and we shall strive to present ourselves between all of the masses of humanity and all of the creations," (ibid., 3) includes within it this sense of heightened external consciousness.

It is possible that the kabbalistic depictions of self-visualization presented above are based on a conception close to that of Plotinus's understanding of the divided soul and the zoharic conception of *ṣelem*, which raise the possibility that part of the soul is on high and observes the physical body. Regarding Ekstein, we may say this with more certainty due to the clear connection he creates between the bifurcated soul and self-visualization.[277] Elevated disembodied imaginal self-visualization allows for self-awareness, which, as was mentioned, according to Ekstein is the path towards the awareness of divinity.[278] Thus, self-visualization is an entrance into esoteric knowledge and the divine reality.

According to Ekstein, imaginal self-visualization techniques, like the autoscopic phenomena of the OBE variety, develop complete self-control to the point of detachment from the ego and its needs. Through imaginal self-visualization, man is able to disengage consciously, not ontologically, from his lower physical part, from "the small matters related to his body's needs,"[279] transcend them, and cling to God. It is precisely this model, which entails the feeling of disembodied consciousness and elevated self-visualization, that is the necessary model for Ekstein's mystical teachings, for it is this feeling that ultimately allows for the detachment from one's ego, total self-awareness, and absolute self-control—matters without which it would be impossible to acquire the longed for mystical union.

The Heautoscopy Model and Its Characterization in Ekstein's Imaginal Self-Visualization Techniques

We have now arrived at a more complex, surprising, and fascinating section of Ekstein's practical teachings. Here he has diverged from the models of autoscopic phenomenon that have been presented in cognitive research and has forged his own unique path. Through the imagery techniques of *raṣo va-shov*, the switching back and forth of imagery (*ḥilufim*), Ekstein was interested in applying these techniques to the OBE model, and consequently adjust them towards the HAS model. The visualization of "exchanges" (*ḥilufim*) will, by its very nature, create a preference for autoscopic phenomenon of the HAS variety. This model allows for transposition and the exchanging of consciousness between the physical figure and the imagined one, such that Ekstein's desired movement of "run-

277 See above subchapter, "The Bifurcated Soul and Self-Awareness."
278 See above the end of the subchapter, "War of Imaginations," and also see above, "Integration (Hitkallelut)."
279 Ekstein, *Tena'ei ha-Nefesh*, 58.

ning and returning" (*raṣo va-shov*) may take place. However, the HAS model being discussed here is entirely different than the one presented above. The HAS model of self-visualization is characterized in the cognitive sciences as creating a sense of confusion and bewilderment, due to the lack of consistency regarding the location of consciousness. In contrast to this characterization, Ekstein, relying on his *raṣo va-shov* method, portrays a model that does not create confusion and may be utilized by man as a preparatory means for absolute self-control. Ekstein is interested in this model first and foremost as an ideal technique for the attainment of self-control:

> It is appropriate for us to utilize these exchanges (*be-ḥilufim*) [of images] also when we are viewing the earth and stars from afar and we are outside of the image, and afterwards we present ourselves in our place, we press (*doḥqim*) ourselves into it and we are within it. So too here, is it fitting to switch the location many times to exit and return, back and forth. These experimentations… also grant us the control so that the mind will be in our control (lit. hands), so that we will be able to steer it and change it as we please, and in order that we will not be bound to any specific vision.[280]

The technique of exchanges (*ḥilufim*), in which man's consciousness changes its location: "And we are outside of the image"—"and we are within it," is also utilized by Ekstein as a solution to a critical and complicated issue, namely, the ability of the imagination to seize man and cause him to immerse himself in emotional dependency. According to Ekstein, through this technique man, "will not be bound to any specific vision." Man's command over his consciousness's location and his ability to switch from the actual image to the imagined image grant him absolute freedom. This freedom is not in the sense of human independence or personal liberty; rather, it is freedom in the divine space. Like God, who is able to create life as he wills, the man who is in total command is able to create his own life and guide it in a controlled manner as he wishes.[281]

K Between Kalonymous Kalman Shapira and Menaḥem Ekstein

While there are substantial similarities between Shapira's and Ekstein's imagery techniques, there are also many distinct differences. Both of them intensively employed imagery techniques and developed complex, rich, and dramatic im-

280 Ibid., 6.
281 Ibid., 19.

agery exercises hitherto unknown in kabbalistic and hasidic literature. Both, in contrast to medieval thought which primarily dealt with the theoretical and philosophical aspects of imagination, did not suffice with mere talk about the "imaginative faculty," but rather offered the reader organized practical techniques as a mode of worship. Both strived to empower religious life and transform it into mystical life in which man experiences divinity in the mundane world. Nonetheless, there are quite a number of differences between them: Shapira's imagery techniques are manifestly religious in character—reiterations of the experience of canonized biblical stories and historical events, experiences of divinity at sacred times, the intensification of anomian religiosity like dance and song, empowerment of prayer and the experience of standing before God, preparation for prophecy, and seeing God. In contradistinction, Ekstein's imagery techniques have a universal character like self-awareness, self-control, ecstasy, and amazement, in which the religious foundation is concealed and is only disclosed through the ultimate principle of integration. Ekstein's conception, like Kook's, sees in self-awareness and self-consciousness a path to divine awareness, allowing for more "neutral" practices that deal with self-consciousness. Indeed, Ekstein's goal too is ultimately religious and even mystical, however the methods which underpin it have a universal and a-religious character. Ekstein's conception of the bifurcated soul and the unity of nature and the divine granted him a fertile ground of natural imagery, whose visualization is meant for a religious purpose: "Europe! How much longer will you not understand, that distancing from faith is distancing from nature as well, from the soul, and from life."[282]

Shapira and Ekstein do not only differ in regard to the imaginal content, but also in regard to the techniques as well. Ekstein uses a collection of images, in quick succession and at times in a *raṣo va-shov* manner, as a technique to develop the flexibility of the mind and the ability to control the imagination itself. Shapira's imagery exercises are advanced in respect to their dramatic aspects, but are nevertheless much simpler, lacking the "exchanges" (*ḥilufim*) and sophistication found in Ekstein's techniques.

Using the models presented in cognitive research I will assert an additional distinction between the imaginal self-visualization techniques of Ekstein and Shapira: the latter's techniques are always the AH model. Even though the imagination serves as an empowering and prophetic factor, the location of man's consciousness does not change and is always in the physical body. There is no clear astral projection in Shapira's teachings. In contrast, Ekstein's techniques are mostly characterized by a global journey between continents, nations, cultures,

282 Ibid., 37.

animals, and plants from an elevated disembodied perspective, in which man's consciousness is external to him. This distinction corresponds with the previous distinction as well: the simplistic nature of Shapira's techniques matches the rudimentary nature of the AH model characterizing his self-visualization techniques, in contradistinction to Ekstein's predilection for complexity, an orientation which manifests itself in his preference for the OBE model for his imaginal self-visualization techniques and the HAS model for his *raṣo va-shov* techniques.

Shapira's imagery techniques have clear roots in kabbalah and hasidism. His originality is expressed by broadening these techniques from static to dynamic, to imagery that is not limited to the viewing of stationary images like in kabbalistic literature, or a simple scene like in most hasidic literature, but are rather characterized by a developing and advanced plot, as in a dream. In contrast, Ekstein's techniques do not have strong precedents in kabbalistic and hasidic literature and there is no doubt that they are slightly more similar to exercises of Far-Eastern origin like *Yoga Vasistha* of Hinduism and the exercises of Paramahansa Yogananda (1893 – 1952) who immigrated in the '20s to the United States and there spread Yoga teachings.[283] Without clear evidence, I am not claiming that there are direct Eastern influences on Ekstein, and perhaps he had no direct knowledge of these practices, as I would just like to note the similarities between them, which are important in their own right.[284] Additionally, the interesting fact should be noted that although the possibility has existed for mapping descriptions of out-of-body experiences in different cultures and ages since antiquity,[285] detailed description of occurrences, whether in a literary aspect or medicinal, primarily appear at the end of the nineteenth century or in the twentieth century.[286] That is to say, Ekstein was not active in a vacuum, but rather developed his imagery techniques in a context of parallel developments.

---

283 *Encyclopedia of Occultism & Parapsychology*, 5th ed., comp. John Gordon Melton (Farmington Hills: Gale Group, 2001), s.v. "Out of the Body Travel." In a different and interesting fashion, see the imagination in the experience of Osho (Rajneesh, born Chandra Mohan Jain) (1931 – 1990), a later figure with universal influence, see Osho, *The Transmission of the Lamp: Talks in Uruguay* (s.l.: s.n., s.a.), http://www.oshorajneesh.com/download/osho-books/world_tour_talks/The_Transmission_of_the_Lamp_(Talks_in_Uruguay).pdf, 30 – 33.

284 See below Pt. 4.

285 See Dean Sheils, "Cross-Cultural Study of Beliefs in Out-of-the-Body Experiences, Waking and Sleeping," *Journal of the Society for Psychical Research* 47 (1978): 697 – 741.

286 Blanke, "Out-of-Body Experience and Autoscopy of Neurological Origin," 244. Also see above chap. 2, subchapter "Empowerment," for the depictions of the astral projection of Robert Allan Monroe and Sylvan Muldoon.

L Imagery Techniques in Twentieth Century Hasidism

While Shapira and Ekstein were indeed unique individuals, they were not entirely alone. The preoccupation with imagery techniques in the twentieth century was not ignored by other hasidic masters. The sixth Ḥabad master, Yosef Yiṣḥaq Schneersohn (1880 – 1950), the Friediker Rebbe, frequently employed imagery techniques both for personal use and as an educational and mystical tool for his audience of Ḥabad ḥasidim. Yosef Yiṣḥaq's imaginative sense is expressed in an extraordinary manner in his monumental work, *Liqquṭei Dibburim*,[287] consisting of 803 pages over four volumes.[288] Research of hasidic literature principally addresses Naḥman of Bratslav's tales as the only collection of original Yiddish textual hasidic stories. However, the writing of Yiddish hasidic stories, without translation, did not conclude with Naḥman of Bratslav, but in fact continued into the twentieth century. Yosef Yiṣḥaq would tell brilliant and unique stories which frequently employed the imaginative faculty. To my knowledge, *Liqquṭei Dibburim* is the largest collection of Yiddish tales by a hasidic master, and its place has been neglected in hasidic scholarship.[289] Yosef Yiṣḥaq stated about himself that, "Often I live anew in my thought and draw different visions that I saw in Lyubavitsh (Lyubavichi) at different times... how the ḥasidim gathered for a *farbrengen* (lit. passed [time], amused oneself; hasidic get-together, in which ḥasidim sang, talked, and listened to the hasidic master) how regular laymen (*ba'alei batim*) and wealthy guests listened to *hasidus* (hasidic teachings)... and I arrived at the fundamental conclusion that the light of hasidism maintains all that is found in its surroundings, and even regarding those for which the light

287 Yosef Yiṣḥaq Schneersohn, *Likkutei Dibburim* (Brooklyn: Kehot, 1955).Translated to Hebrew ibid., *Liqquṭei Dibburim*, trans. Avrohom Chanoch Glitzenshtein, 5 vols. (Brooklyn: Kehot, 1990) Translated into English ibid., *Likkutei Dibburim: An Anthology of Talks by Yosef Yitzchak Schneersohn of Lubavitch*, trans. Uri Kaploun, 5 vols. (Brooklyn: Kehot, 2000).

288 Discourses (*siḥot*) and primarily tales told by Yosef Yiṣḥaq between 1929 – 1950, beginning in Riga, Latvia and concluding in Brooklyn, New York. These tales were first published in 31 separate booklets, some containing only one tale, while others had many more. The first three collections were published in Riga (1933 – 1934); the next seventeen were published in Warsaw (1934 – 1939); the following eighteen were published in New York (1941 – 1955).

289 Gedalyah Nigal devoted one sentence to Yosef Yiṣḥaq as a prolific storyteller; see Nigal, *The Hasidic Tale* (Oxford: *Littman Library*, 2008), 265. Indeed, Nigal references Yosef Yiṣḥaq's work *Sefer ha-Zikhronot* (written originally in Hebrew and translated to Yiddish in 1947) and does not mention his original Yiddish stories in *Liqquṭei Dibburim*. Likewise, this prolific hasidic master who wrote and told numerous stories, unparalleled in hasidic literature, is not mentioned in the rest of Nigal's scholarship, even his detailed lexicon of hasidic stories, ibid., *Hassidic Tales Collectors* (Jerusalem: Carmel, 1995).

of hasidism is only an encompassing light (*or maqif*), hasidism influences them, for they receive a completely different vitality by fulfilling the commandments."[290] In addition to his personal testimony regarding his use of imagery practices, he calls upon his students to do so as well: "In hasidism there are recommendations for a number of matters, matters of the mind and matters of character traits (*midos*)... one of the matters that our fellow ḥasidim (*anshey shlumeynu*) and students of *Hatmimim* (a Ḥabad yeshiva) should train themselves [to do] is: imagery (*ṣiyur*)."[291] Yosef Yiṣḥaq recounts how his forefathers did so as well:

> The Ṣemaḥ Ṣedeq (Menaḥem Mendel Schneersohn) said: "One who has a sense of imagination (*a ḥush in ṣiyur*) is able to easily arrive at repentance, and it is possibile that he will have love and fear in the emotion of the corporeal flesh-heart like the emotion of corporeal love and fear."
>
> When my father said hasidic teachings and spoke of very deep knowledge, like the matter of abstraction (*hafshata*), how an idea is abstract, he would express it so: "When he [someone] understands the matter, after he understands it... he looks at the image (*ṣiyur*) in his mind with the knowledge of one who looks at a pleasant drawing (*ṣiyur*)... the intellectual matter was visualized (*niṣṭaiyer*) in his mind as an example of something like a drawing seen by the eyes."[292]

This sense of imaginal visualization (*ṣiyur*) becomes more sophisticated through the experience of intimacy that occurs at hasidic meetings, and as Yosef Yiṣḥaq conveyed the significance of the *farbrengen*, the meeting between the hasidic master and his followers, as an educational tool in general and as an instrument for the development of the sense of imaginal visualization (*ṣiyur*) in particular:

> In every generation, the *farbrengen* was one of the pillars in the educational structure and teaching of ḥasidim. The sense of imagination is one of the most important forces and senses of the soul, leading to great matters, whether in matters of intelligence or worship, and our forefathers and holy masters greatly valued people with a sense of imagination.[293]

The connection between the imaginative sense and the *farbrengen* is manifested through the hasidic story that the *ṣaddiq* tells his followers. This story awakens the listeners' imagination and even activates it. Yosef Yiṣḥaq accomplished this

---

290 *Liqquṭei Dibburim* (Brooklyn: Kehot, 1990) I:151, *Liqquṭ* 5, sec. 1, *Ḥag ha-Pesaḥ* 5694.
291 Ibid., I:225, *Liqquṭ* 7, *Ḥag ha-Shavu'ot* 5694. The Yiddish original from *Likkutei Dibburim* (Brooklyn: Kehot, 1992), 157.
292 Ibid.
293 Ibid. Original Yiddish edition, 160; Hebrew edition, 228.

through the lengthy stories he recounted. In his stories he weaved complete plots and required his audience to imagine this plot and see it in front of their eyes.[294]

The hasidic master of Tyczyn, Shelomo Aryeh Leib Weinshelbaum (1847–1927), a famous individual in his time in West Galicia, was a son of a simple Jew who acquired his position through his own merit and not due to lineage.[295] He became famous as a spiritual and ecstatic personality, as well as a miracle worker, which led many, Jews and non-Jews alike, to flock to him and wait at his doorstep.[296] Weinshelbaum studied Cordoverian kabbalah and reedited the kabbalistic work *Qol Bokhim: Qinat Setarim* by Abraham Galanti, a Safedian kabbalist of the sixteenth century and a student of Cordovero.[297] He invested most of his efforts in matters of prayer and wrote the book *Hakhanat Lev le-Tefilah* (Preparations of the Heart for Prayer); however it was only published posthumously.[298] This work includes many imagery techniques as tools for prayer preparation and as means for encountering God.[299]

The preoccupation with the imagination also characterizes David Yiṣḥaq Rabinowitz (1898–1979), "The Skolyer Rebbe" (Skala-Podilska), a descendant of Yeḥiel Mikhel of Zlotchov. This hasidic master, who had many kabbalistic customs and behaviors (*hanhagot*), such as wearing only white garments on the sabbath and many other examples,[300] immigrated after World War I to Vienna and

294 See for example a lengthy sequence like this ibid. 228–247 (Hebrew edition).

295 See above Yitzhak Alfasi, ed., *Encyclopedia of Hasidism: Personalities* (Jerusalem: Mossad Harav Kook, 1986), 745–746. A year after his death a biography about him was published, Abe Waks, *Birkhat Shelomoh* (Kraków: M. Lenkowicza Press, 1928).

296 Alfasi, *Encyclopedia of Hasidism*, 745–746, writes that Weinshelbaum attracted numerous people, to the point that they had to wait a number of days in order to meet him, and since there were more guests in Tyczyn than Jewish residents upon the death of Weinshelbaum, "The city was bereft of its primary income and many had to leave the city and look for other forms of income." Interestingly, this fact is written on his tombstone, see Waks, *Birkhat Shelomoh*, 2b: "Thousands and many of our Jewish brethren were sheltered in your holy shadow/ many non-Jews (*goyei ha-areṣ*) flocked to him to receive his blessing." Likewise, his ecstatic prayer and his praise of the kabbalistic work *Qol Bokhim* are found on his tombstone, see ibid. For more regarding his ecstatic prayer see Yari-Wold, *Rzeszow Community*, 232, 481.

297 The book was reprinted in 1914 in Biłgoraj, Poland. It should be noted that in that same year another one of Galanti's books was published *Zekhut Avraham* (on the "Ethics of the Fathers," *Pirqei Avot*), a matter that demonstrates the popularity of Cordoverian kabbalah in hasidism.

298 Shelomo Aryeh Leib Weinshelbaum, *Hakhanat Lev le-Tefilah* (Biłgoraj: s.n, 1927). He began to write the book in 192,1 as is noted in the preface.

299 See for example imagery techniques in ibid., "Preface," 6b, 40a, 73b, 56b, 100b.

300 "Minhagei Qodesh: Minhagei Yom Shabat Qodesh she-Nahag K"Q Maran ADMV"R ZṢVQLLH"H," *Qobeṣ Be'er Yiṣḥaq* 3 (January-February 2001), 77–79.

wrote there in the '20s *Sefer ha-Ḥizyonot* (The Book of Visions), in which he described his dreams and visions. This book is currently concealed in manuscript by the contemporary Skolyer Rebbe in the United States of America.[301]

We analyzed and focused primarily on the imagery techniques of Shapira and Ekstein and not on the other contemporaneous hasidic masters, since the former employed imagery techniques in a more sophisticated manner. Nevertheless, in Yosef Yiṣḥaq Schneersohn's teachings and stories and in Weinshelbaum's imagery exercises, the related imaginative or "drawing" faculties are in accordance with the *ḥasid* (pious person) model of Judah Ha-Levi.[302] The imagination recreates and sensorializes events of religious-experiential character from the historical past. This recreation vitalizes the event and grants a religious fervor to the imagining man. This is not a "creative imagination" like in Shapira's and Ekstein's thought, but is rather an imagination which mimics the external source and recreates it in an experiential manner; an imagination in which the movement goes from the external towards the internal, in contrast to the creative imagination in which the movement is the opposite, going from inside to outside.[303]

---

301 About this manuscript and image of the manuscript's cover, ibid., 18.

302 See above, chap. 1, subchapter "R. Judah Halevi."

303 See Kearney, *The Wake of Imagination*, 167–177; Abrams, *The Mirror and the Lamp*, 52, 58–60. Also, see my own discussion, Daniel Reiser, *Vision as a Mirror: Imagery Techniques in Twentieth Century Jewish Mysticism* (Los Angeles: Cherub Press, 2014), 31–33.

Chapter Seven
War of the "Senses:" Imagination in the Musar Movement

Woe to the imagination, this evil enemy!
—Israel Lipkin, *Iggeret ha-Musar*

Who will restrain them, who will conquer them, who will spur them on towards all [that is] good and beneficial, if not the learning of *musar*, to break the heart and purify it somewhat from its pollution, to arouse the right knowledge for this battle.
—Israel Lipkin, *Or Yisra'el*, 44.

A Introduction

In the mid-nineteenth century, the Musar movement, founded by R. Israel Lipkin of Salant (1810–1883), began to disseminate its message and teachings in Lithuania. This message consisted of the demand for self-transformation.[1] Dov Katz defined this demand as the striving for perfection on three levels: the perfection of one's Torah learning, perfection of one's deeds, and perfection of one's self.[2] The demand for perfection demonstrates the deep sense of lack and inadequacy experienced by followers of this movement. The inadequacy in Torah learning which must be rectified and perfected lies in matters of interpersonal relationships (*bein adam le-ḥaveiro*), whether it be one's theoretical learning or the practical implementation: refraining from anger and slander (*lashon ha-ra*), stealing and deceit, or pursuing righteousness and brotherhood, and just as one beautifies the commandment of the citron (during Sukkot there is a special commandment to acquire a nicer citron), so too one should beautify all domains of one's social life, by speaking nicely, being polite, and having a welcoming face. The

1 Immanuel Etkes, *Rabbi Israel Salanter and the Beginning of the 'Musar' Movement* (Jerusalem: Magnes Press, 1984), 13. On Israel Lipkin and the Musar movement see Mordechai Pachter, *Israel Salanter: Selected Writings* (Jerusalem: Bialik Institute, 1972), 7–67. I have decided to not translate the term "musar" as ethical or moral, (for the issue with this translation see Wolfson, *Venturing Beyond*, 14–16) and instead have chosen the terms self-transformation and self-perfection, or leave it untranslated. This decision is due primarily to the work of Patrick B. Koch, *Human Self-Perfection: A Re-Assessment of Kabbalistic Musar-Literature of Sixteenth-Century Safed* (Los Angeles: Cherub Press, 2015), 1–45.
2 Dov Katz, *The Musar Movement: Its History, Leading Personalities, and Doctrines*, trans. Leonard Oschry (Tel Aviv: Orly Press, 1975) 1:60–64.

https://doi.org/10.1515/9783110535884-010

"perfecting of one's deeds" is the battle against the routineness of fulfilling the commandments. Lipkin wanted to instill life with ritualistic-religious deeds. The "perfection of man" is the demand to eradicate man's destructive forces, egoistic interest and degrading instincts.[3]

Lipkin's primary interest was not theological at all. Theosophic inquiry, the knowledge of the divine, was situated low on his list of priorities and he did not see a religious value or purpose in it. His main concern was the instruction of self-perfection.[4] This pedagogical priority was not only from Lipkin's perspective an urgent mission, but also a clear religious challenge.[5] Immanuel Etkes has demonstrated the connection between Lipkin's disengagement from kabbalistic thought and his manner of discussing the soul's structure and its modes of self-perfection and repair. The kabbalistic conception connected man's soul to metaphysical forces. In contrast, Lipkin severed the two and viewed man's soul as its own self-defined independent entity, whose components and modes of operations have rational explanations.[6] Lipkin's primary innovation, in contradistinction to the medieval musar authors, was "transferring the focus of the problem of Musar from the theological to the psychological realm."[7] The Musar movement had two goals, "the first being the development of a psychological theory explaining the components and dynamics of the psychic mechanism, and second, the development of educational methods based upon this theory, through which one may gain disciplined control over one's psychic life, and thereby over one's behavior in general."[8]

3 Ibid.

4 Etkes, *Rabbi Israel Salanter*, 102–103.

5 Ibid., 104

6 Ibid. Regarding Lipkin's attitude towards kabbalah see, ibid., 103. Also see Mordechai Pachter, "The Musar Movement and the Kabbalah," in *Let the Old Make Way for the New*, eds. D. Assaf and A. Rapoport-Albert (Jerusalem: Zalman Shazar Center, 2009), 1:223–50. Pachter claims that Lipkin did not disapprove of kabbalah and that he did not have a negative attitude towards it. He explains that Lipkin ignored the world of kabbalah due to his total dedication to man's religious-musar education, which he reasoned was not benefitted by kabbalah. More recently, Jonathan Garb has questioned this hypothesis and has offered his own opinion, writing, "The leaders of the Mussar movement... reserved the study of Kabbalah for the select few... As a result, Kabbalah was largely removed from the open discourse of the first generation or two of the movement. However, with the exception of a few important scholars, it was never set aside at any point." Ibid., *Yearnings of the Soul: Psychological Thought in Modern Kabbalah* (Chicago: University of Chicago Press, 2015), 66–67.

7 Immanuel Etkes, *Rabbi Israel Salanter and the Mussar Movement: Seeking the Torah of Truth*, ed. and trans. Jonathan Chipman (Philadelphia: Jewish Publication Society, 1993), 96. This English edition is only used for quotations; all other citations are from the Hebrew edition.

8 Ibid., 97.

In contrast to the hasidic movement, the Musar movement founded by Lipkin was not directed towards or intended for the masses. While this movement's aim was to work towards the rectification of the character traits (*middot*) of the general public and societal rectification,[9] its lofty scholastic demands nevertheless transformed it into an elite movement.[10] Lipkin viewed "fear" in anthropological terms, and portrayed it as a scientific discipline for all intents and purposes, which should be studied and researched extensively and systematically. The first condition of fear according to Lipkin is the knowledge and expertise of all aspects of the Torah. In his opinion, it is impossible to be a worshiper of God (*oved ha-shem*) without being a great scholar of all Torah law.[11] These requirements, after Lipkin's death in the late nineteenth century, in part, allowed for the complicated connection between the Musar movement and the Lithuanian yeshivot: Mir (1815), Kelm (1866), Telshe (1879), Slabodka (1883), Novardok (1896), etc. Some of these yeshivot were established by leading figures of the Musar movement, whereas others were previously established and later infiltrate by the Musar movement.[12] In its beginning, the Musar doctrine was not accepted in every place with great fanfare and caused heated contentions, specifically in 1897.[13] However, with the passage of time, the Musar movement managed to permeate many Lithuanian yeshivot, and from the beginning of the twentieth century Musar became the educational norm in most Lithuanian yeshivot.[14]

---

9 See Samuel Haggai, "Ha-Reqa ha-Hisṭori shel Tenu'at ha-Musar," *Mahanaim* 81 (1963): 70–75.
10 Katz, *The Musar Movement*, 69–70. Also see Etkes, *Rabbi Israel Salanter*, 222–225.
11 Ibid., 246.
12 Regarding the Łomża (Lomza) yeshiva, see Yom-Tov Lewinsky, "The Great Yeshiva in Łomża Fifty Years Ago," in *Memoirs of the Lithuanian Yeshiva*, eds. I. Etkes and S. Tikochinski (Jerusalem: Zalman Shazar Center, 2004), 347–360. Regarding Telshe and Slabodka yeshiva, see respectively ibid., 221–290, 327–346; Shaul Stampfer, *Lithuanian Yeshivas of the Nineteenth Century: Creating a Tradition of Learning*, trans. Lindsey Taylor-Guthartz (Oxford: Littman Library of Jewish Civilization, 2012), 225–336. Regarding ideological characteristics in the Musar movement see Benjamin Brown, "The Rise and Fall of 'the Loftiness of Man' Doctrine: Changes in the Musar Theology of the Slobodka Yeshiva," in *Yeshivot and Study Institutions*, ed. I. Etkes (Jerusalem: Zalman Shazar Center, 2006), 243–272; idem., "Love, Joy, Simplicity and Traditionalism: The Musar Theology of R. Moshe Rosenstein," in *Let the Old Make Way for the New*, eds. D. Assaf and A. Rapoport-Albert (Jerusalem: Zalman Shazar Center, 2009), 251–279.
13 Regarding this polemic against the Musar movement see Dov Katz, *Pulmus ha-Musar* (Jerusalem: Abraham Zioni, 1972); Mordechai Breuer, *The Tents of Torah: The Yeshiva, Its Structure and History* (Jerusalem: Zalman Shazar Center, 2003), 57–60.
14 Breuer, *The Tents of Torah*,57–60.

B The Conception of Imagination in Israel Lipkin of Salant's Teaching

Lipkin's *iggeret ha-mussar* (epistle of musar) begins with a fierce attack against the imagination "this evil enemy;"

> Man is free in his imagination but bound by his intellect. His imagination leads him wildly in the direction of his heart's desire, fearing not the inevitable future, when God will hold him to account for all his deeds, and he will be chastised by severe judgment... Woe to the imagination, this evil enemy. It is in our hands, in our power, to put it far away by turning an attentive ear to the intellect, to pay heed to the truth, to calculate the pleasure gained through transgression against its loss [that is, punishment incurred]. But what shall we do, as the imagination is an overflowing stream in which the intellect drowns, if we do not place it aboard a ship, that is, the excitement of the soul and the storm of the spirit.[15]

Lipkin describes the battle between the imagination and intellect as one in which the intellect must defeat the imagination, just as good must conquer evil. Ostensibly, Lipkin has a negative attitude towards the imagination, as he demands its elimination. The imagination is the root of sin and temptation, it leads man wildly astray, provoking him and diverting him from seeing the future and the consequences of his actions. Nevertheless, other statements made by Lipkin demonstrate a positive relation towards the imagination and its adaption as an instrument for man's self-perfection. In letters written to his students he remarks that, "The power of imagination (*ha-ṣiyur*) is beneficial for musar," and which he exemplified in the following exercise, "One should imagine to himself that if he were the High Priest and needed to enter the Holy of Holies on the Day of Atonement, he would tremble very much in his soul, lest he be injured by the evil at this night... and the heart of the man who delves into this awesome matter shall greatly tremble."[16] The imagination is a key element in the process of man's perfection and acquiring "fear of heaven," which is ultimately man's purpose:

> Now, what is "fear" and how is it acquired? A singular [path] (*aḥat hi*)—the expansion of matters well-known to all: fear of punishment concerning the body and soul, [which is] higher than all the world's foundations. Indeed, knowledge of it alone does not bring man chastisement, as our sages, blessed be their memory, stated in [*b.*] *Shabbat* (31b) "The wicked know that their path leads to death, [but they have fat on their kidneys that prevents that realization from entering their hearts]... Lest you say that it is simply for-

15 As translated in Etkes, *Rabbi Israel Salanter*, 101. Also see Pachter, *Israel Salanter*, 114. Regarding the epistle of musar see Etkes, *Rabbi Israel Salanter*, 215–225.
16 Israel Lipkin, *Or Yisra'el*, ed. I. Blazer (Vilnius: Metz Publishing House, 1900), 27 (Letter 7).

> gotten from them, therefore it is stated 'they approve their end with their own mouths.' (Ps. 49:14) [They are aware of their fate and speak of it, but it does not affect them], see there. And it can only be established through the expansion of the soul's ecstasy, expanding the idea through *sensory depiction*, to arouse the soul through the excitement of the limbs, to draw forth from within it known matters, the punishments of pride and the soul which will not happen to a stranger, but rather if a man himself transgresses, he himself will be punished with a bitter inconsolable punishment.[17]

His distinction between knowing one's day of death and experiencing it, rooted in the talmudic statement, parallels Shapira's distinction as well as his identification of the imagination as an instrument of experience.[18] Per Lipkin, only the expansion of the idea of one's death through "sensory depiction," meaning a visualization done with one's senses, arouses an experience of fear and punishment. The imagination is used as a means by which "fear" is acquired, a matter that cannot be attained through intellectual knowledge about death.

Lipkin called on several occasions for the use of the imaginative faculty in connection to experience in general, and excitement in learning in particular, "[One should] learn with burning lips, with a proper idea, *a broad imagination* (*be-ṣiyur*) broadening all matters, and bring within him proximate *images*, until the heart will become impassioned, to whatever degree."[19] His assertion that "The power of imagination is beneficial for musar" was transformed into a recurring motif in musar literature. His student, R. Isaac Blazer (1837–1907), wrote that, "The power of imagination is very beneficial for musar, to arouse the soul through the excitement of the limbs (*be-rigshat ha-evarim*);"[20] and viewed the imagination as a component of acquiring fear, "And this is the purpose of acquiring fear—it is necessary that the style of learning musar books will be with an excited soul (*be-hitpa'alut ha-nefesh*), a correct heart, a sad voice, [and] burning lips, expanding the idea through sensory depictions."[21]

If this is so, then how are we to understand Lipkin's attitude toward the imagination? Is he a friend or foe? It appears that a phenomenological analysis may yield a solution. An inspection of the characteristics of the concept of "imagination" in the *iggeret ha-mussar* (epistle of musar) shows that the imagination being referred to there is not the same one that we have discussed over

---

17 Ibid., 29. Emphasis mine. The translation of the talmudic portion is based on the Soncino translation.

18 See above chap. 4 "Visualizing the Day of Death."

19 Lipkin, *Or Yisra'el*, 22.

20 Isaac Blazer, "Sha'arei Or," in *Or Yisra'el*, ed. I. Blazer (Vilnius: Metz Publishing House, 1900), 17.

21 Ibid.

the course of this book; there it is not a visual image placed in front of one's eyes. The imagination is characterized in the letter as being absorbed and focused on enjoying the moment, the fixation of the present and divergence of one's thoughts from clear future consequences, "fearing not the inevitable future." The imagination is the drive for momentary satisfaction, he does not calculate the "pleasure gained through transgression against its loss" and therefore it is unconcerned with the future. This characterization is similar to Lipkin's depiction of desire, "The desire breaks forth to love the momentary pleasantry (*ha-arev le-sha'ato*), in order to prevent looking forward, for in the end it will be bitter;"[22] "The evil inclination is the power of man's desire, gazing forth at each momentary pleasantry (*ha-arev le-sha'ato*)... and the good inclination is good sense (*ha-sekhel ha-yashar*) observing and discerning the consequence."[23] Indeed, Immanuel Etkes already indicated that the conception of imagination in the *iggeret ha-mussar* is identical to Lipkin's understanding of desire in his other teachings.[24] Desire, according to Lipkin, is the natural psychic force inscribed in man's soul from childhood, and is characterized by momentary enjoyment and the inability to weigh long-term consequences.[25]

According to Lipkin "man is bound by his rationality." This constriction is the appropriate and desired framework for curbing man's natural inclination to be preoccupied by and give into temporary satisfaction while ignoring the "inevitable future." The intellect is the faculty that enables foresight and the "calculation of the pleasure gained through transgression against its loss [that is, punishment incurred]." This sober vision stirs the fear of future punishment "when God will account for all of his works." In other words, the evaluative intellect wages a battle against the experience of fleeting gratification, and not the imagination in the sense of imagery and visualization. The powerful drive for passing pleasure is referred to as imagination not because of its visual-imagery qualities, but rather since it has imaginary features. While the "evil inclination" is in command, man "imagines" the present as the sole value, neglecting both intellectual considerations and future consequences. Imagination here is not *seeing* a *picture*, but rather *overvaluing* the present situation. Eve imagined, "That the tree was good for eating and a delight to the eyes and that the tree was desirable as a source of wisdom," and only then—"she took of its fruit and ate" (Gen. 3:6). Imagining the tree as "good" and "beautiful" removed the prohibition of eating the fruit from her mind, allowing for the transgression to

22 Pachter, *Israel Salanter*, 117.
23 Ibid., 118.
24 Etkes, *Rabbi Israel Salanter*, 111.
25 Ibid., 107–108.

occur. Like Eve, the mother of all life, man imagines the experience of brief fulfilment, thereby forgetting the future punishment. With the punishment forgotten, the accompanying feeling of fear subsides. Lipkin does not reject the imagination as an instrument for self-perfection—he rejects the positive imagining that accords man momentary gratification, and through which his future is lost.

C Ecstasy and the Battle of the Senses: The Development of the Imagination in the Musar Movement

Lipkin neither thought nor believed for a moment that the intellect can overcome momentary desires, or in his language—the imagination. Lipkin's psychological sensitivity instructed him that the intellect is always the underdog in its battle against the senses, "But what shall we do, as the imagination is an overflowing stream in which the intellect drowns."[26] Yet Lipkin was not resigned. He certainly believed that the intellect could be victorious, albeit only if we "place it aboard a ship," which is "the excitement of the soul and the storm of the spirit." That is to say, only an emotional drive can rescue the intellect and subdue the imagination-desire. This conflict between the imagination and intellect is unlike that found in medieval musar literature.[27] At the same time, it is also dissimilar to that found in Ekstein's teachings, for Lipkin's "negative" imagination is not of a visual variety, nor did he place different imagery exercises against one another. This is a battle between emotions, and, in the terminology of Lipkin's students, a battle of the senses. Only "the excitement of the soul and the storm of the spirit" can contend with desire. The intellect is not meant to compete against desire on its own, but rather through the emotion of fear: "Fear empowers [the intellect] with its power to constrain the strong bonds of desire;"[28] "If through scheming the understanding (*ha-tevunah*) will conjoin with "fear," the sense (*ha-ḥush*) will also change."[29] The challenge of Lipkin's musar doctrine lies in the transforma-

---

26 See above n. 15. Regarding the intellect's lack of reliability and its vulnerability to biased personal interests in the Musar movement, see Tamar Ross, "The Anti-Rationalist Trend in the Musar Movement," in *Alei Shefer: Studies in the Literature of Jewish Thought*, ed. M. Hallamish (Ramat Gan: Bar Ilan University Press, 1990), 145–162. Ross asserts that due to their views, the Musar thinkers were against man's reliance on the intellect for guidance and instruction.
27 See above, chap. 6, "War of Imaginations."
28 Lipkin, *Or Yisra'el*, 29 (Letter 9).
29 Ibid., 24 (Letter 5).

tion of "fear" from an intellectual conviction to an emotional impulse, which will have the force to overcome the desire, the imagination.[30]

The excitement of the soul that Lipkin proposes is ecstasy (*hitpa'alut*). Ecstasy is a powerful emotional drive that outweighs the other impulses. Ecstasy is a state in which one trait overwhelms the psyche and silences the other traits. Ecstasy creates a transformative action, it internalizes knowledge, and changes it from something purely intellectual into a living and burning feeling. Its goal is to transform consciousness into a "sensory force." Without ecstasy, even the learning of musar will remain solely in the realm of consciousness and will not have the capability of guiding the "actions of the limbs." Lipkin differentiated between the learning of musar in depth as a primarily intellectual exercise, and the learning of musar in an ecstatic fashion, transforming the fear of sin from a theological principle into an enrooted attribute of the psyche.[31] After the enrooting of fear in the psyche, it is transformed into an ideal weapon for the intellect to subdue all desires.

Lipkin suggested a number of techniques for the development of ecstasy: the learning of musar literature out loud, singing *nigunim* (melodies) of a melancholic melody and rhythm during learning to arouse the soul, bodily movements, and the repeating of a mantra-like sentence from a musar book or rabbinic passage for an hour accompanied by crying.[32] Blazer reasserted these techniques and emphasized that the purpose of learning musar with these techniques is in order to internalize "fear" in man's psyche "like water, his bones like oil":

> When one reads rabbinic passages and musar books impassioning the heart with the fear of God, blessed is his name, with a voice of grief, sadness, and the ecstasy of the soul, then his heart will be warmed within him and it will storm and excite his soul. All his senses will be excited until these matters will take root in the imagination of his inner heart[33] in order to bring the fear of God to his inner being (*qirvo*). Even more, the learning of musar will sometimes bring him to ecstasy to [the point] of crying, and streams of water will fall from his eyes and his tears will be like the dew of [Mt.] Hermon. Then a new spirit will be given to him and the fear of God will "enter his body like water, his bones like oil." (Ps. 109:18)[34]

---

30 Etkes, *Rabbi Israel Salanter*, 112.

31 Ibid.

32 Ibid., 113 – 115. For more on repetition and recitation (*shinun*) in Lipkin's thought, see Katz, *The Musar Movement*, 1:253; For more on recitation and melancholic melody, ibid., 258 – 259.

33 The Hebrew is taken from Psalm 73:7 *maskiyot levav*, for which the English translation is debated, see JPS 1917 edition for the translation used here, others include "their fancies," JPS New Translation, and "follies" NSRV.

34 Blazer, "Sha'arei Or," 17. It should be noted that Lipkin does not explicitly state that the melody should be sung with a sorrowful voice. Lipkin's locutions ,"a loud and impassioned voice"

Additionally, Lipkin suggested imagery techniques as a tool for bridging the intellect and the senses. Not everything that is absorbed by the intellect is absorbed by the senses. The transformation of intellectual cognition into a powerful emotional experience can be accomplished through the imagination: "Learning... with a proper idea... and to bring within him proximate *images*, until the heart will become impassioned."[35] Lipkin suggests bringing the "idea," meaning the knowledge, to the intellect through "sensory depictions" (*ṣiyurim ḥushim*).[36]

Lipkin's student, R. Simḥah Zissel (Broida) Ziv (1824–1898),[37] known as "the Elder of Kelm," expanded and developed his teacher's distinction between intellectual knowledge and the senses. Like Lipkin, Ziv emphasized the need for ecstasy in the learning of musar works and the insufficiency of intellectual cognition. In his opinion, logical-intellectual activities are not strong enough to overcome the desire implanted within man. It is only through the transformative power of ecstasy that intellectual awareness can become "sensory nature" (*ṭeva ḥushi*).[38] While the techniques that Ziv proposed are no different than those of Lipkin, he further developed the "visual observation,"[39] and taught the use of visual contemplation for the obtainment of fear,[40] "for fear is built upon images (*ṣiyurim*)."[41]

In his essay *Ha-Sekhel ve-ha-Ḥush* (The Intellect and the Sense), he wrote, "And when we contemplate the different faculties of man, the intellectual faculty and the sensory faculty, it appears that most people feel their senses more than their feeling of the intellect (*me-hergesh ha-sekhel*)."[42] Indeed, this is correct so long as the intellectual faculty is not materialized, but "when his intellectual potential force is actualized... the [intellect] is felt much more strongly than the senses."[43] In order to empower the intellectual faculty and impose it on the sensory faculty, man must transform the intellectual faculty into a sensory force, such that the senses thereby are able to battle the senses, the sensory intellect

---

or "burning lips," were interpreted by Blazer as referring to a "sad and melancholic voice," "sorrowful melody," and "crying voice," etc. Also see Katz, *The Musar Movement*, 259 n. 10.

35 Lipkin, *Or Yisra'el*, 22.

36 Katz, *The Musar Movement*, 1:260. Also see Lipkin, *Or Yisra'el*, 29.

37 For more about him see, Geoffrey D. Clausen, *Sharing the Burden: Rabbi Simḥah Zissel Ziv and the Path of Musar* (Albany: State University of New York Press, 2015). On imagination and self-perfection, ibid., 52–55.

38 Katz, *The Musar Movement*, 2:140.

39 Ibid.

40 Ibid., 140–141.

41 Simḥah Zissel Ziv, *ḤḤokhmah u-Musar* (New York: Aber Press, 1957), 383.

42 Ibid., 76.

43 Ibid., 77.

against the sensory desire. Ziv, in fact, claimed that all intellectual understanding is dependent upon living embodied experience: "It is impossible for man to correctly understand any intellectual matter except though sensory immediacy (*hitqarvut le-ḥush*)."[44] This process of "sensory immediacy" is, at times, Shekhinah through imagery techniques. An example of this is Ziv's recommendation to internalize the theological conception of God's greatness through an imagery technique very similar to that of Ekstein—imagery of the world and its contents, of animals and birds, of unique landscapes, and the stars, in which the purpose is to sense the nothingness of man in comparison to the greatness of the creator:

> We must [visually] depict (*le-ṣayair*), that if a man were to see all the existing bulls and all the domesticated animal species together, and all the types of wild animals together, and all of the flies together, all that is in the world, and all the types of birds together, and all the types of creeping things, apart from the heavenly hosts—his existence would be nullified before them, and even more before the creator who created them, *and even more so*, if it would be possible to see all the heavenly hosts and heavens, [like] when King Shekhinah, peace be upon him, saw, in his hymn "Praise the Lord from the heavens, etc." (Ps. 148:1) And contemplate this. And it is enough to recognize God's greatness, each one according to what he is, the great one according to his greatness and the small one according to his smallness, and enough with this.[45]

R. Elijah Eliezer Dessler (1891–1954) stated, in the name of Simḥah Zissel Ziv, a conception that parallels Ekstein's view of "the war of imaginations." The evil inclination uses the imagination and one must fight it with its own weapon—the imagination:

> R. Simḥah Zissel Ziv would ask, "How did the holy patriarchs and all the great ones of the world achieve their level; in what way was their power superior to ours?" And he answered, "They knew the amazing power of the images of the heart. Behold, the evil inclination knows this secret very well, and its warfare is always through depictions and images which ensnare our heart and trap us in its net. We are unable to fight against it, except with its weapon, meaning to multiply images from the side of holiness," as mentioned above. So, the righteous ones always kept in front of their eyes images of the Garden of Eden and the wondrous delight that is in the way of God, and through this they defeated their evil inclinations and withstood all the trials.[46]

---

44 Ibid., 56; Also see *Kitvei ha-Sabba ve-Talmidav me-Qelm* (Bnei Brak: Sifsei Chachamim, 1992), 134–136.

45 Ibid., 252 (the essay "*Derekh le-Ṣiyur Gedulat ha-Shem*").

46 Elijah Eliezer Dessler, *Mikhtav me-Eliyahu*, eds. Aryeh Carmel and Aryeh Halpern (London: Honig and Sons, 1955) 4:252. However, I have not found in Ziv's writings a teaching akin to this oral tradition.

At times, the activation of the imagination is not only a recommendation, but is even a halakhic requirement: "'In every generation a man is bound to regard himself as though he personally had gone forth from Egypt,' (*m. Pesaḥim* 10:5) I was ever perplexed by this, how can a man fulfill this halakhah (law)? And does it not say 'bound,' and in every place that they said bound, it is an obligation, and how can man fulfill this halakhah?"[47] Simḥah Zissel pondered how the sages obligated man "to remember the exodus from Egypt." He solved his quandary by connecting the commandment to remember the exodus from Egypt on Passover with the sages' ultimate recommendation for battling the evil inclination: "He shall remember the day of his death."[48] Similar to Shapira, Ziv interpreted the action of "remembering one's day of death" as an act of the imagination. The inference made from the word "remembering" one's death and the departure from Egypt teaches, according to Ziv, that the obligation of "remembering the exodus from Egypt" is carried out through a simple act of imaginal visualization, and that this activity endows the theological conception of "reward and punishment" with a sensory understanding:

> The very wise man... despite all of [his wisdom,] is not impressed however long the wisdom is in his intellect alone, [un]like the matter in [his] senses... If the sensory awareness is so strong, man must make "reward and punishment" as sensorially immediate as possible (*ṣarikh ha-adam le-qarev sekhar va-onesh kol ma de-efshar la-ḥush*), meaning, to visualize suffering, as if they are actually happening to him God forbid... he shall then visualize in his heart the matter of his own death and not someone else's, like the matter of "he shall remember the day of his death" that our sages spoke of... meaning, he shall remember a [visual] depiction (*ṣiyur*) of the day of his death, and so shall he visualize all types of sufferings, how much he will suffer for transgressing the laws of the Torah, and this is very beneficial for being cautious of sin... and behold the primary [aspect] of the commandments of Passover and remembering the exodus from Egypt is only that he might clarify [for himself] "reward and punishment"... for it has been clarified that the world has a guide and observer... and look, it is at first glance impossible that something from several years ago might make such an impression of excitement upon him, that it is fitting to be excited by it. Therefore, our sages came and advised us, as was mentioned above, to make the sense immediate (*le-qarev el ha-ḥush*), meaning to visualize a true depiction... and through this aforementioned depiction, the memory of the exodus from Egypt will make a strong impression upon him. We find that it is not their intent to obligate [him to be] as if he departed [from Egypt], this is impossible except for the great sages, but rather they came to obligate man to make the miracle of the Exodus sensorially immediate (*le-qarev ha-nes shel yeṣi'at miṣrayim el ha-ḥush*) meaning to visualize the act as if it happen to him in actuality.[49]

47 Ziv, *Ḥokhmat u-Musar*, 55
48 See above chap. 4, subchapter "Visualizing the Day of Death."
49 Ziv, *Ḥokhmat u-Musar*, 56–57 ("A General Essay in Honor of Passover")

The imagination, meaning depiction in Ziv's thought, is utilized as a central path for contemplation and for dwelling on God's deeds, "for contemplation of his abundant mercies and kindnesses is impossible without the power of imagination (*ko'aḥ ha-ṣiyur*)."[50] According to Ziv, the true wise man is the one who *visualizes* what is about to come to pass, he is the one who imagines and views a visual picture of the future:

> "Who is wise? He who discerns what is about to come to pass" (*b. Tamid* 32a)—for through the growth of his power of imagery... precisely through this power, he shall visualize his distant future, like the days of the Messiah, and the world of souls, and the world of resurrection, and the world to come and [the way] he can lose these, may the Merciful One save us, and it is [visually] depicted for him the great and awful Day of Judgment and he is apprehensive about it, and this is the true wise person, and it is wondrous that which our sages said, "Who is wise? He who discerns [lit. sees] what is about to come to pass." And behold it is the power of imagery stands against the world of action, for so is the world of action visualized, and that which is written "and the persons (*ha-nefesh*) that they had acquired in Haran" (Gen. 12:5) is interpreted as implying that they taught them the power of imagery, and through this they were brought close under the wings of the divine presence (*Shekhinah*).[51]

This wise man is the pious one (*ṣaddiq*), for the differentiation between the *ṣaddiq*, who is near to God, and the wicked person, who is distant from the divine, is itself derived from the imaginative faculty:

> Man will understand the ideas of musar, but will not depict them in front of him as living matter. He will understand, but he will not always visualize the matter. And on this point the great ones possessing knowledge are differentiated from the lesser ones. All of greatness is dependent on this alone, and each person who is greater than his fellow, his [power of] imagination is greater than his [fellow's] as well, besides for each person who is greater than his fellow also having greater knowledge. But even in a matter in which their knowledge is equal, the greater one will derive from the knowledge of every matter much more benefit than what the lesser one will acquire, for he will visualize it in front of his eyes.[52]

However, despite what has been stated, most of Simḥah Zissel's teachings which use the imagination as a technique are concerned with visualizing the Day of Judgment, the day of death, etc. The visualization of the future, in Ziv's writings, is not generally meant for the development of the experience of astonishment, communion (*devequt*), or other mystical experiences. The primary emphasis

50 Ibid., 302.
51 Ibid., 66–67.
52 *Kitvei ha-Sabba ve-Talmidav*, 133.

which recurs throughout his work is the fear of or apprehension of "the great and awful Day of Judgment." Even the visualization of the world to come appears in juxtaposition with "[the way] he can lose them:" "he shall visualize his distant future, like the days of the Messiah, and the world of souls, and the world of resurrection, and the world to come and [the way] he can lose these, may the Merciful One save us, and it is [visually] depicted for him the great and awful Day of Judgment and he is apprehensive about it"[53] Ultimately, this visualization of the future is designed and intended to arouse fear and anxiety of the future Day of Judgment. In contrast to Shapira's method of arousing fear, which is intended to develop an empowering experience of communion with God, or exhilaration, at times even mystical,[54] Ziv's initiating of fear is meant to transform fear into "a sensory experience," an experience that can nullify all desires, and only by this might man's proximity to the divine be measured. The sensory fear prevents man from sinning and brings him "under the wings of the divine presence (*Shekhinah*)."[55]

Ziv derives this need from two juxtaposed verses in Ecclesiastes: "It is good to go to a house of mourning," (7:2) "Wise men are drawn to (lit. The heart of wise men are in) a house of mourning." (7:3) If a man is located, physically, in a house of mourning, why does it need to state that his heart is there? Ziv answers this by stating that it is referring to two states. The first is the physical reality in the house of morning, a reality that causes a true sight of the mourner, whereas the second state (the heart of wise men) happens after man leaves the house of mourning. In this case the wise-pious man recreates in his imagination what he saw in the house of mourning:

---

53 Nevertheless, Dessler states a positive visualization of the future in the name of Simḥah Zissel, "So the righteous men, blessed be their memory, always held in front of their eyes [visual] depictions of the Garden of Eden and the wonderful delight found in the path of God and through this they defeated their inclination and withstood all the trials," Dessler, *Mikhtav me-Eliyahu*, 4:252. Yet it should be noted that Dessler refined this passage, and, in contrast to Ziv, developed the imagery techniques in a more positive manner, without a focus on sin or the day of death or judgment. Also see below that according to Dessler it is through the experience of the positive aspect of visualization that man may overcome his desire.

54 See above, chap. 4, subchapter "he Imagination as Intensifying Emotions."

55 Furthermore, see the channeling of visualizing the future, like the messianic days or world to come, for the purpose of experiencing fear from the day of death and the Day of Judgment: "Therefore, the world does not chase after the pleasure of the messianic days and the world to come, for they do not engage with the secret that I have disclosed to them—the secret of imagination (*sod ha-ṣiyur*), and therefore remembering the day of death and fear of the Day of Judgment are strange for man, it is only since he is agitated and empty of the secret of the wisdom of imagination (*me-sod ḥokhmat ha-ṣiyur*)," Ziv, *Ḥokhmat u-Musar*, 66.

> "The heart of wise men are in a house of mourning"... but it is already written "It is good to go to a house of mourning?". However we need both verses "It is good to go"—to see with the senses, and then he shall also visualize, when he is not there, the house of mourning which he saw ... and the difference between the righteous and the wicked man lies only in the power of imagination, for who would not wish for continuous good and that everything will be good, but the wicked man lacks the power of imagination, and not faith as is commonly thought (*ke-sevarat olam*).[56]

Both the righteous man and the wicked man desire good, "for who would not wish for continuous good and that everything will be good," however the righteous man has the capability of visualizing his end, while the wicked man is incapable of doing so. The righteous man is in fact the wise man who sees what is to pass, who through his imaginative faculty perceives the bitter and reckless end of man, while the wicked man does not. Consequently, it is the imagination which differentiates between the righteous and the wicked, with the primary aspect of the imagination consisting of a view of the "dark" future; "a view" that preserves the "fear" in man and endows the intellectualized fear with a powerful emotional impulse.

R. Yeruḥam Halevi Levovitz (1873–1936), a student of both Ziv and R. Natan Ṣevi Finkel ("The Elder from Slobodka"), contributed a decisive musar character to the Mir yeshiva, declaring, "the sensory level is the highest level, and the intellect is dependent on it—'if there is no fear there is no wisdom'—fear is sensory, hence if there is no sensory there is no wisdom, for wisdom without the sensory is nothing."[57] This statement intensifies the need to transform fear into an emotional impulse. This "sensory" impulse serves wisdom, meaning, the intellect, in the war against desire, yet Levovitz grants it a much greater role. In his teachings, Levovitz expanded the role of the imagination, as determined by his predecessor, from a source of fear to a more primal element. The conception of understanding as dependent upon the senses, meaning experience, led him to conceptuale imagination in much broader terms. His interpretation and explanation of the rabbinic statement "Who is wise?" placed in comparison to Ziv's teachings, demonstrates this expansion:

> Since within wisdom there is depicted and dwells all that will come to unfold unfold (*le-hishtaltel*), come to pass, and materialize (*ve-la-ṣei't le-fo'al*, therefore in his being wise—meaning, the power of unfolding (*ha-hishtalshelut*), coming to pass, and materialization of all matters—he must also see now, through his thought, all of the future, and perceive it with clear sight, to feel and sense with the thoughts of his heart as if he is really living

56 Ibid., 58.
57 Yeruḥam Halevi Levovitz, *Ḥaver Ma'amarim* (Vilnius: Krins Publishing, 1939), 430–436.

> in actuality all of the situations that he perceives with his foresight—that everything must be depicted in his wisdom, and consequently now as well he verily sees everything and firmly feels all of the future.[58]

In contrast to Ziv, Levovitz's interpretation does not utilize the element of element, but rather the elementary component of understanding: "What is imagination, meaning the essence and existence of imagination? Wisdom!"[59] Understanding is not "theoretical thought," but rather "situational thinking,"[60] a type of cognition which includes internal experience. Man must be emotionally involved throughout his intellectual efforts, and the wise man must foresee the future in order to experience it in the present, to "feel and sense with the thoughts of his heart as if he is verily living in actuality all of the situations that he beholds with his foresight," an experience which can be acquired through imagery techniques. Furthermore, Levovitz in his teachings expanded "visual depiction" (*ṣiyur*) from the imagination to "illustration" (*hamḥashah*). He explains external acts to be actions which awaken internal experiences, as sensory actions, whose essence are the "secret of imagery" (*sod ha-ṣiyur*):

> "Man is bound to regard himself as though he personally had gone forth from Egypt," (*m. Pesaḥim* 10:5) All of the laws of Passover are derived from this: the Passover Seder (a ritual feast held the first night of Passover), the commandment of "four cups" (drunken during the Seder), etc. At first glance, we will only think of the external [aspects]. For as it is clarified, the entire... foundation of man's service in the world of deeds (*olam ha-ma'aseh*) is only to make "[imagery] depictions," and the one who depicts (*ve-ha-yoṣer*) all [=the Divine] "forms a form" (*ṣar ṣurah*)—in any case it is only through this manner that the "as though he personally had gone forth from Egypt" is constituted," for only through these visualizations, depictions of bitterness and afterwards depictions of freedom, is "as though he personally had gone forth" able to be constituted for man. And that which we clarified in a different place [about] what the sages stated, "for R. Hanina used to say: 'Come, let us go forth to meet the bride, the queen,'" and R. Solomon b. Isaac (Rashi) [commented on "Come, let us go forth"], "Like a man who receives the king," [the talmudic passage continues] R. Yannai would wrap himself [in a prayer shawl] and call out and say, 'Come my bride, come my bride'" (*b. Bava Qama* 32a-b), and would not all the wicked people laugh and mock them [saying], "What is this matter of going out to the field? Does she come from there? And what point of going out to call the Sabbath at all? Is it not seemingly more correct that he should sit in his home in rest and tranquility, and in this way receive

58 Yeruḥam Halevi Levovitz, *Ma'amarei ha-Mashgi'aḥ: Me-Siḥotav shel Rabbeinu ha-Ga'on ha-Ḥasid Maran Yeruḥam Halevi Levovitz* (s.l.: s.n., 2011), 466.
59 Ibid.
60 On the distinction between these two modes of thought, conceptual and situational, see above chap. 4, subchapter, "Intensification of Biblical Stories," specifically Heschel's statements.

> the Sabbath?" However, their claim actually derives from their ignorance regarding the world of deed, for if they knew and understood this principle, they would not have room for this thought. The sages taught that precisely in order to receive the Sabbath one must depict, [and] the manner of the depiction is to go out onto the field. It is only through this depiction that they] receive the Sabbath, and one who is unaware of this principle, behold he is unintelligent and an ignoramus in [regards to] "the secret of depiction" (*sod ha-ṣiyur*).[61]

Imagery techniques that are not directed specifically towards fear can be found in the musar teachings of Elijah Eliezer Dessler, an alumnus of the Kelm yeshiva who served as the spiritual supervisor (*mashgi'aḥ ruḥani*) of Ponevezh yeshiva in Bnei Brak from 1947 until his death in 1953. Dessler was a leading musar figure of the twentieth century, whose teachings, due to their later composition, synthesized different schools of thought found in the Musar movement alongside kabbalistic and hasidic principles. Dessler's uniqueness in comparison to his predecessors lies in his downplaying of fear together with his emphasis on positive subjects as a platform for the imagination. Dessler called for the, "multiplication of tangible (*muḥshim*) depictions of sacred matters in the imaginative faculty, so that we will feel as if [we are] living the wonderous happiness within them."[62] The use of concepts like happiness and delight[63] are an innovation and demonstrate a shifting orientation. Imagery techniques of the world to come that once utilized the cultivation of fear through visualizing "the ways of losing it," are transformed in Dessler's teachings into delightful visualizations.

In Dessler's treatment of art, he states that the role of art is to form an impression upon man's soul. From the discussion of art, whose creativity stems from the imaginative faculty of the creator, he moves on to imagery practices:

> And behold God (lit. the blessed name) placed a spark of artistry in every person, whether it be great or little; and whoever contemplates and visualizes to himself will feel this matter, and it makes an impression on his soul. The ascending (*ha-oleh*) man [a man who constantly improves himself spiritually] will use this, to develop his emotions in his soul. And this is also the case regarding the matter of the power of giving (*ko'aḥ ha-netinah*)... he shall visualize (*yeṣayair*) in his soul the form (*ṣurat*) of his friend and his worries with all of their details and aspects, and then he will feel his friend's suffering and will pity him; similarly in his visual depiction in his soul of his friends great joy and happiness by achieving that

---

61 Yeruḥam Halevi Levovitz, *Da'at Ḥokhmah u-Musar* (New York: Dass Chochmo Umussar Publications, 1966), 130 – 131.

62 Dessler, *Mikhtav me-Eliyahu*, 4:252.

63 See above n. 53.

> required of him—then by his knowing that he can cause much happiness for his friend with his giving, it will ease this giving.[64]

Man must visualize his friend's happiness as he would his agony. This visualization is designed to allow a person, mentally, to open his hand and give actual help to those around him. The "fear" motif is nowhere present here, but rather the utilization of imagery techniques for practical kindness, namely, giving. Moreover, in Dessler's teachings it is difficult to find "fear" or engagement with the "Day of Judgment," even in imagery exercises that deal with the future, as well as the day of death. He seemingly neutralizes the attempt to intensify the experience of the fear of sin, and instead transforms it into a vital force that can stand against the hardships and trials of life. He diverts the discussion from focusing on sin and punishment, and instead concentrates on imagery of death as an element which may endow strength to withstand the present, without an echo of bitter punishments and the like. In his description of R. Aqiva's martyrdom by iron combs (*b. Berakhot* 61b), he discusses the visualization of death:

> How did R. Aqiva merit such a level? Through the power of imagery (*ko'aḥ ha-ṣiyur*). Every day he visualized in his soul the reality of the trial of his soul is being taken, and he continues to accept upon himself the yoke of heaven, and through these visualizations he is able to withstand this difficult trial. We learn from this a wonderful piece of advice for the person who wishs to withstand trials—he should envisage in his imagination many times, before the trial comes, the visual depiction of the trial and his withstanding it, and he should consider in his heart all the reasons and arguments which he utilizes in order to conquer his inclination, and how he is happy in his conquest. And then when the trial really comes and strikes him, he will withstand it. This is tried and tested advice.[65]

Aqiva withstood his harsh and unbearable trial due to his daily use of his imagination. Similarly, Dessler recommends, "tried and tested advice"—that each person should familiarize himself with the utilization of the imagination, a proven matter that will benefit him in his personal struggles.

The usage of the imaginative faculty in the Musar movement reached a height in the teachings of R. Avigdor Miller (1908 – 2001). Miller, an American Jew, traveled to Slabotkė (Slobodka) in 1932 and learned under R. Yiṣḥaq Sher (1880 – 1952) the head of the Slobodka yeshiva at the same time as his father-in-law Finkel, "The Elder of Slobodka." His other primary teacher was R. Avraham Grodzinski (1884 – 1944) the *mashgi'aḥ ruḥani* (spiritual supervisor) of the

64 Dessler, *Mikhtav me-Eliyahu*, 1:45.
65 Dessler, *Mikhtav me-Eliyahu*, 4:252 – 253.

academy, who was killed in a horrific manner in the Holocaust.[66] With the rise of the Nazis, he returned to the United States in 1939 with his wife, who he married in Kaunas in 1935, and his two children who were born there. In the United States, he served as a *mashgi'aḥ ruḥani* in Yeshiva Rabbi Chaim Berlin (in Brooklyn) and for another twenty years in Yeshiva Gedolah Bais Yisroel (in Brooklyn). Miller was known as a prolific writer and authored tens of books in English and Hebrew. He was a gifted orator in English and Yiddish, and thousands of recordings of his talks were produced and sold.[67]

Miller frequently dealt with the concept of "sensory knowledge" or "sensory awareness," and with the battle between intellectual awareness and desire: "The primary aspect of the war against the inclination is the acquirement of a fleshly heart (*lev basar*), meaning the feeling that comes from the power of sensory knowledge (*yedi'ah ḥushit*)."[68] In order to be victorious in this fight and impose awareness on desire, man must "strive for [his learning] to be within his inner emotional experience (*be-kileyotav*, lit. kidneys), meaning that intellectual knowledge will be made [into] sensory and emotional knowledge."[69] Similar to Lipkin, the founder of the Musar movement, Miller emphasized the weakness of the intellect when facing the waves of desire, and the fact that it is not within the intellect's power to overcome the desires unless it receives assistance from the senses:

> And behold men do not live in a world of ideas (*yedi'ot*), but rather in a world of senses. All of man's dealings and experiences are led and influenced by his senses and feelings. The intellect alone does not possess any power in the war of life... the intellectual knowledge by itself, without assistance from the senses or emotions, alone, performs no actions whatsoever and is not worth anything. All the fortresses of the intellect fall before the slightest breeze of a test, for experience is utilized through sense and emotion. All the values of "reward and punishment" remain as mere written letters in a book, but life's desires and wishes, they are living and actual. And the sole advice for the success of spirituality is to live spiritual values and materialize them (*ve-le-hagshimam*), like life—and this is knowledge (*da'at*).[70]

---

66 In an arson attack. See Hillel Seidman, *Ishim she-Hikarti: Demuyot me-Avar Qarov be-Mizraḥ Iropah* (Jerusalem: Mossad Harav Kook, 1970), 10.

67 Regarding him see Avigdor Miller, *Lev Avigdor* (Jerusalem: Hamadpis, 2002), 1–4. Yakir Englander, "Secular Influence on Haredi Thought—The Philosophy of Rabbi Avigdor Miller as Test Case," *Da'at* 71 (2011): 136–139.

68 Miller, *Lev Avigdor*, 57.

69 Ibid., 61.

70 Ibid., 62.

The revitalization and materialization of values,*da'at* (knowledge) in Miller's teachings, is the conjunction of the intellect and the senses, consciousness and experience.[71] The challenge that Lipkin set was expanded in Miller's thought; Lipkin wished to transform "fear" from an intellectual awareness into an emotional impulse, whereas Miller demanded the transformation of all awareness into emotional impulse, so "that intellectual knowledge will be made [into] sensory and emotional knowledge." Miller espoused situational thinking rather than conceptual thinking, a thinking in which the depths of man's very soul are involved, "As it is stated, 'You are present in their mouths, But far from their thoughts." (Jer. 12:2) It speaks here of men who know how and what to speak, and not only this, but also speak [themselves]... they speak well and abundantly. But since their knowledge is far from their interiority—they are not worth anything!"[72] *Da'at* is "sensory knowledge," wisdom that has been transformed into emotional impulse, sensory experience. As far as experience is mixed with knowledge, so is the degree of *da'at* heightened:

> This is the matter: there are levels in the knowledge of matters, differentiated according to the participation of the senses within them. There is intellectual knowledge and there is sensory knowledge. The infant hears from his father that fire burns and he believes with complete faith in his father's words, but he has no sensory knowledge of this. But when he places finger in the fire he then acquires sensory knowledge. The first knowledge did not in fact influence him, but the acquired sensory knowledge will influence him all of his days to be careful. And according to the acuteness of the sensory feeling that there is in knowledge, the level of *da'at* will be ascertained.

The advice for achieving *da'at* is to "live the values", yet, what is the action of "living them?" how is it possible to internalize awareness? Miller responds decisively—through imagination: "*Da'at* is the feeling of visual images (*ṣiyurim*);"[73] "For sensory knowledge is only in visual depictions... for the power of these visual depictions is called *da'at*;"[74] "For *da'at* is predicated on the principle of imagination;"[75] "Among the primary ways to acquire *da'at* is through visualization (*avodat ha-ṣiyurim*). That he will strive to place in his mind (*be-rosho*) clear

71 The principles of his conception of *da'at* are based on the teachings of R. Yosef Yehudah Leib Bloch (1860–1929) the head of Telshe yeshiva, for Bloch's understanding of *da'at*, see Katz, *The Musar Movement*, 5:70–85.
72 Miller, *Lev Avigdor*, 61.
73 Ibid., 173.
74 Ibid., 26–27.
75 Ibid., 28.

images derived from of all his knowledge."[76] Similar to its meaning in Levovitz's teachings, the concept of depiction for Miller is utilized both for imagination and for the act of illustration: "One of the ways of acquiring *da'at* is through visual depiction (*ṣiyur*) and illustration (*hamḥashah*), and this is the concern of the commandment of telling the Exodus story to one's children, and the commandment of remembering the assembly at Mt. Sinai."[77] Nonetheless, in Miller's writings, imagination is superior to illustration in practical aspects. He employs illustration in order to explain the meaning of practical commandments, but he did not design any illustration exercises for his audience. In regards to imagination, on the other hand, Miller saw fit to develop new techniques, which he advised his listeners to use for a number of purposes (and not only the cultivation of fear). His style is characterized by short plots, and in orthographic terms do not exeed one paragraph. Generally speaking, a number of scenes are woven together into a short story: "We shall [visually] depict the High Priest entering before [the holy of holies] on the Day of Atonement, and one person observes him through a window and sees his service ,and he sees that he stands and laughs."[78] These imagined plots are designed to arouse a specific emotion, such as astonishment or the appreciation of the miracles found in simple things:

> We shall depict someone from the generation of the wilderness (*dor ha-midbar*), who only saw manna all days, and when he enters the land of Israel suddenly he sees grain for the first time in his life, how it is planted in the ground, and grows from the earth, and is made into bread. Do his eyes not certainly open with astonishment at the awesome vision, how from a tiny particle and from some dirt with air, sunlight, and water, bread is produced? If so, we find that the manna brought him to contemplate the miracle of bread.[79]

The visualization of God, a halakhicly severe and problematic issue,[80] was extensively discussed in Miller's writings. The "fear of heaven" was defined as the "experience of heaven," meaning the experience of the divine, an experience acquired through imagination. Miller's greatest innovation, in comparison to other musar thinkers, is his insistence that man need not focus on and contemplate "fear", but it is sufficient for him to experience "the heavens," and through this "fear" will be cultivated: "'The fear of heaven'—one must understand that the primary issue is not dependent on the 'fear,' but on the 'heaven,' meaning

---

76 Avigdor Miller, *Sha'arei Orah: Qoveṣ Ma'amarim shel Va'adei Musar* (New York: s.n., 2006), 2:97.

77 Avigdor Miller, *Or Olam* (Arad: s.n., 2002), 2:22.

78 Avigdor Miller, *Torat Avigdor* (Bnei Brak: s.n., 2002), 1:55.

79 Miller, *Sha'arei Orah*, 35.

80 See above chap. 5.

that the primary concern is not what strengthens a person's 'fear,' but that which strengthens [him] in his sense of 'heaven.' However he increases *da'at*, that is, the emotion and sensory depiction, to view himself as standing before God... fear is added in accordance."[81] This conception, which grants preference to the heavens over fear, is directly related to the visualization of God: "For in our being embodied (*basar ve-dam*), and our being limited to corporeal emotions, we are compelled to depict and configure (*ve-lidmot*) the Holy One, blessed be he, in corporeal depictions in order to arouse our thoughts and emotions."[82] Indeed, Miller made multiple imagery techniques for God in different contexts, primarily for the subject of prayer.[83] The importance Miller grants to emotional experience in every conscious action, and the importance of creating an emotional-experiential connection and relationship with God, vindicate the visualization of the divine. He additionally claims that this is the divine will, "as is stated with certainty... the creator may He be blessed, God forfend, has no image or depiction, and it is only a mere image (*dimyon be-alma*) that is depicted. We must nevertheless think, that [even] with all of this, it is God's will that we depict in our thoughts pictures and images (*ve-ṣiyurim*)... in order that our senses and emotions will acquire and feel that we have a relationship with the living and existing God."[84] Sensory knowledge or embodied awareness are so significant as to outweight the issue corporeality, as Miller stated, "It is better for man to corporealize (*she-yagshim*) than to not feel." To be without the experience of God is greater heresy than his corporealization:

> And the prophets envisioned visions and always prophesized with pictures and many corporeal idioms regarding the creator, may he be blessed. At first glance, this raises the question of how they were unconcerned that this would increase the danger of corporealization. And the answer is according to that which has been clarified, that imaginal visualizations are necessary for saving man from the primary danger, namely, that he will remain without a living feeling and sensory awareness (*ve-hakarah muḥashit*) of God's existence. As we clarified, without sensory emotion, the Holy One blessed be he remains, as it were, [just] an abstract idea and human speculation (*ke-sevara be-alma*), and he falls victim to the true danger of heresy, may God have mercy.[85]

Lipkin and his student Ziv utilized the visualization of the future as an instrument for the cultivation of fear in order to overpower desire. For them, visualiza-

---

81 Miller, *Lev Avigdor*, 65.
82 Miller, *Sha'arei Orah*, 65.
83 For example see ibid., 70–71.
84 Ibid., 66.
85 Ibid., 65.

tion of the future is linked to the visualization of the Day of Judgment, and the punishment and sense of awful dread that accompanies it. In contradistinction, Miller directed the visualization of the world to come or the resurrection of the dead towards the development of living experience of "faith," and not only "fear:"

> Furthermore, man is [also] obligated to acquire visual depictions of the other principles and fundamentals of faith, such as the future redemption... and he must similarly acquire a sensory depiction (*ṣiyur muḥshi*) of the resurrection of the dead. And the truth is that if he is unable to acquire a visual depiction of this, then this entire topic is distant for him... and he stands in great danger that, God forfend, his belief in the resurrection of the dead will be lacking, since it is a matter that is very distant from our intellectual depiction. Indeed, the righteous man (*bar levav*) will strive to engrave within himself a living depiction until he will acquire it in his senses. Therefore, he shall depict practical details of this, how the dead will rise in their bodies, and [how] he will encounter his acquaintances that have already set out for their eternal abode, and he will think how he will then perceive all the matters of the world.[86]

Miller's aimed not only to transform fear into a living emotional impulse, but to also develop man's sense of a living belief, in the broadest sense, in all scopes of life. Generally, he utilized the imagination as a means to cultivate a living faith chacterized by emotional experience: "And so there is an obligation to remember and visualize all the miracles that God has done for us over the generations, as it is written, 'Remember the wonders He has done' (Ps. 105:5)... that through them we will have a living depiction of the fundamentals of faith. However, in order that we may have the awaited benefits, we must also, from our perspective, visualize the miracles."[87] According to Miller, the visualization of the resurrection of the dead—"how the dead will rise in their bodies, and [how] he will encounter his acquaintances that have already set out for their eternal abode"—is the fulfillment and realization of one of the thirteen principles of faith. Without the imagination, man is in "true danger of heresy." In the case of heresy against heresy, corporealization against non-experiential faith, Miller decides in favor of a living experiential faith. This decision is based on the broadened conception of *da'at* (knowledge) which he presented, and its place in man's lived experience.

86 Ibid., 95.
87 Ibid., 94.

D Between the Musar Movement and Hasidism

There is much similarity between the imagery techniques developed in the Musar movement and those in hasidism: the visualization of religio-historical events for the purpose of arousing religious passion, the visualization of man's future, as well as the utilization of the imagination as a means for internalization and as an instrument for the development of "situational thinking." With that said, there are also clear differences. The imagination in hasidism is of a more mystical variety. Much emphasis is placed on the experience of the divine and the desire to make it present through imagery techniques. In contrast, the Musar movement places the emphasis on the psychological aspects. The purpose of the imagination is to "place [the intellect] aboard a ship" so that it will not drown in the waves of desire. The purpose of the imaginal-visualization is to provide the intellectual faculty with an emotional impulse, and, in its later development, to transform faith into a lived experience. However, the Musar movement does not place weight on experiencing the divine or its presence, as hasidism does.

The literary styles differ as well: speaking broadly, it is possible to state that the imagery techniques developed in the Musar movement have simple content—concise exercises comprised of a few scenes. There are no imagery techniques spanning multiple pages as in the writings of Shapira, Ekstein, and Schneersohn. These aforementioned hasidic thinkers presented guided imagery techniques which included clear instructions for the audience, a matter that is neither common nor widespread in the Musar movement. In hasidic writings, imagery techniques frequently appear in a commanding tone, with detailed instruction and directions, whether in the spatio-bodily field, such "close your eyes" or in the temporal field, delineating the length and frequency of the exercises.[88] In contradistinction, the Musar movement is characterized more by descriptions of imagery techniques and their importance, and not by the instruction and facilitation of said techniques.

E Conclusion

The utilization of the imagination in the Musar movement began with its founder Israel Lipkin. He employed the imagination as an instrument for the conversion of "fear" from an intellectual to a sensory awareness. This transformation inten-

88 See, for instance, the clear instructions in Ekstein, *Tena'ei ha-Nefesh*, 3–4, 13.

sified and empowered "fear," transforming it into a potent experiential-sensory force possessing the capability to overpower and subdue the desires of man in "the war of senses." Simḥah Zissel Ziv, "the Elder of Kelm," deepened the gap between knowledge and the senses, and instructed to use depictive contemplation in order to acquire "sensory fear." In his musar teachings, imagination became *the criterion* that distinguishes between the righteous and the wicked. With that said, like his teacher, he utilized the imagination as a means of cultivating fear, and generally did not go beyond this area. The primary imagery content in his work is the visualization of the dark future, a vision that bestows an emotional impulse to the intellectual "fear." Yeruḥam Halevi Levovitz expanded the role of the imagination from being a specific instrument for "fear" into a general instrument for understanding. Levovitz claimed that through the imagination, "situational thinking" can be developed. Prominent musar thinkers of the twentieth century, like Elijah Eliezer Dessler and Avigdor Miller, made less of the imagination for cultivating fear, preferring to employ it in a broader fashion for a variety of purposes that attempt to endow man's deeds with religious fervor. The centrality of sensory awareness and experience in the accounts of the Musar movement caused Miller to justify even the visualization of God, despite the halakhic problem of corporeality. God's incorporeality is liable to cause an experiential-disconnect between man and God—assessed by Miller to be a more severe heresy than corporealization.

We thus see that the conceptualization of the imagination underwent development in the Musar movement, together with its practical uses, from being perceived as a means for "fear," to its instrumentalization for understanding, until it became the foundation for faith and the worship of God. It should further be noted that the imagination was not an essential issue at the beginning of the Musar movement, yet in Miller's works, written in the twentieth century, it takes central stage. This development is also reflected in the teachings of R. Shlomo Wolbe (1914–2005),[89] who defined the imagination as the key to faith,

89 A student of Levovitz and son-in-law of Grodzinski. He served as the *mashgi'aḥ ruḥani* at the *Be'er Ya'aqov* yeshiva (between the years of 1949–1982). Afterwards, he founded *Beit ha-Musar* in Jerusalem. He is counted as one of the last ties to pre-Holocaust Musar thinkers and is referred to in the Lithuanian-Haredi sector in Israel as "*Ha-Mashgi'aḥ.*" For more on this personality see Yair Halevy, "Musar, Ḥinukh, Hadrakhah: Ha-Rav Shelomoh Wolbe," in *The Gdoilim: Leaders Who Shaped the Israeli Haredi Jewry*, eds., Benjamin Brown and Nissim Leon (Jerusalem: Magness Press and Van Leer Istitute Press, 2017), 735–765; idem, "Rabbi Shlomo Wolbe and the Musar Revival Efforts in the 'Hashkofe' Yeshiva World," in *From Survival to Consolidation: Change in Israeli Haredi Society and its Scholarly Study*, eds. Kimmy Caplan and Nurit Stadler (Jerusalem: Van Leer Institute, 2012), 55–78. Regarding his view of the intellect, see Garb, *Yearnings of the Soul*, 73–74.

"True imagery is the key to faith... for the blue (*tekhelet*) thread in the *ṣiṣit* (ritual fringes) has the power to arouse an image of the sea, 'and the sea resembles [the color of] heaven, and heaven resembles [the color of] the Throne of Glory' (*b. Soṭah* 17a)—'look at it' (Num. 15:39), may He be blessed!"[90] This development of the imagination, whether in theoretical terms or in practical terms of creating imagery techniques, a development that characterizes the late nineteenth and early twentieth century, is a part of a larger and broader process which will be discussed in the following section.

90 Shlomo Wolbe, *Alei Shur: Gates of Guidance* (Jerusalem: Beit HaMusar 1998), 1:100. Wolbe contrasts "true visual depictions" with "transgressive visual depictions" stating, "On the side of evil, we know that transgressive thoughts (*hirhurei aveirah*) are transgressive visual depictions, and are worse than actual transgression, for the power of depiction is very strong to bring about many deeds," Ibid. In this comparison, it is apparent that the meaning of "depictions" is the imagination. Furthermore, see ibid., 104–105, there he quotes Judah Halevi about the need to visualize key religio-historical events, and prolongs the visualization of "standing at Mt. Sinai" and its impact on man's soul, also see ibid., 107–108.

Section IV: **Adventures of Ideas: West and East**

Introduction: Similar Thought Patterns

Alfred North Whitehead (1861–1947) analyzed Western philosophical traditions in order to understand how Western culture evolved from various ideas that constitute the foundations of this culture in their countless manifestations. These ideas were developed and transformed by central figures, such as ancient Greek philosophers, ancient Israelite prophets, Jesus, Galileo, Newton, and other modern thinkers, ultimately forming Western culture.[1] Whitehead shows how the twentieth century actualized earlier ideas which had ripened slowly for various reasons. Whitehead discussed the complex influence of philosophy, law, and religion on the adventures of ideas,[2] but nevertheless demonstrated that the sociological change was often brought about through scientific-technological developments, such as the industrial revolution, which allowed for the dismantling of the long-criticized institution of slavery.[3]

The adventures of ideas do not only extend historically from past to present, but also culturally and sociologically. That is to say, if we take Whitehead's observations one step further, it stands to reason that different cultures which were exposed to similar religious, political, and social processes will develop comparable and parallel conceptions. Similar conditions naturally produce similar thought patterns and reactions. For instance, talmudic scholars have discussed the parallels between the learning method of the Tosafists (10c.–13c.) and those of contemporary French and German legal scholars. Ephraim Urbach demonstrated that their method was similar to the French scholastic and dialiectic style of the twelfth century.[4] José Faur on this matter has written:

> Franco-German Jewry was particularly sensitive to the flow of events and ideas of their times. The Jew was an integral part of the general environment of the land and was conditioned by the same patterns of thought and feelings that were affecting Medieval France and Germany.[5]

---

1 Whitehead discussed this in *Science and the Modern World* (Cambridge: Cambridge University Press, 1926); idem, *Process and Reality* (New York: Macmillan, 1929); and primarily, idem, *Adventures of Ideas* (New York: The Free Press, 1967).

2 Ibid., 10–25.

3 Ibid., 27–28.

4 Ephraim E. Urbach, *The Tosaphots: Their History, Writings, and Methods* (Jerusalem: Bialik Institute, 1955), 74.

5 José Faur, "The Legal Thinking of Tosafot: An Historical Approach," *Dinei Israel* 6 (1975): xliii.

https://doi.org/10.1515/9783110535884-011

Israel M. Ta-Shma has also discussed how new and changing conditions caused foundational changes in the thought processes of the Tosafists, similar to what developed among the eleventh and twelfth century French and German legalists.[6] Additionally, Norman Solomon has shown that this similar legal thinking continued even into the modern period, and that internal Jewish-legalistic developments from the Tosafist period until the Lithuanian learning method (*lomdus*) of the nineteenth and twentieth century, parallel developments occurring in a non-Jewish context.[7] Needless to say, this example of Franco-German legal thinking developments, which manifested itself within Ashkenazic talmudic study as well as the general population, does not only apply this specific historical case. Similar conditions and circumstances may lead to similar productions and responses across a wide range of fields, whether they be ethical, philosophical, hermeneutical, and even mystical.

Similar imagery techniques began to appear to an astonishing degree in both the East and West at the end of the nineteenth and twentieth century, in Asia, Europe, and the United States, among different religions and cultures. While this fact may point to reciprocal influence and even collaboration, it is unlikely that this was the case. A lack of historical evidence weakens this possibility as the only explanation. In order that there should be no mistake, I believe that when there is proven direct influence it should be presented and noted, but caution should be taken with regard to the question of how such an impact represents wider circles. Even if a certain hasidic thinker would be shown to have contact with an occult movement that does not prove anything regarding the hasidic movement as a whole. The other possible explanation is that these parallel developments stem from similar conditions created by multiple simultaneous processes, without any interaction between the different thinkers. As we have seen similar conditions birth similar thought processes and patterns with practical applications, the path from here to the creation of similar imagery techniques is short. A third possibility may be some combination of the two possibilities delineated above. That is to say, even though there may be no clear direct influence, it is nevertheless impossible to say that there was no connection whatsoever. This possibility augments the idea that similar concepts in different places can appear as responses to similar "field conditions," along with the possibility

6 Israel M. Ta-Shma, *Ritual, Custom and Reality in Franco-Germany, 1100–1350* (Jerusalem: Magnes Press, 1996), 30–34. Also, see idem, *Early Franco-German Ritual and Custom* (Jerusalem: Magnes Press, 1994), 42–48, concerning the similarity between Jewish and German customs of the tenth and eleventh century.

7 Norman Solomon, "Hilluq And Haqira: A Study in the Method of the Lithuanian Halakhists," *Dinei Israel* 4 (1973): lxiv-cvi.

that even if there is no direct mutual knowledge, there are often identical roots that simultaneously affected different movements and organizations in different geographic expanses.

Chapter Eight
"My Heart is in the East and I am at the Ends of the West": Imagery Techniques in Light of the West

A Imagery Techniques in Light of Mesmerism and the Unconscious

Franz Mesmer: His Life, Thought and Influence

Franz Anton Mesmer (1734–1815) was born in February 1734, in the small town of Iznang, close to the German shore of Lake Constance. He studied in Vienna, specializing in medicine, at a time when a mixture of Newtonianism and astrology was accepted by the medical field. In 1774, Mesmer announced his discovery of the "supernal fluid" ("fluidum"), which is found circulating through the whole body; he called this fluid "the agent of nature," which supplies heat, light, electricity, and magnetism. He especially praised this fluid's medical qualities.[1] Mesmer claimed that diseases result from a blockage of the flow of fluidum in parts of the body; he argued that the activity of the fluidum corresponded to that of a "magnet." At the same time, Mesmer claimed that there are people who have the ability to take control of the flow and activity of the fluidum by using "magnetism" (a practice that would eventually be called "mesmerizing" in English), that is, using magnets to massage the "polarities" in the body, and thus overcome the blockage. He would discharge the blockage by inducing some sort of "crisis," sometimes a shock or convulsion, which would restore the person's health, and the harmony between the person and nature.[2] Mesmer called his doctrine "animal magnetism."[3]

1 Robert Darnton, *Mesmerism and the End of the Enlightenment in France* (Cambridge: Harvard University Press, 1968), 3; Catherine L. Albanese, *A Republic of Mind and Spirit: A Cultural History of American Metaphysical Religion* (New Haven: Yale University Press, 2006), 191–192.
2 Darnton, *Mesmerism*, 3–4. Regarding the element of "crisis" in Mesmer's treatments, see Henri F. Ellenberger, *The Discovery of the Unconscious: The History and Evolution of Dynamic Psychiatry* (New York: Basic Books, 1971), 62–63.
3 In German, *Thierischen Magnetismus*; and later in French, *magnétisme animal*. The term "animal" means something with life in it, and does not refer to animals. This is similar to Hebrew, in which the word for animal, *ḥayyah*, shares a common root with the word for vitality, *ḥiyut*.

https://doi.org/10.1515/9783110535884-012

What promoted Mesmer's idea of fluidum most of all were his amazing successes at getting this substance to "work": Mesmer would bring his patients into a sort of epileptic shock, or into a sleepwalking trance, and thus cure them of all sorts of illnesses, from blindness to depression. Mesmer and his students accomplished amazing performances, which held viewers spellbound: they sat in such a way that the patient's legs would be locked between their own and ran their fingers throughout all parts of the patient's body, in search of the poles of the small magnets that together make up the immense magnetic force of the entire body.[4]

In 1774 Mesmer had a huge success in Vienna when he managed to heal Franzl Oesterlin, a young woman of twenty-eight. Franzl had been suffering from hysteria, which was causing her seizures and paralysis. Mesmer instructed her to swallow a solution containing iron and affixed three magnets to her body. Franzl felt a fluid running throughout her body, her paralysis was healed, and her pains were gone.[5] Mesmer quickly became famous throughout Europe. Doctors from throughout the continent sent their patients to Vienna to be treated by him. In addition, Mesmer traveled throughout Europe out of an interest in treating epilepsy, and thus gained additional fame.[6]

After being involved in and charged with a romantic scandal with a blind patient, Maria Theresia Paradis, in Vienna in 1777,[7] Mesmer was forced to leave Vienna, and arrived Paris in 1778.[8] His name preceded him in Paris; by 1780 he had moved on from individual treatment to group treatment, which he conducted with the help of an enormous bathtub (*baquet*) that he set up. Mesmer would treat two hundred people in each group treatment session! Twenty

4 Darnton, *Mesmerism*, 4.

5 Ellenberger, *The Discovery of the Unconscious*, 58–59. We find a description of her recovery in the amazement of Wolfgang Amadeus Mozart (1756–1791), who wrote, in a letter to his father, that Franzl had changed beyond recognition as a result of Mesmer's treatment. See Margaret Goldsmith, *Franz Anton Mesmer: The History of an Idea* (London: Arthur Barker, 1934), 57–59.

6 Goldsmith, *Franz Anton Mesmer*, 75–77. Nonetheless, Mesmer was strongly criticized by scientists in Vienna, see Ellenberger, *Discovery of the Unconscious*, 60.

7 Regarding this whole incident, see Goldsmith, *Franz Anton Mesmer*, 87–101; Vincent Buranelli, *The Wizard from Vienna: Franz Anton Mesmer* (New York: Coward, McCann and Geoghegan, 1975), 75–88.

8 Ellenberger argues that the true reason for Mesmer's departure for Vienna is unclear, and that attributing it to the incident with Paradis is only a hypothesis. Ellenberger prefers to attribute Mesmer's departure to his unbalanced personality, arguing that he had psychopathological problems. See Ellenberger, *Discovery of the Unconscious*, 61. Regarding the development of mesmerism in Germany, see Alan Gauld, *A History of Hypnotism* (Cambridge: Cambridge University Press, 1992), 75–110.

people would stand around the tub, holding onto twenty poles that were attached to the tub; and behind each of these twenty people was a line of another nine patients, each tied together or holding hands, such that the magnetic fluid would be able to flow through them all.[9]

Mesmer's conception was apposite to the French intellectual elite in the late eighteenth century. The science of that period already recognized "invisible" and "amazing" forces and powers in the world. For example, Newton's law of gravity as explicated by François-Marie Arouet (1694–1778); Benjamin Franklin's (1706–1790) discovery of electricity, which was popularized through the lightening poles presented at Paris museums; the invention of the hot air balloon by Joseph-Michel Montgolfier (1740–1810) and Jacques-Étienne Montgolfier (1745–1799), which allowed them to be the first people to fly over Paris. In light of these discoveries and inventions, it is easy to understand the excitement and fanfare that Mesmer's theory received.[10]

In 1784, Louis XVI, king of France, appointed a scientific committee to examine the science of mesmerism and the existence of Mesmer's "fluidum." The committee's conclusion was that there was no proof at all that such a fluid existed.[11] Mesmer, humiliated, left Paris in 1785.[12] Living in Switzerland, he stayed out of the public limelight and became very introverted. In the last year of his life he moved to Meersburg, Germany, and died there on March 5, 1815.[13]

Although Mesmer's theories were rejected, they gained renewed interest posthumously, both in Europe and the United States. Their influence can be seen in the works of nineteenth century French novelists and playwrights, such as Honoré de Balzac (1799–1850) and Victor Hugo (1802–1885).[14] Their writings and characters, who had a certain longing for the wondrous, were influenced by mesmerism. The motif of supernatural "fluidim" runs through Hugo's poems and gives them a glimpse of the paranormal world.[15] American and Euro-

---

9 See Ellenberger, *Discovery of the Unconscious*, 63–64.

10 Darnton, *Mesmerism*, 10. Indeed, Mesmer attempted to explain his theory through the understanding of electricity, see Ellenberger, *Discovery of the Unconscious*, 63.

11 Ibid., 65.

12 Buranelli, *Wizard from Vienna*, 167.

13 Regarding this period of his life, see ibid., 181–188, 199–204.

14 Regarding Balzac and mesmerism, see Ellenberger, *The Discovery of the Unconscious*, 161; concerning Hugo, see Darnton, *Mesmerism*, 127–159.

15 Ibid., 156–159. Also, see Aaron Zeitlin, *The Other Dimension* (Tel Aviv: Yavneh, 1967), 142–146.

pean occult movements were founded on his ideas, and they interpreted them, each in their own way.[16]

Furthermore, mesmeric ideas played a significant role in the development of hypnotism and modern psychology in the late nineteenth and early twentieth centuries. Even in his day, Abbé Faria (1746–1819) laid the foundations for modern hypnotism, based on Mesmer's research. Faria, was a Luso-Goan Catholic monk, and moved to Paris in 1813 to study the phenomenon of "lucid sleep" (*sommeil lucide*).[17] He admitted that Mesmer successfully placed his patients into a state of sleep, however, he claimed that it was not due to magnetic force, but rather from the "concentration" of the patients. According to him, it is easy to put a patient to sleep when he is successfully concentrating on only one matter. Faria would have his patients sit in a comfortable position, and then lean back, relax, close their eyes, remove all distressing thoughts and concentrate on sleep alone. Following this, he would command the patient to sleep. If the patient would not fall asleep or could not remove distracting thoughts, Faria would stretch his fingers, pry them open, and bring them close to the patient's face. This action would force the patient (who was willing to cooperate) to change his focus and to follow the movement of his hands. Through this action Faria succeeded to "grab" the patient's attention and manipulate him to concentrate on the commands given to him.[18]

---

16 Buranelli, *The Wizard from Vienna*, 205–210. Primarily, Spiritualism in Europe and especially America; Christian Science under the leadership of Mary Baker Eddy; New Thought and Theosophy headed by Helena Petrovna Blavatsky. Also, see Ellenberger, *The Discovery of the Unconscious*, 74–85; Goldsmith, *Franz Anton Mesmer*, 236–254.

17 Which was published in his book, José Custódio de Faria, *De la cause du sommeil lucide ou Etude de la nature de l'homme* (Paris: Mme. Horiac, 1819). An English translation, as well as other details about Faria, can be found in Laurent Carrer, *Jose Custodio de Faria: Hypnotist, Priest, and Revolutionary* (Victoria: Trafford, 2004).

18 Buranelli, *The Wizard from Vienna*, 209. Concerning Faria's influence in Europe, see Ellenberger, *The Discovery of the Unconscious*, 75–76. Moshe Idel has discussed the Beshṭ's hypnotic activity as seen from a number of stories collected in *Shivḥei ha-Beshṭ*, see Moshe Idel, "'The Besht Passed His Hand over His Face': On the Besht's Influence on His Followers—Some Remarks," in *After Spirituality: Studies in Mystical Traditions*, ed. Philip Wexler and Jonathan Garb (New York: Peter Lang, 2012), 81–87. Idel discusses cases of the Beshṭ causing changes in his follower's conscious by waving his hand in front of their faces and speaking in a hushed voice with them, actions that are highly similar to those of Faria. Idel mentions the possibility that these stories were written under the influence of mesmerism, see ibid., 95, "It should be mentioned that the idea that it is possible to have such an impact is reminiscent of the theories of the famous Franz Anton Mesmer, active in the last decades of the 18th century in Central and Western Europe, regarding human magnetism." However, Idel rejects this possibility since Mesmer treated groups and not individuals, see ibid. This claim is problematic, as it is entirely based

The royal committee that discredited Mesmer's theories did not deny his successes in putting his patients into a trance, epileptic shock, or sleep; it merely discredited the existence of fluidum. In other words, the committee did not discredit the phenomena that Mesmer demonstrated but only his interpretation of them. Mesmer's undeniable successes thus constituted the harbinger of the "unconscious," the "subconscious," and the power of suggestion. Like Columbus, Mesmer discovered a new world:

> The fateful turning point from exorcism to dynamic psychotherapy was thus reached in 1775 by Franz Anton Mesmer, who has been at times compared to Columbus. Both Columbus and Mesmer discovered a new world, both remained in error for the remainder of their lives about the real nature of their discoveries, and both died bitterly disappointed men.[19]

Mesmer's "discovery" of the unconscious (which was done "unconsciously"), and revelation of parapsychological forces that appeared in his patients when they were under the influence of sleep, together with the element of the relationship between healer and patient, which began to interest people in the wake of Mesmer's treatments, became the basis of hypnosis and Freud's psychoanalysis, which was developed in Vienna in the early twentieth century. These became a springboard for the development of theories of the unconscious or subconscious in modern psychology.[20] Already in the early 1930s, the Jewish Viennese writer Stefan Zweig identified Mesmer and the occult movements as the basis for Freud's theories.[21]

---

on Darnton's work, which only dealt with mesmerism in France, at a later point in Franz Mesmer's life. We have seen that in his earlier stages in Vienna he treated individuals as well. See the beginning of this chapter regarding Mesmer's travels and development of mesmerism between Vienna and France.

19 Ellenberger, *The Discovery of the Unconscious*. 57.

20 Ellenberger, *Discovery of the Unconscious*, 148. Also, see Wouter J. Hanegraaff, *Esotericism and the Academy: Rejected Knowledge in Western Culture* (Cambridge: Cambridge University Press, 2012), 261. Also, see Jeffery J. Kripal, *Authors of the Impossible: The Paranormal and the Sacred* (Chicago: The University of Chicago Press, 2010), 5–35, regarding the role of paranormal and "non-scientific" movements and research in the founding of modern psychology.

21 Stefan Zweig, *Mental Healers: Franz Anton Mesmer, Mary Baker Eddy, Sigmund Freud*, trans. Eden and Ceder Paul (New York: Frederick Ungar, 1932). Regarding Mesmer's role as the founder of the basis of modern psychology, see also: Adam Crabtree, *From Mesmer to Freud: Magnetic Sleep and the Roots of Psychological Healing* (New Haven: Yale University Press, 1993). On Mesmer as the basis for Freud, see also Robert W. Marks, *The Story of Hypnotism* (New York: Prentice-Hall, 1947), 58–97; Jeffrey J. Kripal, *Esalen: America and the Religion of No Religion* (Chicago: University of Chicago Press, 2007), 141.

> After the theory of the fluid had been abandoned, psychological concepts were resorted to, such as the power of the will (Puysegur), or later the idea of psychological forces or nervous energy. During the latter part of the nineteenth century, the view was commonly held by hypnotists and shared by many academic physicians that illness was the result of a lack of nervous energy. Despite its vagueness, this concept was ever present in the first dynamic psychiatry and was ready to be later developed by Janet, Freud, Jung, and others.[22]

Shortly before Mesmer, Emmanuel Swedenborg (1688–1772), an influential Swedish theologian and scientist, wrote an eight-volume Latin work on the "scientific" phenomenon of *influx*,[23] a concept which demonstrates the hidden energy that allows for the existence of the universe,[24] and descends upon the individual in moments of inspiration, in order to empower his vision and writing ability.[25] After intensive study of Hebrew, he practiced Abulafian letter-combination techniques in order to gain divine inspiration.[26]

Indeed, both Mesmer's fluidim and Swedenborg's influx were rejected by several scientists. Nonetheless, their influence on modern psychological theories can be clearly discerned, as Jeffrey Kripal wrote:

---

22 Ellenberger, *Discovery of the Unconscious*, 148. Also, see ibid., 110, "The cumulative experience of several generations of magnetizers and hypnotists resulted in the slow development of a well-rounded system of dynamic psychiatry. These pioneers undertook with great audacity the exploration and the therapeutic utilization of unconscious psychological energies. On the basis of their findings, they elaborated new theories about the human mind and the psychogenesis of illness. This first dynamic psychiatry was an impressive achievement, even more so since it was brought about mostly outside of—if not directly in opposition to – official medicine."

23 Concerning him see Albanese, *A Republic of Mind and Spirit*, 140–144. His work was called *Arcana Coelestia*. For the relation between mesmerism and Swedenborgianism, see George Bush, *Mesmer and Swedenborg: Or, The Relation of the Developments of Mesmerism to the Doctrines and Disclosures of Swedenborg* (New York: John Allen, 1847).

24 Albanese, *A Republic of Mind and Spirit*, 141. Concerning the influence of his conception of *influx* on later metaphysical and astrological movements, see ibid., 170, 175–176, 208, 333; on the American New Thought movement, ibid., 304–305, 395.

25 Kripal, *Esalen*, 139–140. Also, see ibid., regarding fluidim.

26 Ibid., 140. Kripal discusses Swedenborg's letter combination techniques, but does not mention their origin in ecstatic kabbalah, which made their way into Christian Cabala through the work of Egidio da Viterbo (1469–1532), who learned Hebrew and utilized Abulafian techniques, see Marjorie Reeves, "Cardinal Egidio of Viterbo: A Prophetic Interpretation of History," in *Prophetic Rome in the High Renaissance Period*, ed. Marjorie Reeves (Oxford: Oxford University Press, 1992), 97–99. However, Egidio used these techniques as, and not prophetic, hermeneutical means, while Swedenborg seemingly used them for prophetic purposes. Concerning the use of kabbalistic letter combination for mystical and magical purposes among Christian theologians, see Albanese, *A Republic of Mind and Spirit*, 30–35. Concerning the Abulafian works possessed by Egidio, see Idel, "Agideo da Viterbo and the Writings of Abraham Abulafia," and above, chap. 3, n. 65.

> There is a rather clear historical line of development from the European Mesmerists and Swedenborgians, through the Spiritualists of the 1850s and 60s... to the early psychology of religion... Hypnotism, for example, was an early therapeutic technique developed from the magnetized sleep of the Mesmerists, first fully theorized in 1843 by the English physician James Braid.[27]

The intense preoccupation with modern psychology in early-twentieth-century Vienna allowed concepts from mesmerism to become part of European discourse and enter the vocabulary of everyday speech. Although the ideas of "fluidum" and "magnetism" were rejected as scientific concepts, certain circles accepted them as part of European discourse and terminology, albeit not necessarily in their original meaning of an actual hidden fluid that is modulated by a universal magnetic force but rather in the sense of a spiritual, supernatural influence of one person on another. Additionally, James Braid brought the concept of "suggestion" into everyday terminology, referring to the use of unconscious influence to affect the thoughts of others.

Mesmerism and the Jewish World

The teachings of mesmerism, already in their early days in the late eighteenth century, seeped into the European Jewish world, which was naturally influenced, willingly or unwillingly, by the intellectual developments that were occurring

27 Kripal, *Esalen*, 141. James Braid (1795 – 1860), known as the father of modern hypnosis, was a Scottish surgeon and physiologist who personally encountered mesmerism on November 13, 1841. A Swedish mesmerist name Charles Lafontaine (1803 – 1892) demonstrated mesmerism of patients before a crowd in Manchester, and Braid was in the crowd. Braid was convinced that these patients were in an entirely different physical state and different state of consciousness during the mesmerism. At this event, the idea suddenly came to Braid that he had discovered the natural apparatus of psychophysiology that lay behind these authentic phenomena. See William S. Kroger and Michael D. Yapko, *Clinical and Experimental Hypnosis in Medicine, Dentistry, and Psychology* (Philadelphia: Lippincott, Williams, and Wilkins, 2008), 3. This idea resulted in five public lectures that he gave in Manchester later that month. See James Braid, *Neurypnology: Or the Rationale of Nervous Sleep, Considered in Relation with Animal Magnetism* (London: John Churchill, 1843), 2. Braid rejected Mesmer's idea of fluidum and instead came up with a "pure" psychological model, which made use of the concepts "conscious" and "unconscious" and attributed mesmerism's super-normal powers of healing and perception to the intensive concentration that can be caused artificially by hypnosis. Also, see Alison Winter, *Mesmerized: Powers of Mind in Victorian Britain* (Chicago: University of Chicago Press, 1998), 184 – 186, 287-288.

around it.[28] Rabbi Jacob Ettlinger (1798–1871), one of the leaders of Orthodox Jewry in Germany (known as "the *Arukh la-Ner*" after his Talmudic novella of that name), was asked to deal with the following question: is mesmerism "witchcraft" (*kishuf*), and thus forbidden by Jewish law, or is it not? This was not merely a theoretical question but had a real-life application: is it permissible for a Jew to receive treatment "using the power of *magnetisieren*"? This question was addressed to the rabbi in 1852 by the Jewish community of Amsterdam and referred to one of the later transformations of Mesmer's theory of "animal magnetism," namely the theory of hypnosis, which was beginning to develop in the second half of the nineteenth century. The questioner describes a deep hypnotic state in which the patient is under total anesthesia (lack of feeling), and, out of this deep sleep, displays certain supernatural phenomena. For example, the patient, while completely asleep, will describe events that are occurring in some faraway place, of which the patient cannot possibly have any previous information; this phenomenon is called clairvoyance. Ettlinger's response to this question constitutes the first halakhic discussion of mesmerism, as far as I am aware:

> With God's help. Altona, Tevet [5]612 [=January 1852]. To the Jewish community of Amsterdam, may God preserve it, Amen!
>
> *Question:* There is a pious, prominent individual, who has fallen ill, and he has been advised to seek treatment by means of the power that they call *magnetisieren*; this treatment makes the patient asleep, feeling no sensation at all. According to what they tell, the patient undergoes a great change, and becomes a different man. They say that wondrous things happen: the patient can know what is going on far away, can tell what is going on in secret places, and the like. Therefore, this pious man is hesitant to undergo this treatment, for it seems that it uses supernatural spiritual forces, and therefore he is concerned that it involves the working of the Forces of Impurity (*koḥot ha-ṭum'ah*), which any righteous person will avoid. This pious man will follow whatever you instruct him, O rabbi; so, what do you say to do?
>
> *Answer:* I have consulted non-Jewish scholars regarding their opinion of the power of *magnetisieren*—whether it actually causes any changes in nature, as they claim, or not. I have found that their views differ: some say that the whole thing is a complete lie, and nothing actually happens, but rather the patient's imaginative powers are elevated to the point that he thinks he is seeing wondrous things; others say that indeed, the miraculous visions do occur, and they surely must have some natural cause, but we do not understand

---

28 Nevertheless, it should be noted that even before the development of mesmerism one can find Jewish examples of hypnotic activities and certain individuals who had hypnotic abilities, whether knowingly or unknowingly. The difference is that in the wake of mesmerism, modern psychology and psychiatry developed, and these hypnotic phenomena were attributed more and more to the workings of the human soul (the "unconscious") rather than to magic or to the powers of the practitioner. For a discussion of Jews with hypnotic powers from the thirteenth century through the Beshṭ, see Idel, "'The Besht Passed His Hand over His Face,'" 96.

> it … Therefore, in my opinion, even if it is true that we cannot find any natural explanation of how *magnetisieren* can cause such great changes, nonetheless, we do not need to be concerned that it is caused by the Forces of Impurity, for it is clear from the halakhic authorities and the ruling in the *Arba'a Ṭurim* and *Shulhan Arukh* (section *Yoreh De'ah* §155) that one is allowed to receive treatment that is performed by means of a spell (*lahash*) cast by an idolater, as long as it is not certain that the practitioner is actually mentioning the name of a foreign deity as part of the spell … Surely, such a spell has no basis in natural processes, but nonetheless we are not concerned that it might be using the Forces of Impurity; rather, we attribute its working to one of many natural processes that we do not yet understand. So why should we be any more concerned about *magnetisieren*, whose practitioners believe that it is a natural process, not a spiritual one … And thus, there is no halakhic problem with seeking treatment through *magnetisieren*, whose practitioners say that it is a natural process, even though they are unable to understand its natural basis … We cannot forbid such behaviors except where the Torah has explicitly forbidden them. Therefore, in my humble opinion, it is permitted to seek treatment by means of *magnetisieren*, even for a patient who is not deathly ill. And may he receive help from God.
>
> —Jacob the Small [the rabbi's signature, an expression of humility][29]

Thus, Ettlinger permits the use of mesmerism and distinguishes between "magnetism," on the one hand, and "witchcraft" or "a spell," on the other, based on the subjective understanding of the practitioner. If the practitioner truly believes that the treatment operates according to "a natural process," even if there is no convincing scientific explanation, then it is not witchcraft, nor use of "the name of a foreign deity" or "the powers of impurity." Indeed, Mesmer consistently tried to provide scientific explanations for his treatments, even after the scientific community had rejected him; in the last year of his life he wrote a long "scientific" book in which, once again, he explained his theories.[30] Ettlinger's opinion is that the practitioners' attempts to explain the various phenomena naturalistically make these treatments halakhically permissible, and he distinguishes be-

---

29 Jacob Ettlinger, *Binyan Ṣiyyon Responsa*, 1§67. See also Jacob Bazak, *Beyond the Senses: A Study of Extrasensorial Perception in Biblical, Talmudical, and Rabbinical Literature in the Light of Contemporary Parapsychological Research* (Tel Aviv: Dvir, 1968), 42–43.

30 See Franz Mesmer, *Mesmerismus oder System der Wechsel-Beziehungen: Theorie und Andwendungen des Thierischen Magnetismus* (Berlin: In der Nikolaischen Buchhandlung, 1814). This title shows that even in Mesmer's lifetime, his theory was being called "mesmerism," after his own name, and not just "animal magnetism." It is unclear whether Mesmer had advanced the use of this name over the course of his lifetime or, instead, used it only at the end of his days simply because it had become the accepted term among the masses, who preferred to call the theory after the name of its originator and not by its "scientific" name.

tween these practices, on the one hand, and the use of impure forces or names of foreign deities, on the other.[31]

The growing popularity of mesmerism, which, expectedly, aroused great wonder among the masses, was an inspiration also for Jewish writers and inspired powerful literary motifs. Isaac Baer Levinson (1788–1860), one of the pioneering writers of the Jewish Enlightenment (Haskalah) in the Russian Empire, who studied in Galicia in his youth, wrote an anti-hasidic satire that mentions Mesmer and the name of his theory already in the book's subtitle. The book is called: *The Words of the Righteous with the Valley of the Rephaim: It is the vision in the world of Aṣilut, which one of the visionaries ("somnabul", in the vernacular) saw by means of the techniques and mystical tiqqunim of Mesmer ("mesmerism", in the vernacular), which is called magnetismus.* This satire, which was published in Odessa in 1867, includes a description of an Egyptian rabbi named Levai who knows how to use Mesmer's secrets to perform countless wonders. He uses these "*tiqqunim*" (mystical rectifications) to heal several dangerously ill people.[32] This rabbi brings the patients into a hypnotic trance, such that "several sick people, when the sleep falls upon them, see" wondrous visions. While they are asleep, the patients "answer each question, and speak from the World of *Aṣilut*. They speak of what is above [our world] and what is below, of the living and the dead, and of spiritual matters, regarding whatever is asked of them."[33]

Levinson uses the patients' state of hypnotic sleep as a literary tool to reveal the deceit and corruption of the hasidic leaders. At the end of the treatment, the Egyptian rabbi says, "I remove my hands from the patient, to restore him to his original state, for his strength has already become weak."[34] This anti-hasidic satire thus shows acquaintance with mesmerism, which had reached Eastern Europe.

In the second half of the nineteenth century, several Jewish doctors in Western Europe were practicing hypnosis or researching hypnotism, such as Oscar

---

31 A similar attitude toward hypnosis is expressed in a halakhic responsum by Rabbi Moshe Feinstein, a halakhic authority from the second half of the twentieth century; see *Iggerot Moshe Responsa* (Bnei Brak: s.n., 1981), section *Yoreh De'ah*, 3§44: "Regarding your question of whether it is permitted to use hypnotism as a treatment—I have discussed this with people who know a bit about it, and also with Rabbi J. E. Henkin, and we do not see any halakhic problem in it, for there is no witchcraft in it, for it is a natural phenomenon that certain people have the power to bring upon patients with weak nerves or the like."

32 Isaac Baer Levinsohn, *Divrei Ṣaddikim im Emeq Refa'im* (Odessa: s.n., 1867), 1.

33 Ibid.

34 Ibid., 23. The expression "I remove my hand" can be interpreted in two ways: either as a general description of stopping the hypnotic treatment or as literal removal of the healer's hands from before the patient's face.

Berger (1844-1885) and Hippolite Bernheim. Berger, who was a lecturer at Breslau University, specialized in electro-therapeutic treatments, discussed neurological diseases and hypnosis in his opening lecture.[35] Bernheim, a French Jew and lecturer at the University of Strasbourg as well as the Nancy School, was the head of the hypnosis division within the medical department in 1880.[36]

It should be noted that due to the central role that Jews played in the development of mesmerism and hypnotism, anti-Semitic tropes and images were inserted into these concepts. The figure of Svengali in the novel *Tribly*, a modern best-seller,[37] serves to this day as a stereotypical figure of a malicious Jew who controls others through persuasion, fraud, or demonic and impure powers. The author of *Trilby*, George du Maurier, bequeathed for generations to come the identification of the Jew with the mesmerist and hypnotist, which, within the context of his book, are both phenomena negative. The unconscious forces of the mind are connected to black magic and demonic potencies, which were identified since the Middle Ages with Jews. Terrifying and scary supernatural forces are linked to the Jewish person. Du Maurier utilized this ancient image of the Jew (embodied by Svengali) as an evil figure, who bears bad news, together with the figure of the wandering Jew. Henceforth, the evil Jew is transformed into the mesmerist and hypnotist. Evil becomes the master of the unconscious and conscious and is able to control people. The fallen Jew is portrayed in this book in a more devious fashion, the mesmerizing Jew![38]

---

35 *Jewish Encyclopedia Online*, s.v. "Berger, Oscar," last modified September 13, 2017, http://www.jewishencyclopedia.com/articles/3067-berger-oscar.

36 Regarding the Nancy school and Bernheim, see Ellenberger, *The Discovery of the Unconscious*, 85 – 89.

37 George Du Maurier, *Trilby* (New York: Harper and Brothers, 1894).

38 Anna Maria De Bartolo, *Mesmerism and Jewishness in a Novel by George Du Maurier: Trilby* (Soveria Mannelli: Rubbettino, 2002), 10 – 11. Regarding Du Maurier's (1834-1896) simultaneous encounter with mesmerism and Judaism, see ibid., 16 – 17. A brief synopsis: in 1856 he studied painting in Paris for one year and continued his studies in Antwerp, Belgium. During his studies in Antwerp a "tragedy" happened to him, which he defined as the tragedy of his life. One day, suddenly, while he was sitting and painting, he went blind in his left eye due to retinal detachment. During his recovery, he met and connected with a mysterious Jewish figure named Felix Moscheles (1833 – 1917). For Du Maurier, Felix represented a bohemian figure, half-mystic half-artist with a dominant Jewish identity. Felix quickly became material for Du Maurier's works and the subject for his sketches, as Moscheles testifies in his book *In Bohemia With Du Maurier* (1897). Moscheles introduced Du Maurier to mesmerism and they began to practice it. Moscheles writes in his book that they hypnotized a child and made him think that the key in his hand was burning. However, their preoccupation with mesmerism was not for recreational purposes alone, but was rather a real attempt to penetrate the mental world, the world of the unconscious. On the popularity of this book, which earned this fifty-seven-year-old writer recognition after a long

Menaḥem Ekstein, Mesmerism, and Imaginative Technique

Although Ekstein claims to only use terms from within Judaism in his book *Mental Conditions for Achieving Hasidism*,[39] he in fact uses the words "fluidum" and "suggestiya" (i.e., suggestion). For him, "fluidum" is not a liquid, as it is for Mesmer, but a hidden force that is found in the world, that moves from one person to another, and is expressed by means of the influence of one person on another. By means of this hidden force, Ekstein explains the value that hasidism places on gatherings of hasidim; and, above all, he argues that this hidden force is of great value in hasidic teachings:

> It is well known that hasidism places great value on gatherings on Sabbaths and festivals. The reason for this is that it takes account of the influences and forces that pass between people. ... For we often see how when a person is happy, he can bring joy to a whole group of people, simply by appearing among them, without taking any active steps to entertain them; it is as if invisible lines of joy emanate from him and penetrate into their hearts, and thus arouse feelings of joy in them, as well. Similarly, when someone is sad and bitter, he can bring sadness to others simply by being near them, as if clouds of anguish go in front of him and spread out into the hearts of the others. hasidism places great value on this hidden force (*fluidum*),[40] which issues from every individual; for in matters of religion, this force is even more powerful than in other matters.[41]

> How amazed will all the wise men of the world be when they realize that everything that they currently know about these wondrous forces that people receive from and spread to each other (*suggestiya*) are only like a drop from the sea in comparison to what hasidism knows about this.[42]

He explains the influence of the hasidic *rebbe* on his followers as being due to the same hidden force, which emanates from the *rebbe:*

---

career as a cartoonist, see ibid., 25–26, 34–36. On the characterization of the Jew in *Trilby* and its anti-Semitic roots, see ibid., 59–83.

39 Ekstein, *Tena'ei ha-Nefesh*, 1, "In what ways will it be possible for us to study the way of contemplation and reach it? Let us try and strive to give an answer to this question, *an answer that is anthologized from various places in the books of the hasidim*, here arranged systematically" (emphasis added). See also his introduction to the Yiddish version: "In my book, I have made a first attempt to find appropriate definitions and an appropriate style to express the principles of Hasidic thought, so that they can be accessible to the general reader; *everything is taken from primary sources*" (emphasis added).

40 In the second edition of the book (p. 110), and in the third edition (p. 107), the word "fluidum" is removed. However, the word "suggestiya" was left (see second edition, 112; third edition, 110).

41 Ekstein, *Tena'ei ha-Nefesh*, 50.

42 Ibid., 52.

> If we come close to a person that has already freed his soul from all doubts and hesitation by using them for the goodness of his soul, for he has acquired clear, certain knowledge of his Creator, and this true light already shines thoroughly in him—then we necessarily feel the hidden forces that emanate from him. The greater a person is in spirituality and spiritual perfection, the greater and stronger will be the forces that emanate from him. And especially if the people that draw near to him are also trying to free their souls from doubts and uncertainties, then they will have an even greater experience of the light that emanates from those great people.[43]

Ekstein uses this hidden force also to explain hasidic prayer: "If hasidim pray together, and among them are several great individuals, who have already elevated their souls to a high level, then the room will be full of godly lines, as it were, and the spiritual inspiration passes from one person to another—the greater ones influence the lesser ones."[44]

The common factor behind all these terms—fluidum, light, lines, godly lines—is the basically mesmeristic conception that there is a cosmic force in general, and that there are certain skilled people who know how to make use of it to do good things.[45] In Kabbalistic terms, this comes out thus: there are certain men (such as the *rebbe*) who are able to draw forces from on high, "godly lines,"

---

43 Ibid., 50–51. See what he says there about a strong, extraordinary ability to influence others, even against their will, "For there are some extraordinary instances, in which the words remove all veils, and penetrate the heart with great force, even against the will of the listeners. In general, though, the force goes through only to people who are listening intently, and know how to nullify themselves in favor of the speaker, and want his words to influence them." Ekstein shows here that he understands one of the basic principle of psychotherapeutic and psychiatric treatment: that the therapist and the patient need to cooperate for there to be any influence.

44 Ibid., 51.

45 Of course, one can find similar concepts already in antiquity, and in Jewish literature. My point is that the terms that are used to describe these concepts in their modern form are based on Mesmer's teachings and the subsequent development of psychology. We find similar neo-platonic concepts expressed by the Greek word *pneuma* (πνεῦμα) in theurgy and Hellenistic magic, and later in Islamic philosophy and mysticism, translated as "spirituality." This "spirituality" functions as a cosmic force, which is between humanity and God, and we find the idea of humanity's ability to "bring down the spirituality." Regarding all this, and the attitudes toward it of Judah Halevi and Maimonides, see Shlomo Pines, "On the Term Ruḥaniyyot and its Origin and on Judah Halevi's Doctrine," *Tarbiz*, 57, no. 4 (1988): 511–540. On Halevi's Arabic term *mahall* which describes the sense in which a human being may become an abode for the divine, see Diana Lobel, "A Dwelling Place for the Shekhinah," *JQR*, 90, no. 1–2 (1999): 103–125; idem, *Between Mysticism and Philosophy: Sufi Language of Religious Experience in Judah Ha-Levi's Kuzari* (Albany: State University of New York Press, 2000), 120–145.

and use them in this world to draw emanations, in order to emanate them onto others: "The greater ones influence the lesser ones."[46]

Aaron Marcus (1842–1916) was an author, scholar of the Hebrew language, and active member of the Zionist movement in Galicia. He was born and raised in Hamburg, and studied there with the students of Rabbi Isaac Bernays (1792–1849), the rabbi of Hamburg.[47] Marcus was disappointed by the spiritual life of West European Jewry, so in 1862 he moved to Eastern Europe and settled in Cracow. He was enchanted with, and "caught in the net of" hasidism, and became a follower of Rabbi Solomon of Radomsko (1801–1866) and Rabbi David Moses of Czortków (1827–1903).[48] Marcus was a unique individual, and the first to write a modern interpretation of hasidic thought, written, moreover, in German.[49] Mar-

46 The idea of a cosmic force in this sense, and Mesmer's fluid as an "agent of nature," seems to resonate with Henri Bergson's (1859–1941) *élan vital*, a concept translated worldwide as "vital impulse." This impulse, he argued, was interwoven throughout the universe giving life an unstoppable impulse and surge. See Henri Bergson, *Creative Evolution*, trans. Arthur Mitchell (New York: Holt, 1911), 87, 245–246; Jimena Canales, *The Physicist and the Philosopher: Einstein, Bergson, and the Debate that Changed Our Understanding of Time* (Princeton: Princeton University Press, 2005), 7, 282. See ibid., 27–31 about Bergson's *duration* and *élan vital*, and their connection to mystic faith. It is interesting to note that Bergson was a descendant of a Jewish Polish Family which was the preeminent patron of Polish hasidism in the 19th century; see Glenn Dynner, *Men of Silk: The Hasidic Conquest of Polish Jewish Society* (Oxford: Oxford University Press, 2006), 97–113. In 1908, Max Nordau, a Zionist leader, discounted the ideas of Henri Bergson by proclaiming, "Bergson inherited these fantasies from his ancestors, who were fanatic and fantastic 'wonder-rabbis' in Poland" (Ibid., 97). I am grateful to the anonymous referee of *Modern Judaism* who drew my attention to Bergson's *élan vital* and its similarity to the ideas in this paper.

47 On R. Isaac Bernays, see Yehoshua Horowitz, "Isaac ben Jacob Bernays," in *Encyclopaedia Judaica*, 2nd ed. (Detroit: MacMillan Reference USA, 2007), 3:469–470; Isaac Heinemann, "The Relationship between S. R. Hirsch and His Teacher Isaac Bernays," *Zion* 16 (1951): 69–90. It is worth mentioning that Isaac Bernays's granddaughter married Sigmund Freud, see Margaret Muckenhoupt, *Sigmund Freud: Explorer of the Unconscious* (New York: Oxford University Press, 1997), 26 (I would like to thank my friend Gavriel Wasserman for bringing this to my attention). Regarding a Zionist pamphlet that Marcus published, and Theodor Herzl's reaction to the pamphlet, see Herzl's article "Dr. Gidmann's 'National Judaism,'" found in Hebrew on the Ben-Yehuda Project, http://benyehuda.org/herzl/herzl_009.html.

48 See Wunder, *Me'orei Galiṣiyah*, 3:969–971.

49 See Moses Tsinovitsh, "R. Aaron Marcus—The Pioneer of Hasidic Literature," *Ortodoksishe Yugend Bleter* 39 (1933): 7–8; Vili Aron, "Aaron Marcus, the 'German' who became a Hasid," *Yivo Bleter* 29 (1947), 143–148; Yocheved Segal, *The Chasid from Hamburg: A Portrait of Rabbi Aharon Marcus, A Man of Truth, Courage, Genius, and Humility*, trans. Bracha Slae (New York: Feldheim, 2004); Markus Marcus, *Ahron Marcus: Die Lebensgeschichte eines Chossid* (Montreux: David Marcus, 1966). Regarding Marcus's authenticity in his descriptions, see Uriel Gelman, "The Great Wedding in Uściług: The Making of a Myth," *Tarbiz* 80, no. 4 (2013): 574–580. For certain doubts that can be raised about Marcus's reliability, see ibid., 590–594; for further

cus viewed the hasidic teachings of Eastern Europe as a new psychological theory, which brought freshness to Jewish spiritual life. For Marcus, psychological phenomena such as "suggestion" and "autosuggestion" (the ability to convince oneself to the point of influencing the physical) explained the wondrous phenomena that he saw and heard about among the hasidim. When a certain Hasid agreed to die in place of the Sadigura Rebbe, and thus to redeem the latter from death, Marcus explained this as an example of the phenomenon of autosuggestion:

> When the Sadigura Rebbe returned home, he became so weak that the doctors worried that he might die any minute. ... Then his brother, R. Dov of Leova, went out to the people, and said: "O hasidim, do you have anyone among you who is prepared to take upon himself the decree of death that has been decreed upon my brother?"... Immediately, a certain young scholar, R. Mordecai Michel of Lisk, volunteered to rescue the *rebbe* with his own life. One might explain this as being by the power of autosuggestion, but one cannot deny the fact. The volunteer became sick after about a day, invited the members of the burial society, happily bade farewell to his friends, and departed this life. The *rebbe* recovered.[50]

Like Ekstein, Marcus explains the influence of the *rebbe* on his hasidim in terms of the power of suggestion. Marcus presents his readers with a story that he has heard in a first-hand account from the very individual who experienced the suggestive influence of the Sadigura Rebbe, when he met with him:

> I have had the opportunity to observe this phenomenon among reliable personalities. A certain Russian [Jewish] soldier, named Abramowitz, was the son of a border-smuggler... The son was even more coarse and boorish than the father; he had no semblance of any religious feeling. He encountered me in a trading house where he was working, and once told me about his experience: he escaped from Klept,[51] risking his life, along with three other soldiers; after a number of adventures, he arrived at Sadigura, past the Romanian border. "I don't know what happened to me," he said, "but when the Rebbe spoke to me, I broke into uncontrollable tears. I had never cried like this since my childhood." I have no doubt that there wasn't a single spark of religiosity in that man, which could have caused this crying to occur by self-suggestion.[52]

clear mistakes that Marcus made, see Gershon Kitzis, "Aaron Marcus's 'Hasidism,'" *Ha-Ma'ayan*, 21, no. 1 (1981): 64–88.

50 Aaron Marcus, *Hasidism*, trans. Moshe Schoenfeld (Bnei Brak: Neṣaḥ 1980), 242. The German title of the book is *Der Chassidismus: Eine Kulturgeschichtliche Studie* (Pleschen: Jeschurun, 1901).

51 This is evidently the name of a place, but I have not been able to identify it.

52 Ibid., 239.

In other words, Marcus argues that we cannot explain this case as an example of autosuggestion, but only as absolute suggestion (of one individual on another). The Russian Jewish soldier did not have any concealed religious spark with him; hence he could be moved only by the *rebbe*'s direct influence. Marcus recognizes and values Mesmer's theory of magnetism, and writes: "Among all the other evidence … of the validity of 'animal magnetism,' we must note the precise testimony given by the eyewitness 'Vigors' (in his book *The Bible and New Discoveries*, 1868), who has determined without a doubt that we are dealing with a scientific problem in nature … if Napoleon and Mohammed succeeded in gathering hundreds of thousands of people around them, we cannot attribute this to their words, but only to their suggestive powers."[53]

We see a relationship between developments in psychological-hypnotic praxis, on the one hand, and hasidic practice, on the other, in Marcus's descriptions of Rabbi Shalom Rokeah of Belz (1781–1855), who would heal physical and mental ailments by making hand-motions, similar to hypnosis:

> [The Belzer Rebbe] was an expert at treating spiritual diseases and paralyses, which all the doctors had despaired of ever treating. In thousands of cases, his activity was confirmed by Jews and gentiles, nobles and peasants; it aroused the interest of heads of colleges, who subsequently spent many decades trying to explain the phenomenon from the point of view of the new science of psychology, which is influenced by the spiritist approach.[54]

Imagery Techniques and Modern Psychology

The imagery exercises developed by Ekstein cannot be explained purely against the background of mesmerism. Along with "animal magnetism," there was another central factor of influence, namely, developments in the concept of imagination in Western philosophy. As Ellenberger writes:

> Another very important source of the first dynamic psychiatry was the old concept of 'imagination'. At the time of the Renaissance, philosophers and physicians became very interest-

53 Ibid., 385. Also, see ibid., 381–382, about a Jewish woman who underwent hypnotherapy and demonstrated supernatural powers during this treatment, "Dr. Bini Cohen, Bismarck's personal doctor […] hypnotized the wife of R. Gitsh Folk, a Polish Jewish woman, living in Hamburg, who did not know how to read or write German, and had fallen dangerously ill."

54 Ibid., 225. He mentions there that the Belzer *rebbe* performed his treatments by passing his hands over the patient's face. On the Beshṭ's similar techniques, see Idel, "The Besht Passed His Hand over His Face," 79–106.

ed in a power of the mind, Imaginatio, a term that held a much broader meaning than it does today and included what we call suggestion and autosuggestion.[55]

Ekstein's and Shapira's imagery techniques and their multi-scenic creative character should seemingly be understood against this background, that of the "creative imagination," and visual techniques found throughout Jewish mysticism.

In the first chapter I discussed different Western models of imagination. This development directly affected psychology. This affect can be found in Théodule-Armand Ribot's (1839–1916) book *Essai sur l'imagination créatrice* (*Essays on the Creative Imagination*), published in 1900. Ribot uses the philosophically developed conception for psychological ends. This book was even translated into Hebrew under the title *Ha-Dimyon ha-Yoṣer* (*The Creative Imagination*) and was published in Warsaw, Moscow, and New York in 1921.[56] It was distributed by Shtibel (Stybel) Press,[57] and thus was readily available to European readers of Hebrew literature, and perhaps may have played a role in spreading the modern conception of imagination to European Jewry.[58]

---

55 Ellenberger, *The Discovery of the Unconscious*, 110–111.

56 Théodule-Armand Ribot, *The Creative Imagination: Psychological Essay*, trans. Nissan Turov (New York, Warsaw, and Moscow: Shtibel Press, 1921).

57 Shtibel Press (sometimes written as Stybel) was founded by Abraham Joseph Shtibel, with branches in Warsaw, Tel Aviv, Berlin, and New York. This press published the journal *Ha-Tekufah* and was a central platform for Hebrew publications and translations. This press also published kabbalistic works, such as Shmuel Abba Horodezky, *Ha-Mistorin be-Yisra'el*

58 Ribot divides the imagination into two primary categories: the "plastic imagination" and the "diffluent imagination," from which the mystical imagination stems. He writes, "By 'plastic imagination' I understand that which has for its special characters clearness and precision of form; more explicitly those forms whose materials are clear images (whatever be their nature), approaching perception, giving the impression of reality; in which, too, there predominate *associations with objective relations*, determinable with precision. The plastic mark, therefore, is in the images, and in the modes of association of images." Théodule Ribot, *Essay on the Creative Imagination*, trans. Albert H. N. Baron (London: Kegan Paul, Trench, Trübner, 1906), 184. This imagination is obviously used by those involved in the plastic arts, sculptors, painters, and the like (ibid., 187). It is also used by novelists and writers in order to create evoking images through literary form. Ribot writes regarding Hugo, "Thus we are told that 'he never dictates or rhymes from memory and composes only in writing, for he believes that writing has its own features, and he wants to *see the words*'" (ibid., 188–189). Ribot refers to it as an "external imagination," since it emerges from the senses and strives to materialize (ibid., 185). In contrast the "diffluent imagination... consists of vaguely-outlined, indistinct images that are evoked and joined according to the least rigorous modes of association" (ibid., 195). Ribot calls these images, "Emotional abstraction" (ibid., 196). The results of this imagination are within the emotions and, therefore, Ribot sees it as an internal imagination. It "is, trait for trait, the opposite of the plastic imagination... Its creations... act by diffusion and inclusion" (ibid., 197). It has a spontaneous

In the fifth chapter I examined the development of imagery techniques from the beginning of kabbalah until late hasidism. As I wrote, the visual techniques in kabbalah are primarily linguistic in nature, in which one is to visualize the letters of the divine name, whereas in early hasidism the techniques become less linguistic and more scenic, although they remain static. It is only in later hasidism thatthe imagery techniques take on an entirely new character that is qualitatively distinct from its predecessors, that of a multi-scenic plot, akin to a dream or film.[59] It seems to me that we must understand this development against the background of parallel developments in techniques of imagination in Western psychology. Already in studies in the late 1940s, Raphael Straus noted that the changes in the roles of *Ba'alei Shem* (Jewish mystical wonder-workers) must be understood in the context of the development of mesmerism.[60]

---

quality, in which, "an attribute is... arbitrarily selected because it impresses us at the given instant in the final analysis, because it somehow pleases or displeases us" (ibid., 196). This imagination is found in dreams, delusions, and the spirit of the fairy tales. The musical imagination is included in this category as well (ibid., 212). Regarding the composer Schumann he writes, "From the age of eight, he would amuse himself with sketching what might be called musical portraits, drawing by means of various turns of song and varied rhythms the shades of character, and even the physical peculiarities, of his young comrades. He sometimes succeeded in making such striking resemblances that all would recognize, with no further designation, the figure indicated by the skillful fingers that genius was already guiding" (ibid., 215–216). Ribot saw these two imaginations as polar opposites, one internal-emotional and the other external-sensory. However, Ribot also discussed "sub-categories" of imagination, including the mystical imagination (ibid., 221–235). Regarding it, he wrote, "Mystic imagination deserves a place of honor, as it is the most complete and most daring of purely theoretic invention. Related to diffluent imagination, especially in the latter's affective form, it has its own special characters, which we shall try to separate out" (ibid., 221). According to Ribot, "The root of the mystic imagination consists of a tendency to incarnate the ideal in the sensible, to discover a hidden 'idea' in every material phenomenon or occurrence... Its fundamental character... is thus a way of thinking *symbolically*" (ibid., 222; concerning symbolism in kabbalah, see Gershom Scholem, *On the Kabbalah and Its Symbolism*, trans. Ralph Manheim [New York: Schocken Books, 1965], 22–24, 47–53, 87–117). Ribot wrote, "The originality of mystic imagination is found in this fact: It transforms concrete images into symbolic images, and uses them as such. It extends this process even to perceptions, so that all manifestations of nature or of human art take on a value as signs or symbols" (Ribot, *Essay on the Creative Imagination*, 223). Related to symbolism, Ribot discussed its metaphorical expression and extensive use of analogy (ibid., 224–225). What I have quoted is of primary importance for our understanding, while I have also omitted his derogatory tone towards kabbalah, of which he writes of their thought that it is, "a world of unbridled fancy which, in place of human romances, invents cosmic romances" (ibid., 234).

59 See above, chap. 4, subchapter "R. Kalonymous Kalman Shapira's Imagery Techniques and His Imaginal-Literary Style."

60 Raphael Straus, "The Baal-Shem of Michelstadt: Mesmerism and Cabbala," *Historica Judaica*, 8, no. 2 (1946): 135–148.

The "*Ba'al Shem* of Michelstadt," Rabbi Isaac Zekl Leyb Wormser (1768–1847), the rabbi of the city of Michelstadt, Germany, was known for his healing powers. His medical "miracles" won him great popularity in Germany, among both Jews and non-Jews. His private journals, which describe his treatments over a period of two years, list 1500 patients from seven hundred places. Most are women, either during pregnancy or after childbirth, who have been diagnosed with various nervous disorders. His prescriptions for them usually are the recitation of psalms, either by the community or by relatives; giving charity secretly; checking *mezuzot* and *tefillin*; changing the patient's name; wearing gold rings inscribed with the name of Raphael (the angel of healing); wearing white clothes; and occasionally also fasting.[61] Often the *Ba'al Shem* of Michelstadt is asked to give advice about nonmedical matters. His diaries indicate that he believed every physical symptom is psychological in origin.[62]

Karl Grözinger identifies a change in the understanding of the role of the *Ba'al Shem*, which occurred in the eighteenth century—from a healer of physical ailments to a healer of spiritual ailments; from a healer of the body to a healer of the soul. This change is evident in the roles of the *Ba'al Shem* of Michelstadt, of the *Ba'alei Shem* of eighteenth-century Frankfurt, and of the Ba'al Shem Tov (Besht̩, founder of hasidism).[63] Straus maintains that the activities of the *Ba'al Shem* of Michelstadt, and specifically his focus on spiritual healing, must be understood in light of the development of Mesmer's teachings:

> Considering Wormser's interest in scholarship, one can not refer his miracle-healings to old cabbalistic leanings alone. True, in his lifetime the rise of a scientific way of miracle-healing, under the name of 'mesmerism' had created a sensation in Europe. It is unlikely that Wormser should not have learned of Mesmer's 'animalic magnetism' during his stay in Frankfort or Mannheim, and not have combined this then famous theory with his own cabbalistic views.[64]

All this is even more true of Ekstein. It should be borne in mind that Ekstein developed his imagery exercises in a specific place and time—in Vienna, in the years following World War I.

---

61 Ibid., 139–142.

62 Ibid., 143; see examples there and on the subsequent page.

63 Karl E. Grözinger, "Zekl Leib Wormser, the Ba'al Shem of Michelstadt," in *Judaism, Topics, Fragments, Faces, Identities: Jubilee Volume in Honor of Rivka*, ed. Haviva Pedaya and Ephraim Meir (Beer Sheva: Ben-Gurion University of the Negev Press, 2007), 507. See also his book: Karl E. Grözinger, *Der Ba'al Schem von Michelstadt: ein deutsch-jüdisches Heiligenleben zwischen Legende und Wirklichkeit* (Frankfurt: Campus Verlag, 2010).

64 Straus, "Baal-Shem of Michelstadt," 146.

Vienna: Authority and Mysticism

Carl Schorske, in his seminal work *Fin-de-Siècle Vienna: Politics and Culture*, discusses the connection between the "political" and "cultural" dimensions of Vienna at the close of the nineteenth century.[65] Traditional Austrian culture, unlike that of its neighbor Germany, was not concerned with philosophy, ethics, or science; instead Austria was primarily concerned with aesthetics. Vienna's major contribution at the turn of the century was in the realm of the arts: architecture, theater, and music. Art became almost a religion in Vienna, a source of meaning and sustenance for the soul.[66]

Schorske argues that this phenomenon stemmed directly from the political dimension. In the last decade of the nineteenth century, the rise of right-wing, conservative, anti-Semitic influences led to the collapse of liberalism and left the small liberal intellectual community in Vienna shocked and alienated. The strong tendency among the remnants of this liberal upper class was simply to despair of the political situation, and to turn instead toward aesthetic romanticism—and the occult. That is, the world of aesthetics became, for the liberals, a refuge from the rising, racist political reality. Paradoxically, in their very escape from reality to art, this elite group created an impressive high culture.[67] In other words, the extraordinary vibrancy of Viennese culture at the close of the nineteenth century resulted from the weakening of the liberal bourgeoisie, which ended up imitating the aesthetic of the nobility.

Although Schorske's views are not gospel truth nor immune to criticism, they are challenging and have produced great resonance in the scholarly community. Steven Beller argues that Schorske has ignored the Jewish aspect,[68] and that in fact, Viennese high culture around 1900 was effectively Jewish culture. The leading figures in the liberal bourgeois intelligentsia were Jewish, and they constituted the basis of the cultural revival. According to Beller, the Viennese culture was fundamentally Jewish,[69] and the work of Sigmund Freud or

---

65 Carl E. Schorske, *Fin-de-Siècle Vienna: Politics and Culture* (New York: A. A. Knopf, 1980).

66 Ibid., 7–9.

67 Ibid., 3–23. More on the character of Viennese bourgeoisie and the collapse of liberalism, see Allen Janik and Stephen Toulmin, *Wittgenstein's Vienna* (New York: Simon and Schuster, 1973), 33–66.

68 Steven Beller, *Vienna and the Jews, 1867–1938: A Cultural History* (Cambridge: Cambridge University Press 1989).

69 In his book he attempts to define the culture as inherently Jewish, not just as a culture produced by Jews.

Karl Kraus was "nothing other than a culture produced against its Viennese environment."[70] Either way—whether the liberal Viennese group is defined as Jewish or merely as liberal—it fled from the racist "real world" of politics and closed itself off in the realm of aesthetics and art, which, in a certain sense, are the world of imagination and mysticism.

One domain of the world of mysticism and imagination is that of music, which underwent development in Vienna by the Austrian Jewish composer Arnold Schönberg (1874–1951). Schönberg, the leader of the "Composers of the Second Viennese School" and a trailblazer in twentieth-century atonal music, composed music for some poems by the German poet Stefan George (1868–1933). George's absolute adherence to "sacred art," and his mystical sense of humanity's unity with the cosmos, attracted Schönberg's attention. "George's poetry had the synesthetic characteristics appropriate to the artist-priest's mystical unifying function: a language magical in sonority and an imagery rich in color."[71]

The bitter results of World War I intensified the Viennese mood of escape from real life to the world of mysticism and imagination. As Stefan Zweig wrote with his characteristic sharpness:

> How wild, anarchic and unreal were those years, years in which, with the dwindling value of money all other values in Austria and Germany began to slip! ... Every extravagant idea that was not subject to regulation reaped a golden harvest: theosophy, occultism, spiritualism, somnambulism, anthroposophy, palm-reading, graphology, yoga and Paracelsism [paracelsianism]. Anything that gave hope of newer and greater thrills ... found a tremendous market; ... unconditionally prescribed, however, was any representation of normality and moderation.[72]

Interestingly, Zweig characterizes the flight to "every extravagant idea that was not subject to regulation" as a reactionary activity, a response to the sorry state of the country and of politics:

> A tremendous inner revolution occurred during those first post-war years. Something besides the army had been crushed: faith in the infallibility of the authority to which we had been trained to over-submissiveness in our own youth. ... It was only after the

70 See Michael A. Meyer, "Review of Steven Beller 'Vienna and the Jews, 1867–1938: A Cultural History,'" *AJS Review*, 16, no. 1–2 (1991): 236–239. Meyer presents Beller's analysis as being the opposite of Schorske's, but I am not convinced of this.

71 Schorske, *Fin-de-Siècle Vienna*, 348–349. More on Schönberg and his critique of music and society, see Janik and Toulmin, *Wittgenstein's Vienna*, 106–112, 250–256.

72 Stefan Zweig, *The World of Yesterday*, trans. Anthea Bell (Lincoln: University of Nebraska Press, 1964), 301.

> smoke of war had lifted that the terrible destruction that resulted became visible. How could an ethical commandment still count as holy which sanctioned murder and robbery under the cloak of heroism and requisition for four long years? How could a people rely on the promises of a state which had annulled all those obligations, to its citizens which it could not conveniently fulfill?[73]

Obeying authority had been an integral part of Austrian culture. The outcomes of World War I, however, fostered a change: a rebellion against authority and a search for new values. In Zweig's view, this rebellion afforded leverage to the mystical and occult culture that flourished in Vienna after the war. Although Schorske's book does not deal with the postwar period, his theory that the efflorescence of art, imagination, and mysticism marked a flight from the bleak political reality is even more applicable to that era, post-World War I.

Mesmerism and hypnotism already received renewed interest at the turn of the nineteenth century (1880–1920), among Western esoteric societies, as well as Jewish mystics and hasidim. In 1856 a Hebrew book, entitled *Oṣar Ḥokhmah*, by Julius (Yehuda) Barasch was published, which discussed, among other subjects, mesmerism and para-psychology.[74] He explains oneiric and visionary phenomena through mesmerism, in a manner that is unequivocally sympathetic to this theory, "The source of the name "mesmerism" is from the name Mesmer, who was a celebrated physician and was in Vienna and Paris. He was the first to find and discover this knowledge... For those readers who know the languages of the nations, they will find many books, in German (*ashkenazit*), French, English (*beriṭa'it*), and Italian, which speak about this wonderous topic."[75] This book served as an important source for R. Shelomo Ṣevi Shick (1844–1916), from among the disciples and family of R. Moshe Shick (known as, Maharam Shick), for his explanation of para-psychological phenomena found in medieval

73 Ibid., 297–298.

74 Julius Barasch, *Thesaurus Scientiarum*, intro. S. Y. Rapaport (Vienna: Joseph Holzwarte, 1856). This work is only an inkling of his work, of which another 8 booklets can be found at the Jerusalem National Library MS. B 758 38°1893.

75 Ibid., 130–131. One may find non-Hebrew Jewish works that discuss mesmerism and parapsychology as well, such as Moritz Wiener, *Selma Die Jüdische Seherin: Traumleben und Hellsehen Einer Durch Animalischen Magnetismus Wiederhergestellten Kranken* (Berlin: L. Fernbach, 1838). Wiener discusses a woman named Selma, who, through mesmeric therapy, enters into a state of trance and saw things occurring in faraway places, about which she should not have been able to know. For more on this book, see Zeitlin, *The Other Dimension*, 208–210.

rabbinic literature by using mesmeric theories.[76] In 1879, another Hebrew book was published in Vienna under the title *Torat ha-Ḥayyim* (*The Living Torah*), which discusses mesmerism and the "unconscious."[77]

Vienna: The Meeting Place of Hasidic Psychology and Western Psychology

This leads us back to Menaḥem Ekstein's psychology and mystical teachings, which he developed in Vienna after World War I. It must be noted that at the time of the war tens of thousands of Jews came to Vienna as war refugees, most from the frontier cities of the Austrian Empire in Galicia and Bukovina.[78] These refugees brought an East European Jewish spirit to Vienna, a Western city. Among them were many hasidic *rebbe*s, along with their courts. All these *rebbe*s gathered around them a concentration of thousands of hasidim, who continued their East European ways of life almost unchanged and "introduced a new Jewish bloodstream ... into the arteries of the Viennese community."[79]

The encounter of the hasidim of Galicia with the progressive culture of Vienna was fraught.[80] Although secularization and enlightenment had also made inroads in Galicia, hasidic writings indicate that the Western culture of Vienna threatened their traditional lifestyle more considerably. Rabbi Shlomo Hayim Friedman (1887–1972), the *rebbe* of Sadagora, moved to Vienna during World War I and continued to conduct his court there. His sermons from that period have been collected and published as a book, *Ḥayyei Shelomo.*[81] In 1918, he

---

76 Shelomo Ṣevi Shick, *Me-Mosheh ad Mosheh* (Mukachevo: Druck von Kahn and Fried, 1903), 17–20. For example, Solomon ibn Adret's testimony regarding para-psychological phenomena, as found in Solomon ibn Adret, *Responsa*, §548, see Shick, *Me-Mosheh ad Mosheh*, 18.

77 Aharon Paries, *Torat ha-Ḥayyim* (Vienna: Georg Brag, 1880); concerning mesmerism, see ibid., 80–81.

78 Regarding the 77,000 Jewish refugees in Vienna at the time of World War I, see Ungerfeld, *Vienna*, 120–124. On the flow of Jews from Galicia and Bukovina to Vienna, see David Rechter, *The Jews of Vienna and the First World War* (London: Littman Library of Jewish Civilization, 2001), 67–100. According to Rechter's count, 150,000 Jewish refugees arrived in Vienna over the course of World War I. See ibid., 74, 80–82; also, see ibid., 72, where he says that this number increased anti-Semitism. On Jewish immigration before World War I, see Marsha L. Rozenblit, *The Jews of Vienna 1867–1914: Assimilation and Identity* (Albany: State University of New York Press, 1983), 13–45.

79 Ungerfeld, *Vienna*, 129–130. See also Harriet Pass Freidenreich, *Jewish Politics in Vienna 1918–1938* (Bloomington: Indiana University Press, 1991), 138–146.

80 On the tensions between the liberal Austrian Jews and the Orthodox immigrants from Galicia, see Rechter, *Jews of Vienna*, 179–186.

81 Shlomo Hayim Friedman, *Ḥayyei Shelomoh* (Jerusalem: Mehudar, 2006).

gave a sermon for the opening of a new library of traditional Jewish works in Vienna. In it he discusses the uniqueness of hasidism and its ability to rescue the displaced Jews who wander from place to place after the war,[82] and find themselves in Western cities that "defile the soul." Friedman speaks of the powerful influence of the West and the failure of many Jews to resist it, as evident in their abandonment of the Torah and its commandments, especially their violation of the Sabbath. To counteract this trend, Friedman calls on his listeners to open a network of Jewish schools for children:

> And in order to bring Jewish children to the chambers of Torah, we need to establish schools for learning Torah, to which parents will bring their children. We need to stop the flow of hundreds of thousands of Jews to the four corners of the earth, in the aftermath of the war, to places that defile the Jewish spirit and bring them to throw off the yoke of the Torah and its commandments, and, especially, to desecrate the Sabbath.[83]

Thus, in Vienna, Ekstein and many like him were exposed both to a more Western, secular culture than they had known in Galicia (as emerges from Friedman's testimony) and to mystical and occult culture and mentalities, as evident in Stefan Zweig's description of contemporary Vienna. Indeed, mesmerism and hypnosis became topics of renewed interest in Vienna already in the second half of the nineteenth century, both in Western esoteric circles and in Jewish mystical and hasidic circles.

R. Jekuthiel Aryeh b. Gershon Kamelhar, Ekstein's closest teacher, also ended up in Vienna after World War I and later emigrated to the United States.[84] In his book *Dor De'ah*, he explains fundamental hasidic ideas, such as "the ascent of the soul," on the basis of the teachings of mesmerism and principles of psychiatric study that had developed in Vienna:

> It has become clear that the art of somnambulism, which a certain scholar and doctor invented in Vienna in 1776,[85] can numb the body's physical forces; ... and by means of such

---

82 In 1915 there were about 600,000 Jews who were homeless as a result of the war; see Rechter, *Jews of Vienna*, 68.

83 Friedman, *Ḥayyei Shelomoh*, 264. See also his sermons that discuss the tension between the Orthodox immigrants and the Jews of Vienna, the *Ostjuden* and *Westjuden*, ibid., 277: "The Sabbath-desecrators claim that they too are 'good Jews' [...] but those 'good Jews' have torn down, and continue to tear down, the foundations of Judaism, on which the whole structure stands; and without structure, the nation cannot stand" (Vienna, 31st day of the Omer [May 18–19], 1935). On the cultural assimilation of the *Westjuden* of Vienna, see Rozenblit, *Jews of Vienna 1867–1914: Assimilation and Identity.*

84 See Mondshine, *Ha'Tsofeh Le'Doro*, 150–151, 154, 165.

85 That is, Franz Mesmer.

> inventions, wondrous powers of the soul have been discovered, and become known to many through the books of the gentiles. ... And thus we can understand that the hasidic leader's [*ṣaddiq*'s] soul ... has purified all his limbs and uses them as God desires, and while the physical senses do not disturb him...the gates of heaven will be opened for him—in the inner chambers of his heart, which show the wonders of heaven [*hekhalot*], and allow him to hear prophecies about the future. ... This is precisely the "ascent of the soul" that is told about the Ba'al Shem Tov, blessed be the memory of the righteous.[86]

Thus, Vienna was a meeting place between East European hasidic psychology and Western psychology, which was undergoing stages of accelerated development.[87] Here is an appropriate place to mention the 1903 meeting in Vienna between R. Shalom Dovber Schneersohn (1860 – 1920), the fifth *rebbe* of the Ḥabad dynasty, and Sigmund Freud, an encounter that has been discussed in studies by Maya Balakirsky Katz and by Jonathan Garb.[88]

The Hebrew literature that deals with mesmerism, the unconscious, and imagination developed specifically in Vienna, which was also the meeting point of Eastern and Western Europe during Ekstein's time there after World War I. This, and the flourishing of mysticism and rebellion against rationalism, which Zweig describes so well, are significant facts that must constantly be kept in mind when studying Ekstein's concepts.[89] It is reasonable to assume that Ek-

---

86 Jekuthiel Aryeh Kamelhar, *Dor De'ah: Arba'ah Tequfot Ḥasidut Beshṭit be-Shenot Ṭav-Quf–Ṭav-Resh-Qaf* (Ashdod: Makhon Zikhron Qdoshei Polin, 1998), 53. Menachem Ekstein was familiar with Kamelhar's books; he sometimes even funded their publication. See, for example, Kamelhar's acknowledgments to Ekstein for funding the publication of his book *Hasidim Rishonim*, at the end of the preface. Note especially Kamelhar's affectionate words about Ekstein there: "My dear friend Menachem, who restores my soul [cf. Lamentations 1:16], may his light shine, from the city Rzesów." See also Mondshine's theory in *Ha'Tsofeh Le'Doro*, 150, that Kamelhar and Ekstein spent Passover together in 1918 in Vienna.

87 For more discussion of the interface between Eastern and Western Europe at the turn of the century, see the foundational article by Paul Mendes-Flohr, "Orientalism and Mysticism: The Aesthetic of the Turn of the Nineteenth Century and Jewish Identity," *Jerusalem Studies in Jewish Thought* 3, no. 4 (1984): 624 – 681; idem, "Fin-de-siècle Orientalism, the 'Ostjuden' and the Aesthetics of Jewish Self-Affirmation," *Studies in Contemporary Jewry* 1 (1984): 96 – 139.

88 Maya Balakirsky Katz, "An Occupational Neurosis: A Psychoanalytic Case History of a Rabbi," *AJS Review* 34, no. 1 (2010): 1 – 31; Garb, *Shamanic Trance*, 145 – 147.

89 I intend to write at length, elsewhere, about the Hasidic vibrancy and the extensive use of imagination that occurred in immigrant Hasidic communities in Vienna after World War I. To mention one example, Rabbi David Yiṣḥaq Rabinowitz (1898 – 1979), the Rebbe of Skole (Skolye), immigrated to Vienna after World War I where he wrote his *Book of Visions* (in three volumes), in which he describes his imagination and visions; the manuscript is today in the hands of the current Skolye Rebbe in the United States. Regarding this manuscript, see "Minhagei Qodesh: Minhagei Yom Shabat Qodesh she-Nahag K"Q Maran ADMV"R ZṢVQLLH"H," *Qoveṣ Be'er Yiṣḥaq* 3

stein encountered the teachings of mesmerism and the study of the unconscious in Vienna, where he developed his unique imagery techniques, which make use of imagination and visualization to reveal the unconscious layers of the soul.

I have pointed out that Plato's negative attitude toward imagination turned into a positive one in modern philosophy and psychology, which viewed imagination as a productive force, "the creative imagination"; in parallel, psychotherapy developed techniques of imagery, from mesmerism to hypnosis to psychoanalysis. Although the development of imagery techniques in kabbalah and hasidism is not proven to be directly influenced by the development of modern psychiatry, I believe it is impossible to understand such development in hasidism without taking into account the trends in eighteenth-century Europe, which intensified during the nineteenth century and reached a zenith in the early twentieth century.

The rabbinic attitudes toward the phenomenon of "magnetism," as taught by Franz Mesmer, are evidence of the involvement of European Jewry, in the German-speaking areas, with what was going on around them. This involvement makes possible the understanding of imagery techniques among hasidim, against the European background from which the techniques had arisen. Moreover, this European atmosphere forms the background, to a certain extent, for understanding the channeling of such imagery techniques in hasidism to the field of psychotherapy.

B Transformation of Traditional Concepts into Modern Concepts and the Translation of Kabbalah into Psychological Terminology

Gershom Scholem famously wrote that the major feature of hasidism is that "the secrets of the divine realm are presented in the guise of mystical psychology."[90] Nonetheless, as Moshe Idel has demonstrated, this translation of kabbalistic conceptions is not an innovation of hasidism, but can already be found in earlier

(January-February 2001), 77–79. Regarding another encounter between East and West that took place in Vienna that changed the outlook of the Rebbe Israel of Czortków on the writing of historiographical works, see Mondshine, *Ha'Tsofeh Le'Doro*, 153–154.

90 Scholem, *Major Trends*, 341. Also, see idem, *Explication and Implications*, 353–354. Also see Margolin, *The Human Temple*, 26–27, in which he claims that this statement is a reflection of Scholem's understanding of Buber's statement, "Hasidism is the Kabbala become ethos," Martin Buber, *The Tales of Rabbi Nachman*, trans. Maurice Friedman (New York: Horizon Press, 1979), 10.

kabbalistic sources. Abulafia primarily understood the Torah to be discussing spiritual acquisitions and translated the sefirotic realm into human spiritual potencies. Abulafia offered a consistent and ordered psychological interpretation of the *sefirot*, thereby assimilating his opposition's categories and concepts, while drastically transforming their semantic field to include psychological significance.[91] This conception of the *sefirot* as being an integral feature of man[92] is found in the work *Sefer ha-Peli'ah*, and was thereby available to hasidic masters.[93] Also, the kabbalist Joseph ben Shalom Ashkenazi, a contemporary of Abulafia, offered a psychological rendering of the *sefirot*, and did not portray them solely as metaphysical entities, but as correlating to man's corporeal and spiritual potencies. Additionally, he discussed the human sefirotic tree.[94] These tendencies can be found as well in sixteenth and seventeenth century kabbalah, such as that of Abraham Cohen de Herrera and Joseph Solomon Delmedigo, as well as Safedian kabbalah.[95] Although this conception was not central in various formulations of kabbalah, it did exist. Hasidism, rather than innovate, renewed and expanded upon a marginal trend and placed it in the center of spiritual life.[96] That which Abulafia did to theosophic kabbalah, hasidism did to Lurianic kabbalah. The purpose of hasidism, similar to Abulafia, was to reach a state of *devequt* and this goal became a central component of human experience. Dov Baer of Międzyrzecz's students disseminated a psychological kabbalist theosophy in order to create a concrete path of psychological-religious worship.[97]

The hasidic internalization, analyzed extensively by Ron Margolin, did not only affect the sefirotic doctrine, but all realms of religious life.[98] This "internalization" is to some extent a psychological translation of different concepts; by definition, as a mental aspect of the life of a religious person, it is understood that any act of internalization is an act of psychologicalization, an act involving

---

91 Idel, *Hasidism*, 228–229. For a different understanding of Abulafia regarding the *sefirot* and "theosophic kabbalah," cf. Wolfson, *Abraham Abulafia*, 94–177.

92 Idel, *Hasidism*, 229.

93 Ibid., 231.

94 Ibid., 232–233.

95 Ibid., 233 Regarding these Safedian trends, see Margolin, *The Human Temple*, 79–81.

96 Idel, *Hasidism*, 234.

97 Ibid., 235–236. It is important to note that Idel states that the internalization of the sefirotic system as a way of life did not come at the cost of negating their existence, and that the expansion of kabbalistic concepts within man did not neutralize the theosophic aspect, see ibid., 210, 225.

98 Margolin, *The Inner Religion*.

the transformation of various ideas and actions into personal-psychological empowerment.[99]

Cases of hasidic psychologicalization may be found in the twentieth century as well, such as Kalonymous Kalman Shapira's translation of kabbalistic concepts into personal psychological terminology. In *Ḥovat ha-Talmidim* he presents kabbalistic psychology, "It is known from sacred works that a Jew has a [pentapartite] soul (*nefesh, ru'aḥ, neshamah, ḥayyah, u-yeḥidah*),"[100] sefirotic-theosophy, and doctrine of contraction (*ṣimṣum*).[101] In his opinion, kabbalistic sefirotic-theosophy and teachings concerning *ṣimṣum* occur within the individual soul, "Behold, the names of the contracted gradations (*madregot ṣimṣumei*) of *your soul* are already known to you, *nefesh, ru'aḥ*, etc. and the names of the gradations of contraction (*madregot ha-ṣimṣum*) in general, our holy [teachers] have taught to us, that they are ten and they are called *sefirot*";[102] "The Jew himself and his lofty holiness are drawn down and concatenated through his soul (*yeḥidah, ḥayyah, neshamah, ru'aḥ, ve-nefesh*), as well as the worlds of emanation, creation, formation, and doing (*olamot aṣilut, beriyah, yeṣirah, ve-asiyah*)... This means that *each person has part of the worlds* of formation, creation, even emanation, and even though he does not understand them... nevertheless, *they are his*... therefore, the Jew who learns subjects of the world of emanation, creation, and formation—only parts of *his* worlds learn."[103] Nonetheless, Shapira's project regarding this topic is no different than the general project of hasid-

99 It should be noted that Kook identified this internalization as R. Elijah Kramer's (Vilna Gaon) primary opposition towards hasidism, see Abraham Isaac ha-Kohen Kook, *Pinqasei ha-Re'iah* (Jerusalem: Ha-Maḥon al Shem ha-Reṣi'ah Kook ZṢ"L, 2008), 1:6§3: "The basis for the dispute (*ha-maḥloqet*) that the GR"A (Gaon Rabbi Elijah), blessed be his memory, established against the hasidim was primarily that the head of the hasidim [Beshṭ] elevated the intention (*ha-kavvanah*) above the deed. The permit for select individuals (*le-yeḥidei segulah*) to behave at times as they saw fit, departing the path of the Torah, is founded upon the foundation of individual perfection, however, national perfection requires that the deeds and actions will be the main aspect [of religious live]—and the individual, even if he be very great, needs to follow after the community in every matter, which was decided and accepted by the nation, such as the rabbinic rules in the Mishnah and Gemara.

100 Shapira, *Ḥovat ha-Talmidim*, 55a.

101 Ibid., 56a-59a, 78a-79b.

102 Ibid., 56b. Emphasis mine.

103 Ibid., 57a-b. Emphases mine. Even kabbalistic concepts such as *malkhut yisra'el* (kingdom of Israel) and *kenneset yisra'el* (assembly of Israel) undergo a process of psychologization in Shapira's thought, who adds to their theosophic significance personal-mental implications, for concern for human experience is situated at the center of his thought, see ibid., 77b-83a.

ism at large,[104] and is a continuation of traditional hasidic interpretation.[105] Also, Ekstein, similar to Shapira, translated both kabbalistic sefirotic-theosophy and the Lurianic doctrine of *parṣufim* (countenances) into psychological terminology.[106] Nevertheless, Ekstein went a step further—not only did he translate kabbalistic theosophic doctrine into a "mystical psychology," via Scholem, rather he translated it into modern psychological terminology!

Ekstein's universal-psychological language demands interpretation.[107] He does not utilize hasidic or even religious terminology, rather he utilizes a new discourse that characterizes contemporaneous western spiritual movements. An interesting example of this may be found in his use of the term "energy" (*energi'ah*), which, to my knowledge, is not found in contemporaneous hasidic literature. Ekstein writes, "This imagination will greatly increase our souls' ecstasy, it will give us great vitality, joy, *energy*, and renewal (*hitḥadshut*)";[108] "Afterwards we shall go out to our labors with joy, clear thoughts, filled with vitality and energy, we will be able to work in peace and tranquility";[109] "To see the vitality filling everything, to recognize the soul enlivening all of creation, and how this rec-

104 For example, concerning the psychologization of *ṣimṣum* of Lurianic kabbalah in hasidic thought, see Schatz-Uffenheimer, *Hasidism as Mysticism*, 207–212.

105 Except two matters in his thought that were directly influenced by modern psychology and hypnotism, as I will show below.

106 See Ekstein, *Tena'ei ha-Nefesh*, 22–27. Ekstein depicts at length the different combinations between the *sefirot*, which he refers to as joy, fear, glory, victory, and pleasure (correlating to the *sefirot* of *Ḥesed*, *Gevurah*, *Tif'eret*, *Neṣaḥ*, and *Hod*), as well as the groupings of each *sefirah* in modern psychological terminology. *Ḥesed* is grouped with joy, love, delight, and swiftness; *Gevurah* is grouped with anger, hate, and mourning, and so Ekstein continues with the remaining *sefirot*. Furthermore, he emphasizes the affect of the "intellect *sefirot*," *Ḥokhmah*, *Binah*, *Da'at*, on one's traits (*middot*). In his opinion, similar to Shapira, the imagination is an aspect of thought (*maḥshavah*) and is situated within the upper triad of *sefirot*, *Ḥokhmah*, *Binah*, *Da'at* (ibid., 23), and from there influences the lower seven "emotional *sefirot*." From within this conception, Ekstein views the imagination as an "expanding" instrument for the "emotional traits." He writes, "This is the matter of visualization (*ha-ṣiyur*). This visualization stirs joy within man, which he feels in his heart" (ibid.). The action of expanding man's emotional traits is central to Ekstein's thought. Only the "expansion" is able to give man a full internal life, "The feeling of vitality (*hargashat ha-ḥiyut*) is dependent upon the expansion of the ten traits (*eser middot*) within man's soul. Only at the time of expansion and growth will man feel life and joy in their total fullness" (ibid., 27). The Lurianic conception of countenances (*parṣufim*) also undergo a similar process in Ekstein's thought, ibid., 29,31,54.

107 Regarding his universalistic style, which is devoid of religious symbols, see Yechieli, "On the Book *Tena'ei ha-Nefesh le-Hasagat ha-Ḥassidut*," 14–15, 20 Leshem, "Between Messianism and Prophecy," 244–246.

108 Ekstein, *Tena'ei ha-Nefesh*, 6.

109 Ibid., 15.

ognition is able to overflow him (*le-hashpi'a*) with such great joy, vigor (*ra'ananut*), energy, and 'life-will' (*raṣon ḥayyim*)."[110] Energy is not to be understood in its pure scientific sense in this context, but rather in a spiritual sense of renewal and vigor. Nonetheless, it is clear that the choice of using a "scientific" term as an explanation for an emotional phenomenon is influenced by its physical sense, relying on the German scientist Hermann Ludwig Ferdinand von Helmholtz (1821–1894), who discovered the law of the "conservation of energy," which maintains that energy neither disappears, nor is created *ex nihilo*, rather is always changing form. This understanding of energy allowed it to be borrowed from the natural sciences and implemented into the fields of spirituality and religion.[111] His new use of this term expresses a kind of continuous renewal and vigor, for the law of the conservation of energy is based on the discovery that there is neither loss nor disappearance, but only change or renewal in one way or another. The innovative use of the concept of energy by Ekstein is a translation of the kabbalistic concept of *ḥiyyut* (vitality) that had already undergone a hasidic psychological translation.[112] The kabbalistic *ḥiyyut* symbolizes the divine presence in this world as well as the divine element that dwells within man. Hasidism translated this concept into a way of life, a type of fervor for the service of God and the fulfillment of the commandments.[113] Ekstein came and translated this concept into modern terminology—energy. In a sense, Ekstein's translation project is in fact one of secondary translation, translating that which has already been translated.[114]

---

110 Ibid., 42.

111 See Hanegraaff's definition of occult movements as spiritual movements that attempt to scientifically justify their views, Wouter J. Hanegraaff, *New Age Religion and Western Culture: Esotericism in the Mirror of Secular Thought* (Cambridge: Cambridge University Press, 1998), 221–223. Also, see Persico "Jewish Meditation," 310–312.

112 I would like to thank Prof. Ron Margolin who brought this to my attention.

113 Idel, *Hasidism*, 236–238.

114 This "double translation" is to be found later, in the second half of the twentieth century, among many neo-hasidic thinkers, such as Zalman Schachter-Shalomi, see *Yishmru Daat: Chassidic Teachings of the Fourth Turning* (Boulder: OHALAH Rabbinic Fellowship, 2009), 2 (concerning this work, see Shaul Magid, "The Necessary Heresy of Translation—Reflections on the Hebrew Writings of Reb Zalman Schachter-Shalomi," *Spectrum: The Journal of Jewish Renewal* (2007): 19–37), as well as Arthur Green, see idem (Itzik Lodzer), "Response to Robert Goldenberg," *Response: A Contemporary Jewish Review* 2, no. 2 (Fall 1968): 43, "I firmly believe that if Judaism is to speak to certain kinds of religiously sensitive Jews today, new modes of the *translation* of classic Jewish mystical texts must be found"; idem, *Radical Judaism: Rethinking God and Tradition* (New Haven: Yale University Press, 2010), as well as neo-kabbalistic thinkers, especially the Berg family of the Ashlagian school, see Jody Myers, "Marriage and Sexual Behavior in the Teachings of the Kabbalah Centre," in *Kabbalah and Modernity: Interpretations, Transfor-*

A primary example is to be found in his use of the words life (*ḥayyim*) and soul (*neshamah*) as substitutes for the religiously laden term God. Paul Heelas has demonstrated that these aforementioned terms were characteristic of "new spiritual movements,"[115] which infused them with immanentistic meanings.[116] Furthermore, through this terminology, he has distinguished between those movements that identified life with divinity and those who did not do so.[117] We have already discussed Ekstein's gradual propensity to use this term as a substitute for God—whereas in the beginning of his book he uses it selectively, by the end of his work it becomes a primary term.[118] According to Ekstein, being linked to "the life that fills everything" is "the ascent and liberation of the soul," while being disconnected from this life is "the enslavement of the soul." Note, this connection to "life" is through imagery techniques of a universal and non-religious character, visualizations of "creation," such as nature, the sun, and, moon:

> We shall begin by slowly visualizing all of creation... the beautiful images of the splendor of nature, of the land, the sun, the moon, and all of the celestial hosts... There is no doubt in this matter that then we will thoroughly, and always with further clarity, recognize that the vision of the entirety of creation is the link of one's soul to all of life, which fills everything and propels everything, and the vision of the particular, which concerns the body, is a separation from the worldly and filled life. The first is the ascent of the soul, its loftiness and liberty, and the second is [its] contraction, shrinkage, and enslavement.[119]

In Ekstein's opinion, the return to the essence of the soul, which as we have seen is the source of healing for man, occurs through integration with and connection

---

mations, Adaptations, edited by Boaz Huss, Marco Pasi and Kocku von Stuckrad (Leiden: Brill, 2010), 267: "Berg's innovation, however, was to equate the dynamic of the *sefirot* to electrical circuitry or to the atom, with its positively charged protons, negatively charged electrons, and neutral neutrons. (In this case, positive, negative, and neutral do not have any moral implications, and they are all essential.) The left-column *sefirot* are negative energy and identified as Desire to Receive energy. The right-column *sefirot* are positive energy and identified as Desire to Share energy."

115 Paul Heelas, *Spiritualities of Life: Romantic Themes and Consumptive Capitalism* (Oxford: Blackwell Publishing, 2008), 23–30.

116 Ibid., 26–27.

117 Ibid., 27–28

118 See above, chap. 6, subchapter, "Integration *(Hitkallelut)*," and "Between Kalonymous Kalman Shapira and Menaḥem Ekstein."

119 Ekstein, *Tena'ei ha-Nefesh*, 31. Also, see above, chap. 6, subchapter, "War of Imaginations," this quotation is from the context of the battle between two kinds of imagination.

to "life, which fills all the world."[120] The identification between "life" and "God," as well as "faith," in Ekstein's teachings is clear, and is demonstrable from the following sentences, "Europe! How much longer will you not understand, that distancing from faith is distancing from nature as well, from the soul, and from life";[121] "Hasidism elevates man: If the ten powers in his soul have sufficiently developed that he may receive within himself all of creation and become astonished by it—from this same level he will begin to see that all of creation has a soul which sustains it and constantly directs it... and their soul is the creator, blessed be he";[122] "Faith is in the aspect of hearing, however if the ten powers of the soul have already broadened so that they may be enraptured (*le-hitpa'el*) by the leader of the world (*ha-manhig et olamo*) himself, blessed be he, if the consciousness (*mo'aḥ*) has already been cleansed of bodily corporeality by means of always perceiving all of creation (*be-kelal ha-beriyah*)... then man arrives at faith in the aspect of seeing, this faith... is in his soul and is felt throughout his interiority. Hasidism states about this man that he clings (*davuq*) to life, in contrast to one whose faith is limp [and] is separated from the source of life."[123]

Indeed, hasidism as a whole translate the dense kabbalistic terminology into its contemporary psychological language, whereas Ekstein continued this translation project into his own day. He translated these hasidic-translated concepts into modern psychological categories, which are characterized by his engagement with the unconscious, imagery, guided meditation literature,[124] and "universal-spiritualistic" terms. To everything he added imagery techniques in order to instill in the reader a mystical experience, an experience of divine integration. Ekstein's attempt to explain and understand hasidism with new terms, together with his suggested universalistic imagery techniques, which are similar to hypnotic methods, reveal a unique and original thinker, who tried to integrate two modes of thought. This attempt was made self-consciously by Ekstein, as he writes, "In my book, I have made *a preliminary effort* to find suitable definitions and a correct style as to express the principles of hasidism."[125]

120 Ibid., 15–16. Also, see above, chap. 6, subchapter, "Integration (*Hitkallelut*)."
121 Ibid., 37.
122 Ibid., 33.
123 Ibid., 34. For more on the identification between life and God in Ekstein's thought, see Persico, "Jewish Meditation," 240.
124 See above, chap. 6, n. 62
125 Emphasis in the original. Brought as a forward to the Hebrew edition, Ekstein, *Mavoh le-Torat ha-Ḥasidut*, 16. Presumably this preface, being written for the Yiddish translation of his book and published within a Yiddish journal, was written in Yiddish as well. I have been unsuccessful in obtaining the original likely published in *Beys Yankev* 141 or 142 (March-June, 1937).

C The Unconscious and the Occult

Alan Brill has identified the focus on the individual and the unconscious as distinctive features of modernity.[126] Indeed, Tomer Persico emphasized Ekstein's uniqueness in that his techniques focused on the mysterious depths of "consciousness," in accordance with the rise of modern psychological trends.[127] Furthermore, Persico has asserted that the rise of the romantic ethos granted feelings and experiences an authoritative stance, "As Charles Taylor notes, Romanticism granted nature a status of a moral source, and included in this is human nature."[128] Henceforth, praxis is not derived from theology, rather the exact opposite: theology is derived from praxis. This Copernican revolution is a clear marker of modernity. Indeed, Ekstein focuses on the idea of the unconscious and places authoritative import on personal experience. An analysis of Ekstein's thought[129] shows that in his opinion the experience of divinity brings one to certitude of its existence and not contrariwise! Every one of his imagery techniques are meant to disconnect man from his egotistical being, which constitutes a barrier for divine experience and its filling of his consciousness:

> Men are immersed in an awful egoism, individual and national egoism. Men who never learned how to exit their bodies, to exalt themselves towards the "all" and feel with the "all," to rise *towards the source and feel it*... men who have distanced themselves from faith, who have emptied themselves of the awareness of the creator may he be blessed, which is the only thing that can extract them from their individual bodies and teach them to integrate into the "all" and be nullified in it.[130]

Ekstein's book does not attempt to prove the existence of God in a theological manner, but rather provides instruction for the experience of divinity, and from there one can gain certainty regarding his existence.[131] The *raison d'être*

126 Alan Brill, *Thinking God*, 365–369. Also, see ibid. n. 8, 17, 19. Brill writes, based on these studies, that the interest in theories of the unconscious increased considerably between 1730 and 1890.
127 Persico, "Jewish Meditation," 236, 238–245.
128 Ibid., 283.
129 See my detailed analysis, Reiser, "To Fly like Angels," 238–252.
130 Ekstein, *Tena'ei ha-Nefesh*, 36.
131 His work can be fruitfully compared with that of Heschel regarding experience and certainty. As Shai Held has discussed, Heschel's use of language is meant to arouse the unbeliever to belief, for Heschel "the philosopher" understands the epistemological issues of certainty, but Heschel "the believer" is so certain of his own experience. Similar to Ekstein, Heschel's imagery and poetics are not to be understood as purely theological or philosophical arguments, but rath-

of his work, which is filled with imagery techniques that are utterly removed from any type of theology, is to ultimately disconnect from one's ipseitic existence through experiences of wonder and astonishment, which come about through imagery of nature, the animal kingdom, and botanic world, and thereby reach an experience of divine immanence.[132] Additionally, similar to other mesmeric-inspired occult societies,[133] Ekstein believed that all sicknesses and ail-

---

er as windows into a believer's soul. For Held's discussion, see idem, *Abraham Joshua Heschel: The Call of Transcendence* (Bloomington: Indiana University Press, 2013), 52–69.

132 Ekstein, *Tena'ei ha-Nefesh*, 36.

133 Regarding Ekstein's book, Alan Brill wrote, "As I was reading it, I realized that I read these visualizations before. They are from Jean Huston's The Possible Human: A Course in Extending Your Physical, Mental, and Creative Abilities (1982). Jean Huston is a 1980's hero of New Thought incorporating many 1920's classic visualizations in her work. There are similar elements in Alice Baily Shakti Gwain, and Warren Kenton. A quick google search of any of the visualizations yielded dozens of new age sites with the same visualizations. I do not know which works Menachem Ekstein actually read in 1920's Germany, I could not find a list of German New Thought books online" (Alan Brill, "Menachem Ekstein Visions of a Compassionate World—A Post-Hasid?," The Book of Doctrines and Opinions: Notes on Jewish Theology and Spirituality (blog), April 11, 2010, https://kavvanah.wordpress.com/2010/04/11/menachem-ekstein-visions-of-a-compassionate-world-a-post-hasid/). It is unlikely that Ekstein, who in the 1920's was in Vienna, knew about this American movement or was influenced by it, rather it is more likely that this similarity between his techniques and those of the *New Thought*, reflect a certain *zeitgeist* produced by the conception of the "creative imagination."

Phineas Parkhurst Quimby (1802–1866), the father of the American *New Thought* movement, which was further developed by his disciples, met, in the city of Belfast, Maine in 1838, Charles Poyen, a French mesmerist, who came to lecture about mesmerism and to demonstrate it. This was a crucial encounter for him. Quimby was convinced that this phenomenon was real and went on a two-year journey with Poyen, during which he learned about mesmerism. On this journey he met Lucius Burkmar, a young learned man who was interested in hypnotism, and they went on a journey throughout the United States, during which they demonstrated hypnotic techniques, in which Burkmar was hypnotized by Quimby (see Phineas Parkhurst Quimby Resource Center, http://www.ppquimby.com/index.html). Quimby ultimately disavowed the existence of mesmeric fluidum and hidden electric forces that affect other people, and came to the conclusion that thought allows hypnotic phenomena and that thoughts can affect reality (Albanese, *A Republic of Mind and Spirit*, 285). Quimby thought that illness is only a delusion and is in fact an error in thought. At the end of his life he integrated Swedenborgian techniques into his techniques (see Horatio Willis Dresser, *A History of the New Thought Movement* [New York: General Books, 2009], 13–33). Quimby's conceptions led to the creation of the *New Thought* movement, a religious-philosophical movement, which primarily developed in the twentieth-century (Albanese, *A Republic of Mind and Spirit*, 285–289, 300–303). The *New Thought* movement was composed of many different movements, both religious and secular, which claimed that thought affects reality, and therefore emphasized subjects, such as positive thought, self-empowerment, lifeforce, healing, and creative visualization (Ella Wheeler Wilcox, *Heart of the New Thought* [Chicago: The Psychic Research Company, 1902], 20–22, 40–45) This

ments, whether they be physical or spiritual, stem from man's alienation from his true self—again a very modern conception—[134]and that man's return to himself is the cure:

> When will are healing be certain and true? If we shall know to find it in ourselves and in our souls. We must clearly know that all pain and vexation are not the essence of our

---

movement anticipated the immanentistic conceptions of the Separate Intellect or God being found in every place and thing. This immanentistic reality defines man as divine at his foundation and within his essence, and thereby allows for the unity of humankind, since everyone is a spiritual creature. Creative visualization is a basic technique in this movement's teachings, for positive thinking, which was primarily developed by Wallace Delois Wattles (1860–1911), an author and thinker of the *New Thought* movement (see Wallace Wattles, *The Science of Getting Rich* [Holyoke, MA: The Elizabeth Towne Company, 1910]; idem, *The Science of Being Great* [Holyoke, MA: The Elizabeth Towne Company, 1911]). The purpose of creative visualization is to stir new thought and thereby change reality.

Additionally, it should be noted that England acted as a link between European and American mesmerism. A popular wave of mesmerism swept through Victorian England between 1837–1901, see Winter, *Mesmerized*, 255. During this time, mostly public appearances, which fascinated the masses and successfully disseminated mesmerism (ibid., 30–31), and lectures took place (ibid., 112–130). Also, mesmeric journals and institutions were established (ibid., 156–158) at this time. Due to all of these phenomena, Winter refers to mesmerism as the spirit of Victorian England (ibid., 347–348). It is highly plausible that its popularity reached American shores as well, due to the constant contact between the countries. That is to say, not only did mesmerism arrive in America via mesmerists, but most likely through indirect modes as well, since it was "the spirit of the times."

Now, in response to Brill, it does appear that the engagement with visualization found in Ekstein's thought as well as the *New Thought* movement are in fact similar, as Brill stated. Their similarity lies in their use of universalistic imagery, such as the universe, world, creatures, creation, nature, and the like, without directly reverting to religion. Their parallels do not stem from direct mutual influence, but rather from similar backgrounds. Mesmerism and Swedenborgianism, in contrast to hypnotism, advocated for a universal-cosmic force, which is outside of man, that can be transferred to man and from man to his fellow. These types of conceptions are situated at the center of Ekstein's universalistic imagery techniques and in parallel within the *New Thought* movement. The *New Thought* movement, which has roots in Mesmerism and Swedenborgianism as I have shown in this note, accepted the principle of a supernal cosmic power (the Separate Intellect or God) that unites people, and through which the individual can lead their life. An additional similarity that can be found in Ekstein and the *New Thought* movement, is the multi-scenic and dramatic character of their imagery techniques. These conceptions and techniques were empowered by psychological developments, which served both Ekstein and the *New Thought* movement.

134 The most extreme understanding of this conception appears in the American *New Thought* movement, which saw illness as entirely dependent upon one's thought. For more on the influence of mesmerism on the *New Thought* movement, see above n. 16

> souls... Only then is it possible to free and heal ourselves of them, if we shall know how to find the path to return to ourselves and our souls.[135]

Ekstein is not the only person involved in a "new" translation of hasidism. Both Aaron Marcus and Hillel Zeitlin join his efforts to a degree. Zeitlin's book *Be-Pardes ha-Ḥasidut ve-ha-Qabbalah* [The Orchard of Hasidism and kabbalah], and Marcus's book *Der Chassidismus* [Hasidism], previously mentioned, are both prime examples of modern psychological translations of hasidic concepts. Aaron Zeitlin, Hillel Zeitlin's son, intensively dealt with the unconscious and para-psychological phenomena, writing two books on these subjects.[136] A. Zeitlin documented his father's para-psychological experiences, primarily clairvoyant dreams, meaning visions of matters occurring elsewhere, vision received in hypnotic states, and telepathic experiences.[137] Did these experiences affect H. Zeitlin's conception of hasidism and his "translation" project? It would appear so, but this matter requires further research. For now, it is sufficient to state that Zeitlin's mystical experience of astonishment is a cornerstone of his conception of hasidism.[138]

Concerning Shapira, one may find two instances of modern psychological influences—his silencing technique (*hashqaṭah*) and his conception of psychological repression. Shapira, regarding his silencing technique, recommends that one focus on a watch and through this focus empty one's thoughts (silencing of one's mind) as a preliminary stage in the prophetic process:

> Therefore, the main aim is to attain a state of sleep while he is awake, whenever he desires, by silencing his thoughts and wishes that flood man without end... It is also possible to silence [the mind] be staring at a clock for a duration of some time, for this also silences his desires and thoughts. Following the silencing, which must bring some kind of inspiration from above.[139]

---

135 Ekstein, *Tena'ei ha-Nefesh*,15–16. Concerning the return to one's self in Ekstein's thought (as well as Kook's), see above chap. 6, subchapter, "War of Imaginations"; concerning selfhood and returning to one's true essence as a modern phenomenon, see Ronny Miron, *Karl Jaspers: From Selfhood to Being* (Amsterdam: Rodopi, 2012), 81–100.

136 Zeitlin, *The Other Dimension*; idem, *An Expanded Parapsychology* (Tel Aviv: Yavneh, 1973).

137 Idem, *The Other Dimension*, 370–376; idem, *An Expanded Parapsychology*, 313–316. Zeitlin also discusses, among other matters, teletherapy in Yiṣḥaq Halevi Epstein's thought, see idem, *The Other Dimension*, 169–170, as well as parapsychology in hasidic stories, ibid., 170–177 idem, *An Expanded Parapsychology*, 276–278.

138 Regarding astonishment see Zeitlin, *Al Gevul Shenei Olamot*, 18–36; Green, *Hasidic Spirituality for a New Era*, 138–139

139 According to Bein's manuscript, which differs from the printed version. I would like to thank my colleagues and teachers Dr. Zvi Leshem and Prof. Nehemia Polen, who gave me copies

The transition from a state of wakefulness to one of slumber by concentrating on a specific object, in this case a watch, thereby attaining a new state of consciousness, is very similar to hypnotic procedure, as Jonathan Garb has identified.[140] A possible source for this technique may be found in the Hebrew book *Kenneset ha-Gedolah*, published in Warsaw in 1890.[141] This work is a compilation of various articles,[142] including a "science" section containing an article entitled, "Ha-Hipnaṭizmos," (Hypnotism) by Dr. M. A. Zilbershtrom.[143] In this Hebrew article, Zilbershtrom delineates the history of hypnosis, beginning with Franz Mesmer until its current state. He categorizes three levels of hypnotic sleep, writing regarding the first, "It is a state that is called lethargy)*di lethargishe tsushtand*), which man attains through the stimulation of the optic sense, in which he will stare for a known length of time on a single matter... and he will not feel anything, neither in his body, nor in his soul."[144] If we compare Shapira's technique with this description we find a number of parallels. Both Zilbershtrom and Shapira discuss staring at an object, Zilbershtrom as a description and Shapira as instruction. Furthermore, both discuss the feeling of emptiness as a result of this practice. These parallels reinforce the likelihood that hypnotic literature, one way or another, was a major inspiration for Shapira in the development of his silencing technique and possibly for all of his imagery techniques. Natan Ophir has demonstrated an interesting similarity between Shapira's silencing technique and elements found in the "self-remembering" teachings of Georges Ivanovich Gurdjieff (1866–1949) and his pupil Peter Demianovich Ouspensky (1878–1947). Gurdjieff and Ouspensky developed meditation based on self-remembering, liberation from the bounds of daily life, and awareness of internal silence.[145] Ouspensky writes:

---

of the manuscript. For more, see above chap. 5, subchapter, "Silencing Techniques." To my knowledge, this technique is *sui generis* in kabbalah and hasidism; I say this after consulting Prof. Moshe Idel.

140 See Garb, *The Chosen Will Become Herds*, 160–161 n. 18; idem, *Shamanic Trance*, 116–117.

141 Yiṣḥaq Sovelski, ed., *Kenneset ha-Gedolah* (Warsaw: Ḥayyim Kelter, 1889).

142 The subtitle to this collection is: Rabbis Alongside Scholars (*Maskilim*), to Unify the Two Edges and Make Peace between All the Disputes That Are in Our People. The Great People of Our People Worked on It, Rabbis and Scholars (*Ḥakhamim*) Together.

143 M. A. Zilbershtrom, "Ha-Hipnaṭizmos," in *Kenneset ha-Gedolah*, ed. Yiṣḥaq Sovelski (Warsaw: Ḥayyim Kelter, 1889), 41–56.

144 Ibid., 42–43.

145 Natan Ophir, *Quieting the Mind: The Admor of Piaseczno* (Jerusalem: Jewish Meditation Institute Jerusalem, 2009), 12. It should be noted that Ouspensky wrote five lectures in 1934, which were presented at his home in London, and 125 copies were printed in 1940 (see Peter Ouspensky, *The Psychology of Man's Possible Evolution* [New York: Alfred A. Knopf, 1974], publisher's

> I shall try to explain how consciousness can be studied. Take a watch and look at the second hand, *trying to be aware of yourself*, and concentrating on the thought, "I am Peter Ouspensky," "I am now here." Try not to think about anything else, simply follow the movements of the second hand and be aware of yourself, your name, your existence, and the place you are. Keep all other thoughts away.[146]

However, a phenomenological analysis of these techniques, both Shapira's and Ouspensky's, shows that they are in fact contradictory. Shapira states that one must focus on the hour hand, "It is also possible to silence [the mind] by staring at a clock [on the small hand that almost does not move (i. e., the hour hand)] for a duration of some time, for this also silences his desires and thoughts,"[147] while Ouspensky is discussing the *second hand*. Concentrating on the hour hand, which barely moves, empties the mind and consequently, the sense of being, in contradistinction, concentrating on the second hand, which constantly moves, stimulates thought and is intended to intensify a specific thought, bringing about a heightened experience of self-awareness, the sense of being. Ouspensky's technique is kataphatic in nature, meant to cause a certain type of awareness. Shapira's silencing technique is characterized by the lack of self-awareness, "the ego of man opposes inspiration from above… [however, when] he does not have consciousness itself, then it is possible for him to become inspired from above."[148] Contra, Ouspensky's technique, which leads to self-awareness, "'I am Peter Ouspensky,' 'I am now here,'" by following the second hand, thereby emptying one's mind of other thoughts, which *distract and detract from the self*, a result that is the complete opposite of Shapira's intention in his technique, which calls for the forgetting of one's self in order to receive divine inspi-

note). Therefore, it is difficult to see any direct connection between his and Shapira's respective techniques, since in the 1930s Ouspensky's work was yet to be published, and we have no evidence of any personal connection between Shapira and Ouspensky's circle, and once Ouspensky's work was published, Shapira was "imprisoned" in occupied Poland, in addition to the fact that none of the copies were sold. With that said, when I spoke to Ophir, he defended his observation by arguing that the ideas may have been transmitted orally by his disciples. However, it should be noted that even within Ouspensky's thought, his watch technique is quite marginal, a single anecdote that does not repeat itself anywhere else in his books, nor does it appear in Gurdjieff's works.

146 Ouspensky, *The Psychology of Man's Possible Evolution*, 19.

147 Shapira, *Derekh ha-Melekh*, 450 – 451. It should be noted that in the manuscript version the words, "on the small hand that almost does not move," do not appear, rather they appear to be an interpolation of the editor, see above chap. 5, n. 164. However, it should be noted that from the context, both methodologically and textually, the addition is sound and likely reflects Shapira's intent.

148 Ibid., 450.

ration. Nevertheless, despite the differences in these techniques, Ophir's comparison itself shows a certain European *zeitgeist* that developed in the twentieth century.

The topic of psychological repression appears in Shapira's mystical journal *Ṣav ve-Ziruz*.[149] In the fourth entry, Shapira discusses the layers of the soul and calls for the enrooting of "bad traits" and not to ignore them, since ignorance leads to repression, which will ultimately break out, even in old age. Tomer Persico has asserted that it is difficult to understand Shapira's detailed conception of the soul's layers, especially his discussion of psychological repression and outbreak, without recourse to Freud's thought.[150]

The importance of the imaginative faculty did not circumvent the field of medicine, which at the turn of the twentieth century had already begun to include psychological elements. The understanding that the psyche, including the imagination, affects the physical led medical practitioner to take interest in the imagination. Psychological research joined medical studies and showed that emotions in general, and the imagination in particular, are critical tools for changing a patient's state, for better or worse. Utilizing the imagination allows for the overcoming of, and succumbing to, illness. In the medical journal *Der Yidisher Hoyz-Doktor* [The Jewish House Doctor], which was printed in Warsaw in the beginning of the twentieth century, one may find medical articles about the centrality of the imagination in the patient's medical condition, for example, "The imagination is the primary reason for illness" (*der dimyon als sibe fun krank-haytn*).[151] It should be noted that Shapira had some medical background, and perhaps read these local medical journals, thereby becoming exposed to these ideas regarding the imagination's potency.[152]

149 Idem, *Ṣav ve-Ziruz*, 2–7.
150 Persico, "Jewish Mediation," 294.
151 Professor Diyubva, "Der Dimyon als Sibah fun Krankheytn," *Der Yidisher Hoyz-Doktor: A Vekenlikher Zhurnal fir Hoyzlikhe Meditsin aun Gezund-Ferhitung* [The Jewish House Doctor: A Weekly Journal for Domestic Medicine and Healthcare] 22 (June 27, 1913): 11–13. The article continues in following volume (July 4, 1913): 3–5, and concludes in the next volume (July 11, 1913): 8–10. Regarding general publishing trends in Warsaw at this time, see Nathan Cohen, "Distributing Knowledge: Warsaw as a Center of Jewish Publishing, 1850–1914," in *Warsaw. The Jewish Metropolis: Essays in Honor of the 75th Birthday of Professor Antony Polonsky*, ed. Glenn Dynner and François Guesnet (Leiden: Brill, 2015), 180–206; regarding medical literature, although he does not include this journal see, ibid., 201.
152 Regarding his medical knowledge see Reiser, *Sermons from the Years of Rage*, 15–16. It was common for hasidic leaders to practice forms of medicine, from the Beshṭ (Ba'al Shem, meaning healer) until the twentieth century *rebbes*. Another *rebbe* who engaged in medical practices was R. Eliezer of Rzeszów (Rayshe), Ekstein's hometown, see Weinstein, *Reyshe*, 75; Yari-Wold, *Rzes-*

The link between occult movements and Jewish mysticism and mystics has received increased scholarly attention in recent years,[153] include specific occult movements of the late nineteenth century and early twentieth century, such as the Theosophical Society, founded in 1875 by the Russian-German spiritual teacher Helena Petrovna Blavatsky (1831–1891), Henry Steel Olcott (1832–1907), and William Quan Judge (1851–1896), and the Anthroposophical Society founded in 1913 by Rudolf Steiner (1861–1925) after breaking away from the Theosophical Society.

D The Idea of the Unconscious in the Musar Movement

The primary phenomenon discussed in Israel Lipkin's teaching is the gap between intellectual awareness (*ha-yedi'ah*) and emotional experience (*ha-ḥush*).[154] In his later years, he offered an explanation of this phenomenon by distinguishing between "luminous or external forces" (*koḥot me'irim ve-ḥiṣonim*), meaning conscious potencies, and "obscure or internal forces" (*koḥot kahim u-peni'im*), meaning man's subconscious or unconscious.[155] The first explicit discussion of the subconscious appears in a letter, which Etkes dates to 1859:[156]

---

zow Community, 132. On the impact of homeopathy on twentieth century hasidic *rebbes*, see Ira Robinson, "The Tarler Rebbe of Lodz and his Medical Practice: Towards a History of Hasidic Life in Pre-First World War Poland," *Polin* 11 (1998): 53–61. Furthermore, regarding Dr. Ḥayyim David Bernhard, the Rebbe of Zalushin (Działoszyn), who was a certified medical doctor, see Menashe Unger, *Hasidism and Life* (New York: s.n., 1946), 186–191.

153 A prime example is the collected articles in Boaz Huss, Marco Pasi and Kocku von Stuckrad, eds., *Kabbalah and Modernity: Interpretations, Transformations, Adaptations* (Leiden: Brill, 2010). Especially, see Burmistrov Konstantin, "Kabbalah And Secret Societies in Russia (Eighteenth To Twentieth Centuries)," in *Kabbalah and Modernity: Interpretations, Transformations, Adaptations*, eds. B. Huss, M. Pasi, and K. von Stuckrad (Leiden: Brill, 2010) 79–106; Marco Pasi, "Oriental Kabbalah and The Parting of East and West in the Early Theosophical Society," in *Kabbalah and Modernity: Interpretations, Transformations, Adaptations*, eds. B. Huss, M. Pasi, and K. von Stuckrad (Leiden: Brill, 2010), 151–166; Boaz Huss, "'The Sufi Society from America': Theosophy and Kabbalah in Poona in the Late Nineteenth Century," in *Kabbalah and Modernity: Interpretations, Transformations, Adaptations*, eds. B. Huss, M. Pasi, and K. von Stuckrad (Leiden: Brill, 2010), 167–194.

154 See above chap. 7.

155 On Lipkin's understanding of the subconscious, see Etkes, *Rabbi Israel Salanter*, 326–335. Also, see Hillel Goldberg, *Israel Salanter, Text, Structure, Idea: The Ethics and Theology of an Early Psychologist of the Unconscious* (New York: Ktav Publishing House, 1982), specifically, 158–169.

156 Etkes, *Rabbi Israel Salanter*, 328.

> It is called by psychologists (*ḥoqrei koḥot nafshot ha-adam*) clear luminous and obscure forces (*klare un dunkele*), so too in forces of psychological emotional excitement (*be-koḥot hitpa'alut ha-nafshi*), there are luminous (*klar*) and obscure (*dunkele*) forces. The obscure forces are stronger and execute their actions with little arousal. Man's love for his offspring is [from] obscure ones, and most of the time they are not felt by man himself, and with a little arousal it is excited into a burning fire. Man's desires are obscure ones, such that without any arousal, they are almost not felt, and this is their great power to control man.[157]

He writes elsewhere, "Indeed, it will be clarified that when psychologists (*ḥoqrei nefesh ha-adam*) investigated and found that in man's soul there are two types of forces: external and internal… so in man's *middot* (personality traits), within the forces acting upon him there are also two: external and internal, obscure and clear."[158] The distinction between man's external-conscious dimension and his internal-subconscious dimension, is exemplified through a father's unconscious love for his children and the midrashic portrayal of Abraham's tears at the binding of Isaac, an uncontrolled weeping caused by Abraham's subconscious, which happened while he was joyfully preparing to sacrifice his son:

> It is known that the internal acts upon man more than the external, as is seen with the senses. For example, if a man has a beloved student… and this man also has a son, which he hates with perfect hatred (*takhlit sin'ah*), and he actively demonstrated his hatred for him, and behold, it happened when this man fell asleep—behold "A fire went forth from the Lord" (Num. 16:35) and took hold of the son's house as well as the student's house and both of them are in danger. The man the man wakes up suddenly to call for help, to save both the son and student from the blaze; seemingly he will run quickly to save his son first. Why? Because the love for his son, who he hates, is more established within him (*be-penimi'uto*), by its nature, than the external love he has for his student. Therefore, when the man awakes from his sleep, when his external forces are asleep as well, then his internal forces are easily aroused, and they become clarified and overcome the external [forces] and he will run to save his son first.[159]
>
> It is clarified in the words of the *Yalqut* [*Yalqut Shimoni*, Ḥeleq 1, Remez 101], as follows: "Tears flowed and fell from Abraham's eyes until he was covered in tears," and it is further taught there, "The holy one, blessed be he, sees the father binding with all his heart (*be-khol libo*)." Ostensibly, these statements contradict one another—after binding with all his heart, how could so many tears flow from his eyes? However, according to our words, they are both correct, for that which the *Yalqut* stated, "binding with all the heart (*be-khol ha-lev*)," refers to his external forces, which within Abraham were on a higher level, [thereby] overcoming his internal [forces] in his actions; however, the tears flowed from the inner

---

157 Lipkin, *Or Yisra'el*, 25
158 Pachter, *Israel Salanter*, 169.
159 Ibid., 170.

> forced, whose effect upon man's general character is stronger. We clearly learn from this that even Abraham our father, for who was unparalleled in his great awe and righteousness, was nevertheless powerfully acted upon by the inner forces, [causing] tears to come down, even though the action was done in great perfection and with a complete heart, even with joy, as is clarified in the midrash.[160]

A number of writers have stressed that these distinctions between layers of the psyche, such as clear and obscure, external and internal, preceded Freud's similar distinction, claiming that Lipkin predated Freud by decades.[161] However, these claims completely disregard the notion of the existence of an unconscious dimension developed in mesmerism and hypnosis, which predates Freud as well. Pachter and Etkes refuted this claim, noting that Lipkin did not pretend that he was the originator. On the contrary, Lipkin himself explicitly states that his sources are taken from contemporary psychologists,[162] as he wrote, "It is called by psychologists (*ḥoqrei koḥot nafshot ha-adam*)" and "when psychologists (*ḥoqrei nefesh ha-adam*) investigated," and even cited the terms in German in Hebrew letters, "there are luminous (*klar*) and obscure (*dunkel*) forces."[163] The references made by Lipkin to psychological elements in his thought allowed, at a later juncture, for fruitful research comparing Lipkin's thought with psychological theories and treatments.[164]

Aaron Rabinowitz has noted the interesting fact that although Lipkin's disciples (R. Isaac Blazer, R. Simḥah Zissel (Broida) Ziv, and R. Naftali Amsterdam)

---

160 Ibid., 170 – 171.

161 Pachter references Louis Ginzberg, Menahem Glenn, and Dov Katz (ibid., 39 n. 2); Etkes adds R. Yehiel Yaakov Weinberg to this list. This "realization" continues until today, see Mel Gottlieb, "Mussar: A Jewish Psychoethical Model for Our Time," *Conversations: The Journal of the Institute for Jewish Ideas and Ideals* 8 (2010): 39 – 51: "I have come to realize that this insight is similar to Freud's notion of the unconscious (dark, inaccessible) and conscious (more accessible) forces that make up our psyche."

162 Pachter, *Israel Salanter*, 170 – 171; Etkes, *Rabbi Israel Salanter*, 326 – 328.

163 Yizhak Ahren has demonstrated that these German terms have been borrowed from Immanuel Kant's discussion of the subconscious, see ibid.

164 Zvi Erich Kurzweil, "R. Yisra'el me-Salanṭ ve-ha-Tenu'ah ha-Musarit," *Sinai* 47 (1960): 100 – 112; Arnold Rachlis, "The Musar Movement and Psychotherapy," *Judaism* 23 (1974): 337 – 345; Yizhak Ahren, "Rabbi Israel Salanter und das Unbewusste," *Udim* 6 (1975 – 1976): 9 – 11; Aaron Rabinowitz, "The Unconscious: Its Relation to the Judaism-Psychology Dialogue," *Journal of Psychology and Judaism* 13, no. 3 (1989): 149 – 162; Aaron Rabinowitz, "Le-Birur Musag ha-Bilti-Muda be-Tenu'at ha-Musar," in *Samuel Belkin Memorial Volume*, ed. Moshe Carmilly and Hayim Leaf (New York: Yeshiva University, 1981), 36 – 42; idem, "Meqomo shel ha-Bilti-Muda be-Yahadut," *Derakhim le-Emunah be-Yahadut* 23 (1981): 177 – 185; Ya'aqov Alṭman, "Gehinom Petuḥah Lo 'me-Taḥtav'—Tat ha-Hakarah ve-Tiqun ha-Yeṣer: Shiṭatah shel 'Tenu'at ha-Musar' le-mul Etgarei ha-Pesiko'analizah," *Tzohar* 30 (2007): 89 – 98.

frequently used terms such as *sekhel* (intellect) and *ḥush* (sense), and *sekhel* and *hitpa'alut* (excitement), they did not ascribe these ideas to obscure-internal or luminous-external forces.[165] They did maintain that the soul is made of multiple strata, but their statements are have no theoretical basis in the distinctions delineated by Lipkin regarding the different forces within man.[166] Rabinowitz raises the possibility that the omission of the "internal and external forces," the conscious and subconscious, in the works of Lipkin's disciples may lie in the controversy regarding the Musar movement in the days of his student Isaac Blazer. Due to this controversy, "The Musar masters were compelled… to be less revolutionary in their thought, in order to prevent the possibility of accusations that they were innovating things without precedent."[167] Additionally, we may claim that the deletion of psychological terminology also precludes the suspicion that Lipkin's thought has contributions from non-Jewish sources. The accusation is not only that Lipkin innovated, but that he did so utilizing external sources.[168] Following (Rabbi) Dov Katz's groundbreaking treatment of the Musar movement, in which he suggested that Lipkin's thought contains "non-religious elements," a modern apologist, the educator Prof. Zvi Erich Kurzweil, wrote a critique stating, "Rabbi Katz's opinion, depicting R. Israel Salanter's approach as bordering "autosuggestion," which is constructed upon the approach of the French scholar Émile Coué (1867–1926), should not be accepted, since autosuggestion has no religious foundation and is characterized by the belief in the possibility of mechanistic psychological influence, which has nothing to do with R. Israel Salanter's approach."[169] This modern criticism, written in 1960, demonstrates why the Musar masters, active in the nineteenth century, were so concerned about revealing their sources, ultimately concealing them. Nonetheless, it should be noted that this concern weakened over time, and twentieth century Musar thinkers, such as Elijah Eliezer Dessler and Avigdor Miller, were unconcerned with making use of the terminological distinction between conscious and subconscious. Dessler wrote of the "subconscious" (*tat ha-hakarah*), while Miller referred to it as "the sleeping and concealed intellect" (*ha-sekhel ha-yashen ve-ha-ne'alam*) or "the concealed depths of his heart":

---

165 Rabinowitz, "Le-Birur Musag ha-Bilti-Muda be-Tenu'at ha-Musar," 37–38; idem, "Meqomo shel ha-Bilti-Muda be-Yahadut," 183.
166 Rabinowitz, "Le-Birur Musag ha-Bilti-Muda be-Tenu'at ha-Musar," 38.
167 Ibid., 40.
168 Also, see above chap. 6, regarding Ekstein's insistence on the Jewishness of his sources.
169 Kurzweil, "R. Yisra'el me-Salanṭ," 109.

In order to overcome passions and desires, one should activate the *subconscious* itself. This may be acheived through several ways. One of them is to use images (*be-ṣiyurim*), for thinkink with detailed images touchs the subconscious and has great effect there, and this is what the great Musar masters said, that the words of *musar* need to be explained to the body. The intent is to explain to the aspect of the body within the soul, meaning the animal soul (*ha-nefesh ha-behemit*), and this matter may be acheived through the use of the power of imagery (*ko'aḥ ha-ṣiyur*).[170]

Sensory knowledge is only in images (*be-ṣiyurim*). All that a man acquires through his senses, whether ocular, aural, olfactoric, or gustatory, are all absorbed into his mind forever. Sometimes the absorbed image (*ha-ṣiyur*) is an image (*temunat*) of a man or object alone, and sometimes the image (*ha-temunah*) is absorbed together with the sounds of words which he or another spoke at the time of seeing this same person or object, and sometimes with the image (*ha-temunah*) is absorbed together with a haptic (*hargashat mishush*), olfactoric, or gustatory feeling. It is possible that the image (*she-ha-temnuah*) is forgotten by him, meaning that he no longer sees it before his eyes in *his awoken intellect* (*be-sikhlo ha-er*), however, by no means is the image (*ha-temunah*) erased, and it is not lost forever, rather it sinks into the depths of *his sleeping and concealed intellect* (*sikhlo ha-yashen ve-ha-ne'alam*). Sometimes fifty years (*yuval shanim*) will pass, in which he will not see this same man or object, and when he sees him a second after this time, suddenly the image (*ha-temunah*) will stir within *the concealed depths of his heart* and will arise and be situated before his eyes. He compares the man standing before him with the image that has jumped from the depths of his heart, and he says this is him (*ploni*)! Along with the imag,e the other sensory feelings, which he had at that time, are stirred as well, meaning that the voice of the same man (*oto ploni*) rings in his ears, and that which he spoke fifty years ago (*yuval shanim*) and that which he will speak [now], and perhaps he will remember the touch of his hand (*masos yado*) as well as his smell, whether perfumed or putrid. And no injury, inflicted by the man or object, is ever forgotten.[171]

It is interesting that the subconscious, according to both of them, is explicitly linked to the imagination. Dessler calls for the affecting of the subconscious through the imagination, "For thought within detailed images touch the subconscious," while Miller describes the "sinking" of the image within the subconscious, until one day this image will burst forth, "However, by no means is the image (*ha-temunah*) erased... rather it sinks into the depths of his sleeping and concealed intellect (*sikhlo ha-yashen ve-ha-ne'alam*). And sometimes fifty years (*yuval shanim*) will pass... [and] suddenly the image (*ha-temunah*) will stir within the concealed depths of his heart."

The practical aspects emerging from Lipkin's perception of the unconscious in his teachings must still be examined.

---

170 Elijah Eliezer Dessler, *Mikhtav me-Eliyahu* (Bnei Brak: Sifsei Chachamim, 2009), 35.
171 Miller, *Lev Avigdor*, 26–27.

- Aaron Rabinowitz demonstrated that there are significant differences between Lipkin and contemporary psychological schools regarding the practical utilization of the subconscious. The multi-layered structure of the psyche, conscious and subconscious, allowed Lipkin to suggest a psychological theory for the "war of the senses." The source of the evil inclination is within the internal forces of the subconscious, and their defeat will be brought about through the transformation of the positive external forces into internal ones as well. The purpose of learning musar with fervor (*be-hitlahavut*) is to convert conscious external forces, like the intellect, into internal ones, thereby defeating the desires. While psychological schools of all varieties want to bring the unconscious to light, Lipkin desired the exact opposite, to bring the conscious to the unseen.[172]
- Zvi Erich Kurzweil indicated clear parallels between Lipkin and modern psychoanalytic views. Lipkin differentiated between the "subjugation" and "rectification" of the evil inclination, meaning, between the non-engagement with or repression of sin and the transformation or sublimation of it into good. Lipkin preferred sublimation over repression, since he reasoned that man is not able to constantly repress his desires and that these "subjugated personality traits" (*ha-middot ha-kevushot*) may "poison the intellectual faculty" (*eres be-ko'aḥ ha-sekhel*). The attempt to eradicate the evil inclination through its rectification is similar to the modern psychoanalytic view that claims that psychological repression (*Verdrängung*) leads to negative results. The poison injected into man's psyche through the "subjugated personality traits" resembles the negative results discussed by psychoanalysis.[173] This psychological understanding is different than many hasidic psychological approaches. For example, Shneur Zalman of Liadi, the founder of Ḥabad hasidism, preferred the subjugation of desire (*itkafya*), in order to rectify it (*ithaphka*). Shneur Zalman uses the zoharic terms[174] of *itkafya* and *ithaphka* (subjugation and transformation) in order to distinguish between the worship of the intermediate man (*benoni*) and that of the righteous man (*ṣaddiq*), between the worship of common people and that of select individu-

172 Rabinowitz, "Le-Birur Musag ha-Bilti-Muda be-Tenu'at ha-Musar," 40. For different positions regarding the emergence of the unconscious in Lipkin's teachings and psychological theories, ibid., 40 – 41; idem, "Meqomo shel ha-Bilti-Muda be-Yahadut," 182. Furthermore, for the distinctions between the musar movement and psychoanalysis, see idem, "The Unconscious: Its Relation to the Judaism-Psychology Dialogue."
173 Kurzweil, "R. Yisra'el me-Salanṭ," 107.
174 *Zohar* 2:128.

als.[175] This distinction recognizes the different levels of worship that are dependent upon each person's character. Shneur Zalman states that, "There are two kinds of spiritual repose before him, blessed be he. The first is from the complete nullification of the other side (*biṭṭul ha-siṭra aḥara le-gamrei*) and its transformation from bitter to sweet, from dark to light, (*ve-ithappekha mi-meriru le-mitqa u-me-ḥashokha li-nehora*) by righteous men (*ṣaddiqim*). And the second, when the *siṭra aḥara* is subdued (*itkafya*), while it is still at its strongest and most powerful, raising itself like an eagle, and from there, God lowers it due to the arousal from below (*it'aruta diltata*) of the intermediate men (*beinonim*)."[176] The first path is similar to that recommended by Lipkin. In contrast, the second path of *itkafya* (subjugation), the path of exerting control over the evil inclination and not transforming it into good, is recommended for most people. Shneur Zalman called for every person (*benoni*) to defer the evil inclination that is revealed in his own nature and to conquer it, rather than to struggle with it directly and nullify it, "Even if lustful thoughts (*hirhurei ta-avot*) and other alien thoughts befall him... He should not pay them heed, rather he should remove his thought (*yasi'aḥ da'ato*) from them for now. Also, he should not be foolish as to engage in the raising of the traits of the alien thought (*be-ha'ala'at ha-middot shel ha-maḥshavah zarah*), as is known, for these words were only said for righteous men (*ṣaddiqim*)."[177] Although this path of subjugation, rather than nullification, entails a constant battle with the evil inclination, Shneur Zalman was unconcerned by this struggle and saw it as part of the divine plan for man, "This is the trait of the intermediate (*middat ha-beinonim*) and their worship, to conquer the [evil] inclination and lustful thoughts (*ve-ha-hirhur*) arising from the heart to the brain (*le-mo'aḥ*), and completely remove his mind (*u-le-hasi'aḥ da'ato*) from them and reject them with both hands... Therefore, man should not be depressed or very troubled (*al yipol lev adam alav, ve-lo year levavo me'od*), even if all his days will be in this battle, for perhaps this is why he was created and this is his worship, to constantly subjugate the other side (*le-akhepeya le-siṭra aḥara tamid*)."[178] In contradistinction, Lipkin believes that man is unable to live in a state of constant battle, "It is difficult for man to utilize the trait of strength (*be-mid-*

175 Regarding the terms *itkafya* and *ithaphka*, see Moshe Hallamish, "The Theoretical System of R. Shneur Zalman of Liady (Its Sources in Kabbalah and Hasidism)" (Ph.D. thesis, Hebrew University, 1976), 374–382; Wolfson, *Open Secret*, 94–103.

176 Shneur Zalman of Liadi, *Tanya*, part 1, chap. 27.

177 Ibid., chap. 28.

178 Ibid., chap. 27.

dat ha-gevurah), to suffer a burden and constant pain. For this man will search for advice and a trick (*aṣeh ve-taḥbulah*) on how to rectify his soul's traits and forces, whether a little or a lot."[179] The subjugation, which is a kind of repression, will eventually break forth, such that there is no other option than to eradicate the evil inclination itself by transforming it into good, "When man will transform his soul's forces… into good, to the point that the evil force will be uprooted from him, and will neither be seen, nor found in his being at all."[180] Even Freud did not develop his conception of repression in a vacuu—his conception was founded upon mesmerism and developments in hypnosis. A goal of hypnotherapy was to raise repressed feelings from the patient's unconscious and treat them directly.[181]

– One of the techniques that Lipkin suggested in order to achieve emotional excitement (*hitlahavut*) was the mantric-like repetition of a specific sentence from musar literature or rabbinic work for a lengthy period of time.[182] Dov Katz compared this technique with that of the French psychologist, Émile Coué de la Châtaigneraie (1867–1926), who developed "positive autosuggestion" and maintained that man's energies are affected by this repetition.[183] As previously mentioned, Kurzweil criticized this opinion due to the non-religious nature of autosuggestion.[184] However, his criticism is unclear for two reasons. First, Katz never claimed that Lipkin based his conception upon that of Coué, rather he only demonstrated that there are parallels, just as Kurzweil himself did regarding psychoanalysis.[185] Second, since Lipkin himself refers to modern psychological conceptions, as shown above, the fact that autosuggestion is "non-religious," which should be understood as non-Jewish from the context, does not demonstrate that Lipkin would be averse to it. Furthermore, Coué's thought is not entirely original and is based on mesmerism and hypnosis. Coué studied hypnosis with Hippolite

179 Lipkin, *Or Yisra'el*, 82.

180 Ibid., 42.

181 See Crabtree, *From Mesmer to Freud*. Furthermore, see Lancelot Law Whyte, *The Unconscious Before Freud* (New York: Basic Books, 1960).

182 See above chap. 7, subchapter, "Ecstasy and Battle of the Senses: The Development of the Imagination in the Musar Movement."

183 Katz, *The Musar Movement*, 1:254.

184 Kurzweil, "R. Yisra'el me-Salanṭ," 109. See the beginning of this subchapter.

185 Historically speaking Lipkin could not have based his "mantra" technique on Coué's thought, since his theory of autosuggestion was only developed after Lipkin's death. Coué's book, *Self-Mastery Through Conscious Autosuggestion*, was published in French and English in 1922, as well as German in 1923.

Bernheim,[186] and therefore, his thought is another link in the research and analysis of the unconscious.[187]

186 See above, subchapter "Mesmerism and the Jewish World."
187 See Ellenberger, *The Discovery of the Unconscious*, 842. Also, see Coué, *Self-Mastery Through Conscious Autosuggestion* (New York: American Library Service, 1922), 5–15, in which he discusses hypnotism and the imagination.

Chapter Nine
"A Voice Calls from the East:" Imagery Techniques in Light of the East

The *mundus imaginalis* (world of imagination) is mentioned both in kabbalistic and Sufi literature, as a mediating world between the corporeal and spiritual realm.[1] Moshe Idel claims that, due to this parallel, this concept was appropriated into the teachings of R. Isaac of Acre (a student of Nathan ben Sa'adyahu Harar, from Abulafia's ecstatic kabbalah circle) from Sufism and that this circle was proximate to Sufism.[2]

The Sufi master, Abū ʿAbd Allāh Muḥammad ibn ʿAlī ibn Muḥammad ibn ʿArabī, commonly referred to as Ibn 'Arabī (1165–1240), developed the conception of the imagination and brought it to new heights. In his opinion, human consciousness is dependent upon the imagination. The imagination is the creator of our reality, not as a false entity, but as a reflection and mirror of true existence. True entities belong to the divine realm and the imagination is the mirror through which these entities are seen.[3] The Islamic scholar Henry Corbin (1903–1978) focused his scholarship on Ibn 'Arabī's teachings, coined the term *imaginaire*, and situated it within modern discourse.[4]

Corbin was a phenomenologist of religion, specifically religious consciousness, who first and foremost opposed all static conceptions. Corbin's metaphysics renounce the false security of faith in something permanent and stable. According to him, this type of faith, whether it be in the humanities, sciences, art, politics, and even life itself—creates an idol, a false god. In contradistinction, the imagination is perpetually and constantly moving and thereby creates a symbol,

---

1 Sara Sviri, *The Sufis: An Anthology* (Tel Aviv: Tel Aviv University, 2008), 527; Idel, *Studies in Ecstatic Kabbalah*, 73–89. For more on connections between kabbalah and Sufism see Gershom Scholem, "Note on a Kabbalistical Treatise on Contemplation," *Melanges offerts à Henry Corbin*, ed. Seyyed Hossein Nasr (Teheran: Tehran UP, 1977), 665–670; Moshe Idel, *Ascensions on High in Jewish Mysticism: Pillars, Lines, Ladders* (Budapest: Central European University Press, 2005) 51–54. On the appearance of the concept of *mundus imaginalis* see idem, "R. Judah Hallewa and his *Ẓofenat Pa'aneah*," *Shalem* 4 (1984): 132–133. Also see Wolfson, *Through a Speculum*, 61–62; idem, *Language Eros Being*, xvii, 189; Corbin, *Creative Imagination*, 190–195.

2 Idel, *Studies in Ecstatic Kabbalah*, 73–89.

3 Sviri, *The Sufis*, 527; Corbin, *Creative Imagination*, 218–219, 272–273; Elliot R. Wolfson "*Imago Templi* and the Meeting of the Two Seas: Liturgical Time-Space and the Feminine Imaginary in Zoharic Kabbalah," *RES: Anthropology and Aesthetics* 51 (2007): 123–124.

4 See above, intro., n. 47; Steven M. Wasserstrom, *Religion after Religion: Gershom Scholem Mircea Eliade and Henry Corbin at Eranos* (Princeton: Princeton University Press, 1999), 147–148.

https://doi.org/10.1515/9783110535884-013

an icon. The idol is impermeable and does not allow for transcendence, whereas the icon allows a vision and sight of transcendence:

> The ambiguity of the Image comes from the fact that it can be either an idol (Gr. *eidolon*) or an icon (Gr. *eikon*). It is an idol when it fixes the viewer's vision on itself. Then it is opaque, without transparency, and remains at the level of that from which it was formed. But it is an icon, whether a painted image or a mental one, when its transparency permits the viewer to see through it to something beyond it, and because what is beyond can be seen only through it. ...Idolatry consists in immobilizing oneself before an idol because one sees it as opaque, because one is incapable of discerning in it the hidden invitation that it offers to go beyond it. Hence, the opposite of idolatry would not consist in breaking idols, in practicing a fierce iconoclasm aimed against every inner or external Image; it would rather consist in rendering the idol transparent to the light invested in it. In short, it means transmuting the idol into an icon.[5]

Corbin claims that the main characterization of Western philosophy is the chasm between "thought" and "being." In Western philosophy two types of knowledge are presented—sensory perception and logical comprehension, in which the sensory conception does not necessarily affect the logical conception, and whereas the intellect does not inevitably affect man ontologically. Corbin challenged this view and asserted that there is a third type of knowledge, an intermediate knowledge between the intellect and the sense—the "Active Imagination," which appears in Sufi literature.[6] According to this view, man has primary access to spiritual and religious phenomena, which is not mediated through the intellect or senses, but rather through the third source of knowledge—the Active Imagination, a source of knowledge neglected in Western philosophy which "has been left to the poets:"

> Between the sense perceptions and the intuitions or categories of the intellect there has remained a void. That which ought to have taken its place between the two, and which in

5 Henry Corbin, "Theophanies and Mirrors: Idols or Icons?" trans. J. A. Pratt and A. K. Donohue, *Spring Journal: An Annual of Archetypal Psychology and Jungian Thought* (1983), 1–2 idem, *La Philosophie Iranienne Islamique Aux XVII et XVIII Siecles* (Paris: Buchet Chastel, 1981), 358, 363–364. Regarding the difference between an idol and icon in Corbin's thought and its significance for the study of religious consciousness, see Tom Cheetham, *All the World an Icon: Henry Corbin and the Angelic Function of Beings* (Berkeley: North Atlantic Books, 2012), 5–6, 16, 182–188; idem, *The World Turned Inside Out: Henry Corbin and Islamic Mysticism* (Woodstock: Spring Journal Books, 2003), 141–148.
6 Cheetham, *The World Turned Inside Out*, 43–50.

> other times and places did occupy this intermediate space, that is to say the *Active Imagination*, has been left to the poets.[7]

Corbin clarifies that his utilization of the concept of imagination is not in its common use as fantasy or fiction, but as an objective and authentic source of knowledge:

> Here we shall not be dealing with imagination in the usual sense of the word: neither with fantasy, profane or otherwise, nor with the organ which produces imaginings identified with the unreal; nor shall we even be dealing exactly with what we look upon as the organ of esthetic creation. We shall be speaking of an absolutely basic function, correlated with a universe peculiar to it, a universe endowed with a perfectly 'objective' existence and perceived precisely through the Imagination.[8]

According to Corbin, the imagination allows access to a world in which the intellect and senses are unified. Without the imagination, religious phenomena in general and religious experience in particular would be impossible! Through the imagination, man perceives "icons" and religious meanings therein, which allow him a glimpse of transcendence:

> Unlike common knowledge, which is effected by a penetration of the sense impressions of the outside world into the interior of the soul, the work of prophetic inspiration is a projection of the inner soul upon the outside world. The Active Imagination guides, anticipates, molds sensory perception; that is why it transmutes sensory data into symbols. The Burning Bush is only a brushwood fire if it is merely perceived by the sensory organs. In order that Moses may perceive the Burning Bush and hear the Voice calling him 'from the right side of the valley'—in short, in order that there may be a theophany—an organ of trans-sensory perception is needed... This theophanic perception is accomplished in the "*ālam al-mithāl*," whose organ is the theophanic Imagination.[9]

The Active Imagination is necessary in order to verify reality and understand numerous personal experiences, including dreams, visions, and prophetic revelation.[10] The imagination, as a source of knowledge, allows access to a world of

7 Henry Corbin, *Spiritual Body and Celestial Earth: From Mazdean Iran to Shī'ite Iran*, trans. N. Pearson (Princeton: Princeton University Press, 1989), vii.

8 Henry Corbin, *Creative Imagination in the Sufism of Ibn 'Arabī*, trans. R. Manheim (Princeton: Princeton University Press, 1969), 3. Regarding imagination as objective knowledge see Roberts Avens, *Imagination as Reality: Western Nirvana in Jung, Hillman, Barfield and Cassirer* (Dallas: Spring Publications, 1980).

9 Corbin, *Creative Imagination*, 80.

10 Concerning imagination and prophetic revelation in Corbin's thought see Tom Cheetham, *Green Man, Earth Angel: The Prophetic Tradition and The Battle for the Soul of the World*, Albany:

true existence, an objective world which Corbin, inspired by the Islamic concept of *ālam al-mithāl*, which appears in the mystical doctrine of Ibn 'Arabī and others, calls the imaginal world or *mundus imaginalis.*[11]

The Active Imagination in Corbin's thought is not only a source of knowledge and an intermediary between the *logos* and the senses, but is also primarily a "creative imagination."[12] The imagination is both the epistemological awareness of an object and is simultaneously that which creates it! Corbin demonstrates this primarily in the realm of prayer in which the imagination creates the divine revelation:

> Prayer takes on a meaning which would have been profoundly repugnant not only to Ibn 'Arabī but to Sufism in general. For prayer is not a request for something: it is the expression of a mode of being, a means of existing and of *causing to exist*, that is, a means of causing the God who reveals Himself to appear, of 'seeing' Him, not to be sure in His essence, but in the *form* which precisely He reveals by revealing Himself by and to that form. This view of Prayer takes the ground from under the feet of those who, utterly ignorant of the nature of the theophanic Imagination as Creation, argue that a God who is the 'creation' of our Imagination can only be 'unreal' and that there can be no purpose in praying to such a God. For it is precisely because He *is* a creation of the imagination that we pray to him, and that He exists. Prayer is the highest form, the supreme act of the Creative Imagination. ...the *Prayer of Man* accomplishes this theophany because in it and through it the 'Form of God' (*ṣūrat al-Ḥaqq*) becomes visible to the heart.[13]

The visualization of God during prayer causes the same imaginal God to disclose himself to the imaginer. According to Corbin, prayer in its essence is not supplication, even if it is full of supplications. Prayer in its essence, "is the expression of a mode of being, a means of existing and of *causing to exist.*" Prayer, based on man's imagination, creates divine revelation, for "through it the 'Form of God' (*ṣūrat al-Ḥaqq*) becomes visible to the heart." God, "epiphanizes Himself insofar as He is the God *whom* and *for whom* we pray."[14] Furthermore, Corbin emphasizes the fact that the imagination takes shape in works of art and science, as well

State University of New York Press, 2005); idem, *After Prophecy: Imagination, Incarnation, and the Unity of the Prophetic Tradition* (New Orleans: Spring Publications 2007), 97–138.

11 Concerning the *ālam al-mithāl* in Islam see Fazlur Rahman, "Dream, Imagination and 'Alam AlMithal,'" *Islamic Studies* 3 (1964): 167–180, also for its place in Corbin's thought see Cheetham, *The World Turned Inside Out*, 66–83.

12 Regarding the connection between the Active Imagination and the Creative Imagination see Cheetham, *All the World an Icon*, 18–20, 159–181.

13 Corbin, *Creative Imagination*, 248.

14 Ibid.

as modern parapsychological performances, and thus its creative power is actualized.[15]

Indeed, although Corbin only disseminated his scholarship on Islam and the imagination throughout Europe mainly in the second half of the twentieth century, nonetheless, there is no doubt that there were already, non-mature, prior ideological structures in the beginning of the twentieth century which brought the Sufi conception of the imagination to Europe. In the late nineteenth and early twentieth century it is possible to identify an incursion of Sufi doctrines and practices in Europe, and with them the importance of the imagination, both in the philosophical and practical (as well as mystical, psychological, and medical) realm. William James presented them in his work, which was published already in 1902.[16] Thinkers at the periphery of hasidism, like Hillel Zeitlin, who was concomitantly in contact with hasidic leaders and public Jewish figures, quotes James in his books and writings that were published in Poland and Europe in Hebrew and Yiddish.[17] This is one example of the possible dissemination of Sufism among European Jewry, through James's work.[18]

Not only did Sufism gain a foothold in Europe at the turn of the nineteenth century, but so did techniques from the Far East. Surprisingly, there was a widespread and detailed knowledge of Eastern mystical techniques from India, and even Tibet, in hasidic circles already from the beginning of the nineteenth century. Evidence for this can be found in books like, *Me'ora'ot Ṣevi: Sipur Ḥalomot Qeṣ Hafla'ot* (Lemberg: J. Rosanes Press, 1804), which was presumably written by R. Yisra'el Yafeh, who published *Shivḥei ha-Beshṭ*. This literary style also appeared in non-hasidic books (which were in any case available for all) like the book *Sefer Shevilei Olam* (1822) and *Masa'ei Yisra'el* (1859).[19] This literature re-

---

15 Ibid., 222.

16 See James, *The Varieties of Religious Experience*, 402–406.

17 Zeitlin calls James's composition a "wondrous book" and about him writes that, "James is almost the only person who has found the scientific key to unlock religion's gates." Zeitlin, *Al Gevul Shenei Olamot*, 13 (translation from Green, *Hasidic Spirituality*, 126).

18 For Heschel's relationship with and slight influence on Corbin, specifically through the concepts of "religion of sympathy" and "theology of pathos," see Paul B. Fenton, "Henry Corbin and Abraham Heschel," in *Abraham Joshua Heschel: Philosophy, Theology and Interreligious Dialogue*, eds., Stanisław Krajewski and Adam Lipszyc (Wiesbaden: Harrossowitz, 2009), 102–111. On his relationship with Gershom Scholem, see Wasserstrom, *Religion after Religion*, 52–66. Elliot Wolfson in his scholarship has made extensive use of Corbin's concepts like *imaginative presence* and developed others like the *imaginal body* in order to conceptualize the formless form of the divine see Wolfson, *Through a Speculum*, 8, 63, 108.

19 Shimshon Bloch, *Sefer Shevilei Olam* (Żółkiew: Menerhoffer, 1822); Israël Joseph Benjamin, *Eight Years in Asia and Africa*, trans. David Gordon (Lyck: Defus Tsvi Hirsch Petsall, 1859). Re-

veals extremely intimate knowledge of Eastern and African religions and makes it accessible to a wider audience.[20] Indeed, our attention should also be drawn to the remarkable fact that modern colonialism and imperialism (which peaked at the end of the nineteenth and beginning of the twentieth century), which revealed and brought the West to the East, ultimately created a cultural encounter between them. This encounter also brought the East to the West, such that Eastern conceptions, methods, and practices were spread into the heart of Western culture, which until this day is still engaged with this encounter and is in dialogue with it.[21]

In this context it should be noted that the scholar of religion, Mircea Eliade (1907–1986), was in India for his studies between the years 1928 and 1931 at Calcutta University (now Kolkata) and half a year in an ashram in Rishikesh in the Himalayan area.[22] His time in the Far East engendered his doctoral thesis on In-

garding these works see Tomer Persico, "Be-Darkhei No'am: Ha-Neyu Eij ke-Haṭma'ah shel Etos Noṣri be-Yahadut Bat Zemanainu," *Akdamot* 24 (2010): 72–75 and the footnotes there.

20 The anonymously authored *Me'ora'ot Ṣevi* (Lemberg: J. Rosanes Press, 1804) was written against Sabbateanism. The book prosaically describes Sabbatei Ṣevi's deeds in comparison to Far Eastern and African rituals performed by pagan priests. On Eastern Indian religious rituals, ibid., 16a; For parallels between the biblical *soṭah* ritual (the trial of a wife suspected of adultery) with Indian, Japanese, and African religious customs, see ibid., 19b-20a; For the Tibetan ritual of creating an artificial anthropoid (*golem*) see ibid., 20b; For Indian pagan medicine ibid., 32a-b; For religious rituals in Kenya (*qandjz*), ibid., 26b-27a. The book *Masa'ei Yisra'el* investigates the Jewish communities of Asia and Africa and other congregations that the author identifies as parts of the lost ten tribes. Israël Joseph Benjamin embarked on his journey on February 1, 1846 from Moldavia to Turkey and from there to Palestine. He left Palestine in January 1848 (ibid., 10) for Damascus through the Lebanese mountains and from there to the villages of Kurdistan, Baghdad, Persia, and India (ibid., 10–80). The second half of the book details his journey to North Africa (ibid., 102–134): Egypt, Tripoli, Tunis, Algeria, Morocco. Shimshon Bloch's book, *Shevilei Olam*, is a geographical and historical work without any focus on religion or Judaism. Nevertheless, it depicts religious rituals (in India, ibid., 44b-47a; in Tibet ibid., 73). In this book there is a description of Asia and Asian culture (Turkey, Arabia, Persia, India, China, Tibet, Japan) and Africa (the subchapters, "Northern Africa," "Middle Africa," and "Southern Africa"). On page 61 he describes the Jews of the land of Kush (Ethiopia) who are called Falasha (Beta Israel).

21 For the influence of Far Eastern techniques on Europe see Colin Campbell, *The Easternization of the West: A Thematic Account of Cultural Change in the Modern Era* (Boulder: Paradigm Publishers, 2007); Although colonialism began in the fifteenth century, it was only with the technological ability of quick transportation, brought about by the industrial revolution of the mid-nineteenth century, that the encounter between West and East was enriched and through which the East became central in the West.

22 Mircea Eliade, *Yoga: Immortality and Freedom*, (Princeton: Princeton University Press, 1970), xx.

dian Yoga. This composition constituted a preliminary stage in his understanding of Indian spirituality and his philosophical focus on techniques, which was later incorporated in his book *Yoga: Immortality and Freedom.*[23] These studies and his concentration on techniques, which were published in Europe in the first half of the twentieth century, were not only used as academic resources, but also changed the modes of thinking about the East and allowed for yogic and similar techniques to enter the European consciousness.[24]

The terms that Eliade disclosed to the West became a fertile ground for innovative thought and the formation of new techniques. Eliade's introduction of the concept of *Karma*, "The law of universal causality which connects man with the cosmos,"[25] to the West, constituted a possible setting for the development of imagery techniques of a universal and cosmological character. Additionally, Indian techniques, like Yoga, emphasized the necessity for human initiation together with its practical side.[26] This conception parallels that found in hasidism, also predicated upon human initiative and the necessity of developing and searching for techniques. Another spiritual resource that Eastern techniques presented was the need for a spiritual guide. Man does not learn Yoga alone, he is dependent on instruction from a guru.[27] Similarly, the imagery techniques that I have presented in this study are characterized by guidance, where the "guru," is the hasidic *ṣaddiq.*[28] It should be noted that Yoga, unlike Sāmkhya, is theistic since it posits the existence of God (Iśvara) and stresses meditative techniques (in contrast to Sāmkhya, which sees metaphysical knowledge as the sole means for salvation).[29] Most likely its theistic nature facilitated its permeation, to the extent that there was, into different religious circles. Furthermore, the con-

---

23 Idem, "The Comparative History of Yoga Techniques" (Ph.D. diss., Bucharest University, 1933); idem, *Techniques du Yoga* (Paris: Gallimard, 1948).

24 Eliade's goal, as he himself stated, was not solely academic. Eliade intentionally brought the Eastern conceptions to the West in order to disseminate them and influence Western conceptions.

25 Eliade, *Yoga*, 3.

26 Ibid., 5.

27 Ibid.

28 Although, in Yoga the emphasis is on oral learning from the guru, face to face, while the imagery techniques that I have presented in this work are transferred graphically, through books. Nonetheless there is a clear common denominator being the precise instruction and guidance passed from master to pupil, while in Yoga it is verbal and in hasidism it is textual. However, with its introduction to the West, Yoga changed as well. As soon as it was spread throughout the West through popular publication, it too (like hasidism) was transformed from an oral tradition to a textual one.

29 Eliade, *Yoga*, 7.

cepts of *biṭṭul ha-yesh* (the nullification of something) and *biṭṭul ha-ani* (self-annihilation) are found in Yoga,[30] as well as hasidism, a correlation which can allow for the proliferation of Yoga and its measured absorption in hasidic thought.[31]

In his studies Eliade dealt with imagery techniques developed in Tibet. In Tibetan Tantra, imagination and imagery techniques play a central role as enablers of meditation.[32] Moreover, he highlighted the fact that "Indian psychology" was well aware of hypnosis and attributed it to a temporary state of concentration.[33] This particular identification of Yoga techniques and modern hypnotic techniques amplified Yoga's popularity and its absorption in Europe, specifically when hypnosis reached maturity. According to Eliade:

> The ideal of Yoga, the state of *jivan-mukti*, is to live in an 'eternal present,' outside of time. 'Liberated in life', the jivan-mukta no longer possesses a personal consciousness—that is, a consciousness nourished on his own history—but a witnessing consciousness, which is

---

30 Ibid., 33–34.

31 I am not ignoring the very real differences between Yoga and Judaism, specifically hasidism. The purpose of Yoga is to liberate man from this world see ibid., xx, "One of India's greatest discoveries: that of consciousness as witness, of consciousness freed from its psychophysiological structures and their temporal conditioning, the consciousness of the 'liberated' man, of him, that is, who have succeeded in emancipating himself from temporality and thereafter knows the true, inexpressible freedom;" meaning that the primary goal of Indian philosophy is the absolute liberation of man, and its mystical techniques are designed for that goal. This liberation is done through the negation of this world, see ibid., 5, 35. Implications of this conception are the techniques whose purpose are to empty one's consciousness, ibid., 77. This emptying is the opposite, generally speaking, of what is characteristic of hasidic techniques, which fill consciousness with all types of images and visualizations, and do not attempt to empty it. On the relation of hasidism to this world see chap. 3, subchapter, "Two Models of Prophecy," regarding positive and negative mysticism. Regarding Kook's relation to Buddhism and its sources see Amir Mashiach, "Rabbi Kook and Buddhism," *Da'at* 70 (2011): 81–96. Also see ibid., 83 n. 8 for Eliezer Goldman's list of sources concerning Kook's exposure to European thought. Mashiach claims that Kook's main sources for Buddhism and Eastern wisdom come from Schopenhauer's (ibid., 87–89) and Nietzsche's (ibid., 90–93) works, and that he knew their work primarily through Fabius Mieses's book *History of Modern Philosophy* (Leipzig: s.n., 1887). Also see ibid., 84 for R. David Cohen (*Rav Ha-Nazir*) relation to Buddhism. For our purposes, if Kook and Cohen were exposed to Buddhism, whether in a roundabout manner are by mistake as Mashiach claims, there is no reason that other Jewish thinkers who were in Europe at the same time would not have similarly been exposed as well. It also makes no difference if the exposure was in order to attack these doctrines or to be influenced by them, what is important for our purposes is that they were exposed.

32 Eliade, *Yoga*, 207–212; Also see that these imagery exercises have universal content, just like those of Menaḥem Mendel Ekstein's.

33 Ibid., 78–79.

> pure lucidity and spontaneity… Yoga takes over and continues the immemorial symbolism of initiation; in other words, it finds its place in a universal tradition of the religious history of mankind.[34]

The aspiration for eternal life is not in the sense of physical immortality, but rather supra-temporal life. This life is one of the annihilation of personal consciousness, comprised of its own experiences, and the acquirement of an alternative consciousness—of "pure lucidity and spontaneity." Eliade terms this consciousness a "witnessing consciousness," a conception that is similar to the philosophical underpinnings of Menaḥem Mendel Ekstein's autoscopic imaginal visualization techniques, in which man observes himself from an external viewpoint.[35]

European interest in the East at the turn of the century had a weighty impact on Jewish identity. In Western Europe, assimilation, which had already taken root, brought with it a loss of identity and feelings of inferiority. The younger Jewish generation was drawn towards Orientalism and found for itself a place of self-definition within this complex process. Paul Mendes-Flohr discussed the renewed interest of Jewish youth, at the turn of the nineteenth century, in Indian, Buddhist, and Islamic mystical teachings, as well as a renewed interest in the mystical tradition of medieval Christianity.[36]

Eastern culture, which before the turn of the century was viewed as inferior, suddenly became quite attractive.[37] The invalidation of the moral and material promise of the Enlightenment, primarily by the philosophies of Schopenhauer and Nietzsche, contributed to the veneration of the East.[38] The *Ostjuden* (Oriental Jews) were now able to feel a renewed sense of self-satisfaction while the East was granted a new positive image.[39] One may find organizations, like the Bar

---

34 Ibid., 363.

35 For an interesting comparison of tantric and kabbalistic views see Idel, *Mystical Experience*, 215 n. 82, also see his comment that a fruitful comparison may be made between Tibetan Yoga and theurgical kabbalah, idem, *Kabbalah: New Perspectives*, 396 n. 76. For a comparison of Abulafian prophecy techniques and Yoga idem, *Mystical Experience*, 24–26, 39–40. For more on kabbalah, Yoga, and Tantra see Garb, *Manifestations of Power*, 23–24, 253, 277. On the image of "fire" as a hasidic expression for language (the words of the righteous, "all their words are a blazing fire") and similar tantric parallels see Garb, *Shamanic Trance*, 85.

36 Paul R. Mendes-Flohr, "Fin-de-Siècle Orientalism, the *Ostjuden*, and the Aesthetics of Jewish Self-Affirmation," in *Divided Passions: Jewish Intellectuals and the Experience of Modernity*, ed. Paul R. Mendes-Flohr (Detroit: Wayne University Press, 1991), 77–132; idem, "Orientalism and Mysticism," 624–681.

37 Ibid., 625

38 Ibid., 625–628.

39 Ibid., 631–633.

Kochba Association in Prague, and volumes, like *Von Judentum* (1913), which cultivated a transformed sense of Jewish pride and increased interest in Eastern spirituality and mysticism. Martin Buber was officially appointed in 1908 to be the spiritual guide of the Bar Kochba Association, which called for a Jewish renaissance. Buber's lectures delivered to this association elaborated on the mystical quality of hasidism and compared the hasidic spirituality with different mystical traditions, like Indian, Chinese, Finnish, Celtic, and Persian. Hasidism, according to Buber, expresses the authentic "oriental" nature of the Jew,[40] and he presented it as an "oriental myth."[41]

This European *zeitgeist*, influenced by the East and the West, modern psychology and philosophy, serves as a specific setting for the understanding of the development of imagery techniques of the nineteenth and twentieth century found in hasidism as well as the Musar movement. The development of imagery techniques in Jewish mysticism, from linguistic techniques in the early kabbalah to visual techniques, focusing on individual scenes, in early hasidism, and finally to the imaginal visualization of entire plots in later hasidism, did not occur in a vacuum. This development should be seen as part of a more encompassing and universal process, even when there is no proof of direct influence, and all the more so where there is. Jewish figures developed imagery techniques against the background of parallel developments and sometimes as a reaction to them, travelers in the *Adventures of Ideas.*

40 Ibid., 634–641.

41 Ibid., 664–665. On the anti-rationalistic atmosphere at the turn of the nineteenth century, see Maor, *A New Secret Doctrine*, 28–30, 32–36, 158–165. Also regarding the new appeal of the East, ibid., 38–39,122–123, 213.

Afterword

> Faith must be in *Anokhi* (I), meaning, in God's very entity, and not to grasp him intellectually (*lo le-hasigo*); on the contrary it is forbidden to investigate and examine him. A Jew must only have some grasp and *vision of it* (*aḥizah ve-ra'ayah bo*). For example, the prophet said, "I beheld my Lord" (Is. 6:1)... God created and emanated some kind of spiritual sight and this is what was for the prophet... however, no Jew is exempt from this vision... it is only that the prophet had many prophetic visions and the intermediate man (*benoni*), nevertheless, needs a small portion of it. I am not speaking now from only knowledge (*yedi'ah*) and emotion, rather more than them—from *actual vision!* Prophetic vision that is within all of Israel, for they are disciples of the prophets... My intention in this is *the imagination.* Man believes that his imagination is null and void, for he sees it as a delusion (*mas'ot shav*), folly, and false, but in truth the imagination is the action and vision of the soul, as it truly is (*ke-she-hi le-aṣmah*).[1]

In the postmodern age in which the imagination precedes reality and is of central importance, the development of imagery techniques, from the beginning of kabbalah in the twelfth century until forms of twentieth century Jewish mysticism, should be paid heed. Linguistic imagery techniques developed into multi-scenic and dramatic imagery techniques, filled with imagery and plot, similar to dreams and cinema, "Scene after scene will pass in front of our spiritual eyes like in a *Kino* (cinema)."[2] This development was part and parcel of a wider development, in which the imagination expanded in many different dimension, both philosophical as well as practical, within Western philosophy, psychology, psychiatry, and studies—both in the East and West. At the turn of the nineteenth century (1880–1920) the imagination was understood in certain circles as a unique source of knowledge, able to decipher and epistemologically know reality, and as a medium that allows for an understandings beyond linear logic.

A common element in different mysticisms is the intensification and empowerment of religious life and the experience of the sublime within the specific context of each religion. Naturally, Jewish mysticism intensified the "bodily commandments," meaning the rituals performed in the physical realm, which are the heart of Judaism. The imagination served a number of hasidic thinkers as an intensifier of both nomian and anomian experiences, thereby allowing one to sense the divine presence and encounter God. The driving force behind the de-

1 Shapira's sermon on the eve of Rosh Hashanah 1924. See Ḥayyim Barukh Tesher, *Yehudah me-Ḥoqeqei, Igerot ha-R"B, Derekh ha-Melekh: Ḥadash me-Ketav Yad* (Brooklyn: s.n., 2006), 15–16. Emphasis mine.

2 Ekstein, *Tena'ei ha-Nefesh*, 8. Also, see above chap. 6, subchapter, "*Raṣo va-Shov* (Running and Returning): Numerous Scenes and Their Successive Progression."

https://doi.org/10.1515/9783110535884-014

velopment of these imagery techniques was the mystical and personal need of certain spiritual figures to experience communion with the divine. Additionally, the imagination served to some extent as a means for the development of ecstatic prophecy, which influences and causes change in reality. Even in the Lithuanian Musar movement, a tremendous development can be discerned regarding the utilization of imagery practices and techniques, from the internalization of fear (*yir'ah*) to the internalization of faith. While in the Musar movement there is no emphasis on the experience of the divine presence, as there is in hasidism, the imagination nonetheless served as a means of intensifying and empowering faith in the twentieth century, transforming it into a living experience. Furthermore, the imagination allowed for the illustration of the divine, which created a spectrum of enormous tensions, between the desire to see God and the prohibition in doing so. It is along this spectrum that mystical and religious consciousness oscillate, manifesting in both hasidism and the Musar movement.

The elements and foundations of different imagery techniques—whether they be mystical, emotionally empowering, religiously intensifying, modern self-expression, or the acquiring of suprarational understandings—are carried out through autonomous human initiative. Man must exert himself and attempt "to fly like angels."[3] Imagery techniques are the essence of man and the source of his vitality, as Ekstein wrote, "Those standing outside of hasidism... refer to the masters of this movement as masters of hallucination and fantasy, chasing after images (*dimyonot*)... however... these images, hallucinations, and fantasies... are man's essence, a man who knows to live, disclose, and bring to light all the hidden treasures in his soul."[4]

---

3 Shapira, *Mevo ha-She'arim*, 59a. Also, see above chap. 4, subchapter, "R. Kalonymous Kalman Shapira's Imagery Techniques and His Imaginal-Literary Style."
4 Ekstein, *Tena'ei ha-Nefesh*, 30.

Bibliography

Primary Rabbinic, Kabbbalistic, Hasidic Sources

Aaron ben Asher of Karlin. *Beit Aharon.* Jerusalem: A. Schwortz, 1965. [Hebrew]
Abrams, Daniel, ed., *The Book Bahir: An Edition Based on the Earliest Manuscripts.* Introduction by Moshe Idel. Los Angeles: Cherub Press, 1994. [Hebrew]
Abulafia, Abraham. *Sefer Ḥayyei ha-Olam ha-Ba.* Jerusalem: Amnon Gross, 1999
Alter, Yehudah Leib of Ger. *Sefat Emet.* Or Eṣion: Ha-Maḥon ha-Torani Or Eṣion, 2011. [Hebrew]
Azulai, Abraham. *Ḥesed le-Avraham.* Jerusalem: Sha'ar Ha-Shamayim, 1996. [Hebrew]
Azulai, Abraham. *Or ha-Ḥamah.* Bnei Brak: Yahadut, 1972. [Hebrew]
Azulai, Ḥayyim Joseph David. *Birkei Yosef.* Jerusalem: s.n., 2001. [Hebrew]
Azulai, Ḥayyim Joseph David. *Midbar Qedemot.* Modi'in Illit: Ahavat Shalom, 2008. [Hebrew]
Baḥya ben Asher. *Commentary on the Torah.* Edited by Hayyim Dov Chavel. Jerusalem: Mossad HaRav Kook, 1972. [Hebrew]
Barukh ben Avraham of Kosov. *Na'im ve-Neḥmad: Yesod ha-Emunah.* Józefów: Barukh Zetzer's Press, 1884. [Hebrew]
Bernstein, Meir of Radom. *Sefer Oraḥ Mishor.* Warsaw: s.n., 1900.
Birth Certificate for Kalonymous Kalman Shapira, July 13, 1889, Registration No. 53, Grodzisk Mazowiecki Birth Registry Book of 1889.
Birth Certificate for Menaḥem Mendel Ekstein, December 21, 1884, Mic. no. 553/62, The Polish National Archive of Rzeszów.
Blazer, Isaac. "Sha'arei Or." In *Or Yisra'el.* Edited by Isaac Blazer. Vilnius: Metz Publishing House, 1900. [Hebrew]
Bloch, Shimshon. *Sefer Shevilei Olam.* Żółkiew: Menerhoffer, 1822. [Hebrew]
Bornsztain, Shmuel. *Shem me-Shemu'el.* Jerusalem: Eastern Books Press, 1992. [Hebrew]
Bosker, Ben-Zion, ed., *Abraham Isaac Kook: The Lights of Penitence, Lights of Holiness, The Moral Principles, Essays, Letters, and Poems.* Translated by ben-Zion Bosker. New York: Paulist Press, 1978.
Cordovero, Moses. *Pardes Rimmonim.* Jerusalem: Yarid ha-Sefarim, 2000. [Hebrew]
Correspondence from Menaḥem Mendel Ekstein to Jekuthiel Aryeh Kamelhar, Jekuthiel Aryeh ben Gershon Kamelhar Personal Archive, ARC. 4°1517, National Library in Jerusalem, Israel.
Da Fano, Menaḥem Azariah. *Ma'amar Tiqqunei Teshuvah.* In *Ma'amarei ha-RaM"A me-Fano.* Vol. 3. Jerusalem: Yismaḥ Lev—Torat Mosheh, 2003. [Hebrew]
De Vidas, Elijah. *Re'shit Ḥokhmah ha-Shalem.* Edited by Ḥayyim Yosef Waldman. Jerusalem: Or ha-Musar, 2000. [Hebrew]
Deblitzki, Seraya. *Beino Shenot Dor ve-Dor.* Bnei Brak: s.n., 2006. [Hebrew]
Dessler, Elijah Eliezer. *Mikhtav me-Eliyahu.* Edited by Aryeh Carmel and Aryeh Halpern. London: Honig and Sons, 1955; Jerusalem: Sifriyati, 1992; Bnei Brak: Sifsei Chachamim, 2009. [Hebrew]
Dov Baer of Międzyrzecz. *Maggid Devarav le-Ya'aqov.* Brooklyn: Kehot, 2010. [Hebrew]
Eibenschütz, David Solomon. *Sefer Arvei Naḥal ha-Shalem.* Jerusalem: Maḥon Giv'ot Olam, 2004. [Hebrew]

https://doi.org/10.1515/9783110535884-015

Ekstein, Menaḥem Mendel. *Mavoh le-Torat ha-Ḥasidut.* Tel Aviv: Neṣaḥ Publishing, 1960. [Hebrew]
Ekstein, Menaḥem Mendel. *Tena'ei ha-Nefesh le-Hasagat ha-Ḥassidut.* Vienna: Union Press-Appel Brothers, 1921; Beitar Ilit: Makhon Even ha-Shetiya"h, 2006. [Hebrew]
Ekstein, Menachem. *Visions of a Compassionate World: Guided Imagery for Spiritual Growth and Social Transformation.* Translated by Yehoshua Starett. New York: Urim Publications, 2001.
Elijah ben Solomon Zalman. *Seder Olam im Perush ha-GR"A.* Warsaw: Israel Alapin Press, 1876. [Hebrew]
Elijah of Wiskitki, *Ezor Eliyahu.* Warsaw: s.n., 1885. [Hebrew]
Epstein, Kalonymus Kalman Halevi. *Sefer Ma'or ve-Shemesh ha-Shalem.* Breslau: s.n., 1842; Jerusalem: Or ha-Sefer, 1994. [Hebrew]
Ettlinger, Jacob. *Binyan Ṣiyyon Responsa.* Altona: Gebrüder Bonn, 1868. [Hebrew]
Feinstein, Moshe. *Iggerot Moshe Responsa.* Bnei Brak: s.n., 1981. [Hebrew]
Frankel, Ḥayyim, and David Ḥayyim Zilbershlag, eds. *Zikharon Qodesh le-Ba'al Esh Qodesh.* Jerusalem: Va'ad Ḥasidei Pi'asechna—Grodzhisq, 1994. [Hebrew]
Friedman, Benjamin of Miszkolc. *Tif'eret Avot.* Tel Aviv: s.n., 1966. [Hebrew]
Friedman, Shlomo Hayim. *Ḥayyei Shelomoh.* Jerusalem: Mehudar, 2006. [Hebrew]
Halevi, Judah. *Sefer ha-Kuzari.* Edited by A. Tzifroni. Tel Aviv: Mahbarot Lesifrut, 1989. [Hebrew]
Hallamish, Moshe. *Kabbalistic Commentary of Rabbi Yoseph ben Shalom Ashkenazi on Genesis Rabbah.* Jerusalem: Magnes Press, 1984. [Hebrew]
Ḥarlap, Jacob Moses ben Zebulun. *Mei Marom.* Vol. 6. Jerusalem: Bet Zevul, 1982. [Hebrew]
Ḥayyim Berish ben Ya'aqov ha-Kohen. *Sefer Ṭov Me'od.* Jerusalem: Gushtzineni Press, 1889. [Hebrew]
Hirsch, Aaron ben Ẓevi ha-Kohen of Opatow. *Or ha-Ganuz le-Ṣaddiqim.* Zhovkva: Rabin-Stein Press, 1800; Warsaw: J. Unterhendler Press, 1887. [Hebrew]
Horowitz, Isaiah. *Shnei Luḥot ha-Berit: Asarah Ma'amarot.* Haifa: Yad Ramah, 1997. [Hebrew]
Horowitz, Meir. *Responsa Imre No'am.* Krakow: Josef Fisher Publishing, 1888. [Hebrew]
Jacob ben Asher. *Ṭur.* Vilna: s.n., 1923. [Hebrew]
Judah ben Samuel he-Ḥasid, *Sefer Ḥasidim.* Edited by Judah Wistinetzki and Jacob Freimann. Berlin: H. Itzkowski, 1891. [Hebrew]
Kagan, Israel Meir. *Mishneh Berurah.* Jerusalem: Or ha-Ḥayyim, 2018. [Hebrew]
Karo, Joseph. *Shulḥan Arukh.* Jerusalem: s.n., 1992. [Hebrew]
Katz, Jacob Joseph ben Ẓevi Ha-Kohen of Polonnoye. *Ben Porat Yosef.* Brooklyn, s.n., 1976. [Hebrew]
Keter Shem Ṭov. Lemberg: s.n., 1851; New York: Otzar Hasidim Press, 1987. [Hebrew]
Kitvei ha-Sabba ve-Talmidav me-Qelm. Bnei Brak: Sifsei Chachamim, 1992. [Hebrew]
Kohen, David (Ha-Nazir). *Mishnat ha-Nazir.* Jerusalem: Nezer David, 2005. [Hebrew]
Kohen, David (Ha-Nazir). *Qol ha-Nevu'ah.* Jerusalem: Nezer David, 2002. [Hebrew]
Kohen, David (Ha-Nazir). *The Voice of Prophecy.* Jerusalem: Mossad Harav Kook, 1970. [Hebrew]
Koidanover, Tsevi Hirsch. *Qav ha-Yashar.* Frankfurt am Main: s.n., 1705. [Hebrew]
Kook, Abraham Isaac ha-Kohen. *Ma'amarei ha-Ra'ayah: Qoveṣ Ma'amarim.* Jerusalem: Mossad Harav Kook, 1984. [Hebrew]
Kook, Abraham Isaac ha-Kohen. *Olat Re'iyah.* Jerusalem, Mosad Harav Kook, 1996. [Hebrew]

Kook, Abraham Isaac ha-Kohen. *Orot ha-Emunah*. Jerusalem: Mossad Harav Kook, 1945. [Hebrew]
Kook, Abraham Isaac ha-Kohen. *Orot ha-Qodesh*. Vol. 1. Jerusalem: Mossad Harav Kook, 1994. [Hebrew]
Kook, Abraham Isaac ha-Kohen. *Orot ha-Teshuvah*. Jerusalem: Mossad HaRav Kook, 1994. [Hebrew]
Kook, Abraham Isaac ha-Kohen. *Orot*. Jerusalem: Mossad Harav Kook, 1985. [Hebrew]
Kook, Abraham Isaac Hakohen. *Orot*. Translated by Bezalel Naor. Spring Valley: Orot; New Milford, CT: Maggid Books, 2014.
Kook, Abraham Isaac ha-Kohen. *Pinqasei ha-Re'iah*. Jerusalem: Ha-Maḥon al Shem ha-Reṣi'ah Kook ZṢ"L, 2008. [Hebrew]
Kook, Abraham Isaac ha-Kohen. *Shemonah Qevaṣim*. Jerusalem: Mossad Harav Kook, 2004. [Hebrew]
Lainer, Mordekhai Yosef of Izbica. *Mei ha-Shilo'aḥ*. Bnei Brak, 2005. [Hebrew]
Lauterbach, Jacob Z., ed. and trans., *Mekhilta de-Rabbi Ishmael*. 2 Vols. 1933. Reprint, Philadelphia: The Jewish Publication Society, 2004.
Levenson, Alter Ḥayyim. *Sefer Tiqqun Olam*. Warsaw: Feder Brothers Publishing, 1932. [Hebrew]
Levi Yiṣḥaq of Berditchev, *Qedushat Levi*. Jerusalem: s.n., 1993. [Hebrew]
Levovitz, Yeruḥam Halevi. *Da'at Ḥokhmah u-Musar*. New York: Dass Chochmo Umussar Publications, 1966. [Hebrew]
Levovitz, Yeruḥam Halevi. *Ḥaver Ma'amarim*. Vilnius: Krins Publishing, 1939. [Hebrew]
Levovitz, Yeruḥam Halevi. *Ma'amarei ha-Mashgi'aḥ: Me-Siḥotav shel Rabbeinu ha-Ga'on ha-Ḥasid Maran Yeruḥam Halevi Levovitz*. s.l.: s.n., 2011. [Hebrew]
Lipkin, Israel. *Or Yisra'el*. Edited by Isaac Blazer. Vilnius: Metz Publishing House, 1900. [Hebrew]
Me'ora'ot Ṣevi: Sipur Ḥalomot Qeṣ Hafla'ot. Lemberg: J. Rosanes Press, 1804. [Hebrew]
Miller, Avigdor. *Lev Avigdor*. Jerusalem: Hamadpis, 2002. [Hebrew]
Miller, Avigdor. *Or Olam*. Arad: s.n., 2002. [Hebrew]
Miller, Avigdor. *Sha'arei Orah: Qoveṣ Ma'amarim shel Va'adei Musar*. Vol. 2. New York: s.n., 2006. [Hebrew]
Miller, Avigdor. *Torat Avigdor*. Vol. 1. Bnei Brak: s.n., 2002. [Hebrew]
"Minhagei Qodesh: Minhagei Yom Shabat Qodesh she-Nahag K"Q Maran ADMV"R ZṢVQLLH"H." *Qobeṣ Be'er Yiṣḥaq* 3 (January-February 2001): 77–79. [Hebrew]
Morgenstern, Yiṣḥaq Me'ir. *Yam ha-Ḥokhmah*. Jerusalem: Makhon Yam ha-Ḥokhmah, 2008. [Hebrew]
Moses ben Maimon (Maimonides). *The Eight Chapters of Maimonides on Ethics*. Edited and translated by Joseph I. Gorfinkle. New York: Columbia University Press, 1912.
Moses ben Maimon (Maimonides). *The Guide of the Perplexed*. Edited and translated by Shlomo Pines. 2 vols. Chicago: University of Chicago Press, 1963.
Moses ben Maimon (Maimonides). *Mishneh Torah*. Vols. 12. Bnei Brak: Hotsa'at Shabse Frankel, 1975–2001. [Hebrew]
Moses ben Maimon (Maimonides). *Moreh Nevukhim*. Annottated by Judah Even Shemuel. Jerusalem: Mossad Harav Kook, 2005. [Hebrew]
Moses ben Maimon (Maimonides). *Moreh Nevukhim*. Edited and translated by Michael Schwarz. 2 vols. Tel Aviv: Tel Aviv University Press, 2002. [Hebrew]

Moses Ḥayyim Ephraim of Sudlikov. *Degel Maḥaneh Efrayim*. Jerusalem: s.n., 1997.
Naḥman of Bratslav. *Ḥayyei Moharan*. Jerusalem and Tel Aviv: Yisroel Ber Odesser Fund, s.a. [Hebrew]
Naḥman of Bratslav. *Liqquṭei MoHaRaN*. Jerusalem: s.n., s.a. [Hebrew]
Naḥman of Bratslav. *Siḥot ha-Ran*. Jerusalem: Ḥasidei Bereslev, 1995. [Hebrew]
Natan of Nemirov. *Liqquṭei Halakhot*. Jerusalem: s.n., 1974. [Hebrew]
Palaggi, Ḥayyim. *She'elot u-Teshuvot Ḥayyim be-Yad*. Izmir: s.n., 1873. [Hebrew]
Paries, Aharon. *Torat ha-Ḥayyim*. Vienna: Georg Brag, 1880. [Hebrew]
Pesiqta Zuṭrata (Leqaḥ Ṭov). Edited by Solomon Buber. Vilna, s.n., 1880. [Hebrew]
Phineas of Korzec. *Midrash Pinḥas*. Biłgoraj: N. Kronberg, 1930. [Hebrew]
Pseudo-Baḥya. *Sefer Torat ha-Nefesh*. Edited by D. Broyde. Paris: Levinsohn-Kilemnik, 1896. [Hebrew]
Rabinowitz, Zadok ha-Kohen. *Divrei Sofrim*. Jerusalem: s.n., 2005. [Hebrew]
Rabinowitz, Zadok ha-Kohen. *Maḥshavot Ḥaruṣ*. Jerusalem: s.n., 2005. [Hebrew]
Rabinowitz, Zadok ha-Kohen. *Peri Ṣaddiq le-Ḥanukah*. Jerusalem: s.n., 2005. [Hebrew]
Rabinowitz, Zadok ha-Kohen. *Peri Ṣaddiq*. Jerusalem: s.n., 2005. [Hebrew]
Rabinowitz, Zadok ha-Kohen. *Quntres Sefer ha-Zikhronot*. Jerusalem: s.n., 2005. [Hebrew]
Rabinowitz, Zadok ha-Kohen. *Resisei Lailah*. Jerusalem: s.n., 2005. [Hebrew]
Rubin, Joseph David. *Aṣei ha-Levanon*. s.l.: s.n., 1899.
Ṣava'at ha-Ribash. New York: Kohet, 1998. [Hebrew]
"Ṣava'at Rebi Yeḥiel me-Aleksander." In *Ṣava'at ve-Hanhagot me-ha-Beshṭ ve-Talmidav*, 203. Bnei Brak: Maḥshevet, 1987. [Hebrew]
Schneersohn, Dov Baer. *Ma'amerei Admor ha-Emṣa'i: Qunṭresim*. Brooklyn: Kehot, 1991. [Hebrew]
Schneersohn, Dov Baer. *Perush ha-Millot*. Brooklyn: Kehot, 1993. [Hebrew]
Schneersohn, Dov Baer. *Torat Ḥayyim: Shemot*. Brooklyn: Kehot, 2003. [Hebrew]
Schneersohn, Yosef Yiṣḥaq. *Likkutei Dibburim*. Brooklyn: Kehot, 1955. [Yiddish]
Schneersohn, Yosef Yiṣḥaq. *Liqquṭei Dibburim*. Translated by Avrohom Chanoch Glitzenshtein. 5 vols. Brooklyn: Kehot, 1990. [Hebrew]
Schneersohn, Yosef Yitzchak. *Likkutei Dibburim: An Anthology of Talks by Yosef Yitzchak Schneersohn of Lubavitch*. Translated by Uri Kaploun, 5 vols. Brooklyn: Kehot, 2000.
Shapira, Avraham Elimelekh. *Mishnat Ḥakhamim*. Jerusalem: Sheneur Zalman Grossman, 1934. [Hebrew]
Shapira, Kalonymous Kalman. *Benei Maḥshavah Ṭovah*. MS Ḥabad Library 1192/27. Printed edition, Jerusalem: Va'ad Hasidei Piasetzna, 1970. [Hebrew]
Shapira, Kalonymous Kalman. *Derashah*. Warsaw: Ḥevrei ha-Qehilah ha-Ivrit de-Pi'aceşna, 1936. [Yiddish]
Shapira, Kalonymous Kalman. *Derekh ha-Melekh*. Jerusalem: Va'ad Hasidei Piasetzna, 1995. [Hebrew]
Shapira, Kalonymous Kalman. *Esh Qodesh*. Jerusalem: Va'ad Hasidei Piasetzna, 1960. [Hebrew]
Shapira, Kalonymous Kalman. *Hakhsharat ha-Avreikhim*. Jerusalem: Va'ad Hasidei Piasetzna, 1962. [Hebrew]
Shapira, Kalonymous Kalman. *Hovat ha-Talmidim*. Warsaw: Feder Press, 1932. [Hebrew]

Shapira, Kalonymous Kalman. *Kalonymous Kalman Shapira to Avraham Mosheh Gribstein.* MS Ring. II/432. Mf. ZIH-806, p. 4; Jewish Historical Institute, Warsaw, *Ringelblum Archive.* [Hebrew]
Shapira, Kalonymous Kalman. *Mavo ha-She'arim.* Jerusalem: Va'ad Hasidei Piasetzna, 1962. [Hebrew]
Shapira, Kalonymous Kalman. *Ṣav ve-Ziruz.* Jerusalem: Va'ad Hasidei Piasetzna, 1962. [Hebrew]
Shapira, Kalonymous Kalman. *Shelosh Derashot.* Tel Aviv: Merkaz Hasidei Koźnic, 1985. [Hebrew]
Shick, Shelomo Ṣevi. *Me-Mosheh ad Mosheh.* Mukachevo: Druck von Kahn and Fried, 1903.
Shneur Zalman of Liadi, *Liqquṭei Torah.* Brooklyn: Kehot, 1999 [Hebrew]
Shneur Zalman of Liadi, *Torah Or.* Brooklyn: Kehot, 1991. [Hebrew]
Shneur Zalman of Liadi. *Liqquṭei Amarim: Tanya.* Jerusalem: Heiḥal Menaḥem, 1997. [Hebrew]
Sirkis, Joel. *Bayit Ḥadash.* Jerusalem: s.n., 1959. [Hebrew]
Solomon ibn Adret. *Responsa.* Bnei Brak: 1958–1965. [Hebrew]
Soloveitchik, Ḥayyim ha-Levi. *Ḥiddushei Rabbeinu Ḥayyim ha-Levi: Ḥiddushim ve-Bi'urim al ha-Rambam.* Brest: Yehoshu'a Qlein, 1936. [Hebrew]
Soroski, Aharon. "Me-Toldot ha-ADMO"R ha-Qadosh Maran Rabi Kalonimus Kalmish Shapira ZṢ"L me-Pi'aschenah." In Kalonymous Kalman Shapira, *Esh Qodesh.* Edited by Aharon Soroski, i-xxviii. Jerusalem: Sifra Press, 1960. [Hebrew]
Tesher, Ḥayyim Barukh. *Yehudah me-Ḥoqeqei, Igerot ha-R"B, Derekh ha-Melekh: Ḥadash me-Ketav Yad.* Brooklyn: s.n., 2006. [Hebrew]
Tyrer, Ḥayyim ben Solomon of Czernowitz. *Sefer Be'ar Mayyim Ḥayyim ha-Shalem.* Jerusalem: s.n., 1992. [Hebrew]
Tyrer, Ḥayyim ben Solomon of Czernowitz. *Sidduro shel Shabbat.* Jerusalem: Makhon Beer Hayim, 1995. [Hebrew]
Vital, Ḥayyim. *Eṣ Ḥayyim.* Jerusalem: s.n., 1910. [Hebrew]
Vital, Ḥayyim. *Liqquṭei Torah—Ṭa'amei ha-Miṣvot.* Jerusalem: Yahadut Ha-Torah, 1988. [Hebrew]
Vital, Ḥayyim. *Peri Eṣ Ḥayyim.* Jerusalem: s.n., 1986. [Hebrew]
Vital, Ḥayyim. *Sefer Sha'arei Qedushah ha-Shalem.* Tel Aviv: Amnon Gross, 2005. [Hebrew]
Vital, Ḥayyim. *Sha'ar ha-Kavvanot.* Jerusalem: s.n., 2002. [Hebrew]
Waks, Abe. *Birkhat Shelomoh.* Kraków: M. Lenkowicza Press, 1928. [Hebrew]
Weinberg, Avraham. *Yesod ha-Avodah.* Jerusalem: Yeshivat Beith Avraham., 1989. [Hebrew]
Weinshelbaum, Shelomo Aryeh Leib. *Hakhanat Lev le-Tefilah.* Biłgoraj: s.n., 1927. [Hebrew]
Weisblum, Elimelekh of Lizhensk. *No'am Elimelekh.* Jerusalem: Yarid Hasfarim, 1995. [Hebrew]
Weisblum, Elimelekh of Lizhensk. *Sefer Tsetil Katan.* Kisvárda: s.n., 1925. [Hebrew]
Wolbe, Shlomo. *Alei Shur: Gates of Guidance.* Jerusalem: Beit HaMusar 1998. [Hebrew]
Yalqut Shim'oni. 1878. Reprint, Jerusalem: s.n., 1960. [Hebrew]
Ziv, Simḥah Zissel. *ḤḤokhmah u-Musar.* New York: Aber Press, 1957. [Hebrew]

Philosophical and Secondary Sources

Abrams, Daniel. "Defining Modern Academic Scholarship: Gershom Scholem and the Establishment of a New (?) Discipline." *The Journal of Jewish Thought and Philosophy* 9 (2000): 267–302.

Abrams, Meyer H. *The Mirror and the Lamp: Romantic Theory and the Critical Tradition.* New York: Oxford University Press, 1953.

Viterbensis, Ægidius. *Libellus de Litteris Hebraicis.* Translated by Yehuda Liebes. Jerusalem: Carmel, 2013. [Hebrew]

Afterman, Adam. "Afterword: A New Paradigm in Kabbalah Research." In Moshe Idel, *Enchanted Chains: Techniques and Rituals in Jewish Mysticism.* Translated by Miri Scharf, 221–232. Jerusalem: Shalom Hartman Institute, 2015. [Hebrew]

Afterman, Adam. *"And They Shall Be One Flesh": On the Language of Mystical Union in Judaism.* Leiden: Brill, 2016.

Afterman, Adam. *Devequt: Mystical Intimacy in Medieval Jewish Thought.* Los Angeles: Cherub Press, 2011. [Hebrew]

Afterman, Adam. *The Intentions of Prayers in Early Ecstatic Kabbalah: A Study and Critical Edition of an Anonymous Commentary to the Prayers.* Los Angeles: Cherub Press, 2004. [Hebrew]

Ahren, Yizhak. "Rabbi Israel Salanter und das Unbewusste." *Udim* 6 (1975–1976): 9–11

Albanese, Catherine L. *A Republic of Mind and Spirit: A Cultural History of American Metaphysical Religion.* New Haven: Yale University Press, 2006.

Alfasi, Yitzhak, ed., *Encyclopedia of Hasidism: Personalities.* Jerusalem: Mossad Harav Kook, 1986. [Hebrew]

Alfasi, Yitzhak. *The Kingdom of Wisdom: The Court of Ropczyce-Dzików.* Jerusalem: Carmel, 1994. [Hebrew]

Alṭman, Ya'aqov. "Gehinom Petuḥah Lo 'me-Taḥtav'—Tat ha-Hakarah ve-Tiqun ha-Yeṣer: Shiṭatah shel 'Tenu'at ha-Musar' le-mul Etgarei ha-Pesiko'analizah." *Tzohar* 30 (2007): 89–98. [Hebrew]

Altmann, Alexander. "Qedushah Hymns in the Ancient Hekhalot Literature." *Melilah* 2 (1946): 1–24. [Hebrew]

Altshuler, Mor. *The Messianic Secret of Hasidism.* Leiden: Brill, 2006.

Amsel, Meir, ed., *Ha-Maor: Rabbinical Bi-Monthly Journal* 35, no. 2 (December/January 1982–1983). [Hebrew]

Aristotle. "On Memory and Recollection." In *On the Soul. Parva Naturalia. On Breath.* Translated by W. S. Hett, 281–307. Loeb Classical Library. Cambridge: Harvard University Press, 1935.

Aristotle. "On the Soul." In *On the Soul. Parva Naturalia. On Breath.* Translated by W. S. Hett, 2–203. Loeb Classical Library. Cambridge: Harvard University Press, 1935.

Aron, Vili. "Aaron Marcus, the 'German' who became a Hasid." *Yivo Bleter* 29 (1947): 143–148. [Yiddish]

Arzy, Shahar, and Moshe Idel. Kabbalah: *A Neurocognitive Approach to Mystical Experiences.* New Haven: Yale University Press, 2015.

Arzy, Shahar, Moshe Idel, Theodor Landis, and Olaf Blanke. "Speaking With One's Self: Autoscopic Phenomena in Writings from the Ecstatic Kabbalah." *Journal of Consciousness Studies* 12, no. 11 (2005): 4–29.

Assaf, David. "'A Girl! He Ought to be Whipped': The Hasid as *Homo Ludens*." In *Let the Old Make Way for the New: Studies in the Social and Cultural History of Eastern European Jewry Presented to Immanuel Etkes*. Edited by David Assaf and Ada Rapoport-Albert, 121–150. Jerusalem: Zalman Shazar Center, 2009. [Hebrew]

Avens, Roberts. *Imagination as Reality: Western Nirvana in Jung, Hillman, Barfield and Cassirer.* Dallas: Spring Publications, 1980.

Bar Lev, Roni. *The Avant-garde Faith of Rabbi Nachman of Breslov.* Ramat Gan: Bar-Ilan University Press, 2017. [Hebrew]

Barasch, Julius. *Oṣar Ḥokhmah be-Lashon Avar.* Jerusalem—The National Library of Israel MS Heb. 38°1893. [Hebrew]

Barasch, Julius. *Thesaurus Scientiarum*, intro. S. Y. Rapaport. Vienna: Joseph Holzwarte, 1856.

Bar-Levav, Avriel. "The Concept of Death in *Sefer ha-Ḥayyim. The Book of Life*. by Rabbi Shimon Frankfurt." PhD thesis, Hebrew University, 1997. [Hebrew]

Bar-Levav, Avriel. "Death in the Thought of the Kabbalist Rabbi Naftali Hakohen Katz." Master's thesis, Hebrew University, 1990. [Hebrew]

Bar-Levav, Avriel. "Story, Ritual and Metaphor: Comprehending the Day of Death as a Spiritual Exercise and the Internal War in Jewish Ethical Literature." In *Peace and War in Jewish Culture*. Edited by Avriel Bar-Levav, 145–163. Jerusalem: Zalman Shazar Center, 2006. [Hebrew]

Bar-Yosef, Hamutal. "Feierberg, Mordekhai Ze'ev." *YIVO Encyclopedia of Jews in Eastern Europe*. Accessed November 1, 2017. http://www.yivoencyclopedia.org/article.aspx/Feierberg_Mordekhai_Zeev.

Bazak, Jacob. *Beyond the Senses: A Study of Extrasensorial Perception in Biblical, Talmudical, and Rabbinical Literature in the Light of Contemporary Parapsychological Research*. Tel Aviv: Dvir, 1968. [Hebrew]

Bein, Leibel. *From the Notebook of a Hassidic Journalist*. Translated by Mordekhai Selifoy. Jerusalem: s.n., 1967. [Hebrew]

Beller, Steven. *Vienna and the Jews, 1867–1938: A Cultural History.* Cambridge: Cambridge University Press 1989.

Benjamin, Israël Joseph. *Eight Years in Asia and Africa*. Lyck: Defus Tsvi Hirsch Petsall, 1859.

Ben-Shlomo, Joseph. "Afterword." In Rudolf Otto, *Rational Factor in the Idea of the Divine and Its Relation to the Rational*. Translated by Miryam Ron, 199–202. Jerusalem: Carmel Publishing, 1999. [Hebrew]

Bergman, Samuel Hugo. *A History of Modern Philosophy from the Enlightenment to Kant.* Jerusalem: Mosad Bialik, 1978. [Hebrew]

Bergman, Samuel Hugo. *A History of Philosophy: Jacobi, Fichte, Schelling*. Jerusalem: Bialik Institute, 1984. [Hebrew]

Bergson, Henri. *Creative Evolution*. Translated by Arthur Mitchell. New York: Holt, 1911.

Berman, Feigue. "Hasidic Dance: An Historical and Theological Analysis." PhD diss., New York University, 1999.

Blanke, Olaf, and Christine Mohr. "Out-Of-Body Experience, Heautoscopy, and Autoscopic Hallucination of Neurological Origin: Implications for Neurocognitive Mechanisms of Corporeal Awareness and Self-Consciousness." *Brain Research Reviews* 50, no. 1 (2005): 184–199.

Blanke, Olaf, and Shahar Arzy. "The Out-of-Body Experience: Disturbed Self-Processing at the Temporo-Parietal Junction." *The Neuroscientist* 11, no. 1 (2005): 16–24.
Blanke, Olaf, and Thomas Metzinger. "Full-Body Illusions and Minimal Phenomenal Selfhood." *Trends in Cognitive Sciences* 13, no. 1 (2009): 7–13.
Blanke, Olaf, Theodor Landis, Laurent Spinelli, and Margitta Seeck. "Out-of-body Experience and Autoscopy of Neurological Origin." *Brain: A Journal of Neurology* 127, no. 2 (2004): 243–258.
Bloch, Chaim. *Heikhal le-Divrei ḤZ"L u-Pitgameihem.* New York: Pardes and Shaulson, 1948.
Blumenthal, David R. *Philosophic Mysticism: Studies in Rational Religion.* Ramat Gan: Bar-Ilan University Press, 2006.
Bowers, Margaretta, and Shmuel Glasner. "Auto-Hypnotic Aspects of the Cabbalistic Concept of Kavanah." *Journal of Clinical and Experimental Hypnosis* 6 (1958): 50–70.
Boyarin, Daniel. *Carnal Israel: Reading Sex in Talmudic Culture.* Berkeley: University of California Press, 1993.
Braid, James. *Neurypnology: Or the Rationale of Nervous Sleep, Considered in Relation with Animal Magnetism.* London: John Churchill, 1843.
Breuer, Mordechai. *The Tents of Torah: The Yeshiva, Its Structure and History.* Jerusalem: Zalman Shazar Center, 2003. [Hebrew]
Brill, Alan. "Menachem Ekstein Visions of a Compassionate World—A Post-Hasid?." The Book of Doctrines and Opinions: Notes on Jewish Theology and Spirituality. Blog. April 11, 2010.
https://kavvanah.wordpress.com/2010/04/11/menachem-ekstein-visions-of-a-compassionate-world-a-post-hasid/.
Brill, Alan. *Thinking God: The Mysticism of Rabbi Zadok of Lublin.* New York: Yeshiva University Press, 2002.
Brown, Benjamin. "Love, Joy, Simplicity and Traditionalism: The Musar Theology of R. Moshe Rosenstein." In *Let the Old Make Way for the New.* Edited by David Assaf and Ada Rapoport-Albert, 251–279. Jerusalem: Zalman Shazar Center, 2009. [Hebrew]
Brown, Benjamin. "The Rise and Fall of 'the Loftiness of Man' Doctrine: Changes in the Musar Theology of the Slobodka Yeshiva." In *Yeshivot and Study Institutions.* Edited by Immanuel Etkes, 243–272. Jerusalem: Zalman Shazar Center, 2006. [Hebrew]
Buber, Martin. *Hasidism and Modern Man.* Translated by Maurice Friedman and introduction by David Biale. Princeton: Princeton University Press, 2016.
Buranelli, Vincent. *The Wizard from Vienna: Franz Anton Mesmer.* New York: Coward, McCann and Geoghegan, 1975.
Burke, Edmund. *A Philosophical Enquiry into the Origin of Our Ideas of the Sublime and Beautiful.* Oxford: Oxford University Press, 1987.
Bush, George. *Mesmer and Swedenborg: Or, The Relation of the Developments of Mesmerism to the Doctrines and Disclosures of Swedenborg.* New York: John Allen, 1847..
Campbell, Colin. *The Easternization of the West: A Thematic Account of Cultural Change in the Modern Era.* Boulder: Paradigm Publishers, 2007.
Canales, Jimena. *The Physicist and the Philosopher: Einstein, Bergson, and the Debate that Changed Our Understanding of Time.* Princeton: Princeton University Press, 2005.
Carrer, Laurent. *Jose Custodio de Faria: Hypnotist, Priest, and Revolutionary.* Victoria: Trafford, 2004.

Cheetham, Tom. *After Prophecy: Imagination, Incarnation, and the Unity of the Prophetic Tradition.* New Orleans: Spring Publications 2007.
Cheetham, Tom. *All the World an Icon: Henry Corbin and the Angelic Function of Beings.* Berkeley: North Atlantic Books, 2012.
Cheetham, Tom. *Green Man, Earth Angel: The Prophetic Tradition and The Battle for the Soul of the World*, Albany: State University of New York Press, 2005.
Cheetham, Tom. *The World Turned Inside Out: Henry Corbin and Islamic Mysticism.* Woodstock: Spring Journal Books, 2003.
Chernetzky, Binyamin. *Midot u-Ma'asim: Si'aḥ Ḥinukhi.* Tel Aviv: Beth Yaakov Publishing, 1992. [Hebrew]
Clausen, Geoffrey D. *Sharing the Burden: Rabbi Simḥah Zissel Ziv and the Path of Musar.* Albany: State University of New York Press, 2015.
Cohen, Adir. *To Dream with Open Eyes (Guide): Bibliotherapy, Guided Imagery, Creative Writing.* Tel Aviv: Mishkal, 1995. [Hebrew]
Cohen, Nathan. "Distributing Knowledge: Warsaw as a Center of Jewish Publishing, 1850–1914." In *Warsaw. The Jewish Metropolis: Essays in Honor of the 75th Birthday of Professor Antony Polonsky.* Edited by Glenn Dynner and François Guesnet, 180–206. Leiden: Brill, 2015.
Copenhaver, Brian, and Daniel Stein Kokin. "Egidio da Viterbo's Book on Hebrew Letters: Christian Kabbalah in Papal Rome." *Renaissance Quarterly* 67, no. 1 (2014): 1–42.
Copleston, Frederick Charles. *History of Philosophy.* Vol. 7, *Fichte to Nietzsche.* Mahwah: Paulist Press, 1963.
Corbin, Henry. *Creative Imagination in the Sufism of Ibn 'Arabi.* Translated by Ralph Manheim. Princeton: Princeton University Press, 1969.
Corbin, Henry. *La Philosophie Iranienne Islamique Aux XVII et XVIII Siecles.* Paris: Buchet Chastel, 1981.
Corbin, Henry. "*Mundus Imaginalis*, or the Imaginary and the Imaginal." In *Swedenborg and Esoteric Islam.* Translated by L. Fox, 1–33. West Chester: Swedenborg Foundation, 1995.
Corbin, Henry. "*Mundus Imaginalis:* or the Imaginary and the Imaginal." Translated by Ruth Horine. *Spring* (1972): 1–13.
Corbin, Henry. "Theophanies and Mirrors: Idols or Icons?." Translated by J. A. Pratt and A. K. Donohue. *Spring Journal: An Annual of Archetypal Psychology and Jungian Thought* (1983): 1–2.
Corbin, Henry. *Spiritual Body and Celestial Earth: From Mazdean Iran to Shīʿite Iran.* Translated by Nancy Pearson. Princeton: Princeton University Press, 1989.
Corbin, Henry. *Swedenborg and Esoteric Islam.* Translated by Leonard Fox. West Chester: Swedenborg Foundation, 1995.
Coué, Émile. *Self-Mastery Through Conscious Autosuggestion.* New York: American Library Service, 1922.
Crabtree, Adam. *From Mesmer to Freud: Magnetic Sleep and the Roots of Psychological Healing.* New Haven: Yale University Press, 1993.
Dan, Joseph. *On Sanctity: Religion, Ethics, and Mysticism in Judaism and Other Religions.* Jerusalem: Magnes Press, 1997. [Hebrew]
Dan, Joseph. "Research in Jewish Mysticism and Corresponding Phenomena in Other Religions." In *Studies in Judaica: Collected Papers of the Symposium in Honour of the*

Sixtieth Anniversary of the Institute of Jewish Studies. Edited by Moshe Bar-Asher, 137–143. Jerusalem: Hebrew University of Jerusalem, 1986. [Hebrew]

Darnton, Robert. *Mesmerism and the End of the Enlightenment in France.* Cambridge: Harvard University Press, 1968.

Davidson, Herbert. "The Active Intellect in the Cuzari." *Revue des études juives* 131 (1972): 351–396.

Davidson, Herbert A. *Alfarabi, Avicenna, and Averroes, on Intellect: Their Cosmologies, Theories of the Active Intellect, and Theories of Human Intellect.* Oxford: Oxford University Press, 1992.

Davila, James R. *Hekhalot Literature in Translation: Major Texts of Merkavah Mysticism.* Leiden: Brill, 2013.

De Bartolo, Anna Maria. *Mesmerism and Jewishness in a Novel by George Du Maurier: Trilby.* Soveria Mannelli: Rubbettino, 2002.

De Faria, José Custódio. *De la cause du sommeil lucide ou Etude de la nature de l'homme.* Paris: Mme. Horiac, 1819.

Deleuze, Giles. *Cinema 2: The Time-Image.* Translated by Hugh Tomlinson and Robert Galeta. London: The Athlone Press, 1989.

Derrida, Jacques. *Dissemination.* Translated by Barbara Johnson. London: The Athlone Press, 1981.

Dimyon Nove'a. "Home Page." Accessed February 6, 2018. http://www.dimyonovea.com

Dresser, Horatio Willis. *A History of the New Thought Movement.* New York: General Books, 2009.

Du Maurier, George. *Trilby.* New York: Harper and Brothers, 1894.

Dynner, Glenn. *Men of Silk: The Hasidic Conquest of Polish Jewish Society.* Oxford: Oxford University Press, 2006.

Einat-Nov, Idit. "The Sublime and the Image of the Divine in Psalms and some Genres of Medieval Spanish Hebrew Liturgical Poetry." *Jerusalem Studies in Hebrew Literature* 21 (2007): 221–264. [Hebrew]

Elior, Rachel. *Freedom on the Tablets: The Mystical Origins and Kabbalistic Foundations of Hasidic Thought.* Tel Aviv: Ministry of Defense, 1999. [Hebrew]

Elior, Rachel. *Heikhalot Literature and Merkavah Tradition: Ancient Jewish Mysticism and its Sources.* Tel Aviv: Yediʿot Aharonot, 2004. [Hebrew]

Elior, Rachel. *The Paradoxical Ascent to God: The Kabbalistic Theosophy of Habad Hasidism.* Translated by Jeffrey Green. Albany: State University of New York Press, 1993.

Ellenberger, Henri F. *The Discovery of the Unconscious: The History and Evolution of Dynamic Psychiatry.* New York: Basic Books, 1971.

Elman, Yaakov. "The History of Gentile Wisdom According to Zadok Hakohen of Lublin." *Journal of Jewish Thought and Philosophy* 3, no. 1 (1993): 153–187.

Elqayam, Avraham. "Eretz ha-Zevi: Portrayal of the Land of Israel in the Thought of Nathan of Gaza." In *The Land of Israel in Modern Jewish Thought.* Edited by Aviezer Ravitsky, 128–185. Jerusalem: Yad ben-Zvi Institute, 1998. [Hebrew]

Encyclopaedia Hebraica, s.v. "Epstein, Zalman." [Hebrew]

Encyclopedia of Occultism & Parapsychology. 5th ed. Compiled by John Gordon Melton. Farmington Hills: Gale Group, 2001.

Englander, Yakir. "Secular Influence on Haredi Thought—The Philosophy of Rabbi Avigdor Miller as Test Case." *Da'at* 71 (2011): 133–165. [Hebrew]

Erlanger, Yitzhaq Moshe. *Quntresei Ḥasidut: Inyanei Shabbat Qodesh.* Jerusalem: Ha-Makhon le-Iyun be-Ḥasidut, 2007. [Hebrew]
Etkes, Immanuel. *Rabbi Israel Salanter and the Beginning of the 'Musar' Movement.* Jerusalem: Magnes Press, 1984. [Hebrew]
Etkes, Immanuel. *Rabbi Israel Salanter and the Mussar Movement: Seeking the Torah of Truth.* Edited and translated by Jonathan Chipman. Philadelphia: Jewish Publication Society, 1993.
Even-Shoshan. Abraham. *The New Dictionary—The Combined Version.* Jerusalem: Kiryat-Sefer, 1997. [Hebrew]
Faur, José. "Imagination and Religious Pluralism: Maimonides, Ibn Verga, and Vico." *New Vico Studies* 10 (1992): 36–51.
Faur, José. "The Legal Thinking of Tosafot: An Historical Approach." *Dinei Israel* 6 (1975): xliii-lxxii.
Faur, José. "Maimonides on Imagination: Towards a Theory of Jewish Aesthetics." *The Solomon Goldman Lectures* 6 (1994): 89–104.
Feierberg, Mordekhai Ze'ev. *Le'an.* Tel Aviv: Kneset, s.a. [Hebrew]
Fenton, Paul B. "Henry Corbin and Abraham Heschel." In *Abraham Joshua Heschel: Philosophy, Theology and Interreligious Dialogue.* Edited by Stanisław Krajewski and Adam Lipszyc, 102–111. Wiesbaden: Harrossowitz, 2009.
Fenton, Paul B. "The Literary Legacy of the Descendants of Maimonides." *Pe'amim* 97 (2004): 17–21. [Hebrew]
Fenton, Paul B. "Some Remarks on Dance in Hassidism." In *Judaism, Topics, Fragments, Faces, Identities: Jubilee Volume in Honor of Rivka.* Edited by Haviva Pedaya and Ephraim Meir, 277–291. Beer-Sheva: ben Gurion University Press, 2007. [Hebrew]
Fine, Lawrence. "Recitation of Mishnah as a Vehicle for Mystical Inspiration: A Contemplative Technique Taught by Hayyim Vital." *Revue des études juives* 141 (1982): 183–199.
Fishbane, Eitan P. *As Light Before Dawn: The Inner World of a Medieval Kabbalist.* Stanford: Stanford University Press, 2009.
Fishbane, Michael A. "To Jump for Joy: The Rites of Dance According to R. Nahman of Bratzlav." *Journal of Jewish Thought & Philosophy* 6 (1997): 371–387.
Forman, Robert K. C. "What Does Mysticism Have To Teach Us About Consciousness?." *Journal of Consciousness Studies* 5, no. 2 (1998): 185–201.
Forverts. New York. March 30, 1940. [Yiddish]
Freidenreich, Harriet Pass. *Jewish Politics in Vienna 1918-1938.* Bloomington: Indiana University Press, 1991.
Freidnazen, A.G., ed., *Beys Yankev: Literarishe Shrift far Shul un Heym, Dint di Enyonim fun Beys Yankev Shuln un Organizatzies Bnos Agudas Yisroel in Poyln 1924–1939.* [Yiddish]
Freidnazen, A.G., ed., *Beys Yankev: Ortodoksisher Familien-Zhurnal Argan fun der Tsentrale Bnos Agudas Yisroel in Poyln: Lodzh, Varshe, Kroke.* [Yiddish]
Freud, Sigmund. "Thoughts for the Times on War and Death." In *The Standard Edition of the Complete Psychological Works of Sigmund Freud.* Vol 14. Translated and edited by James Strachey, 275–300. London: Hogarth Press, 1955.
Friedhaber, Zvi. "'Riqudei ha-Miṣvah': Toldoteihem ve-Ṣuroteihem." *Dukhan* 7 (1966): 75–85. [Hebrew]
Fuchs, Uziel. "Miriam the Prophetess and the Rebbe's Wife: The Piaseczner Rebbe's Sermons on Miriam the Prophetess." *Masekhet* 3 (2005): 65–76 [Hebrew]

Garb, Jonathan. *The Chosen Will Become Herds: Studies in Twentieth-Century Kabbalah.* Translated by Yaffah Berkovits-Murciano. New Haven: Yale University Press, 2005.
Garb, Jonathan. "In Honor of Moshe Halbertal's book *By Way of Truth: Nahmanides and the Creation of Tradition.*" Lecture, Van Leer Institute, Jerusalem, Israel, May 27, 2007. https://www.academia.edu/8016459/In_honor_of_Moshe_Halbertal_By_Way_of_Truth_-Nahmanides_and_the_Creation_of_Tradition.
Garb, Jonathan. *Manifestations of Power in Jewish Mysticism: From Rabbinic Literature to Safedian Kabbalah.* Jerusalem: Magnes Press, 2005. [Hebrew]
Garb, Jonathan. "Shame as an Existential Emotion in Modern Kabbalah." *Jewish Social Studies: History, Culture, Society* 21, no. 1 (2015): 89–122.
Garb, Jonathan. "Trance Techniques in the Kabbalah of Jerusalem." *Pe'amim* 70 (1997): 47–67. [Hebrew]
Garb, Jonathan. *Shamanic Trance in Modern Kabbalah.* Chicago: University of Chicago Press, 2011.
Garb, Jonathan. *Yearnings of the Soul: Psychological Thought in Modern Kabbalah.* Chicago: University of Chicago Press, 2015.
Gauld, Alan. *A History of Hypnotism.* Cambridge: Cambridge University Press, 1992.
Gavarin, Martel. "The Conception of Time in the Works of Rabbi Azriel." *Jerusalem Studies in Jewish Thought* 6, no. 3–4 (1987): 309–336 [Hebrew]
Gefen, Shem Tov. *Dimensions, Prophecy, and Geology.* Jerusalem: Mosad Harav Kook, 1974. [Hebrew]
Gefen, Shem Tov. *Prophecy and Purity, or Mathematical Philosophy of Infinity.* Cairo: Ḥayyim Vidal, 1923. [Hebrew]
Gelman, Uriel. "The Great Wedding in Uściług: The Making of a Myth." *Tarbiz* 80, no. 4 (2013): 574–580. [Hebrew]
Geshuri, Meir S. "Ha-Beshṭ Mefu'naḥ ha-Nigun ha-Ḥasidi." *Mahanayim* 46 (1960): 105–108. [Hebrew]
Geshuri, Meir S. *Music and Dance in Hassidism.* 5 vols. Tel Aviv: Neṣah, 1955. [Hebrew]
Geshuri, Meir S., ed. *La-Ḥasidim Mizmor.* Jerusalem: Ha-Teḥiyah, 1936. [Hebrew]
Gliker, Yohanan. "Imagination in Aristotle's Soul Doctrine." PhD diss., Hebrew University, 1948. [Hebrew]
Goldberg, Hillel. *Israel Salanter, Text, Structure, Idea: The Ethics and Theology of an Early Psychologist of the Unconscious.* New York: Ktav Publishing House, 1982.
Goldsmith, Margaret. *Franz Anton Mesmer: The History of an Idea.* London: Arthur Barker, 1934.
Gottlieb, Ephraim. *Studies in Kabbalistic Literature.* Edited by Joseph Hacker. Tel Aviv: Tel Aviv University, 1976. [Hebrew]
Gottlieb, Mel. "Mussar: A Jewish Psychoethical Model for Our Time." *Conversations: The Journal of the Institute for Jewish Ideas and Ideals* 8 (2010): 39–51.
Govrin, Michal. "Théatre Sacré: Contemporain: Théories et Pratiques." PhD diss., Université de Paris III, 1976.
Green, Arthur. *Hasidic Spirituality for a New Era: The Religious Writings of Hillel Zeitlin.* New York: Paulist Press, 2012.
Green, Arthur. *Radical Judaism: Rethinking God and Tradition.* New Haven: Yale University Press, 2010.

Green, Arthur (Itzik Lodzer). "Response to Robert Goldenberg." *Response: A Contemporary Jewish Review* 2, no. 2 (Fall 1968): 43–44.

Green, Arthur. *Tormented Master: A Life of Rabbi Nahman of Bratslav.* Tuscaloosa: The University of Alabama Press, 1979.

Gries, Ze'ev. *Conduct Literature (Regimen Vitae): Its History and Place in the Life of Beshtian Hasidism.* Jerusalem: Bialik Institute, 1990. [Hebrew]

Gries, Ze'ev. "Jewish Time and Jewish Identity." *Da'at* 68/69 (2010): 311–321. [Hebrew]

Grözinger, Karl E. *Der Ba'al Schem von Michelstadt: Ein deutsch-jüdisches Heiligenleben zwischen Legende und Wirklichkeit.* Frankfurt: Campus Verlag, 2010.

Grözinger, Karl E. "Zekl Leib Wormser, the Ba'al Shem of Michelstadt." In *Judaism, Topics, Fragments, Faces, Identities: Jubilee Volume in Honor of Rivka.* Edited by Haviva Pedaya and Ephraim Meir, 501–510. Beer Sheva: ben-Gurion University of the Negev Press, 2007. [Hebrew]

Hadari, Yeshayahu. "*Shnei Kohanim Gedolim.*" In *Me'at latzadik: Anthology on Rabbi Tzadok Hacohen.* Edited by Gershon Kitsis, 77–95. Jerusalem: Bayit, 2000. [Hebrew]

Hadas, Moses, ed., *Solomon Maimon: An Autobiography.* New York: Schocken Books, 1947.

Ha-Derekh: Itonah ha-Merkazi shel ha-Histadrut ha-Olamit Agudat Yisra'el. Zurich 6–7 (February-March 1920); Vienna 3, no. 6 (February-March 1921); Vienna 6, no. 2 (April-May 1924); Vienna 6, no. 3 (May-June 1924). National Library of Israel. [Hebrew]

Haggai, Samuel. "Ha-Reqa ha-Hisṭori shel Tenu'at ha-Musar." *Mahanaim* 81 (1963): 70–75. [Hebrew]

Hakham, Amos. "Maḥol ve-Riqud be-TaNa"KH." *Mahanayim* 48 (1960): 30–32. [Hebrew]

Halbertal, Moshe. *By Way of Truth: Nahmanides and the Creation of Tradition.* Jerusalem: Shalom Hartman Institute, 2006. [Hebrew]

Halbertal, Moshe. "Opening Remarks." Presented at Studies in Kabbalah Research: An International Conference in Honor of Prof. Moshe Idel and Prof. Yehuda Liebes at the Van Leer Institute, Jerusalem, Israel, July 10, 2012. [Hebrew]

Halevy, Shoshana. *The First Hebrew Books Printed in Jerusalem in the Second Half of the Nineteenth Century (1841–1890).* Jerusalem: ben-Zvi Institute, 1975. [Hebrew]

Halevy, Yair. "Musar, Ḥinukh, Hadrakhah: Ha-Rav Shelomoh Wolbe." In *The Gdoilim: Leaders Who Shaped the Israeli Haredi Jewry.* Edited by Benjamin Brown and Nissim Leon, 735–765. Jerusalem: Magness Press and Van Leer Istitute Press, 2017. [Hebrew]

Halevy, Yair. "Rabbi Shlomo Wolbe and the Musar Revival Efforts in the 'Hashkofe' Yeshiva World." In *From Survival to Consolidation: Change in Israeli Haredi Society and its Scholarly Study.* Edited by Kimmy Caplan and Nurit Stadler, 55–78.. Jerusalem: Van Leer Institute, 2012. [Hebrew]

Hallamish, Moshe. "The Theoretical System of R. Shneur Zalman of Liady. Its Sources in Kabbalah and Hasidism." PhD diss., Hebrew University, 1976. [Hebrew]

Hanegraaff, Wouter J. *Esotericism and the Academy: Rejected Knowledge in Western Culture.* Cambridge: Cambridge University Press, 2012.

Hanegraaff, Wouter J. *New Age Religion and Western Culture: Esotericism in the Mirror of Secular Thought.* Cambridge: Cambridge University Press, 1998.

Har'el, Ze'ev. *In the Warmth of the Holy Fire.* Digital media. Directed by Ze'ev Har'el. Yad Binyamin, Israel: Torat ha-Ḥayyim, 2008. https://www.youtube.com/watch?v=i0a2Mh8UFkk.

Harvey, Warren Zev. "Judah Halevi's Synthetic Theory of Prophecy and a Note on the Zohar." *Jerusalem Studies in Jewish Thought* 13 (1996): 141–156. [Hebrew]
Harvey, Warren Zev. "Three Theories of the Imagination in 12th-Century Jewish Philosophy." In *Intellect et Imagination dans la Philosophie Médiévale*. Edited by Maria Cândida Pacheco and José F. Meirinhos, 287–302. Turnhout: Brepols, 2002.
Heelas, Paul. *Spiritualities of Life: Romantic Themes and Consumptive Capitalism*. Oxford: Blackwell Publishing, 2008.
Heinemann, Isaac. "The Relationship between S. R. Hirsch and His Teacher Isaac Bernays." *Zion* 16 (1951): 69–90. [Hebrew]
Held, Shai. *Abraham Joshua Heschel: The Call of Transcendence*. Bloomington: Indiana University Press, 2013.
Hellner-Eshed, Melila. *A River Flows from Eden: The Language of Mystical Experience in the Zohar*. Tel Aviv: Am Oved, 2005. [Hebrew]
Henn, Thomas Rice. *Longinus and English Criticism*. Cambridge: Cambridge University Press, 1934.
Hershkowitz, Isaac. "Rabbi Kalonymus Kalmish Shapira, The Piasechner Rebbe His Holocaust and Pre-Holocaust Thought, Continuity or Discontinuity?." Master's thesis, Bar-Ilan University, 2004. [Hebrew]
Herzl, Theodor. "Dr. Gidmann's 'National Judaism.'" http://benyehuda.org/herzl/herzl_009.html. [Hebrew]
Heschel, Abraham Joshua. "Did Maimonides Believe That He Attained the Rank of a Prophet?." In *Louis Ginsberg Jubilee Volume*. Edited by Saul Lieberman et al., 159–188. New York: American Academy for Jewish Research, 1945.
Heschel, Abraham Joshua. *God in Search of Man: A Philosophy of Judaism*. New York: Farrar, Straus and Giroux, 1955.
Heschel, Abraham Joshua. *The Prophets*. New York: Harper and Row, 1962.
Heschel, Abraham Joshua. *The Sabbath: Its Meaning for Modern Man*. New York: Farrar, Straus and Giroux, 1951.
Hollenback, Jess Byron. *Mysticism: Experience, Response, and Empowerment*. University Park: Pennsylvania State University Press, 2000.
Holtzman, Avner. "Shiloaḥ, Ha." *The YIVO Encyclopedia of Jews in Eastern Europe*. Accessed November 1, 2017. http://www.yivoencyclopedia.org/article.aspx/Shiloah_Ha-.
Ḥomet, Avraham, ed., *Ṭorne: Kiym un Khurbn fun a Yiddisher Shtot* [*Tarnów: The Establishment and Destruction of a Jewish City*]. Tel Aviv: Landsmanshafṭn fun Torne Yiddn, 1954. [Yiddish]
Horowitz, Yehoshua. "Isaac ben Jacob Bernays." In *Encyclopaedia Judaica*, 2nd ed. Detroit: MacMillan Reference USA, 2007.
Huss, Boaz, Marco Pasi, and Kocku von Stuckrad, eds., *Kabbalah and Modernity: Interpretations, Transformations, Adaptations*. Leiden: Brill, 2010.
Huss, Boaz. "Ask No Questions: Gershom Scholem and the Study of Contemporary Jewish Mysticism." *Pe'amim* 94–95 (2003): 57–72. [Hebrew]
Huss, Boaz. "Ask No Questions: Gershom Scholem and the Study of Contemporary Jewish Mysticism." *Modern Judaism* 25, no. 2 (2005): 141–158.
Huss, Boaz. "Jewish Mysticism in the University, Academic Study or Theological Practice." *Zeek* (December 2007). Assessed August 8, 2016, http://www.zeek.net/712academy.

Huss, Boaz. “Madame Théon, Alta Una, Mother Superior: The Life and Personas of Mary Ware (1839–1908).” *ARIES: Journal for the Study of Western Esotericism* 15 (2015): 210–246.

Huss, Boaz. “‘Paying Extra’: A Response to Shaul Magid.” *Zeek* (March 2008). Assessed August 8, 2016, http://www.zeek.net/803huss/.

Huss, Boaz. “Religionization of Non-Christian Cultures and the Formation of New Secularities.” Paper presented at the the final symposium of the ANR-DFG Neoreligitur Research Program: De-secularization and New Religiosities through the prism of the Turkish Case, Paris, France, October 2017. https://www.academia.edu/35249861/Religionization_of_Non-Christian_Cultures_and_the_Formation_of_New_Secularities

Huss, Boaz. “The Mystification of the Kabbalah and the Modern Construction of Jewish Mysticism.” *BGU Review* (Summer 2008). Accessed August 8, 2016, http://in.bgu.ac.il/en/heksherim/2008/Boaz-Huss.pdf.

Huss, Boaz. “The Mystification of the Kabbalah and the Myth of Jewish Mysticism.” *Pe‘amim* 110 (2007): 9–30. [Hebrew]

Huss, Boaz. “The Theologies of Kabbalah Research.” In *Jewish Thought and Jewish Belief.* Edited by Daniel J. Lasker, 33–54. Be’er Sheva: ben-Gurion University Press, 2012. [Hebrew]

Huss, Boaz. “Theologies of Kabbalah Research.” *Modern Judaism* 34, no. 1 (2014): 3–26.

Huss, Boaz. *Sockets of Fine Gold: The Kabbalah of R. Shimo’n Ibn Lavi.* Jerusalem: Magnes Press, 2000. [Hebrew]

Huss, Boaz. “‘The Sufi Society from America’: Theosophy and Kabbalah in Poona in the Late Nineteenth Century.” In *Kabbalah and Modernity: Interpretations, Transformations, Adaptations.* Edited by Boaz Huss, Marco Pasi, and Kocku von Stuckrad, 167–194. Leiden: Brill, 2010.

Huss, Boaz. *The Question About the Existence of Jewish Mysticism: The Genealogy of Jewish Mysticism and the Theologies of Kabbalah Research.* Tel Aviv: Van Leer Institute and Hakibbutz Hameuchad, 2016. [Hebrew]

Idel, Moshe. *Abraham Abulafia: An Ecstatic Kabbalist.* Lancaster: Labyrinthos, 2002.

Idel, Moshe. “Abraham J. Heschel on Mysticism and Hasidism.” *Modern Judaism* 29, no. 1 (2009): 80–105.

Idel, Moshe. *Absorbing Perfections: Kabbalah and Interpretation.* New Haven: Yale University Press, 2002.

Idel, Moshe. “Agideo da Viterbo and the Writings of Abraham Abulafia.” *Italia* 2 (1981): 48–50. [Hebrew]

Idel, Moshe. *Ascension on High in Jewish Mysticism: Pillars, Lines, Ladders.* Budapest: Central European University Press, 2005.

Idel, Moshe. *Ben: Sonship and Jewish Mysticism.* London: Continuum, 2007.

Idel, Moshe. “The *Besht* as a Prophet and Talismanic Magician.” In *Studies in Jewish Narrative: Presented to Yoav Elstein.* Edited by Avidov Lipsker and Rella Kushelevsky, 121–145. Ramat Gan: Bar Ilan University Press, 2006. [Hebrew]

Idel, Moshe. “‘The Besht Passed His Hand over His Face’: On the Besht’s Influence on His Followers—Some Remarks.” In *After Spirituality: Studies in Mystical Traditions.* Edited by Philip Wexler and Jonathan Garb, 79–106. New York: Peter Lang, 2012.

Idel, Moshe. “Conceptualizations of Music in Jewish Mysticism.” In *Enchanting Powers: Music in the World’s Religion.* Edited by Lawrence E. Sullivan, 159–188. Cambridge: Harvard University Press, 1997.

Idel, Moshe. "Definitions of Prophecy—Maimonides and Abulafia." *Da'at* 64–66 (2009): 1–36 [Hebrew]
Idel, Moshe. "*Ganz Andere:* On Rudolf Otto and Concepts of Holiness in Jewish Mysticism." *Da'at* 57–59 (2006): v-xliv.
Idel, Moshe. *Golem: Jewish Magical and Mystical Traditions on the Artificial Anthropoid.* Albany: State University of New York Press, 1990.
Idel, Moshe. "'Forever, Lord, Your Word is Firm': Studies in the Early Doctrine of the Baal Shem Tov and Its Development in Hasidism." *Kabbalah* 20 (2009): 219–286. [Hebrew]
Idel, Moshe. *Enchanted Chains: Techniques and Rituals in Jewish Mysticism.* Los Angeles: Cherub Press, 2005.
Idel, Moshe. *Hasidism: Between Ecstasy and Magic.* Albany: State University of New York Press, 1995.
Idel, Moshe. "History of Kabbalah and History of the Jews." *Theory and Criticism* 6 (1995): 137–148. [Hebrew]
Idel, Moshe. "'Hitbodedut' qua 'Concentration' in Ecstatic Kabbalah." *Da'at* 14 (1985): 35–82. [Hebrew]
Idel, Moshe. "Hitbodedut as Concentration in Jewish Philosophy." *Jerusalem Studies in Jewish Thought* 7 (1988): 39–60. [Hebrew]
Idel, Moshe. "Hitbodedut: On Solitude in Jewish Mysticism." In *Einsamkeit: Archäologie der literarischen Kommunikation VI.* Edited by Aleida Assmann and Jan Assmann, 189–212. Munich: Fink, 2000.
Idel, Moshe. "Inner Peace through Inner Struggle in Abraham Abulafia's Ecstatic Kabbalah." *The Journal for the Study of Sephardic & Mizrahi Jewry* 2, no. 2 (March 2009): 62–97.
Idel, Moshe. "Intention and Colors: A Forgotten Kabbalistic Responsum." In *Tribute to Sarah: Studies in Jewish Philosophy and Mysticism Presented to Sara O. Heller Wilensky.* Edited by Moshe Idel, Devorah Dimant, and Shalom Rosenberg, 1–14. Jerusalem: Magnes Press, 1994. [Hebrew]
Idel, Moshe. *Kabbalah and Eros.* New Haven: Yale University Press, 2005.
Idel, Moshe. "Kabbalah and Music." In *Judaism and Art.* Edited by D. Cassuto, 275–289. Ramat Gan: Bar Ilan University, 1989. [Hebrew]
Idel, Moshe. *Kabbalah: New Perspectives.* New Haven: Yale University, 1988.
Idel, Moshe. *Language, Torah, and Hermeneutics in Abraham Abulafia.* Translated by Menahem Kallus. Albany: State University of New York Press, 1989.
Idel, Moshe. "The Magical and Theurgic Interpretation of Music in Jewish Sources from the Renaissance to Hassidism." *Yuval: Studies of the Jewish Music Research Centre* 4 (1982): 33–62 [Hebrew]
Idel, Moshe. *Messianic Mystics.* New Haven: Yale University Press, 1998.
Idel, Moshe. "*Milhemet ha-Yetzarim:* Psychomachia in Abraham Abulafia's Ecstatic Kabbalah." In *Peace and War in Jewish Culture.* Edited by Avriel Bar Levav, 99–143. Jerusalem: Zalman Shazar Center, 2006. [Hebrew]
Idel, Moshe. "Modes of Cleaving to the Letters in the Teachings of Israel Baal Shem Tov: A Sample Analysis." *Jewish History* 27, no. 2–4 (2013): 299–317
Idel, Moshe. "Music and Prophetic Kabbalah." *Yuval* 4 (1982): 150–169.
Idel, Moshe. *The Mystical Experience in Abraham Abulafia.* Jerusalem: The Hebrew University Magnes Press, 2002. [Hebrew]

Idel, Moshe. *The Mystical Experience in Abraham Abulafia*. Translated by Jonathan Chipman. Albany: State University of New York Press, 1988.
Idel, Moshe. *Nocturnal Kabbalists*. Jerusalem: Carmel, 2006. [Hebrew]
Idel, Moshe. "Old and New in the Study of Kabbalah." *Zion* 54, no. 4 (1989): 493–508. [Hebrew]
Idel, Moshe. "On Judaism, Jewish Mysticism and Magic." In *Envisioning Magic: A Princeton Seminar and Symposium*. Edited by Peter Schäfer and Hans G. Kippenberg, 195–214. Leiden: Brill, 1997.
Idel, Moshe. "On Prophecy and Early Hasidism." In *Studies in Modern Religions, Religious Movements, and the Bābī Bahā'ī Faiths*. Edited by Moshe Sharon, 41–75. Leiden: Brill, 2004.
Idel, Moshe. "On the Land of Israel in Medieval Jewish Mystical Thought." In *The Land of Israel in Medieval Jewish Thought*. Edited by Moshe Hallamish and Aviezer Ravitzky, 193–214. Jerusalem: Yad Izhak ben-Zvi, 1991. [Hebrew]
Idel, Moshe. "On the Language of Ecstatic Experiences in Jewish Mysticism." In *Religions: The Religious Experience*. Edited by Matthias Riedl and Tilo Schabert, 43–84. Würzburg: Königshausen & Neumann, 2008.
Idel, Moshe. "The Parable of the Son of the King and the Imaginary Walls in Early Hasidism." In *Judaism: Topics, Fragments, Faces, Identities: Jubilee Volume in Honor of Rivka Horwitz*. Edited by Haviva Pedaya and Ephraim Meir, 87–116. Beer Sheva: ben Gurion University of the Negev Press, 2007.
Idel, Moshe. "Performance, Intensification and Experience in Jewish Mysticism." *ARCHÆVS* 13 (2009): 95–136.
Idel, Moshe. "Prayer, Ecstasy, and 'Alien Thoughts' in the Religious Experience of the Besht." In *Let the Old Make Way for the New: Studies in the Social and Cultural History of Eastern European Jewry*. Edited by David Assaf and Ada Rapoport-Alpert, 57–120. Jerusalem: Zalman Shazar Center, 2009. [Hebrew]
Idel, Moshe. "R. Judah Hallewa and his *Ẓofenat Pa'aneah*." *Shalem* 4 (1984): 119–148. [Hebrew]
Idel, Moshe. "Rabbi Abraham Abulafia, Gershom Scholem and Rabbi David Ha-Kohen. ha-Nazir." *Jerusalem Studies in Jewish Thought* 19 (2005): 819–834. [Hebrew]
Idel, Moshe. *Rabbi Menahem Recanati the Kabbalist*. Jerusalem: Schocken, 1998. [Hebrew]
Idel, Moshe. "Rabbi Nathan ben Sa'adiah Harar, Author of Sha'arei Tzedek and His Influence in the Land of Israel." *Shalem* 7 (2002): 47–58. [Hebrew]
Idel, Moshe. "Sabbath: On Concepts of Time in Jewish Mysticism." In *Sabbath: Idea, History, Reality*. Edited by Gerald J. Blidstein, 57–93. Beer Sheva: ben Gurion University Press of the Negev, 2004.
Idel, Moshe. *Studies in Ecstatic Kabbalah*. Albany: State University of New York Press, 1988.
Idel, Moshe. "Time and History in Kabbalah." In *Jewish History and Jewish Memory: Essays in Honor of Yosef Hayim Yerushalmi*. Edited by Elisheva Carlebach, John M. Efron, and David N. Myers, 153–188. Hanover Brandeis University Press, 1998.
Idel, Moshe. "Universalization and Integration: Two Conceptions of Mystical Union in Jewish Mysticism." In *Mystical Union in Judaism Christianity and Islam: An Ecumenical Dialogue*. Edited by Moshe Idel and Bernard McGinn, 27–57. New York: Continuum, 1996.

Idelsohn, Abraham Z. "Ha-Neginah ha-Ḥasidit (Al Pi ha-Sifrut ha-Ḥasidit ve-Neginotehah)." In *Sefer Hashanah: The American Jewish Yearbook*. Edited by Menahem Ribalov and Zevi Scharfstein, 74–87. New York: Hoṣa'at ha-Histadrut ha-Ivrit be-Ameriqah, 1931. [Hebrew]
Idelsohn, Abraham Z. *Jewish Music: Its Historical Development*, intro. Arbie Orenstein. 1929. Reprint, New York: Dover Publications, 1992.
Jacobs, Louis. "The Uplifting of Sparks in Later Jewish Mysticism." In *Jewish Spirituality: From the Sixteenth-Century Revival to the Present*. Edited by Arthur Green, 99–126. New York: Crossroad, 1987.
Jacobson, Yoram. *From Lurianic Kabbalism to the Psychological Theosophy of Hasidism*. Tel Aviv: Ministry of Defense, 1984. [Hebrew]
Jacobson, Yoram. *The Hasidic Thought*. Tel Aviv: Ministry of Defense Press, 1986. [Hebrew]
Jacobson, Yoram. "The Rectification of the Heart: Studies in the Psychic Teachings of R. Shneur Zalman of Liadi." *Teudah* 10 (1996): 359–409. [Hebrew]
James, William. *The Varieties of Religious Experience*. New York: Longmans, Green, and Co., 1902.
Janik, Allen, and Stephen Toulmin. *Wittgenstein's Vienna*. New York: Simon and Schuster, 1973.
Jewish Encyclopedia Online, s.v. "Berger, Oscar." Last modified September 13, 2017. http://www.jewishencyclopedia.com/articles/3067-berger-oscar.
Jones, Rufus Matthew. *Studies in Mystical Religion*. London: Macmillan, 1909.
Kadari, Adiel. "Thought and Halakhah in Maimonides' Laws of Repentance." PhD thesis, ben Gurion University of the Negev, 2000. [Hebrew]
Kamelhar, Jekuthiel Aryeh, ed., *Ohel Mo'ed* 1 (1898) [Hebrew]
Kamelhar, Jekuthiel Aryeh. *Dor De'ah: Arba'ah Tequfot Ḥasidut Beshṭit be-Shenot Tav-Quf–Tav-Resh-Khaf*. Ashdod: Makhon Zikhron Qdoshei Polin, 1998. [Hebrew]
Kamelhar, Jekuthiel Aryeh. *Ḥasidim Rishonim: Dor Dorim*. Vác: s.n., 1917. [Hebrew]
Kant, Immanuel. *Critique of the Power of Judgment*. Edited by P. Guyer and translated by P. Guyer and E. Matthews. Cambridge: Cambridge University Press, 2000.
Kaplan, Aryeh. *Jewish Meditation: A Practical Guide*. New York: Schocken Books, 1995.
Kaplan, Aryeh. *Meditation and Kabbalah*. Boston: WeiserBooks, 1985.
Kasher, Hannah. "Disciples of Philosophers as 'Sons of the Prophets' (Prophecy Manuals among Maimonides' Followers)." *Jerusalem Studies in Jewish Thought* 14 (1998): 73–85 [Hebrew]
Katz, Dov. *The Musar Movement: Its History, Leading Personalities, and Doctrines*. Tel Aviv: Orly Press, 1975. [Hebrew]
Katz, Dov. *Pulmus ha-Musar*. Jerusalem: Abraham Zioni, 1972. [Hebrew]
Katz, Maya Balakirsky. "An Occupational Neurosis: A Psychoanalytic Case History of a Rabbi." *AJS Review* 34, no. 1 (2010): 1–31.
Katz, Steven T. "The Conservative Character of Mysticism." In *Mysticism and Religious Tradition*. Edited by Steven T. Katz, 3–60. Oxford: Oxford University Press, 1983.
Katz, Steven T. "General Editor's Introduction." In *Comparative Mysticism: An Anthology of Original Sources*. Edited by Steven T. Katz, 3–22. New York: Oxford University Press, 2013.
Katz, Steven T. "Language, Epistemology and Mysticism." In *Mysticism and Philosophical Analysis*. Edited by Steven T. Katz, 22–74. New York: Oxford University Press, 1978.
Katzburg, David Zvi, ed., *Tel Talpios* 6 (1898). [Hebrew]

Kaufmann, Yehezkel. *The History of Israelite Religion*. Jerusalem: Bialik Institute, 1972. [Hebrew]
Kearney, Richard. *The Wake of Imagination: Toward a Postmodern Culture*. Minneapolis: University of Minnesota Press, 1988.
Kellner, Menachem. "Maimonides and Gersonides on Mosaic prophecy." *Speculum* 52, no. 1 (1977): 62–79.
Kierkegaard, Søren. *Practice in Christianity*. Translated by Howard V. Hong and Edna H. Hong. Princeton: Princeton University Press, 1991.
Kitzis, Gershon. "Aaron Marcus's 'Hasidism.'" *Ha-Ma'ayan* 21, no. 1 (1981): 64–88. [Hebrew]
Klein-Braslavy, Sara. "Identification of Nahash and Samael in the Guide of the Perplexed." *Da'at* 10 (1983): 9–18. [Hebrew]
Klein-Braslavy, Sara. *Maimonides' Interpretation of the Adam Stories in Genesis: A Study in Maimonides' Anthropology*. Jerusalem: Magnes Press, 1986. [Hebrew]
Koch, Patrick B. *Human Self-Perfection: A Re-Assessment of Kabbalistic Musar-Literature of Sixteenth-Century Safed*. Los Angeles: Cherub Press, 2015.
Konstantin, Burmistrov. "Kabbalah and Secret Societies in Russia. Eighteenth to Twentieth Centuries." In *Kabbalah and Modernity: Interpretations, Transformations, Adaptations*. Edited by Boaz Huss, Marco Pasi, and Kocku von Stuckrad, 79–106. Leiden: Brill, 2010.
Koren, Israel. "Martin Buber—From Ecstasy to the Mysticism of Life." *Kabbalah* 5 (2000): 371–410.
Koren, Israel. *The Mystery of the Earth: Mysticism and Hasidism in the Thought of Martin Buber*. Leiden: Brill, 2010.
Krassen, Miles. *Uniter of Heaven and Earth: Rabbi Meshullam Feibush Heller of Zbarazh and the Rise of Hasidism in Eastern Galicia*. Albany: State University of New York Press, 1998.
Kreisel, Howard. "Halevi' s Influence on Maimonides: A Preliminary Appraisal." *Maimonidean Studies* 2 (1992): 95–121.
Kreisel, Howard. *Prophecy: The History of an Idea in Medieval Jewish Philosophy*. Dordrecht: Kluwer Academic Publishers, 2001.
Kripal, Jeffery J. *Authors of the Impossible: The Paranormal and the Sacred*. Chicago: The University of Chicago Press, 2010.
Kripal, Jeffrey J. *Esalen: America and the Religion of No Religion*. Chicago: University of Chicago Press, 2007.
Kroger, William S., and Michael D. Yapko. *Clinical and Experimental Hypnosis in Medicine, Dentistry, and Psychology*. Philadelphia: Lippincott, Williams, and Wilkins, 2008.
Kurzweil, Zvi Erich. "R. Yisra'el me-Salanṭ ve-ha-Tenu'ah ha-Musarit." *Sinai* 47 (1960): 100–112. [Hebrew]
Lamm, Norman. *The Religious Thought of Hasidism*. Hoboken: Ktav, 1999.
Landau, Bezalel. "Ha-Maḥol ve-ha-Riqud be-Tenu'at ha-Ḥasidut." *Mahanayim* 48 (1960): 54–62. [Hebrew]
Lederberg, Netanel. *Sod HaDa'at: Rabbi Israel Ba'al Shem Tov, His Spiritual Character and Social Leadership*. Jerusalem: Rubin Mass, 2007. [Hebrew]
Leibowitz, Yeshayahu. *Body and Mind: The Psycho-Physical Problem*. Tel Aviv: The Ministry of Defense, 1989. [Hebrew]
Leshem, Zvi. "Between Messianism and Prophecy: Hasidism According to the Piaseczner Rebbe." PhD diss., Bar-Ilan University, 2007. [Hebrew]

Leshem, Zvi. "Flipping into Ecstasy: Towards a Syncopal Understanding of Mystical Hasidic Somersaults." *Studia Judaica* 17 (2014): 157–183.
Leshem, Zvi (Blobstein). "Iyunim be-Shiṭato ha-Ruḥanit shel ha-ADMO"R me-Pi'asechne." Master's thesis, Touro College, 2002. [Hebrew]
Leshem, Zvi. "Piaseczna Rebbe's Quieting Tune." YouTube video, 2:44. From 2007 by Rav Zvi Leshem and his students at Yeshivat Bat Ayin. Posted November 16, 2016. https://www.youtube.com/watch?v=zoDCpYHaoxE.
Levinger, Jacob S. *Maimonides as Philosopher and Codifier.* Jerusalem: Bialik Institute, 1989. [Hebrew]
Levinsky, Yom Tov. "Riqud, Ma'ase'ah, Zemer be-Torat ha-Ḥasidut." *Mahanayim* 46 (1960): 98–103. [Hebrew]
Levinsohn, Isaac Baer. *Divrei Ṣaddikim im Emeq Refa'im.* Odessa: s.n., 1867. [Hebrew]
Levitas-Bivas, Yaara. "Imagination in the Thought of R. Nahman of Bratslav." Master's thesis, Bar-Ilan University, 2007. [Hebrew]
Lewinsky, Yom-Tov. "The Great Yeshiva in Łomża Fifty Years Ago." In *Memoirs of the Lithuanian Yeshiva.* Edited by Immanuel Etkes and Shlomo Tikochinski, 347–360. Jerusalem: Zalman Shazar Center, 2004. [Hebrew]
Liebes, Yehuda. "Naḥman of Bratslav and Ludwig Wittgenstein." *Dimmui* 19 (2001): 9–13 [Hebrew]
Liebes, Yehuda. *Studies in the Zohar.* Translated by Arnold Schwartz, Stephanie Nakache, and Penina Peli. Albany: State University of New York Press, 1993.
Lobel, Diana. "A Dwelling Place for the Shekhinah." *Jewish Quarterly Review*, 90, no. 1–2 (1999): 103–125.
Lobel, Diana. *Between Mysticism and Philosophy: Sufi Language of Religious Experience in Judah Ha-Levi's Kuzari.* Albany: State University of New York Press, 2000.
Longinus. *On the Sublime.* Translated by A.O. Prickard. Oxford: Clarendon Press, 1926.
Longinus. *On the Sublime.* Translated by Yoram Bronowski. Tel Aviv: Sifriat Poalim, 1982. [Hebrew]
Longinus. "On the Sublime." Translated by W. Hamilton Fyfe. In *Aristotle, Longinus, Demetrius. Poetics. Longinus: On the Sublime. Demetrius: On Style*, 143–306. Loeb Classical Library. Cambridge: Harvard University Press, 1995.
Lurie, Yuval. *Tracking the Meaning of Life: A Philosophical Journey.* Haifa: Haifa University Press, 2001. [Hebrew]
Magid, Shaul. "Associative Midrash: Reflections on a Hermeneutical Theory in *Likkutei MoHaRan.*" In *God's Voice from the Void: Old and New Studies in Bratslav Hasidism.* Edited by Shaul Magid, 15–66. Albany: State University of New York Press, 2002.
Magid, Shaul. *From Metaphysics to Midrash: Myth, History, and the Interpretation of Scripture in Lurianic Kabbala.* Bloomington: Indiana University Press, 2008.
Magid, Shaul. "Is Kabbala Mysticism? Another View." *Zeek* (March 2008). Assessed August 8, 2016, http://www.zeek.net/803huss/.
Magid, Shaul. "The Necessary Heresy of Translation—Reflections on the Hebrew Writings of Reb Zalman Schachter-Shalomi." *Spectrum: The Journal of Jewish Renewal* (2007): 19–37.
Maimon, Dov. "Rabbinical Judaism and Islamic Mysticism: The Limits of a Relationship." *Akdamot* 8 (1999): 43–72. [Hebrew]

Maor, Zohar. *A New Secret Doctrine: Spirituality, Creativity and Nationalism in the Prague Circle*. Jerusalem: Zalman Shazar Center, 2010. [Hebrew]

Marcus, Aaron. *Der Chassidismus: Eine Kulturgeschichtliche Studie*. Pleschen: Jeschurun, 1901. [German]

Marcus, Aaron. *Hasidism*. Translated by Moshe Schoenfeld. Bnei Brak: Neṣaḥ 1980. [Hebrew]

Margolin, Ron. *The Human Temple: Religious Interiorization and the Structuring of Inner Life in Early Hasidism*. Jerusalem: Magnes Press, 2005. [Hebrew]

Margolin, Ron. *Inner Religion: The Phenomenology of Inner Religious Life and Its Manifestation in Jewish Sources. from the Bible to Hasidic Texts*. Ramat Gan: Bar-Ilan University Press; Jerusalem: Shalom Hartman Institute, 2011. [Hebrew]

Mark, Natan. "Daqṭor Ya'aqov Na'kht: Le-Milo'at Ḥeṣi Yovel le-Avodato ha-Sifrutit." *Ha-Tsefirah*, March 16, 1928. [Hebrew]

Mark, Zvi. *Mysticism and Madness in the Work of R. Nahman of Bratslav*. Tel Aviv: Am Oved; Jerusalem: Shalom Hartman Institute, 2004. [Hebrew]

Mark, Zvi. *Mysticism and Madness: The Religious Thought of Rabbi Nachman of Bratslav*. London: Continuum, 2009.

Marks, Robert W. *The Story of Hypnotism*. New York: Prentice-Hall, 1947.

Markus Marcus, *Ahron Marcus: Die Lebensgeschichte eines Chossid*. Montreux: David Marcus, 1966.

Marmur, Michael. "Heschel's Rhetoric of Citation: The Use of Sources in *God in Search of Man*." PhD diss., Hebrew University, 2005.

Mashiach, Amir. "Rabbi Kook and Buddhism." *Da'at* 70 (2011): 81–96. [Hebrew]

Matanky, Eugene D. "The Mystical Element in Abraham Joshua Heschel's Theological-Political Thought." *Shofar: An Interdisciplinary Journal of Jewish Studies* 35, no. 3 (2017): 33–55.

Mayse, Ariel Evan. "The Sacred Writ of Hasidism: Tanya and the Spiritual Vision of Rabbi Shneur Zalman of Liady." In *Books of the People: Revisiting Classic Works of Jewish Thought*. Edited by Stuart W. Halpern, 109–156. New York: Straus Center and Yeshiva University Press, 2017.

Mazor, Yaakov, and Edwin Seroussi. "Towards a Hasidic Lexicon of Music." *Orbis Musicae* 10 (1990/1991): 118–143.

Mazor, Yaakov, and Moshe Taube. "A Hassidic Ritual Dance: The *Mitsve Tants* in Jerusalemite Weddings." *Yuval* 6 (1994): 164–224.

Mazor, Yaakov. "Koḥo shel ha-Nigun be-Hagut ha-Ḥasidit ve-Tafkidav be-Havai ha-Dati veha-Ḥevrati." *Yuval* 7 (2002): 25–36. [Hebrew]

Mendes-Flohr, Paul R. "Fin-de-Siècle Orientalism, the *Ostjuden*, and the Aesthetics of Jewish Self-Affirmation." In *Divided Passions: Jewish Intellectuals and the Experience of Modernity*. Edited by Paul R. Mendes-Flohr, 77–132. Detroit: Wayne University Press, 1991.

Mendes-Flohr, Paul. "Fin-de-siècle Orientalism, the 'Ostjuden' and the Aesthetics of Jewish Self-Affirmation." *Studies in Contemporary Jewry* 1 (1984): 96–139.

Mendes-Flohr, Paul. "Orientalism and Mysticism: The Aesthetic of the Turn of the Nineteenth Century and Jewish Identity." *Jerusalem Studies in Jewish Thought* 3, no. 4 (1984): 624–681 [Hebrew]

Mesmer, Franz. *Mesmerismus oder System der Wechsel-Beziehungen: Theorie und Andwendungen des Thierischen Magnetismus*. Berlin: In der Nikolaischen Buchhandlung, 1814.

Meyer, Michael A. "Review of Steven Beller 'Vienna and the Jews, 1867–1938: A Cultural History.'" *AJS Review* 16, no. 1–2 (1991): 236–239.
Mieses, Fabius. *History of Modern Philosophy.* Leipzig: s.n., 1887. [Hebrew]
Miller, Samuel, ed., *Apiryon* 1 (1924) [Hebrew]
Miron, Ronny. *Karl Jaspers: From Selfhood to Being.* Amsterdam: Rodopi, 2012.
Mirsky, Yehudah. *Rav Kook: Mystic in a Time of Revolution.* New Haven and London: Yale University Press, 2014.
Mondshine, Yehoshua. *Ha'Tsofeh Le'Doro: Rabbi Yekuthiel Aryeh Kamelhar, His Life and Works.* Jerusalem: Rubin Mass, 1987. [Hebrew]
Monk, Samuel Holt. *The Sublime: A Study of Critical Theories in XVIII-Century England* (1935. Reprinted, Ann Arbor: University of Michigan Press, 1960.
Monroe, Robert A. *Journeys Out of the Body.* New York: Doubleday, 1977.
Moscheles, Felix. *In Bohemia with Du Maurier.* New York: Harper and Brothers, 1897.
Muckenhoupt, Margaret. *Sigmund Freud: Explorer of the Unconscious.* New York: Oxford University Press, 1997.
Myers, Jody. "Marriage and Sexual Behavior in the Teachings of the Kabbalah Centre." In *Kabbalah and Modernity: Interpretations, Transformations, Adaptations.* Edited by Boaz Huss, Marco Pasi, and Kocku von Stuckrad, 259–282. Leiden: Brill, 2010.
Nacht, Jacob, Zalman Epstein, and Yitzchak Leib Baruch. *Sefer ha-Shabbat.* 1936. Reprint, Tel Aviv: Dvir, 1971. [Hebrew]
Epstein, Zalman. "Ḥazon ha-Shabbat." In Jacob Nacht, Zalman Epstein, and Yitzchak Leib Baruch, *Sefer ha-Shabbat.* http://benyehuda.org/epstein/008.html. [Hebrew]
Naor, Bezalel. *Lights of Prophecy.* New York: Union of Orthodox Jewish Congregations of America, 1990.
Niborski, Yitskhok. *Dictionary of Hebrew and Aramaic Words in Yiddish.* Paris: Medem, 2012.
Nigal, Gedalyah. *Hassidic Tales Collectors.* Jerusalem: Carmel, 1995. [Hebrew]
Nigal, Gedalyah. *The Hasidic Tale.* Oxford: Littman Library, 2008.
Ogren, Brian, ed., *Time and Eternity in Jewish Mysticism: That Which is Before and That Which is After.* Leiden: Brill, 2015.
Ophir, Natan. *Quieting the Mind: The Admor of Piaseczno.* Jerusalem: Jewish Meditation Institute Jerusalem, 2009. [Hebrew]
Osho, *The Transmission of the Lamp: Talks in Uruguay.* s.l.: s.n., s.a. http://www.oshorajneesh.com/download/osho-books/world_tour_talks/The_Transmission_of_the_Lamp_(Talks_in_Uruguay).pdf
Otto, Rudolf. *Mysticism East and West: A Comparative Analysis of the Nature of Mysticism.* Translated by Bertha L. Bracey and Richenda C. Payne. New York: Macmillan, 1932.
Otto, Rudolf. *Religious Essays: A Supplement to 'The Idea of the Holy'.* Translated by Brian Lunn. Oxford: Oxford University Press, 1931.
Otto, Rudolf. *The Idea of the Holy: An Inquiry into the Non-rational Factor in the Idea of the Divine and Its Relation to the Rational.* Translated by John W. Harvey. Oxford: Oxford University Press, 1958.
Ouspensky, Peter. *The Psychology of Man's Possible Evolution.* New York: Alfred A. Knopf, 1974.
Pachter, Mordechai. *Israel Salanter: Selected Writings.* Jerusalem: Bialik Institute, 1972. [Hebrew]

Pachter, Mordechai. “The Kabbalistic Foundation of the Faith-Heresy Issue in Rav Kook’s.” *Da’at* 47 (2001): 69 – 100. [Hebrew]

Pachter, Mordechai. “The Musar Movement and the Kabbalah.” In *Let the Old Make Way for the New.* Edited by David Assaf and Ada Rapoport-Albert, 223 – 50. Jerusalem: Zalman Shazar Center, 2009. [Hebrew]

Pachter, Shilo. “Shemirat Habrit: The History of the Prohibition of Wasting Seed.” PhD diss., Hebrew University, 2006. [Hebrew]

Pasi, Marco. “Oriental Kabbalah and The Parting of East and West in the Early Theosophical Society.” In *Kabbalah and Modernity: Interpretations, Transformations, Adaptations.* Edited by Boaz Huss, Marco Pasi, and Kocku von Stuckrad, 151 – 166. Leiden: Brill, 2010.

Pedaya, Haviva. “Shabbat, Shabbetai and the Diminution of the Moon: Sabbath, Sign and Image.” *Eshel Beer-Sheva* 4 (1996): 143 – 197. [Hebrew]

Pedaya, Haviva. “Sight, Fall, Song: The Longing for a Vision of God and the Spiritual Element in Early Jewish Mysticism,” *Asufot* 9 (1995): 237 – 277. [Hebrew]

Pedaya, Haviva. “Two Types of Ecstatic Experience in Hasidism.” *Da’at* 55 (2005): 73 – 108.

Pedaya, Haviva. *Vision and Speech: Models of Revelatory Experience in Jewish Mysticism.* Los Angeles: Cherub Press, 2002. [Hebrew]

Persico, Tomer. “Be-Darkhei No’am: Ha-Neyu Eij ke-Haṭma’ah shel Etos Noṣri be-Yahadut Bat Zemanainu.” *Akdamot* 24 (2010): 72 – 95. [Hebrew]

Persico, Tomer. “Jewish Meditation: The Development of a Modern Form of Spiritual Practice in Contemporary Judaism.” PhD diss., Tel Aviv University, 2012. [Hebrew]

Persico, Tomer. *The Jewish Meditative Tradition.* Tel Aviv: Tel Aviv University Press, 2016. [Hebrew]

Phineas Parkhurst Quimby Resource Center. http://www.ppquimby.com/index.html.

Piekarz, Mendel. *The Beginning of Hasidism: Ideological Trends in Derush and Musar Literature.* Jerusalem: Bialik Press, 1978. [Hebrew]

Piekarz, Mendel. *Between Ideology and Reality: Humility, Ayin, Self-Negation and Devekut in Hasidic Thought.* Jerusalem: Bialik Press, 1994. [Hebrew]

Piekarz, Mendel. *Ideological Trends of Hasidim in Poland During the Interwar Period and the Holocaust.* Jerusalem: Bialik Institute, 1990. [Hebrew]

Piekarz, Mendel. *The Literature of Testimony as a Historical Source of the Holocaust and Three Hasidic Reflections to the Holocaust.* Jerusalem: Bialik Institute, 2003. [Hebrew]

Pines, Shlomo. “On the Term Ruḥaniyyot and its Origin and on Judah Halevi’s Doctrine.” *Tarbiz*, 57, no. 4 (1988): 511 – 540. [Hebrew]

Piron, Mordechai. “Ha-Riqud ve-ha-Zemer be-Tequfat ha-Talmud.” *Mahanayim* 48 (1960): 34 – 39. [Hebrew]

Plato. *The Republic.* Translated by Paul Shorey. Loeb Classical Library. 2 vols. Cambridge: Harvard University Press, 1930, 1935.

Polen, Nehemia. *The Holy Fire: The Teachings of Rabbi Kalonymus Kalman Shapira, the Rebbe of the Warsaw Ghetto.* Northvale: Jason Aronson, 1994.

Polen, Nehemia. “Sensitization to Holiness: The Life and Works of Rabbi Kalonymos Kalmish Shapiro.” *Jewish Action* (Winter 1989 – 1990): 30 – 33.

Polen, Nehemia. “The Spirit Among the Sages: *Seder Olam*, the End of Prophecy, and Sagely Illumination.” In *“It’s Better to Hear the Rebuke of the Wise than the Song of Fools” (Qoh 7:5). Proceedings of the Midrash Section, Society of Biblical Literature, Volume 6.* Edited by W. David Nelson and Rivka Ulmer, 83 – 94. Piscataway: Gorgias Press, 2015.

Professor Diyubva. "Der Dimyon als Sibah fun Krankheytn." Pts. 1, 2, and 3. *Der Yidisher Hoyz-Doktor: A Vekenlikher Zhurnal fir Hoyzlikhe Meditsin aun Gezund-Ferhitung* [The Jewish House Doctor: A Weekly Journal for Domestic Medicine and Healthcare] 22 (June 27, 1913): 11–13; 23 (July 4, 1913): 3–5; 24 (July 11, 1913): 8–10. [Yiddish]

Qorman, Ya'aqov. Shapira's disciple. Interviewed by the author, May 2010.

Qoveṣ Histadruti shel Agudat Yisra'el, 5672–5683. Vienna: Lishkat ha-Merkaz shel Agudat Yisra'el ha-Olamit, 1923. [Hebrew]

Rabinowitz, Aaron. "Le-Birur Musag ha-Bilti-Muda be-Tenu'at ha-Musar." In *Samuel Belkin Memorial Volume.* Edited by Moshe Carmilly and Hayim Leaf, 36–42. New York: Yeshiva University, 1981. [Hebrew]

Rabinowitz, Aaron. "Meqomo shel ha-Bilti-Muda be-Yahadut." *Derakhim le-Emunah be-Yahadut* 23 (1981): 177–185. [Hebrew]

Rabinowitz, Aaron. "The Unconscious: Its Relation to the Judaism-Psychology Dialogue." *Journal of Psychology and Judaism* 13, no. 3 (1989): 149–162.

Rabinowitz, Alexander Ziskind (Azar). "Keter Torah." In *Ha-Maḥshavah ha-Yisra'elit.* Edited by Elhanan Kalmanson. Jerusalem: s.n., 1920.

Rachlis, Arnold. "The Musar Movement and Psychotherapy." *Judaism* 23 (1974): 337–345.

Rafel, Dov. *Prophecy Through the Lens of Jewish Thought.* Jerusalem: Amanah, 1971. [Hebrew]

Rahman, Fazlur. "Dream, Imagination and 'Alam AlMithal,'" *Islamic Studies* 3 (1964): 167–180.

Rahman, Fazlur. *Prophecy in Islam.* London: Allen & Unwin, 1958.

Rapaport-Albert, Ada. "God and the Zaddik as the Two Focal Points of Hasidic Worship." *History of Religions* 18, no. 4 (1979): 296–325.

Rechter, David. *The Jews of Vienna and the First World War.* London: Littman Library of Jewish Civilization, 2001.

Reeves, Marjorie, ed. *Prophetic Rome in the High Renaissance Period.* Oxford: Oxford University Press, 1992.

Reeves, Marjorie. "Cardinal Egidio of Viterbo: A Prophetic Interpretation of History." In *Prophetic Rome in the High Renaissance Period.* Edited by Marjorie Reeves,91–109. Oxford: Oxford University Press, 1992., 97–99

Reeves, Marjorie. *The Influence of Prophecy in the Later Middle Ages.* Oxford: Clarendon Press, 2000.

Reines, Alvin. "Maimonides' Concept of Mosaic Prophecy." *Hebrew Union College Annual* 40–41 (1969): 325–361.

Reiser, Daniel. "'To Fly like Angels": Imagery or Waking Dream Techniques in Hasidic Mysticism in the First Half of the Twentieth Century." PhD diss., Hebrew University, 2011. [Hebrew]

Reiser, Daniel. "Historicism and/or Phenomenology in The Study of Jewish Mysticism: Imagery Techniques in the Teachings of Rabbi Kalonymus Kalman Shapira as a Case Study." *Modern Judaism* 36, no. 1 (2016): 1–16.

Reiser, Daniel. *R. Kalonymus Kalman Shapira: Sermons from the Years of Rage.* 2 vols. Jerusalem: Herzog Academic College / World Union of Jewish Studies / Yad Vashem, 2017. [Hebrew]

Reiser, Daniel. "'To Rend the Entire Veil': Prophecy in the Teachings of Rabbi Kalonymous Kalamish Shapira of Piazecna and its Renewal in the Twentieth Century." *Modern Judaism* 34, no. 3 (2014): 334–352.

Reiser, Daniel. "Self-Imagery, Hasidism and Cognition," *BDD: Journal of Torah and Scholarship* 31 (2016): 111–126. [Hebrew]
Reiser, Daniel. *Vision as a Mirror: Imagery Techniques in Twentieth Century Jewish Mysticism.* Los Angeles: Cherub Press, 2014. [Hebrew]
Reiser, Daniel. "Voicedness and Audio." In *Hasidism: Anthology.* Edited by Rela Kushlavsky. Ramat Gan: Bar-Ilan University Press, forthcoming. [Hebrew]
Ribot, Théodule-Armand. *The Creative Imagination: Psychological Essay.* Translated by Nissan Turov. New York, Warsaw, and Moscow: Shtibel Press, 1921. [Hebrew]
Ribot, Théodule. *Essay on the Creative Imagination.* Translated by Albert H. N. Baron. London: Kegan Paul, Trench, Trübner, 1906.
Robinson, Henry Wheeler. "Hebrew Psychology." In *The People and the Book: Essays on the Old Testament.* Edited by Arthur S. Peake, 353–375. Oxford: Clarendon Press, 1925.
Robinson, Ira. "The Tarler Rebbe of Lodz and his Medical Practice: Towards a History of Hasidic Life in Pre-First World War Poland." *Polin* 11 (1998): 53–61.
Rosenberg, Shalom. "The Return to the Garden of Eden: Remarks for the History of the Idea of the Restorative Redemption in the Medieval Jewish Philosophy." In *The Messianic Idea in Jewish Thought: A Study Conference in Honour of the Eightieth Birthday of Gershom Scholem.* Edited by Shmuel Re'em, 37–86. Jerusalem: Israel Academy of Sciences and Humanities, 1982. [Hebrew]
Rosenberg, Shimon Gershon. *"A Memorial of the First Day": High Holiday Sermons.* Efrat: Yeshivat Siach Yitzhak, 2001. [Hebrew]
Rosenberg, Shimon Gershon. *A Time of Freedom: Discourses for Pesach.* Edited by Yishai Mevorach. Alon Shevut: The Institute for the Advancement of Rav Shagar's Writings, 2010. [Hebrew]
Rosenberg, Simeon Gershon. "Faith and Language According the Admor ha-Zaqen of Habad from the Philosophical Perspective on Language of Wittgenstein." In *On Faith: Studies in the Concept of Faith and Its History in the Jewish Tradition.* Edited by Moshe Halbertal, David Kurzweil, and Avi Sagi, 365–387. Jerusalem: Keter, 2005. [Hebrew]
Rosenberg, Shimon Gershon. *Return, O My Soul: Divine Grace or Human Free Will.* Efrat: Yeshivat Siach Yitzhak, 2003. [Hebrew]
Rosenberg, Shimon Gershon. *We Walk in Fervor.* Efrat: Yeshivat Siach Yitzhak, 2008. [Hebrew]
Rosenzweig, Franz. *The Star of Redemption.* Translated by Barabra E. Galli. Madison: The University of Wisconsin Press, 2005.
Ross, Tamar. "The Anti-Rationalist Trend in the Musar Movement." In *Alei Shefer: Studies in the Literature of Jewish Thought Presented to Rabbi Dr. Alexandre Safran.* Edited by Moshe Hallamish, 145–162. Ramat Gan: Bar Ilan University Press, 1990. [Hebrew]
Rozenblit, Marsha L. *The Jews of Vienna 1867–1914: Assimilation and Identity.* Albany: State University of New York Press, 1983.
Rubenstein, Shahar. "Prophecy in the Teachings of R. Abraham ben ha-RaMBaM." Master's thesis, Hebrew University, 2009. [Hebrew]
Russ-Fishbane, Elisha. *Judaism, Sufism, and the Pietists of Medieval Egypt: A Study of Abraham Maimonides and His Times.* Oxford: Oxford University Press, 2015.
Sartre, Jean Paul. *The Psychology of Imagination.* Translated by Bernard Frechtman. New York: Washington Square Press, 1966.
Schachter-Shalomi, Zalman. *Yishmru Daat: Chassidic Teachings of the Fourth Turning.* Boulder: OHALAH Rabbinic Fellowship, 2009. [Hebrew]

Schatz-Uffenheimer, Rivka. *Hasidism as Mysticism: Quietistic Elements in Eighteeth-Century Hasidic Thought*. Translated by Jonathan Chipman. Princeton: Princeton University Press, 1993.
Schiller, Friedrich. *On the Sublime*. Translated by William F. Wertz. Last modified October 29, 2016. https://www.schillerinstitute.org/transl/trans_on_sublime.html.
Scholem, Gershom. *Explications and Implications: Writings on Jewish Heritage and Renaissance*. Tel Aviv: Am Oved, 1982. [Hebrew]
Scholem, Gershom. *Kabbalah*. Jerusalem: Keter, 1974.
Scholem, Gershom. *Major Trends in Jewish Mysticism*. New York: Schocken Books, 1954.
Scholem, Gershom. *On the Kabbalah and Its Symbolism*. Translated by Ralph Manheim. New York: Schocken Books, 1965.
Scholem, Gershom. *On the Mystical Shape of the Godhead: Basic Concepts in the Kabbalah*. Translated by Joachim Neugroschel. New York: Schocken Books, 1991.
Scholem, Gershom. *The Messianic Idea in Judaism*. New York: Schocken Press, 1971.
Scholem, Gershom. "Note on a Kabbalistical Treatise on Contemplation." *Melanges offerts à Henry Corbin*. Edited by Seyyed Hossein Nasr, 665–670. Teheran: Tehran UP, 1977.
Schorske, Carl E. *Fin-de-Siècle Vienna: Politics and Culture*. New York: A. A. Knopf, 1980.
Schwartz, Dov. *Faith at the Crossroads: A Theological Profile of Religious Zionism*. Translated by Batya Stein. Leiden: Brill, 2002.
Schwartz, Dov. "The Fourteenth Century Jewish Neoplatonic Circle on Mosaic Prophecy." *Journal of Jewish Thought and Philosophy* 2 (1992): 97–110.
Schwartz, Dov. "On the Conception of Prophecy of R. Isaac Polcar, R. Solomon Alconstantin and Spinoza." *Asufot* 4 (1990): 57–72. [Hebrew]
Schwartz, Dov. "Psychological Dimensions of Mosaic Prophecy—Imagination and Intellect." In *Moses the Man—Master of the Prophets: In the Light of Interpretation throughout the Ages*. Edited by Moshe Hallamish, et al., 251–283. Ramat-Gan: Bar-Ilan University Press, 2010. [Hebrew]
Schweid, Eliezer. *The Classic Jewish Philosophers: From Saadia through the Renaissance*. Translated by Leonard Levin. Leiden: Brill, 2008.
Schweid, Eliezer. *From Ruin to Salvation*. Tel Aviv: Hakibbutz Hameuchad, 1994. [Hebrew]
Schweid, Eliezer. "Mysticism and Judaism According to Gershom Scholem." *Jerusalem Studies in Jewish Thought* 2 (1983): 5–88. [Hebrew]
Schweid, Eliezer. *Prophets for Their People and Humanity: Prophecy and Prophets in 20th Century Jewish Thought*. Jerusalem: Magnes Press, 1999. [Hebrew]
Seeman, Don. "Ritual Efficacy, Hassidic Mysticism and 'Useless Suffering' in the Warsaw Ghetto." *Harvard Theological Review* 101 (2008): 465–505.
Segal, Yocheved. *The Chasid from Hamburg: A Portrait of Rabbi Aharon Marcus, A Man of Truth, Courage, Genius, and Humility*. Translated by Bracha Slae. New York: Feldheim, 2004.
Seidman, Hillel. *Ishim she-Hikarti: Demuyot me-Avar Qarov be-Mizraḥ Iropah*. Jerusalem: Mossad Harav Kook, 1970. [Hebrew]
Shapiro, Malkah. *The Rebbe's Daughter: Memoir of a Hasidic Childhood*. Translated by Nehemia Polen. Philadelphia: The Jewish Publication Society, 2002.
Shear-Yashuv, Aharon. "The Harmony between Maimonides, Kabbalah and Kant According to Rabbi Shem Tov Gefen." *Da'at* 64–66 (2009): 343–350. [Hebrew]

Sheilat, Yitzhak. "The Uniqueness of Israel: Comparing the Kuzari and Maimonides." *Ma'aliyot* 20 (1999): 275–288. [Hebrew]
Sheils, Dean. "Cross-Cultural Study of Beliefs in Out-of-the-Body Experiences, Waking and Sleeping." *Journal of the Society for Psychical Research* 47 (1978): 697–741.
Shonkoff, Sam Berrin. "Sacramental Existence and Embodied Theology in Buber's Representation of Ḥasidism." *Journal of Jewish Thought and Philosophy* 25 (2017): 131–161.
Shor, Avraham Avishai. "Maran Rebi Aharon ha-Gadol, Zekhuto Yagen Aleinu Amen, ve-Ḥavurat ha-Ḥasidim be-Qarlin." *Beit Aharon ve-Yisrael* 51 (1994): 153–160. [Hebrew]
Solomon, Norman. "Hilluq And Haqira: A Study in the Method of the Lithuanian Halakhists." *Dinei Israel* 4 (1973): lxiv-cvi.
Soloveitchik, Joseph B. *Halakhic Man.* Translated by Lawrence Kaplan. Philadelphia: The Jewish Publication Society, 1983.
Soloveitchik, Joseph B. *On Repentance: The Thought and Oral Discourses of Rabbi Joseph B. Soloveitchik.* Edited and translated by Pinchas H. Peli. New York: Paulist Press, 1984.
Sorabji, Richard. *Aristotle on Memory.* Chicago: University of Chicago Press, 2006.
Stampfer, Shaul. *Lithuanian Yeshivas of the Nineteenth Century: Creating a Tradition of Learning.* Translated by Lindsey Taylor-Guthartz. Oxford: Littman Library of Jewish Civilization, 2012.
Steinsaltz, Adin. *The Thirteen Petalled Rose.* Jerusalem: Maggid Books, 1996. [Hebrew]
Straus, Raphael. "The Baal-Shem of Michelstadt: Mesmerism and Cabbala." *Historica Judaica*, 8, no. 2 (1946): 135–148.
Strikovsky, Aryeh, ed., *Daf le-Tarbut Yehudit* 278 (December 2009). [Hebrew]
Sviri, Sara. *The Sufis: An Anthology.* Tel Aviv: Tel Aviv University, 2008. [Hebrew]
Ta-Shma, Israel M. *Early Franco-German Ritual and Custom.* Jerusalem: Magnes Press, 1994. [Hebrew]
Ta-Shma, Israel M. *Ritual, Custom and Reality in Franco-Germany, 1100–1350.* Jerusalem: Magnes Press, 1996. [Hebrew]
Theon, Eliezer Mordekhai. *The Gate to the Secrets of Contemplation.* Jerusalem: Argaman Circle, 1995. [Hebrew]
Tishby, Isaiah, and Joseph Dan. "Hasidism—Doctrine and Literature." *Encyclopaedia Hebraica.* Vol. 17. Jerusalem and Tel Aviv: Encyclopaedia Publishing Co., 1965. 810–811. [Hebrew]
Tishby, Isaiah. *The Wisdom of the Zohar: An Anthology of Texts.* Translated by David Goldstein. 3 Vols. London: Littman Library, 1991.
Tsinovitsh, Moses. "R. Aaron Marcus—The Pioneer of Hasidic Literature." *Ortodoksishe Yugend Bleter* 39 (1933): 7–8. [Yiddish]
Uffenheimer, Benjamin. *Classical Prophecy: The Prophetic Consciousness.* Jerusalem: Magnes Press, 2001. [Hebrew]
Uffenheimer, Benjamin. *Early Prophecy in Israel.* Jerusalem: Magnes Press, 1973. [Hebrew]
Uffenheimer, Benjamin. "Prolegomena to the Problem of Prophetic Ecstasy." *Sefer Bar-Ilan* 22–23 (1988): 45–62. [Hebrew]
Uffenheimer, Benjamin. "Rudolf Otto's Approach and the Prophetic Consciousness." *Beit Mikra* 38, no. 1 (1983): 1–13. [Hebrew]
Underhill, Evelyn. *Mysticism: A Study in the Nature and Development of Spiritual Consciousness.* 1911. Reprint, Mineola: Dover Publications, 2002.
Unger, Menashe. *Hasidism and Life.* New York: s.n., 1946. [Yiddish]

Ungerfeld, Moshe (Agaf). *Vienna*. Tel Aviv: Naḥum Dreemer Publishing, 1946. [Hebrew]
Ungerfeld, Moshe. "Y. L. Barukh (Ḥamishim Shanah le-Pe'ulato ha-Sifrutit)." *Moznaim* 1, no. 6 (1947): 135–136. [Hebrew]
Urbach, Ephraim E. *The Sages: Their Concepts and Beliefs*. Jerusalem: Magnes Press, 1975. [Hebrew]
Urbach, Ephraim E. *The Tosaphots: Their History, Writings, and Methods*. Jerusalem: Bialik Institute, 1955. [Hebrew]
Urbach, Ephraim E. *The World of the Sages: Collected Studies*. Jerusalem: Magnes Press, 2002. [Hebrew]
Wacks, Ron. *The Flame of the Holy Fire: Perspectives on the Teachings of Rabbi Kalonymous Kalmish Shapiro of Piaczena*. Alon Shevut: Tevunot, 2010. [Hebrew]
Wacks, Ron. "Nevu'ah ve-Ḥasidut be-Torato shel ha-Rebi me-Pi'asechnah." In *Prophesy, O Son of Man: On the Possibility of Prophecy*. Edited by Odeya Tzurieli, 39–52. Jerusalem: Rubin Mass, 2006. [Hebrew]
Wacks, Ron. "The Technique of Guided Imagination in the Thought of R. Kalonymos Kalman Shapira of Piasecno." *Kabbalah* 17 (2008): 233–249. [Hebrew]
Wasserstrom, Steven M. *Religion after Religion: Gershom Scholem Mircea Eliade and Henry Corbin at Eranos*. Princeton: Princeton University Press, 1999.
Wattles, Wallace. *The Science of Being Great*. Holyoke: The Elizabeth Towne Company, 1911.
Wattles, Wallace. *The Science of Getting Rich*. Holyoke: The Elizabeth Towne Company, 1910.
Weinstein, Berish. *Reyshe: Poeme*. New York: Ignatov Fund, 1947. [Yiddish]
Weiss, Joseph G. "Beginnings of Hasidim." *Zion* 16 (1951): 88–103 [Hebrew]
Weiss, Joseph G. *Studies in Braslav Hasidism*. Jerusalem: Bialik Institute, 1974. [Hebrew]
Weiss, Joseph G. *Studies in Eastern European Jewish Mysticism*. Edited by David Goldstein with an introduction by Joseph Dan. Oxford: Littman Library of Jewish Civilization, 1985.
Werblowsky, R. J. Zwi. *Joseph Karo: Lawyer and Mystic*. Philadelphia: Jewish Publication Society of America, 1977.
Wertheim, Aaron. *Law and Custom in Hasidism*. Translated by Shmuel Himelstein. Hoboken: Ktav, 1992.
Whitehead, Alfred North. *Adventures of Ideas*. New York: The Free Press, 1967.
Whitehead, Alfred North. *Process and Reality*. New York: Macmillan, 1929.
Whitehead, Alfred North. *Science and the Modern World*. Cambridge: Cambridge University Press., 1926
Whyte, Lancelot Law. *The Unconscious Before Freud*. New York: Basic Books, 1960.
Wiener, Moritz. *Selma Die Jüdische Seherin: Traumleben und Hellsehen Einer Durch Animalischen Magnetismus Wiederhergestellten Kranken*. Berlin: L. Fernbach, 1838. [German]
Wilcox, Ella Wheeler. *Heart of the New Thought*. Chicago: The Psychic Research Company, 1902.
Winter, Alison. *Mesmerized: Powers of Mind in Victorian Britain*. Chicago: University of Chicago Press, 1998.
Wittgenstein, Ludwig. *Tractatus Logico-Philosophicus*. Translated by D. F. Pears and B. F. McGuinness. London: Routledge, 1974.
Wolfson, Elliot R. *A Dream Interpreted Within a Dream: Oneiropoiesis and the Prism of Imagination*. New York: Zone Books, 2011.

Wolfson, Elliot R. *Abraham Abulafia—Kabbalist and Prophet: Hermeneutics, Theosophy, and Theurgy*. Los Angeles: Cherub Press, 2000.

Wolfson, Elliot R. "Afterword: To Pray after Praying/To Dance with No Feet." In Aubrey L. Glazer, *Mystical Vertigo: Contemporary Hebrew Poetry Dancing Over the Divide*, 267–273. Boston: Academic Studies Press, 2013.

Wolfson, Elliot R. *Alef, Mem, Tau: Kabbalistic Musings on Time, Truth, and Death*. Berkeley: University of California Press, 2006.

Wolfson, Elliot R. *Along the Path: Studies in Kabalistic Myth, Symbolism, and Hermeneutics*. Albany: State University of New York Press, 1995.

Wolfson, Elliot R. "The Body in the Text: A Kabbalistic Theory of Embodiment." *Jewish Quarterly Review* 95, no. 3 (2005): 479–500.

Wolfson, Elliot R. "The Cut That Binds: Time, Memory, and the Ascetic Impulse." In *God's Voice from the Void: Old and New Studies in Bratslav Hasidism*. Edited by Shaul Magid, 103–154. Albany: State University of New York Press, 2002.

Wolfson, Elliot R. "Exchange: Open Secret in the Rearview Mirror." *AJS Review* 35, no. 2 (2011): 401–418.

Wolfson, Elliot R. "Fore/giveness On the Way: Nesting in the Womb of Response." *Graven Images: A Journal of Culture, Law and Sacred* 4 (1998): 153–169.

Wolfson, Elliot R. "From My Flesh I Would Behold God: Imaginal Representation and Inscripting Divine Justice, Preliminary Observations." *The Journal of Scriptural Reasoning* 2, no. 3 (2002), http://jsr.shanti.virginia.edu/back-issues/vol-2-no-3%C2%97-september-2002-a-harmony-of-opposing-voices/from-my-flesh-i-would-behold-god-imaginal-representation-and-inscripting-divine-justice-preliminary-observations/

Wolfson, Elliot R. "From Sealed Book to Open Text: Time, Memory, and Narrativity in Kabbalistic Hermenutics." In *Interpreting Judaism in a Postmodern Age*. Edited by Steven Kepnes, 145–178. New York: New York University Press, 1996.

Wolfson, Elliot R. *Giving Beyond the Gift: Apophasis and Overcoming Theomania*. New York: Fordham University Press, 2014.

Wolfson, Elliot R. "The Hermeneutics of Visionary Experience: Revelation and Interpretation in the *Zohar*." *Religion* 18 (1998): 311–345.

Wolfson, Elliot R. "Iconic Visualization and the Imaginal Body of God: The Role of Intention in the Rabbinic Conception of Prayer." *Modern Theology* 12 (1996): 137–162.

Wolfson, Elliot R. "Images of God's Feet: Some Observations on the Divine body in Judaism." In *People of the Body: Jews and Judaism from an Embodied Perspective*. Edited by Howard Eilberg-Schwartz, 143–181. Albany: State University of New York Press, 1992.

Wolfson, Elliot R. "Imagination and the Theolatrous Impulse: Configuring God in Modern Jewish Thought." In *The Cambridge History of Jewish Philosophy: The Modern Era*. Edited by Martin Kavka, Zachary Braiterman, and David Novak, 663–703. Cambridge: Cambridge University Press, 2012.

Wolfson, Elliot R. "*Imago Templi* and the Meeting of the Two Seas: Liturgical Time-Space and the Feminine Imaginary in Zoharic Kabbalah." *RES: Anthropology and Aesthetics* 51 (2007): 121–135.

Wolfson, Elliot R. "Judaism and Incarnation: The Imaginal Body of God." In *Christianity in Jewish Terms*. Edited by Tikva Frymer-Kensky et al., 239–253. Boulder: Westview Press, 2000.

Wolfson, Elliot R. *Language, Eros, Being: Kabbalistic Hermeneutics and Poetic Imagination.* New York: Fordham University Press, 2005.
Wolfson, Elliot R. *Luminal Darkness: Imaginal Gleanings from the Zoharic Literature.* Oxford: Oneworld Publications, 2007.
Wolfson, Elliot R. "Merkavah Traditions in Philosophical Garb: Judah Halevi Reconsidered." *Proceedings of the American Academy for Jewish Research* 57 (1990–1991): 203–235.
Wolfson, Elliot R. *Open Secret: Postmessianic Messianism and the Mystical Revision of Menaḥem Mendel Schneerson.* New York: Columbia University Press, 2009.
Wolfson, Elliot R. "Phantasmagoria: The Image of the Image in Jewish Magic from Late Antiquity to the Early Middle Ages." *Review of Rabbinic Judaism: Ancient, Medieval and Modern* 4 (2001): 78–120.
Wolfson, Elliot R. "The Problem of Unity in the Thought of Martin Buber." *Journal of the History of Philosophy* 27, no. 3 (1989): 423–444.
Wolfson, Elliot R. "Suffering Eros and Textual Incarnation: A Kristevan Reading of Kabbalistic Poetics." In *Towards a Theology of Eros: Transfiguring Passion at the Limits of Discipline.* Edited by Virginia Burrus and Catherine Keller, 341–365. New York: Fordham University Press, 2006.
Wolfson, Elliot R. *Through a Speculum that Shines: Vision and Imagination in Medieval Jewish Mysticism.* Princeton: Princeton University Press, 1994.
Wolfson, Elliot R. *Venturing Beyond: Law and Morality in Kabbalistic Mysticism.* Oxford: Oxford University Press, 2006.
Wolfson, Elliot R. "Weeping, Death, and Spiritual Ascent in Sixteenth-Century Jewish Mysticism." In *Death, Ecstasy, and Other Worldly Journeys.* Edited by Daniel Collins and Michael Fishbane, 209–247. Albany: State University of New York Press, 1995.
Wolfson, Harry Austryn. "The Internal Senses in Latin, Arabic, and Hebrew Philosophic Texts." *Harvard Theological Review* 28, no. 2 (1935): 69–133.
Wolfson, Harry Austryn. "Maimonides on the Internal Senses." *Jewish Quarterly Review* 25 (1935): 441–467.
Wunder, Meir. *Me'orei Galiṣiyah: Encyclopedia of Galician Rabbis and Scholars.* Jerusalem: Institute for the Commemoration of Galician Jewry, 1978–2005. [Hebrew]
Ya'el Levin, "Ha-ADMO"R she-Nigen ba-Kinor ve-Ḥadal im Histalqut Ra'aiyato." *Daf le-Tarbut Yehudit* 273 (2007): 39. [Hebrew]
Yari-Wold, Moshe, ed., *Rzeszow Community: Memorial Book.* Tel Aviv: Former Residents of Rzeszow in Israel and the USA, 1967. [Hebrew]
Yechieli, Netanel. "On the Book *Tena'ei ha-Nefesh le-Hasagat ha-Ḥassidut* by R. Menaḥem Ekstein, May God Avenge His Blood: Hasidic Psychological Worship Assisted by the Imaginative Faculty." Seminar paper, Hebrew University of Jerusalem, 1998. [Hebrew]
Yifrach, Yehuda. "The Elevation of Foreign Thoughts in the Tradition of R. Israel Baal Shem Tov." Master's thesis, Bar Ilan University, 2007. [Hebrew]
Zeitlin, Aaron. *An Expanded Parapsychology.* Tel Aviv: Yavneh, 1973. [Hebrew]
Zeitlin, Aaron. *The Other Dimension.* Tel Aviv: Yavneh, 1967. [Hebrew]
Zeitlin, Hillel. *Al Gevul Shenei Olamot.* Tel Aviv: Yavneh, 1965 [Hebrew]
Zeitlin, Hillel. *Be-Pardes ha-Ḥasidut ve-ha-Qabbalah.* Tel Aviv: Yavneh, 1965. [Hebrew]
Zeitlin, Hillel. *Ḥasidut le-Shiṭotehah u-Zeramehah.* Warsaw: Sifrut, 1910. [Hebrew]
Zeitlin, Hillel. "Mafte'aḥ le-Sefer ha-Zohar—Ḥeleq Sheni." *Ha-Tequfah* 9 (1921): 265–330. [Hebrew]

Zilbershtrom, M. A. "Ha-Hipnaṭizmos." In *Kenneset ha-Gedolah*. Edited by Yiṣḥaq Sovelski, 41–56. Warsaw: Ḥayyim Kelter, 1889. [Hebrew]

Zinqover, S. M. "ben ha-melekh ve-ha-ḥakham." *Qoveṣ le-Torah ve-Ḥasidut: Mevo'ei ha-Naḥal* 37 (1981): 35–37. [Hebrew]

Zohar, Ze'ev. *Sefer ha-Yovel ha-Esrim ve-Ḥamishah shel Beit ha-Sefer ha-Tikhon ve-ha-Seminar le-Gananot ve-le-Morot "Beit Ya'aqov" be-Tel Aviv 1936–1961*. Tel Aviv: Beth Yaakov Publishing, 1961. [Hebrew]

Zweig, Stefan. *Mental Healers: Franz Anton Mesmer, Mary Baker Eddy, Sigmund Freud*. Translated by Eden and Ceder Paul. New York: Frederick Ungar, 1932.

Zweig, Stefan. *The World of Yesterday*. Translated by Anthea Bell. Lincoln: University of Nebraska Press, 1964.

Index of Persons

Abulafia, Abraham 4, 6f., 9, 64, 71, 78, 81, 84, 93, 128–130, 134, 137, 149, 160, 206, 214f., 234f., 239, 268–270, 273, 276, 303f., 307, 353, 374, 396, 404
Al-Hujwiri 61
Albotini, Judah 56, 79, 134
Allan Monroe, Robert 62, 313
Aristotle 19f., 35, 39, 204, 268

Bein, El'azar 163, 242, 383
Bein, Leibel 100, 101f, 242
Benei Maḥshavah Ṭovah 84, 91, 94f., 102–104, 116, 123, 132f., 140, 145, 154, 164, 169, 176–178, 181f., 184, 188–190, 210, 218, 226f., 229, 240, 246
Bornsztain, Shmuel 161f., 177
Buber, Martin 7, 73f., 142, 198, 275, 278, 280, 288, 373, 405

Corbin, Henry 12, 24, 396–400
Cordovero, Moses 108f., 129, 134f., 159, 164, 180, 195, 235, 270, 316

Dan, Joseph 18, 130, 214, 234
Derrida, Jacques 21f.
Dessler, Elijah Eliezer 201, 327, 330, 333f., 341, 390f.

Egidio da Viterbo 81, 353
Ekstein, Menaḥem 13, 48, 170, 250–262, 264–267, 270–274, 276–280, 287–294, 296–302, 304f., 308–314, 317, 324, 327, 340, 359f., 362–364, 366, 370–373, 376–383, 386, 390, 403f., 406f.
Eliade, Mircea 13, 68, 157, 396, 401–404
Elior, Rachel 25, 75, 156f., 187, 275, 277
Etkes, Immanuel 120, 318–321, 323, 325, 387, 389
Ettlinger, Jacob 355f.

Faur, José 32, 34–36, 48, 345
Feierberg, Mordekhai Ze'ev 207f.
Fichte, Johann Gottlieb 21
Finkel, Natan Ṣevi („The Elder from Slobodka") 331, 334
Forman, Robert K. C. 53, 55, 241
Foucault, Michel 30, 40f.
Freud, Siegmund 178, 352f., 361, 367, 372, 386, 389, 394

Garb, Jonathan 2, 4, 8f., 11, 29, 53, 56, 61, 63–66, 86f., 143, 146f., 155f., 184f., 187, 191, 215, 241, 280, 319, 341, 351, 372, 384, 404
Gefen, Shem-Tov 84, 96

Halevi, Judah 7, 23, 26–30, 41, 46–48, 82, 105, 109, 206, 208, 214, 244, 304, 317, 342, 360, 383
Harvey, Warren Zev 26, 28, 30, 37, 283
Heidegger, Martin 21
Herder, Johann Gottfried 17, 30
Hershkowitz, Isaac 99, 191–193
Heschel, Abraham Joshua 36, 46, 70–72, 89, 120, 147, 162, 165, 190, 198f., 234, 249, 281, 284, 286–289, 332, 380f., 400
Hollenback, Jess Byron 53, 61–64, 86f., 90, 189, 197
Huss, Boaz 53, 57–60, 79, 241, 378, 387

Ibn Arabi 12, 24, 396, 399
Idel, Moshe 1–4, 6–12, 18, 23f., 54–57, 60, 64–66, 68, 71, 78, 81, 84, 95, 108, 114–116, 128–131, 133f., 137, 143f., 149, 152, 155–157, 160–162, 173, 187, 189, 191, 206, 214f., 217, 221, 234f., 239f., 263, 268f., 275–277, 295, 300, 302–308, 351, 353, 355, 363, 373f., 377, 384, 396, 404
Isaac of Acre 78, 134, 235, 396
Ivanovich Gurdjieff, Georges 384

Jacobson, Yoram 25, 45, 75, 149, 173, 182, 212, 237, 277, 279

James, William 53, 57, 178, 233, 284, 354, 400

Kamelhar, Jekuthiel Aryeh ben Gershon 253 f., 261 f., 290, 371 f.
Kant, Immanuel 17, 20 f., 25, 30, 84, 282 f., 288 f., 389
Katz, Steven 24, 53 f., 56, 179 f., 318, 320, 325 f., 336, 372, 389 f., 394
Kaufmann, Yehezkel 69 f., 199
Kearney, Richard 17–21, 25, 30, 40, 268, 317
Kierkegaard, Søren 21, 172, 176
Kook, Abraham Isaac ha-Kohen 36, 53, 77, 84, 184, 198–200, 203–206, 208, 224, 248, 274, 279, 312, 316, 335, 375, 383, 403

Leshem, Zvi 88, 92, 99–103, 105, 107, 110–112, 119, 123 f., 131, 135 f., 146, 181, 191–193, 229, 241 f., 376, 383
Levovitz, Yeruḥam Halevi 331–333, 337, 341
Liebes, Yehuda 2, 81, 114 f., 161, 194, 286
Lipkin, Israel of Salant 184, 318–326, 335 f., 338, 340, 387–394
Locke, John 21, 30
Longinus 281 f., 284, 288 f.
Luria, Isaac 9, 110, 118, 163, 169, 180, 208, 236, 270, 275

Maimonides 23, 26, 28, 31–42, 44–48, 76, 82, 84, 122, 127–129, 136, 151, 159, 173, 182, 199, 206 f., 213 f., 220 f., 224, 227, 232, 236, 268–270, 273, 292 f., 303, 360
Maimuni, Abraham 82 f.
Marcus, Aaron 361–363, 383
Margolin, Ron 29, 54, 67, 72–75, 78 f., 90, 199, 270, 373 f., 377
Mark, Zvi 42–46, 135, 256, 352
Mazor, Yaakov 119, 131
Mesmer, Franz 348–357, 359–361, 363, 366, 369, 371, 373, 384, 394
Mevorach, Yishai 286, 289
Miller, Avigdor 334–339, 341, 390 f.
Moscatto, Yehudah 129
Moses of Kiev 79
Muldoon, Sylvan 62, 313

Naḥman of Bratslav 23, 41, 121 f., 135, 138, 188, 209, 228, 286, 314
Nietzsche, Frederick 21, 286, 403 f.

Ophir, Natan 241, 384–386
Or ha-Ganuz (Hidden Light) 155, 215–217, 300
Otto, Rudolf 67–70, 72–74, 283
Ouspensky, Peter 384 f.

Pachter, Mordechai 44, 204, 318 f., 321, 323, 388 f.
Pedaya, Haviva 5–8, 24, 68, 72, 79 f., 118, 120, 125, 143, 154 f., 166, 199, 219 f., 224 f., 231, 366
Persico, Tomer 107, 260, 293, 377, 379 f., 386, 401
Plato 18–21, 31, 39, 268, 373

Rabinowitz, David Yiṣḥaq 316, 372
Rabinowitz, Zadok ha-Kohen of Lublin 198, 200–205, 208, 221, 224, 248
Rosenberg, Shimon Gershon 6, 29 f., 32–35, 45–47, 156 f., 182, 198, 201, 286, 289

Sartre, Jean Paul 21, 35, 40, 221 f., 225
Schatz-Uffenheimer, Rivka 25, 73–75, 173, 376
Schelling, Friedrich Wilhelm Joseph 21
Schneersohn, Shalom Dovber 372
Schneersohn, Yosef Yiṣḥaq 314–315, 317, 340
Scholem, Gershom 2 f., 5, 53 f., 56, 60, 68, 70, 72–74, 84, 90 f., 114 f., 156, 173, 214, 263 f., 294, 303 f., 365, 373, 376, 396, 400
Schorske, Carl 367–369
Schweid, Eliezer 74, 82–85, 89, 198–200
Shapira, Kalonymous Kalman 9 f., 48, 63, 76, 83–96, 99–107, 109–117, 122–126, 131–133, 135–142, 144–156, 160, 162–166, 168–178, 180–197, 199, 207–214, 216–218, 220, 226–249, 262, 265, 304,

311–314, 317, 322, 328, 330, 340, 364f., 375f., 378, 383–386, 406f.
Shimon Ibn Lavi 78
Shneur Zalman of Liadi 25, 45, 75, 138, 159, 181–183, 187, 211, 277, 300, 392f.

Taylor, Charles 320, 380
Théon, Max (Eli'ezer Mordekhai) 241
Tishby, Isaiah 130, 263, 303f

Uffenheimer, Benjamin 10, 67–74, 187, 199
Underhill, Evelyn 53, 56

Wacks, Ron 84, 91, 93, 99, 105–108, 110–114, 147, 152, 175, 192f., 209, 214, 236, 241
Weinshelbaum, Shelomo Aryeh Leib 316f.
Weiss, Joseph 37, 71, 135, 149, 214
Wertheim, Aaron 131
Whitehead, Alfred North 345
Wittgenstein, Ludwig 285f., 367f.
Wolbe, Shlomo 341f.
Wolfson, Elliot R. 2, 5, 7, 9, 11f., 18, 21f., 28f., 35, 39–41, 44f., 53f., 56, 60, 62, 68, 75, 87, 108, 119, 121, 140f., 143f., 147, 155f., 158–161, 168, 177f., 223, 235, 275, 277f., 280, 302, 318, 374, 393, 396, 400

Zeitlin, Aaron 350, 383, 369
Zeitlin, Hillel 177, 194, 259, 263, 284–288, 383, 400
Ziv, Simḥah Zissel 326–332, 338, 341, 389
Zweig, Stefan 352, 368f., 371f.

Subject Index

Alien Thoughts 24, 149 f., 238, 241, 259, 268 f., 393
Amazement 138, 281, 286, 289, 312, 349
Anomian techniques 8 f., 116 f., 142, 189
Antinomian 8 f., 73
Antisemitism 199
Anxiety 79, 178, 183, 185 f., 189, 217, 282, 286, 330
Astral Projection 62, 312 f.
Autoscopy 170, 302, 305, 308, 313
– Self-Visualization 170, 302, 310
Avodah be-Gashmiyut (corporeal worship) 131, 270

Bifurcated Soul 262–265, 267, 299, 302 f., 309 f., 312
Biṭṭul (self-nullification) 73, 75, 120, 176, 237, 260, 272, 274, 277 f., 393, 403
Breathing 65

Christianity 83, 172, 223, 269, 276, 404
Conceptual thinking 147, 171, 336
Corporealization 220 f., 223–226, 230–232, 235, 338 f., 341

Dance 8, 112, 116–126, 130–132, 142, 170, 189, 208, 296, 312
Day of Death 145, 176–182, 252, 265, 322, 328–330, 334
Devequt (Communion) 2 f., 5, 10, 12, 29, 36, 47, 56, 78 f., 131, 134 f., 143 f., 152, 173, 193, 195, 215 f., 260, 273, 276–278, 286, 291, 329, 374
Distress 5, 11, 34, 69, 71, 82, 104, 122, 132, 147, 154, 170, 173–178, 181–185, 189 f., 210, 215, 217, 226 f., 229 f., 251, 273, 282, 290, 319, 337 f., 375, 378, 390
Divine names 6, 9–11, 66, 108, 128, 160, 215, 234–240, 248

Ecstasy (*Hitpa'alut*) 2 f., 7, 24, 63, 65, 67–72, 74, 87, 90, 96, 105, 111, 114, 121, 124–127, 131, 137 f., 149, 151, 171, 175–177, 202, 208, 210 f., 215, 226, 228 f., 234, 239 f., 245–247, 249, 257, 259, 266, 275, 281, 284, 288–293, 304, 312, 321 f., 324–326, 328, 350, 376, 388, 390, 394
Empowerment 11, 13, 35, 39, 47, 53–56, 60 f., 63–66, 86–88, 90, 96, 107, 115, 139 f., 142–146, 148–152, 160, 170 f., 173–175, 178, 185, 189 f., 197, 211, 274, 280, 312 f., 332, 375, 381, 406
Energy 38, 46 f., 154, 245, 353, 376–378
Exteriorization 62

Faith 1–3, 29, 41, 45–48, 55, 58, 69, 71, 83–86, 92 f., 105, 112, 167 f., 204, 221, 227, 243, 262, 264, 267, 280, 286, 288, 291, 312 f., 331, 336, 339–341, 361, 368, 379 f., 390, 396, 406 f.
Fire 11, 85, 87 f., 91, 99–102, 104 f., 107 f., 112 f., 121, 124, 145, 147, 152, 155, 175, 185–188, 192–194, 196, 209, 221, 227, 229, 236, 241, 295, 336, 388, 398, 404

Gilui ha-Nefesh (Revelation of the soul) 209–212

Hanukkah 120, 167–170, 254
Heaven 62, 71, 79, 87, 89–91, 104, 108, 112, 121, 125, 132, 137, 139, 146, 150–153, 163 f., 168 f., 171 f., 174, 186, 194, 208, 216–218, 226 f., 232–234, 239, 243, 248, 291 f., 321, 327, 334, 337 f., 342, 372
Historicism 114, 191, 211
Hitbodedut (concentration, solitude) 4, 116, 133–137, 142, 189, 215, 220
Hithapkhuyot 120 f., 123–125
Hitkallelut (integration) 173, 275 f., 310, 378 f.
Hypernomian 9, 160

Illustration 219, 332, 337, 407

Imagery 4, 6 f., 10 – 12, 29 f., 34, 49, 54, 103, 108, 110 – 112, 114, 116 f., 133, 137, 141 f., 148, 150, 153, 155, 164 f., 169 – 172, 174, 176, 181, 185 – 187, 190 f., 194 f., 213, 216, 229, 235, 238 f., 241, 246 f., 258, 260, 264, 266 – 268, 272, 274, 278, 289 f., 293 – 295, 297, 299 – 302, 308 – 310, 312 f., 315, 317, 323 f., 327, 329, 332 – 334, 341 f., 363, 366, 368, 373, 379 – 382, 391, 403, 406 f.
Imagery Techniques 5 – 13, 17 f., 23, 30, 49, 60, 64, 96, 103, 107 – 117, 125, 136 f., 141 f., 146 f., 149 f., 152, 154 – 156, 160, 162 f., 165, 168 – 170, 173, 175, 178, 180, 183 f., 186 – 191, 195, 207, 216 – 218, 220, 232, 235, 239, 241, 243 – 245, 247 f., 250, 258, 262, 270 f., 274, 278 – 280, 292 – 294, 299 – 302, 308 – 314, 316 f., 326 f., 330, 332 – 334, 338, 340, 342, 346, 348, 363 – 365, 373, 378 – 382, 384, 396, 402 f., 405 – 407
– linguistic 10 f, 108, 110, 216 f, 236, 406
– Multi-scenic 6, 7, 10, 12, 148, 153, 169, 171, 195, 239, 364, 365, 382 f
– Plot 6, 10 – 12, 106, 169, 195, 200, 239, 309, 313, 316, 337, 365, 405 f.
Imaginal 2, 6 – 8, 10, 12, 21, 24 f., 28 – 30, 43, 49, 104 – 107, 110 f., 113, 124 f., 132 f., 137, 140 f., 143 – 146, 148, 150, 152, 165, 167, 169 – 172, 187 f., 195, 197, 204 f., 214, 222 – 226, 228, 230 – 232, 235 f., 239, 245, 247 f., 266, 288 f., 295, 302 – 305, 309 f., 312 f., 315, 328, 338, 340, 365, 399 f., 404 f., 407
Imaginal World 12, 24, 396, 399
– World of Imagination 368, 396
Imagination 5 – 8, 11 – 13, 17 – 25, 27 – 49, 61 – 65, 85, 99, 103 – 109, 111 – 117, 124 – 126, 133, 137, 139 – 142, 144 – 146, 148 f., 151, 154, 156, 163, 166 f., 170, 172 f., 176, 181 – 183, 185 – 189, 195 f., 198, 200, 202, 204 – 210, 213 f., 218 – 225, 227, 229 – 231, 234 f., 237 – 242, 244 – 250, 259, 265 – 273, 276, 278 f., 281, 288 – 290, 293, 295, 298 f., 301 – 304, 308 – 313, 315 – 318, 321 – 334, 336 f., 339 – 342, 363 – 365, 368 f., 372 f., 376, 378, 383, 386, 391, 394 – 400, 403, 406 f.
– Creative imagination 12 f., 20 f., 23 – 25, 28, 30, 34 – 36, 47 – 49, 195, 198, 317, 364 f., 373, 381, 396, 398 f.
– in Western Philosophy 18 – 23
– in Jewish Thought 23 – 49
– Lamp Model 195
– Mirror Model 195
– within Imagination 167, 234, 239
Imaginative Faculty 26 – 30, 32 f., 35 – 48, 79, 148 f., 153, 155, 166, 183, 189, 203 – 208, 213 f., 218, 221, 224, 235, 237, 240, 245, 267 – 269, 272, 277, 279, 289, 295 – 297, 312, 314, 322, 329, 331, 333 f., 386
Impassioned (*Hitlahavut*) 29 f., 32, 34, 45 – 47, 113, 138, 153, 155, 175 f., 190, 195 f., 198, 201, 207, 246 f., 317, 322, 325 f., 341, 377, 392
Islam 12, 24, 32, 35, 276, 399 f.
Isolation 4, 133 – 137, 215, 220

Kavvanot (Intentions) 8 – 10, 71, 108, 159, 207, 236, 240, 279, 302

Life 21, 23, 29, 46, 54 f., 59, 64, 66, 69, 71, 73 f., 85, 101, 107, 112 – 114, 118 f., 122 – 124, 130, 134 f., 147, 157, 159, 165, 171 – 175, 179, 184 f., 189 f., 196, 199, 201, 204 – 206, 220, 234, 241 f., 246 f., 253, 256, 259, 261 f., 264, 266, 269 – 271, 273 – 275, 279 – 281, 286 f., 289, 291, 294, 298, 301, 311 f., 318 f., 324, 334 f., 337, 339, 348, 350, 352, 355 f., 358, 361 f., 368, 370, 374, 376 – 379, 381 f., 384, 387, 396, 403 f., 406
Light 3, 7 f., 11, 18, 20, 33 f., 55, 60, 62, 78 – 80, 86 – 93, 113, 120, 134, 138, 155, 161 – 165, 167 – 170, 192 – 194, 197, 201, 203 – 206, 209, 216 f., 232, 235 f., 239, 250, 252, 254 f., 258, 267, 273 f., 277, 280, 282, 287 f., 291, 300, 303, 307, 314 f., 348, 350, 356, 360, 366, 372, 392 f., 396 f., 407

Maḥshavah (Thought) 53, 93, 96, 103–107, 109, 111f., 117, 126, 139, 168f., 181, 183, 186, 188, 213f., 217f., 226f., 229–231, 240, 246–249, 258, 292f., 376, 393
Melody 8, 42f., 100, 112, 120, 126, 131–133, 142, 175, 229, 250, 325f.
Mesmerism 12, 348–359, 363, 365f., 369–373, 381f., 389, 394f.
Midrash 37, 40, 46f., 91, 100, 119, 149, 200, 207, 243, 273, 287, 389
Modern psychology 351f., 354f., 363, 376, 405
Mussar Movement 319
Mystical Techniques 1f., 8, 13, 56, 64, 66, 189, 206, 215, 400, 403
Mysticism 1–10, 12f., 18, 22, 25, 27, 29, 41–46, 49, 53–75, 81f., 86f., 90, 96, 110, 115, 128f., 135, 143, 152, 156, 160, 173, 177f., 187, 189–191, 197, 199, 203, 207, 211, 214, 225, 233, 235, 241, 275–277, 285–288, 293f., 304, 317, 360, 364, 367–369, 372, 376, 387, 396f., 403–406

Nefesh Geluyah (A Revealed Soul) 209, 244
Nomian techniques 8, 145

Opposites 43, 172, 365

Para-psychology 369
Passover 165–167, 254, 328, 332, 372
Prayer 6–10, 24, 62, 71, 92, 94, 101, 108f., 113, 116–118, 131, 134–140, 142–144, 149–155, 163, 170, 174, 177, 179–181, 184, 186f., 189, 196, 199, 210, 216, 223, 227, 232–235, 237, 241, 251, 257, 312, 316, 332, 338, 360, 399
Prophecy 3, 13, 26–30, 32–36, 38–43, 45–48, 60, 63–72, 74–86, 88–96, 99, 102f., 105, 107f., 111–113, 119, 123, 126–128, 131, 134–137, 144, 146, 149, 154f., 166, 171, 181, 191–193, 198–209, 211–217, 219, 227, 229f., 239–245, 248f., 264, 268, 278, 292f., 295, 303, 312, 376, 399, 403f., 407
Prophet 9, 26–29, 32–34, 36, 38, 40–43, 64f., 67–72, 75–78, 80–96, 113, 127f., 140, 146f., 166, 185, 197–202, 204, 213–215, 218, 220, 229–232, 239, 243, 248f., 295, 303–305, 338, 345, 406
Prophetic Kabbalah 4, 9, 12, 65f., 71, 78, 108, 128f., 133f., 155, 217, 235, 268, 302, 304, 353, 396
Psychologization 3, 264, 375f.

Running and returning (*raṣo va-shov*) 160, 183, 225, 231, 294, 296f., 299f., 302, 310–313, 406

Sabbath 62, 100, 102, 107, 118, 122, 129, 156f., 160–165, 170, 189, 216, 226, 245, 251f., 256, 316, 332f., 359, 371
Ṣaddiq 3, 6f, 46f, 64, 88f, 92, 105f, 108–110, 112, 121–122, 146–147, 191–197, 231, 329, 402,
Secularism 190f.
Seeking God 173f.
Self-Awareness 112f, 207f, 238, 242, 259–267, 273–274, 309–310, 312, 385
Self-Consciousness (*see* Self-Awareness)
Self-Empowerment 171, 173f, 280f, 381f
Self-Sacrifice 104, 123f., 186f., 208
se'udah shelishit 163–165, 245
Silencing 56, 64, 66, 100, 175, 237f., 241–244, 383–385
Simḥat Torah 118f., 121, 123, 125f.
Situational thinking 147, 332, 336, 340f.
Song 6, 62, 72, 80, 116–118, 123, 126, 131–133, 136f., 151, 153, 155, 162–164, 166, 185, 189, 195, 200, 210, 219f., 250, 312, 365
Speaking Out Loud 137–139, 142
Sublime 18, 29, 55, 58, 77, 88, 110, 204, 212, 266, 281–284, 286–289, 406
Substitution 137, 232
Sufism 12, 24, 82f., 396, 398–400

Technique 1–4, 6–13, 23, 25, 30f., 48f., 54, 56–58, 62, 64–66, 78, 83–85, 93, 95f., 101, 107–118, 120f., 126–131, 133–135, 137–139, 141–145, 148, 150, 152f., 155f., 160, 163–167, 169–175, 177–179, 181–183, 185–187, 190f., 193–197, 200, 206–208, 213–217,

219 f., 226, 229, 232, 234–246, 258, 260, 262, 264–267, 270–272, 274, 278, 280, 289 f., 292–302, 304 f., 308–313, 315, 317, 321, 324–327, 329, 333 f., 337, 340, 348, 353 f., 357–359, 363–366, 373, 380–387, 394, 400–405, 407
The Technique of „Negative Commandments" (*Lav*) 300
Theurgy 9, 68, 129, 360
Time 7–11, 17, 22, 27, 32, 44, 48 f., 60, 62, 76, 80–83, 85 f., 88, 91, 93, 100–102, 104–106, 110 f., 114, 117–119, 121–124, 127 f., 131 f., 136, 138 f., 146, 149, 151–162, 164 f., 167–172, 175 f., 178–180, 182, 184, 187, 197, 200–205, 207, 209, 211, 219 f., 226 f., 229, 232–234, 241–246, 248, 250, 254, 256, 260 f., 263–265, 269, 271, 275, 279, 289, 293 f., 297–299, 301, 311 f., 314, 316, 320, 324, 327 f., 330, 334, 337, 345, 348, 352, 361, 363, 366, 370, 372, 375 f., 382–386, 388–391, 394, 396, 398, 401, 403
– Cyclical time 157 f., 160
Torah Study 7 f., 112, 114, 131, 134, 142–146, 149, 159, 170, 174, 189, 201, 371

Unconscious 72, 106, 142, 178, 242, 247, 260, 348–355, 358, 361, 364, 370, 372 f., 379 f., 383, 387–392, 394 f.

Vienna 101, 252, 254–256, 260, 298, 316, 348–352, 354, 366–373, 381
Visualization 5–7, 10 f., 47, 61, 103–110, 117, 124 f., 132 f., 140 f., 143–145, 148 f., 151–155, 165 f., 170 f., 173, 176 f., 180–182, 187 f., 194–197, 200, 213, 216, 218–227, 231 f., 235–241, 243, 245, 248, 263–266, 273, 278, 290, 295–305, 307, 309–313, 315, 322 f., 328–330, 332–334, 336–342, 373, 376, 378, 381 f., 399, 403–405
– Visualizing God 108, 139, 144, 218, 225, 232, 239 f.
– Visualizing the Tetragrammaton 6, 10, 216
Vitality 45, 160, 182, 206, 315, 348, 376 f., 407

Waking Dream 4, 54, 62 f., 106 f., 169, 217, 239, 295
Weeping 4, 124 f., 127, 139, 148, 150, 154, 167, 174, 176–178, 210, 325, 362, 388 f.
World to come 24, 104, 160–162, 172 f., 189, 192, 220, 242, 250, 329 f., 333, 339
Writing 3, 22, 27, 33, 41, 60–62, 69–71, 76 f., 81–84, 86, 91, 93, 103–108, 110–116, 121 f., 128–131, 134, 136–138, 140–142, 151, 156, 161, 163, 177, 181 f., 185, 187, 191 f., 194 f., 197, 205, 207, 209, 214, 217, 226, 235, 241, 247, 256, 259, 268 f., 276, 282 f., 285, 287, 289, 294, 302, 308, 314, 318 f., 327, 329, 337, 340, 345, 350, 353, 364, 370, 373, 377, 383 f., 400

www.ingramcontent.com/pod-product-compliance
Lightning Source LLC
Chambersburg PA
CBHW031409230426
43668CB00007B/257
9783110710496